MANAGEMENT INTERNATIONAL
CASES, EXERCISES, AND READINGS

Dorothy Marcic
Metropolitan State University

Sheila M. Puffer
Northeastern University

West Publishing Company
Minneapolis/St. Paul   New York   Los Angeles   San Francisco

WEST'S COMMITMENT TO THE ENVIRONMENT

In 1906, West Publishing Company began recycling materials left over from the production of books. This began a tradition of efficient and responsible use of resources. Today, up to 95% of our legal books and 70% of our college texts and school texts are printed on recycled, acid-free stock. West also recycles nearly 22 million pounds of scrap paper annually—the equivalent of 181,717 trees. Since the 1960s, West has devised ways to capture and recycle waste inks, solvents, oils, and vapors created in the printing process. We also recycle plastics of all kinds, wood, glass, corrugated cardboard, and batteries, and have eliminated the use of Styrofoam book packaging. We at West are proud of the longevity and the scope of our commitment to the environment.

Production, Prepress, Printing and Binding by West Publishing Company.

 TEXT IS PRINTED ON 10% POST CONSUMER RECYCLED PAPER  PRINTED WITH SOY INK

Chapter 1
Developing global consciousness:
Competitiveness and culture

Chapter 2
Cross-cultural awareness and sensitivity

cases and exercises:

Chapter 3
Ethics

cases and exercises

Readings

Chapter 4
Human resource management

cases and exercises

readings

Chapter 5
Managing a diverse workforce

cases and exercises

Readings

Chapter 6
Multinational parent-subsidiary and joint venture relationships

cases and exercises

Chapter 7
Strategy

cases and exercises

Readings

Chapter 9
European and North American integration

cases and exercises

Readings

Epilogue:
The future

exercise

Appendices

To my sister, Janet Mittelsteadt

—D.M.

To Ken and Ellen Puffer

—S.P.

Introduction

We live in a world beset with chaos, one involved in a massive revolution of the economic order. As Nichols said, "we are mid-stride between an old and a new era, and we have not yet found our way. We know the old no longer works; the new is not yet formed clearly enough to be believed."

Gone is the day when companies could do business in a small geographic area. Today, firms are often required to get supplies in one country, ship them somewhere else for assembly, then market in a multitude of locations, each with its own local distributor and sales force. Organizations without the ability to function across national borders will not thrive as we move into the twenty-first century. Success nowadays requires cross cultural awareness and sensitivity, knowledge of legal systems in other countries, language skills, ability to negotiate in various settings, a keen understanding of political risk and the dangers/opportunties involved, and global strategic thinking.

This book seeks to help the student of international management grasp some of the essentials of doing business in a global economy. Current articles explore important issues in this field. Students then are given the opportunity to apply these concepts through the use of case studies and experiential exercises. Each chapter has a variety of the three elements – readings, cases and exercises. We have tried, as much as possible, to give a balance between these elements.

Although primarily written as a text supplement for an International Management course, the book can also be used alone, supplemented with other readings or cases. In addition, it can be used for courses in international business, cross-cultural awareness, and even international relations.

Not only are business organizations faced with borderless commerce, but this book was written in a way not dissimilar to that of many of these new companies who simultaeously operate in numerous geographical and cultural locations.

International Management: Not just the title of this book, but also an apt metaphor for the project which produced this book. When we agreed to work on this book, we were happy about the prospect of working together, but wary of the distance factor. Based on different continents thousands of miles apart (with six time zones separating us), we experienced first-hand the complexities of managing internationally. Dorothy was in exotic Prague in the Czech Republic, experiencing the transition from command to market economies. Meanwhile, Sheila was in familiar Boston trying to keep up with the latest developments on NAFTA and GATT. Except for one early-stage meeting at a conference in Slovakia, we had to work sight unseen and became fellow travellers, so to speak, on the "information superhighway"– mostly through BITNET (how did we ever live without it?) and overnight mail (to Prague it means half-week).

Yes, we had a bumpy ride on the potholes between Central Europe and the United States. We quickly gave up telephoning after the endlessly buzzing busy signals, hollering over static which sounded like someone crunching aluminum foil in your ear, puzzling over what was about to be said when the line would go dead, as well as waking each other up at odd hours (due to time differences) because that was the only time to get a line through. Faxes were not better, we discovered, after trying for days sometimes to get a line through, but then what would appear at the other end were waves and squiggles, requiring multiple copies to be fed through the ever tempermental international phone lines.

After getting the e-mail accounts to talk to each other, communication eased up some, but still not without difficulties. We got used to working late at night and leaving half a dozen messages for the other to read upon rising in the morning. Eventually, we found the limits, though, when Sheila e-mailed about the 20th version of the table of contents and INTERNET jumbled up the selections resembling something like a bowl of spaghetti. To top it off, Sheila's computer died in the last weeks of the project, while online midsentence to Dorothy.

In the end, our communication heroes which shuttled last minute articles and updates from Boston to Prague were the US Postal Service and Ceska Posta (which delivered one package at 8:30 PM, something which caused Dorothy's Czech friend Ludek to remark, "Well, I'm impressed.")

Besides navigating our way through the precarious international communication systems, we also learned that managing internationally requires additional resources and deliberate redundancies in order to meet deadlines and produce high-quality work. Both of us agreed to working on solving various problems in the hope that at least one would be successful. This turned out to be a good srategy in order to meet our production deadline. We also both had the good fortune of having institutional support as well as that from numerous individuals who played a major role in this project.

Acknowledgements

A book of this sort cannot be completed without the support of many people. We both would like to take the opportunity to show our appreciation for all those who have given us so much help.

To my colleagues at Metropolitan State University I offer sincere appreciation, particularly to former Dean David Crockett who had the generosity to give me research support in the early stages of this project when I was still in Minnesota. Others who offered assistance and support include Ken Zapp, Barbara Gorski (who gave professional and friend-support), Barbara Keinath, Gary Seiler and Nancy Johnson. And finally, I cannot write this without deeply thanking administrative assistant Gloria Mitchell, who did so much for me, even after I was transplanted to Prague, often mailing me huge packages or faxing me urgent information. She is one of those living angels. At the Czechoslovak Management Center Dean Bill Pendergast has consistently offered me help and encouragement on various projects, including this one. Carol Pendergast, Director of Faculty development, was always there for me and gave me hope and encouragement to keep hanging in there. In addition, Michael Cakrt taught me a great deal about cross-cultural teaching and understanding, as did Dagmar Glaukofova, who became my friend, as well. I would not have had the opportunity to live international management without the support of the Fulbright Commission and the helpful people there – Dr. Vaclav Aschenbrener, Hanna Ripkova and Vera Moravova. Other people, colleagues and friends, in the Czech Republic, who have helped me a great deal include Marketa Glancova, Venus Jahanpour, Maya Čurhová, Ludek Miller, Marie Miller (who ran my house while I finished the book) and my very dear friend Ivan Sterzl.

People in my life who have consistently been encouraging, helpful, confrontative in a positive way, and just generally supportive (often offering multitudes of prayers) are Margaret Clayton, Stephen and Najla Birkland, Debby and Bob Rosenfeld, Rose Presser, May Hoffman Ballerio, Greg and Gail Edwards, George Starcher, Diane Casbolt, Peter Khan, and Maxine and Mark Rossman. And I cannot forget Peter Vaill, whose regular bitnotes are like taking a post-doctoral seminar in organization theory.

Finally, I wish to thank my family – my sister, Janet Mittelsteadt, who offered continuous encouragement to me, and to my three children, who were mostly patient about the long hours spent on this book. Of course, I must mention that towards the end of the project my youngest, Elizabeth (age 7) announced she wanted to be a check-out clerk in a grocery store when she grows up, so she wouldn't have to work all the time like her mom. After some reality checks about life with bar codes, she decided she would be a doctor, because at least she would be helping people. My thanks to all three daughters, to Roxanne, Solange, and Elizabeth, the real joys of my life.

Dorothy Marcic
Prague, December 1993

I wish to gratefully acknowledge the support of the College of Business Administration at Northeastern University as well as the assistance of students Jennifer Sherwin and Wilson Yi who so ably worked on production detail of the manuscript under tight deadlines. The students in MGT 4446, International Business Management and Operations, engaged in interesting discussions of many of the selections during the Fall 1993 quarter at Northeastern, and gave valuable feedback on the book. Finally, Hugh, Douglas and Carol readily took in stride that another book was part of the family's agenda.

Sheila Puffer
Boston, December 1993

People who helped with the manuscript itself include Monte Hanson who diligently edited the next to last draft of the book, which means about 70% of what you read here is improved by his touch. Steve Danforth was Dorothy's assistant in Minnesota and did much of the early organization and correspondence work, as well as offering useful advice. The final lay-out and design was wonderfully done by Julie Hänsel, at Communication/design in Prague. We were helped by several rounds of proof-reading, done by Sara Brock, Chuck Sabatos as well as Rich Reilly.

Lastly we are both grateful to the contributors who have written such interesting and relevant material and who granted us permission to publish their work. We also want to thank our colleagues at West Publishing who worked closely with us and encouraged our efforts, in particular Esther Craig (who has now worked with Dorothy for eight years), who has been so patient, and Dick Fenton, who from the start believed in the project and did what was necessary to get it off the ground.

In addition, we would like to thank those colleagues who reviewed two earlier drafts of this book and gave useful and insightful feedback. They are Steven K. Paulson of University of North Florida, Art Whately of New Mexico State University, Gregory K. Stephens of Texas Christian University, Ray Montagno of Ball State University, Robert C. Losik, John A.C. Stanbury for Indiana Unversity, A.G. Homan of Golden Gate University, Abdul Rasheed of University of Texas as Arlington, Sheila Adams of University of North Carolina-Wilmington, Richard Baldwin of Cedarville College, George Gore, of University of Cincinnati, Golpira Eshghi of Bentley College, and Duane Kujawa of University of Miama in Florida.

Any ideas for future editions, or prospective cases/exercises, can be sent to us in care of West Publishing, College Division, 610 Opperman Drive, St. Paul, MN 55164.

Chapter 1   introduction

Developing global consciousness: competitiveness and culture

To perform effectively in the growing international business environment, managers need to develop a global consciousness. In particular, they need to become aware of two critical features of the international arena: competitiveness and culture. In striving to regain the competitive edge in world markets, leading American companies realize that understanding other cultures is a valuable asset that can be a source of competitive advantage.

The first step in developing cultural awareness is to question the values and assumptions of one's own culture. The exercise, *A way of getting at American values,* provides an opportunity to do so by generating a list of American proverbs and examining the values that underlie them. These values provide insight into the American character and help explain typical American attitudes and behaviors. The *"As if"* exercise goes a step further by considering what a society would be like if it believed in various values that are not widely held in the United States. It is useful to think about the impact of such values on sources of work and life satisfaction, the work ethic, power relations and conflict resolution. Next comes an exercise, *Cultural stereotypes* which helps us to look at the assumptions we hold about various ethnic or cultural groups. The fourth exercise, *Dimensions of national culture and effective leadership patterns,* focuses on work-related values such as the degree of uncertainty avoidance in risk taking and power distance in hierarchical relationships that is preferred by individuals. These dimensions have been found to differentiate business practices in many countries. After completing the questionnaire that measures your own scores on these work-related values, you should consider the reasons for your scores and think of situations you have encountered that confirm or disconfirm your scores. The work-related values are discussed in more detail in the reading, *Cultural constraints in management theories.* The reading also shows how the concept and practice of management vary around the world, with illustrations from Germany, Japan, France, Africa, Russia and others. In addition, the reading concludes with three notable characteristics of American management that do not necessarily apply to other countries or regions. This discussion is another way of "getting at American values" and understanding culture as a framework for developing global consciousness.

Competitiveness, the second component of global consciousness, is discussed in two readings and an exercise. In *Global corporate competition: Is the American Firm an Endangered Species?*, a thirty-year analysis of global competition shows that

America has yielded its leading position to Asian and European firms in many industries. In banking, for example, U.S. firms had dominated for years, but in 1990 not a single American bank appeared on the elite list of the top twelve. The reading explores the causes of America's decline in global markets and concludes by questioning whether the decline will continue and how important its impact is on the U.S. economy. One answer to these questions is provided in the note, *The theory of competitive advantage,* which contains a framework for guiding countries to make their industries internationally competitive. The theory is based on the premise that innovation and continuous improvement are key mechanisms for increasing productivity, which in turn enhances a country's standard of living and international competitive position. Four interrelated determinants constitute a model of national competitive advantage. The Case 1 exercise, *Alcot Sato Machine Tool Company,* brings the issue of international competitiveness to the firm level. In this in-basket exercise, you are asked to put yourself in the position of a CEO in an industry that U.S. firms dominated for decades, but that has been overtaken by Japanese and European competitors. You have returned from a trip to find correspondence from Japan, Russia and Germany that can affect your competitive position and require action. An understanding of competitiveness and culture will assist in making sound decisions.

Chapter 1

Developing global consciousness: competitiveness and culture

1. A way of getting at American values[1]

purpose

To understand the foundation of the American value system.

group size

Any size.

time required

35 minutes.

exercise schedule

1 Complete list (pre-class)

Students fill out proverb list below. (Optional: May be done in class; allow 10 minutes.)

	unit time	total time
2 Group discussion (optional)	15 min	15 min

Groups of four or five people compile lists of proverbs and determine values relevant for each proverb. Each group develops a list of the most prominent values that come from these proverbs.

| **3 Class discussion** | 20 min | 20+ min |

Instructor asks groups to present their proverbs and writes them on the board. Class discusses how they relate to the American system of values. Students from other countries comment on their own value systems.

---

1 Adapted from Robert Kohls in *Intercultural Sourcebook* by David S. Hoopes and Paul Ventura (eds.), Society for Intercultural Education, Training and Research, 1979. Used with permission.

Proverbs and axioms

In the space below, write any proverb you have heard over and over. To the right of the proverb, write the value the proverb is espousing. Two are shown as examples. If you are doing this exercise outside class, you may ask other people to help you think of the proverbs and values.

Proverb	Value
1 A penny saved is a penny earned	Diligence
2 Don't cry over spilled milk	Practicality
3	
4	
5	
6	
7	
8	
9	
10	

2. "As if..." exercise[2]

purpose

To explore the effect of various value systems and beliefs on the structure of societies.

group size

Any number.

time required

50+ minutes.

exercise schedule

		unit time	total time
1	**Triads develop**	**20 min**	**20 min**

Groups of three persons are assigned one of the premises listed below and are to consider what a society would be like if it were based on that premise.

		unit time	total time
2	**Groups report**	**20+ min**	**40+ min**

Triads report on their hypothetical societies; other groups react.

		unit time	total time
3	**Discussion**	**10+ min**	**50+ min**

Instructor leads a discussion on the relationship between values and the way a society is designed and functions.

---

2 Adapted from Robert Kohls in *Intercultural Sourcebook* by David S. Hoopes and Paul Ventura (eds.), Society for Intercultural Education, Training and Research, 1979. Used with permission.

assignment

What would a society be like IF it believed implicitly...

1 in reincarnation and karma?

2 that all other people are infidels?

3 that all events in the world are determined by fate?

4 in the passive approach to life as preferable to action?

5 that certain ethnic or racial groups are intellectually inferior and emotionally immature?

6 that old people should be revered and honored?

7 that aesthetic values are supremely important and should determine every major issue in life?

8 that group rights are more important than individual rights?

9 that women are superior to men?

3. Cultural stereotypes[3]

purpose

To understand the prevalence (and negative effects of) common stereotypes

group size

Any number of groups of 3-6 members, preferably mixed with any cultural or ethnic groups.

time required

20 minutes or more.

exercise schedule

1 Complete sentences   **pre-class**

2 Small groups discuss (optional)   **20 min**

Groups of 3-6 members try to achieve consensus on the stereotypes of various cultural groups.

3 Class discussion   **20+ min**   **20 min**

Instructor leads discussion on common stereotypes. Were there similarities between the various groups? What were the differences? How can stereotypes impede productive business relationships?

Stereotype questionnaire

Use one word to describe the following groups:

1. The English.

2. The French.

---

3 Adapted from *Do's and Taboos Around the World* by Roger E. Axtell. Copyright 1990 John Wiley & Sons, Inc. Reprinted with permission of John Wiley & Sons, Inc.

3. Norwegians.

4. Latins.

5. Japanese.

6. Italians.

7. Chinese.

8. Africans.

9. Middle Easterners.

10. Americans.

11. Our neighbor to the north: Canada.

   a. One word to describe the people.

   b. Who is the current prime minister?

   c. Name three Canadian historical figures.

   d. List four Canadian provinces.

   e. Main language.

   f. Type of government.

   g. Relationship to England.

h. Name of currency and relationship to U.S. dollar.

i. Main exports to U.S.

12. Our neighbor to the south: Mexico.

a. One word to describe the people.

b. Who is the current president?

c. Name three Mexican historical figures.

d. List three states of Mexico.

e. Main language.

f. Type of government.

g. Relationship to Latin America.

h. Name of currency and relationship to U.S. dollar.

i. Main exports to U.S.

4. Dimensions of national culture and effective leadership patterns: Hofstede revisited[4]

purpose
To measure value systems.

group size
Any number.

time required
20 minutes.

exercise schedule

		unit time	total time
1 **Preparation**			
Complete inventory.			
2 **Class discussion**		20+ min	20+ min
Instructor leads a discussion on Hofstede's value system.			

In the questionnaire below, please indicate the extent to which you agree or disagree with each statement. For example, if you strongly agree with a particular statement, circle the 5 next to the statement.

1 = strongly disagree

2 = disagree

3 = neither agree nor disagree

4 = agree

5 = strongly agree

4 By Peter Dorfman, *Advances in International Comparative Management*, vol. 3, pages 127-150. Copyright 1988 by JAI Press Inc. Used with permission.

Questionnaire 2[5]

		strongly agree				strongly disagree
1	It is important to have job instructions spelled out in detail so that employees always know what they are expected to do.	1	2	3	4	5
2	Managers expect employees to closely follow instructions and procedures.	1	2	3	4	5
3	Rules and regulations are important because they inform employees what the organization expects of them.	1	2	3	4	5
4	Standard operating procedures are helpful to employees on the job.	1	2	3	4	5
5	Instructions for operations are important for employees on the job.	1	2	3	4	5
6	Group welfare is more important than individual rewards.	1	2	3	4	5
7	Group success is more important than individual success.	1	2	3	4	5
8	Being accepted by the members of your work group is very important.	1	2	3	4	5
9	Employees should pursue their own goals only after considering the welfare of the group.	1	2	3	4	5
10	Managers should encourage group loyalty even if individual goals suffer.	1	2	3	4	5

5 By Peter Dorfman, *Advances in International Comparative Management*, vol. 3, pages 127-150. Copyright 1988 by JAI Press Inc. Used with permission.

11	Individuals may be expected to give up their goals in order to benefit group success.	1 2 3 4 5
12	Managers should make most decisions without consulting subordinates.	1 2 3 4 5
13	Managers should frequently use authority and power when dealing with subordinates.	1 2 3 4 5
14	Managers should seldom ask for the opinions of employees.	1 2 3 4 5
15	Managers should avoid off-the-job social contacts with employees.	1 2 3 4 5
16	Employees should not disagree with management decisions.	1 2 3 4 5
17	Managers should not delegate important tasks to employees.	1 2 3 4 5
18	Managers should help employees with their family problems.	1 2 3 4 5
19	Managers should see to it that employees are adequately clothed and fed.	1 2 3 4 5
20	A manager should help employees solve their personal problems.	1 2 3 4 5
21	Management should see that all employees receive health care.	1 2 3 4 5
22	Management should see that children of employees have an adequate education.	1 2 3 4 5

23   Management should provide legal assistance
     for employees who get into trouble with the law.   1   2   3   4   5

24   Managers should take care of their employees
     as they would their children.   1   2   3   4   5

25   Meetings are usually run more effectively
     when they are chaired by a man.   1   2   3   4   5

26   It is more important for men to have a
     professional career than it is for women to
     have a professional career.   1   2   3   4   5

27   Men usually solve problems with logical
     analysis; women usually solve problems with
     intuition.   1   2   3   4   5

28   Solving organizational problems usually
     requires an active, forcible approach, which
     is typical of men.   1   2   3   4   5

29   It is preferable to have a man, rather than
     a woman, in a high-level position.   1   2   3   4   5

Background work values[6]

Geert Hofstede examined international differences in work-related values and came up with the four dimensions: power distance, uncertainty avoidance, individualism and masculinity. Below are brief definitions of each of the four dimensions.

POWER DISTANCE (PD) measures human inequality in organizations, looking at the boss's decision-making style, employees' fear of disagreeing with the superior, and how subordinates prefer a boss to make decisions. Power distance assesses the interpersonal power or influence between lower- and higher-ranking employees, as perceived by the less powerful one. Essentially, it looks at how less powerful people validate the power structure. Cultures with a low score tend to respect individuals, strive for equality and value happiness. Those with a high score look to servitude and tact of lesser individuals, while allowing great privileges to those with influence. Other characteristics of low-scored cultures are that managers tend to consult subordinates when making decisions, perceived work ethic is stronger, close supervision is evaluated negatively by subordinates, and employees are cooperative. High scorers are less likely to have managers consult subordinates, and employees are reluctant to trust each other.

UNCERTAINTY AVOIDANCE (UA) explains each society's Search for Truth and the anxiety people feel in a situation with conflicting values or unstructured outcomes. Cultures with high uncertainty avoidance try to minimize the anxiety with a thorough set of strict laws and behavior norms. To ease the discomfort on the philosophical level, there is a belief in One Truth, the One Way. Low uncertainty avoidance cultures tend to have fewer rules and more acceptance of diversity of thought and behavior. Organizations, too, try to avoid uncertainty by creating rules, rituals and technology that give the illusion of predictability. Even group decision-making, however, is a means for avoiding risk because no one is held accountable. Countries that have low UA tend to have less emotional resistance to change, a stronger achievement motivation, a preference for managerial careers over specialist fields, and hope for success. On the other hand, countries with high UA tend to have more emotional resistance to change, weaker achievement motivation, a preference for specialist careers over managerial, and a fear of failure.

INDIVIDUALISM (I) looks at the degree to which people are part of groups or on their own. In collective societies, everyone is born into a strong clan of uncles, aunts and cousins (even third and fourth) who are part of one unit. Each person contributes to the group and at some time receives care from the group. Loyalties are to the group above everything else. In more individualistic societies, people are more or less on their own and are expected to take care of themselves and their immediate family. In collective countries (with a low I score), there is often an emotional dependence on the company, managers aspire to conformity and orderliness, group decisions are considered better than individual ones, and managers value security in their work. In societies with a high I score, though, there is more emotional independence from the

---

6 By Peter Dorfman, *Advances in International Comparative Management*, vol. 3, pages 127-150. Copyright 1988 by JAI Press Inc. Used with permission.

company; managers aspire to leadership and variety; managers seek input from others, but individual decisions are still seen as better; and managers value autonomy in their work.

MASCULINITY (M) versus its opposite, femininity, examines how roles are distributed between the sexes. The predominant pattern of socialization worldwide is for men to be more assertive and women to be more nurturing. In countries with high M scores, the successful manager is seen as more male – aggressive, competitive, just and tough – and not as feminine – soft, yielding, intuitive and emotional (as the stereotypes define it). In countries with high M scores, earnings, recognition and advancement are important to employees, work is more central to people's lives, achievement is defined in terms of wealth and professional success, people prefer more salary rather than fewer working hours, "Theory X" gets some acceptance, and there is higher job stress. In societies with low M scores, on the other hand, cooperation and security are valued by employees, work is less central to people's lives, achievement is defined in terms of human interactions, people prefer fewer working hours rather than more salary, "Theory X" is less accepted, and there is lower job stress.

Table 1
Culture Dimension Scores for Ten Countries[7]

PD = Power Distance; ID = Individualism; MA = Masculinity; UA = Uncertainty Avoidance; LT = Long Term Orientation

H = top third, M = medium third, L = bottom third (among 53 countries and regions for the first four dimensions; among 23 countries for the fifth)

	PD	ID	MA	UA	LT
USA	40 L	91 H	62 H	46 L	29 L
Germany	35 L	67 H	66 H	65 M	31 M
Japan	54 M	46 M	95 H	92 H	80 H
France	68 H	71 H	43 M	86 H	30'L
Netherlands	38 L	80 H	14 L	53 M	44 M
Hong Kong	68 H	25 L	57 H	29 L	96 H
Indonesia	78 H	14 L	46 M	48 L	25'L
West Africa	77 H	20 L	46 M	54 M	16 L
Russia	95*H	50*M	40*L	90*H	10*L
China	80*H	20*L	50*M	60*M	118 H

* estimated

7 Excerpted from Geert Hofstede, *Academy of Management Executive,*7(1), 1993, 81-94. Used with permission.

5. Alcot Sato Machine Tool Company[8]

Additional topics covered: joint ventures, cross-cultural issues,
foreign competition and protectionism.

George Alcot leaned back in his leather chair. Gazing across the massive oak desk
and through a big picture window, he watched the dismal drizzle obscure the
building across the street. He reflected that Cincinnati in late winter was indeed a
dreary place. As CEO of Alcot Sato, Inc., George spent several weeks a year traveling to the company's subsidiaries abroad. He had just come back from his latest
round of visits and was both encouraged and dismayed by what he had found. The
weather seemed to foster reflection and reminiscences. George began to think about
the beginnings of grandfather Alcot's machine tool business in the 1890s.

Back in the "olden days," so the Alcot family history went, Samuel Eliot Alcot
joined many other Cincinnati-based entrepreneurs in founding a small machine tool
company making metalworking lathes for an industrializing America. "Well,"
George mused, "we had about 70 years to do things the way Grandpa did. But now
the machine tool business is truly international." The Alcot Company, like other
U.S. machine tool companies, enjoyed an environment almost free from foreign
competition in the half-century before World War II and the two decades that
followed. U.S. technology was pre-eminent and was particularly strong after World
War II left Japan and German industry in ruins. In the mid-1960s, U.S. machine tool
exports from companies like Alcot were more than four times imports. Those
machines that were imported were cheap and shoddy in quality. Designed for special
and simple jobs, the imports did not eat into principal U.S. markets.

In 1980, Alcot's world changed. The Japanese made a major commitment to develop
their machine tool business worldwide. The National Machine Tool Builders'
Association (the U.S. trade association, a lobbying organization) began to worry.

Gloomily, George remembered what the Japanese thrust into the world market
meant when the 1981 recession hit. Sales of U.S.-made machine tools dropped 65
percent and most producers went into debt. About 25 percent of the small producers
went out of business. By 1984, sales of U.S.-made tools were running at less than
half the 1980 level. Although the National Machine Tool Builders' Association
lobbied furiously for protection through quotas, the Reagan administration was not
inclined to help. The plight of the American machine tool industry was underscored
in a report of the National Research Council. In 1983, the Council reported that
"the American industry is beginning to lag behind in technological leadership to the
Japanese and West German industries. ... American machine tool builders are
significantly behind in the organization and technology utilized in the production
processes." (*The Wall Street Journal*, Sept. 4, 1984, p. 25).

---

3 By Heidi Vernon-Wortzel, Northeastern University. Used with permission.

The Japanese threat was brought home to Alcot and other U.S. machine tool makers such as Cincinnati Milacron and Houdaille Industries. Japan's Mazak Corporation, the U.S. subsidiary of Japan's largest machine tool maker, Yamazaki Machinery Works, built a fully automated plant in Florence, Kentucky. This new plant was far more modern than its Ohio-based neighbors and was likely to outproduce them with products that were "state-of-the-art." The computer-controlled lathes and machining centers produced by Mazak were, themselves, made under the control of a sophisticated central computer.

George did not sit idly by when the industry began to change. In the early 1980s, realizing that the Japanese were in the machine tool business to stay, Alcot sold 51 percent of the company to Sato Milling Machine, Ltd., a Japanese machine tool builder. The company, now known as Alcot Sato Milling Machine, Inc., continued to make lathes, but it assembled Sato-designed machining centers that used Japanese parts. In 1983, Alcot Sato established a plant in Singapore that sold highly auto-mated lathes built by a West German manufacturer. The company also had a small plant in Taiwan. By 1985, none of the machines made by Alcot were made by one nationality. The machining centers assembled in the United States had half U.S. and half Japanese parts and labor. The German-designed lathes were assembled in the United States using some locally made parts and electronic controls. The Singapore plant made lathes designed by Alcot Sato (U.S.) but contained parts made in the U.S., Japan and Singapore. The Singapore plant, in 1986, began production on a small machining center designed by Sato (Japan) containing Japanese parts. The Taiwanese and Japanese plants made machining centers. The Japanese parent company conducted business on its own as well as with Alcot Sato.

By 1991, the machine tool business had changed dramatically. The U.S. auto industry, a huge machine tool customer, was in a slump and Japanese competition was increasing. Some companies began to look for new markets in Western and Eastern Europe. Litton Industries, for example, won a huge contract for machine tools used in making engines, transmissions, and brake systems for Ford Motor in Britain. Giddings & Lewis, Inc. tried to drum up business in Eastern Europe and the disintegrating Soviet Union.

With a sigh, George turned to his in-basket full of letters and memos that his secretary, Peter, had left while he had been on his travels. How would George respond most effectively to the problems and opportunities posed by these letters?

Mr. George E. Alcot
Chief Executive Officer
Alcot Sato Machine Tools
Cincinnati, Ohio

Dear Mr. Alcot:

Allow me to introduce myself. My name is Alexsander Nobokov. I represent a major machine tool factory in Kazan, which is located 800 miles east of Moscow at the head of the Volga River. Our capacity is huge and we have highly skilled workers. We are seeking an American company as a joint venture partner.

I should tell you a little about the new opportunities that exist between our two countries. In 1988, the U.S. sold slightly more than $1 million in tools to our country while the West Germans topped $500 million. American tool manufacturers would benefit by having operations in the Soviet Union and especially Kazan.

In 1987, our government established a new policy to encourage joint ventures in the Soviet Union. Now joint ventures are protected under Soviet legislation as are their intellectual property rights. We also allow the Western partner to select top management. As of April 1, 1989, the Soviet Union granted direct international trade rights to all Soviet enterprises as long as they did not require hard currency. By the end of March 1989, more than 300 Western firms had entered joint ventures, 90 percent of which were capitalized at less than $10 million. We know that the political situation is not entirely clear, but it will not affect foreign investment.

Many American and European firms continue to approach us with propositions. Perhaps you are familiar with the joint venture Khomatek. In this joint venture, the Soviet partner is Sergo Orzhonikidze Machine Tool Works. The West German partner is Heinemann Maschinen-und-Anlagaenbau GmbH. This company makes lathes, machine tools, and flexible production models. It is doing extremely well and we expect that others like it will also succeed.

We hope that you will respond to this letter and begin talks on a possible joint venture.

Sincerely yours,

Alexsander Nobokov

TO: George E. Alcot, CEO
FROM: James L. Gordon, Marketing Director
RE: Staffing of Marketing Department

As you know, we are entering our recruitment period for marketing department personnel. I have spent considerable time on the phone with Yoshi Yawasaki, director of marketing of Sato Milling. We seem to have a problem that neither of us can resolve. I would like to hire two recent MBA graduates as marketing trainees for our products in Asia. Yoshi is convinced that we should hire two young men who will be graduating from Tokyo University this June. He tells me that the Japanese will understand Asian culture better and will be able to communicate more effectively with our subsidiaries in Singapore and Taiwan. He acknowledges that the MBAs are far more proficient in marketing theory and quantitative aspects but thinks that a longer training period will more than make up for initial lack of skills. He would like to put the two men through a rotating two year training period, moving them through all of the operations in Japan and elsewhere.

My own view is that the MBAs will be able to help us in six months. I do not think that Japanese language skills will be any particular benefit. In Singapore and Taiwan, most of the people with whom they will deal speak English. Since they will be working in the U.S. eventually, I think the Americans will fit in better. By the way, one of the American MBAs is a woman.

I would appreciate your feedback as soon as possible.

Mr. George E. Alcot
CEO
Alcot-Sato, Inc.
Cincinnati, OH

Dear Mr. Alcot:

I am writing to you for support as we lobby for trade relief. As you know, the machine tool industry has suffered greatly from the vast quantities of European and Japanese machine tool imports. May 1990 statistics showed that orders for lathes, grinders, milling machines, machining centers, and boring mills were $137.6 million, down by 7 percent from 1989. Although orders for metal-forming presses were up from 1989, they were down from last month.

If we listen to Congress, it is apparent that defense spending is going to be cut. Defense-oriented aerospace concerns will soon have a great deal of excess capacity, discouraging them from buying new machinery. With the circumstances in Eastern Europe and the Soviet Union, we cannot be sure of what our national security needs will be.

We also see that producers of cars, trucks, and automotive parts are ordering slowly because their own sales are sluggish. With the economy in this general recession we are particularly vulnerable to foreign competition.

As you know, we have had a "voluntary restraint agreement" (VRA) with Japan and Taiwan for the past five years. This agreement, which is now almost at its end, must be renewed. We at the NMTBA want this agreement to be renewed even though it is incomplete and excludes imports from Germany and Switzerland.

We think that Congress should give American companies some protection from foreign competition. We rely on your contribution to help us continue our essential work.

Sincerely yours,

John McDaniels
National Machine Tool
Builders' Association

Mr. George E. Alcot
CEO
Alcot Sato, Inc.
Cincinnati, OH

Dear Mr. Alcot:

I am the organizer of the Hanover European Machine Tool Fair. I would like to invite your company to take exhibition space at our fair. The space will cost $35 a square meter, a small price to pay for access to the 35,000 visitors we expect this year. We hope your firm will join us and will take advantage of the superb advertising opportunity that this fair offers.

Sincerely yours,

Hans Mann
127 Domstrasse
Hanover, Germany

assignment

Prepare an answer for each letter.

Cultural constraints in management theories[9]

Executive overview

Management as the word is presently used is an American invention. In other parts of the world, not only the practices but the entire concept of management may differ, and the theories needed to understand it may deviate considerably from what is considered normal and desirable in the United States. The reader is invited on a trip around the world, and both local management practices and theories are explained from the different contexts and histories of the places visited: Germany, Japan, France, Holland, the adopted countries of the overseas Chinese, Southeast Asia, Africa, Russia, and finally mainland China.

A model in which worldwide differences in national cultures are categorized according to five independent dimensions helps in explaining the differences in management found, although the situation in each country or region has unique characteristics that no model can account for. One practical application of the model is in demonstrating the relative position of the U.S. versus other parts of the world. In a global perspective, U.S. management theories contain a number of idiosyncrasies not necessarily shared by management elsewhere. Three such idiosyncrasies are mentioned: a stress on market processes, a stress on the individual, and a focus on managers rather than on workers. A plea is made for an internationalization not only of business, but also of management theories, as a way of enriching theories at the national level.

Alice's croquet-playing problems are good analogies to attempts to build culture-free theories of management. Concepts available for this purpose are themselves alive with culture, having been developed within a particular cultural context. They have a tendency to guide our thinking toward our desired conclusion.

In my view

Lewis Carroll's *Alice in Wonderland* contains the famous story of Alice's croquet game with the Queen of Hearts.

> Alice thought she had never seen such a curious croquet-ground in all her life; it was all ridges and furrows; the balls were live hedgehogs, the mallets live flamingoes, and the soldiers had to double themselves up and stand on their hands and feet to make the arches.

You probably know how the story goes: Alice's flamingo mallet turns its head whenever she wants to strike with it, her hedgehog ball runs away, and the doubled-up soldier arches walk around all the time. The only rule seems to be that the Queen of Hearts always wins.

As the same reasoning may also be applied to the arguments in this article, I had better tell you my conclusion before I continue – so that the rules of my game are understood. In this article, we take a trip around the world to demonstrate that there are no such things as universal management theories.

---

9   Excerpted from Geert Hofstede, *Academy of Management Executive,*7(1), 1993, 81-94. Used with permission.

Dorothy Marcic and Sheila Puffer, *Management International,* West Publishing, 1994.

Germany

Elements of the medieval guild system have survived in historical continuity in Germany until the present day. In particular, a very effective apprenticeship system exists both on the shop floor and in the office, which alternates practical work and classroom courses. At the end of the apprenticeship, the worker receives a certificate, the Facharbeiterbrief, which is recognized throughout the country. About-two thirds of the German worker population hold such a certificate and a corresponding occupational pride. In fact, quite a few German company presidents have worked their way up from the ranks through an apprenticeship. In comparison, two-thirds of the worker population in Britain have no occupational qualification at all.

> The manager is not a cultural hero in Germany. If anybody, it is the engineer who fills the hero role. Frederick Taylor's *Scientific Management* was conceived in a society of immigrants – where large number of workers with diverse backgrounds and skills had to work together. In Germany, this heterogeneity never existed.

Business schools are virtually unknown in Germany. Native German management theories concentrate on formal systems. The inapplicability of American concepts of management was quite apparent in 1973, when the U.S. consulting firm of Booz, Allen and Hamilton, commissioned by the German Ministry of Economic Affairs, wrote a study of German management from an American viewpoint. The report is highly critical and writes among other things that "Germans simply do not have a very strong concept of management." Since 1973, from my personal experience, the situation has not changed much. However, during this period, the German economy has performed in a superior fashion to the U.S. in virtually all respects, so a strong concept of management might have been a liability rather than an asset.

> The highly skilled and responsible German workers do not necessarily need a manager, American-style, to "motivate" them. They expect their boss or Meister to assign their tasks and to be the expert in resolving technical problems. Comparisons of similar German, British and French organizations show the Germans as having the highest rate of personnel in productive roles and the lowest both in leadership and staff roles.

Japan

The American type of manager is also missing in Japan. In the United States, the core of the enterprise is the managerial class. The core of the Japanese enterprise is the permanent worker group, workers who for all practical purposes are tenured and who aspire to lifelong employment. They are distinct from the non-permanent employees – most women and subcontracted teams led by gang bosses to be laid off in slack periods. University graduates in Japan first join the permanent worker group and subsequently fill various positions, moving from line to staff as the need occurs while being paid according to seniority rather than position. They take part in Japanese-style group consultation sessions for important decisions, which extend the decision-making period but guarantee fast implementation afterwards. Japanese are to a large extent controlled by their peer group rather than by their manager.

Three researchers from the East-West Center of the University of Hawaii, Joseph Tobin, David Wu and Dana Danielson, did an observation study of typical preschools in three countries: China, Japan and the United States. Their results have been published both as a book and as a video. In the Japanese preschool, one teacher handled twenty-eight four-year-olds. The video shows one particularly obnoxious boy, Hiroki, who fights with other children and throws teaching materials down from the balcony. When a little girl tries to alarm the teacher, the latter answers, "What are you calling me for? Do something about it!" In the U.S. preschool, there is one adult for every nine children. This class has its problem child too,

Glen, who refuses to clear away his toys. One of the teachers has a long talk with him and isolates him in a corner, until he changes his mind. It doesn't take much imagination to realize that managing Hiroki thirty years later will require a different process from managing Glen.

There are no secrets of Japanese management, however; it is even doubtful whether there is such a thing as management, in the American sense, in Japan at all. The secret is in Japanese society; and if any group in society should be singled out as carriers of the secret, it is the workers, not the managers.

American theories of leadership are ill-suited to the Japanese group-controlled situation. During the past two decades, the Japanese have developed their own "PM" theory of leadership, in which P stands for performance and M for maintenance. The latter is less a concern for individual employees than for maintaining social stability. In view of the amazing success of the Japanese economy in the past thirty years, many Americans have sought the secrets of Japanese management, hoping to copy them.

France

The manager, U.S.-style, does not exist in France either. In a very enlightening book, unfortunately not yet translated into English, the French researcher Philippe d'Iribarne (1989) describes the results of in-depth observation and interview studies of management methods in three subsidiary plants of the same French multinational: in France, the United States and Holland. He relates what he finds to information about the three societies in general. Where necessary, he goes back in history to trace the roots of the strikingly different behaviors in the completion of the same tasks.

The French do not think in terms of managers versus non-managers but in terms of cadres versus non-cadres; one becomes cadre by attending the proper schools and one remains it forever; regardless of their actual task, cadres have the privileges of a higher social class, and it is very rare for a non-cadre to cross the ranks.

He identifies three kinds of basic principles (logiques) of management. In the U.S., the principle is the fair contract between employer and employee, which gives the manager considerable prerogatives, but within limits. This is really a labor market in which the worker sells his or her labor for a price. In France, the principle is the honor of each class in a society that has always been and remains extremely stratified, in which superiors behave as superior beings and subordinates accept and expect this, conscious of their own lower level in the national hierarchy but also of the honor of their own class.

The conflict between French and American theories of management became apparent in the beginning of the twentieth century, in a criticism by the great French management pioneer Henri Fayol (1841-1925) on his U.S. colleague and contemporary Frederick W. Taylor (1856-1915). The difference in career paths of the two men is striking. Fayol was a French engineer whose career as a cadre superieur culminated in the position of President-Directeur-General of a mining company. After his retirement, he formulated his experiences in a path-breaking text on organization: *Administration industrielle et generale,* in which he focused on the sources of authority. Taylor was an American engineer who started his career in industry as a worker and attained his academic qualifications through evening studies. From chief engineer in a steel company, he became one of the first management consultants.

Taylor was not really concerned with the issue of authority at all; his focus was on efficiency. He proposed to split the task of the first-line boss into eight specialisms, each exercised by a different person; an idea which eventually led to the idea of a matrix organization.

Taylor's work appeared in a French translation in 1913, and Fayol read it and showed himself generally impressed but shocked by Taylor's "denial of the principle of the Unity of Command" in the case of the eight-boss system.

Seventy years later, Andre Laurent, another of Fayol's compatriots, found that French managers in a survey reacted very strongly against a suggestion that one employee could report to two different bosses, while U.S. managers in the same survey showed fewer misgivings. Matrix organization has never become popular in France as it has in the United States.

Holland

In terms of management theories, both motivation and leadership in Holland are different from what they are in the United States. Leadership in Holland presupposes modesty, as opposed to assertiveness in the United States. No U.S. leadership theory has room for that. Working in Holland is not a constant feast, however. There is a built-in premium on mediocrity and jealousy, as well as time-consuming ritual consultations to maintain the appearance of consensus and the pretense of modesty. There is unfortunately another side to every coin.

In my own country, Holland, or as it is officially called, the Netherlands, a study by Philippe d'Iribarne found the management principle to be a need for consensus among all parties, neither predetermined by a contractual relationship nor by class distinctions but based on an open-ended exchange of views and a balancing of interests. In terms of the different origins of the word "manager," the organization in Holland is more menage (household), while in the United States it is more manege (horse drill).

At my university, the University of Limburg at Maastricht, every semester we receive a class of American business students who take a program in European Studies. We asked both the Americans and a matched group of Dutch students to describe their ideal job after graduation, using a list of twenty-two job characteristics. The Americans attached significantly more importance than the Dutch to earnings, advancement, benefits, a good working relationship with their boss, and security of employment. The Dutch attached more importance to freedom to adopt their own approach to the job, being consulted by their boss in his or her decisions, training opportunities, contributing to the success of their organization, fully using their skills and abilities, and helping others. This list confirms d'Iribarne's findings of a contractual employment relationship in United States, based on earnings and career opportunities, against a consensual relationship in Holland. The latter has centuries-old roots; the Netherlands was the first republic in Western Europe (1609-1810) and a model for the American republic. The country has been and still is governed by a careful balancing of interests in a multiparty system.

The overseas Chinese

Among the champions of economic development in the past thirty years we find three countries mainly populated by Chinese living outside the Chinese mainland: Taiwan, Hong Kong and Singapore. Moreover, overseas Chinese play a very important role in the economies of Indonesia, Malaysia, the Philippines and Thailand, where they form an ethnic minority. If anything, the "little dragons" – Taiwan, Hong Kong and Singapore – have been more economically successful than Japan, moving from rags to riches and now counted among the world's wealthy industrial countries. Yet very little attention has been paid to the way in which their enterprises have been managed. *The Spirit of Chinese Capitalism* by Gordon Redding (1990), the British dean of the Hong Kong Business School, is an excellent book about Chinese business. He bases his insights on personal acquaintance and in-depth discussions with a large number of overseas Chinese businesspeople.

Overseas Chinese American enterprises lack almost all characteristics of modern management. They tend to be small, cooperating for essential functions with other small organizations through networks based on personal relations. They are family-owned, without the separation between ownership and management typical in the West, or even in Japan and Korea. They normally focus on one product or market, with growth by opportunistic diversification;

in this, they are extremely flexible. Decision-making is centralized in the hands of one dominant family member, but other family members may be given new ventures to try their skills on.

Overseas Chinese prefer economic activities in which great gains can be made with little manpower, like commodity trading and real estate. They employ few professional managers, except their sons and sometimes daughters who have been sent to prestigious business schools abroad, but who upon return continue to run the family business the Chinese way.

The origin of this system, or – in the Western view – this lack of system, is found in the history of Chinese society, in which there were no formal laws, only formal networks of powerful people guided by general principles of Confucian virtue. The favors of the authorities could change daily, so nobody could be trusted except one's kinfolk – of whom, fortunately, there used to be many, in an extended family structure. The overseas Chinese way of doing business is also very well-adapted to their position in the countries in which they form ethnic minorities, often envied and threatened by ethnic violence.

Chinese American enterprises are low-profile and extremely cost-conscious, applying Confucian virtues of thrift and persistence. Their size is kept small by the assumed lack of loyalty of non-family employees, who, if they are any good, will just wait and save until they can start their own family business.

Overseas Chinese businesses following this unprofessional approach command a collective gross national product of some 200 to 300 billion U.S. dollars, exceeding the GNP of Australia. There is no denying that it works.

Management transfer to poor countries

Four-fifths of the world's population live in countries that are poor.

After World War II and decolonization, the stated purpose of the United Nations and the World Bank has been to promote the development of all the world's countries in a war on poverty. After forty years, it looks very much like we are losing this war. If one thing has become clear, it is that the export of Western – mostly American – management practices and theories to poor countries has contributed little or nothing to their development. There has been no lack of effort and money spent for this purpose: Students from poor countries have been trained in this country, and teachers and Peace Corps workers have been sent to the poor countries. If nothing else, the general lack of success in economic development of other countries should be sufficient argument to doubt the validity of Western management theories in non-Western environments.

If we examine different parts of the world, the development picture is not equally bleak, and history is often a better predictor than economic factors for what happens today. There is a broad regional pecking order with East Asia leading. The little dragons have passed into the camp of the wealthy; then follow Southeast Asia (with its overseas Chinese minorities), Latin America (in spite of the debt crisis), South Asia; Africa always trails behind. Several African countries have only become poorer since decolonization.

Regions of the world with a history of large-scale political integration and civilization generally have done better than regions in which no large-scale political and cultural infrastructure existed, even if the old civilizations had decayed or been suppressed by colonizers. It has become painfully clear that development cannot be pressure-cooked; it presumes a cultural infrastructure that takes time to grow. Local management is part of this infrastructure, it cannot be imported in package form. Assuming that, with so-called modern management techniques and theories, outsiders can develop a country has proven a deplorable arrogance. At best, one can hope for a dialogue between equals with the locals, in which the Western partner acts as the expert in Western technology and the local partner as the expert in local culture, habits and feelings.

Russia and China

The crumbling of the former Eastern bloc has left us with a scattering of states and would-be states of which the political and economic future is extremely uncertain. The best predictions are those based on a knowledge of history because historical trends have taken revenge on the arrogance of the Soviet rulers who believed they could turn them around by brute power. One obvious fact is that the former bloc is extremely heterogeneous, including countries traditionally closely linked with the West by trade and travel, like the Czech Republic, Hungary, Slovenia and the Baltic states, as well as others with a Byzantine or Turkish past; some having been prosperous, others always extremely poor.

The industrialized Western world and the World Bank seem committed to helping the ex-Eastern bloc countries develop, but with the same technocratic neglect for local cultural factors that proved so unsuccessful in the development assistance to other poor countries. Free-market capitalism, introduced by Eastern-style management, is supposed to be the answer from Albania to Russia.

Let me limit myself to the Russian republic, a huge territory with some 140 million inhabitants, mainly Russians. We know quite a bit about the Russians as their country was a world power for several hundreds of years before communism, and in the nineteenth and twentieth centuries it has produced some of the greatest writers in world literature. If I want to understand the Russians – including how they could for so long support the Soviet regime – I tend to re-read Lev Nikolayevich Tolstoy. In his most famous novel, *Anna Karenina* (1876), one of the main characters is a landowner, Levin, whom Tolstoy uses to express his own views and convictions about his people. Russian peasants used to be serfs; serfdom had been abolished in 1861, but the peasants, now tenants, remained as passive as before. Levin wanted to break this passivity by dividing the land among his peasants in exchange for a share of the crops; but the peasants only let the land deteriorate further. Here follows a quote:

> (Levin) read political economy and socialistic works…but, as he had expected, found nothing in them related to his undertaking. In the political economy books – in (John Stuart) Mill, for instance, whom he studied first and with great ardour, hoping every minute to find an answer to the questions that were engrossing him – he found only certain laws deduced from the state of agriculture in Europe; but he could not for the life of him see why these laws, which did not apply to Russia, should be considered universal. …Political economy told him that the laws by which Europe had developed and was developing her wealth were universal and absolute. Socialist teaching told him that development along those lines leads to ruin. And neither of them offered the smallest enlightenment as to what he, Levin, and all the Russian peasants and landowners were to do with their millions of hands and millions of acres, to make them as productive as possible for the common good.

Citing Tolstoy, I implicitly suggest that management theorists cannot neglect the great literature of the countries they want their ideas to apply to. The greatest novel in Chinese literature is considered Cao Xueqin's *The Story of the Stone,* also known as *The Dream of the Red Chamber,* which appeared around 1760. It describes the rise and fall of two branches of an aristocratic family in Beijing, who live on adjacent plots in the capital. Their plots are joined by a magnificent garden with several pavilions in it, and the young, mostly female members of both families are allowed to live in them. One day, the management of the garden is taken over by a young woman, Tan-Chun, who states:

> I think we ought to pick out a few experienced trustworthy old women from among the ones who work in the Garden – women who know something about gardening already – and put the upkeep of the Garden into their hands. We needn't ask them to pay us rent; all we need ask them for is an annual share of the produce. There would be four advantages in this arrangement. In the first place, if we have people whose sole occupation is to look after trees and flowers and so on, the condition of the Garden will improve gradually year after year and there

In the summer of 1991, the Russian lands yielded a record harvest, but a large share of it rotted in the fields because no people were to be found for harvesting. The passivity is still there, and not only among the peasants. And the heirs of John Stuart Mill (whom we met before as one of the early analysts of "management") again present their universal recipes, which simply do not apply.

will be no more of those long periods of neglect followed by bursts of feverish activity when things have been allowed to get out of hand. Secondly, there won't be the spoiling and wasteage we get at present. Thirdly, the women themselves will gain a little extra to add to their incomes which will compensate them for the hard work they put in throughout the year. And fourthly, there's no reason why we shouldn't use the money we should otherwise have spent on nurserymen, rockery specialists, horticultural cleaners and so on for other purposes.

As the story goes on, the capitalist privatization – because that is what it is – of the garden is carried through, and it works. When in the 1980s Deng Xiaoping allowed privatization in the Chinese villages, it also worked. It worked so well that its effects started to be felt in politics and threatened the existing political order; hence the knockdown at Tienanmen Square of June 1989. But it seems that the forces of privatization are getting the upper hand again in China. If we remember what Chinese entrepreneurs are able to do once they have become overseas Chinese, we shouldn't be too surprised. But what works in China – and worked two centuries ago – does not have to work in Russia, not in Tolstoy's days and not today. I am not offering a solution; I only protest against a naive universalism that knows only one recipe for development, the one supposed to have worked in the United States.

A theory of culture in management

Management is not a phenomenon that can be isolated from other processes taking place in a society. During our trip around the world, we saw that management interacts with what happens in the family, at school, in politics and government. It is obviously also related to religion and to beliefs about science. Theories of management always had to be interdisciplinary, but if we cross national borders they should become more interdisciplinary than ever.

Our trip around the world is over and we are back in the United States. What have we learned? There is something in all countries called "management," but its meaning differs to a larger or smaller extent from one country to the next, and it takes considerable historical and cultural insight into local conditions to understand its processes, philosophies and problems. If already the word may mean so many different things, how can we expect one country's theories of management to apply abroad? One should be extremely careful in making this assumption, and test it before considering it proven.

Conclusion

This article started with *Alice in Wonderland*. In fact, the management theorist who ventures outside his or her own country into other parts of the world is like Alice in Wonderland. He or she will meet strange beings, customs, ways of organizing or disorganizing and theories that are clearly stupid, old-fashioned or even immoral – yet they may work, or at least they may not fail more frequently than corresponding theories do at home. Then, after the first culture shock, the traveler to Wonderland will feel enlightened, and may be able to take his or her experiences home and use them advantageously. All great ideas in science, politics and management have traveled from one country to another and been enriched by foreign influences. The roots of American management theories are mainly in Europe – with Adam Smith, John Stuart Mill, Lev Tolstoy, Max Weber, Henri Fayol, Sigmund Freud, Kurt Lewin and many others. These theories were replanted here and they developed and bore fruit. The same may happen again. The last thing we need is a Monroe Doctrine for management ideas.

Global corporate competition:
Is the large American firm
an endangered species?[10]

This article provides a thirty-year overview of global corporate competition. In large measure, it is an update through 1990 of findings presented in the article, "Global Corporate Competition: Who's Winning, Who's Losing, and the R&D Factor as One Reason Why," published in the Strategic Management Journal (Franko 1989a). Like the recent film, *Naked Gun 2 1/2*, the results turn out to be "more than a sequel." Alas, those results – at least from the perspective of U.S.-headquartered big business firms – are vastly less amusing than the aforementioned film.

U.S. dominance of the world banking industry is but a dim memory, with no U.S. bank on the list of top 12 by assets and only one – Citibank at number 18 – among the leading 25.

The 1960-80 erosion of the global position of large U.S. industrial and banking enterprises documented two years ago not only continues, it appears to have accelerated during the late 1980s. Indeed, the erosion of the U.S. corporate position – or, if one prefers, the rise of non-U.S. enterprises – has begun to be noticeable in high-tech and resource-based sectors, such as computers and office equipment, aerospace, pharmaceutical, and paper and forest products – areas seemingly immune from declines in U.S. dominance even during the mid-1980s.

Propelled by computer downsizing, small copiers and a monopoly on fax machines, the Japanese onslaught of computers and office equipment appears stronger than ever. Airbus continues to do more than irritate Boeing and McDonnell-Douglas in aerospace. Heavy electrical and telecommunications equipment are more and more dominated by European firms, as Japan and, more recently, South Korea consolidate the non-U.S. hold on consumer electronics. BMW joins the "top 12" for the first time in autos and trucks, and European firms also seize the high road to 1992 in paper and non-ferrous metals.

Winners and losers

While firm-based data on winners and losers in rankings and "world market share" constitute an imperfect scorecard, over time they do help keep score. In very broad outline, the story told by the numbers in Tables 1 and 2, industry by industry, is as follows.

Aerospace. American firms are still dominant, with a nearly 80 percent world market share in 1990. The rise of British Aerospace and Rolls Royce may be exaggerated by those firms' recent acquisitions outside of their main industry (Rover cars by British Aerospace, and Northern Engineering, a turbine firm, by Rolls Royce). Still, the decline in U.S. position since the mid-1980s is consistent with the end of the U.S. defense-contract boom, with Rolls Royce's technology-led gains in the jet engine business, and with British Aerospace's participation in the European Airbus consortium – whose worldwide sales prowess, if not profit success, is now uncontested.

Autos and Trucks. The mid-1980s resurgence in the competitive position of the U.S. auto producers may well have been ephemeral. The world market share of Detroit's Big Three has fallen from 50 percent in 1986 to 38 percent in 1990 – both figures a far cry from the two-

10 Excerpted from Lawrence G. Franko, *Business Horizons*, Nov./Dec. 1991, 14-22. Used with permission.

thirds share enjoyed by U.S. firms in 1970 and the total dominance of the 1960s. The appearance of BMW on the list of the top 12 in 1990 seems symptomatic of a German, if not wider European, ability to exploit the model and market opportunities of 1992 and beyond. And the American firms are faced with a continuous gnawing away of their domestic position by Japanese transplants at home.

Banking. Much of the blame for the decline in the world position of U.S. banks can be laid macroeconomic factors, such as the (much) higher savings rates in Japan and Europe, as well as to the manifest absurdities of American banking law restraining interregional and financial services expansion by U.S. banks. Notwithstanding this, it is hard to escape the feeling that it took some special managerial genius for American banks to go from global dominance (67 percent of the assets of the world's top 12) in the 1970s to no presence at all by 1990. One clue may lie in the fact that the only U.S. bank still to be among the top 25 was also the only U.S. bank that seriously built a multinational presence within foreign markets when the opportunity was available. (Regarding the benefits to Citibank of being "global," see Lascelles 1991.)

Chemicals. Last year, 1992 saw the disappearance from the top 12 of Union Carbide, and thence the first truly notable realignment of rankings since the mid-1970s, when each of the three German giants overtook DuPont. The fruits of the Bhopal disaster, however, only accelerated a broader U.S. decline long signaled by a low level of R&D investment relative to industry peers and the distractions of unrelated diversifications.

Computers and Office Equipment. As already noted, the Japanese challenge to the U.S. is alive and well. Massive dominance by giant U.S. firms has been replaced by fragmentation among industry segments at home and a strong Asian incursion. But the large U.S. firms that have maintained their leadership position, especially Hewlett Packard and DEC, have notably maintained their R&D investments relative to sales revenues at levels in the industry reached only by Japan's Fujitsu among the big 12. All of the large firms, to be sure, also face attack on another front from smaller U.S. firms such as Apple, Compaq and Sun Microsystems. Whether these smaller U.S. firms will in turn grow large enough to pick up the slack of U.S.-company world market share lost by the declines of IBM and Unysis, and the departures from the list of CDC and Honeywell, remains to be seen.

Electrical Equipment and Electronics. The Japanese have won in consumer electronics and are being joined by the South Koreans. Were it not for General Electric, U.S. firms would have exited the list of the world's top 12 by 1988. The Europeans, especially Asea Brown Boveri of Sweden and Switzerland and Siemens of Germany, appear to be relegating GE (and Westinghouse) to also-ran status in heavy electrical equipment. On global competition in telecommunications, see Yoffie and Vietor 1991.) The diversifiers – or, as Peter Lynch of Magellan Fund fame used to put it, deworsifiers" – ITT, RCA and the UK's General Electric, are long gone from the majors.

The telecommunications equipment part of France's Alcatel alone is larger than the equipment division of AT&T. (The equipment part of AT&T itself is not large enough to make the top 12 list, although it used to be on it in the 1970s as Western Electric. That was before AT&T allowed itself, among other things, to be pre-empted in digital switching systems in its home market by Canada's Northern Telecom.

All is not necessarily lost for the U.S. electronics industry. Motorola is among the top 25 in the world; Intel ranks thirty-fifth. But they do not yet rival the non-Americans in scale and scope.

Food and Beverage Products. In spite of the best efforts of the leveraged buyout movement in the U.S. – which, as Alfred Chandler has noted (1990), especially affected and afflicted this sector of American industry – sales rankings show American firms (just) holding onto their historic

---

8   Excerpted from Lawrence G. Franko, *Business Horizons*, Nov./Dec. 1991, 14-22. Used with permission.

majority of world sales in these businesses. The departing Beatrice and Dart and Kraft have been replaced by Conagra and a transformed Philip Morris. Indeed, the "new news" is the rise of Continental European groups such as France BSN and Italy's Feruzzi. Renewed European market growth and future promise appear to have called forth renewed entrepreneurial dynamism.

Iron and Steel. Asia has won; big U.S steel is no more. Indeed, U.S. firms, no longer large enough to be among the top 12, are largely exiting the business, selling out to the Japanese or both. And "mini-mills" are just that relative to the impact this industry once had on U.S. economic activity, employment and incomes.

Petroleum Products.
For the first time, U.S. companies accounted for less than half of the world market in 1990. The era of the "seven sisters" is no more; Royal Dutch Shell, not Exxon, is now the world's largest oil enterprise; third-world National Champions joined the list; and French-company discoveries in the North Sea, dynamism and acquisitions have altered the industry.

Non-Ferrous Metals. The surprise here is a resurgent Germany, with the world market share of Metallgesellschaft, Degussa, Preussag and VIAG advancing rapidly during the 1980s to 44 percent by the end of 1990. The U.S. at 16 percent maintains its activity through Alcoa Reynolds in aluminum, but the days of dominance in copper are no more.

Industrial and Farm Equipment. The battering taken by Caterpillar in the early 1980s appears to have stopped; Deere is even back to number seven in the world rankings, after starting out the decade in sixth place, then falling to eleventh in 1986. The U.S.-firm share holds in the upper 20s, but the major successes during the 1980s were Japanese and Korean.

Paper and Forest Products. The stimulus of 1992 is visible again, with the Swedes leading the charge to consolidate their position in the EC through vertical and horizontal integration. In 1990, the "world market share" of Swedish firms reached 18 percent, while that of U.S. companies dropped to 62 percent. Some American firms, notably International Paper, have also been going global by entering the European market, but they appear to be following, not leading.

Pharmaceutical. In pharmaceuticals, U.S. companies also slipped just below half of the "world market share" of the 12 largest companies in 1990 for the first time. Notable was the reappearance of a UK firm on the list, SmithKline-Beecham, albeit due to the UK's Beechat taking over the American SmithKline. Not withstanding the influence of acquisition, this development does seem to reflect a broader surge of UK-firm activity in the world pharmaceutical industry; on recent growth form, it would not be a surprise to welcome Britain's Glaxo (number sixteen by our count, which includes Ciba-Geigy and the Pharma divisions of Bayer and Hoechst, not included in Fortune's ranking) to the top 12 in the near future. The appearance of Procordia of Sweden on the list also appears to realistically reflect a notable R&D dynamism in health care of firms based in that country.

Textiles. It was fashionable in the early 1980s to assert that the scale advantages of U.S. textile mills, plus the eternal appeal of Levi Strauss' blue jeans, would maintain the U.S. dominance of this industry. But something happened that halved the U.S. share of the "world industry" from 41 percent to 21 percent during the 1980s. Part of what happened was the rise of large Korean and Turkish producers; part was a lack of eternal appeal for Levis; and part may have been leveraged buyouts of formerly leading U.S. textile producers and a subsequent lack of investment therein.

Tires. As noted in my 1989 SMJ article, the handwriting had been on the wall for the U.S. tire industry for several years, even though the world market share figures (at 50 percent in both 1980 and 1986) showed a deceptive stability in the U.S. firms' global position. Too little R&D, too little presence in non-U.S. markets of more rapid market growth and leading-edge technological development, and too much conglomeration by Uniroyal, Goodrich, General, Firestone and even (so far) survivor

Goodyear caused the decline of the U.S. share of this industry to play out during the decade of the 1980s like a slow-motion Greek tragedy. The late 1980s LBOs of the terminally ill patients, and subsequent sales of the carcasses to France's Michelin, Japan's Bridgestone and Germany's Continental extracted the last bit of "shareholder value" from once-leading companies, but neither the LBOs nor the foreign acquisitions drove the underlying dynamic of the U.S. demise. Thus, the U.S. representation is down to one firm, itself a bit of a conglomerate struggling with a useless, unsalable pipeline activity, doing less R&D than at least two of its rivals, and without great presence in many of the growth markets of the new Europe and the newly industrializing countries.

Possible causes

There is a rich agenda of possible causes of the shifts in the global position of large firms based in different countries summarized in Table 1. Although statistical analyses along the lines of those undertaken for the 1970s are yet to be done, many of the hypotheses discussed therein retain their validity.

It seems no accident, for example, that in the computer and office equipment industry the survivors and gainers in rank through 1990 tended to have above-average R&D intensity (R&D-to-sales ratios) during the 1980s, whereas those who dropped off the list were of low R&D intensity, unrelated diversifiers, or both. Likewise, firms that were above average in R&D intensity in the early 1980s maintained or improved their rankings in aerospace, electrical equipment and pharmaceuticals, whereas firms neglecting R&D either slipped (American Home Products declined from third to eighth in pharmaceuticals), or dropped off (Westinghouse in electrical equipment, Warner-Lambert in pharmaceuticals).

The conglomerate, unrelated diversifiers of the 1970s, disproportionately of U.S. provenance and especially prevalent in electrical equipment and tires, also largely disappeared during the 1980s – both from the "world's largest" lists and, frequently, altogether. Focus, on the other hand, was related to success.

A global spread into foreign growth markets and lower-cost production sites appeared to count, too. The American firms surviving at or near the top of the computer, aerospace, chemical, auto, paper, pharmaceutical and tire industries had foreign sales percentages – and therefore access to non-U.S. growth markets – well above the majority of those leaving the top rank.

The late 1980s resurgence in European company dynamism so noticeable from Table 1, and so different from the Asian-dominated results through 1986 presented in the 1989 SMJ article, surely has much to do with the replacement of "Eurosclerosis" with "Europe 1992" and after-the Berlin-Wall European market dynamism. Those American (and Japanese) firms that had already built a marketing and production network capable of accessing renewed European growth and dynamism could now grow with the new Europe; those U.S. firms and banks (several of whom withdrew from Europe just in time for the Euro-boom) that looked mainly to their domestic market could not.

Intriguingly, there is not much evidence here for blaming leveraged buyouts or "the financial excesses of the 1980s" for declines in U.S.-company dominance. LBOs were not much of a feature in most of the industries, especially the higher-technology industries, surveyed here. They affected large U.S. companies principally in food products – therein "restructuring" or moving around parts of companies apparently without great effect on world rankings by country of headquarters (although France's BSN was able to expand its European activities by buying pieces of what once had been RJR-Nabisco) – and in tires. But in tires, the (strategic) deed was almost surely done. Perhaps the LBOs hastened the process through industrial euthanasia; perhaps the LBOs had a more ecological function, like wolf packs killing weak caribou – and recycling their meat into "shareholder value" – before death from natural causes occurred. To blame the LBO practitioners for not "saving" Uniroyal-Goodrich seems a little like blaming ordinary mortals for their inability to resurrect the dead.

Will the waning of the large American firm continue? Perhaps some respite is possible: The "deworsified" conglomerates of the 1970s are already LBO'd, restructured or deceased. Still, some of the American firms appearing at or near the top of the electrical equipment, aerospace and chemicals rankings do not seem to be giving the priority to R&D they once did.

There are still some domestically oriented U.S. firms that could become unviable as others' technologies, costs or market locations provide competitive advantage – which is a longish way of saying that the fears of Chrysler's eventual demise often expressed in the business press are hardly irrational.

Does the waning of the large American-headquartered firm matter? Pundits like Robert Reich (1991) would have one believe not, or not very much. After all, the newly dominant non-U.S. firms can and do contribute to U.S. productivity and economic growth by setting up efficient plants in the U.S., like Honda's and Nissan's transplants. Or they can acquire U.S. firms or factories and (potentially) render U.S. capital and labor more productive (Bridgestone's acquisition of Firestone? Michelin's of Uniroyal-Goodrich? Beecham's takeover of SmithKline? Hoechst and Celanese? Bayer's extensive U.S. activities? Schneider and Square D? St. Gobain and Norton? Rhone-Poulenc and Rorer? Samsung's investment in Zenith Electronics?) With such a long and growing list, the U.S. had better hope so.

Yet even if all those good productivity effects happen, losses of U.S. headquarters do matter. The most highly skilled (and highly paid) jobs are nearly universally located at headquarters. It is not for nothing that headquarters cities are more culturally dynamic than "branch-plant towns." (Boston-area pundits and professors will begin to notice this as Wang, never having quite made it to the world's top 12 in computers, quietly disappears into the bureaucracy of IBM.) Headquarters also is where tax-allocation decisions among countries are made. Perhaps even more important, R&D activities and jobs are concentrated at headquarters: The "transnational" corporation with R&D and decision-making jobs broadly dispersed among countries is, in the real world, a mythological beast, far more discussed than observed.

Others may argue – or hope – that small firms will ride to the rescue of U.S. industry and employment. But the success of the Japanese, Europeans and Koreans argues that the relationship of scale and scope to cost and risk reduction, and ultimately to global competitiveness, has yet to be repealed. Small firms matter in the aggregate not when they are small, but when, through technological, capital, and human investment, they become large, globally dominant enterprises and create large numbers of well-paying jobs during the past thirty years. European, Japanese and newly industrializing countries' firms have been performing this transformation more effectively than have their American counterparts.

References

A.P. Chandler, "Underinvestment in America: Is There a Short-Term Investment Perspective?" Unpublished draft manuscript, Harvard Business School, 1990.

L.G Franko, "Global Corporate Competitiveness: Who's Winning, Who's Losing, and the R&D Factor as One Reason Why," *Strategic Management Journal* (1989a) 449-474.

L. G. Franko, "Unrelated Diversification and Global Corporate Performance," in A. R. Negandhi and A. Savara (eds.), *International Strategic Management* (Lexington, Mass.: Heath-Lexington Books, 1989b)

D. Lascelles, "Global Strategy Banking on Boulevards to Build the Business," *The Financial Times,* Management Page, July 24, 1991.

R. Reich, "Who Is Us?" *Harvard Business Review,* January-February 1990, pp. 53-64.

"Special Report/The Global 500," *Fortune,* 1991.

D. Yoffie and R. Vietor, "International Trade and Competition in Glogal Telecommunications." Unpublished manuscript, Harvard Business School, 1991.

Table 1
Changes in "World Market Share" in Major Industries, 1960-1990

	Numbers of Firms					% of Sales				
	'60	'70	'80	'88	'90	'60	'70	'80	'88	'90
AEROSPACE										
USA	9	9	9	9	9	85	88	81	84	79
France	0	1	2	1	1	3	6	5	5	4
UK	3	2	1	2	2	15	9	6	11	17
AUTOS AND TRUCKS										
USA	6	4	3	3	3	83	66	42	44	38
Japan	0	3	3	3	3	0	12	17	21	23
Germany	2	2	2	2	3	7	11	14	15	21
France	2	1	2	2	2	4	4	15	10	10
Italy	1	1	1	1	1	3	4	10	7	8
UK	1	1	1	1	0	3	4	3	0	0
Sweden	0	0	0	0	0	0	0	0	3	0
BANKING (% of total assets)										
Japan	0	0	2	8	7	0	0	15	71	66
France	0	2	4	2	3	0	12	37	14	21
Germany	0	0	1	1	1	0	0	8	7	7
UK	3	2	1	0	1	22	15	15	0	6
USA	6	6	3	1	0	61	67	26	8	0
Italy	0	1	0	0	0	0	6	0	0	0
Canada	3	0	0	0	0	17	0	0	0	0
CHEMICALS										
Germany	3	3	3	3	3	18	27	36	39	39
USA	8	5	4	4	3	68	40	31	29	23
UK	1	1	1	1	1	14	11	10	10	11
Italy	0	1	1	1	1	0	9	7	6	6
France	0	1	1	1	1	0	6	5	6	7
Norway	0	0	0	1	1	0	0	0	5	5
Japan	0	0	1	0	1	0	0	5	0	4
Netherlands	0	1	1	1	1	0	7	0	5	5
COMPUTERS/OFFICE EQUIPMENT										
USA	7	9	8	6	6	95	90	86	74	70
Japan	0	1	2	3	4	0	3	7	18	23
Italy	1	1	1	1	1	3	5	4	4	4
UK	1	1	1	1	0	2	2	3	3	0
France	0	0	0	1	1	0	0	0	3	3
ELECTRICAL EQUIPMENT/ELECTRONICS										
Japan	2	3	3	5	6	8	17	21	42	47
South Korea	0	0	0	2	1	0	0	0	13	11
USA	6	5	5	1	1	71	59	44	12	11
Germany	2	2	1	1	1	10	12	11	11	10
Netherlands	1	1	1	1	1	8	9	11	9	8
France	0	0	2	1	1	0	0	12	7	7
UK	1	1	0	0	0	4	5	0	0	0
Sweden/Switz.	0	0	0	1	1	0	0	0	6	7
FOOD AND BEVERAGE PRODUCTS										
USA	9	10	8	7	7	62	67	50	51	52
UK	1	1	3	3	2	24	25	36	28	23
Switzerland	1	1	1	1	1	10	8	14	17	15
Italy	0	0	0	0	1	0	0	0	0	6
France	0	0	0	0	1	0	0	0	0	3
Canada	1	0	0	0	0	4	0	0	0	0
Japan	0	0	0	1	0	0	0	0	5	0
IRON AND STEEL										
Japan	1	4	4	5	5	5	30	31	43	44
Germany	2	3	2	2	3	11	21	24	20	26
France	0	0	1	1	1	0	0	5	12	12

Australia	0	1	0	1	1.	0	7	0	6	8
UK	1	1	1	1	1	5	12	7	6	6
South Korea	0	0	0	0	1	0	0	0	0	5
USA	*7*	*3*	*3*	*2*	*0*	*74*	*31*	*26*	*12*	*0*
Netherlands	0	0	1	0	0	0	0	7	0	0
Luxembourg	1	0	0	0	0	5	0	0	0	0

NON-FERROUS METALS

Germany	1	1	2	4	4	8	10	18	34	44
USA	*8*	*5*	*3*	*2*	*2*	*63*	*39*	*21*	*16*	*16*
France	1	2	1	1	1	7	19	16	11	13
Canada	2	2	2	2	2	22	18	14	20	12
UK	0	2	1	1	1	0	14	11	7	7
Japan	0	0	1	2	1	0	0	7	10	5
Switzerland	0	0	1	0	1	0	0	7	0	4
Belgium	0	0	1	0	0	0	0	6	0	0

NON-ELECTRICAL MACHINERY (INDUSTRIAL AND FARM EQUIPMENT)

USA	*5*	*6*	*5*	*3*	*3*	*37*	*51*	*41*	*28*	*26*
Germany	4	3	2	3	3	42	28	23	26	25
Japan	0	1	1	3	3	0	7	6	21	23
South Korea	0	0	1	1	1	0	0	9	15	17
UK	0	1	1	1	1	0	7	5	5	5
France	1	0	1	1	1	7	0	12	6	5
Canada	1	1	1	0	0	8	6	5	0	0
Sweden	1	0	0	0	0	6	0	0	0	0

PAPER AND PAPER PRODUCTS

USA	*10*	*9*	*8*	*8*	*7*	*86*	*81*	*66*	*73*	*62*
Sweden	0	0	1	1	2	0	0	7	8	18
Canada	1	1	0	0	1	6	5	0	0	8
New Zealand	0	0	0	1	1	0	0	0	7	7
Finland	0	0	0	0	1	0	0	0	0	6
Germany	0	0	1	1	0	0	0	10	6	0
UK	1	2	2	0	0	8	14	17	0	0
Japan	0	0	0	1	0	0	0	0	6	0

PETROLEUM PRODUCTS

USA	*10*	*10*	*7*	*7*	*5*	*77*	*78*	*61*	*59*	*47*
Netherlands	1	1	1	1	1	17	16	15	18	18
UK	1	1	1	1	1	6	6	9	11	10
Italy	0	0	1	1	1	0	0	5	6	7
France	0	0	1	1	2	0	0	5	5	10
Brazil	0	0	0	1	1	0	0	0	4	4
Venezuela	0	0	1	0	1	0	0	4	0	4

PHARMACEUTICALS

USA	*10*	*9*	*7*	*7*	*6*	*87*	*70*	*55*	*52*	*49*
Switzerland	2	3	3	3	3	13	30	32	35	30
Germany	0	0	2	1	1	0	0	13	6	6
UK	0	0	0	0	1	0	0	0	0	9
Japan	0	0	0	1	0	0	0	0	7	0
Sweden	0	0	0	0	1	0	0	0	0	6

TEXTILES

Japan	1	5	3	5	5	7	32	21	42	42
USA	*7*	*5*	*5*	*3*	*3*	*58*	*44*	*41*	*18*	*21*
UK	2	2	2	2	2	19	23	22	18	16
South Korea	0	0	1	1	1	0	0	8	10	11
Turkey	0	0	1	1	1	0	0	8	11	10
Netherlands	1	0	0	0	0	10	0	0	0	0
Italy	1	0	0	0	0	6	0	0	0	0

TIRES

Japan	0	1	2	3	3	0	3	10	33	32
France	1	1	1	1	1	6	8	18	19	19
USA	*6*	*5*	*7*	*2*	*1*	*76*	*69*	*50*	*23*	*19*
Italy	1	1		1	1	7	9		15	14
UK	1	1	1	0	0	11	9	18	0	0
Germany	0	1	1	1	1	0	3	4	10	9
Australia	0	0	0	0	1	0	0	0	0	7

Table 2
Largest 12 Companies Worldwide in 15 Industries:
Sales in $Billion and "World Market Share" of "Total Industry Sales," 1980 and 1990

	1980	%		1990	%
IND. & FARM EQUIPMENT			**IND. & FARM EQUIPMENT**		
Caterpillar	8.60	0.14	Mitsubishi Heavy Industries	16 40	0.12
Schneider	7.60	0.12	Mannesmann	15 09	0.11
Mannesmann	7.22	0 12	Daewoo	22.26	0.17
Gutehoffnungshutte	6.91	0.11	Tenneco	14.89	0.11
Hundai	5.54	0.09	Caterpillar	11 54	0.09
Deere	5.47	0.09	MAN	10.83	0.08
Dresser Industries	4.02	0.07	Deere	7.88	0.06
Ishikawajima-Harima Heavy Ind.	3.60	0.06	Hoesch	6.43	0.05
FMC	3.48	0.06	Schneider	6.80	0.05
Combustion Eng.	3.15	0.05	Komatsu	7.83	0.06
Massey Ferguson	3.13	0.05	Kawasaki Heavy Industries	6.38	0.05
BICC	2.98	0.05	BCC	6.53	0.05
TOTAL	61.70	1.00	TOTAL	132.86	1.00
NON-FERROUS METALS			**NON-FERROUS METALS**		
Pechiney	9.03	0.16	Preussag	14.99	0.14
Rio Tinto Zinc	6.50	0.11	Pechiney	14 12	0.13
Alcan Aluminum	5.22	0.09	Viag	12.17	0.11
Alcoa	5.15	0.09	Metallgesellschaft	11.9	0.11
Metallgesellschaft	5.08	0.09	Alcoa	10.8	0.01
Degussa	4.85	0.08	Alcan	8.85	0.08
Alusuisse	4.12	0.07	Degussa	8.26	0.08
Nippon Mining	3.94	0.07	RTZ	7.20	0.07
Reynolds	3.65	0.06	Reynolds	6.08	0.06
Metallurgie H.O.	3.36	0.06	Mitsubishi Metal	5.58	0.05
Kaiser	3.22	0.06	Noranda (ex. forest)	4.68	0.04
Inco	3.02	0.05	Alusuisse	4.56	0.04
TOTAL	57.14	1.00	TOTAL	109.32	1.00
CHEMICALS			**CHEMICALS**		
Hoechst	16.48	0.13	BASF	29.18	0.14
Baver	15.88	0.12	Hoechst	27.75	0.13
BASF	15.28	0.12	Bayer	26.06	0.12
Du Pont	13.65	0.10	Imperial Chemical Industries	23.35	0.11
Imperial Chemical Industries	13.29	0.10	Du Pont (ex. Conaco)	22.06	0.01
Dow Chemical	10.60	0.08	Dow Chemical	20.01	0.09
Union Carbide	9.99	0.08	Rhône-Poulenc	14.47	0.07
Montedison	9.10	0.07	Montedison	13.03	0.06
DSM	7.51	0.06	Norsk Hydro	9.87	0.05
Rhone-Polenc	7.16	0.05	AKZO Group	9.51	0.04
Monsanto	6.57	0.05	Monsanto	9.05	0.04
AKZO Group	6.27	0.05	Mitôsubishi Kasei	8.22	0.04
TOTAL	131.78	1.00	TOTAL	212.56	1.00
IRON & STEEL			**IRON & STEEL**		
Thyssen	15.24	0.16	Thyssen	21.45	0.15
Nippon Steel	13.10	0.14	Nippon Steei	21.1t	0.15
U.S. Steel	12.49	0.13	Usinor-Sacilor	17.64	0.12
Krupp-Konzern	7.67	0.08	Krupp	9.70	0.07
Estel	7.05	0.07	Sumilomo Metal	12.78	0.09
British Steel	6.77	0.07	Broken Hill Proprietary	10.83	0.07
Bethlehem Steel	6.70	0.07	NKK	10.25	0.07
NKK	5.93	0.06	Kobe Steel	9.44	0.07
Armco	5.68	0.06	Kawasaki Steel	8 65	0.06
Sumitomo Metal	5.56	0.06	British Steel	8.45	0.06
Usinor-Sacilor	5.15	0.05	Pohang Iron & Steel	7.00	0.05
Kawasaki Steel	5.02	0.0S	Hoesch	7.83	0.05
TOTAL	96.36	1.00	TOTAL	145.23	1.00
AEROSPACE			**AEROSPACE**		
United Technologies	12.30	0.20	Boeing	27.60	0.18
Boeing	9.40	0.15	United Technologies	21.78	0.14
Rockwell	6.90	0.11	British Aerospace	19.33	0.13
McDonnell-Douglas	6.06	0.10	McDonnell-Douglas	16.35	0.11
Lockheed	5.40	0.09	Allied-Signal	12.40	0.08
General Dynamics	4.74	0.08	General Dynamics	10.18	0.07

Company	Value	Share	Company	Value	Share
Textron	3.64	0.06	Lockheed	9.98	0.07
British Aerospace	3.31	0.05	Textron	7.92	0.05
Aerospatiale	3.12	0.05	Rolls Royce	6.62	0.04
Rolls Royce	2.93	0.05	Aerospatiale	6.47	0.04
Martin Marietta	2.62	0.04	Martin Marietta	6.14	0.04
Dassault Aviation	2.55	0.04	Northrop	5.49	0.04
TOTAL	62.97	1.00	TOTAL	150.26	1.00

BANKING | | | **BANKING** | | |

Company	Value	Share	Company	Value	Share
Citicorp	114.92	0.10	Sumitomo	407.91	0.10
Bank America	111.62	0.10	Dai-Ichi	426.86	0.10
Banque Nationale de Paris	107.28	0.10	Mitsubishi	412.78	0.10
Credit Agricole	105.91	0.09	Mitsui	407.50	0.10
Credit Lyonnais	98.15	0.09	Sanwa	401.47	0.10
Societe Generale	90.16	0.08	Fuji	398.32	0.10
Barclay's	88.62	0.08	Credit Agricole	302.98	0.07
Dai-Ichi	88.52	0.08	Banque Nationale de Paris	289.75	0.07
Deutsche Bank	88.47	0.08	Industrial Bank of Japan	289.18	0.07
National Westminster	82.59	0.07	Credit Lyonnais	285.24	0.07
Mitsubishi	76.43	0.07	Deusche Bank	267.70	0.00
Chase Manhanan	76.20	0.07	Barclay's	260.05	0.06
TOTAL	1,128.87	1.00	TOTAL	4,149.74	1.00

COMPUTER & OFFICE EQUIPMENT | | | **COMPUTER & OFFICE EQUIPMENT** | | |

Company	Value	Share	Company	Value	Share
IBM	26.20	0.42	IBM	69.02	0.36
Xerox	8.20	0.13	Xerox	18.38	0.10
Sperry	4.78	0.08	FUjjLSU	17.97	0.09
NCR	3.32	0.05	Hewlett Packard	13.23	0.07
Hewlett Packard	3.10	0.05	Digital Equipment	13.09	0.07
Burroughs	2.86	0.05	Canon	12.21	0.06
CDC	2.75	0.04	Unisys	10.11	0.05
Fujitsu	2.62	0.04	Sharp	9.93	0.05
Olivetti	2.54	0.04	Olivetti	7.54	0.04
Digital Equipment	2.37	0.04	Bull	6.41	0.03
Canon	1.85	0.03	NCR	6.40	0.03
ICL	1.67	0.03	Ricoh	5.96	0.03
TOTAL	62.26	1.00	TOTAL	190.24	1.00

AUTOS & TRUCKS | | | **AUTOS & TRUCKS** | | |

Company	Value	Share	Company	Value	Share
GM	57.70	0.23	GM	110.80	0.19
Ford	37.10	0.15	Ford	81.84	0.14
Fiat	25.16	0.10	Toyota	64.52	0.11
Renault	18.98	0.08	Daimler-Benz	54.26	0.09
Volkswagen	18.34	0.07	Fiat	47.75	0.08
Daimler-Benz	17.11	0.07	Volkswagen	43.71	0.08
Peugeot	16.85	0.07	Nissan	40.22	0.07
Toyota	14.23	0.06	Chrysler	26.97	0.05
Nissan	13.85	0.06	Renault	30.05	0.05
Mitsubishi Heavy Industries	11.0	0.04	Peugeot	29.38	0.05
Chrysler	9.2	0.04	Honda	27.07	0.05
British Leyland	6.6	0.03	BMW	17.29	0.03
TOTAL	246.21	1.00	TOTAL	573.85	1.00

ELECTRICAL | | | **ELECTRICAL** | | |

Company	Value	Share	Company	Value	Share
GE	24.96	0.15	Hitachi	50.69	0.13
ITT	18.53	0.11	GE	44.88	0.11
Philips	18.40	0.11	Samsung	45.04	0.11
Siemens	17.60	0.11	Matsushita Electric Ind.	43.52	0.11
Matsushita Electric Ind.	13.60	0.08	Siemens	39.23	0.10
Hitachi	12.87	0.08	Philips	30.87	0.08
Western Electric	12.03	0.07	Toshiba	30.18	0.07
CGE	10.85	0.07	Asea Brown Boveri	27.71	0.07
Thomson-Brandt	8.60	0.05	Alcatel-CGE	26.46	0.07
Westinghouse	8.51	0.05	NEC	24.39	0.06
Toshiba	8.15	0.05	Mitsubishi Electric	21.23	0.05
RCA	8.01	0.05	Sony	20.93	0.05
TOTAL	162.17	1.00	TOTAL	405.13	1.00

FOOD & BEVERAGE | | | **FOOD & BEVERAGE** | | |

Company	Value	Share	Company	Value	Share
Unilever	26.43	0.26	Philip Morris	44.32	n.19
Nestlé	14.62	0.14	Unilever	39.97	0.19
Dart & Kraft	9.41	0.09	Nestlé	33.36	0.17
Beatrice	8.29	0.08	Pepsi Co.	17.80	0.14

Pepsi Co.	5.98	0.06		Conagra	15.52	0.07
General Foods	5.96	0.06		Grand Metropolitan	14.77	0.06
Coca-Cola	5.90	0.06		Ferruzi	13.97	0.06
Consolidated Food	5.34	0.05		Sara Lee (Cons. Foods)	11.65	0.05
Grand Metropolitan	5.10	0.05		Anheuser Busch	10.75	0.05
Associated British Food	5.00	0.05		Coca-Cola	10.41	0.05
Ralston Purina	4.88	0.05		BSN	9.72	0.04
Greyhound	4.70	0.05		Archer-Daniels-Midl;Ind	7.89	0.03
TOTAL	101.67	1.00		TOTAL	230.13	1.00

PAPER & FOREST PRODUCTS

PAPER & FOREST PRODUCTS

International Paper	5.04	0.11		International Paper	12.96	0.14
Georgia-Pacific	5.02	0.11		Georgia-Pacific	12.67	0.13
Flick Group	4.64	0.10		Stora Kopparbergs Berg.	11.07	0.12
Weyerhaeuser	4.50	0.10		Weyerhaeuser	9.02	0.09
Bowater	4.09	0.09		Noranda	8.12	0.09
Champion International	3.75	0.08		Fletcher Challenge	7.13	0.07
Statsforetag Group	3.34	0.07		Kimberly-Clark	6.45	0.07
Reed International	3.31	0.07		Repola	6.04	0.06
Crown Zellerbach	3.07	0.07		Stone	5.77	0.06
Boise Cascade	3.02	0.07		James River	5.42	0.06
Mead	2.71	0.06		Scon	5.39	0.06
Regis	2.70	0.06		Svenska Cellulosa	5.33	0.06
TOTAL	45.19	1.00		TOTAL	95.38	1.00

PETROLEUM PRODUCTS

PETROLEUM PRODUCTS

Exxon	103.10	0.20		Royal Dutch/Shell	107.20	0.18
Royal Dutch/Shell	77.10	0.15		Exxon	105.89	0.18
Mobil	59.50	0.11		British Petroleum	59.54	0.10
Texaco	51.20	0.10		Mobil	58.77	0.10
British Petroleum	48.00	0.09		ENI	41.76	0.07
Chevron	40.50	0.08		Texaco	41.24	0.07
ENI	27.20	0.05		Chevron	39.26	0.07
Gulf	26.50	0.05		Elf Aquitaine	32.94	0.06
Standard of Indiana	26.10	0.05		Amoco	29.28	0.08
CFP	23.90	0.05		Total-CFP	23.59	0.04
Atlantic Richfield	23.70	0.05		Petróleos de Venezuela	23.47	0.04
Petróleos de Venezuela	18.82	0.04		Petrobras	20.47	0.04
TOTAL	525.62	1.00		TOTAL	583.41	1.00

PHARMACEUTICALS

PHARMACEUTICALS

Ciba-Geigy	7.11	0.17		Ciba-Geigy	14.48	0.14
Johnson & Johnson	4.84	0.11		Johnson & Johnson	11.23	0.11
American Home Products	3.80	0.09		Bristol-Myers Squibb	10.51	0.10
Hoffmann-La Roche	3.50	0.08		Sandoz	8.90	0.09
Warner-Lambert	3.48	0.08		SmithKline Beecham	8.64	0.09
Bristol Meyers	3.16	0.07		Merck	7.82	0.08
Pfizer	3.03	0.07		Hoffmann-La Roche	6.96	0.07
Sandoz	2.93	0.07		American Home Products	6.92	0.07
Hoechst	2.80	0.07		Pfizer	6.60	0.07
Merck	2.79	0.07		Procordia	6.34	0.06
Bayer	2.70	0.06		Hoechst	6.22	0.06
Lilly (Eli)	2.56	0.06		Abbon	6.21	0.06
TOTAL	42.70	1.00		TOTAL	100.83	1.00

TIRES

TIRES

Goodyear	8.44	0.20		Bridgestone	12.40	0.21
Michelin	7.73	0.18		Michelin	11.52	0.19
Dunlop	7.51	0.18		Goodyear	11.45	0.19
Firestone	4.85	0.11		Pirelli	8.46	0.14
Goodrich	3.08	0.07		Continental	5.30	0.09
Bridgestone	3.02	0.07		Pacific Dunlop	3.88	0.06
Uniroyal	2.30	0.05		Sumitomo Rubber	3.79	0.06
GenCorp	2.22	0.05		Yokahama Rubber	2.96	0.05
Continental	1.7~	0.01		TOTAL	59.77	1.00
Yokohama Rubber	1.12	0.03				
Armstrong	0.40	0.01				
Cooper						
TOTAL	42.73	1.00				

TEXTILES 1980

TEXTILES

Courtauld	3.97	0.16		Toray Industries	6.05	0.12
Burlington	2.90	0.12		Hyosung	5.26	0.11
Levi Strauss	2.80	0.11		HaciOmerSabanci	5.13	0.10

Kanebo	2 06	0.08	Kanebo	4.63	0.09
Haci Omer Sabanci	1.98	0.08	Courtaulds	4.33	0.09
Hyosung	1 9S	0.08	Levi Strauss	4.25	0.08
J.P. Stevens	1.92	0.08	Teijin	4.11	0.08
Toyobo	1.73	0.07	Toyobo	3.69	0.07
Coats Patons	1.60	0.06	Wickes	3.65	0.07
Unitika	1 57	0.06	Coats Viyella	3.29	0.07
Armstrong World	1.32	0.05	Unitika	2.62	0.05
West Point Pepperel	1.25	0.05	VF	2.96	0.06
TOTAL	25.07	1.00	TOTAL	49.97	1.00

Summary of
the theory of competitive advantage[11]

We start from the premise that the only meaningful concept of competitiveness at the national level is that of efficiency of productivity, i.e., the value of the output produced by a unit of labor or capital. Hence, a nation's standard of living in the modern age depends on its aggregate capacity to achieve a high level of efficiency of productivity, and to increase it over time. From this frame of reference, contrary to classical economic theory, the theory of competitive advantage of nations maintains that "(a) nation's competitiveness depends on the capacity of its industry to innovate and upgrade." Companies gain advantage against the world's best competitors because of pressure and challenge. They benefit from having strong domestic rivals, aggressive home-based suppliers and demanding local customers. In a world of increasingly global competition, the role of the nation has grown.

Various differences in national values, culture, economic structures, institutions and histories all contribute to the competitive success of a nation.

Although companies in a given country can benefit from technological breakthroughs, innovation more typically is manifested in incremental, mundane advances in product design, in production processes, in new marketing approaches. Information that competitors either do not have or do not seek plays a large role in innovation.

> Once a firm achieves competitive advantage through innovation, it needs to sustain it by relentless improvement. Competitors will eventually overtake any company that stops innovating and improving. Hence, holds the theory, the only way to sustain a competitive advantage is to constantly upgrade it, moving toward more sophisticated approaches.

Additionally, however, in order to maintain competitive advantage a company must adopt a global approach to strategy, and often must endeavor to make its own existing advantage obsolete – before someone else does.

The theory advances four interrelated attributes of a nation, cited as determinants of national competitive advantage, that encourage its companies to establish and maintain competitive edge through innovation and improvement. These determinants are: 1) factor conditions; 2) demand conditions; 3) related and supporting industries; and 4) firm strategy, structure and rivalry.

Factor conditions relate to factors of production in a nation, such as the availability of needed, skilled labor or the condition of pertinent infrastructure elements. In all sophisticated industries, a nation does not inherit production factors such as skilled labor or scientific base, but rather it creates such factors. Far more important than the stock of such factors at a given moment in time which a given nation enjoys is the rate and efficiency with which it can create, upgrade and deploy them vis-a-vis specific industries. Because the factors that are most specific to a given industry's particular needs are most scarce, require the most sustained investment to create, and hence also are the most difficult for competitors to duplicate, such factors are the only ones that directly support competitive advantage.

---

11 Adapted from Michael Porter, *The Competitive Advantage of Nations*. New York: Free Press, 1990.

In fact, selective disadvantages in the more basic infrastructure factors can actually prod a company to innovate and upgrade, by way of competition, and thereby achieve competitive advantage. This can only happen when two conditions coincide, however. First, the selective disadvantage in question must give a message about circumstances that will spread to other countries, thus equipping the company deriving that message to innovate in advance of foreign rivals. Second, other conditions in the "diamond" of national competitiveness must be favorable.

Related and supporting industries include auto suppliers in a nation to its various firms, and its other, related industries that are internationally competitive. Access to components and machinery is important. But still more significant to international competitiveness is the "clustering" of related suppliers and end-users geographically, and the extent to which these "network" with each other in an ongoing exchange of ideas and innovations.

Firm strategy, structure and rivalry mean those conditions in a country that govern or influence how companies are created, organized and managed, as well as how domestic rivalry is conducted. It is the convergence of management practices and organizational modes favored in a country, on one hand, and the sources of competitive advantage in a given industry, on the other hand, that result in international competitiveness in a specific industry. Strong, local rivals stimulate creation and persistence of competitive advantage internationally.

According to this theory, then, government's proper role should be as a catalyst and prompter of a country's companies to move to higher levels of competitive performance. Successful government policies therefore are those that are largely indirect, rather than participatory, creating an environment conducive to companies' gaining and maintaining competitive advantage. The theory includes quite a number of recommendations both to governments and to a nation's companies to maximize international competitiveness.

Demand conditions refer to the home-market demand in a country for a firm's products or services. Home demand is conducive to international competitiveness when such demand gives internationally competing, local companies a clearer picture of emerging buyer needs, and where demand pressures companies toward innovation and to become more sophisticated than foreign rivals.

Cross-cultural awareness and sensitivity

This chapter takes a closer look at the topic of culture that was introduced in Chapter 1. The focus is on the characteristics of several cultures in Asia and Europe and the implications for doing business in those cultures. In Chinese, Indian and American Values a number of similarities and differences in the value systems of these cultures are explored by rating a set of values in terms of their importance for each culture. Ratings are then compared to those made by a large number of people from each culture. Likewise, some similarities and differences between Japanese and American cultures are illustrated in a set of five experiential exercises entitled *Understanding Japan.* These exercises provide an opportunity to experience the dynamics of Japanese group behavior, consensual decision–making, Zen meditation and the meaning of symbols, as well to learn some interesting facts about Japanese society.

Several selections involve negotiations. *The East-West game* is a role play between members of an Eastern and a Western culture who negotiate over a national treasure in the Eastern culture. The role play underscores the importance of cultural sensitivity in cross-cultural negotiations. *An exercise in international negotiations* calls for researching a particular culture and identifying dominant values and corresponding behaviors. The final task of the exercise is to devise a strategic negotiating response for each behavior. The objective is to develop a causal model that shows how one negotiating team's cultural values lead to behaviors that can be interpreted by the other team and serve as the basis for formulating a strategic response. The reading, *Insights into international negotiations,* provides useful background information for both *The East-West game* and *An exercise in international negotiations.* It describes the pitfalls of American negotiators unskilled in cultural sensitivity and contrasts them with the characteristics and behaviors of Americans who were successful in cross-cultural negotiations.

Two short cases and a reading provide a look at business and culture in the Republic of China (Taiwan). The reading, *A linkage between Confucianism and the Chinese family firm in the Republic of China,* contains background information on the five human relationships in Confucianism and how they affect the structure and management of Chinese family businesses. The case, *Lao Bao's,* deals with problems of executive succession when Bao Sr., the respected founder with "an iron head and a Buddha heart," planned to step down. In *Duo Tsai Paint Company,* the founder, Victory Chao, died suddenly and conflicts arose among his children who each inherited a share of the firm. While the first case revolves around who the successor will be, the second case involves the conflicting perspectives and strategies of the four inheritors of the business.

The concluding reading on cross-cultural awareness and sensitivity, *A Miss Manners guide to doing business in Europe,* offers seven practical tips for Americans to avoid offending Europeans in business relationships. Although American culture is closer to that of European countries than to Asian and other cultures, Americans who are mindful of European traditions and attitudes toward time and competition are in a superior position to gain the trust and confidence of European counterparts. This reading is useful for analyzing cases on European firms in later chapters such as the Swedish case, *Saab-Scania's niche strategy* (in Chapter 7); the Italian case, *Bieffebi, S.P.A.* (in Instructor's Manual); the Dutch case, *KNP, N.V.*, also in Chapter 7; and the British case, *Cadbury Schweppes, PLC*, in Chapter 9. Obtaining additional information about these cultures can help determine how the advice in the *Miss Manners* reading applies to the customs and traditions in each country.

Chapter 2
Cross cultural awareness and sensitivity

6. Chinese, Indian and American values[1]

purpose

To learn some differences between Chinese, Indian and American value systems.

group size

Any number of groups of five to eight people.

time required

20+ minutes.

exercise schedule

1   complete rankings (pre–class)

Students rank the 15 values for either Chinese and American orientations or for Indian and American systems. If time permits, all three can be done.

		unit time	total time
2	**small groups (optional)**	**15 min**	**15 min**

Groups of five to eight members try to achieve consensus on the ranking values for both Chinese and American cultures.

3	**group presentations (optional)**	**15 min**	**30 min**

Each group presents its rankings and discusses reasons for making those decisions.

4	**discussion**	**20+ min**	**50 min**

Instructor leads a discussion on the differences between Chinese and American value systems and presents the correct rankings.

---

1 Copyright 1993 by Dorothy Marcic. Adapted from the Michael Harris Bond (ed.) book, *The Psychology of the Chinese people, Hong Kong*: Oxford University Press, 200 Madison Ave., NY 10016, 1986. The selection used here is a portion of "Chinese Personality and its Change" by Kuo-Shu Yang, pp. 106-170. Used with permission.

Background

In the 1950s and '60s, a number of value–orientation studies were conducted using university students in various countries. The data presented here come from some studies that used the Edwards Personal Preference Schedule. Groups tested included 1,504 Americans, 2,876 Chinese and 288 Indian students.

Value rankings

Rank each of the 15 values below according to what you think they are in the Chinese, Indian (from India) and American cultures. Use "1" as the most important value for the culture and "15" as the least important value for that culture.

Value	American	Chinese	Indian
Achievement			
Deference			
Order			
Exhibition			
Autonomy			
Affiliation			
Intraception			
Succorance			
Dominance			
Abasement			
Nurturance			
Change			
Endurance			
Heterosexuality			
Aggression			

Some definitions

Succorance: Willingness to help another or to offer relief.

Abasement: To lower oneself in rank, prestige or esteem.

Intraception: The other side of extraception, where one is governed by concrete, clearly observable physical conditions. Intraception, on the other hand, is the tendency to be governed by more subjective factors, such as feelings, fantasies, speculations and aspirations.

Internal/external locus of control

Consider American and Chinese groups. Which one would be more internal locus of control (tend to feel in control of one's destiny, that rewards come as a result of hard work, perseverance and responsibility)? Which one would be more external (fate, luck or other outside forces control destiny)?

Machiavellianism

This concept was defined by Christie and Geis as the belief that one can manipulate and deceive people for personal gain. Do you think Americans or Chinese would score higher on the Machiavellian scale?

Discussion questions

1 What are some main differences between the cultures? Did any pattern emerge?

2 Were you surprised by the results?

3 What behaviors could you expect in business dealings with Chinese (or Indians) based on their value system?

4 How do American values dictate Americans' behaviors in business situations?

7. Understanding Japan: a series of exercises[2]

related topics

Cultural influences on business.

International aspects of organizational behavior.

group size

Any number of people.

time required

Exercise 1   35 minutes.

Exercise 2   30 minutes.

Exercise 3   Two class sessions of 45 minutes each.

2 By Bill Van Buskirk, La Salle University, Philadelphia. Used with permission.

Dorothy Marcic and Sheila Puffer, *Management International,* West Publishing, 1994.

Exercise 1:[3]
Japanese group dynamics

purpose

To explore the differences between Japanese and American culture, values and behaviors. To explore the implications of these differences for management effectiveness.

exercise schedule

		unit time	total time
1	**Introduction**	**5 min**	**5 min**

Five to seven people volunteer to participate in an experiment. Once these people are selected, they leave the room for about five minutes. While the volunteers are out, the rest of the class is told what to watch for in the group exercise. The four variables are: membership, leadership, communication and status. Brief descriptions are included in the **appendix** of this book.

		unit time	total time
2	**task**	**10 min**	**15 min**

The volunteers are invited to re-enter the room. They sit in a circle of chairs arranged in the middle of the room. The professor tells the group that it must do what Japanese automatically do whenever they are in a new situation. Their task is to "find your rightful place in this group." The professor then sits down in the group. Group members attempt to accomplish this task until the professor announces time is up.

		unit time	total time
3	**class discussion**	**20 min**	**35 min**

The class discusses the dynamics of the exercise from the standpoint of what each individual was attempting to observe.

---

3   By Bill Van Buskirk, La Salle University, Philadelphia. Used with permission.

Exercise 2:
Interesting facts about Japan

goal

To stimulate discussion about differences between Japan and the United States.

exercise schedule

		unit time	total time
1	**dyads discuss**	**10 min**	**10 min**

Students select from the list three facts that are the most "unusual." Dyads discuss their selection.

2	**class discussion**	**20 min**	**30 min**

Students ask the professor questions about their selections. Professor provides contextualization for the selections and links them up to management topics.

Interesting facts about Japan[4]

Birth–control pills are legal, abortion is legal.

There is a 95 percent conviction rate for major crimes.

Japan has 1/20 the crime rate of the United States.

Superiors resign if their subordinates engage in wrongdoing.

The Shinto religion has about 80,000 gods.

Dependency is a sign of health. Independence is considered a kind of sickness.

Most prime ministers (and company presidents) are in their 60s and 70s.

Bosses often introduce their subordinates to prospective marriage partners.

All titles in Japanese companies mean the same thing across companies.

Japanese verbs have two tenses, past and non–past.

Japanese people literally do not know what words to use in a conversation
until the hierarchical relationship between the speakers is clarified.

Compulsory retirement is often at age 55.

Japanese people have the longest life expectancy in the world.
For women it is close to 80.

The company budgets for after–work entertaining exceed
the entire defense budget of Japan.

Most Japanese can't stand our food.

Fifteen–hour workdays are common.

There are 4,000 characters in the average Japanese person's alphabet.

Japan is a country of 120 million people on a land mass the size of California.

Land in Tokyo sometimes sells for several thousand dollars a square foot.

In large Japanese companies, there are over a million suggestions a year
for improvement of operations.

Japan has more than ten times as many industrial robots
in operation than does the United States.

---

4   By Bill Van Buskirk, La Salle University, Philadelphia. Used with permission.

Dorothy Marcic and Sheila Puffer, *Management International,* West Publishing, 1994.
*All rights reserved. May not be reproduced without written permission of the publisher.
For more information, contact West Publishing, Publications Dept., 610 Opperman Drive,
St. Paul, MN 55164.*

Exercise 3:[5]
Japanese decision–making exercise (Ringi/Nemawashi)

goals

1 To give students the opportunity to work through a meaningful task in the manner of Japanese consensual decision making.

2 To compare their own experiences of group decision making with the Japanese approach.

preparation
(optional)

Background reading: chapter 3 of *The False Promise of the Japanese Miracle*, by P. Sethi, N. Namiki and C. Swanson.

exercise schedule

	unit time	total time
1 introduction	**5 min**	**5 min**

Instructor explains the processes of Ringi and Nemawashi and sets up the structure of the exercise. Group composition includes group leaders (Kacho) and student manager (Bucho).

	unit time	total time
2 primary groups meet	**20 min**	**25 min**

Groups of four to six members design a final exam format that is likely to be a valuable learning tool and basis of evaluation.

	unit time	total time
3 secondary groups meet	**20 min**	**45 min**

New groups of four to six members continue with assignment as above, using what was discussed in primary groups as a basis. These are called secondary groups (Kacho). After this session, groups can meet in whatever way they want. The professor will give guidance during one or two open–ended class sessions. Outside class meetings occur at the instigation of the group leaders and the student manager.

---

5 By Bill Van Buskirk, La Salle University, Philadelphia. Used with permission.

4   whole class decides   **30 min (new class)**

Generation of a Ringi document specifying the content of the exam. Document must be signed by all students in the class. Instructor discusses what problems, if any, this document might cause with university administration.

5   evaluation   **15 min**   **45 min**

Evaluation of the exercise. How much did it resemble the descriptions of Ringi and Nemawashi found in the literature? What difficulties did we encounter? Were those difficulties likely to be present in the Japanese context? If so, how would they likely be managed? This evaluation may be done in the context of class discussions and as part of the final exam.

8. The East-West game
(Emperor's pot)[6]

purpose

To explore dynamics of cross–cultural interactions when one group wants something from the other.

group size

An even number of groups with 10 to 19 people in each group.

time required

One class period of 90 minutes, or two class periods of 50 minutes each.

exercise schedule

		unit time	total time
1	**groups form**	**5 min**	**5 min**

Students are assigned a group, either "West" or "East." If the class is large enough to have more than one East/West group, each East group is paired with a West group. Within each group, role assignments are made. Participants within each group decide who will play which role.

		unit time	total time
2	**groups prepare**	**30+ min**	**35 min**

Groups discuss what their culture and behaviors will be like and they practice various interactions. This part may be done the class before, or assigned as a group project for outside class.

		unit time	total time
3	**role play**	**20 min**	**55 min**

A delegation from the East visits the West group, while simultaneously a delegation from the West visits the East group.

		unit time	total time
4	**debrief**	**20+ min**	**75 min**

Instructor leads a discussion on what occurred. What was it like to play a part in your culture? How different was it from your own culture? How well did the West group do in asking the favor of the East group? Were members sensitive to cultural differences? How can cultural insensitivity get in the way of business negotiations?

---

6 Adapted from "The Experiment in International Living" in *The Intercultural Sourcebook* by David S. Hoopes and Paul Ventura (eds.), Society for Intercultural Education, Training and Research, 1979. Prepared with the assistance of Toby S. Frank and Sheila Ramsey. Used with prmission.

East group[7]

Your group represents an ancient Eastern culture. You are poor but proud.

A highly treasured artifact is in your possession. It dates back to A.D. 400. It is a national treasure, in fact THE national treasure. Culturally, you cannot give it up under any circumstances. The other side (West) wants it. Their delegation is under strong pressure from the West to return with the artifact. (You may wish to identify one key behavior that, if demonstrated by the West, will win the treasure.)

However, it is in the nature of your culture to be very agreeable, to be very polite, to try always to answer affirmatively, whether you mean it or not. You never come out directly with a flat negative in the negotiations. You never tell their delegates that they will never get the artifact. You dissemble if necessary; you seem to agree and go along, because culturally you never wish to offend.

Situational note: The West will be sending delegates to your culture to find a way to persuade you to relinquish the national treasure. You will observe their style and make notes on your assumptions, based on the way they behave and talk in your culture during the Phase II negotiations. At the same time (Phase II), a delegation of your people will visit the West (to their embassy, let's assume), where their officials will try to persuade some of your people on their home ground.

Culturally, it is important for you to avoid strong, direct eye contact with the delegates or visitors from the West. You look them in the eye, but never a fixed, hard, direct look of any duration.

Typically, even your negotiating team (your delegates to the West) will practice the ancient art of dealing through a third party. Example: One of you has the role of Chief Spokesman (a senior scholar and official), who may act as one of your delegates to the West, or may negotiate at home with the delegates from the West. And while he will do some of the talking in either situation, he will defer often to one of the other members of your group, allowing that other person to carry on some, if not most, of the conversation with the other side. The West will not understand what dynamic is operating here, but that is its problem.

Your list of cultural values follows. A staff person in your room will help with questions during the Phase I planned period. During that time, you will sort out your various roles, decide who and how many should go to the West, and who should remain in the East to negotiate with the West delegates. You should decide on your approach in Phase II.

---

7 Adapted from "The Experiment in International Living" in *The Intercultural Sourcebook* by David S. Hoopes and Paul Ventura (eds.), Society for Intercultural Education, Training and Research, 1979. Prepared with the assistance of Toby S. Frank and Sheila Ramsey. Used with prmission.

Dorothy Marcic and Sheila Puffer, *Management International*, West Publishing, 1994.

Roles:

Chief Spokesman

Minister of Education and Culture

Security Officer

Political Officer

Protocol Officer

Information Officer

Recorder: to list all the assumptions and values of other side

Astrologer/timekeeper: to keep each phase exactly on schedule

GOD (Group Organizational Director):
the overall organizer of East

Most Honored Grandmother

Spokesman #2 (most honored)

Advisers: all others

East cultural traits

(These are the items governing your behavior)

WE Performance is conditioned by role in society, as opposed to individualism.

OVERLAPPING EGO Expectations/morality of community more important than those of the individual. Individual always in social role. Cannot do anything to conflict with group.

FORM Outward form is of major importance. Manners extremely important. Must participate in activities considered important by group, even if one disagrees.

PASSIVISM Confucian idea of endurance is prevalent. Acceptance of fate, life, etc.

PRAGMATISM Confucian or community morality is applied to social issues and problems.

PROGRESS Change is both negative and positive. Technical change is necessary; social change is bad.

NATURE Nature is considered beautiful/good. Conformity to rule of nature considered good.

EFFICIENCY Considered less important than higher values such as form, face, conformity to custom.

TIME Not precisely measured, except in business/science. Time not a primary consideration. The present, not the future, is given utmost consideration.

HISTORY History is seen as a cyclical phenomenon rather than a linear progression.

HUMILITY Humility is related to social status. One never takes advantage of one's rank. One must always defer to another of higher social rank, must always try to appear humble. Persons of higher rank must even make attempts to defer to and honor special inferiors.

DISCIPLINE Pre–school: much freedom, little discipline. School age: discipline begins at home and from teachers in school. Considered a function of the school system at this age rather than a function of the parents. Adulthood: many responsibilities to family and community. Old age: great freedom, shown much respect, considered to have great wisdom.

MOBILITY Important because of duties to family and community.

WORK A means to an end rather than an end in itself. Has no value in itself.

MONEY Saving for the sake of saving is seldom considered a virtue. Some attitudes toward money involve concepts of "face" – i.e., spending an entire year's income for elaborate ceremonies, wedding, etc., to increase or maintain family prestige. Price is regarded as an index of quality.

AGE Great reverence for age, which means wisdom, authority, great perspective on life. Age brings certain privileges (a girl is not a woman until married and a mother). One always uses honorific terms when addressing an elder.

EDUCATION A discipline and a reflection on family prestige. Means of raising whole family's status. Confucian idea of education to create the true gentleman.

AUTHORITY Confucian values stress the cautions. Obedience to authority. Individual rights bear little consideration. Vertically organized hierarchy regarded as most orderly and harmonious.

MORAL SUPERIORITY A moral smugness stemming from a conviction that East's people are a special people with a set of values and conditions that have made them unique.

instructions   Only to be read by West group

West group[8]

Your group represents an authentic Western culture. You are rich and powerful.

A highly treasured artifact is in the possession of the East. It is a most valuable part of their ancient cultural heritage, and although they are a poor country, they will be reluctant to give it up. You have been assigned the task, however, by your national museum, with strong urging from the government itself, to obtain this national treasure for your country's own collection. Money is no problem.

Situational note: When told, you will send your delegation to the East. While they are negotiating, this team will also be recording observations about the ways in which the Easterners operate and making assumptions about them. At the same time, a delegation from the East will come to the West. During the visit you will try to persuade their delegates about the merits of your case for the artifact and to simultaneously find out from them what the price might be, etc.

Thus your task is to assemble a delegation and send it to the East. You decide who goes, how many, what approach they should use ... as long as the approach appears to you to be compatible with the cultural values listed on the next page. In plainest terms, your group has been sent to the East to bring back the artifact at whatever cost, although you cannot come right out and say this during negotiations with the East. They are known as shrewd traders, even though they are relatively poor, but you have been instructed to operate on the supposition that "every man has his price."

Culturally, it is important for you and your negotiators to figure out which approaches are acceptable on the other side, in order to smooth out the path to your objective of gaining the artifact. At the same time, you should try to stay within the value system defined for you in the next pages.

Typically, you tend to be success–oriented, hard–working and efficient; you plan ahead and try to use time productively.

Your list of cultural values follows. There will be a staff person in your room to help with questions during the Phase I planning period. During that time, you will sort out, consult the value list, decide who and how many should go to the East to negotiate, and who and how many should remain in the West to negotiate with their delegation.

8 Adapted from "The Experiment in International Living" in *The Intercultural Sourcebook* by David S. Hoopes and Paul Ventura (eds.), Society for Intercultural Education, Training and Research, 1979. Prepared with the assistance of Toby S. Frank and Sheila Ramsey. Used with prmission.

Roles:

Curator of National Museum (expert on Oriental Art)

Diplomatic Officer

Public Relations person

CIA agent posing as an Area Studies specialist

Journalist

Chief of your task group (forceful administrator)

Recorder: to list all assumptions, values, etc., of other side

Timekeeper: to keep each phase of exercise exactly on schedule

GOD (Group Organizational Director): organizer of the West

Advisers: all others

West cultural traits

(These are the items governing your role behavior)

"I" Ego–centrism

INDIVIDUALISM Self–reliance. Initiative expected from each. Status achieved by own efforts. Economic, social, political equal opportunity regarded as right of individual. Achievement is good and requires competitiveness. Competition expected.

SOCIAL CONFORMITY Outward conformity to opinions of others and to dress has certain value in society.

ACTIVISM Being active, especially in face of uncertainty, is a virtue. Achievement and goal–oriented activities are strongly stressed.

PRAGMATISM Practical ingenuity applied to social as well as materialistic problems.

PROGRESS Change in itself is good. Improvement, especially personal, is a duty. Man is supposed to work in order to control nature.

EFFICIENCY Applies not only to machines but to social organizations and personalities.

TIME Precisely measured and must be used productively and efficiently.

HISTORY Seen as a linear progression.

AGGRESSIVENESS Ambition, competition, self–assertiveness to achieve success are emphasized. High status, once attained, does not confer right to treat lower class as "inferior." Personal excelling is good, but empty boasts and boasting about success are bad.

DISCIPLINE Pre–school: discipline from parents. School age: increased freedom and responsibility. Adulthood: time of greatest freedom. Old age: considered less productive, less active, an epoch of incapability, less freedom.

MOBILITY Great physical and social mobility seen as good.

WORK Valued as an end in itself. Personal effort and energy output are good. Laziness is bad.

MONEY An economic tool, plus a yardstick for social status, influence and power satisfaction.

YOUTH Highly valued. Old people wish they were young again. Elders feel outmoded by rapid change.

EDUCATION Means to an end. Reflections on family prestige. Means to attain skill, money, status.

AUTHORITY Rules/law generally obeyed, but don't like to be ordered to obey. Authorities must not infringe upon individual rights. Mild suspicion of authority.

MORAL SUPERIORITY A moral smugness stemming from convictions that West's people are a special people with a set of values and conditions that have made them unique.

9. Critical incidents in cross-cultural understanding[9]

purpose

To explore various cross-cultural situations and problems that can occur when working with other cultures.

group size

Any number of groups of three to four members.

time required

50 minutes.

exercise schedule

1   Complete answer sheet (pre-class)

Students read all critical incidents and fill in the answer sheet.

	unit time	total time
2 Small group discussions	**20 min**	**20 min**

Groups of three or four people discuss several of the incidents (instructor will assign them). If there is more time, groups may do all nine incidents. Each group tries to

       a) achieve consensus on the rating

       b) give a mutually agreeable reason for the rating, and

       c) an acceptable substitute action in the incident.

	unit time	total time
3 Class discussion	**30 min**	**50 min**

Groups present their outcomes and instructor leads a discussion on acceptable and effective behaviors in other cultures.

---

9 Adapted from Henry Holmes and Stephen Guild in *International Sourcebook*, by David S. Hoopes and Paul Ventura (eds.), Society for Intercultural Education, Training and Research, 1979. Used with permission.

Critical incidents

1 Juan had recently been assigned to live in a remote district in Central America and carry out a health survey. Because he was friendly and had been educated in the city, village people often came to his house to visit in the evening, some of them staying quite late. Juan, however, was accustomed in the city to having time to himself. Also, his treks to other villages made him tired, so these late visits became a burden. On this particular night, exhausted, he finally tells them, "Excuse me, please, Uncles, but I am tired and have to sleep now."

2 Kumar works in a Pakistani mill managed by a European. Recently he has been late getting to work in the afternoon and has been scolded by his boss. Today, having finished lunch, he realizes he had better walk quickly, for fear of being late to the mill again. As he approaches the mill, he sees Indru, a man from his home village and one of his best friends, coming toward him. Indru is just visiting from the village and has time for a chat and a drink, something Kumar would ordinarily (in their own village) welcome as a matter of course, whatever the time of day. Now, however, as they exchange greetings, Kumar breaks off the conversation politely but abruptly and hurries off to work.

3 My father was an important chief in our province during the colonial period, so I used to accompany him to important functions. One of these was the coronation of our Sultan. When the Sultan entered the great hall, everyone else stood. But the British officials quickly sat down. I was shocked; it reminded me how our roles are mainly for show, while they have all the power. I am a mature civil servant now and have been able to send my three oldest children to England to study.

4 Mindo was a new teacher in this Southeast Asian village. The school yard needed improvement and Mindo knew that the students could fix things if they were properly organized. Ordinarily, manual labor was not done by educated people, but the school couldn't afford to hire laborers. Mindo found, though, that the students almost enjoyed the work if they could do it in large groups. Eventually, the job was nearly done and Mindo, who liked to encourage independence, assigned particular individuals to separate areas of the school. One of them, assigned to dig a trench near the edge of the school yard, refused to work and asked to go home. Mindo was angry and perplexed.

5 I am president of the local school association in a district where residents are mostly poor and members (like me) of a minority group. Many of these people want our school to have teachers from the same minority group, because they are afraid our culture will be overcome by the ways of the majority. The city education officials who administer our district insist that it is they who must select teachers for us because the quality of education is the hope of our people.

6 After going to school abroad for five years, Sutira returned to Nepal, where her large extended family lived in the capital city. When Sutira told her father that she wanted to find an apartment with a friend in another part of the city, he was troubled. He had plenty of room, and besides, she was part of the family. Her education was a thing of prestige to the family. Sutira felt she wanted her own life, however, and proceeded to find a new place, even though it cost her much of her savings.

7 As I do my work, I do my best to introduce in local villages the idea of freedom and democracy. Most rural people are locked into an age-old authoritarian system; I think I can show them a better way. I constantly look for local leaders who see things as I do, so together we can work to change the system.

8 Mr. Subramaniam is a senior Indian government official, who was attending a conference in a European capital. Lonely one evening at the hotel, he saw a European seated nearby in the lounge and struck up a conversation. The man, a Mr. West, was unfamiliar with India, but was nonetheless amiable and expressed interest in Mr. Subramaniam. During the conversation, a friend of Mr. West's passed by. Mr. West introduced the friend, Mr. Norton, to Mr. Subramaniam. Mr. Norton said he could have dinner with Mr. West the following evening. Mr. West accepted enthusiastically. Neither man asked Mr. Subramaniam if he would like to go, however. Mr. Subramaniam, feeling unwanted and ashamed, asked to be excused and left immediately.

9 Jeanne was a teacher in a rural area overseas. One of her students, whose father was an influential political leader, had done little work during the term. Jeanne had felt obligated to turn in a failing grade for her. The headmaster called Jeanne in and asked her to reconsider the failing grade. She refused.

10. An exercise in international negotiations[10]

> *"The reliability of an opposing bargainer*
> *is always a factor that must be considered.*
> *The Soviets are known to carry out the letter*
> *of an agreement, but to take advantage*
> *of every possible loophole they can find.*
> *The Chinese, on the other hand, will go out*
> *of their way to honor both the letter*
> *and the spirit of what is decided."*
>
> President Jimmy Carter
> "Negotiations: The Alternative to Hostility," 1984

purpose

To explore various cultural differences and problems that can occur when negotiating with other cultures.

group size

Any number of groups of two to five members.

time required

40 minutes or more.

preparation required

Read "Insights into international negotiations" later in this chapter.

exercise schedule

1   Study model (previous class)

Instructor explains model and groups discuss.

2   Research culture (outside class)

Each group thoroughly researches assigned culture, identifying three dominant values and corresponding behaviors.

	Unit time	Total time
3 Work on model in or outside class	**20+ min**	

Devise strategic negotiating responses for each of the five behaviors.

4 Groups present	**20+ min**	**20+ min**

Some or all groups present their strategic negotiating responses, as well as part, or all, of the V-B-S model.

---

10 By Dr. Arthur Whately, from *Training for the Cross-Cultural Mind.* SIETAR, Washington, D.C., 1979. Used with permission.

	Unit time	Total time
5 Class discussion	**20+ min**	**40+ min**

Instructor leads discussion on cultural differences and their relevance in negotiations.

Procedures

1   In teams of two to five, study the following material entitled "The Value, Behavior and Strategic Response Model for International Negotiations." Discuss this model within your group to ensure that each member understands how the model works.

2   The team is to choose one culture to study. Once the culture is chosen, the team is to research and identify three dominant values of the culture and their corresponding behaviors. Discuss these values within your group to ensure that each member understands each value and the nature of the behavior it produces. For example, if the culture emphasizes a present time perspective (as opposed to a future or past time perspective), we can predict that negotiators from that culture will not be in a hurry to finalize negotiations, will change from topic to topic easily even though the previous topic has been left unresolved, and will introduce topics for discussion unrelated to the negotiations.

3   Now that five values and corresponding behaviors from the country have been identified, your team is to devise a strategic negotiating response for each of the five behaviors. Organize your answer into a causal model to show how cultural values lead to behaviors that, in turn, provide strategic information for the opposing party. Use the V–B–S worksheet provided to show your work.

The Value, Behavior and Strategic Response Model for international negotiations[11]

Traditionally, the practice of international negotiations has relied on the concept of competitive advantage. If a firm had a price, market, capital or product advantage, negotiations would likely be influenced in that firm's favor. For example, during the first 70 years of this century, firms in the United States had a decided advantage over much of the world in terms of the availability of financial capital. Consequently, U.S. firms used access to cheap and plentiful capital as a position of strength in the international negotiations process. If negotiations with a firm in one country were going poorly, the U.S. firm could threaten to take its products and services to another country because it had the financial strength. Now, however, due to the worldwide availability of capital, technology and information, it is increasingly difficult for a firm to gain a competitive advantage on the basis of these traditional factors.

If negotiating with the mainland Chinese, the dominant cultural value that will emerge is the concept of "face" (Kindel, 1988). The Chinese culture distinguishes two types: lien and mein–tzu. Lien is learned through moral behavior, such as fulfilling one's obligation. Mien–tzu is reputation based on personal effort. Acquiring wealth or education through hard work is an example.

Professor Irby Kindel (1988) has developed an international negotiations model that uses "styles of offer" as the source for competitive advantage rather than some traditional factor. This model is called V–B–S Model. Its most unique feature is the application of cultural understanding directly into the negotiating process. The steps in the model are to first identify the important cultural Values (V) of the opposing party. This requires extensive research to gain the necessary understanding of basic values. Second, based on knowledge about the opposition's cultural values, identify the expected Behaviors (B) that are most likely to occur. And third, now that we know the values and their corresponding behaviors, what Strategies (S) do we want to use to effectively counter the behaviors?

The predictable Chinese behavior stemming from the cultural value of "face" would be to continuously check with superiors to show respect (lien), to negotiate every detail through exhaustive effort (mein–tzu), and to compromise/agree at some point (lien).

Given these predictable Chinese behaviors, expect and plan for a rather long negotiation period, resist insulting or embarrassing the Chinese negotiator under any circumstance, and "give face" by fulfilling obligations and giving praise.

References

Casse, Pierre. *Training for the Cross-Cultural Mind*, SIETAR, Washington, D.C., 1979.

Graham, J. and Herberger. Business negotiations in Japan, Brazil and the U.S. *Journal of International Business Studies*, 14, Spring/Summer 1983, 47-62.

Kindel, Thomas. Negotiations between East and West: A cultural format. Presented at the International Symposium in Pacific-Asian Business, January 1988, Honolulu, Hawaii.

11 By Dr. Arthur Whately, from *Training for the Cross-Cultural Mind*. SIETAR, Washington, D.C., 1979. Used with permission.

The V-B-S Worksheet[12]

Country chosen:

1 Dominant value (briefly describe):

Corresponding behaviors stemming from this value (describe in detail):

Strategies designed to effectively respond to the behaviors (describe in detail):

2 Dominant value (briefly describe):

Corresponding behaviors stemming from this value (describe in detail):

Strategies designed to effectively respond to the behaviors (describe in detail):

3 Dominant value (briefly describe):

Corresponding behaviors stemming from the value (describe in detail):

Strategies designed to effectively respond to the behaviors (describe in detail):

---

12 By Dr. Arthur Whately, from *Training for the Cross-Cultural Mind.* SIETAR, Washington, D.C., 1979. Used with permission.

11. Lao Bao's[13]

See "A linkage between Confucianism and the Chinese family firm in the Republic of China" later in this chapter for background to the case.

In 1948, Bao, a young military officer, arrived on Taiwan from mainland China, as part of the withdrawal of the nationalist army retreating from the communists. For several years, Bao filled a minor government post. In 1950, he resigned from his position and founded a company to produce processed food, Lao Bao's Company. Bao's company primarily manufactured canned products: sardines, pork, bamboo shoots, water chestnuts, star fruit, preserved bananas, pineapple, sugarcane. His market efforts initially focused on domestic buyers. Bao, like many other Chinese entrepreneurs, inherited the traditional agricultural work ethics – hard work, frugality, perseverance in the face of hardship and future–orientation.

In the 1960s, the national government on Taiwan promoted exports. Following this lead, Bao traveled to most of the Southeast Asian countries, and ultimately to the U.S. He succeeded in establishing a network of manufacturing representatives for his products. Aided by the government in the 1950s and benefitting from the national economic policies during the 1960s and 1970s, Lao Bao's Company grew and prospered and by 1989 had sales of NT $5 billion.

Bao Sr. has always been a conscientious boss who has good relationships with his employees, especially his top executives and managers. His subordinates described him as a person with "iron head and Buddha heart." They often chatted among themselves about how lucky they were to work for Bao. He had tried to avoid giving the impression of favoritism toward his son, so as not to irritate the other senior managers, many of whom had helped Bao Sr. to found the firm. Bao Jr., younger than the other Vice Presidents and senior managers, referred to them as "uncles."

In 1959, Bao and his wife were blessed by the birth of a son, Bao Jr. Mrs. Bao, who had five years of accounting training and experience in a small business while still on the mainland, became a housewife after her marriage to Bao. In 1983, at the age of 24, Bao Jr. graduated from the most prestigious university in Taiwan, Taiwan University, with a degree in Economics. Although he had frequently played in his father's company since infancy, he officially joined the firm upon graduation. From the inception of his involvement in Lao Bao's Company, young Bao proved himself to be a reasonably competent executive. Initial assignments involved him in the manufacturing department of the company. Later assignments exposed him to financial and marketing activities. His marketing responsibilities ultimately exposed him to all of the major sales agents representing the firm in the various countries where the firm did business. In 1988, Bao Sr. sent his son to the United States to study at Columbia University. He completed his MBA two years later and, after an extended trip to California, he returned to resume his duties in the company. He rose rapidly in his father's company, through a succession of promotions, such that by 1991 he was the Vice President of the sales department at Lao Bao's Company. At that time, Bao Sr. was Chairman of the company; King, Fu was President and Ling, Lia Fa was the

---

13 By Agnes Syu, Assistant Professor, Philadelphia College of Textiles & Science, Philadelphia, Pennsylvania. Used with permission.

Dorothy Marcic and Sheila Puffer, *Management International*, West Publishing, 1994.

Executive Vice President and Chief Financial Officer. There were four other Vice Presidents in the company, in addition to Bao Jr.

Despite Bao Sr.'s best effort, senior managers felt that Bao Jr.'s succession to his father was inevitable. Furthermore, Chairman Bao, now 66 years old, had been suffering from severe lung disease for two years and was expected to announce his retirement soon.

The firm was shocked by the resignation of President King, Executive Vice President Ling and three other senior managers over a short time period of three months. It was heard later that King, Ling and two others had founded a new firm, partial competitors to Lao Bao's Company. Lao Bao, fearing further defections from his senior management staff, announced that he would continue as the head of the firm.

Discussion Questions:

1 What explains the resignation of these managers?

2 What were the advantages of Chairman Bao's decision to remain as the head of the firm? Were there any disadvantages?

3 Was there any alternative to Chairman Bao's continuation as the head of the firm?

4 According to Wu Lun, what problems do you see in Lao Bao's Company? If you were Chairman Bao, what would you do to overcome these? How feasible are your solutions under the behavioral principles of Wu Lun?

12. Duo Tsai Paint Company[14]

See "A linkage between Confucianism and the Chinese family firm in the Republic of China" later in this chapter for background to the case.

In 1963, Chao decided to return to Taiwan to establish his paint–manufacturing firm. From its very beginning, the company was very successful due to Chao's expertise in all the latest technology in his industry. Initially, the firm concentrated on the manufacture of architectural coatings, i.e, interior and exterior house paint. By 1967, the firm had begun production of industrial coatings for metal products such as cars and appliances, etc.

Duo Tsai Paint Company was founded by Victory Chao in 1964, to produce paint products for residential home and industrial facilities, e.g. automobile, machinery, farm implements, etc. The company was under the supervision of Chao and grew successfully in Taiwan.

In 1960, at the age of 30, Chao received his Ph.D. in physical polymer chemistry, the chemistry of plastics, from Oxford University in England. He specialized in latex emulsion film formers used in the manufacture of paints. Upon completion of his degree, he traveled to the United States to visit a colleague who had gone to school with him in England. He was invited to a lunch with his friend and his friend's boss, the V.P. of Research and Development for one of American's largest paint companies. Before the lunch was concluded, Chao had received and accepted an offer to work as researcher with the firm. Within a few years, Chao had distinguished himself as one of the most innovative paint chemists in the industry.

Chao's wife died in 1989 after suffering several years from colon cancer. They had three sons and one daughter. All are married. The sons and the son–in–law are managers of the firm. Background information for the children is contained in Table 1. Although all his children were born abroad, except the youngest son, Chao was strict in educating them in traditional Chinese family values. He was pleased to see that the relationships among his children were very close–knit. One thing that Chao noticed about his children after their return from their college educations, in the U.S., was that they had become much more individualistic and reserved. On one occasion, he was surprised while over-hearing this conversation between his youngest son, Kuo, and second–oldest son, Ming. Ming: "Why don't you have San San (Kuo's wife) take off this year from work to take care of An An (Kuo's first child), so that you would not be so stressful yourself?" Kuo: "It's not your business."

Chao had always been a dynamic, energetic individual with excellent health. Even with his busy schedule, he never stopped practicing taichichuan (also known as "shadow boxing") every morning. After his daily taichi ritual, while bathing preparatory to work, he collapsed and died instantly. The doctor diagnosed that his death was due to a cerebral hemorrhage.

His three sons and the daughter each inherited one–fourth of the firm. The oldest son, Chung

---

14 By Agnes Syu, Assistant Professor, Philadelphia College of Textiles & Science, Philadelphia, Pennsylvania. Used with permission.

Chao, became Chairman of the firm, replacing his father. Serious disagreements soon emerged over how best to run the firm. What was the best future goal for the firm?

The son–in–law wanted the firm to diversify. It seemed like this division might lead to the splitting of the firm, which could be avoided only by the realization of the heirs that to split it would destroy it, and with it, its value. Chung Chao has been contemplating the situation of the firm for over a month. He knows that a decision will have to be made in the coming week.

Discussion Questions:

1 What management problems are involved, according to the traditional Chinese culture or Confucius' teaching, when there are multiple heirs, as in the Duo Tsai Paint Company?

2 Are there any constraints on the leadership style that the eldest son, Chung Chao, as Chairman of the firm, may use?

3 What is your perception as to whether the heirs should split the firm or not? Explain the reasons that underlie your view.

4 If you were hired as a consultant, what suggestions would you propose for the future management structure/actual authority delegation network for the Duo Tsai Paint Company, if it decides to continue rather than split? Are your suggestions feasible under the behavioral principles of Wu Lun?

5 Do the behavioral principles of Wu Lun provide any guideline for dealing with this problem? Can you think of any way to deal with the limitations of Wu Lun when it is applied to the family firm?

13. International Negotiation Case[15]

When cultures collide

Kiel AG, a multinational conglomerate, is based in Switzerland and owns companies all over Europe. In 1988, Kiel's management developed a special interest in the construction boom in the southeastern United States.

Through an American business broker, Kiel learned about Georgia–based Edwards Engineering Inc. (EEI) as a possible acquisition target. EEI, a middle–sized construction company, had 60 employees and $12 million in annual revenues. Joseph Edwards, founder, president and sole shareholder of the company, wanted to retire and sell his interest, preferably to someone who would actively maintain the business.

Early contacts were promising. Kiel's tentative offer was not far from Edward's asking price, and Edwards was assured that Kiel would keep the company intact. As negotiations progressed, Kiel was tempted to proceed with only an informal audit of EEI. But, because of Edwards' zeal for selling and his openness and friendly approach to negotiations, an approach not understood by Kiel, the latter reluctantly hired an American Big Eight accounting firm to conduct an intensive pre–acquisition audit of its target. When the audit was concluded, a date was set for the final face–to–face negotiations.

Herbert Kiel, Kiel's president, came to the U.S. to personally conduct negotiations. He brought the company's financial controller, the head of Kiel's international real estate development division (under whose jurisdiction EEI would fall after the merger) and the company's Swiss lawyer. He also hired an American lawyer from a small Georgia firm to serve as local counsel. Edwards was represented by a large regional corporate law firm.

> Initially, both sides thought that they were close to agreement on all major issues. But after a day or two in negotiations, it became clear that they were growing further apart.

Seemingly minor issues kept blossoming into major ones. After four frustrating days, talks broke off and the Kiel group went home. Both sides were left with a negative impression, not only of each other but of the entire process of transatlantic acquisitions.

Neither side was sure what went wrong. Each wanted to make the deal, took what it thought was a fair opening position, and was encouraged by the other's opening proposals. In addition, all participants were on their best negotiating behavior. So what happened?

---

15 Abridged by Dr. Arthur Whately from Robert M. Bryan and Peter C. Buck, "When Customs Collide: The Pitfalls of International Acquisitions." *Financial Executive*, 5 (3) May/June 1989, 43-46. Used with permission.

Worlds Apart

Experienced international negotiators know this scenario is as common as it is baffling. In conducting a post–mortem, they suggest examining the behavior of each side from the cultural perspective of the other. In a deal like the one between EEI and Kiel, a number of potential trouble spots exist.

> The Swiss, accustomed to the gamesmanship and ritual characterizing European negotiations, did not know what to make of Edwards. They wavered between thinking him naive and worrying that his apparent openness was a ploy to hide some serious problem.

In his typical American way, Edwards was forthright and open. He was candid about the strengths and weaknesses of his company, and responded quickly to every request for information. Given this openness, he found the expensive and time–consuming pre–acquisition audit unnecessary and even a little insulting. In either case, esteem for Edwards and his company diminished. His impatience with the audit magnified Kiel's concern. On the other hand, Edwards was put off by the Kiel team's lengthy, polite, but unresponsive answers to his questions. They impressed him as secretive, often huddling for whispered consultations in German. Their wary response to his requests to inspect documents further alienated him.

As negotiations proceeded, Edwards displayed characteristic American pragmatism, quickly modifying his proposals and demands to respond to Kiel's concerns. Kiel proceeded in a more formal fashion, refusing to modify some positions "on principle," yet conceding other points completely. Edwards viewed Kiel as arbitrary and stubborn; Kiel viewed Edwards as "slippery" and unreliable.

Questions for Discussion:

1   What are the underlying cultural differences that are causing the conflict between these two parties?

2   Could a different approach to negotiations be taken here? Discuss briefly.

3   Using the theory of successful negotiations presented in "Insights Into international negotiations" in this chapter, briefly describe how each party can improve its negotiating behavior.

Different behaviors or tactics Edwards could take:

Insights into international negotiations[14]

Business negotiations are always a sensitive and complex activity involving a variety of skills, including planning for the negotiation meeting, accurate and effective communications with the other party, judgment regarding offers and counter offers, and anticipating the responses of the other party. Additional skills are required when negotiations involve people from other cultures. Differences in culture translate into different values and perceptions regarding the negotiation process. Americans may value promptness – "Let's get down to business" – while negotiators from other cultures will see promptness as unnecessary and the rush to get down to business as rude and overlooking social relationships. The international negotiator can use a set of skills to overcome the special problems created by international negotiations. These skills are described below (Casse, 1979):

1 To be able to view the world as others see it and to understand their behavior from their perspective. For example, mainland Chinese negotiators may need to confer often with their superiors during a negotiation meeting. They are not allowed to make major decisions without approval from their superiors. Thus, delays during the session are frequent and the time to complete a project is often viewed as excessive unless the opposing party is willing to view the world as the Chinese see it.

2 To be able to show the other party the advantages of accepting your proposal. For example, many American companies have established maquiladora (twin–plant) operations in Mexico. The advantage to the American firms is obvious: the availability of low–cost Mexican labor, which is approximately $9 a day. Parts are shipped to Mexico, assembled by hand, and the final product is then exported all over the world. American firms negotiating to locate a twin plant in Mexico must establish in the eyes of the Mexican negotiator the advantages of having the firm as a maquila. Stable employment, on–the–job training and supervisory training are some items Mexican negotiators find attractive.

3 To be able to respond to unpredicted demands and ambiguous situations without undue stress. For example, American negotiators tend to focus on one issue at a time in the negotiations – providing factual support for the issue and emphasizing its merits. Syrian negotiators, however, will seek to broaden the scope of the issue into areas seemingly irrelevant to the Americans, such as the historical value of their civilization. Such an ambiguous move will often generate confusion and frustration on the part of the unaware American negotiator. Rather than get upset,

---

14 By Arthur Whately from "Training for the Coss–Cultural Mind." SIETAR, Washington, D.C., 1979. Used with permission.

the appropriate response is to understand the Syrian's love of his country's long history and how such a long history can make the issues in the negotiations seem small and insignificant by comparison.

4 To be able to communicate your ideas so that the other party understands them. For example, the concept of compromise is foreign to Russian culture and language. If used at all, it has a derogatory connotation. Given that Russians negotiate from an ideological as well as practical position, to compromise means to violate their ideology. For Americans to be successful negotiating with Russians, they will have to negotiate the entire issue as a whole. If this is not possible, it may be permissible to engage in a form of bartering where there is a direct and equal exchange of goods on a quid pro quo basis.

> Largely because of the economic success the United States has experienced this century, Americans tend to view the world from a highly ethnocentric perspective – our way of doing business is the only way, our products are superior, and our management practices are the best.

5 To be sensitive to the cultural background of the other party. For example, when negotiating with Arabs, it is insulting to inquire about the well – being of their wives – a very private matter – or to offer something to another using the left hand, which historically is used for cleaning oneself.

American negotiators do not come by these skills naturally and often tend to be ethnocentric. Ethnocentric behaviors on the part of American negotiators have been summarized by Graham and Herberger (1983) as follows:

- **I can go it alone.** Many Americans think they can handle any negotiating situation by themselves.

- **Just call me John.** Americans emphasize informality and equality when dealing with others. They try to make others comfortable by playing down the status distinctions.

- Americans aren't very talented at speaking **foreign languages** and therefore miscommunicate frequently, not bothering to learn the language of their opposing negotiator.

- Americans like to **get to the point**, lay their cards on the table, stop beating around the bush, stop wasting time.

- **Silence is not 'golden'** to Americans. They talk frequently and expect others to do so as well.

- **One thing at a time.** Americans usually like to negotiate one issue at a time, sequentially.

- **I am what I am.** Changing one's mind is unusual for Americans.

If they are insensitive to the cultural characteristics of the other party or unaware of their own cultural predispositions, international negotiators are likely to fail. To reduce the prospects of failure, a set of negotiation skills should be part of every negotiator's mindset. These skills were identified in a large research project conducted in1976 on American negotiators and designed to distinguish between the "successful" negotiator as contrasted to the "average" negotiator. Successful negotiators were those who were rated as successful by both parties, were known to be successful based on their track record, and had a low failure rate. A total of 48 successful negotiators were studied by observing their behaviors and analyzing the recordings of 102 separate negotiating sessions.

The skills and characteristics of these successful negotiators were found to be quite different from the average negotiators. In terms of planning for the negotiation meetings, important findings were:

- Successful negotiators considered a wider range of outcomes (5.1 outcomes or options per issue) than did the average negotiator (2.6 outcomes or options per issue).

- Successful negotiators focused the negotiations on areas of common interest three times as often (38 percent of comments on areas of possible agreement or common ground) as did the average negotiator (11 percent of comments on areas of possible agreement or common ground).

- Successful negotiators were twice as likely to emphasize the long term (8.5 percent of comments) as compared to the average negotiator (4 percent of comments).

- Successful negotiators were significantly more likely to establish a range of possible outcomes or points of agreement then were average negotiators, who were most likely to specify a fixed outcome (example: "The price we want is $3.89 per unit").

- Successful negotiators were more flexible in terms of how negotiations proceeded than were average negotiators. Negotiable items were not linked to one another as often by successful negotiators. Average negotiators would attempt to make the outcome of one item contingent upon the outcome of a prior item, and so on.

Successful negotiators were found to more frequently set aside time after the negotiation meeting to review what had gone on, what was learned, and what was likely to occur during the next meeting.

Once negotiations began, other important behavioral differences between the successful and average negotiators were found. For example, successful negotiators were five times less likely during negotiations to use irritating words or phrases (example: "I am making you a generous offer") than were average negotiators: 2.3 irritating comments per hour of face–to–face speaking time vs. 10.8, respectively.

Successful negotiators were also slower to make counter proposals than were average negotiators: 1.7 vs. 3.1 counter proposals per hour of face–to–face speaking time, respectively. A third way that successful negotiators were found to be different from average negotiators was the number of reasons they gave to justify their position: Successful negotiators pose fewer reasons (1.8) for their position than do average negotiators (3.0). This finding runs counter to the commonly held notion that the more reasons one can produce to support a position, the better the chances for success.

These findings suggest ways to behave during the negotiation process to increase the chances of having a successful negotiation outcome.

References

Casse, Pierre. *Training for the Cross-Cultural Mind*, SIETAR, Washington, D.C., 1979.

Graham, J. and Herberger. Business negotiations in Japan, Brazil and the U.S. *Journal of International Business Studies*, 14, Spring/Summer 1983, 47-62.

Kindel, Thomas. Negotiations between East and West: A cultural format. Presented at the International Symposium in Pacific-Asian Business, January 1988, Honolulu, Hawaii.

A linkage between Confucianism and the Chinese family firm in the Republic of China[17]

Hofstede and Bond (1988) discovered a cultural link to economic phenomena, finding that Confucian dynamism was strongly associated with economic growth in 22 countries during the period 1965 to 1985. Confucian dynamism is basically the behavioral dimensions that are based on Confucius' teaching regarding human relationships, social structure, virtuous behavior and work ethics. Among the 22 countries, the so-called Five Dragons – Singapore (7.6 percent, #8), the Republic of China (ROC) on Taiwan (7.2 percent, #2), South Korea (6.6 percent, #4), Hong Kong (6.1 percent, #1), and Japan (4.7 percent, #3), hold the top five positions in economic growth (average annual GNP growth rate, in percentage), and number 8, 2, 4, 1 and 3 in positions for Confucian dynamism, respectively.

The ROC holds second position both in average annual GNP growth rate (7.2 percent) and in Confucian dynamism among the 22 countries, suggesting a positive relationship between Confucius' teaching and economic growth. Confucianism has been a major immigrant cultural teaching to the cluster of the Five Dragons, except for the ROC, which is along with the People's Republic of China the heir of Confucianism.

> Traits of these enterprises include a diligent and frugal working style; endurance of hardship; employment of untrained and unskilled workers; giving low priority to financial, management and marketing planning; assuming low profit; and a family-oriented management style.

The family firm in the ROC

In the mid–1980s, ROC economic policies favored big trading companies (both in public and private sectors) so that they might be internationally competitive. Big trading companies are important for the expansion of export market, and for facilitating imports of raw materials and intermediate goods at low cost. Because of Japanese success with their big trading companies, other countries, such as Korea and Singapore, instituted efforts to form big manufacturing and trading companies. The ROC government mirrored this trend. In the process, ROC economic policy makers discovered a unique economic phenomenon: 98 percent of domestic firms are medium or small enterprises holding 70 percent of the job market, 80 percent of export production, and 65 percent of national production; and most of these are family firms (Cheng, 1987).

Their working offices or production factories are often located in the living rooms of the owners' homes or apartments. Small firms typically have one to 50 workers while medium enterprises have less than 250 workers. More than half have a single owner, the rest operating as partnerships (Cheng, 1987). One trait associated with these enterprises is the nepotistic style of management most obvious in family firms.

---

17 By Agnes Syu, Assistant Professor, Philadelphia College of Textiles & Science, Philadelphia, Pennsylvania. Used with permission.

A common trait of family firms in the ROC is that they do not last too long. In the United States, the average life of family firms is 24 years, and 30 percent of these firms can be traced down to the third generation. In Singapore, only 4 percent of family firms are operated by the third generation (Lee, 1986). This phenomenon supports an old Chinese saying, "Good businesses don't last more than the third generation."

Confucianism and the Chinese family firm

Confucius' Teaching and the Development of Wu Lun

The Chinese family system in the ROC and Confucius' (551 B.C .– 479 B.C.) teachings are inseparable, since most of his teachings were built upon family relationships. Confucius created a blueprint that envisions a world in which harmony, equality, justice and universal brotherhood prevail (similar to the utopian world) (Waley, 1938). To reach this world, one must first cultivate and discipline oneself, then, govern one's family, then, govern one's nation; only then, is one able to settle and bring peace to the world (Ye, 1987). The family is the primary organizational unit with which an individual associates in learning how to reach this world.

In the micro concept of the family, Confucius followed and continued early Chinese cultural development. The Book of Change (600 B.C.) describes the ancient Chinese observation of the development nature and the sequence of human relationships:

These observations suggest that one needs to develop "the way" of getting along with the others called Jen Lun. Lun is "the way" of getting along with the others while Jen, in this context, means human. Therefore, the purpose of life for human beings on earth is to seek "the way" to get along with other people. For example, respecting and obeying older people is "the way" to get along with the elderly. If one does not follow this mode of behavior, his or her behavior is considered to be inappropriate.

Confucius extended Jen Lun by defining five basic human relationships, and principles for each relationship, called Wu Lun. These are master/follower, father/son, husband/wife, older brother/younger brother, and friends. For each relationship, certain behavioral principles must be followed to ensure a harmonious society. Confucius perceived that the practice of these principles was a result of "jen." Jen, as used here, means one's unselfishness and ability to measure other people's feelings by one's own, or one's "goodness" (Waley, 1938). As one Chinese scholar describes, "Jen" is love (Lo, 1974).

The association of "Jen" with the five basic human relationships and their principles can be expressed by a Wu Lun Chart (Figure 1). "Jen" is placed in the center of the concentric circles to stress the central idea of the development of Wu Lun. The middle and outer circles represent the five basic human relationships and their principles. The Wu Lun Chart is used to conceptualize the development of basic human relationships. One's performance of the principles of Wu Lun can be described as projections of one's love for those who are in relationships with oneself.

The emergence of family firms in the ROC can be attributed to two major factors: the improvement of personal wealth, enabling individuals to participate economically, and the fact that the family has always been the center of Eastern society. While a family functions according to social and personal motives instead of formal structures and systems, family firms simultaneously perform social and economic roles. This causes conflicts within a family and between the family and the firm in the ROC.

"First, there are heaven and earth, so there are living things; there are living things, so there are man and woman; there are man and woman, so there are husband and wife; there are husband and wife, so there are father and son; there are father and son, so there are master and follower; there are master and follower, so there is seniority (or hierarchy); there is seniority, so there is distinction between right and wrong behavior" (Ye, 1987).

Figure 1

The Wu Lun chart[18]

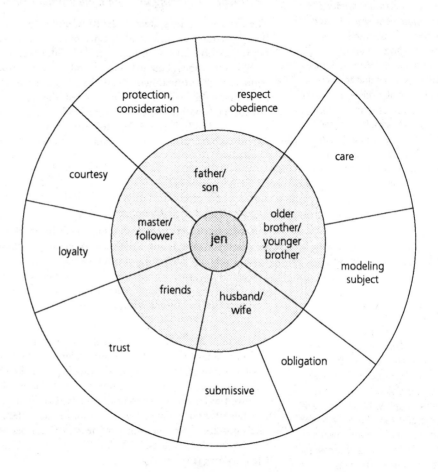

The center circle represents the central idea of the development Lun (i.e., love);
the middle circle represents the five basic human relationships;
the outer circle represents the behavioral principal each basic relationship set.

---

18 By Agnes Syu, Assistant Professor, Philadelphia College of Textiles & Science, Philadelphia, Pennsylvania. Used with permission.

Wu Lun and the Chinese Family Firm

Thus, following Wu Lun, a good person is required, in private family life, to obey and respect one's parents and to protect and be considerate of one's children. Men must oblige their wives, model themselves after their older brothers, and care for their younger brothers. Women must be submissive to their husbands. In public (including the work place), people must be courteous to followers and loyal to masters, and trust their friends.

Three out of the five basic human relationships are family relationships. Confucius believed that one who came from a healthy family (who knows "the way") would be a good influence on others as he/she entered society. Thus, family eduction is essential for the individual and basis for the development of all relationships in society.

One thing obvious about Wu Lun is that it suggests that Chinese society is paternalistic. In fact, Confucius almost always used only the male versions of language to define family relationships. In all family relationships, the relationship of father/son is considered to be the most important, and devotion of a son to his father is perceived to be the most important element of morality and conduct. This paternal character is expressed most vividly in the Chinese system of inheriting property.

When this inheritance system is carried to the level of the family firm, the son of the owner would be expected to inherit the firm. However, as long as the father who owns the firm lives, he is respected as the highest authority in the firm, and the son would not take charge or outdo his father. If the entrepreneur of the first generation has only one son, then that son will be the certain heir. If the son succeeds in investing his inheritance, the firm will probably grow. If the son is not successful in the business, instead of passing down the firm to other relatives, the owner will probably sell the firm. There is always a rare chance that a "like father, like son" situation will happen for more than three or four generations. This is the logic of the Chinese saying, "Good businesses don't last more than the third generation."

If the entrepreneur has several sons, each son would have an equal share in the inheritance. Referring to Wu Lun principles, a father would pass down his assets or properties equally among his sons to show his "consideration" or fairness for each son. In such a case the sons might end up splitting the inheritance because it complicates the family relationships. The split might be postponed, however, if it would cause devaluation of the property and the value of the firm. In the modern reality of the ROC, second–generation owners would rather adopt collective management and operation than split the family firm (Hsu, l986).

The inheritance system in Chinese culture is patriarchical. When a father passes down his assets and properties to his son, it is considered to be an expression of his "love" or "consideration and protection" for his son. On the other hand, a son recognizes his obligation and duty for the inheritance. He would try hard to continue what his father was not able to finish to show his devotion to his father.

Collective management of Chinese family firms creates a problem, that is, the emergence of a dual relationship among the brothers as elder brother and younger brother, and as co–owners. In Wu Lun, the relationship of older brother/younger brother has always been described as the relationship between one's hands and feet. However, this close relationship embeds some weaknesses when it is translated to the level of co–ownership. For example, Chinese men and women have learned since their youth that their family property will eventually be split and that each seeks his or her own independence after he or she reaches adulthood. They thus see the present family as a temporary organization. This causes ambivalence for the heirs of the family firm. They question whether they should behave in a way such as to secure their own highest personal benefit or to relinquish control of their own share to their family in order to show their care or honor for their brothers.

In contrast, when the second generation adopts a collective management style, the internal family command network becomes horizontal. Not only is the power of the leadership decentralized, but it also requires frequent coordination, negotiation, and consultation among the heirs. In this case, cliques are likely to be formed since each heir tries to secure his personal benefit in the firm. The relationship among brothers (heirs) is very unstable and vulnerable, similar to a business partnership. The operation of the family firm can be seriously interrupted and damaged due to incongruent goals, disunited command, and a weak power structure – a disharmonious family relationship. In such circumstances, the teaching of Wu Lun principles is an insufficient guide for the family relationships.

The inheritance system of the Chinese family firm can cause problems not only within the family but also between the family (the heirs) and the firm (senior managers). It is common that the senior managers are the pioneers and followers of the founder of a family firm. According to Confucian teaching, the junior owes respect to the senior, and obedience is applicable, before the inheritance, to the relationship between the young heir and the senior managers. However, once the inheritance takes place, the seniority order is reversed between the young heir and the senior managers. The young heir becomes the master of the senior managers, while psychologically, both actors are preoccupied by the previous seniority order. These senior managers are usually more experienced and older but their positions become lower than those of the heir. It is common that the senior managers are not convinced that the young heirs are experienced enough or capable of managing the family firm. They lose motivation for their devotion to the firm, due to an inevitable feeling of debasement. On the other hand, the young heir is also facing a role conflict situation. Although officially the leader of the firm, he needs to be very careful in his behavior. If he acts as an authority figure, like his father, he would be criticized for being arrogant in front of senior employees, seriously violating the Wu Lun principle. If he acts as submissive to and respectful of the senior managers as a junior should be, he would be perceived as an incompetent leader in the eyes of the other workers.

> The second problem of collective management is its inefficiency and disunity. While the father is still alive, he holds the highest authority, both in the family and firm. The command network in the family system is top–down. The father does not need to solicit opinions for decision–making or worry about challenge from others. There is no problem of a dual relationship (master/follower and father/son) between the father and the son, because in Wu Lun, the behavioral principle of master/follower is included in the father/son relationship. The father spends little time worrying about family members' opinions, and hence is able to strive wholeheartedly for the goals of the firm.

Those owners of the family firms who recognize that they can pass down their ownership and properties, but not management ability and leadership quality, to their son(s) will try to prepare their son(s) in their education and apprenticeship. However, it can only decrease, not eliminate, the degree of conflict resulting from the reversed seniority in the firm. This confusion in the new relationship of the heir and the senior management can interrupt the regular operation of the firm, especially at the beginning of the inheritance. To settle this problem, almost every family firm has to go through a transitional period. In spite of the problems with the Chinese inheritance system, 99 percent of family enterprises in the ROC were passed down to the owners' son(s) (Lee, 1986).

> Another common characteristic of the Chinese family firms is the closed style of management, which only allows the closest relatives to be in charge. A study found that the Chinese family firm in the Philippines can be expressed by three concentric circles. The innermost circle must be the owner's family members (Hsu, 1986). This phenomenon is probably the most vulnerable point of the Chinese family firm, because experienced and competent people usually leave the firm upon the realization that they could never enter the "family core." All important decisions are made by the "family core," which acts as a control, allowing family relationships to easily conform to the working situation. This characteristic is the major barrier to growth of the family firm. After all, a family has a limited number of members, and not all of them are guaranteed to be successful in operating a firm.

The Japanese writing of "family" is the same as the Chinese writing but is pronounced differently. Both see family as a "concept of continuity," but in different ways. The Chinese envision the continuity of family as the continuity of strain and family name, but not property. The Japanese perceive that the individual's life is limited, but that family and property continue; thus, their concept of the continuity of family is the continuity of family name and property, but not strain (Hsu, 1986).

If we examine the Wu Lun chart, it will be easier to understand why the Chinese family firm has such a closed style of management. Sixty percent of the Wu Lun principles emphasize the learning of family members' relationships. As a family extends its function into a business organization, this 60 percent is enlarged to an 80 percent share in the "pie" of basic human relationships because the relationship of master/follower is replaced by the family relationships. The "family core" is actually a defense mechanism that is developed in relating to the non–family members who work in the family firm. This characteristic is somewhat different from Japanese family firms, which share a similar cultural background with the Chinese.

"Home" is a more proper word to describe the Japanese family relationship than "family," because anyone who lives in the "home" is legitimate for purposes of continuing the life of the "home." Thus on heir can be an adopted son, son–in–law or even a housekeeper. Consequently, there are more choices for selecting the heir, and the "family core" is more tolerant of those who are not from the same strain but who are seen as members of the family. The Japanese see family as providing continuity for common benefit. Therefore, when this concept of family is extended to the unit of enterprise or national organization, the whole organization or nation becomes a large family.

In contrast to the characteristic of the Chinese family's equal share of inheritance, the Japanese family allows only one person to be the successor to all inheritance (Lee, 1986). This person is usually the oldest son. The other sons, if there are any, need to leave the firm or become stockholders or followers of the oldest son (1986). The Japanese family firm works the same way as their family system. Each enterprise has only one heir. The name of the firm cannot be changed nor can the property be split. Therefore, the life of most Japanese family firms continues.

References

Cheng, W. L. 1987. Strategies for the medium and small enterprises in dealing with economic changes. *Leader Journal*, 27: 11–13. Taipei, Taiwan.

Cheng, W. L. 1987. Problems of the medium and small enterprises. *Leader Journal*, 27: 18–25. Taipei, Taiwan.

Hofstede, Geert, and Bond, M. H. 1988. The Confucius connection: from cultural roots to economic growth. *Organizational Dynamics*. Spring: 5–21.

Hsu, K. A. 1987. *Central Daily News*. September 1: 1. Taipei, Taiwan.

Hsu, S. J. 1986. Family and enterprise. *Commonwealth Journal*. August: 30. Taipei, Taiwan.

Lee, Yi Wuan. 1986. Right is from man, leadership is from God. *Commonwealth Journal*. October: 158–160. Taipei, Taiwan.

Lo, Kuwang. 1974. *Philosophy of Life*. Taipei, Taiwan: Taiwan Publication.

Waley, E. 1938. *The Analects*.

Ye, G. Y. 1987. *Application of Book of Change*. Taipei, Taiwan: Li Min Cultural Enterprise Inc.

A Miss Manners guide to doing business in Europe[19]

In Europe, the concept of 1992 is now under way. The beginning of European unity has been fraught with all the anticipated problems and more, but the engine is running and the economic machinery is beginning to work. Meanwhile, American business is watching, waiting and readying itself for increased competition, aware that the staples of automobiles and airlines will be challenged but also licking its proverbial chops at the economic prospects that a united Europe presents: a $4 trillion market economy!

Doing business in Europe will be easy, American businesspeople assume, not just because of standardized parts and fewer trading restrictions but also because "these are our kinds of folk." China has 25 percent of the people in the world, but the customs, cultures and world views of Far Eastern cultures are foreign to Americans. It is difficult for Americans to think like "them." Not so the Europeans, the American businessperson assumes. Once you overcome the language barriers, you have the same kind of people Americans are. After all, we share the same ancestry.

To be sure, Americans and Europeans are relatives both metaphorically and in terms of much of their cultural heritage. But over time these two continents have grown apart along critical dimensions, and efforts to do more business together may not be as shock-free as many American businesspeople expect. True, the cultural differences between the United States and Europe are far less pronounced than are those between Western and Eastern cultures, but important differences do exist. American businesspeople must adjust and adapt their behavior to these subtle differences if they have any hope of attaining success within this new merger of nations. What follows is a "Miss Manners" guide to social and business etiquette in Europe. Its purpose is to help American businesspeople avoid some common social and cultural gaffes when initiating business contacts in Europe. We hope it will help.

> In 1869, Mark Twain published *Innocents Abroad*, a collection of essays describing his travels in Europe, Egypt and the Holy Land. A better title for the work might have been *Ignorants Abroad*, for in many ways, Twain set the tone for American behavior abroad for the next 125 years.

Be innocent, not arrogant

Twain proudly describes what 100 years later would become known as the "Ugly American": a town group that people enjoyed wearing inappropriate clothing for a country's culture and "talked loudly at the table sometimes...and got what we conveniently could out of a franc." The essays end with a patriotic fervor that could only greatly offend Twain's European hosts:

"We always took care to make it understood that we were American – Americans! ...The people of those foreign countries are very, very ignorant...people stared at us everywhere, and we stared at them. We generally made them feel rather small, too, before we got done with them, because we bore them down with America's greatness until we crushed them."

---

19 By John Hill and Ronald Dulek, *Business Horizons*, July-August 1993, 48-53. Used with permission.

Dorothy Marcic and Sheila Puffer, *Management International*, West Publishing, 1994.
*All rights reserved. May not be reproduced without written permission of the publisher.
For more information, contact West Publishing, Publications Dept., 610 Opperman Drive,
St. Paul, MN 55164.*

Twain inevitably stretched reality with his own unique brand of poetic license. However, beneath the veneer is more than a modicum of national chauvinism.

Mark Twain's excesses can, of course, be attributed to a youthful country's need to assert its individuality against "Mother Europe." But teenage America is now grown up, and it is time to establish mature adult relationships.

One key to doing this involves an appreciation of the parents and what they have experienced. Europeans love the past – and with due cause. The history of the United States pales in comparison with that of the countries forming the European Community. This area's long, complex history and the distinguished traditions that have evolved from it cannot be easily discarded. That history influences and affects the present. Understanding history and traditions is therefore an integral part of understanding the E.C. today.

U.S. businesspeople should therefore be receptive to European history and culture. They should inquire about, study, express interest in and ask questions about traditions and political events. All questions are fair if they are asked sincerely and express genuine interest. One of the best ways to demonstrate such sincerity is to listen carefully when a business host describes traditions, places or events. For just as Americans take pride in showing and telling visitors about Concord, Lexington and Gettysburg, European hosts enjoy showing and telling visitors about local and national places of historical interest. And educated Europeans are excellent and amusing raconteurs!

Recognize that different social systems cause different views of material worth

Henry James' *The American* tells of the self-made, wealthy American, Christopher Newman, who aspires to marry a beautiful Parisian widow. The widow's relatives veto the marriage because Newman is not a nobleman, even though he is affluent. In many ways, James' story describes the basic difference between nineteenth-century European and American social systems. The differences between the two have lessened but not disappeared in the 115 years that have passed since the publication of James' novel.

European class systems are more rigid than their American counterparts. They are based on hereditary criteria and family pedigree. The social class into which a person is born is probably the one in which that person will die. Moving between social classes is difficult. The primary catalyst for social mobility tends to be educational achievement, although even that does not ensure social progression.

The American social class system, on the other hand, is fluid. It is based on a system of self-reliance; Americans idolize and praise the self-made person. James' main character in *The American*, Christopher Newman (a.k.a. the New Man), symbolizes the notion that humankind determines its own worth in society, and that economic criteria – income, wealth, material possessions – measures worth. Money is power within the American social system; money brings class, prestige and social status.

The equation of money with social status drives American materialism. A material possession denotes status. Americans pay close attention to the cars they drive, the neighborhoods in which they live and the cost of their possessions. Compliments about houses and possessions are taken kindly by Americans, and monetary values of goods are frequently discussed. Electronic and labor-saving gadgets bring not only efficiency (a characteristic to be mentioned later), but they also demonstrate material worth. How else can one explain paying $200 for a fountain pen? Or $3,000 for a watch that keeps time less accurately than one available for $12.50?

So in dealing with Europeans, American businesspeople are advised not to comment on their hosts' possessions unless they truly appreciate them. Appreciation should come from the objects' age, beauty or form, not from its price. The past is revered and should not be cast aside lightly. Compliments should come from the heart, for Europeans find few things as insulting as a superficial comment. Social platitudes are easy to spot. Never praise things as a matter of course, only if they deserve it.

Problems arise when Americans abroad start attaching material values to most of what they see. Americans will often compliment Europeans on their possessions, even speculating about the price or cost of such possessions. Historic structures such as Windsor Castle are often praised with the words, "Can you imagine what that would cost to build today?"

Although European hosts can usually turn a blind eye to such comments, they are much less forgiving when such comments refer to their personal possessions. American visitors customarily compliment hosts' homes and possessions. In Europe such pleasantries can embarrass hosts. First, Europeans know that in most cases what they own is likely to be less noteworthy than what is found in the average American household. The compliment therefore appears hollow and superficial. Second, Europeans are not as likely to value an object because of its dollar value. Objects are appreciated for their age, beauty, form – or because they have been in the family for years.

For Europeans, then, material possessions are inadequate indicators of an individual's worth. Social longevity is more meaningful. Only after a family has been in a particular social class for one or two generations can it consider itself of that social class. Economic criteria that give individuals rapid vertical social mobility are less relevant. The length of time one has been in a class is more important than the material possessions that propelled one there.

View business relationships as marathons, not wind sprints

A good first impression is essential to most Americans. They work from the adage, "You never get a second chance to make a good first impression." Americans therefore tend initially to overwhelm Europeans. "Gushy" is how one international expert describes it.

Americans want to become acquainted with people as quickly as possible. To this end, they are quick to use first names. Such cutting through formalities is efficient, saves time and establishes at least a superficial social rapport. The idea that social bonding activities are time-consuming and involve forming friendships is anathema to most U.S. businesspeople. However, this is the way Europeans develop relationships. British reserve and German and Swiss formality are all apparent in initial meetings, providing listeners time to size up the speaker. Europeans want to become well–acquainted with someone before establishing social bonds. They want to know the "real" person, including observations of the person's integrity, honesty and, of course, social standing.

After a while, the ice melts, and over tea or coffee conversations blossom. This is when Europeans come to know Americans and try to establish rapport, by sharing intimate family details or even pet gripes about their own or American society. This is customarily where Americans "dry up" or become evasive. They worry about opinions or impressions that may alienate people, or intimacies that may come back to haunt them at a future time. They "back off."

So it is easy to see how a social impasse can occur. Americans regard conversation as a sprint. They run into it rapidly, quickly establishing what they perceive as social rapport. Europeans view conversation as a marathon. They start slowly but pick up the tempo once the formal preliminaries end. This often occurs about the same time Americans run out of conversation. Either way, it is easy to see why liaisons between Europeans and Americans can falter.

One topic to be especially aware of is politics – a favorite pastime all over the world but especially in Europe. Businesspeople can expect to find themselves having to defend U.S. foreign policy. Educated Europeans are well–versed in world affairs but rarely let politics stand in the way of friendship. Hence, Americans should be ready to handle political and world–event discussions on an intellectual rather than a patriotic level. Most Europeans do not take their politicians as seriously as Americans; political satires are national pastimes, although one must always be vigilant and monitor the body language being communicated.

> The antidote for Americans abroad is reserve. Exercise restraint when first meeting people. Avoid rushing into using first names. Europeans generally prefer to be addressed by their formal titles (Mr., Ms., Dr.) for quite a while after being introduced. Further, Americans should let conversations develop naturally. Ask questions. Strive for sincerity and remember that Europeans are not interested in the superficial public relations person.

Forget Vince Lombardi; remember Eddie "the Eagle" Edwards

Most societies have competitive elements within them, but the degree of societal competitiveness varies. The United States is the most market–forces oriented country in the world; its corporations are among the world's most competitive. Unfortunately, American competitiveness does not stop in the boardroom. Rivalries between groups and individuals are part of Americana. Its citizens desire to be first in almost everything. Why else would a country unleash an entourage of NBA professional basketball players to participate in the Olympics? The quote attributed to legendary football coach Vince Lombardi characterizes much of the American view of competition: "Winning isn't everything, it's the only thing."

Teamwork and sociability are ingrained into European lifestyles. Their major sports – among them soccer, rugby and cricket – all have strong team orientations. In many ways, these sports resemble some American sports, particularly basketball, but European sports have fewer pre-planned, choreographed plays. Often, sports are played for the fun of playing, with the emphasis on winning less pronounced; witness international cricket matches, which are played six hours per day for five days but are still declared draws if both sides fail to complete two innings each.

> American competitive behavior abroad often seems out of place. Because European social systems are more staid, with relatively little vertical movement, there are few reasons for people and groups to compete against each other. Mobility is not an option. Competition between individuals is emphasized less and is sometimes even grounds for social ostracism.

In business situations, American competitiveness surfaces when agreements are being formalized. The United States has more than 750,000 lawyers (70 percent of the world's total); one of their primary purposes is to ensure that contracts are water-tight. Loopholes or fine–print provisions are viewed as ways to wriggle out of obligations. If one does find a loophole, it is socially acceptable – "good business" – to take advantage of it.

Business relationships in Europe have a more relaxed atmosphere. In most foreign markets, business and social relationships are intertwined. Americans want objectivity in their commercial relationships so they can sever them with a minimal of social inconvenience if things get rough; many Europeans (with the exceptions of Germans, Swiss and some Scandinavians) like to build up the social sides of business relationships. The contract that is then formed is social, not business – but it is as binding as any legal contract. Because U.S. businesspeople have a desire to avoid subjectivity and personal interplay within their commerce, they often appear cold and aloof.

American businesspeople in Europe, then, are advised to control their competitive juices and to set aside their win-at-all-cost philosophy. Europeans like to win, but the world does not collapse if they do not. In a sense, the symbol for European competition might be Eddie Edwards, the Olympic skier who represented England in the ski-jump competition in the 1988

Olympics. Eddie quickly became an Olympic everyman, with the world holding its breath hoping not that Eddie would win, but that he would land safely. Eddie's prayer before jumping, "May I survive," in many ways symbolizes the European concept of competition: One does not have to be competitively superior, only a competitive survivor.

View change as good, but not godly

American businesspeople are renowned for their hustle, for not letting grass grow under their feet. They constantly change things – themselves, their images, homes, products, services, the way they do things. To Americans, change is good; change is improvement. The spate of recent bestselling business books exemplifies America's love affair with change. Peters and Waterman, Peters and Allen, and Terrence Deal have elevated change into an American deity. Change, each writer argues, is vital to corporate America's survival.

This respect for the past and for tradition is not just a societal feature for Europeans; it pervades thinking at the individual level as well. The result is that for Americans to question the status quo or to suggest change is often a lose-lose situation. For one thing, European hosts may have already tried some of the American suggestions and concluded that the present methods are optimal. Even if they have not tried American methods, it is likely that European hosts are so traditional they would not accept an outsider's suggestions for change anyway.

European countries and companies do not so easily discard their long and proud histories. Patience and an established way of doing things are virtues, not weaknesses. Change occurs only after its implications are fully examined and understood – and even then reluctantly. These are cautious, conservative societies in which one needs a reason to change.

The best way to administer change in traditional societies such as Europe's is to make it occur behind the scenes. Change never occurs in a public, face-to-face confrontation. Rather, Americans should suggest a new idea in private to an individual or to a small group of individuals; the suggestions should be made in a calm, placid, quiet manner. If the idea takes (and it often does if it makes the local managers look progressive), the originator of the suggestion should not be surprised to receive little or no public credit for the concept. But that person will have gained the confidence of a handful of important managers, each of whom will repay this favor gradually by speaking favorably to others in a low-key, subtle manner. The European networking system is subtle and quiet, but effective.

Use a Walden, not a Greenwich, approach to time

The Europeans view time as important, but few are obsessed by it. They are not, of course, as indifferent to it as the people of Latin America – where to arrive less than 15 minutes late is rude – but they are still not as fastidious about it as Americans. In a rather ironic twist, Greenwich – the symbol of precision – is found in Europe. Henry David Thoreau, a man with a European vision of time, was born in America. In the midst of the business-driven, go-go-go age of the nineteenth century, Thoreau walked calmly beside his pond and purportedly observed, "Time is but the stream I go a-fishing in."

Thoreau, taken as a European, symbolizes the basic difference between the European and American concepts of time. The difference exists in the terms "precise" and "pressed". Europeans are generally precise; they are as on–time as most Americans. Americans are pressed; they are on-time but hurrying to remain so. Pressed behavior exists among Americans because they equate time with efficiency. Efficiency leads to higher productivity, creating more goods and generating more wealth. Moreover, time is money.

Based on these equations, Americans strive to maximize their use of time. In the business world, this means calling on more customers more quickly, talking business over all meals, and conducting business over late–night drinks in a bar. Lost time is lost opportunity.

The notion of pressed time is most clearly evidenced in American tourists abroad. Tours that promise to show 12 countries in six days receive amazing support. Perhaps most frightening of all, after having completed such whirlwind tours, participants declare themselves "pretty international."

Americans' concept of "pressed time" proves most damaging by the public behavior that surrounds a business transaction. They often complain loudly about lackadaisical service in shops, hotels and restaurants and they imply or openly state that slow service demonstrates that foreigners are lazy and inefficient. Often, business-people voice these complaints in front of their European hosts. In doing so, they inadvertently insult not only the locals providing the service but also the hosts who identify with and understand the different pace of their own country.

Patience, then, is a virtue. Americans must be tolerant when service levels fall short of American standards. They should take their cues from locals who know when to become annoyed and when to register protests. (See what happens when subway trains are very late in Paris.) Accept the level of service and keep the comments down until you reach the confines of the hotel room. If there is any complaining to do, let the locals do it.

Prepare to do business in Europe

Every experienced traveler knows that a trip is more enjoyable and meaningful when one has done one's homework in advance – that is, having read something about the place to be visited. Likewise, American businesspeople will find advance preparation beneficial to their business interests in Europe. At the very least, Americans should prepare to do business in Europe by studying the countries' histories, current events and cultural heritages. These efforts will be rewarded by a broadened ability to ask intelligent questions and initiate conversations with European hosts on matters of mutual interest.

For business people, the Department of Commerce's excellent *Overseas Business Report's* provides sound commercial information, as does its *Foreign Economic Trends and Their Implications for the United States*. For those seeking cultural information about gestures, attitudes, diets, visiting protocols, customs and the like, Brigham Young University's Culturegram Series is a "must buy." At about $30 for 100 countries, it provides excellent value.

Hector St. John Crevecoeur's *Letters from An American Farmer*, originally published in 1782, praised American virtues such as thrift and hard work, diligently tracing the ties that exist between Europe and the young American nation. Crevecoeur knew that the adolescent America had to establish its own identity before it could develop a mature relationship with its European parent. Yet at the same time, Crevecoeur saw "a secret communion among good men throughout the world: a mental affinity connecting them by a similitude of sentiments."

The beginning of EC 92 gives American businesspeople an opportunity to re–establish this "similitude of sentiments." Americans can do business in Europe effectively and efficiently. Europeans do not shun competition – their economic unification demonstrates that. But adopting American-style competition does not mean adopting American attitudes on all other fronts. Eventually, Western Europe may become more like the United States, but until that actually occurs, Americans must compete on European terms and remember European perspectives or be prepared for failure. American businesspeople must not land on European shores striving to create little Americas. They must instead respect European traditions and cultures and bring this respect and understanding to all of their business and personal dealings.

References

Culturegram Series, Brigham Young University, David M. Kennedy Center for International Studies, Provo, Utah, 84602.

J Hector St. John Crevecoeur, *Letters From An American Farmer* (Garden City, New York Doubleday & Company, 1976).

Mark Twain, *The Innocents Abroad*, or The New Pilgrims' Progress (New York Literary Classics of the United States, 1984).

"Unlikely Ski Jumper Lands, Hard, in Calgary," *New York Times*, February 13, 1988. pp. 51, 55.

Ethics

Attitudes toward business ethics vary more widely around the world than business practices and procedures, which have tended to become more standardized in many countries and industries. Ethics emanate from deep-seated values about appropriate behavior and therefore do not change readily. *The globalization of business ethics: Why America remains distinctive* describes violations of business ethics around the world. It also explains "the ethics gap" between the United States and other countries by offering several reasons why Americans are more preoccupied with business ethics than other nationalities. One reason, the greater regulation of business in the U.S., is described in detail in *The Foreign Corrupt Practices Act: Revisited and amended.* The article outlines the antibribery provisions and accounting controls mandated by the Foreign Corrupt Practices Act of 1977 and the 1988 amendments passed in the Omnibus Trade and Competitiveness Act. These legislative documents provide guidelines for conducting business ethically, but many situations fall into "gray areas" that require careful interpretation and judgment.

The complex issues that arise in international business often create ethical dilemmas for Americans. An exercise, *Bribery in international business,* presents a series of situations around the world that require decisions about respecting U.S. law, observing cultural practices in the host country, and making trade-offs between ethical behavior and profits. *Chicago Medical Supplies Corp.* and *A different situation* raise issues of ethics versus profits. The first case deals with explaining unusually high sales figures in India, and the second one involves unseemly practices in maintaining sales in Japan. *H.B. Fuller in Honduras: Street children and substance abuse* extends business ethics to the societal level by exploring the social responsibility of an American firm selling glue that is misused by glue sniffers, including children, in Honduras.

Ethics

14. Bribery in international business[1]

purpose

To discuss issues related to ethical behavior in international business dealings.

group size

Any number of groups of 4-6 members.

time required

One class period.

preparation required

Students read mini-cases and decide what action should be taken in each one. Also read the article on Foreign Corrupt Practices Act, later in this chapter.

Cases

1 You are driving to a nearby country from your job as a manager of a foreign subsidiary. In your car are a number of rather expensive gifts for family and friends in the country you are visiting. When you cross the border, the customs official tells you the duty will be equivalent to $200. Then he smiles, however, hands back your passport and quietly suggests you put a smaller sum, say $20, in the passport and hand it back to him.

What do you do?

2 You have been hired as an independent consultant on a United States development grant. Part of your job involves working with the Ministry of Health in a developing country. Your assignment is to help standardize some procedures to test for various diseases in the population. After two weeks on the job, a higher-level manager complains to you that money donated by the World Health Organization to the ministry for purchasing vaccines has actually been used to buy expensive computers for top-ranking officials.

What do you do?

Dorothy Marcic and Sheila Puffer, *Management International*, West Publishing, 1994.
All rights reserved. May not be reproduced without written permission of the publisher. For more information, contact West Publishing, Publications Dept., 610 Opperman Drive, St. Paul, MN 55164.

3 You have been trying for several months to privatize what was formerly a state-owned business. The company has been doing well and will likely do better in private hands. Unfortunately, the paperwork is slow and it may take many more months to finish. An official who can help suggests that if you pay expenses for him and his family to visit the parent company in the United States (plus a two-week vacation at Disney World and in New York City), the paperwork can be completed within one week.

What do you do?

4 One of your top managers in a Middle Eastern country has been kidnapped by a terrorist group that has demanded a ransom of $2 million, plus food assistance for refugees in a specified camp. If the ransom is not paid, they threaten to kill him.

What do you do?

5 On a business trip to a developing country, you see a nice leather briefcase (which you badly need) for a reasonable price in the local currency (the equivalent of $200 on the standard exchange rate). In this country, however, it is difficult for the locals to get U.S. dollars or other hard currency. The shop clerk offers you the briefcase for $100 if you pay in U.S. dollars.

What do you do?

6 You are the manager of a foreign subsidiary and have brought your car with you from the U.S. Because it is a foreign-purchased car, you must go through a complicated web of lines and bureaucracy (and you yourself must do it – no one can do it for you), which takes anywhere from 20 to 40 hours during business hours. One official tells you, however, that he can "help" if you "loan"him $100 and buy him some good U.S. bourbon.

What do you do?

7 Your company has been trying to get foreign contracts in this developing country for several months. Yesterday, the brother-in-law of the Finance Minister offered to work as a consultant to help you secure contracts. He charges one and one-half times more than anyone else in a similar situation.

What do you do?

8 You have been working as the director of the foreign subsidiary for several months. This week, you learned several valued employees have part-time businesses that they run while on the job. One of them exchanges foreign currency for employees and visitors. Another rents a few cars to visitors. And so on. You are told this has been acceptable behavior for years.

What do you do?

9 As manager of a foreign subsidiary, you recently discovered your chief of operations has authorized a very convoluted accounting system, most likely to hide many costs that go to his pocket. Right now, you have no real proof, but rumors are circulating to that effect as well. This chief, however, has close ties to officials in the government who can make or break your company in this country.

What do you do?

10 You have been hired to do some management training in a developing country. The costs of the program are almost entirely covered by a U.S. government agency. The people responsible for setting up one of the programs in a large company tell you they want the program to be held in a resort hotel (which is not much more expensive than any other) in a beautiful part of the country. Further, because they are so busy with all the changes in their country, they cannot come to a five-day program, which is what has been funded. Could you please make it a little longer each day and shorten it to three days? You would get paid the same.

What do you do?

11 You have been hired by an investment firm funded by U.S. dollars. Your job is to fund companies in several former communist countries. If you do not meet your quota for each of three months, you will lose your job, or at least have your salary severely cut back. One of the countries is still run by communists, though they have changed the name of their political party. They want you to fund three companies that would still be tightly controlled by the state. You know they would hire their relatives to run those companies. Yet, if you don't fund them, no other opportunities will exist for you in this country.

What do you do?

12 Your new job is to secure contracts with foreign governments in several developing countries. One of your colleagues takes you aside one day to give you "tips" on how to make sure you get the contracts you are after. He tells you what each nationality likes to hear, to soothe their egos or other psychological needs. For example, people in one country like to be told they will have a better image with the U.S. government if they contract with your company (of course, this is not true). If you tell them these things, he says, they will most definitely give you the contracts. If not, someone in another company will tell them similar things and they will get the contracts.

What do you do?

13 You have been asked to be on the board of directors of a large telecommunications company about to be privatized. The two main organizers of the project, former government officials, have asked that their names not be used until after all the governmental approval is set, as they were are concerned with being accused of using undue influence in other privatization projects.

What do you do?

14 You are the manager of a foreign company in a country where bribery is common. You have been told an important shipment has arrived but it will take up to six months to clear the paperwork. However, you were informed casually that a "tip" of $200 would cut the time to three days.

What do you do?

15. Chicago Medical Supplies Corporation: Explaining sales in India[2]

Related topics covered: corruption, bribery, whistle-blowing.

Chicago Medical Supplies Corporation was a privately owned company that sold medical devices, such as diagnostic and therapeutic catheters, to hospitals and practicing doctors. This corporation had existed for about 15 years and was growing rapidly. Sales reached approximately $200 million in 1991. Chicago Medical serves four major medical specialties – cardiology, radiology, gastroenterology and urology – through separate product divisions. Each of these divisions had its own sales forces and marketing teams. Manufacturing, research and development, financing, and accounting were shared between the divisions. The company's sales were worldwide, with subsidiaries in France, Germany and Japan.

> This deal would be very beneficial to Chicago Medical, giving the company the opportunity to expand. On the other hand, Chicago Medical employees were under tremendous pressure from the owners to be among the top performers in their industry. The owners wanted to drive profits as high as possible so that the company would be at the pinnacle of its success and the market when the decision of whether to buy was made in seven years.

The medical devices industry is not the same as pharmaceuticals or medical equipment; its sole function is to produce tools necessary for medical procedures. Demand for medical devices shifts with the health of the economy, but the fluctuation is minimal in comparison with other industries.

The deal

With the rapid growth of the medical devices industry, Chicago Medical Supplies Corporation expanded rapidly. After several years of swift and successful expansion, Chicago Medical reached a point where it couldn't generate working capital internally and had exhausted financing from banks. The owners of Chicago Medical did not want to go public with stocks and similar financing, fearing loss of control and equity. Accordingly, they began searching for an investor, thus enabling them to continue their expansion. After an in-depth search, the company found an interested major player in the pharmaceuticals industry. This corporation, one of the elite Fortune 500, had the finances that Chicago Medical needed.

The two companies' managements made a deal stating that the pharmaceutical corporation would invest a limited amount of capital in Chicago Medical. In seven years, the investor would have the option of buying the firm or allowing it to continue as a privately owned corporation. At the end of the seven years, an appro-

2 By Kara Stull under the direction of Lynne M. H. Rosansky, Ph.D. Used with permission. Names and details have been disguised. ©Babson College, 1992.

Dorothy Marcic and Sheila Puffer, *Management International*, West Publishing, 1994.
All rights reserved. May not be reproduced without written permission of the publisher. For more information, contact West Publishing, Publications Dept., 610 Opperman Drive, St. Paul, MN 55164.

priate price for Chicago Medical would be determined by multiplying the average after-tax profits of 1990 and 1991 by the acquiring company's price-earnings ratio.

Steve Jensen

Steve Jensen received his doctorate in management from Harvard in 1981. He taught in a local university for several years and then got involved with the medical devices industry.

Steve was a happily married family man. He and his wife had their first child in 1987 and planned to have more. Steve's only regret was that he could not spend as much time as he wanted with his family due to the requirements of his job.

Steve entered Chicago Medical as a product manager in the gastroenterology division, but one year after the International Division was established, he was offered a position there in sales management. In the International Division, Jensen's title was Director of Export Sales. The job consisted of working with approximately 100 independent distributors in 65 countries for the purpose of achieving sales targets. The predetermined sales targets were $12 million in 1988, $15 million in 1989, and $19.5 million in 1990. Jensen was also responsible for building the distributor network and meeting expense targets.

The scenario

India was categorized in the C group from the time that Jensen had started in export sales. This country had always operated in the same manner, with several small independent distributors all working for Chicago Medical on a non-exclusive basis. Since the distributors in India were ranked in the C group and had never given Chicago Medical much sales, India was not a priority for Jensen.

Chicago Medical's international distributors and country markets were prioritized in three different groups: A, B and C. At the end of each year, the sales from the four divisions would be compared and ranked in descending order. A was the high priority group of six to twelve distributors that received the maximum effort and support from Chicago Medical. The B group of another twelve distributors received considerable support, but less than the A group. The C group received whatever support Chicago Medical could give after the two higher-priority classes.

Surprisingly, on an August afternoon, Steve Jensen received a phone call from Jamal, the president of one of these Indian distributors. Jamal expressed his desire to become the exclusive Indian distributor for Chicago Medical. Jensen was hesitant at first, but when Jamal demonstrated his dedication by attending a worldwide training meeting in Chicago, Jensen saw the aggressiveness imperative in a great salesman. It was these qualities that led Jensen to grant Jamal the position as the sole Chicago Medical distributor in India. Furthermore, Jamal had demonstrated great perseverance by continually staying in contact with Jensen and reassuring him that "he was the man" who would turn India into one of the company's biggest country markets (sales figures). His desire to commit himself and his steadfast determination convinced Jensen to give Jamal the exclusive contract.

During that year, Jensen was happy to see that Jamal was aspiring to the goals they had set and was working extremely hard. Jensen was pleased with Jamal's work and had noticed that the sales figures for India had increased by 100 percent. But despite the growth and Jamal's efforts, India still remained a low- to middle-priority country in the ranking system.

The next years held many surprises for Steve Jensen. After the next full year's sales figures came out, Jensen was astonished by the numbers for India. India's sales had increased by approximately $400,000, especially in cardiology. Due to Jamal's hard work, the country had moved into the top echelon of the B distributors. But this was not the end of Jamal's success. With the next sales figures, India moved into the A class and would now be a high-priority country. Jensen felt that it was time for Jamal to come to Chicago Medical and give a presentation on the market size, future prospects, key physicians, marketing and sales plans, and plans for covering all of India, a large and internally diverse nation.

The following year even more substantial orders were placed, amounting to nearly $1 million. When Jensen saw these figures, he was amazed. He was aware of Jamal's persistence and aggressiveness when it came to sales, but this large an increase was very impressive.

The following spring, Jamal came to the United States and gave his presentation to several important members of the International Department, including Steve Jensen. Jamal's presentation was thoroughly complete, excluding no details. Nevertheless, there was one part of Jamal's presentation that puzzled Jensen. When Jamal had discussed the market and forecasted sales figures, Jensen realized that the actual numbers were very different from what they should have been. Jamal listed the market for the product as X, but when he listed the forecasted sales dollars, sales exceeded the market for the product (See Exhibit 1). Steve was not sure what this meant. He thought that maybe the recent success in India had Jamal embellishing when it came down to actual dollars or that maybe it was just a simple error. At any rate, Jensen waited for the two men to be alone to ask the questions he had concerning these numbers.

Steve sat back and listened as Jamal explained that there are key physicians and players whom he works with directly. For each order of considerable size, a certain percentage of its dollar value was given to people by Jamal. Furthermore, a great deal of India's medical supplies are funded by the Indian government, so Jamal was greasing the palms of everyone down the line – government officials, customs agents, accounting clerks, purchasing agents and local physicians. This was the answer that Steve Jensen did not want to hear. The first thing that entered his mind was that they were violating the Foreign Corrupt Practices Act. He knew that this matter would take a lot of thinking and consultation with colleagues at Chicago Medical. So he bid farewell and told Jamal that he would be in touch.

On Jamal's last day at Chicago Medical, Steve Jensen asked him about the market for the product and the unmatched forecasted sales dollars. Jamal seemed quite uneasy at first, but then responded with a straightforward answer: "This is a very unusual situation, Steve. In India, business is done very differently than it is here in the United States."

Jensen's decision

Steve Jensen was in very uncomfortable and unfamiliar territory. For the past two years, he had done exceptionally well in the International Department, and he looked all the better with the surprise of India moving from a class C to class A distributor. But now he was faced with an ugly situation. If Steve blew the whistle on Jamal, he would lose a substantial amount of sales dollars for the company. With the internal pressure at Chicago Medical to have top performance in all areas, Steve could lose his job. On the other hand, if Steve was caught letting Jamal do business the way Jamal said it is done in India, he could face unthinkable penalties under the Foreign Corrupt Practices Act.

> Steve Jensen knew that he was in a situation where any choice he made would have unfavorable ramifications. If he blew the whistle on Jamal, he would most likely lose his job. If he let things go on as they were, he could go to jail or be blackballed from the business world.

Steve went to several colleagues, including his boss, and received the same response from everyone: Chicago Medical wants sales any way it can get them. Jensen's boss was frank with him. He told him that he would not admit knowing or supporting him if anything were uncovered concerning the Foreign Corrupt Practices Act. In addition, Steve knew he could lose his job if he failed to meet his specified quotas. So now Steve found himself in a Catch-22.

Steve Jensen was well-educated, adequately experienced in public relations, and knowledgeable in the management field. As Director of Export Sales, Jensen was very successful, always meeting or exceeding his monthly quotas. In spite of Steve's education and experience, however, he found himself in an uncomfortable situation – one that might lead him to break federal law.

Questions

1 What should Steve do?

2 How can Steve avail himself of "whistleblower protection" regulations? Will this protection safeguard Steve's career, or just this job for now?

3 Does the Foreign Corrupt Practices Act impose criminal penalties for what should be known, or only for what is actually known? Should the law penalize someone for having inquired? Has this legislation fostered a corporate culture of "plausible deniability"?

Exhibit 1
Jamal's forecasted market and sales plan

DIVISION	PRODUCT	EXPECTED MARKET	EXPECTED SALES
CARDIOLOGY	A	$300,000	$350,000
CARDIOLOGY	B	$300,000	$380,000
CARDIOLOGY	C	$400,000	$420,000
CARDIOLOGY	D	$350,000	$400,000
CARDIOLOGY	E	$300,000	$300,000
RADIOLOGY	F	$100,000	$120,000
RADIOLOGY	G	$100,000	$100,000
RADIOLOGY	H	$150,000	$150,000
RADIOLOGY	I	$ 85,000	$100,000
RADIOLOGY	J	$ 50,000	$ 75,000
GASTRO/UROLOGY	K	$180,000	$180,000
GASTRO/UROLOGY	L	$ 90,000	$100,000
GASTRO/UROLOGY	M	$120,000	$130,000
GASTRO/UROLOGY	N	$100,000	$100,000
GASTRO/UROLOGY	O	$ 85,000	$100,000

16. A different situation: Maintaining sales in Japan[3]

preparation suggested:

background on The Foreign Corrupt Practices Act (see article later in this chapter)

While Jane Welch was growing up in Texas, she was an excellent student. Her parents and teachers thought of her as "college capable." In fact, she never seriously considered any option other than college. She majored in marketing because one of her goals was, in her own words, "not to get stuck in civil service like my dad did. Private industry is the place for me, where I have more of an opportunity to be promoted on my own merits and not necessarily on seniority." Jane entered college and, as usual, did well scholastically.

One day during the spring semester of her senior year, Jane talked with one of her marketing professors, Dr. Mayfield, about her career goals. Dr. Mayfield suggested that perhaps Jane should look into the exporting business. Dr. Mayfield said he had a friend in Memphis who was a vice president in a cotton exporting firm, Cotton Belt Exporting. Things fell into place and Jane received and accepted an offer of a job in the firm.

As college graduation neared, Jane began to interview with a number of companies. The college placement counselor advised Jane to make a list of what she would find desirable and undesirable in a job. One of the items on her list was that the company and its product or goal had to be socially justifiable. This item came to mind because many of her classmates were going to work for oil companies. In spite of the oil companies' slightly higher pay scale, Jane believed she would not want to work for a company that sold a non-renewable resource.

Another requirement on her list was that she wanted to travel in her job. Her family had traveled in the United States on vacations when she was a child, and she had been to Mexico and Canada. But she wanted to see something of other parts of the world. Although Jane did not care to live in another country, she did think that a job that took her periodically to other countries for short trips would be desirable.

For the first couple of years, Jane's responsibilities included traveling throughout the southern United States and California buying cotton from farmers and gins. But the company promised that once she had proven herself in a couple of positions, she would be promoted to dealing directly with people in foreign countries. After about six years and two positions in the firm, she was promoted to Manager of Export Sales to Japan.

---

3 By Paul N. Keaton and Patricia A. Watson-Kuentz. Used with permission.

Jane also became acquainted with the mechanics of selling cotton to Japan. She learned that disagreements between cotton sellers in the United States and cotton buyers in Japan were arbitrated to a large degree by two associations, one in the U.S. (the American Cotton Shipping Association) and one in Japan (the Cotton Trade Association). The two associations agreed on many rules for trade. When rules conflicted, the cotton contracts themselves specified which rules would apply.

On one trip to Japan, Jane heard rumors from importers that the Cotton Trade Association was contemplating some rule changes in the near future that could affect her company's ability to trade with Japan. She visited the association, but her usual contact was on vacation in Hawaii, so she had to see another gentleman, Mr. Kodama. Mr. Kodama said that he know little about the pending changes, but he intimated that, although he was a busy man, for a small fee he could probably find out "many" details. Jane left the office promising to get back to Mr. Kodama.

It took Jane some time to become accustomed to dealing with Japanese businesspeople, but in doing so she became fascinated by the differences in customs. She learned that just because Mr. Tanaka said "yes" while Jane was talking to him did not mean that he agreed. Instead, he meant merely that he understood what was being said. Each trip to Japan was a learning experience.

Jane considered her options. She decided that although she opposed paying for information, the urgency of the situation and the probable need for immediate action dictated that she should make an exception this time. The next day, she returned to Mr. Kodama's office with an envelope containing 22,170 yen (equivalent to about $100), which was, she had heard, the going rate for such payments.

Mr. Kodama told Jane that a middle-level government official, Mr. Nakamura, was pressuring the cotton importing people to diversify their sources of cotton in order to reduce Japan's dependency on one country. The association reacted by considering rule changes that would encourage importers to buy from sources other than their largest ones. Since the United States was the largest supplier of cotton to Japan, this action was certain to reduce the total amount of cotton it could sell to Japan.

Jane checked with her company, and her boss approved Jane's suggestion that she do some lobbying while she was in Japan. After obtaining the appropriate introductions, Jane arranged to have lunch with Mr. Nakamura. At the restaurant, Jane explained her company's situation, giving Mr. Nakamura facts about the promise of larger crops in the United States, reduced prices because of technological advances in production and improved strains of cotton. After much discussion, Mr. Nakamura indicated that, having given some thought to the specifics of the problem, he believed hc could see Jane's side of the argument.

Later in the conversation, Mr. Nakamura discussed the increasing cost of living, especially because his son had been admitted to Harvard. He wondered if Jane's company might see fit to give the boy some type of scholarship. According to the Harvard catalog, his son would need about $20,000 a year to attend school. Mr. Nakamura subtly (but unmistakably) intimated that financial aid to his son might help him see the cotton situation more clearly.

Jane found herself in a dilemma. She had rationalized the payments for information, but somehow this situation seemed different.

Questions

1 Is there a difference between the legal and the ethical in business practice?

2 Does American law (e.g. theForeign Corrupt Practices Act) say anything relevant to the situation Jane faces?

3 How responsive should Americans be to cultural differences that may approve of or even encourage business practices that would be frowned upon or outlawed in the U.S.?

4 How does an individual resolve conflicts between personal values and "commonly accepted practices"?

5 Would the situation be different if something other than money were requested?

17. H.B. Fuller in Honduras: Street children and substance abuse – when there is no answer but "no"[4]

Additional topics covered: Social responsibility in business, charitable programs by businesses

In the summer of 1985, the following news story was brought to the attention of an official of the H.B. Fuller Company in St. Paul, Minnesota.

Glue Sniffing Among Honduran Street Children

Honduras: Children Sniffing their Lives Away

An Inter Press Service Feature

By Peter Ford

Tegucigalpa, July 16, 1985 (IPS) – They lie senseless on doorsteps and pavements, grimy and loose-limbed, like discarded rag dolls.

Some are just five or six years old. Others are already young adults, and all are addicted to sniffing a commonly sold glue that is doing them irreversible brain damage.

Roger, 21, has been sniffing "Resistol" for eight years. Today, even when he is not high, Roger walks with a stagger, his motor control wrecked. His scarred face puckers with concentration, his right foot taps nervously, incessantly, as he talks.

Since he was 11, when he ran away from the aunt who raised him, Roger's home has been the streets of the capital of Honduras, the second-poorest nation in the western hemisphere after Haiti.

Roger spends his time begging, shining shoes, washing car windows, scratching together a few pesos a day, and sleeping in doorways at night.

Sniffing glue, he says, "makes me feel happy, makes me feel big. What do I care if my family does not love me? I know it's doing me damage, but it's a habit I have got, and a habit's a habit. I cannot give it up, even though I want to."

No one knows how many of Tegucigalpa's street urchins seek escape from the squalor and misery of their daily existence through the hallucinogenic fumes of "Resistol." No one has spent the time and money needed to study the question.

But one thing is clear, according to Dr. Rosalio Zavala, Head of the Health Ministry's Mental Health Department, "These children come from the poorest slums of the big cities. They have grown up as illegal squatters in very disturbed states of mental health, tense, depressed, aggressive."

---

4 By Norman E. Bowie and Stephanie A. Lenwy, University of Minnesota. Used with permission.

"Some turn that aggression on society, and start stealing. Others turn it on themselves, and adopt self-destructive behavior."...

But he understands the attraction of the glue, whose solvent, toluene, produces feelings of elation. "It gives you delusions of grandeur, you feel powerful, and that compensates these kids for reality, where they feel completely worthless, like nobodies."

From the sketchy research he has conducted, Dr. Zavala believes that most boys discover Resistol for the first time when they are about 11, though some children as young as five are on their way to becoming addicts.

Of a small sample group of children interviewed in reform schools here, 56% told Zavala that friends introduced them to the glue, but it is easy to find on the streets for oneself.

Resistol is a contact cement glue, widely used by shoe repairers, and available at household goods stores everywhere...

In some states of the United States, glue containing addictive narcotics such as toluene must also contain oil of mustard – the chemical used to produce poisonous mustard gas – which makes sniffing the glue so painful it is impossible to tolerate. There is no federal U.S. law on the use of oil of mustard, however...

But even for Dr. Zavala, change is far more than a matter of just including a chemical compound, such as oil of mustard, in a contact cement.

"This is a social problem," he acknowledges. "What we need is a change in philosophy, a change in social organization."

Resistol is manufactured by H.B. Fuller S.A., a subsidiary of Kativo Chemical Industries, S.A., which in turn is a wholly owned subsidiary of the H.B. Fuller Company of St. Paul, Minnesota.[1] Kativo sells more than a dozen different adhesives under the Resistol brand name in several countries in Latin America for a variety of industrial and commercial applications. In Honduras the Resistol products have a strong market position.

Three of the Resistol products are solvent-based adhesives designed with certain properties that are not possible to attain with a water-based formula. These properties include rapid set, strong adhesion and water resistance. These products are similar to airplane glue or rubber cement and are primarily intended for use in shoe manufacturing and repair, leatherwork and carpentry.

Edward Sheehan writes in Agony in the Garden (1989: 46):

Even though the street children of each Central American country may have a different choice of a drug for substance abuse, and even though Resistol is not the only glue that Honduran street children use as an inhalant, the term "Resistolero" stuck and has become synonymous with all street children, whether they use inhalants or not. In Honduras, Resistol is identified as the abused substance.

Resistol. I had heard about Resistol. It was a glue, the angel dust of Honduran orphans ... In Tegucigalpa, their addiction had become so common they were known as los Resistoleros.

Honduras

The social problems that contributed to widespread inhalant abuse among street children can be attributed to the depth of poverty in Honduras. In 1989, 65 percent of all households and 40 percent of urban households in Honduras were living in poverty, making it one of the poorest countries in Latin America.[2] Between 1950 and 1988, the increase in the Honduran gross domestic product (GDP) was 3.8 percent, only slightly greater than the average yearly increase in population growth. In 1986, the Honduran GDP was about $740 per capita and has only grown slightly since. Infant and child mortality rates are high, life expectancy for adults is 64 years, and the adult literacy rate is estimated to be about 60 percent.

Honduras has faced several economic obstacles in its efforts to industrialize. First, Honduras lacks abundant natural resources. The mountainous terrain has restricted agricultural productivity and growth. In addition, the small domestic market and competition from more industrially advanced countries has prevented the manufacturing sector from progressing much beyond textile and agricultural processing industries and assembly operations.

The key to the growth of the Honduran economy has been the production and export of two commodities: bananas and coffee. Both the vagaries in the weather and the volatility of the commodity markets have made the foreign exchange earned from these products very unstable. Without consistently strong export sales, Honduras has not been able to buy sufficient energy and other productive input to allow the growth of its manufacturing sector. Honduras has also had to import basic grains (corn and rice) because the country's traditional staples are produced inefficiently by small farmers using traditional technologies with poor soil.

In the 1970s, the Honduran government relied on external financing to invest in the physical and social infrastructure and to implement development programs intended to diversify the economy. Government spending increased 10.4 percent a year from 1973. By 1981, the failure of many of these development projects led the government to stop financing state-owned industrial projects. The public-sector failures were attributed to wasteful administrative mismanagement and corruption. Left with little increase in productivity to show for these investments, Honduras continues to face massive budgetary deficits and unprecedented levels of external borrowing.

Rural-to-urban migration has been a major contributor to urban growth in Honduras. The urban population grew at more than twice the rural population rate in the 1970s. This migration has increased in part as a result of a rapid growth rate in the rural population together with the move by large landholders to convert forest and fallow land necessary for subsistence agriculture to pasture and cotton land. As more and more land was enclosed, an increasing number of landless looked to the cities for a better life.

The government deficit was further exacerbated in the early 1980s by increasing levels of unemployment. By 1983, unemployment reached 20-30 percent of the economically active population, with an additional 40 percent of the population underemployed, primarily in agriculture. The rising unemployment, falling real wages and low level of existing social infrastructure in education and health care contributed to the low level of labor productivity found in the Honduran economy in the early 1980s. Unemployment benefits were very limited, and only about 7.3 percent of the population was covered by social security.

Tegucigalpa, the capital of Honduras, has had one of the fastest population increases among Central American capitals, growing by 178,000 between 1970 and 1980, with a projected population of 975,000 by the year 2000. Honduras' second-largest city, San Pedro Sula, is projected to have a population of 650,000 by the year 2000.

The slow growth in the industrial and commercial sectors has not been adequate to provide jobs for those moving to the city. The migrants to the urban areas typically move first to cuarterias (rows) of connected rooms. The rooms are generally constructed of wood with dirt floors, and they are usually windowless. The average household contains about seven persons, who live together in a single room. For those living in the rooms facing an alley, the narrow passageway between building serves both as a sewage and waste disposal area and as a courtyard for as many as 150 persons.

Although more than 70 percent of the families living in cuarterias had one member with a permanent salaried job, few could survive on that income alone. For stable extended families, this income is supplemented by entrepreneurial activities such as selling tortillas. Given migratory labor, high unemployment and income insecurity, many family relationships are unstable. Often the support of children is left to mothers. Children are frequently forced to leave school and bolster the family income through shining shoes, selling newspapers or guarding cars, which can bring in essential income. If the mother has become sick or dies, some children are also abandoned to the streets.

Kativo Chemical Industries S.A.

Kativo celebrated its 40th anniversary in 1989. It is now one of the 500 largest private corporations in Latin America. In 1989, improved sales in most of Central America were partially offset by a reduction in sales in Honduras.

Walter Kissling, the chairman of the board of Kativo and Senior Vice President for International Operations for H.B. Fuller, has the reputation of giving the country managers of Kativo a high degree of autonomy. Local managers often have to respond quickly because of unexpected currency fluctuations. He comments that "In Latin America, if you know what you are doing, you can make more money managing your balance sheet than by selling products" (Schine, 1987). The emphasis on managing the balance sheet in countries with high rates of inflation has led Kativo management to develop a distinctive competence in finance.

In spite of the competitive challenge of operating under unstable political and economic conditions, in its annual report (1989:8), the management of Kativo stressed the importance of going beyond the bottom line in its statement that:

> Kativo is an organization with a profound philosophy and ethical conduct, worthy of the most advanced firms. It carries out business with the utmost respect for ethical and legal principles and its orientation is not solely directed to the customer, who has the highest priority, but also the shareholders, and communities where it operates.

In the early 1980s, Kativo, which was primarily a paint company, decided to enter the adhesive market in Latin America. The strategy was to combine Kativo's marketing experience with H.B. Fuller's products. Kativo found the adhesive market potentially profitable in Latin America because of the lack of strong competition.

Kativo's initial concern in getting into the adhesives market was to build market share. Resistol was the brand name for all adhesive products including the water-based school glue.

Kativo and the street children

In 1983, Honduran newspapers carried articles about police arrests of "Resistoleros," street children who drugged themselves by sniffing glue. In response to these newspaper articles, Kativo's Honduras advertising agency, Calderon Publicidad, informed the newspapers that Resistol was not the only substance abused by Honduran street children and that the image of the manufacturer was being damaged by using a prestigious trademark as a synonym for drug abusers. Moreover, the glue-sniffing problem was not caused by something inherent in the product but was a social problem. For example, on one occasion they complained to the editor requesting that he "make the necessary effort to recommend to the editorial staff that they abstain from using the brand name Resistol as a synonym for the drug, and the adjective Resistolero as a synonym for the drug addict."

> Beto had proven his courage and his business creativity when he was among 105 taken hostage in the Chamber of Commerce building in downtown San Pedro Sula, Honduras, by guerrillas from the communist Popular Liberation Front. Despite firefights between the guerrillas and government troops, threats of execution, and being used as a human shield, Beto had sold two clients (fellow hostages) who had previously been buying products from Kativo's chief competitors! Beto also has a reputation for emphasizing the importance of "making the bottom line," an important part of the Kativo corporate culture.

The man on the spot was Kativo Vice President Humberto Larach ("Beto"), a Honduran, who headed Kativo's North Adhesives Division. Nine countries including all of Central America, Mexico, the Caribbean and two South American countries, Ecuador and Columbia, reported to him. (See Figure 1) He had become manager of the adhesives division after demonstrating his entrepreneurial talents managing Kativo's paint business in Honduras.

By the summer of 1985, more than corporate image was at stake. As a solution to the glue-sniffing problem, social activists working with street children suggested that oil of mustard, allyl isothiocyanate, could be added to the product to prevent its abuse. They argued that a person attempting to sniff a glue with oil of mustard added would find it too powerful to tolerate. Sniffing it has been described as getting an "overdose of horseradish." An attempt to legislate the addition of oil of mustard received a boost when Honduran Peace Corps volunteer Timothy Bicknell convinced a local group called the "Committee for the Prevention of Drugs at the National Level" of the necessity of adding oil of mustard to Resistol. All members of the committee were prominent members of Honduran society.

Beto, in response to the growing publicity about the "Resistoleros," requested staff members of H.B. Fuller's U.S. headquarters to look into the viability of oil of mustard as a solution, with special attention to side effects and whether the oil was required or used in the U.S. H.B. Fuller's corporate industrial hygiene staff found from 1983 toxicology reports that oil of mustard was a cancer-causing agent in tests run with rats. A 1986 toxicology report from the Aldrich Chemical Company described the health-hazard data of allyl isothiocyanate as:

Future generations of Hondurans will be in danger of turning into human parasites, without a clear awareness of what is harmful to them. But if drugs and ignorance are to blame, it is even more harmful to sin by indifference before those very beings who are growing up in an environment without the basic advantages for a healthy physical and mental existence. Who will be the standard bearer in the philanthropic activities that will provide Honduras with the education necessary to combat drug addiction? Who will be remiss in their duty?

Acute Effects

May be fatal if inhaled, swallowed, or absorbed through skin.

Carcinogen.

Causes burns.

Material is extremely destructive to tissue of the mucous membranes and upper respiratory tract, eyes and skin.

Prolonged contact can cause:

Nausea, dizziness and headache.

Severe irritation or burns.

Lung irritation, chest pain and edema, which may be fatal.

Repeated exposure may cause asthma.

In addition, the product had a maximum shelf life of six months.

To the best or our knowledge, the chemical, physical and toxicological properties have not been thoroughly investigated.

In 1986, Beto contacted Hugh Young, president of SAFE (Solvent Abuse Foundation for Education) and gathered information on programs SAFE had developed in Mexico. Young, who believed that there is no effective deterrent, took the position that the only variable approach to substance abuse was education, not product modification. He argued that reformulating the product is an exercise in futility because "nothing is available in the solvent area that is not abusable." With these reports in hand, Beto attempted to persuade Resistol's critics, relief agencies, and government officials that adding oil of mustard to Resistol was not the solution to the glue-sniffing problem.

During the summer of 1986, Beto had his first success in changing the mind of someone in the press. Earlier in the year, Mary Kawas, an independent writer and journalist, wrote an article sympathetic to the position of Timothy Bicknell and the Committee for the Prevention of Drugs in Honduras. In June, Beto met with her and explained how both SAFE and Kativo sought a solution that was not product-oriented but that was directed at changing human behavior. She was also informed of the research on the dangers of oil of mustard (of which additional information had been obtained). Kawas then wrote a new article. In this article she said:

Education is the solution for drug addiction

By Marie J. Kawas

La Ceiba – A lot of people have been interested in combating drug addiction among youths and children, but few have sought solutions, and almost no one looks into the feasibility of the alternatives that are so desperately proposed...

Oil of mustard (allyl isothiocyanate) may well have been an irresponsible solution in the United States of America during the sixties and seventies, and the Hondurans want to adopt this as a panacea without realizing that their information sources are out of date. Through scientific progress, it has been found that the inclusion of oil of mustard in products which contain solvents, in order to prevent their perversion into use as an addictive drug, only causes greater harm to the consumers and workers involved in their manufacture...

Education is a primordial instrument for destroying a social cancer. An effort of this magnitude requires the cooperation of different individuals and organizations...

A company document states that: "We want to be more than just bricks, mortar, machines and people. We want to be a company with recognized values, demonstrating involvement and commitment to the betterment of the communities we are a part of." Later that year, the Honduran community affairs committees went on to make contributions to several organizations working with street children.

At first, Beto did not have much success at the governmental level. In September of 1986, Dr. Rosalio Zavala, head of the Mental Health Division of the Honduran Ministry of Health, wrote an article attacking the improper use of Resistol by youth. Beto was unsuccessful in his attempts to contact Dr. Zavala. He had better luck with Mrs. Norma Castro, governor of the State of Cortes, who after a conversation with Beto became convinced that oil of mustard had serious dangers and that glue sniffing was a social problem.

Beto's efforts continued into the new year. Early in 1987, Kativo began to establish Community Affairs Councils, as a planned expansion of the worldwide company's philosophy of community involvement. These employee committees had already been in place in the U.S. since 1978.

A company document stated the purpose of community affairs councils:

- *To educate employees about community issues.*
- *To develop understanding of, and be responsive to, the communities near our facilities.*
- *To contribute to Kativo/H.B. Fuller's corporate presence in the neighborhoods and communities we are a part of.*
- *To encourage and support employee involvement in the community.*
- *To spark a true interest in the concerns of the communities in which we live and work.*

In June 1988, Dr. Alvarado asked the Congressional Committee to reject the legislation proposed by the five congressmen. Alvarado was given 60 days to present a complete draft of legislation. In August 1988, Dr. Alvarado retired from his position. With his resignation, Kativo lost its primary communication channel with the Congressional Committee on Health. This was critical because Beto was relying on Alvarado to help ensure that the legislation reflected the technical information that he had collected.

In March 1987, Beto visited Jose Oqueli, Vice-Minister of Public Health, to explain the philosophy behind H.B. Fuller's Community Affairs Program. He also informed him of some of the health hazards of oil of mustard, and they discussed the cultural, family and economic roots of the problem of glue sniffing among street children.

In June of 1987, PRIDE (Parents Resource Institute for Drug Education) set up an office in San Pedro Sula. The philosophy of this organization is that through adequate parental education on the drug problem, it is possible to deal with the problems of inhalant abuse. PRIDE is a North American organization that had taken international Nancy Reagan's "just say no" approach to inhalant abuse. Like SAFE, PRIDE took the position that oil of mustard was not the solution to glue sniffing.

Through PRIDE, Beto was introduced to Wilfredo Alvarado, the new head of the Mental Health Division in the Ministry of Health. Dr. Alvarado was an adviser to the Congressional Committee on Health and was in charge of preparing draft legislation and evaluating legislation received by Congress. Together with Dr. Alvarado, Kativo staff worked to prepare draft legislation to address the problem of inhalant-addicted children. At the same time, five Congressmen drafted a proposed law that required the use of oil of mustard in locally produced or imported solvent-based adhesives.

The company did not have an active lobbying or government monitoring function in Tegucigalpa, the capital, which tends to be isolated from the rest of the country. (In fact, the company's philosophy has generally been not to lobby on behalf of its own narrow self-interest.) It took over two months for Beto to learn of Alvarado's departure from government. When the legislation was passed in March, he was completely absorbed in reviewing strategic plans for the nine country divisions that report to him.

On March 30, 1989, the Honduran Congress voted the legislation drafted by the five congressmen into law. (See Appendix C for text of legislation.)

Beto, located in San Pedro Sula, had no staff support to help him monitor political developments. He did this in addition to his daily responsibilities. His ability to keep track of political developments were made more difficult by the fact that he travels about 45 percent of the time outside of Honduras.

After the law was passed, Beto spoke to the press about the problems with the legislation. He argued:

This type of cement is utilized in industry, in crafts, in the home, schools and other places where it has become indispensable; thus by altering the product, not only will the drug addiction problem not be solved, but rather, the country's development would be slowed.

In order to put an end to the inhalation of Resistol by dozens of people, various products which are daily necessities would have to be eliminated from the marketplace. This is impossible, since it would mean a serious setback to industry at several levels...

There are studies that show that the problem is not the glue itself, but rather the individual. The mere removal of this substance would immediately be substituted by some other, to create the same hallucinogenic trip for the person who was sniffing it.

H.B. Fuller: The corporate response

In late April 1986, Elmer Andersen, H.B. Fuller Chairman of the Board, received the following letter:

4/21/86

Elmer L. Andersen

H.B. Fuller Co.

Dear Mr. Anderson:

I heard part of your talk on public radio recently, and was favorably impressed with your philosophy that business should not be primarily for profit. This was consistent with my previous impression of H.B. Fuller Co. since I am a public health nurse and have been aware of your benevolence to the nursing profession.

However, on a recent trip to Honduras, I spent some time at a new home for chemically dependent "street boys" who are addicted to glue sniffing. It was estimated that there are 600 of these children still on the streets in San Pedro Sula alone. The glue is sold for repairing tennis shoes and I am told it is made by H.B. Fuller in Costa Rica. These children also suffer toxic effects of liver and brain damage from the glue...

Hearing you on the radio, I immediately wondered how this condemnation of H.B. Fuller could be consistent with the company as I knew it before and with your business philosophy.

Are you aware of this problem in Honduras, and, if so, how are you dealing with it?

That a stockholder should write the 76-year-old Chairman of the Board directly is significant. Elmer Andersen is a legendary figure in Minnesota. He was responsible for the financial success of H.B. Fuller from 1941-1971 and his values, reflected in his actions as CEO, are embodied in H.B. Fuller's mission statement. (For a brief corporate history of H.B. Fuller, see Appendix C.)

The H.B. Fuller corporate mission is to be a leading and profitable worldwide formulator, manufacturer and marketer of quality specialty chemicals, emphasizing service to customers and managed in accordance with a strategic plan.

H.B. Fuller mission statement

H.B. Fuller is committed to its responsibilities, in order of priority, to its customers, employees and shareholders. H.B. Fuller will conduct business legally and ethically, support the activities of its employees in their communities, and be a responsible corporate citizen.

Anderson also served a brief term as governor and was extraordinarily active in civic affairs. In 1990, he was elected Minnesotan of the Year and thousands of citizens attended his 80th birthday, which was celebrated on the steps of the State Capitol in St. Paul.

It was also Elmer Andersen who as President and CEO made the decision that foreign acquisitions should be managed by locals. Kativo Chemical Industries Ltd. was acquired in 1967. Concerning the purchase, Elmer Andersen said:

> We had two objectives in mind. One was directly business-related and one was altruistic. Just as we had expanded in America, our international business strategy was to pursue markets where our competitors were not active. We were convinced that we had something to offer Latin America that the region did not have locally. In our own small way, we also wanted to be of help to that part of the world. We believed that by producing adhesives in Latin America and by employing only local people, we would create new jobs and help elevate the standard of living. We were convinced that the way to aid world peace was to help Latin America become more prosperous (H.B. Fuller Co., 1986:101-102).

Vice President for Corporate Relations Dick Johnson understood that this problem crossed functional and divisional responsibilities. Given H.B. Fuller's high visibility as a socially responsible corporation, the glue-sniffing problem had the potential for being a public-relations nightmare. The brand name of one of H.B. Fuller's products had become synonymous with a serious problem. Additionally, Dick understood that this was an issue larger than product misuse: It had social and community ramifications. The issue is substance abuse by children, whether the substance is a H.B. Fuller product or not. As a part of the solution, a community-relations response was required. Therefore, he invited Karen Muller to join him on his trip to Honduras.

Three years later, the Resistol issue was raised dramatically and visibly for a second time directly by a stockholder. On June 7, 1989, Vice President for Corporate Relations Dick Johnson received a call from a stockholder whose daughter was in the Peace Corps in Honduras. Her question was how can a company like H.B. Fuller claim to have a social conscience and continue to sell Resistol which is "literally burning out the brains" of children in Latin America?

Johnson was galvanized into action. This complaint was of special concern because he was about to meet with a national group of socially responsible investors who were considering including H.B. Fuller's stock in their portfolio. Fortunately Karen Muller, Director of Community Affairs, had been keeping a file on the glue-sniffing problem. Within 24 hours of receiving the call, Dick had written a memo to CEO Tony Anderson.

In that memo Dick had articulated some basic values that had to be considered as H.B. Fuller wrestled with the problem. Among these values were the following.

1 *H.B. Fuller's explicitly stated public concern about substance abuse*

2 *H.B. Fuller's "Concern for Youth" focus in its community-affairs projects*

3 *H.B. Fuller's reputation as a socially responsible company*

4 *H.B. Fuller's history of ethical conduct*

5 *H.B. Fuller's commitment to the intrinsic value of each individual*

Whatever "solution" was ultimately adopted would have to be consistent with these values. In addition, Dick suggested a number of options, including that H.B. Fuller withdraw from the market or alter the formula to make Resistol a water-based product so sniffing could no longer be an issue.

As they returned from their trip to Honduras, Karen and Dick had the opportunity to reflect on what they had learned. They agreed that removing Resistol from the market would not resolve the problem. However, the problem is extremely complex. The use of inhalants by street children is a symptom of Honduras' underlying economic problems – problems which have social, cultural, and political aspects as well as simply economic dimensions.

Tony responded by suggesting that Dick create a task force to find a solution and a plan to implement it. Dick decided to accept Beto's invitation to travel to Honduras to view the situation firsthand.

Karen recalled a memo she had written about a year earlier directed to Beto. In the memo, she had articulated her version of a community-relations approach as distinguished from the government-relations approach that Beto had been following. In that memo Karen stated:

> This community relations process involves developing a community-wide coalition from all those with a vested interest in solving the community issue – those providing services in dealing with the street children and drug users, other businesses, and the government. It does require leadership over the long-term both with a clear set of objectives and a commitment on the part of each group represented to share in the solution...

In support of the community-relations approach Karen argued that:

1 *It takes the focus and pressures off H.B. Fuller as one individual company.*

2 *It can educate the broader community and focus on the best solution, not just the easiest one.*

3 *It holds everyone responsible, the government, educators, H.B. Fuller's customers, legitimate consumers of our product, social service workers and agencies.*

4 *It provides H.B. Fuller with an expanded good image as a company that cares and will stay with the problem – that we are willing to go the second mile.*

5 *It can depoliticize the issue.*

6 *It offers the opportunity to counterbalance the negative impact of the use of our product name Resistol by reidentifying the problem.*

Resistol appeared to be the drug of choice for young street children. However, the street children seemed to obtain the drug in a number of different ways. There was no clear pattern and hence, the solution could not be found in simply changing some features of the distribution system. Children might obtain the glue from legitimate customers, small shoe repair stalls, by theft, from "illegal" dealers or from third parties who purchased Resistol from legitimate stores but who then sold the product to children. For some persons the sale of Resistol to children could be profitable.

Karen and Dick left for a four-day trip to Honduras on September 18. Upon arriving they were joined by Beto, Oscar Sahuri, General Manager for Kativo's adhesives business in Honduras, and Jorge Walter Bolanos, Vice-President Director of Finance. Karen had also asked Mark Connelly, a health consultant from an international agency working with street children, to join the group. They began the process of looking at all aspects of the situation. Visits to two different small shoe-manufacturing shops and a shoe supply distributor helped to clarify the issues around pricing, sales, distribution and the packaging of the product.

A visit to a well-run shelter for street children provided insight into the dynamics of substance abuse among this vulnerable population in the streets of Tegucigalpa and San Pedro Sula. At a meeting with the officials at the Ministry of Health, the issue of implementing the oil of mustard law was reviewed and the Kativo managers offered to assist the committee as it reviewed the details of the law. In both Tegucigalpa and San Pedro Sula, the National Commission for Technical Assistance to Children in Irregular Situations (CONATNSI), a countrywide association of private and public agencies working with street children, organized meetings of its members at which the Kativo managers offered an explanation of the company's philosophy and the hazards involved in the use of oil of mustard.

> Honduran street children include children from a wide variety of circumstances. Some are true orphans, while others are abandoned. Some are runaways, while others are working the streets to help augment their parents' insufficient income. Children doing street jobs or begging usually earn more than the minimum wage. Despite this, children who work the street for money are often punished if they bring home too little. This creates a vicious circle because the children would rather be on the street than home – a situation that increases the likelihood that they will fall victim to drug addiction. The problems of the street children are exacerbated by the lack of opportunities for young people and by the fact that the regulations concerning school attendance are not enforced. In addition, the police sometimes abuse street children.

Resistol was available in small packages, which made it more affordable. However, the economic circumstances of a country like Honduras made small packages economically sensible.

The government had a reputation for being unstable. As a result, there was a tendency for people working with the government to hope that new policy initiatives would fade away within a few months. Moreover, in government there is a large amount of turnover of officials, little knowledge of H.B. Fuller and its corporate philosophy, and a great desire for a quick fix. (See Appendix for a brief background on Honduran politics.) Although it was on the books for six months by the time of their trip, the law requiring oil of mustard in Resistol still had not been implemented. Moreover, the country was only three months away from major national elections. During meetings with government officials, it appeared to Karen and Dick that no further actions would be taken as current officials waited for the outcome of the election.

Kativo company officers Jorge Walter Bolanos and Humberto Larach discussed continuing the government-relations strategy, hoping that the law might be repealed or modified. They also were concerned with the damage dome to H.B. Fuller's image. Karen and Dick thought the focus should be on community relations. From their perspective, efforts directed toward changing the law seemed important but would do nothing to help with the long-term solution to the problems of the street children and substance abuse.

Much of the concern for street children is found in private agencies. The chief coordinating association is CONATNSI, created as a result of a seminar sponsored by UNICEF in 1987. CONATNSI is under the direction of a General Assembly and a Board of Directors elected by the General Assembly. It began its work in 1988. Its objectives include: a) improving the quality of services, b) promoting interchange of experiences, c) coordinating human and material resources, d) offering technical support, and e) promoting research. Karen and the others believe that CONATNSI has a shortage of both financial and human resources. Yet this association appeared to be well-organized and emerged as a potential intermediary for the company.

As a result of their trip, they know that a community-relations strategy will be extremely complex and risky. H.B. Fuller is committed to a community-relations approach to this problem, but what would a community-relations solution look like in Honduras? The H.B. Fuller mission statement does not provide a complete answer. It does indicate that H.B. Fuller has responsibilities to its Honduran customers and employees regarding oil of mustard. But what additional responsibilities does it have? What impact can one company have in solving a complex social problem? How should the different emphases in perspective of Kativo and its parent, H.B. Fuller, be handled? What does corporate citizenship require in situations like this?

Endnotes

1 The Subsidiaries of the North Adhesives Division of Kativo Chemical Industries, S.A., go by the name "H.B. Fuller (Country of Operation)," e.g. H.B. Fuller S.A. Honduras. To prevent confusion with the parent company, we will refer to H.B. Fuller S.A. Honduras by the name of its parent, "Kativo."

2 The following discussion is based on *Honduras: A Country Study,* 2nd edition, James D. Rudolph, editor (Washington, D.C.: Department of the Army, 1984).

Unless otherwise indicated, all references and quotations regarding H.B. Fuller and its subsidiary Kativo Chemical Industries S.A. are from company documents.

The authors express their deep appreciation to the H.B. Fuller company for providing access to company documents and personnel relevant to this case.

References

Acker, Alison, *The Making of a Banana Republic,* Boston: South End Press, 1988.

Rudolph, James D., Editor, *Honduras: A Country Study,* 2nd ed., Washington, D.C.: Department of the Army, 1984.

H.B. Fuller Company, *A Fuller Life: The Story of H.B. Fuller Company: 1887-1987,* St. Paul, H.B. Fuller Company, 1986.

Schine, Eric, "Preparing for Banana Republic U.S." *Corporate Finance* (December, 1987).

Sheehan, Edward, *Agony in the Garden: A Stranger in Central America,* Boston: Houghton Mifflin, 1989.

The globalization of business ethics:
Why America remains distinctive[5]

In a number of important respects, the increased globalization of the economies of the United States, Western Europe and Japan is making business practices more uniform. The structure and organization of firms, manufacturing technologies, the social organization of production, customer relations, product development, and marketing are all becoming increasingly similar throughout the advanced industrial economies. One might logically think that a similar trend would be taking place with respect to the principles and practices of business ethics.

The unusual visibility of issues of business ethics in the United States lies in the distinctive institutional, legal, social and cultural context of the American business system. Moreover, the American approach to business ethics is also unique: It is more individualistic, legalistic and universalistic than in other capitalist societies.

This is occurring, but only very slowly. Business ethics have not yet globalized; the norms of ethical behavior continue to vary widely among capitalist nations. During the last decade, highly publicized incidents of misconduct on the part of business managers have occurred in virtually every major industrial economy. These scandals have played an important role in increasing public, business and academic awareness of issues of business ethics in the United States, Western Europe and Japan. Yet the extent of both public and academic interest in business ethics remains substantially greater in the United States than in other advanced capitalist nations. While interest in business ethics has substantially increased in a number of countries in Europe, and to a lesser extent in Japan, no other capitalist nation approaches the United States in the persistence and intensity of public concern with the morality of business conduct.

Recent business scandals

Much of the current surge in public, business and academic interest in business ethics in the United States can be traced to the scandals associated with Wall Street during the 1980s. Characterized by one journalist as "the most serious corporate crime wave since the foreign bribery cases of the mid-1970s," these abuses began with money-laundering by the Bank of Boston in 1986 and check-kiting by E.F. Hutton in 1987. They went on to include violations of insider-trading regulations by Paul Thayer, who received a five-year jail term; Dennis Levine and the so-called "yuppie five"; and Ivan Boesky, who was fined $100 million and sentenced to prison for three years. Half of all the cases brought by the SEC alleging illegal use of stock market information since 1949 were filed during a five-year period in the middle of the 1980s.

In 1988, "junk-bond king" Michael Milken and his firm, Drexel Burnham, were indicted for violating federal securities laws and regulations. Both subsequently paid large fines and Milken was sentenced to prison for ten years, subsequently reduced to two. At about the same time, the public became aware of widespread evidence of fraud in the savings and loan industry. A number of bankers were indicted and convicted, including Charles Keating Jr., head of one of the nation's largest savings and loan associations. In 1991, Salomon Brothers admitted that it had committed "irregularities and rule violations in connection with its submission of bids in certain auctions of Treasury securities."[1] Two managing directors were suspended and the investment bank's Chairman and Chief Executive, John Gutfreund, was forced to resign after admitting that he had known of the firm's misconduct but had neglected to report it.

---

5 Excerpted from David Vogel. Copyright 1992 by The Regents of the University of California. Reprinted from the *California Management Review*, 35(1), Fall 1992, 30-49. By permission of the Regents.

Much of the recent increase in interest in business ethics outside the United States can also be attributed to various business scandals that came to light in Europe and Japan during roughly the same timeperiod. In 1982, an American company that had acquired a leading British member of Lloyd's found "undisclosed financial commitments and funds missing from the firm's reinsurance subsidiaries."[2] In 1985, another major scandal struck London's insurance market: 450 individual members of Lloyd's lost $180 million underwriting policies organized by agents who were alleged to have stolen some of the funds. At about the same time in London, "a wave of suspicious price movements in advance of takeover bids ... prompted concern that insider trading is spreading."[3] In 1987, Geoffrey Collier, a top trader at Morgan Grenfell Group PLC, was indicted for illegally earning more than $20,000 on two mergers involving his prestigious investment banking firm.

In 1991, another prominent British businessmen, Robert Maxwell, was implicated in a number of wide-ranging abuses, including the looting of a large pension fund and deceptive record-keeping designed to conceal the insolvency of various firms that he controlled. Maxwell died under mysterious circumstances shortly before his "massive international confidence game" – involving large numbers of respectable British and American banks and accounting firms – became public.[6] It was subsequently revealed that Maxwell had plundered a total of £450 million from various pension funds he controlled.

The same year, Ernest Saunders, the chief executive of Guinness, a major British-based alcoholic beverages company, was accused of attempting to illegally prop up the price of his company's shares in order to help support its bid for the Distillers beverages group. Saunders was arrested and spent a night in jail. He was subsequently forced to sell many of his possessions, including his spacious home in Buckinghamshire, to meet legal costs, and all of his remaining assets were frozen. Saunders' trial did not begin for another three and half years, making the "Guinness Affair" the most prolonged financial scandal in the history of the City of London. In 1990, Saunders was found guilty of having helped engineer the stock's "fortuitous rise" and was sentenced to five years in prison. Three other prominent executives were also found guilty in what has been described as the "financial trial of the century."[4] The Guardian noted, "The six-month trial has lifted the lid on the seamy side of the City, exposing a sordid story of greed, manipulation and total disregard for takeover regulations."[5]

Japan, too, has recently experienced a considerable number of business-related scandals. In the spring of 1987, one of the subsidiaries of the Toshiba Corporation was discovered to have sold advanced milling equipment to the Soviet navy to be used for making submarine propellers, in violation of both Japanese law and an international treaty restricting the export of military-related technology to communist-bloc countries. Both the Chairman and President of the company were forced to resign. Shortly thereafter, numerous cases of influence-peddling by the Recruit Company become public: A press report revealed that the firm had given shares at below-market prices to a number of prominent politicians in the ruling Liberal Democratic Party in exchange for various political favors. A number of politicians were forced to resign and the Chairman of Recruit, Hisashi Shinto, along with several of his fellow executives, were indicted on bribery charges. On October 9, 1990, Shinto was convicted: He was fined $170,000 and given a two-year prison term, which was suspended due to his age.

Sumitomo Bank, Japan's second largest, had lent more than $1 billion to an Osaka trading company headed by a former official of the bank, who then squandered nearly $2 billion in "shady deals." In another major banking scandal, a number of Japan's most prestigious

In 1991, another major scandal surfaced in Japan. Nomura Securities and Nikko Securities, two of Japan's major brokerage firms, admitted to having lent more than $250 million to a well-known underworld organization. Tax authorities revealed that the same two firms had been secretly reimbursing large clients for stock market loses; other firms were subsequently implicated in this practice as well. (See Nomura case in Chapter 6).

financial institutions, including the Industrial Bank of Japan Ltd., were linked to a scheme involving $2.5 billion in fraudulently obtained loans. In the spring of 1992, former Chisan Co. Chairman Hirotomo Takai was sentenced to four years in prison and fined $3.8 million dollars for evading $25.6 million in taxes, "the largest-ever tax fraud by an individual."[7] And in 1992, Sagawa Kyubin, a mob-related company, was revealed to have donated more than $17 million to a number of prominant Japanese politicians, including three former Prime Ministers and two current Cabinet members.

Three important business-related scandals have also occurred in Australia. In July 1989, five prominent businessmen, including Ian Johns, the former managing director of an Australian merchant bank, were arrested and charged with insider trading. The following month, Laurie Connell, a prominent Perth financier, was charged with making false statements in the annual report of Rothwells, the merchant bank that collapsed in 1988. In 1990, George Herscu, the bankrupt Australian property magnate, was sentenced to five years in jail for bribing a state government minister. Two years later, Alan Bond, one of Australia's most successful entrepreneurs – his fortune is estimated at $7.6 billion – was sentenced to two and one-half years in prison for fraud.

The response

As a response, in part, to these numerous cases of business misconduct, the level of public, business and academic interest in issues of business ethics increased throughout much of the industrialized world. While interest in this subject was largely confined to the United States during the 1970s, during the 1980s it spread to a number of other capitalist nations as well. In 1983, the first chair in business ethics was established in Europe at the Netherlands School of Business; a second was established at another Dutch university three years later, and four more have been founded subsequently in other European countries. In 1986, the Lord Mayor of London organized a formal conference on company philosophy and codes of business ethics for 100 representatives from industry and the professions. The following year, a group of 75 European business managers and academics established the European Business Ethics Network (EBEN); its first conference was held in 1987, and four more have been held since, most recently in Paris in 1992. In 1987, the first European business ethics journal, *Ethica Degli Affari,* was published, in Italy.

Since the mid-1980s, two ethics research centers have been established in Great Britain, in addition to one each in Belgium, Spain, Germany and Switzerland.[8] Interest in business ethics is also increasing in Japan, though on a much smaller scale. In 1989 and 1991, the Institute of Moralogy sponsored international ethics conferences in Kashiwa City, Chiba Ken, Japan.

In America, each new disclosure of business misconduct prompts a new wave of public indignation, accompanied by numerous articles in the business and popular press which bemoan the general decline in the ethical conduct of managers and seek to explain "what went wrong" in the most recent case.

The "Ethics Gap"

Notwithstanding these initiatives, the "ethics gap" between the United States and the rest of the developed world remains substantial. By any available measure, the level of public, business and academic interest in issues of business ethics in the United States far exceeds that in any other capitalist country. Nor does this gap show any sign of diminishing: While interest in the subject in Europe has increased in recent years, its visibility in America has increased even more.

Ethics disclosures are frequently followed by Congressional hearings featuring politicians demanding more vigilant prosecution of white-collar criminals; shortly thereafter, regulatory standards are tightened, penalties

The most important reason why there appears to be so much more white-collar crime in the United States is that there are so many more laws regulating business in the United States to be broken. Moreover, regulations governing business tend to be more strictly enforced in the United States than in other capitalist nations. In addition, thanks to more aggressive journalism, as well as to government disclosure requirements, business misdeeds are more likely to be exposed in the United States.

are increased, and enforcement efforts are strengthened. Executives, in turn, make speeches emphasizing the importance of good ethical behavior for business success, using the most recent round of indictments and associated business failures to demonstrate the "wages of sin." Business educators then re-emphasize the need for additional instruction in ethics, often receiving substantial sums of money from various businessmen to support new educational programs. The most recent scandal then becomes the subject of a case, to be taught in an ever-increasing number of business ethics courses designed to assist the next generation of managers in avoiding the pitfalls of their predecessors. When a new scandal occurs – as it invariably does – the cycle begins anew.

No comparable dynamic has occurred in other capitalist nations, where public interest in business ethics tends to be episodic rather than cumulative: thus, only in America are the 1980s referred to as a "decade of greed."

The importance of issues of business ethics in the United States likely lies in the distinctive institutional, legal, social and cultural context of the American business system. In brief, Americans are more concerned with the ethics of business because they have higher expectations of business conduct. Not only is more business conduct considered unethical in the United States, but unethical behavior is more likely to be exposed, punished and therefore become a "scandal" in America than in other capitalist nations.

Legal vulnerability

Another distinctive feature of the contemporary legal environment of business in the United States is the relatively large exposure of both individual executives and corporations to legal prosecution. As recently as two decades ago, the prosecution of individuals for white-collar crime in the United States was relatively rare. On occasion, high-status individuals were sentenced to prison; for example, in 1938, Richard Whitney, who had been President of the New York Stock Exchange, was found guilty of embezzlement and sentenced to five years in federal prison. In the early 1960s, a handful of senior managers from General Electric and Westinghouse received light prison sentences after they were found guilty of price-fixing.

However, this began to change in the early 1970s when, in connection with Watergate, a number of high-status individuals were sentenced to prison. By the end of the decade, what began as a trickle had become a flood.

Public expectations

The high expectations of business conduct in the United State are not confined to the legal system. They also are reflected in the way many Americans invest and consume. For example, "ethical investment" funds in the United States enable individuals and institutions to make their investment strategy consistent with their political/social values either by avoiding investments in firms they judge to be behaving irresponsibly or by increasing their holdings of the stocks and bonds of firms that are acting "socially responsible." While such

"Businessmen spent more time in jail for price-fixing in 1978 than in all the 89 years since the passage of the Sherman Antitrust Act."[9] Sixty-five percent of the individuals convicted of security law violations during the 1980s received jail sentences.

On balance, during the last 15 years, more corporate officers and prominent businessmen have been jailed or fined in the United States than in all other capitalist nations combined. Likewise, the fines imposed on corporations in the United States have been substantially greater than in other capitalist nations. While the penalties for white-collar crime also have increased outside the United States, over the last decade the magnitude of the difference between the legal vulnerability of corporations and individual managers in the United States and those in other capitalist nations has increased. This development both reflects the high standards that exist for corporate conduct in the United States and also serves to re-enforce the perception that business misconduct is more pervasive in the United States.

Business ethics in the United States has been strongly affected by the "tradition of liberal individualism that ... is typical of American culture."[11] Not surprisingly, a frequent characteristic of business ethics cases developed in the United States is that they require the individual to decide what is right on the basis of his or her own values. While the company's goals and objectives or the views of the individual's fellow employees are not irrelevant, in the final analysis they are not intended to be decisive. Indeed, they may often be in conflict.

funds exist in a number of European countries – including Britain and the Netherlands – they both originated and remain much larger in the United States. The same is true of the use of various social criteria to screen investments by institutional investors. For example, in no other capitalist nation have so many institutional investors divested themselves of shares of firms with investments in South Africa.

Business values

Ironically, it may be precisely because the values of "business civilization" are so deeply ingrained in American society that Americans tend to become so upset when the institutions and individuals whom they have looked up to – and whose values and success they have identified with – betray their trust. More generally: "In the United States ... the single all-pervasive 'ought' rampages widely beyond the control of the 'is.' The result is a unique and ever-present challenge ... posed by the gap between the ideals by which the society lives and the institutions by which it functions."[34] Because the public's expectations of business conduct are so high, the invariable result is a consistently high level of public dissatisfaction with the actual ethical performance of business.

An important key to understanding the unique interest of Americans in the subject of business ethics lies in America's Protestant heritage: "The United States is the only country in the world in which a majority of the population has belonged to dissenting Protestant sects."[10] This has important implications for the way in which Americans approach the subject of business ethics. By arguing that one can and should do "God's work" by creating wealth, Protestantism raised the public's expectations of the moral behavior of business managers. Thus, thanks in part to the role played by Reformed Protestantism in defining American values, America remains a highly moralistic society. Compared to the citizens of other capitalist nations, Americans are more likely to believe that business and morality are, and should be, related to each other, that good ethics is good business, and that business activity both can and should be consistent with high personal moral values.

Key differences in business ethics

The United States is distinctive not only in the intensity of public concern with the ethical behavior of business, but also in the way in which business ethics are defined. Americans tend to emphasize the role of the individual as the most critical source of ethical values, while in other capitalist nations relatively more emphasis is placed on the corporation as the locus of ethical guidance. Second, business ethics tends to be much more legalistic and rule-oriented in the United States. Finally, Americans are more likely to consider their own ethical rules and standards to be universally applicable.

By contrast, "In European circumstances it is not at all evident that managers, when facing a moral dilemma, will navigate first and foremost on their personal moral compass."[12] Rather, managers are more likely to make decisions based on their shared understanding of the nature and

One possible outcome of the tension between the interests and values of the company and those of the individual employee is whistle-blowing. Critics of business in the United States have urged increased legal protection for whistle-blowers – and, in fact, some regulatory statutes in the United States explicitly protect those who publicly expose violations of various policies.

One French manager, whose firm had recently been acquired by an American company, stated:

I resent having notions of right and wrong boiled down to a checklist. I come from a nation whose ethical traditions date back hundreds of years. Its values have been transmitted to me by my church and through my family. I don't need to be told by some American lawyers how I should conduct myself in my business activities.[15]

scope of the company's responsibilities. The ultimate moral expectations of a company are shaped by the norms of the community, not the personal values or reflections of the individual. The latter has been labeled "communicative" or "consensual" business ethics.[13]

By contrast, the idea that there could even be such a tension between the individual and the organization is thoroughly alien to Japanese business culture, where whistle-blowers would be regarded more as traitors than heroes. Only a handful of European countries have laws protecting whistle-blowers. And few non-American firms have established formal mechanisms, such as the appointment of ombudsmen, to enable employees to voice their moral concerns about particular corporate policies. Workers in many other capitalist nations may well feel a greater sense of loyalty toward the firms for which they work, and a greater respect for those in authority.

The popularity of codes of ethics in the United States meets with little response in Europe, America's individualism does not correspond to the social traditions of Europe. These large differences make fruitless all desire to imitate the other's steps.[14]

Henri-Claude de Bettignies, who teaches business ethics at INSEAD, adds:

Some European leaders perceive corporate codes of conduct as a device which deresponsibilizes the individual. ... He does not have to think for himself, he just needs to apply the codes of conduct which he has learnt and which – through training – have programmed him to respond in a certain "corporate" way.[16]

By contrast, European firms appear to place greater emphasis on informal mechanisms of social control within the firm. Indeed, European managers frequently profess astonishment at the apparent belief of many American executives, as well as government officials, that a company's adoption of a code can actually alter the behavior of its employees.

Conclusion

Regulatory rules and standards, especially within the European Community and between the United States and Western Europe, are certainly becoming more similar. For example, a strengthening of environmental regulation has occurred in virtually all capitalist nations, while legal restrictions on insider trading – a decade ago largely confined to the United States – are now the norm in Europe. Similarly, a number of European nations have recently enacted legislation banning sexual harassment. The prosecution of white-collar criminals has also recently increased in Europe. In 1989, the first Swede to be found guilty of insider trading was sentenced to five years in prison. Not only are many American legal norms and standards of corporate conduct being adopted in other capitalist nations, but as globalization proceeds and

All these dimensions are, in fact, interrelated. To summarize the American approach: business ethics is about individuals making moral judgments based on general rules that treat everyone the same. By contrast, business ethics in Europe and Japan has more to do with managers arriving at decisions based on shared values, often rooted in a particular corporate culture, applied according to specific circumstances and strongly affected by the nature of one's social ties and obligations.

world commerce is increasingly driven by multinational firms, these firms may well come to adopt common ethical standards. These developments are important. But they continue to be overshadowed by the persistence of fundamental national differences in the ways in which business ethics is defined, debated and judged.

While much has been written on differences in the laws and business norms of developed and less-developed nations, the equally important contrasts in the way in which ethical issues are discussed and defined among the developed nations has been all but ignored.[17] Significantly, among the hundreds of ethics cases developed for use in management education in the United States and Europe, only one – Toshiba Machine Company – contrasts differences in ethical norms between two advanced industrial nations.[18] We need a better appreciation of the differences in the legal and cultural context of business ethics between the United States and other capitalist nations, and between Western and Asian economies as well, if managers are to work effectively in an increasingly integrated global economy.

Endnotes

1   "The Salomon Shocker: How Bad will It Get?" *Business Week,* August 26, 1991, p. 36.

2   Barnaby Feder, "Overseeing Insurance Reform at London's Venerable Mart:" *New York Times,* January 8, 1984, p. 6.

3   Gary Putka, "British Face Finance-Industry Scandals Just as They Move to Deregulate Markets:" *Wall Street Journal,* August 12, 1985, p. 20.

4   Robert Rice and Richard Waters, "Fraud of Office Drops Charges in Third Guinness Case," *Financial Times,* February 9, 1992, p. 1.

5   *The Guardian,* August 28, 1990, p. 1.

6   "An Honor System Without Honor:" *Economist* December 14, 1991, p. 81.

7   "Top Tax-Evader Gets Four-Year Sentence," *Japan Times Week International Edition.* May 11-17, 1992, p. 2.

8   Henk J. L. van Luijk. "Recent Developments in European Business Ethics," *Journal of Business Ethics,* 9: 538.

9   Nick Galluccio, "The Boss in the Slammer," *Forbes,* February 5, 1979. p. 61.

10 Samuel P. Huntington, *American Politics: The Promise of Disharmony* (Cambridge, MA: Harvard University Press. 1981), p. 15.

11 van Luijk, op. cit., p. 542.

12 Ibid.

13 Ibid, pp. 543-544.

14 Antoine Kerhuel, "De Part et D'Autre De L'Atlantique" [David Vogel translation].

15 This statement was made at an executive training session at IMD in the fall of 1991 that the author taught.

16 Henri-Claude de Bettignies, "Ethics and International Business: A European Perspective," paper presented at the Tokyo Conference on the Ethics of Business in a Global Economy, Kashiwa-shi, Japan, September 10-12, 1991, p. 11.

17 The handful of exceptions includes: Catherine Langlois and Bodo Schegelmilch, "Do Corporate Codes of Ethics Reflect National Character? Evidence from Europe and the United States," *Journal of International Business Studies* (Fourth Quarter 1990), pp. 519-539; van Luijk, op. cit., pp. 537-544; Ernest Gundling. "Ethics and Working with the Japanese: The Entrepreneur and the Elite Course," *California Management Review.* 33/3 (Spring 1991): 25-39; Joanne Ciulla, "Why Is Business Talking about Ethics?" *California Management Review,* 34/1 (Fall 1991): 67-86.

18 Toshiba Machine Company, Harvard Business School #388-197.

The Foreign Corrupt Practices Act: Revisited and amended[6]

U.S. business has operated under the provisions of the Foreign Corrupt Practices Act (FCPA) for nearly 12 years. Scant attention was paid to the fact that one section of the lengthy Omnibus Trade and Competitiveness Act signed by President Reagan August 23, 1988, amended the FCPA. Although there had been several failed attempts to change the act over the years, this was the first substantive change in the FCPA since its passage in 1977.

The amendment of FCPA received little notice in the media or the business community. This lack of reaction is in striking contrast to the swirl of attention and controversy that surrounds the original legislation. In 1977, the passage of the FCPA was the source of much anxiety and apprehension in the U.S. business community. These anxieties were based on legitimate grounds. While some provisions of the act were straightforward and compliance requirements easily understood, other provisions of the act were framed in nebulous, vague and ill-defined terms that made it impossible for firms to ensure they were in compliance. There was great fear that the vaguely defined terms of the Act might be unreasonably interpreted and would become the basis for continuing harassment from the federal agencies assigned responsibilities for its enforcement, i.e., the Securities and Exchange Commission (SEC) and Department of Justice.

In retrospect, some of the rhetoric attendant to passage of the FCPA seems overblown, exaggerated and bordering on hysteria. For the most part, U.S. business has successfully navigated the uncertainties of the FCPA. A large measure of credit must go to publicly held companies that shouldered significant compliance costs documenting, evaluating and changing, when necessary, internal control systems. The worst-case scenarios foreseen by doomsayers in 1977-79 have not come to pass and now, given the new amendments, seem less likely to occur in the future.

Certainly, a more descriptive title than "FCPA" could have been found for the law; one that more accurately reflected the substantive content of the legislation. Pundits have asserted that the title of the law is a misnomer, that is, organizations that are neither foreign nor corrupt are subject to the dictates of the law. Indeed, a corporation may violate the provisions of the FCPA without having any foreign business and without seeking to corrupt any official.

Given the occasion of its first amendment, it seems apropos to do a retrospective on the FCPA. The purpose of this article is to review the circumstances leading to the passage of the act, survey its major provisions, and finally review the recently enacted amendments.

Background of the FCPA

Prohibitions against foreign bribery and mandates relating to control and record keeping are inexorably interconnected in the act and in the events that led to its passage. The FCPA is the child of political scandal. The findings of the Watergate Special Prosecutor provided the impetus for the legislation. During his investigations, the prosecutor found that many corporations had made substantial, illegal contributions during the 1972 presidential election campaign. In many instances, these contributions were made possible by off-the-books slush funds that were maintained by corporations. Follow-up investigations in 1976 and 1977 by the SEC into corporate slush funds and "voluntary" disclosures by publicly traded companies revealed that instances of undisclosed, questionable or illegal corporate payments, both domestic and foreign, were widespread.

6   By O. Ronald Gray. *Business and Society,* Spring 1990, 11-17. Reprinted with permission of Sage Publications.

Dorothy Marcic and Sheila Puffer, *Management International,* West Publishing, 1994.
All rights reserved. May not be reproduced without written permission of the publisher.
For more information, contact West Publishing, Publications Dept., 610 Opperman Drive,
St. Paul, MN 55164.

More than 400 United States corporations including such notables as American Airlines, American Telephone and Telegraph, Colgate-Palmolive Co., Exxon, Firestone, Gulf, International Telephone and Telegraph (ITT), Lockheed and Textron admitted having made kickbacks, bribes or other questionable payoffs. In many cases, company records were deliberately falsified or otherwise manipulated to obscure the nature of the transactions. It was the SEC's position that the illegal payments and falsifications of books were made possible because internal corporate accounting controls were ineffective or easily subverted.

The payments brought to light were previously unknown to auditors, directors, shareholders, and, if one believes their testimony, members of the senior management of corporations making such payments. A favored defense by corporate officers was ignorance that such payments were being made and/or such payments were unauthorized and directly contrary to corporate policy. The effect of these disclosures was to shake the public's confidence and trust in the integrity of business leadership hard on the heels of the Watergate political crisis. On a larger scale, these revelations contributed to a rising tide of public cynicism, skepticism, and disillusionment which President Carter characterized as a national "malaise." Given the scope of the scandal, the Congress was compelled to respond. On December 19, 1977, after nearly three years of hearings and debate, the Congressional response to the scandal – the FCPA – became law. The ultimate objective of the FCPA was to reinforce the existing system of corporate disclosure and enhance public confidence in the securities markets.

The FCPA as enacted

It is clear from a review of the legislative history that the FCPA was enacted to proscribe illegal payments to foreign officials and the internal accounting control provisions, as well as the record-keeping requirements for publicly held companies were included in the act to help accomplish that purpose.

Congress attempted to prevent corporate bribery of foreign officials by three basic provisions of the FCPA: accounting requirements, criminalization of foreign bribery and enforcement.

The accounting provisions

The accounting provisions are applicable to all companies under SEC jurisdiction. Hence, the act's provisions dealing with accurate books and records, and accounting controls are far-ranging in scope. They are universal requirements that cover all transactions, not simply those related to overseas business activities or corrupt practices.

Section 102 of the FCPA amended 13(b) of the Securities Exchange Act of 1934 to require firms regulated by the SEC to "make and keep records, books, and accounts, which, in reasonable detail, accurately and fairly reflect the transactions and dispositions of the assets" of the firms. This provision thus prohibited the "disguising" of questionable payments to persons overseas and prohibited secret slush funds- that is "inaccurate books, off-the-book accounts and related practices" (SEC Release No. 14478, February 16, 1978).

Section 102 of the FCPA further amended section 13(b) of the Securities Act of 1934 to require firms regulated by the SEC to devise and maintain a system of internal accounting controls sufficient to provide reasonable assurances that:

(1) transactions of the firm are executed in accordance with management's general or specific authorization

(2) transactions are recorded as necessary to (1) permit preparation of financial statements in conformity with generally accepted accounting principles or any other criteria applicable to such statements, and (2) to maintain accountability for assets

(3) access to assets is permitted only in accordance with management's general or specific authorization

(4) the afforded accountability for assets is compared with the existing assets at reasonable intervals and appropriate action is taken with respect to any differences.

In and of themselves, the accounting requirements are not radical. To the contrary, the FCPA adopted the generalized objectives almost verbatim from the American Institute of Certified Public Accountants (AICPA) Statement of Auditing Standards (SAS) No. 1, Section 320.28, definition of accounting controls. Hence, it seems fair to say that the act simply endorsed private-sector accounting standards and incorporated them into federal securities law.

Both of the act's accounting provisions are modified by the key term "reasonable." Unfortunately, an explicit materiality standard was not incorporated into the accounting provisions, and "reasonable" was left undefined. To further frustrate the compliance problem, the SEC refused to issue interpretive rulings concerning the application of the FCPA to specific transactions (SEC Rel. No. 14478, Feb. 16, 1978). As a consequence, a great deal of concern arose in the business, legal and accounting worlds as to the true implication of the accounting provisions for publicly held companies.

While the FCPA provides no specific guidance on how to meet the "reasonable assurance" requirement, neither does it require any specific action on the part of publicly held companies. In fact, given that the concepts incorporated into the law had been in existence for some time in the private sector, the accounting provisions of the FCPA might have been relatively noncontroversial. In fact, the effect of accounting requirements on well-managed and controlled companies should have been minimal. The compliance burden should have fallen on those public companies that lacked effective control with the consequential impact of leveling public company control systems; i.e., raising companies with deficient control systems to the standard of their better-managed public company peers.

Unfortunately, the phraseology adopted from the SAS lacked sufficient specificity to serve as an effective standard for enforcement purposes. The wording of the accounting provisions made it difficult, if not impossible, for corporate officers to determine on an objective basis whether their companies were in compliance with the law. Evaluating the sufficiency of an internal control system is a difficult judgmental task in any circumstance, but given the lack of any objective criteria in the FCPA and the unwillingness of the SEC to provide interpretive guidance, the problem was further compounded. Consequently, there was a great deal of confusion regarding the adequacy of record keeping and internal control systems and what constituted compliance with the act's accounting provisions. Corporate officers expressed grave concerns about prosecution as the result of what they might consider immaterial errors in corporate records and weakness in internal control.

While the standards of the accounting provisions were characterized by members of the business community as "ambiguous" or "vague," the penalties for their violation were crystal-clear. Penalties for violations of the accounting requirements were the same as for other violations of the Securities Exchange Act. Section 32(a) of the exchange act provided for a fine of not more than $10,000 or imprisonment for not more than five years upon conviction.

As a consequence of the uncertainties surrounding compliance with the accounting provisions of the FCPA, companies were very cautious in assuring compliance. During 1978-81, there was a great flurry of activity on the part of many publicly held companies to document existing accounting information systems, change systems to address weaknessses, establish or expand internal audit department, increase the number and responsibilities of independent directors, and create audit subcommittees of the board of directors. The irony is that the companies that least needed improvement in their systems were the very companies that most zealously attempted to assure compliance. The unintended economic consequence of the accounting provisions may well have been a diversion of corporate resources from more profitable, productive utilization. Certainly, resources were directed to control systems without being scrutinized as aggressively and dispassionately as before the FCPA.

Foreign Bribery

The "reason to know" provision attached responsibility regardless of whether the U.S. business intended to have the third person make an improper payment. Many exporters were very concerned because they asserted they had no idea when they might be found to have "reason to know" about a bribe paid by an agent without their authorization. U.S. businesses strongly held that the "reason to know" or negligence standard was too vague and motivated an excessive caution which adversely effected export sales. Moreover, it was asserted that this standard discriminated against small companies that, lacking offices abroad, operate through foreign agents.

The FCPA specifically prohibits domestic firms, whether registered with the SEC or not, from bribing a foreign official, a foreign political party, party official or candidate for the purpose of obtaining or maintaining business. Under Sections 103 and 104 of the FCPA, criminal penalties are provided for any firm regulated by the SEC or for any other domestic concern that uses the mails or interstate commerce "corruptly" in furtherance of an offer or payment of money or anything of value to a "foreign official" for the purpose of influencing such person in his decision-making or in the use of his influence to affect governmental decisions to assist the firm in obtaining or retaining business.

In addition to prohibiting such bribes directly by a firm or by any of its employees, officers, agents or directors acting on its behalf, the act also addressed so-called third-party bribery by prohibiting the payment of money to any person by a firm if the firm "knew" or had "reason to know" that a portion or all of such payment was to be used to bribe a foreign official for his influence in obtaining or retaining business (S. Rept. 95-114, p.1).

There are exceptions to the bribery prohibitions. Not all payments to employees of foreign governments were considered by Congress to be illegal bribes under the FCPA. First, the definition of "foreign official" within the act excludes those employees of foreign governments "whose duties are essentially ministerial or clerical" (section 103(b) and 104(d)(1) of FCPA of 1977). Second, the legislative history of the act states specifically that the act was not intended to cover minor payments such as "payments for expediting shipments through customs or placing a transatlantic telephone call, securing required permits, or obtaining adequate police protection, transactions which may involve even the proper performance of duties" (S. Rept. 95-114, p. 10).

The penalties for violations of the bribery provision of the FCPA include fines for the firm or corporation of up to $1 million and fines of up to $10,000 or imprisonment of up to five years or both for individuals.

Enforcement

Two federal agencies are involved in the enforcement and administration of the FCPA. The record keeping and accounting control provisions of the FCPA, requiring fair and accurate accounting of corporate transactions and expenditures by U.S. publicly held companies are under the authority of the SEC. The SEC also has civil authority to enforce the prohibitions against foreign bribery by U.S. publicly held companies. The enforcement of the criminal penalties for corporate "bribery" of foreign officials are primarily under the authority of the Department of Justice, which also has the authority to bring civil actions against domestic concerns whose securities are not registered with the SEC.

1988 amendments to FCPA

Since its passage, there have been persistent and continuing efforts to address perceived deficiencies of the act. During the period following the 1980 presidential election when the Republican Party held the majority in the Senate, there were two unsuccessful efforts to amend the FCPA. In early 1981 and again in early 1983, the Senate attempted to remedy some of the uncertainties associated with the FCPA. Each time, the amendments were passed by the Senate only to die in the Democrat-controlled House.

The amendment to the FCPA that finally passed as a section of the Omnibus Trade and Competitiveness Act of 1988 attempts to resolve many of the uncertainties inherent in the original legislation by clarifying various provisions of the act. In addition, the amendment consolidates most of the enforcement responsibility for bribery violations into the Department of Justice and increases the civil and criminal penalties for violating the F(C-PA

> The amendment acknowledges that it is unrealistic to expect a minority owner to exert a disproportionate degree of influence over the accounting practices of an investee, and that the amount of influence that an owner can exercise may vary from case to case. Any company that can demonstrate good-faith efforts to use its influence to promote compliance with the accounting provisions by its investee will be presumed to have complied with its responsibilities under the act.

The accounting provisions amendments

The FCPA amendment defined the terms "reasonable detail" as used in the record keeping requirement and "reasonable assurances" as used in the internal control systems by reference to a prudent-man test. According to the amendment, "reasonable detail" and "reasonable assurances" mean such level of detail and degree of assurance as would satisfy prudent officials in the conduct of their affairs. The prudent-man standard was adopted to clarify that the FCPA does not require an unrealistic degree of exactitude or precision. While an explicit cost-benefit test was not included in the amendment, the concept of reasonableness implicitly contemplates the weighing of a number of factors, including the costs of compliance.

The FCPA was silent on the issue of the legal responsibility of a publicly held company for compliance by its domestic and foreign subsidiaries with the accounting requirements. The amendment addressed this issue in this manner: Minority shareholders (controlling 50 percent or less of the voting power) will be in compliance with the accounting provisions if they make a good-faith effort to influence the subsidiary/investee to comply with the FCPA. The amendment requires a parent to use its influence to the extent reasonable under the circumstances. What is reasonable under the circumstances is affected by the relative degree of the issuer's ownership of the domestic or foreign firm and the laws and practices governing the business operation of the country in which such firm is located.

The amendment limits future criminal liability to intentional actions to circumvent the internal accounting control system or falsify the company books. Specifically, no criminal liability will be imposed for failing to comply with the FCPA's accounting provisions unless a person knowingly circumvents a system of internal accounting controls or knowingly falsifies books, records or accounts. Inadvertent errors of either omission or commission will not be treated as violations of the FCPA accounting provisions.

Criminalization of foreign bribery

The bribery provisions continue to cover both direct and indirect payments to foreign officials. For payments made through third parties, the "reason to know" standard for payments has been eliminated and the "knowing" standard modified. This is a significant modification of the act; one that should be welcomed by U.S. exporters. Under the act,

Many types of payments continue to be excluded from the FCPA's definition of bribery. The act clarifies the traditional exclusion for "grease payments" by stating that they include payments to foreign officials for expediting or securing "routine governmental action" such as obtaining documentation to do business, processing papers, providing police protection, scheduling inspections related to transit of goods, and providing phone service, power and water. These exclusions should reduce the disadvantage U.S. corporations have in relationship to foreign corporations, which are allowed to make such payments in other countries.

"knowing" is defined to entail the substantial certainty or conscious disregard of a high probability that the third-party payment will become a bribe. Hence, management will not be permitted to use a "head-in-the-sand" or "deliberate ignorance" approach to avoiding responsibility. Criminal liability is applied for firms and individuals who make payments to third parties while "knowing" that the payment will be used by the third party for purposes barred by the act.

Additional types of payments also are officially legitimized. They include payments that are lawful under the foreign government's written laws and regulations or that are reasonable and bona fide expenses, such as travel and lodging, directly related to promoting products or performing or executing contracts. If a U.S. company can demonstrate that its payments fell only into these categories, it will have a complete defense to any Justice Department prosecution under the FCPA.

Enforcement

The civil and criminal penalties for violating the FCPA have been increased. Criminal penalties have been increased from $1 million to $2 million for companies, and from $10,000 to $100,000 for individuals. The maximum imprisonment remains five years. A civil penalty of $10,000 for individuals has been established and may not be paid by the company.

The amendment consolidates within the Justice Department all jurisdiction for enforcing the anti-bribery provisions of the FCPA. The SEC remains responsible for civil enforcement of the books and records and internal accounting control provisions.

Summary and conclusion

The FCPA has been very influential over the last 12 years. The accounting control provisions of the FCPA provided the impetus for publicly held corporations to document their control systems, change systems to address identified weaknesses, establish or expand internal audit departments, create audit committees, and increase the number of independent board members. Independent auditors have responded to the FCPA by placing a greater emphasis on evaluating their clients' control systems. Assessment of client's control structure including the control environment is now a required phase of every audit. This evolution in audit practice is at least partially attributable to the FCPA.

The FCPA represents the most significant expansion of SEC authority since the establishment of the commission in 1934. Fortunately, the SEC of the 1980s has not been characterized by zealous activism. To date, the powers granted by the act have not been fully exercised. That is not to say, however, that some future SEC will not aggressively and creatively use the powers of the FCPA to extend its grasp to aspects of business practices, procedures, and conduct that have not been previously subject to regulation. The recently enacted amendments clarifies much of the ambiguity surrounding terms of the original legislation, and consequently reduces the potential for abuse of power. However, the FCPA places potent powers in the hands of the SEC and it is likely that some future administration will choose to use them.

References:

American Institute of Certified Public Accountants, *Statement of Auditing Standards No. 1,* Section 320, 1977.

Foreign Corrupt Practices Act of 1977, 91 Stat. 1494 8, 1977.

Maher, Michael W. "The Impact of Regulation on Controls: Firm's Response to the Foreign Corrupt Practices Act." *The Accounting Review*, October 1981, pp. 751-770.

Moser, S. Thomas. "The Foreign Corrupt Practices Act of 1977: An Auditor's Perspective." *The CPA Journal,* May 1978, pp. 71-75.

Omnibus Trade and Competitiveness Act, Public Law 100-418, Sec.5003. 100th Congress, 2nd Session, 1988.

Omnibus Trade and Competitiveness Act, Legislative History, House Conference Report No. 100-576, 100th Congress, 2nd Session, 1988.

SEC Release No. 14478, February, 1978.

Schechtman, Daniel. "SEC Commentary: Chairman Indicates SEC Policy on Accounting Provisions of FCPA." *The CPA Journal,* June 1981, pp.70-71.

U.S. Senate Report No. 114, 95th Congress, 1st Session, 1977

Human resource management

Talented and motivated people are key any firm's business success, and they play an even more crucial role in the complex web of international business relationships. Yet, many firms have paid a dear price for failing to devote sufficient attention to selecting, training, and motivating people who work in international positions. One study found, for instance, that a mere four percent of the time spent on creating international joint ventures was typically spent on human resources issues.

A basic starting point in successful international human resource management practices is to develop a program for selecting people who are predisposed to international assignments and socializing them to help them cope with the inevitable culture shock of working in a foreign country as well as the re-entry shock upon returning home. In *Ellen Moore in Bahrain,* a young western woman manager encounters the challenges of managing a financial services operation in the Middle East, including the Islamic religion and cultural traditions toward women. She must make a career decision of compromising her values or her career when she is unexpectedly denied a position involving frequent travel to Saudi Arabia. Ellen Moore's suitability for international assignments can be assessed using the *International Orientation Scale,* and her responses can be compared with your own. Responses can also be examined in light of the difficulties encountered by nearly 500 graduates of international business programs in their international assignments, as reported in *Entry shock, culture shock: socializing the new breed of global managers.* The article also provides eight guidelines to help companies establish sound human resources practices for employees working in international assignments.

Developing compensation plans that are fair to internationally-based executives and appropriate to the company and the host country is a complex task that has been given insufficient attention in many firms. *Executive compensation in the international arena: Back to the basics* warns of the unexpected consequences that can occur when American incentive plans are applied abroad without taking into account issues specific to the host country including its culture and laws, as well as the needs and preferences of the executives assigned abroad. The article also advocates cash-incentive plans and stock-based plans as part of compensation packages for international executives.

Two selections examine human resources practices in the context of different economic systems. *Comrade's dilemma* is an interactive exercise that contrasts the methods of organizing and motivating workers in a centrally planned economy and a market-based economy. Those playing the role of planners and managers in the exercise make decisions within the constraints of each economic system and direct workers to produce various quantities and varieties of goods. The exercise illustrates some of the advantages and disadvantages of centrally planned versus market-based economies, and suggests that managers in countries that are transforming from central planning to free enterprise face major challenges in changing their own attitudes and behaviors as well as those of their employees. How one company has successfully introduced western human resources practices in a formerly communist country is described in *Management education and employee training at Moscow McDonald's*. McDonald's applied the human resources practices it uses worldwide to train Russians to become managers and crew members of the Moscow restaurant, their largest operation in the world. In its Russian joint venture, McDonald's of Canada painstakingly selected and trained local people to operate the restaurant and carefully developed incentives that would appeal to their Russian staff members. Being one of the first western ventures to hire large numbers of Russians, McDonald's learned how to deal with the complexities and restrictions of the centrally planned, communist system and was an innovator in introducing western management methods and human resources practices to Russia.

Chapter 4
Human resource management

18. Ellen Moore in Bahrain[1]

Topics covered: Women in Middle East organizations

Management in Islamic countries

> *"The General Manager had offered me a choice of two positions in the Operations area. I had considered the matter carefully and was about to meet with him to tell him I would accept the Accounts Control position. The job was much more challenging than the Customer Services post, but I knew I could learn the systems and procedures quickly, and I would have a great opportunity to contribute to the success of the Operations area."*

In November 1989, Ellen Moore was just completing her second year as an expatriate manager at the offices of a large American financial institution in Manama, Bahrain. After graduating with an M.B.A. from a leading business school, Ellen had joined her husband, who was working as an expatriate manager at an offshore bank in Bahrain. Being highly qualified and capable, she had easily found a demanding position and had worked on increasingly complex projects since she had begun at the company. She was looking forward to the challenges of the Accounts Control position.

Ellen Moore

Ellen graduated as the top female student from her high school when she was 16 and immediately began working full-time for the main branch of one of the largest banks in the country. By the end of four years, she had become a corporate accounts officer and managed more than 20 large accounts.

> "I remember I was always making everything into a game, a challenge. One of my first jobs was filing checks. I started having a competition with the woman at the adjacent desk who had been filing for years, except she didn't know I was competing with her. When she

1 By Gail Ellement, Martha Maznevski and Henry W. Lane. In Lane/DiStefano, *International Management Behavior*, 2d ed, 1992, Boston, MA: PWS-Kent Publishing Company. Used with permission.

Dorothy Marcic and Sheila Puffer, *Management International*, West Publishing, 1994.
All rights reserved. May not be reproduced without written permission of the publisher. For more information, contact West Publishing, Publications Dept., 610 Opperman Drive, St. Paul, MN 55164.

realized it, we both started competing in earnest. Before long, people used to come over just to watch us fly through these stacks of checks. When I moved to the next job, I used to see how fast I could add up columns of numbers while handling phone conversations. I always had to do something to keep myself challenged."

While working full-time at the bank, Ellen achieved a Fellowship in the Institute of Bankers after completing demanding courses and exams. She went on to work in banking and insurance with one of her former corporate clients from the bank. When she was subsequently promoted to manage their financial reporting department, she was both the first female and the youngest person the company had ever had in that position.

Since she had begun working full-time, Ellen had been taking courses towards a bachelor's degree at night at one of the city's universities. In 1983 she decided to stop working for two years to complete her degree. After she graduated with a major in accounting and minors in marketing and management, she entered the M.B.A. program.

"I decided to go straight into the M.B.A. program for several reasons. First, I wanted to update myself. I had taken my undergraduate courses over ten years and wanted to obtain knowledge on contemporary views. Second, I wanted to tie some pieces together as my night-school degree left my ideas somewhat fragmented. Third, I wasn't impressed with the interviews I had after I finished the bachelor's degree. And fourth, I was out of work anyway. Finally, my father had already told everyone that I had my M.B.A., and I decided I really couldn't disappoint him."

Just after Ellen began the two-year M.B.A. program, her husband was offered a position with an affiliate of his bank, posted in Bahrain, beginning the next spring. They sat down and examined potential opportunities that would be available for Ellen once she completed her M.B.A. They discovered that women could work and assume positions of responsibility in Bahrain and decided they could both benefit from the move. Her husband moved to Bahrain in March, while Ellen remained to complete her M.B.A. Ellen followed, with degree in hand, 18 months later.

Bahrain

Bahrain is an archipelago of 33 islands that are located in the Persian Gulf (see Figure 1). The main island, Bahrain, comprises 85 percent of the almost 700 square kilometers of the country and is the location of the capital city, Manama. Several of the islands are joined by causeways, and in 1987 the 25 kilometer King Fahd Causeway linked the principal island to the mainland of Saudi Arabia, marking the end of island isolation for the country. In 1971, Bahrain gained full independence from Britain, ending a relationship that had lasted for almost a century. Of the population of more than 400,000 people, about one-third were foreigners.

Bahrain has had a prosperous history. Historically, it has been sought after by many countries for its lush vegetation, fresh water, and pearls. Many traditional crafts and industries were still practiced, including pottery, basket making, fabric weaving, pearl diving, (fishing boat) building, and fishing. Bahrain was the pearl capital of the world for many centuries. Fortunately, just as the pearl industry collapsed with the advent of cultured pearls from Japan, Bahrain struck its first oil.

The Bahrain government had been aware for several years that the oil reserves were being seriously depleted. It was determined to diversify the country's economy away from a dependence on one resource. Industries established since 1971 included aluminum processing, shipbuilding, iron and steel processing, and furniture and door manufacturing. Offshore banking began in 1975. Since Bahrain nationals did not have the expertise to develop these industries alone, expatriates from around the world, particularly from Western Europe and North America, were invited to conduct business in Bahrain. By the late 1980s, the country was a major business and financial center, housing many Middle East branch offices of international firms.

Since the 1930s, the oil industry had been the largest contributor to Bahrain's gross national product. The country was the first in the Persian Gulf to have an oil industry, established with a discovery in 1932. Production at that time was 9,600 barrels a day. Eventually, crude output reached over 40,000 barrels a day. Bahrain's oil products included crude oil, natural gas, methanol and ammonia, and refined products such as gasoline, jet fuels, kerosene, and asphalt.

Expatriates in Bahrain

Since Bahrain was an attractive base from which to conduct business, it was a temporary home to many expatriates. Housing compounds, schools, services, shopping and leisure activities all catered to many international cultures. Expatriates lived under residence permits, gained only on the basis of recruitment for a specialist position that could not be filled by a qualified and available Bahraini citizen.

To Ellen, one of the most interesting roles of expatriate managers was that of teacher. The Arab nations had been industrialized for little more than two decades and had suddenly found themselves needing to compete in a global market. Ellen believed that one of her main reasons for working in Bahrain was to train its nationals to take over her job eventually.

"Although it was outside of office policy, I held 'Ellen's Introduction to Computers' after office hours, just to get people comfortable with the machines and to teach them a few basics."

"Sometimes the amount of energy you had to put into the teaching was frustrating in that results were not immediately evident. I often worked jointly with one of the Bahraini managers, who really didn't know how to develop projects and prepare reports. Although I wasn't responsible for him, I spent a great deal of time with him, helping him improve his work. Initially there was resistance on his part, because he was not prepared to subordinate himself to an expatriate, let alone a woman. But eventually he came around and we achieved some great results working together."

"The inequality among nationalities was one issue I found very difficult to deal with during my stay in Bahrain. The Third World immigrants were considered to be the lowest level possible in the pecking order, just slightly lower than

"Usually the teaching part was very interesting. When I first arrived in the office, I was amazed to see many staff members with microcomputers on their desks, yet they did not know the first thing about operating the equipment. When I inquired about the availability of computer courses, I was informed by a British expatriate manager that 'as these were personal computers, any person should be able to use them, and as such, courses aren't necessary.' It was clear to me that courses were very necessary when the computer knowledge of most employees consisted of little more than knowing where the on/off switch was located on a microcomputer."

nationals from countries outside the Gulf. Gulf Arabs, being of Bedouin origin, maintained a suspicious attitude towards "citified" Arabs. Europeans and North Americans were regarded much more highly. These inequalities had a major impact on daily life, including the availability of jobs and what relations would develop or not develop between supervisors and subordinates. Although I was well acquainted with the racial problems of North America, I haven't seen anything compared to the situation in Bahrain. It wasn't unusual for someone to be exploited and discarded, as any expendable and easily replaceable resource would be, because of their nationality."

The range of cultures represented in Bahrain was vast. Expatriate managers interacted not only with Arabic nationals, but also with managers from other parts of the world, and with workers from developing countries who provided a large part of the unskilled labor force.

Although many expatriates and their families spent their time in Bahrain immersed in their own cultural compounds, social groups, and activities, Ellen believed that her interaction with the various cultures was one of the most valuable elements of her international experience.

Managing in Bahrain

Several aspects of the Middle Eastern culture had tremendous impact on the way business was managed, even in Western firms located in Bahrain. It seemed that the concept of "time" differed between Middle Eastern and Western cultures. Schedules and deadlines, although sacred to Western managers, commanded little respect from Bahraini employees. The two areas that had the most impact on Ellen's managing in a company in Bahrain were the Islamic religion and the traditional attitude towards women.

It seemed to Ellen, for example, that "truth" to a Bahraini employee was subject to an Arab interpretation, which was formed over hundreds of years of cultural evolution. What Western managers considered to be "proof" of an argument or "factual" evidence could be flatly denied by a Bahraini; if something was not believed, it did not exist.

Islam[2]

Most Bahrainis are practicing Muslims. According to the Muslim faith, the universe was created by Allah, who prescribed a code of life called Islam, and the Qur'an is the literal, unchanged Word of Allah preserved exactly as transcribed by Muhammad. Muhammad's own acts as a prophet form the basis for Islamic law and are second in authority only to the Qur'an.

"Certainly the Muslim religion had a tremendous impact on my daily working life. The first time I walked into the women's washroom at work I noticed a tap about three inches off the floor over a drain. I found this rather puzzling; I wondered if it was for the cleaning crew. When a woman came in, I asked her about the tap, and she explained that before going into the prayer room, everyone had to wash all uncovered parts of their bodies. The tap was for washing their feet and legs.

2 "Residents in Bahrain," Vol. 1, 1987. *Gulf Daily News*, pp. 61-63.

"One time I was looking for one of my employees, Mohammed, who had a report due to me that afternoon. I searched for him at his desk and other likely spots throughout the office, but to no avail; he just wasn't around. I had difficulties with Mohammed's work before, when he would submit documents long after deadlines, and I was certain he was attempting to slack off again. I bumped into one of Mohammed's friends and asked if he knew Mohammed's whereabouts. When he informed me that Mohammed was in the prayer room, I wasn't sure how to respond. I didn't know if this prayer room activity was very personal and if I could ask questions, such as the length of time one generally spends in prayer. But I needed to know how long Mohammed would be away from his desk. Throwing caution to the wind, I asked the employee how long Mohammed was likely to be in prayers and he told me it usually takes about 10 minutes.

"During Ramadan, the hours of business are shortened by law. It is absolutely illegal for any Muslim to work past 2 o'clock in the afternoon, unless special permits are obtained from the Ministry of Labor. Unfortunately, business coming in to an American firm does not stop at 2, and a majority of the non-Muslim workers are required to take up the slack."

The five Pillars of Islam are belief, prayer, fasting, giving alms, and pilgrimage. Muslims pray five times a day. During Ramadan, the ninth month of the Islamic calendar, Muslims must abstain from food, drink, smoking, and sexual activity from dawn until dusk in order to master the urges that sustain and procreate life. All Muslims are obliged to give a certain proportion of their wealth in alms for charitable purposes; the Qur'an stresses that the poor have a just claim on the wealth of the prosperous. Finally, if possible, all Muslims should make a pilgrimage to Mecca during their lives, in a spirit of total sacrifice of personal comforts, acquisition of wealth, and other matters of worldly significance.

Unlike religion in Western civilization, Islam permeates every function of human endeavor. There does not exist a separation of church, state and judiciary. Indeed, in purist circles, the question does not arise. The hybrid systems existing in certain Arab countries are considered aberrations created by Western colonial influences. Accordingly, to function successfully, the expatriate must understand and learn to accept a very different structuring of a society.

"It wasn't that I felt I didn't have the right to know where my employee was or how long he would be away; I just wasn't certain my authority as a manager allowed me the right to ask questions about such a personal activity as praying."

Women in Bahrain

Bahrain tended to be more progressive than may Middle Eastern countries in its attitude towards women. Although traditions were strong, Bahraini women had some freedom. For example, all women could work outside the home, although the hours they could work were restricted both by convention and by the labor laws. Bahraini women were permitted to wear a variety of outfits, from the conservative full-length black robe with head scarf, which covers the head and hair, to below-the-knee skirts and dresses without head covering.

"Arab women who sincerely want change and more decision-making power over their own lives face an almost impossible task, because the male influence is perpetuated not only by men but also by women who are afraid to alter views they understand and with which they have been brought up all their lives. I once asked a female co-worker why one of the women in the office, who had previously been 'uncovered,' was now sporting a scarf over her head. The response was that this woman had just been married, and although her husband did not request that she become 'covered,' she personally did not feel as though she was a married woman without the head scarf. So she simply asked her husband to demand that she wear a scarf on her head. It was a really interesting situation; some of the more liberal Bahraini women were very upset that she had asked her husband to make this demand. They saw it as negating many of the progressive steps the women's movement had made in recent years."

Women could only work if their husbands, fathers, or brothers permitted them, and they could not take potential employment away from men. Work outside the home was to be conducted in addition to, not instead of, duties performed inside the home, such as child rearing and cooking. Most women who worked held secretarial or clerical positions; few worked in management.

Although Bahrainis had been exposed to Western cultures for the two decades of industrial expansion, they were still uncomfortable with Western notions of gender equality and less traditional roles for women.

"One day a taxi driver leaned back against his seat and, while keeping one eye on the road ahead, turned to ask me, 'How many sons do you have?' I replied that I didn't have any children. His heartfelt response of 'I'm so sorry' and the way he shook his head in sympathy were something my North American upbringing didn't prepare me for. Although Bahrain is progressive in many ways, attitudes on the role of women in society run long and deep, and it is quite unlikely these sentiments will alter in the near, or even distant, future.

"Another time I was greeted with gales of laughter when I revealed to the women in the office that my husband performed most of the culinary chores in our household. They assumed I was telling a joke, and when I insisted that he really did most of the cooking, they sat in silent disbelief. Although these women have successful business careers – as clerks, but in the workforce nonetheless – they believe women should perform all household tasks without the assistance of their husbands. The discovery that this belief holds true in Bahrain is not remarkable, as I know many North American and European businesswomen who believe the same to be true. What is pertinent is these women allow themselves to be completely dominated by the men in their lives."

"The one concept I faced daily but never accepted was that my husband was regarded as the sole decision-maker in our household. He and I view our marriage as a partnership in which we participate equally in all decisions. But when the maintenance manager for our housing compound came by, repairs were completed efficiently only if I preceded my request with, 'My husband wants the following to be completed.' It's a phrase I hated to use because it went against every rational thought I possess, but I frequently had to resort to it."

"My taxi driver's response typifies the attitude projected toward women, whether they are expatriates from Europe or North America or Bahrainis. Women are meant to have children, preferably sons. "

"One woman spoke up and informed the group that she didn't think her husband even knew where the kitchen was in their house, let alone would ever be caught touching a cooking utensil. The group nodded in agreement."

These attitudes also affected how Ellen was treated as a manager by Bahraini managers:

"One manager, I'll call him Fahad, believed that women were capable of fulfilling only secretarial and coffee-making functions. One day I was sitting at my desk, concentrating on some documents. I didn't notice Fahad having a discussion with another male manager nearby. When I looked up from my papers, Fahad noticed me and immediately began talking in French to the other manager. Although my French was a bit rusty, my comprehension was still quite serviceable. I waited for a few moments and then broke into their discussion in French. Fahad was completely dismayed. Over the next few years, Fahad and I worked together on several projects. At first, he was pompous and wouldn't listen to anything I presented. It was a difficult situation, but I was determined to remain above his negative comments. I ignored his obvious prejudice towards me, remained outwardly calm when he disregarded my ideas, and proceeded to prove myself with my work. It took a lot of effort and patience but, in time, Fahad and I not only worked out our differences, but worked as a successful team on a number of major projects. Although the situation has a happy ending, I really would have preferred to have directed all that energy and effort toward more productive issues."

Bahraini nationals were not the only ones who perpetuated the traditional roles of women in society. Many of the expatriates, particularly those from Commonwealth countries, tended to view their role as "the colonial charged with the responsibility to look after the developing country." This was reflected in an official publication for new expatriates that stated: "Wives of overseas employees are normally sponsored by their husbands' employers, and their Residence Permits are processed at the same time..."[3] However, wives were not permitted to work unless they could obtain a work permit for themselves.

"The first question I was often asked at business receptions was, 'What company is your husband with?' When I replied that I worked as well, I received the glazed-over look, because they assumed I occupied myself with coffee mornings, beach, tennis, and other leisure activities as did the majority of expatriate wives."

"Social gatherings were always risky. At typical business and social receptions the men served themselves first, after which the women selected their food. Then women and men positioned themselves on opposite sides of the room. The women discussed "feminine" topics, such as babies and recipes, whereas the men discussed the fall (or rise) of the dollar and the big deal of the day. At one Bahraini business gathering, I hesitated in choosing sides: Should I conform and remain with the women? But most of these women did not work outside their homes, and, consequently, they spoke and understood very little English. I joined the men. Contrary to what I expected, I was given a gracious welcome.

"However, on another occasion, I was bored with the female conversation, so I ventured over to the forbidden male side to join a group of bankers discussing correspondent banking courses. When I entered the discussion, a British bank general manager turned his nose up at me. He motioned towards the other side of the room and told me I should join the women. He implied that his discussion was obviously over my head. I quickly informed him that although I personally had found the banking courses difficult to complete while holding a full-time banking position, I not only managed to complete the program and obtain my Fellowship but at the time was the youngest employee of my bank ever to be awarded the diploma. The man did a quick turnabout, was thoroughly embarrassed and apologized profusely. Although it was nice to turn the tables on the man, I was more than a little frustrated with the feeling that I almost had to wear my resume on my sleeve to get any form of respect from the men, whether European, North American or Arab."

---

3 "Resident in Bahrain," Vol. 1, 1987, *Gulf Daily News*, p. 57.

A small percentage of Bahraini women had completed university degrees in North America and Europe. While residing in these Western cultures, they were permitted to function as did their Western counterparts. For example, they could visit or phone friends when they wished without first obtaining permission. After completing their education, many of these women were qualified for management positions; upon returning to Bahrain, however, they were required to resume their traditional female roles.

Ellen discovered that, despite being a woman, she was accepted by Bahrainis as a manager as a result of her Western nationality, her education, and her management position in the company.

> "Many of my male Arab peers accepted me as they would any expatriate manager. For example, when a male employee returned from a vacation, he would typically visit each department, calling upon the other male employees with a greeting and a handshake. Although he might greet a female co-worker, he would never shake her hand. However, because of my management position in the company and my status as a Western expatriate, male staff members gave me the same enthusiastic greeting and handshake normally reserved for their male counterparts."

Ellen also found herself facilitating Bahraini women's positions in the workplace.

> "Because I was the only female in a senior management position in our office, I was often asked by the female employees to speak to their male supervisors about problems and issues they experienced in their departments."

The government of Bahrain introduced legislation that restricted the amount of overtime hours women could work. Although the move was being praised by the (female) Director of Social Development as recognition of the contribution women were making to Bahraini industry, Ellen saw it as further discriminatory treatment restricting the choices of women in Bahrain. Her published letter to the editor of the Gulf Daily News read:

"The notion of pink M.B.A. diplomas for women and blue for men is very real. Although any M.B.A. graduate in North America, male or female, is generally considered to have attained a certain level of business sense, I had to constantly 'prove' myself to some individuals who appeared to believe that women attended a special segregated section of the university with appropriately tailored courses."

"I also had to provide a role model for the women because there were no female Bahraini managers. Some of them came to me not just to discuss their career issues but to discuss life issues. There was just no one else in a similar position for them to talk to. On the other hand, male managers would ask me to discuss sensitive issues, such as hygiene, with their female staff members."

> "... How the discriminatory treatment of women in this regulation can be seen as recognition of the immense contribution women make to the Bahrain workforce is beyond comprehension. Discrimination of any portion of the population in the labor legislation does not recognize anything but the obvious prejudice. If the working women in Bahrain want to receive acknowledgment of their indispensable impact on the Bahrain economy, it should be through an increase in the number of management positions available to qualified women, not through regulations limiting the hours they work. All this regulation means is that women are still regarded as second-class citizens who need the

strong-arm tactics of the government to help them settle disputes over working hours. Government officials could really show appreciation to the working women in Bahrain by making sure that companies hire and promote based on skill rather than gender. But there is little likelihood of that occurring."

The letter was signed with a pseudonym, but the day it was published one of Ellen's female employees showed her the letter and claimed, "If I didn't know better, Ellen, I'd think you wrote this letter."

When Ellen first arrived in Bahrain, she had great expectations that she would work somewhere she could make a difference. She received several offers for positions and turned down, among others, a university and high-profile brokerage house. She decided to take a position as a Special Projects Coordinator at a large American financial institution.

> "In fact, the records will show I was actually hired as a "Financial Analyst," but this title was given solely because at that time the government had decided that expatriate women shouldn't be allowed to take potential positions away from Bahraini nationals. The expertise required as a Financial Analyst enabled the company to obtain a work permit for me, as I had the required experience and academic credentials, although I performed few duties as an analyst."

In her special projects role, Ellen learned a great deal about international finance. She conducted efficiency studies on various operating departments. She used her systems expertise to investigate and improve the company's microcomputer usage, and she developed a payroll program that was subsequently integrated into the company's international systems. She was a member of the Strategic Review Committee, and produced a report outlining the long-term goals for the Middle East market, which she then presented to the Senior Vice President of Europe, Middle East and Africa.

After one year, Ellen was rewarded for her achievements by a promotion to Manager of Business Planning and Development, a position that reported directly to the Vice President and General Manager. She designed the role herself and could be creative and quite influential in the company. During her year in this role, she was involved in a diverse range of activities. She managed the Quality Assurance Department, coordinated a product launch, developed and managed a senior management information system, was an active participant in all senior management meetings, and launched an employee newsletter.

The first position was for Manager of Accounts Control, which covered the Credit, Collection, and Authorization departments. The Manager's role was to ensure that appropriate information was used to authorize spending by clients, to compile results on client payment, and to inform management of nonpayment issues. The Manager also supervised in-house staff and representatives in other Gulf countries for the collection of withheld payments.

The second post was Manager of Customer Services, New Accounts, and Establishment

At the end of her second year in Bahrain, Ellen was informed that two positions in operations would soon be available. The General Manager, a European expatriate, asked if she would be interested in joining the area. She had previously worked only in staff positions and quickly decided to accept the challenge and learning experience of a line post. Both positions were in senior management, and both were responsible for approximately 30 employees.

Services. The Manager's role was to ensure that new clients were worthy and that international quality standards were met in all Customer Service activity. The Manager also worked with two other departments - Marketing, to ensure that budgets were met, and Sales, to manage relationships with the many affiliate outlets of the service.

After speaking with the two current Managers and considering the options carefully, Ellen decided that she would prefer working in the Accounts Control area. The job was more oriented to financial information, the Manager had more influence on operations at the company, and she would have the opportunity to travel to other countries to supervise staff. Although she was not familiar with the systems and procedures, she knew she could learn them quickly. Ellen went into her meeting with the General Manager excited about the new challenges.

Ellen meets with the general manager

Ellen reminded the General Manager of the pride the company took in its quality standards and how senior management salaries were in part determined by assuring quality in their departments. Although the company was an equal opportunity employer in its home country, the United States, she believed the spirit of the policy should extend to all international offices.

Ellen told the General Manager she had decided to take the Accounts Control position and outlined her reasons. Then she waited for his affirmation and for the details of when she would begin.

"I'm afraid I've reconsidered the offer," the General Manager announced. "Although I know you would probably do a terrific job in the Accounts Control position, I can't offer it to you. It involves periodic travel into Saudi Arabia, and women are not allowed to travel there alone." He went on to tell Ellen how she would be subject to discriminatory practices, would not be able to gain the respect of the company's Saudi Arabian clients, and would experience difficulty traveling there.

Ellen was astonished. She quickly pointed out to him that many businesswomen were representatives of American firms in Saudi Arabia. She described one woman she knew who was the sole representative of a large American bank in the Eastern Province of Saudi Arabia. The woman frequently traveled there alone. She explained that other women's experiences in Saudi Arabia showed professional men there treated professional women as neither male nor female, but as businesspeople. Besides, she continued, the company had no other candidates for either position.

The General Manager informed her that his decision reflected his desire to address the interests of both herself and the company. He was worried, he said, that Ellen would have trouble obtaining entry visas to allow her to conduct business in Saudi Arabia and that the customers would not accept her. Also, if there were ever any hostile outbreaks, he believed she would be in danger, and he could not live with that possibility.

Ellen stated that, as a woman, she believed she was at lower risk of danger than her Western male counterparts, since, in the event of hostility, the Saudi Arabians would most likely secure her safety. There was much greater probability that a male representative of the firm would be held hostage.

The General Manager was adamant. Regardless of her wishes, the company needed Ellen in the Customer Service position. New Accounts had only recently been added to the department, and the bottom-line responsibility was thus doubled from what it had been in the past. The General Manager said he wanted someone he could trust and depend on to handle the pressure of New Accounts, which had a high international profile.

Ellen was offered the Customer Service position and then dismissed from the meeting. In frustration, she began to consider her options.

Take the customer service position

The General Manager obviously expected her to take the position. It would mean increased responsibility and challenge. Except for a position in high school where she managed a force of 60 student police, Ellen had not yet supervised more than four employees at any time in her professional career. On the other hand, it went against her values to accept the post, because it had been offered as a result of gender roles when all consideration should have been placed on competence. She knew she had the abilities and qualifications for the position.

> She viewed the entire situation as yet another example of how the business community in Bahrain had difficulty accepting and acknowledging the contributions of women to international management, and she didn't want to abandon her values by accepting the position.

Fight back

There were two approaches that would permit Ellen to take the matter further. She could go to the General Manager's superior, the Senior Vice President of Europe, Middle East, and Africa. She had several dealings with him in the past and had once presented a report that impressed him. But she wasn't sure she could count on his sympathy regarding her traveling to Saudi Arabia, as his knowledge of the region was limited and he generally relied on local management's decisions on such issues. She could consider filing a grievance against the company. Provisions in Bahraini Labor Law would have permitted this option in her case. She understood, however, that the Labor Tribunals, unlike those held in Western countries, did not try cases based on precedents or rules of evidence. In other words, the judge would apply a hodgepodge of his own subjective criteria to reach a decision.

Stay in the business planning and development job

Although the General Manager had not mentioned it as an option, Ellen could request that she remain in her current position. It would mean not giving in to the General Manager's prejudices. Since she had been considering the two Operations positions, though, she had been looking forward to moving on to something new.

Leave the company

Ellen knew she was qualified for many positions in the financial center of Bahrain and could likely obtain work with another company. She was not sure, though, whether leaving her present company under these circumstances would jeopardize her chances of finding work elsewhere. Furthermore, to obtain a post at a new company would require a letter of permission from her current employer, who, as her sponsor in Bahrain, had to sanction her move to a new employer who would become her new sponsor. She was not sure that she would be able to make those arrangements, considering the situation.

Ellen's superior did not have the same attitude towards his employees. As she considered her options, Ellen realized that no move could be made without a compromise either in her career or her values. Which choice was she most willing to make?

"I always tell my employees: 'If you wake up one morning and discover you don't like your job, come to see me immediately. If the problem is with the tasks of the job, I'll see if I can modify your tasks. If the problem is with the department or you want a change, I'll assist you in getting another position in the company. If the problem is with the company, then I'll help you write your resume.' I have stated this credo to all my employees in every post I've held. Generally, they don't believe that their manager would actually assist with resume writing, but when the opportunity arises, and it has, and I do come through as promised, the impact on remaining employees is priceless. Employees will provide much more effort towards a cause that is supported by someone looking out for their personal welfare."

Bahrain's Persian Gulf location is economically as well as militarily strategic.

19. Comrade's dilemma:
From communism to free enterprise[4]

purpose

1 To offer participants an opportunity to experience simulated economies under communism and free enterprise.

2 To demonstrate different types of incentives and controls in the two economies and the problems/opportunities faced in changing from a command economy to a free enterprise system.

group size

A minimum of 17, maximum of 50.

time required

Two 50-minute class periods, or about 120 minutes in one class.

materials needed

1 A pad of paper for all participants.

2 A watch or clock that accurately measures five-minute intervals.
room arrangement

A room large enough to accomodate three work groups, with each participant having a desk or other writing surface.

exercise schedule:

(see next page)

---

4 By John E. Oliver and Julia T. Connell, Valdosta State College, Valdosta, Georgia.
Used with permission.

part one – command economy

1   Introduction   5 min   5 min

Instructor gives brief overview of the exercise and divides class into two groups of approximately equal size.

Group I: One group is The Workers, who turn to Appendix and read "Directions for Workers."

Group II: The other is the state group and is subdivided further into two group, each of which reads "Directions for State" from the Appendix. One of the State groups is Military. The other is Planning Group, which reads "Five Minute Plan Form" in the Appendix.

Group members read over roles and prepare to play.

2.   Round I   5 min   10 min

Groups play roles. Instructor calls time after five minutes. Workers give the State their list of needs, and State gives Workers their initial assignment and production quotas, as well as the first Five Minute Plan.

3   Round II   5 min   15 min

Groups work for five more minutes. State reviews lists of worker needs and prepares a second Five Minute Plan with new assignments and quotas for Workers. Workers produce the products requested in the first Five Minute Plan. At the end of the five minutes, State receives all products produced by Workers and gives Workers the new, second Five Minute Plan with revised assignments and quotas.

4   Round III   5 min   20 min

Groups work for five more minutes, during which time Workers produce according to their new assignments while State determines how to distribute what has been produced. At the end of the time, State collects all production.

5   Distribution   5 min   25 min

State determines how to distribute what has been produced, how to eliminate surpluses and shortages, and how to assign quotas for the beginning of the next round. All this happens while Workers go on a Five Minute Vacation.

6   Round IV   5 min   30 min

State gives workers a third Five Minute Plan and distributes to Workers their allocation of products. Workers produce for five minutes while State prepares the fourth Five Minute Plan. At the end of time, State collects Worker production and gives Workers new assignments.

7. Round V   5 min   35 min

Workers produce while State determines how to distribute what has been produced and creates a fifth Five Minute Plan. At the end of five minutes, State distributes to Workers products previously collected, while Workers give State their production. Finally, State gives Workers the last Five Minute Plan.

8. Round VI   5 min   40 min

Workers produce according to the fifth Five-Minute Plan while State distributes accumulated production. At the end of time, State collects production and distributes it.

9. Discussion   10+ min   50 min

Entire group assembles to discuss experience. What has been produced should not be destroyed; all participants are to keep what has been distributed. This is their total wealth, even though some products, such as food, have theoretically been consumed. Workers exiled to Siberia should be brought back for the discussion.

Discussion questions:

How did you feel about the role you played?

Why were Workers asked to produce twice what they needed?

How well were the Workers' needs filled?

Were priorities set correctly in the Five Minute Plans?

Did workers become more or less productive as the game progressed?

Did the quality of what was produced change during the exercise?

Did you like the economy? Why or why not?

If you could change the economy, what would you do?

part two – free market enterprise

1   Introduction   5 min   5 min

Instructor explains that the Chief Comrade has decided to change the economy from communist to free enterprise. Students begin Part Two with same roles as in Part One, but may change roles after section begins. Everyone reads "Directions for free Enterprise" in the Appendix.

2   Role play   35 min   40 min

Students begin to play roles under free enterprise sysem. At the end of 35 minutes, participants stop role-playing and add up their wealth.

3   Group discussion   10+ min   50 min

Questions:

How did you feel playing the roles in the Free Enterprise economy?

How well were Worker needs filled?

Did Workers become more or less productive as the game progressed?

Did the quality or features of what was produced change during the exercise?

What did you like and not like about this economy?

Did you create an/or accumulate more wealth under 35 minutes of communism or 35 minutes of free enterprise?

If you were the Grand Comrade, what would you advise a communist economy to do in order to increase productivity and society's well-being (be specific)?

Do you think people in a communist economy would require "training" in how to behave in a free enterprise economy?

20. Management education
and employee training at Moscow McDonald's[5]

McDonald's is one of the largest fast food chains in the world. Founded in the 1950s in the United States, it has expanded worldwide and has become a household word. After fourteen years of negotiations McDonald's succeeded in opening a restaurant and processing plant in Moscow in 1990. The focus of this article is the management education and employee training practices adopted at Moscow McDonald's. This material is presented following an overview of the start-up of operations in Russia.

Background on the Moscow Operation

The joint venture (JV) was created in April 1987. The agreement was signed between McDonald's Restaurants of Canada and the firm, Mosrestauranservice (a "trust" *obedinenie*, under the Moscow City Council). In accordance with existing legislation, the JV had to be registered with the USSR Ministry of Finance. Moscow McDonald's was registered December 15, 1988 and was assigned registration number 159 (i.e., it was one of the first JVs). The USSR Ministry of Finance registered invested capital (ystavnoi fond) of 14 million rubles (approximately $20 million on the official exchange rate prevailing at the time). The Soviet partner's share was 51 per cent, the Canadians' share, 49. The Canadian partners agreed not to take profits out of the country, but to reinvest them in a chain of twenty restaurants in Moscow. To ensure a high quality of work at Moscow McDonald's, McDonald's Restaurants of Canada invested a total of $50 million (including their contribution to the initial invested capital). Forty million dollars was allocated for design and construction, equipment, and training personnel for the processing plant. Ten million dollars was used for design and construction, equipment, and personnel training for the restaurant in Pushkin Square (currently operational) and Ogarova Street in Moscow.

The creation of the JV was the culmination of twenty years of negotiations that began during the Montreal Olympics in 1976 at the initiative of George Cohan, president and CEO of McDonald's Restaurants of Canada, Limited. They had wanted to open a restaurant in Moscow for the 1980 Olympics, but were not successful. The negotiations were protracted and went on and off over the years, and did not always go smoothly. One of the reasons was that the members of the negotiating team changed several times, hence continuity was lost.

The management of Moscow McDonald's is run by the executive committee (direktsia) headed by a general director (who must be a Canadian citizen) and a deputy general director (a Soviet citizen). Currently the head office is located in the Minsk Hotel in downtown Moscow. Initially they rented two rooms, however, with the growth of the number of personnel, they now occupy an entire floor.

The general director reports to the board (upravlenie) of the JV which makes the key decisions. The board consists of two Soviets and two foreign members who have voting rights, and two Soviets and two foreign representatives who have no voting rights. Unanimity is

5 By Sheila M. Puffer and Oleg S. Vikhansky. Reprinted by permission from European Management Journal, Vol. 11 (1), March 1993, 102-107, Pergamon Press Ltd. Oxford, England.

Dorothy Marcic and Sheila Puffer, *Management International,* West Publishing, 1994.

required for all decisions. The chairperson of the board must be a Soviet citizen, the deputy chairperson a representative of the Canadian side.

The processing plant

The main differentiation in the conditions of working in the USSR from other countries was the construction of a food processing and distribution plant. This plant is the only one of its kind in McDonald's worldwide system.

The food processing plant became operational in mid-January 1990. It is one of the most modern food processing facilities in Europe. Equipment was imported from fifteen countries. For example, the milk processing equipment was from Sweden, the potato processing equipment from the Netherlands, the baking systems from the U.S., Sweden, Canada and other countries.

The floor space of 10,000 square meters contains processing lines for meat, milk, baking. There is a shop for potato processing, mayonnaise, ketchup, cheese, etc. There are several quality control laboratories, and strict sanitation standards are observed. The daily processing capacity is 55,981 kilograms, one million hamburger buns, 72,000 kg. of potatoes, 90,000 liters of milk, and 127,740 slices of cheese.

The restaurant

The first restaurant of the Moscow McDonald's joint venture opened January 31, 1990. The restaurant is located on Pushkin Square, in the center of Moscow, the city's historical and cultural center. This location is one of the factors contributing to the great popularity of the restaurant for Moscovites and visitors.

The founders of the JV anticipated that they would serve 10,000 to 15,000 customers a day. On opening day 30,000 people showed up. This set a world record for McDonald's for an opening day (this was surpassed by the opening of the restaurant in Beijing, China several months later). This turned out to be their slowest day. In the first year of operation an average of 45,000 customers a day visited the restaurant.

Moscow McDonald's is not only the most visited restaurant in the McDonald's worldwide system, it is also the largest. The floor space is 2,200 square meters. It includes 700 seats and 27 cash registers. Although customers are served on average within less than one minute, they must wait in line to enter the restaurant for thirty minutes to one hour. Recently the waiting time has decreased.

Selection of managers

During the start-up phase McDonald's drew upon the expertise of their employees from around the world. Initially there were 45 western managers from various countries. This number was gradually reduced, so that by March 1991, only seven remained. By June 1991, this number should be reduced to four. All these managers were replaced by Soviets.

Initially McDonald's hired 28 managers, but within the first year, the number increased to 40 because of high customer demand and the need to increase the work force nearly twofold.

The first four managers selected for the highest positions were in their early thirties and had supervisory experience in the restaurant business in the USSR. Georgii Smoleevskii had ten years' experience in public catering, including managing a staff of 350 in a Moscow restaurant. He studied economics at the Soviet Trade Institute and pursued graduate studies in food catering.

Mikhail Shelesnov's background included supervising seven food establishments, which he toured daily. He received two degrees from the Moscow Higher Technical School and studied the economics of retail trade at the Plekhanov Institute of the Economy, also in Moscow.

Khamzat Khazbulatov was formerly assistant manager of the prestigious Budapest restaurant in Moscow, where he managed a staff of 650. His responsibilities included approving new menu items, overseeing service and kitchen operations, and training of new employees. His previous experience included managing another restaurant and working as a chef for the Food Service Center. He received a degree in food service technology engineering from the Plekhanov Institute. He was chosen as manager of the Moscow restaurant because he was the best student in Canada and won the coveted "Archie" award. He was then promoted to deputy general director of the entire Soviet operation.

Vladimir Zhurakovskii worked for ten years for Tiajpromexport, an exporter of metallurgical equipment for the Ministry of External Relations. His work there included a four-year assignment in Pakistan. Mr. Zhurakovskii was educated in blast furnace engineering at the Moscow Steel and Alloys Institute.

Selection of crew members

The success of the operation in the first year was due in large part to the personnel policies conducted with Soviet workers. The human resources system enabled the JV to avoid many of the problems typically encountered by many JVs that seriously harm their operations when they use a large number of Soviet workers.

First, Moscow McDonald's JV based their recruitment on a broad solicitation of applications and a competition. This was in marked contrast to the hiring practices of other JVs which consisted of one of two practices: either hiring personnel already employed by the Soviet JV partner, or hiring people based on patronage and influence and personal contacts. These latter practices did not guarantee the best workers. Workers from the Soviet JV partner were often either unable or unwilling to work according to international standards. Not only did they need to be retrained with respect to their skills, but their work attitudes also needed to be changed.

Moscow McDonald's placed a single advertisement in Moscow newspapers soliciting applications. By the fall of 1989, when they started to hire workers, they had received approximately 27,000 applications. This created a base for selecting the most energetic, motivated, intelligent and outgoing young men and women. When the restaurant opened they had a staff of 630. Within a year the staff nearly doubled, to 1,100. The overall number of workers in the restaurant, the processing plant and the administrative offices increased to 1550. The positive aspect of holding a hiring competition was not only that the administration could select the best of this large number of applicants, but also the competition itself motivated the young people even more to work in the JV, and developed a feeling of pride in them and a higher degree of satisfaction with having been hired.

The criteria used in the initial screening of applications included the following: The applicant had to have a telephone in order to be reached easily (in the USSR, telephones are not as widely available as in the U.S. - 10% of the people have access). They needed to live within a half-hour of the restaurant. Five thousand applicants met these criteria and each one was interviewed. Two assistant managers interviewed everyone and both had to agree in order for the candidate to be considered further. Candidates then had a second interview with the Canadian managers.

Following its practice widely used in its U.S. restaurants, McDonald's decided to hire Moscow teenagers as crew members. Whereas the motivation for hiring teenagers in the U.S. is largely for economic reasons (crew members initially earn slightly above the minimum wage), in the USSR the primary reason was to hire people with no prior work experience. The idea was that it would be easier to instill McDonald's work habits and standards in people who knew no other way to work than to disabuse people of unacceptable work habits they had acquired in previous jobs.

The majority of young people hired were between 18 and 27 years old. For many of them it was their first job. This was unusual because in the USSR teenagers seldom worked and there are labor laws protecting them. (For example, they must have time off to write exams, etc.) Initially 40 percent of the workers were hired on a full-time basis. By March 1990 the management changed it to 80 percent. The reason was that it was difficult for teenagers to study and work at the same time.

McDonald's human resources philosophy and methods

McDonald's used the same philosophy about human resources that it uses all over the world, such as McDonald's is one big family, and McDonald's cares about their workers' lives at work and outside work. This had a very big influence on their relations with their workers. The young people were very pleased and proud to wear the McDonald's uniform. They like the fact that, regardless of their position, they all call each other by their first name. They like to wear their nametag on their chest. They like to talk with customers with a smile, as if playing a theatrical role. There is nothing like this in Soviet management. This uniqueness strengthens the feeling of being special and exceptional and correspondingly has a positive impact on their work attitude. The McDonald's JV regularly conducts various events to recognize specific milestones and achievements of the workers. In addition, crew meetings, attended by crew members and management, are held every three months. This strengthens the feeling of family, and is a very strong motivator.

A big motivator is monthly social events such as boat trips on the Moscow River, sporting events, attending cultural events, and other forms of recreation paid for by the joint venture. To celebrate Hallowe'en (which is not observed in the USSR), the Canadian staff decorated the restaurant and had a Hallowe'en party, complete with costumes. It was an interesting and fun cross-cultural event.

Organization of work

An important aspect of human resources management for Soviet workers is the system of how the work is organized. The well-defined organization of work with the clear division of responsibilities (job description) and accountability makes it easier for people to do their jobs, simplifies communication between workers, and creates a better work atmosphere.

Modern equipment also made their work easier and simplified various operations. The cleanliness of the operation (sanitation standards) also played a big motivating role, as did the modern design of the facilties. Cleanliness and aesthetics made work more attractive, especially for those who had previous experience in Soviet enterprises and organizations.

Compensation system

The compensation system played an exceptionally important role in motivating the Soviet work force because wages were substantially higher than the average Soviet wage. Crew members were paid two rubles an hour when the restaurant first opened (This was increased in April 1991 in response to the general price increases announced by the Soviet government). This enabled young people to earn two and half times the average national salary. Substantially higher wages than the national average were also paid to office staff and people who worked in the processing facilities. The people worked in the restaurant were paid more than those in the processing plant. However, the plant workers were paid higher wages than in other typical Soviet factories and worked in attractive surroundings. The plant was built in a Moscow suburb where many people previously did not have steady jobs and had to commute to other areas for work. Hence they were glad to get a steady job close to home.

Another important aspect of the compensation system was free health benefits at high quality private clinics and hospitals, free vacations at recreation areas (health spas, seaside resorts), and free meals while on the job.

Crew members receive wage increases of 15 to 25 cents an hour for mastering various tasks and meeting performance targets (product and service quality, time spent filling orders).

McDonald's also arranged for employees to order (at the employees' expense) groceries from other suppliers. This was to help them cope with the food supply problems they encountered. However, the company strictly enforced the policy of firing employees who committed theft of company property.

McDonald's uses competitions and contests to encourage good performance. Teams compete to win prizes. Contests are organized at the store, regional, national and international level. The crowning glory is the annual international competition. The best crews from around the world have a cook-off at a choice location (e.g., in 1984 McDonald's sponsored a cooking olympics in Los Angeles to parallel the Olympic Games held there at the same time). Participants win a trip, prizes and are treated like VIPs.

Training methods

McDonald's applied the same training methods in its Moscow operation that it uses world-wide. We will describe these methods, evaluate their success in the first year of operation, and assess the possibilities for the future.

Training managers

Twenty-eight managers were selected who worked in the restaurant industry. All of them studied in Toronto from 3 to 8 months in order to prepare them for future positions of managers and assistant manager of various outlets in the USSR. In 1989 the managers of the production processing line were trained in Western Europe where the equipment came from - to operate the equipment (Sweden, Holland, Germany). Eighty-five workers in the restaurant studied in Moscow and joined the management ranks.

The four people selected to become managers of the Moscow McDonald's operation received the same training as all McDonald's managers. The goal was for them to apply the same management techniques in the Moscow restaurant that are used in McDonald's 10,500 restaurants around the world. The managers were sent for training for 5 months to McDonald's Institute of Hamburgerology in Toronto, Ontario, Canada. The 1,000-hour training program included classroom instruction, equipment maintenance techniques, and on-the-job training in restaurant management. This program gave them practical experience in all facets of McDonald's restaurant operations from making hamburgers to motivating crew members.

The managers spent an additional two weeks at McDonald's worldwide training center, Hamburger University, in Oakbrook, Illinois, U.S.A. There, along with 235 other managers from different countries, they participated in a course in advanced restaurant operations.

Training crew members

The crew members received the standard McDonald's training program. In the United States McDonald's is often the first job that young people take, and the company's training practices are a solid foundation that can serve a person well in any type of employment. Many American employers value prospective candidates who have excelled at McDonald's because they recognize that these people have acquired good work habits.

One of the first things new employees do is watch a videotape that explains the work habits and attitudes expected of McDonald's crew members. Employees learn, for example, the essentials of personal grooming: to keep their hair neat, take a bath before coming to work (in Moscow there is a shower on the premises), wear a clean uniform, and wash their hands before handling food. They are taught the importance of discipline and responsibility: they must report to work on time, meet strict standards of quality and timeliness in filling food orders and other tasks. They are also instilled with a sense of initiative: when a co-worker needs help, they should not hesitate to pitch in, even if it is not their official task. Crew members also learn the basics of customer relations: to reach the counter before the customer appears, look the customer in the eye, greet him or her with a smile, and suggest additional items for purchase.

A fundamental aspect of McDonald's human resources philosophy is to give employees a sense of pride in doing a job well and being recognized for their achievements.

McDonald's has well-developed procedures for evaluating, rewarding and disciplining crew members. McDonald's policy on disciplinary action is focused on teaching and correction rather than on punishment. Employees receive instruction on how to perform tasks they are not doing well. Rarely is poor performance cause for dismissal. Firing is used as a last resort, and is reserved for such serious violations as swearing at customers or theft.

Moscow training program for crew members

Training of crew members began on January 9, 1990. Every crew person received 60 hours of training, which included serving "practice" customers such as their parents and members of the media.

Career advancement

McDonald's has a policy of promotion from within. The company views opportunities for career advancement as a way of motivating the work force. Within the first year of operation more than thirty crew members were promoted to management.

Take for example, the case of Ivan, who was hired as a maintenance person. He graduated from the Moscow Aviation Institute, one of the most presitigious institutes of higher education in the USSR. He had studied to become a spaceship designer. However, he saw McDonald's ad in the newspaper and applied. For the first three months he worked as a maintenance man on the night shift, and then was promoted to coordinator of the maintenance crew. Shortly thereafter, he was promoted to second assistant, and now he is assistant manager. He aspires to be a store manager. This illustrates the career opportunities available at McDonald's however, it is important to keep in mind that Ivan was perhaps atypical in light of his fine education and personal capabilities. Ivan is glad to have been promoted, he likes to work with people, and he is happy to be a member of the McDonald's family, but at the same time he defines himself as Russian. Ivan thinks that people are the same around the world, that Russians are just like Canadians.

Discussion Questions

1   Why did the Canadians invest more than their share of the ownership warranted?

2   How do you view the long negotiations? What are the advantages and disadvantages and the causes for the lengthy negotiations?

3   What are the reasons why McDonald's built a food processing plant?

4   What impact can this food processing plant have on the Soviet economy?

5   What other influence can the Pushkin Square location have on the work of Moscow McDonald's? That is, what problems might the location pose?

6   What factors influence the waiting time to enter Moscow McDonald's? That is, what factors might influence MM's popularity?

7   What problems and challenges might the international start-up team have faced in training Soviet employees? What techniques would be most useful to solve these problems?

8   Why is the clear definition of job responsibilities at McDonald's motivating for Soviet workers?

9   Why was modern equipment and facilities an effective motivator?

10   Why is the practice of helping employees place orders for their own groceries important?

11   What problems might McDonald's encounter in the future if it keeps the same training program in its Soviet restaurants that it has worldwide?

12   What problems could be created by attitudes like Ivan's that there is little difference between Russians and Westerners?

13   How will McDonald's reconcile their need for people to feel like members of the McDonald's family, while at the same time respecting employees' needs to be recognized as Russians?

14   What will be Ivan's attitude toward working at McDonald's when there are 20 restaurants in Moscow? How should McDonald's deal with these changes?

15   What problems should McDonald's anticipate given that 80 percent of its workforce is employed full time?

21. The International Orientation Scale[6]

purpose

To examine the ability of people to adjust to a new culture.

group size

Any number of groups of four to six members.

time required

40 minutes.

preparation required

Read the background, the case study, answer the questions and complete the sample inventory.

exercise schedule

1   Preparation (pre-class)

Read the background on the scale, the case study "Office Supplies International," complete the ratings and questions, and fill out the self-assessment inventory.

2   Group discussions (optional)

Groups of four to six people discuss their answers to the case study questions and their own responses to the self-assessment.

		Unit time	Total time
3	**Class discussion**	**20+ min**	**20+ min**

Instructor leads a discussion on the International Orientation Scale and the difficulties and challenges of adjusting to a new culture. Why do some people adjust more easily than others? What can you do to adjust to a new culture? What can you regularly do that will help you adjust in the future to almost any new culture?

---

6   By Paula M. Caligiuri, Dept. of Psychology, Pennsylvania State University. Used with permission.

Background on the International Orientation Scale[7]

Tung (1981) found that the most frequent reason expatriates terminate their assignments early is the inability of their spouses to adjust to different physical and cultural environments. The second most important reason for expatriate failure is that the expatriates themselves can't adjust to different physical and cultural environments. Clearly, adjustment is the critical factor in determining whether expatriates succeed in their overseas assignment. There are two broad categories to consider in cross-cultural adjustment: the characteristics of the person and the characteristics of the host country environment. Although the effects of the environment are great, many employees have no choice in deciding the country to which they are transferring. Since the demands of the host countries cannot be changed – only assessed – this study focuses on predicting individuals who would be best suited to go abroad.

One of the best ways to assess personal characteristics is by assessing actual behaviors. Behaviors related to the personal characteristics that are necessary for cross-cultural adjustment may include: studying a foreign language, eating at foreign restaurants, and having foreign friends.

The International Orientation Scale or the IOS (Caligiuri, 1992) was developed on the premise that potential expatriates exhibit certain behaviors before going overseas. Those behaviors can predict their future level of cross-cultural adjustment. The IOS has four dimensions: international attitudes, participation in cultural activities, foreign experiences and comfort with differences. The first dimension is attitudinal, whereas the last three are behavioral.

The first dimension is international attitudes. This dimension is characterized by one's thoughts and feelings toward people of other cultures and toward cross-cultural experiences. People with positive international attitudes want foreign experiences (such as taking an overseas assignment or hosting a foreign exchange student). Additionally, they consider foreign experiences a high priority in their lives and the lives of their families. At a community level, they support cultural involvement and appreciation (e.g. teaching foreign languages in elementary schools).

The second dimension is foreign experiences. This dimension (along with the other behavioral dimensions) measures the extent people have sought out and participated in foreign experiences. One of the behavioral indices of people's international orientation is whether they elect to study a foreign language. In some educational systems, foreign language study is required. This dimension, however, requires outside interest, rather than mere fulfillment of a requirement. For example, if a job applicant for a multinational corporation has foreign language study on his or her resume, it would be helpful in a job interview to ask why the language courses were taken, how much they were enjoyed, how much was retained, etc. The other behavioral index in this dimension is foreign travel. Again, this is not a "more is better" index. Even though a person who seeks out foreign travel (e.g. a study-abroad

People who score well on international attitudes are fascinated by other cultures and will have a greater likelihood of succeeding abroad because they would approach the foreign experience with an open mind and a positive attitude.

---

7 By Paula M. Caligiuri, Dept. of Psychology, Pennsylvania State University. Used with permission.

semester) might have a greater international orientation, it is also possible that the type of experience abroad may have been very "American." In other words, one can be abroad and still have very little contact with host nationals or the host country's culture (e.g. stay in Westernized hotels, associate only with other Americans). As with language study, the appropriate follow-up interview questions can determine an individual's foreign experience.

The third dimension of the International Orientation Scale is comfort with differences. This dimension assesses the differences among one's friends. Very simply, if one chooses to become close with only those people who are very similar to him or her, chances are he or she is not very comfortable with the differences of others. This dimension is critical when determining to what extent someone will adjust to interacting with host nationals. An extreme negative case of this would be a person who is a bigot, (e.g. intolerant of any differences). The more typical case is the person who attended a culturally homogeneous school, lived in a non-ethnic community, or maintains close friendships with people who have similar personal profiles.

A person who is low on contact with differences has friends and acquaintances with similar backgrounds: education level, race, religious affiliation, age, and socioeconomic status. The opposite, and more appropriate person to go abroad, is someone who has friends and acquaintances who differ significantly.

The last dimension of the International Orientation Scale is participation in cultural events. This dimension assesses one's intellectual curiosity for foreign cultures. Someone who is more likely to adjust to living abroad will embrace the experience as an opportunity to experience cultural activities first hand. A person who has a high score on this dimension will show a strong interest in culture through his or her cultural activities. For example, he or she will enjoy eating at foreign restaurants, going to art galleries, concerts and museums. Additionally, he or she is more likely to keep abreast of world events through watching the world news or reading the newspaper.

Reliability and validity of the International Orientation Scale

The International Orientation Scale has a Cronbach's alpha (a measure of internal consistency) of 0.81. The IOS demonstrated criterion-related validity evidence for a sample of study abroad students who had completed the IOS prior to going abroad, and adjustment scales upon returning. Given that cross-cultural adjustment is a multi-dimensional construct, two facets of adjustment were measured. The first was general adjustment. It was measured by a 25-item scale and had a Cronbach's alpha of 0.84. The second was interaction adjustment, or level of interaction. This was measured by an eight-item scale and had a Cronbach's alpha of 0.80. A dimension of the IOS (international attitudes), an adjective profile and a measure of country difficulty predicted general adjustment, with a R-square of 0.24. Another dimension of the IOS (comfort with differences) and a measure of foreign language adequacy predicted interaction adjustment with a R-square of 0.25. These regression analyses support the theoretical base for using the International Orientation Scale to predict cross-cultural adjustment prior to actually going abroad.

Case study:
Office Supplies International – marketing associate[8]

Jonathan Fraser is a marketing associate for a large multi-national corporation, Office Supplies International (OSI), in Buffalo, New York. He is being considered for a transfer to the International division of OSI. This position will require that he spend between one and three years living abroad in any one of the OSI's three foreign subsidiaries: OSI-France, OSI-Japan or OSI-Australia. This transfer is considered a fast track career move at OSI, and Jonathan feels honored to be in the running for the position.

Jonathan has been working for OSI since he graduated with his bachelor's degree in marketing ten years ago. He is married and has lived and worked in Buffalo all his life. Jonathan's parents are first-generation German-Americans. His grandparents, although deceased, spoke only German at home and upheld many of their traditional ethnic traditions. His parents, although quite "Americanized," have retained some of their German traditions. In order to communicate better with his grandparents, Jonathan took German in high school, but never used it because his grandparents had passed away.

Both Sue and Jonathan are excited about the potential transfer and accompanying pay raise. They are, however, also feeling apprehensive and cautious. Neither Sue nor Jonathan has ever lived away from their families in Buffalo, and Sue is concerned about giving up her newly re-established career. Their daughter Janine has just started school, and Jonathan and Sue are uncertain whether living abroad is the best thing for her at her age.

In college, Jonathan joined the German club and was a club officer for two years. His other collegiate extra-curricular activity was playing for the varsity baseball team. Jonathan still enjoys playing in a summer softball league with his college friends. Given his athletic interests, he volunteered to be the athletic programming coordinator at OSI, where he organizes the company's softball and volleyball teams. Jonathan has been making steady progress at OSI. Last year, he was named marketing associate of the year.

His wife, Sue, is also a Buffalo native. She teaches English literature at a high school in one of the middle-class suburbs of Buffalo. Sue took five years off from teaching after she had a baby, but returned to teaching this year when Janine, their 5-year-old daughter, started kindergarten. She is happy to be resuming her career. One or two nights a week, Sue volunteers her time at the

---

8   By Paula M. Caligiuri, Dept. of Psychology, Pennsylvania State University. Used with permission.

city mission where she works as a career counselor and a basic skills trainer. For fun, she takes both pottery and ethnic cooking classes.

Using the three-point scale below, try to rate Jonathan and Sue as potential expatriates. Write a sentence or two on why you gave the ratings you did.

Rating scale

1 Based on this dimension, this person would adjust will to living abroad.

2 Based on this dimension, this person may or may not adjust well to living abroad.

3 Based on this dimension, this person would not adjust well to living abroad.

Jonathan's International Orientation

rating dimension   **rating and reason for rating**

International Attitudes

Foreign Experiences

Comfort with Differences

Participation in Cultural Events

Sue's International Orientation

rating dimension   **rating and reason for rating**

International Attitudes

Foreign Experiences

Comfort with Difference

Participation in Cultural Events

Discussion Questions: Case Study

1 Imagine that you are the international human resource manager for OSI. Your job is to interview both Jonathan and Sue to determine whether they should be sent abroad. What are some of the questions you would ask? What critical information do you feel is missing? It might be helpful to role play the three parts and evaluate your classmates responses as Jonathan and Sue.

2 Suppose France is the country where they would be sent. To what extent would your ratings change? What else would you change about the way you are assessing the couple?

3 Now answer the same questions, except this time they are being sent to Japan. Repeat the exercise for Australia.

4 For those dimensions that you rated Sue and Jonathan either 2 or 3, (indicating that they might have a potential adjustment problem), what would you suggest for training and development? What might be included in a training program?

5 Reflect on your own life for a moment and give yourself a rating on each of the following dimensions. Try to justify why you rated yourself as you did. Do you feel that you would adjust well to living abroad? What might be difficult for you?

rating dimension	rating and reason for rating France, Spain, Australia (or other)
International Attitudes	
Foreign Experiences	
Comfort with Differences	
Participation in Cultural Events	

6 Generally, what are some of the potential problems a dual career couple might face? What are some solutions to those problems?

7 How would the various ages of children affect the expatriate's assignment? At what age should the children's international orientations be assessed along with their parents?

Self-Assessment
International Orientation Scale (Caligiuri, 1992)[9]

The following sample items are taken from the International Orientation Scale. Answer each question and give yourself a score for each dimension. The highest possible score for any dimension is 20 points.

Dimension 1: International attitudes

Use the following scale to answer question Q1 through Q4.

1	*Strongly agree*
2	*Agree somewhat*
3	*Maybe or unsure*
4	*Disagree somewhat*
5	*Strongly disagree*

Q1.   Foreign language skills should be taught (as early as) elementary school.

Q2.   Traveling the world is a priority in my life.

Q3.   A year-long overseas assignment (from my company) would be a fantastic opportunity for my family and me.

Q4.   Other countries fascinate me.

Total Dimension 1 _____

Dimension 2: Foreign experiences

Q1.   I have studied a foreign language.

1	Never
2	For less than a year
3	For a year
4	For a few years
5	For several years

---

9 By Paula M. Caligiuri, Dept. of Psychology, Pennsylvania State University. Used with permission.

Q2.   I am fluent in another language.

1	I don't know another language.
2	I am limited to very short and simple phrases.
3	I know basic grammatical structure and speak with a limited vocabulary.
4	I understand conversation on most topics.
5	I am very fluent in another language.

Q3.   I have spent time overseas (traveling, studying abroad, etc.).

1	Never
2	About a week
3	A few weeks
4	A few months
5	Several months or years

Q4.   I was overseas before the age of 18.

1	Never
2	About a week
3	A few weeks
4	A few months
5	Several months or years

Total Dimension 2   _____

Dimension 3: Comfort with differences

Use the following scale for questions Q1 through Q4.

1	*Quite similar*
2	*Mostly similar*
3	*Somewhat different*
4	*Quite different*
5	*Extremely different*

Q1.   My friends' career goals, interests and educations are...

Q2.   My friends' ethnic backgrounds are...

Q3.   My friends' religious affiliations are ...

Q4.   My friends' first languages are ...

Total Dimension 3   _____

Dimension 4: participation in cultural events

Use the following scale to answer questions Q1 through Q4.

Q1.   I eat at a variety of ethnic restaurants (e.g. Greek, Polynesian, Thai, German).

Q2.   I watch the major networks' world news programs.

Q3.   I attend ethnic festivals.

Q4.   I visit art galleries and museums.

Total Dimension 4   _____

Self-assessment discussion questions:

Based on your responses to Question 5 of the Case Study Discussion section, do any of these scores surprise you?

Would you like to improve your international orientation?
If so, what could you do to change various aspects of your life?

Entry shock, culture shock:
Socializing the new breed of global managers[10]

Recent graduates in the field of international business face not only the entry shock of making the transition from school to work, but also the culture shock of working in foreign countries or with joint ventures and foreign subsidiaries. Using survey data collected from 459 recent recipients of masters degrees in international business, this article explores the special problems new entrants into the field of international business face in their first few jobs and suggests organizational strategies for more effectively socializing these new global managers.

Difficulties encountered during entry shock and culture shock

For most respondents, their early job assignments had provided significant amounts of personal development. They had opportunities to develop new work skills, to travel and learn about new cultures, to have much more autonomy and responsibility in their jobs than they had had in school, to work with people from other countries, and to dramatically increase their standard of living over their student days.

The positive reactions to these jobs, however, were tempered somewhat by the surprises and disappointments they faced trying to launch their careers in international business. Three underlying themes emerged from the study participants' reactions. First, these new global managers had difficulties in the labor market. They had trouble finding jobs overseas, and in many cases, finding domestic jobs which utilized their knowledge of foreign language and foreign affairs. Second, many participants noted that their corporations did not really understand what managers with a career focus in international business could actually contribute on a day-to-day basis, and, therefore, had more difficulty utilizing these managers effectively. Third, many participants noted that their organizations did a poor job in managing their career paths, often delaying their initial expatriate assignments and then having no positions readily available for them when they returned from overseas.

The comments from participants suggested that they faced six difficulties in particular during their early career transitions. Each of these difficulties is reviewed in more detail below. Table III briefly summarizes those difficulties, indicates the percentages of respondents who experienced those difficulties, and provides quotes illustrating the problems faced by these new global managers.

1. Many new graduates in the international business find it very difficult to find jobs in their chosen field, especially challenging meaningful expatriate assignments.

Besides being genuinely interested in international affairs, foreign cultures, and multinational corporations, many students who enter international business programs do so because they believe a specialization in international business will be an advantage in the job market as

10 Daniel C. Feldman and Holly B. Tompson, *Human Resource Management* 1992, 31(4), 345-362. Copyright 1993 by John Wiley & Sons, Inc. Reprinted by permission of John Wiley & Sons, Inc.

Dorothy Marcic and Sheila Puffer, *Management International,* West Publishing, 1994.
All rights reserved. May not be reproduced without written permission of the publisher.
For more information, contact West Publishing, Publications Dept., 610 Opperman Drive,
St. Paul, MN 55164.

well. Given the amount of corporate rhetoric concerning the need to globalize business, not to mention the amount of popular press attention paid to this issue, the students' optimism about their chosen career path does not seem foolhardy. Unfortunately, the reality for many of these students is that there are relatively few overseas jobs for graduates who have less than five years' work experience.

Participants cited several reasons for their difficulties in lining up expatriate assignments. One is the recent recession, which has led to fewer transfers of employees both domestically and internationally. Another reason is the increased use of host nationals rather than expatriates as a means of decreasing the costs of doing international business. A third reason is that many organizations have decided to develop their expatriate talent in senior managers rather than in junior managers:

Although I sought and still seek an international position, I have found no companies interested in my international experience. The only work I was able to obtain was purely domestic. Having kept in close contact with over 50 of my classmates, I found that many of them were not able to obtain international business positions either. Despite the globalization of business, many Americans are not interested in hiring people with international backgrounds.

Although my company speaks of being a global first and the need for its managers to be global in their thinking, they do not back it up with the development of their employees. It has been very difficult to get an overseas assignment with my firm despite the fact that we have offices all over the world and the supposed commitment of the firm to make all of its employees more international.

2. Many new entrants into the field of international business find that companies value their specific technical skills rather than their foreign language skills and foreign affairs knowledge.

Even after these internationally trained managers have obtained positions, many of their employers are not quite sure how best to utilize them. Participants commented repeatedly that for many of their employers, the world is divided into clearly demarcated areas of functional expertise: finance, marketing, production. However, it is apparently much less clear to corporate employers in which specific areas an international business student has specialized competence:

Many U.S. firms don't know how to use you. They have never had anybody with Japanese language ability (or experience living in Japan) before so they don't have a well thought out place for you. They know it's important but don't know how to value Japanese language and cultural knowledge .

I have found that foreign language and international business experience are not the key hiring qualifications for overseas positions. Rather, specific skills are given higher priority.

3. Although respondents knew intellectually that conducting business in the international arena was more difficult than conducting business domestically, many recent graduates are still surprised by just how uncertain and complex working with, or for, multinational organizations could be.

Webber (1976) noted that one of the greatest shocks for new graduates was the uncertainty involved in real-world decision-making, which was not present in casework in college. Perfect information is unavailable; there is no one right answer; all problems can't be solved in a 90-minute class period. This uncertainty is even greater in the international arena. Political events (e.g., changes in governments), economic events (e.g., currency fluctuations), and labor difficulties (e.g., mass labor strikes) limit the predictability of doing business in a multinational environment:

There are often more variables and uncertainties which must be analyzed and more considerations which need to be made. ... The problem is that many of these variables cannot be foreseen and many are out of your control.

Having a career in a foreign organization can be quite frustrating for an American as foreign management styles can be quite different. ... The demands on one's personal life are higher, and the decisions are often more complex...

4. Instead of finding that international assignments give them a competitive advantage in moving up the organizational hierarchy, many graduates are discovering that international assignments can take them off the fast track to the top.

Many respondents noted that taking expatriate assignments took them out of the information loop and "off the road" to the top of the organization. This is the same "out of sight, out of mind" problem noted by Feldman and Thomas (1991, 1992). Although organizations often give lip service to the importance of international experience in terms of advancement, when promotion decisions are being made it is often more advantageous to be at headquarters than in a foreign subsidiary on assignment (Harris, 1986; Black & Mendenhall, 1990). While this problem may resolve itself over the next ten years as more and more organizations become multinational in focus, at the present time this is a real and immediate frustration to new entrants into the field:

Seems like those on foreign assignments become out of sight on the domestic front. ... We are cut off from the rest of the organization. ... Opportunities for advancement are limited...

For most American companies, an international assignment is a backwater. Taking an overseas assignment can put your career movement and exposure to high-level executives on hold.

5. The difficulties of managing dual-career marriages in an international arena are much greater than expected.

When Webber wrote his article in 1976, the problems of dual-career couples were just beginning to gain attention in the careers literature. Now, the already difficult problems of managing dual-career marriages are exacerbated by the necessity of dealing with the additional constraints imposed by moving internationally. Another major change since Webber's 1976 article is that the percentage of dual-career couples has increased dramatically over the last fifteen years (Gallos, 1989). Moreover, there are increasing numbers of female expatriates (Jelinek & Adler, 1988), so that the "spouse problem" is now one that affects men as well as women:

There is certainly limited flexibility when you're married and your spouse has a career.

Being a dual-career international couple is almost impossible. Compromise is essential. No overseas assignment can be considered without thinking about derailing the other partner's career.

6. Even after expatriates return from their international assignments, they are surprised that their expertise is underutilized, and they often have no specific job assignments waiting for them.

Rosalie Tung (1984, 1988) and others have noted that many expatriates often get left in "permanent exile" because their companies have no domestic assignments for them upon return. Even the expatriates who do return home for their next tour of duty are sometimes put into "holding patterns" when they return, waiting weeks and sometimes even months for new permanent assignments (Feldman, 1991; Moran, 1988; Murry, 1978). While this type of political maneuvering is difficult for experienced managers, it is especially troubling for early-career individuals, as their comments suggest:

U.S. employers are very myopic when it comes to selecting an internationally experienced candidate for a domestic slot. Too many times, I've seen U.S. businesses pay lip service to those with international experience. ... I am stuck in international assignments now for better or worse.

My company does not have a good record of finding positions for expatriates returning to the U.S. Most end up leaving the company within one year. ... Most of the expatriates in my firm believe that even if the company fails to find them a challenging job, with their experience they could find other work fairly easily. My belief is that the company is wasting valuable assets. Hopefully I won't be one of them.

For a variety of reasons, then, graduating students are often ill-prepared for the careers in international business that they are entering. First, the business media rhetoric regarding the demand for students in international business is frequently inconsistent with the actual demand in the labor market. Whether this softer demand is due to the recession, the general trend toward downsizing and the elimination of middle management positions, or the increased use of host nationals, there are fewer job opportunities for new entrants than might be expected from reading business journals and periodicals.

In addition, business schools themselves often given students unrealistic expectations concerning both the ease of obtaining jobs in international business and the competitive advantage holders of international business degrees will have in the marketplace. Moreover, university programs in international business often emphasize language skills and culture studies in their current curricula at the expense of functional business training; it is this functional business training which seems to be particularly critical in obtaining challenging first job assignments.

Another issue is the changing nature of career paths in international business itself. Rather than being sent overseas relatively early in their careers for an extended expatriate assignment in one country, the new breed of global managers now may have to wait five to seven years for overseas assignments. In addition, many job assignments in international business today do not involve the traditional expatriate assignment in one foreign country, but consist instead of shorter travel assignments and liaison work with multiple foreign countries conducted from domestic headquarters. Neither students' expectations nor business school curricula seem to have adjusted fully to these new realities.

Lastly, for new graduates to make the transitions successfully from school to work and from domestic assignments to foreign assignments (and back again), it is critical that organizations manage their career paths systematically and thoughtfully. Unfortunately, the career development many recent graduates receive from their employers is inadequate or incomplete. For this reason, the next section of this article suggests alternatives to improve the socialization of the new breed of global managers.

Socializing the new breed of global managers

Despite the wide array of positions held by study respondents, there was remarkable consistency in the recommendations they made for the improvement of the human resource management of global managers. One theme which emerged was the need to improve the balance between corporations' traditional focus on technical and functional job assignments and new entrants' desires for international exposure and experience. A second theme was the need for more logical and orderly career pathing – domestic assignments which prepare managers for upcoming expatriate assignments, coupled with repatriate assignments which utilize recently acquired overseas experience. A third theme was the need for more career support for new global managers in terms of realistic job previews, mentoring, and assistance for spouses and families.

Eight specific policy recommendations for improving the socialization and development of these new global managers are discussed below. Table III presents the percentages of respondents who currently work for corporations which already have these recommended policies in place; it also presents illustrative quotes from respondents on the need for these HR policies.

1. Give newcomers realistic career previews as well as realistic job previews.

The importance of giving new recruits realistic job previews has long been recognized (Wanous, 1992). These realistic job previews can help potential employees make the decision to remove themselves from the applicant pool if the jobs offered are a poor fit; they can also vaccinate newcomers against the inevitable disappointments new jobs can bring.

In the case of young international managers, there is a need for realistic career previews as well. Since corporations vary so widely in how they view international business career paths, they need to give prospective applicants a better sense of what the typical career path in their own organization looks like. Potential employees who are uncomfortable with their future career paths in a corporation can then self-select out, and those who remain will have less uncertainty about what lies ahead. Several comments of respondents reinforced this suggestion:

My biggest problem was knowing what kind of job responsibilities to expect. ... More should be done to define the objectives in the overseas assignment and to come to some sort of mutual agreement on how to implement these objectives...

In my position, I talk to many new graduates in international business, and I believe many are being misled and oversold as to the availability of international positions, especially expatriate assignments...

2. Provide newcomers with technical training to build upon and enhance their international background.

A potential competitive disadvantage new graduates in international business may have relative to mainline MBA students is less depth in some functional area like finance, marketing, or operations. While the language skills, international affairs knowledge, and cultural studies knowledge may in the long run be very useful, in the short run new global managers have to compete on technical excellence.

To retain the expertise and talent of young global managers in the long run, then, multinational firms may need to provide additional functional training for these recent hires in the short run. Otherwise, as the quotes below suggest, organizations will continually try to make tradeoffs between two unattractive staffing alternatives.

At my firm (a bank), I was actually told by several managers within different lending departments that "we don't want those international types – all they know how to do is entertain." ... My peers and younger associates felt that I should not be on an equal par with them because I didn't have domestic real estate experience...

The problem arises from the fact that the market, in general, is not aware that individuals (with degrees in international business) even exist in the first place. When needs arise to staff foreign operations, companies must choose between a manager who knows the business but doesn't know the culture or an (international business) graduate who knows the culture but not the business...

3. In early domestic assignments, provide opportunities for future global managers to learn about international finance, international marketing, or some other international functional area.

Although most recent graduates in international business initially begin their careers in domestic jobs, their enthusiasm and commitment to their employers could still be engaged by providing opportunities to gain expertise in some aspects of international operations. Moreover, this expertise in international business can be developed in numerous innovative ways in domestic assignments, such as being sent overseas on short temporary assignments, serving as a liaison with foreign operations, or handling domestic sales for foreign clients.

I believe you will find a large percentage (of my classmates) have not had expatriate assignments. Nonetheless, many of us are engaged in international business on a daily basis and accomplish what we need to do with short trips, telephone calls, faxes, modems, video-conferencing, etc. ... What I've done may not fit into any nice neat career path, (but) those who adapt the fastest and the best survive...

I am currently employed in Washington, D.C., at (a major federal agency). It is a very good place to work, and once in a while I get some international exposure – meeting with representatives from other governments and discussing the relative merits/disadvantages of our budgeting systems.

4. Early in their careers, provide opportunities for future global managers to work with, or manage, a multicultural workforce.

Developing interpersonal skills, particularly in the context of managing others, is a critical step in the socialization of all young managers (Schein, 1978; Van Maanen, 1976; Louis, 1980; Feldman, 1981). However, organizations can still provide opportunities for new hires to work with foreign nationals even outside the context of traditional expatriate assignments. Moreover, these opportunities would help new entrants master their skills in communicating with, and managing, a culturally diverse workforce:

The high point of (this assignment) has been a lot of contact with people of many cultures and national origins. ... I've seen some very complex and interesting international business problems.

The high point of this job is international travel, the opportunity to meet people who come from different cultural perspectives, the opportunity to learn the best from each new place, the ability to begin to understand all people no matter what language they speak.

5. Build some type of meaningful, challenging expatriate assignment into their career paths within the first 3-5 years.

As the comments of participants frequently indicated, more and more organizations are delaying assigning new hires to their first expatriate assignments. For some organizations, this is out of temporary economic necessity; for others, it is a deliberate corporate strategy; for still others, it is a result of haphazard human resource planning.

However, if the expatriate assignment is delayed too long, organizations may lose the continued commitment of young managers hoping to build careers in international business. For most new global managers, though, the expatriate assignment is a sign of corporate investment in their careers and a portent of the future. Without even a relatively short-term expatriate assignment (1-3 years) on the horizon, many study participants who are 3-5 years out of school are clearly more focused on looking for new jobs than on building careers with their current employers:

I finally left my (first) employer because I was frustrated with the firm's general financial problems, the bureaucracy, and the lack of support, respect, and opportunities for people in international business.

With a degree in international business and not much previous work experience, you're really in a hard spot (in the job market). ... No one wants to hire you. ... I am now back in the job market (after three years in a domestic job) ...

6. Develop mentor relationships between expatriates and people in the corporate headquarters for the purpose of social support, information exchange, and general advice.

A great number of respondents mentioned how critical it was to have a mentor during their socialization into the organization, and particularly as they made their transitions into, and back home from, their first expatriate assignments. In the domestic career development literature, the need for mentors has already been highlighted (Kram, 1985). Mentors provide technical support, social support, counseling, political advice, and other kinds of information that help newcomers master the subtleties and minefields of their first few jobs. In the international arena, the need for mentors is even greater (Feldman & Thomas, 1991, 1992). Mentors are vital as information links during overseas assignments, and are often indispensable in terms of lining up good repatriate assignments for people currently serving overseas:

The importance of a mentor is even greater for people working abroad. Future career opportunities are often a result of the existence of such a mentor. Organizations should train someone in personnel to be responsible for the relocation (of expatriates) in order not to lose sight of international personnel.

Mentors from the head office need to be appointed and, if necessary, visit in the field or bring the person back to the head office more frequently. ...Occasionally it feels like the Gulag out here, even though I enjoy my work.

7. Plan ahead for a specific assignment for the returning expatriate, and provide opportunities for the expatriate to use the knowledge and skills learned overseas.

Many organizations inadvertently lose their investment in young global managers by not having definite repatriate assignments for them upon their return or by not utilizing the skills and expertise developed overseas (Feldman, 1991; Black & Gregersen, 1990; Mendenhall,

Dunbar, & Oddou, 1987). Frustrated by the lack of reasonable repatriate assignments, young global managers are much more likely to leave their employers.

The frustration of returning repatriates seems to emerge for three reasons. First, many young managers view the expatriate assignment as a rite of passage; after they have survived their overseas assignments, they are more anxious than ever to advance quickly up the organizational ladder. Second, while expatriate assignments are often exciting and lucrative, they also involve considerable hard work and personal sacrifice; upon return, these young managers want to see their efforts rewarded and feel their sacrifices were worthwhile. Third, many expatriates view how corporations handle their repatriate assignments as an indication of how seriously (and systematically) the organization is going to manage the careers of internationally oriented personnel; if organizations mishandle the repatriate assignment, repatriates often conclude that their employers are not really serious about commitments to their careers.

Distress at the lack of careful, thoughtful career planning for repatriates is reflected in the following comments:

Most companies are poor when repatriating you to your home country after an extended stay overseas – there is plenty of support when you leave, practically none when you return.

In my personal experience, I had a very difficult time when coming back after my overseas assignment. I was hired abroad, and coming back meant opening up a space for me within the organization. The lack of company plans and support programs during the adjustment period made it hard for me to cope with the repatriation shock.

8. Ensure that international managers are not relegated to the "slow track" because of their overseas assignments.

Perhaps the greatest paradox facing new entrants to the field of international business is that the career path that, in theory, should be the fast track to the top; the career path that takes them overseas for a series of assignments can be the slow path or even can be an impediment to corporate advancement in practice. Despite the good intentions of many corporations, most of the study participants felt that their employers were failing in keeping international managers on track for advancement:

My present company does not really recognize the difficulties involved in operating in an international environment – the communications problems, the variations in ways of doing business, etc. I expect that this will change over time, but I am not sure I will stay to see it. It's frustrating!

My advice: enter international business for the exceptional personal rewards. It may not be the fastest route to the top; (but) relax, enjoy the experience, and leave the rat race at home!

Implications for human resource management

As more and more business students head for careers in international business and more and more corporations become multinational in structure and strategy, the pressure to improve the integration of this new breed of global managers into organizations will intensify. This article highlights some of the important issues multinational corporations need to address in managing the careers of these valuable human resources.

Because the media and business schools frequently give students unrealistic expectations concerning the careers they have chosen, it is critical that multinational corporations give prospective job candidates not only realistic job previews but also realistic career previews as well. In addition, while the value of global managers to the firm is high in the long run, many multinational corporations are having trouble utilizing these individuals in the short run. To retain a cadre of young internationally oriented managers, organizations need to provide them with both more functional training and more exposure to multinational business problems in the first few years of their careers.

The changing nature of the career paths in international business will require new methods of designing the jobs of these global managers as well. Exposure to international business issues, foreign cultures, and multicultural workforces will need to be built into most job assignments, not just into expatriate assignments. In addition, organizations are going to have to provide more opportunities for these international managers to participate in strategic and operational planning decisions in which their international perspectives are relevant. This involvement is vital to sustaining these individuals' continued employment and commitment to their firms.

While many multinational corporations have improved their capacities to manage the physical logistics of international moves, they have lagged in their ability to provide social support for expatriates and repatriates. Better programs are needed to ensure frequent communication between international managers and their domestic counterparts and to ensure that these global managers receive opportunities for supportive and helpful mentoring. Moreover, many multinational firms have inadvertently allowed their global managers to fall off the fast track to the top into "career cul-de-sacs" (Feldman & Thomas, 1992), career paths with no visible direction and no visible exit from their frustration. Multinational firms need to work harder to provide logical sequences of job assignments for global managers and to facilitate these managers' career growth and career advancement. For organizations serious about developing a multinational managerial workforce, these career development issues must be a high priority in the years ahead.

Writing about his frustrations with his own early career experiences in international business, one of our respondents noted:

Even in this day and age and even with Fortune 500 companies, it is difficult to convince recruiting departments and managers of the benefit of hiring a student with multicultural sensitivity, who is bilingual, who has international exposure and real knowledge of international business over a person with a (traditional) MBA. It leads one to question: Is there really a career in international business?

This article suggests some steps organizations can take to ensure that the answer to that question will be yes.

References

Adler, N. J., & Bartholomew, S. (1992). Managing globally competent people. *Academy of Management Executive, 6,* 52-65.

Black, J. S., & Gregersen, H. B. (1990). Expectations, satisfaction, and intent to leave of American managers in Japan. *Journal of International Business Studies, 19,* 277-294.

Black, J. S., & Mendenhall, M. (1990). Cross-cultural training effectiveness: A review and theoretical framework for future research. *Academy of Management Review, 15,* 113-136.

Feldman, D. C. (1981). The multiple socialization of organization members. *Academy of Management Review, 6,* 309-318.

Feldman, D. C. (1991). Repatriate moves as career transitions. *Human Resource Management Review, 1,* 163-178.

Feldman, D. C., & Thomas, D. C. (1991). From Desert Shield to Desert Storm: Life as an expatriate during the Persian Gulf War. *Organizational Dynamics, 20,* 37-47.

Feldman, D. C., & Thomas, D. C. (1992). Career issues facing expatriate managers. *Journal of International Business Studies, 23,* 271-294.

Gallos, J. V. (1989). Exploring women's development: Implications for career theory, practice, and research. In M. B. Arthur, D. T. Hall and B. S. Lawrence (Eds.), *Handbook of career theory.* Cambridge, UK: Cambridge University Press.

Harris, P. R. (1986). Employees abroad: Maintain the corporate connection. *Personnel Journal, 65,* 107-110.

Jelinek, M., & Adler, N. J. (1988). Women: World-class managers for global competition. *Academy of Management Executive, 2,* 11-19.

Kotter, J. P. (1975). *The first year out.* Unpublished manuscript, Harvard Business School. Boston: Harvard Business School Division of Research.

Kram, K. E. (1985). *Mentoring at work.* Glenview, IL: Scott Foresman.

Louis, M. R. (1980). Career transitions: Varieties and commonalities. *Academy of Management Review, 5,* 329-340.

Maruyama, M. (1992). Changing dimensions in international business. *Academy of Management Executive, 6,* 88-96.

Mendenhall, M. E., Dunbar, G., & Oddou, G. R. (1987). Expatriate selection, training, and career pathing. *Human Resource Management, 26* (3), 331-345.

Moran, R. T. (1988). Corporations tragically waste overseas experience. *International Management, 43,* 74-75.

Murry, J. (1978). International personnel repatriation: Culture shock in reverse. *Michigan State University Business Topics, 21,* 29-33.

Schein, E. H. (1978). *Career dynamics: Matching individual and organizational needs.* Reading, MA: Addison-Wesley.

Tung, R. L. (1984). *Key to Japan's economic strength: Human power.* Lexington, MA: Lexington Books/D. C. Heath.

Tung, R. L. (1988). *The new expatriate.* Cambridge, MA: Ballinger Press.

Van Maanen, J. (1976). Breaking in: Socialization to work. In R. Dubin (Ed.), *Handbook of work organization and society* (pp. 67-130). Chicago: Rand McNally.

Wanous, J P. (1992). *Organizational entry.* Reading, MA: Addison Wesley

Webber, R. A. (1976). Career problems of young managers. *California Management Review, 18,* 11-33.

Executive compensation in the international arena: Back to the basics[11]

To avoid problems associated with "global" executive compensation programs, companies must address issues specific to the country, culture, laws and executives involved.

Executive compensation is receiving unprecedented attention these days--partially as a result of the new Securities and Exchange Commission (SEC) disclosure requirements (and the pressure this is putting on corporate boards and compensation committees) and partially in reaction to poor corporate performance and related downsizings. Unfortunately, companies are not giving the same attention to international executive compensation programs. The fact is, companies and their boards of directors pay considerably less attention than they should to the cross-border aspects of executive compensation plans--that is, when plans apply to executives in more than one country.

But no matter where the company or the executive is located, companies must keep in mind the most fundamental tenet of executive compensation--it simply makes good business sense to pay attention to the tools being used to induce executives to perform in the best interests of the company. Plans, whether cross-border or domestic, must focus on the right issues and be viewed as achievable by the executives they are designed to motivate. This deceptively simple statement is the key to effective executive compensation programs--and one that, on an international basis, too often goes unheeded.

For many companies, this oversight is characterized by the practice of simply shipping their domestic executive compensation programs abroad. All too often, the result is a compensation program that does not comply with each country's tax code and other laws and regulations, and worse, is ineffective for motivating the type of performance by executives in other countries that will translate into superior company performance. The troubles often continue as the company's compensation professionals "patch up" the programs, especially stock-related ones, just to make them "legal" in terms of local tax and legal regulations around the world.

For the most part, these patches do nothing to address the more fundamental question of how effective the program is, and may actually exacerbate the program's ineffectiveness in meeting the company's goals and objectives. The development of a truly effective global executive compensation plan begins at the planning stage. The process of designing executive compensation for international executives follows the same design steps as for domestic programs--who the plan will cover, the amount of pay at risk, and so on. But to be truly effective, additional issues need to be addressed. Beyond the obvious tax and legal issues lie differences in culture, business practices and so on that impact how and how well executives do their jobs. Such global plans must address a number of specific issues, including these:

---

11 By Ranae M. Hyer. Reprinted, by permission of publisher, from *Compensation and Benefits Review*, Mar/April 1993 © 1993 American Management Association, New York, 49-54. All rights reserved.

How should the goals and targets be established?

Should goals be set in a common currency (e.g., U.S. dollars) or in the currency of the country where the executive is working?

Should goals be set on a pretax or after-tax basis?

Should competitive levels of payouts be established for each country or should similar business results yield similar amounts of incentive compensation no matter what the location?

If payouts are based on percentages, should they be related to base salary, total cash compensation, or what?

We will discuss two perspectives of these issues – setting the goals or measures and setting the payout levels – and examine some issues inherent in stock-based incentive plans. This overview of executive compensation in the international arena offers insight on some key nuts and bolts and uses case studies to demonstrate how companies can design truly effective executive compensation programs for international executives.

Setting the goals

To effectively motivate desired performance, any executive compensation plan – whether domestic or internationa – must first define what the company wants to accomplish and link those accomplishments to individual executive performance goals that will consistently benefit the company. The process for developing goals and the criteria for establishing goals are the same for both domestic and cross-border plans – that is, they should be measurable, achievable, and clear. The primary difference is that certain issues unique to the international arena must be addressed – the earlier in the design process, the better.

While the company must evaluate various issues in designing cross-border plans, we will look at just the following three aspects of goal setting to illustrate the complexity the international arena brings to the development of such programs.

The currency in which the goals are set.

Whether goals are set on a pretax or after-tax basis.

Whether goals should include a measure of overall corporate performance or simply the performance at the locations for which the executive is responsible.

Currency

Any plan that covers executives in more than one country involves issues that are relatively more complex than plans in a single country. For example, if the U.S. parent is using profitability as a primary performance measure, the first question should revolve around the currency in which the company measures profitability for each executive in the plan. Should it be in U.S. dollars or the currency of the country or countries for which the executive is responsible? The answer usually depends on whether the executive has control over foreign exchange.

For example, if the treasury function at corporate headquarters manages foreign exchange risk, assigning U.S. dollar goals to the executive managing a European operation or a single, foreign-country operation probably makes little sense. In some years, the executive may reap a windfall; in other years, the executive may be significantly penalized for hedging decisions made elsewhere. The better solution may be to set executives' goals in local currency and assign to the corporate treasury separate goals that measure those executives' effectiveness in managing the cross-border currency risk.

On the other hand, if the executive heading a European or South American operation sits on the corporate management team and fully participates in the resource and risk allocation decisions, then it may be perfectly (or at least reasonably) appropriate to measure performance in U.S. dollars.

The answers to these hypothetical situations appear blatantly obvious. Nonetheless, the issue of currency rarely comes up in a purely domestic incentive plan. So, if a company simply exports its U.S. plan globally, all goals will inevitably be stated in U.S. dollars. One high-technology company that acquired operations throughout Europe initially planned to export its U.S. plan to Europe with performance goals in U.S. dollars, even though its U.S. headquarters treasury office managed all foreign exchange risk. Fortunately, the compensation manager saw the potential problem, and the company established targets in local currency. This seemingly simple plan change allowed the company to hold its German manager accountable for suboptimal performance as measured in deutschemarks, rather than paying out a substantially larger bonus that resulted simply from a strengthening German currency.

Some companies are tempted to resolve currency issues by ensuring to the extent possible that international executives are given authority for managing currency risk. If the country manager is given this authority, at least in part, to ensure full performance measurement, the company must understand the implicit risk of permitting the manager to "play" in the currency markets. More than a few companies have experienced major foreign exchange losses when managers, to meet their current year's performance targets, speculated in the currency markets to make up for less-than-stellar operations.

A preferable approach is to determine what authorities for managing currency exist and make sense and then establish plans that permit performance goals to be set in currency consistent with the executive's actual authority. It is essential to point out the risks inherent in including foreign exchange in the plan goals, and the company must be willing and able to accept those risks. Then, of course, the company needs reporting systems that can track the performance goals and results in multiple currencies.

Pretax or after-tax goals

Once again, there are no hard-and-fast rules for pre- or after-tax goal setting. It all depends on who has responsibility for setting tax policy and determining the level of aggressiveness with which the company wants to operate. If tax positions are determined centrally in the finance department, it is advisable to set the goals on a pretax basis. Incentive compensation for effective tax planning would then be reserved for the finance department.

Conversely, if the country or regional manager has clearly defined responsibility for tax decisions, it is reasonable to measure performance on an after-tax basis. This is not as atypical as it may appear. Most other countries' tax rates are higher than, and their tax rules significantly different from, those in the United States. In addition, if the foreign unit is an acquisition, the knowledge and application of tax rules in that jurisdiction may have been handled locally for some time, particularly if the new owner is just entering international business.

Again, as with foreign exchange, decentralized tax administration has inherent risks for the company. The extent to which the executive is measured on an after-tax basis may provide an incentive to take more aggressive tax positions. This could, of course, lead to unanticipated consequences in future tax audits. Therefore, it is imperative to consider the actual delegations as they exist, while also pointing out the implications of assigning after-tax goals.

Several years ago, a large international financial institution implemented an incentive plan with after-tax goals. As a result, the company paid large bonuses to its executives for what appeared to be high levels of after-tax earnings attributable to very aggressive tax positions. Unfortunately, a few years later, the company ended up going around the world, checkbook in hand, paying taxes and large penalties in countries where the aggressive positions taken by the long-gone managers were ultimately determined to be inappropriate by the local tax authorities.

If a company is going to pay bonuses on after-tax profitability, it must be aware of the risks and be willing to take them. If it is not comfortable with these risks, paying executives on a pretax basis is clearly the better option.

Goals and corporate performance

While it can be argued, and often is, that paying executives below the very top management positions on the basis of corporate performance tends to reward or penalize them for results that are beyond their control, this policy does pay them for something that shareholders understand.

For international executives, the primary issue is how much of their bonuses should be based on performance that they may see as being almost totally beyond their control. (By the way, a similar argument can be made for or against paying U.S. executives a significant amount of their incentive compensation based on results unrelated to the performance of the U.S. company.) Here, particularly, there are no "cookbook" answers. In developing the plan, balance must be achieved between what is good for the whole and what can be related specifically to the executive's efforts.

If the world were pure, perhaps some elaborate system could be established to track the ultimate consequence of each management decision and its relative contribution to the success of the company. Minus such a system, the balance between local and corporate (not to mention regional or divisional) performance will remain a matter of judgment. In establishing a global incentive plan, it is essential to consider the implications of the local/corporate balance and not simply to assume that what works in the United States will work everywhere.

It is usually considered preferable to have all executives at similar levels receive the same mix of local/corporate goals. Multinational companies, however, may want to consider varying this mix by region or country or balancing them with a regional component that is related to the total amount of business generated in the area for the company. For example, a medical-technology company with worldwide operations has had payouts based on a goal mix of 75% unit performance/25% corporate performance. It is currently considering changing that to reflect the portion of business or resources each country or region represents. So, for example, if the UK generated 10% of the company's global business, 10% of the UK manager's bonus would be subject to corporate performance. The company is still considering a number of alternatives before it finalizes its plan.

Setting the payouts

Having considered some of the complexities of setting meaningful performance goals for cross-border executive incentive plans, let us now turn to some issues involved in setting appropriate payout levels. As mentioned earlier, the questions come down to whether there should be similar payouts for similar performance or whether payouts should be locally competitive. In the latter case, how does the company determine what is "competitive"?

Not only are most U.S. companies rather ethnocentric in their view of what motivates (or at least what should motivate) desired behavior, but they are also rather egalitarian by global standards. It is certainly not unheard of for U.S. companies to establish both performance goals and target payouts in U.S. dollars. The question is whether common payout levels provide enough or too much incentive compensation.

At the very least, the company should consider relating payouts for local nationals to the same percentage of pay that the payout amount represents to the U. S. executive. Thus, if a salary grade M executive in the United States receives a bonus of 25% of base salary for achieving targeted performance, any grade M executive around the world would be eligible for the same bonus.

Taking a U.S. incentive plan and exporting it globally, even if the plan is based on a percentage of base salary, can still have rather unexpected consequences. For example, French executives are not accustomed to having a lot of their total pay at risk, so exporting a U.S. plan with target payouts of 25% to 50% or more of base salary can produce some real consternation. One high-technology company encountered some unexpected costs because it had to pay incentives on top of already fully competitive total compensation. But the company also found that reducing base pay and replacing it with greater incentive opportunities not only was demotivating to its French executives, but also brought up some legal issues specific to that country.

For most companies, a better approach would be to involve international executives at the beginning of the design process – just as many companies involve executives in developing a domestic plan. Letting these executives, be they from France or any other country, bring up their concerns and comment on the relative motivational value of various alternatives is essential to these executives' support and buy-in of the program.

By global standards, the U.S. is a low-tax, low-benefit, high-cash paying country. Typical U.S. executives receive a higher percentage of their lifetime remuneration in cash – specifically base salary, incentive compensation, and proceeds from stock-related plans – and make their own decisions on the relative levels of retirement, medical benefits, housing, and current discretionary spending. Such benefits are mandated by government or national union in many European countries.

With this in mind, taking a U.S. incentive plan and exporting it globally, even if done as a percentage of base salary, can still be problematic. For example, in some countries with very high tax rates, the executive actually receives very little of the bonus after taxes. He or she will often push to have the bonus converted into some other form of more "tax effective" compensation, such as automobiles, or even, perhaps, to have it paid "offshore."

Also, it is quite likely that base salary represents a much smaller portion of total employment costs, because perquisites – e.g., cars for personal use and housing subsidies – are much more common in other countries, particularly in Europe, than they are in the United States. As a result, relating the bonus to base salary may provide less meaningful amounts. There are even jurisdictions that might look upon a bonus as regular pay and not permit the company to pay less in future years. Or, the worst nightmare of all, some countries might require that bonus to be paid similarly to all executives at the same level.

This is not meant to scare U.S. companies away from establishing global executive incentive compensation plans. Quite the contrary. Such plans have been successfully introduced and used in locations where, up until a few years ago, even senior-level executives were paid largely on an "age-wage" basis. The trick is to take the time to examine carefully local total compensation practices and address the questions on amount and form of payment in the early design stages of any cross-border plan. Companies need to involve international executives in program development, listen to their perspectives, and challenge whether the executives' opinions are simply a reflection of the "old ways" or represent meaningful cultural differences important for motivating the future global executives.

Keep in mind that in many countries, U.S. firms have been able to attract highly talented local national staff even when they are competing for top talent against successful local corporations. Part of the reason for this may be the U.S. system of differentiating pay on the basis of performance, most particularly basing incentive compensation on some measure of the executive's contribution to the company.

Stock-based plans

Finally, let us look briefly at the most common type of corporate performance-related executive incentive plans: stock-based plans. These are often the core or sole type of long-term incentive in most companies. In fact, in high technology companies, such plans often reach far beyond the executive and managerial ranks.

It may be possible to address the issues of regulatory requirements and tax effectiveness, or to develop phantom-type plans in locations where real options or restricted plans will not work. The process is not simple. It requires careful research on a country-by-country basis, and it is usually expensive. To ensure its legality, the technical issues need to be addressed before a stock-based plan can be implemented in another country. Nonetheless, in most jurisdictions, some form of stock-related compensation can nearly always be implemented – and with good results.

Regardless of whom they cover, the question is whether these plans can be effectively exported. The answer, in this case, goes beyond the appropriateness of implicit performance goals to the individual, and even beyond how individual target levels are established. It goes all the way to whether the form of payout – stock – is applicable around the world. Tax implications, currency controls and securities regulations aside, the bottom line is whether or not a stock-based plan for executives in other countries has the same, or even somewhat the same, incentive value as it does to U.S. executives.

Conclusion

Cash-incentive plans or stock-based plans can and, in many cases, should be used in other countries. To avoid the all-too-prevalent problems associated with so-called "global" executive compensation programs, companies must seriously and carefully address the issues specific to the country, culture, laws and executives in question, while meeting the company's business needs. And it should be done sooner, rather than later – that is, in the early design phases of any plan that is likely to be used across country borders.

Clearly, incentive plans do motivate executive performance. So companies must take extreme care in structuring global executive compensation programs to ensure that their programs are motivating the right kind of performance. Not only must the plans focus on the right issues, but they must be relevant in terms of goals, payouts and form. While this is often a complex task, the potential benefits are substantial.

Table 1
Characteristics of the Sample

Mean Age: 32

% Male: 67

% Marned: 62

% of Married Respondents with Children: 65

% in First Job Out ot School: 27

Year of Graduation:	1977-1982	24%
	1983-1985	24%
	1986-1987	17%
	198-1989	17%
	1990-1992	18%

Job Tenure:	0-l year	46%
	1-2 years	25%
	2-3 years	16%
	over 3 years	13%

Functional Area:	30%	Marketing
	10%	Import/export business or sales
	40%	Accounting/finance
	20%	HRM, R&D, computer science, operations management, or public relations

Industry:	25%	Manufacturing, operations management, energy
	23%	Consumer products, pharmaceutical, clothing, or electronics
	19%	Financial services, real estate
	17%	Education, government, or health services
	9%	Communications, computer, or software
	7%	Food services agriculture, construction transportation, entertainment, or the arts

Organizational Unit:	38%	Headquarters of parent corporation
	28%	Headquarters of a subsidiary
	9%	Regional offices of a subsidiary

Table 2
Difficulties Encountered in Entry Shock and Culture Shock

% Agree	Difficulty
90	Recent graduates have difficulty finding entry-level jobs in international business.
	My company has determined it is more cost effective to hire people living witihin the foreign country. Expatriate packages are now rare and only offered to upper-level management. This makes it difficult to receive international experience early in your career.
77	Companies value recent graduates more for their technical skills than for their language skills and foreign affairs knowledge.
	I have found that foreign language and international business experience are not the key hiring qualifications for overseas positions. Rather, specific skills are given higher priority.
60	Conducting business in an international context is much more uncertain and complex than it is in the domestic context.
	My difficulties: the different speed in which business is conducted, the different importance of time in general, and communications problems because of cultural barriers.
42	International assignments can take managers off the fast track to the top of the organization.
	Career advancement is best staying in the U.S. I tend to have the opinion that except for the very largest companies, people outside headquarters lose the visibility and career opportunities that might open up.
52	The difficulties of managing dual-career marriages in the context of international business are great.
	International life and a fast career can be very demanding on your personal life... therefore, the "I love international business" has to come from both the husband and the wife.
55	Companies often do not know how to utilize the knowledge young expatriates develop on their assignments, and often do not have specific plans for repatriates upon their return.
	(My company) handled my repatriation badly... We cope by knowing that if the experience abroad isn't appreciated by our company, it will be recognized in the job market. By not planning ahead, and by not offering the repatriate a good assignment on return, my company loses a fair percentage of expatriates returning to U.S. headquarters.

Table 3
Recommendations for Socializing New Global Managers

% Currently Working In Organizations Using HR Practice	Recommendation
72	Give newcomers realistic career previews as well as realistic job previews.
	A (potential) employee and personnel should sit down and talk about future goals, plans, opportunities, and the desires of each. That way, plans could be modified as needed.
46	Provide newcomers with technical training to build upon and enhance their international background.
	Most organizations do not have a formal training program for international managers, and most managers are not well prepared for international assignments. They end up learning on the job. That is not entirely negative, but many initial mistakes could be avoided if formal training were available.
61	In early domestic assignments, provide opportunities for future global managers to learn about international finance, international marketing, or some other international functional area.
	Despite my frustration (at not getting an expatriate assignment), I am amazed at how much international business I am handling from the U.S. In a little over a year I have had deals all over the world – Africa, the Middle East, South America, North America, and Europe.
50	Early in their careers, provide opportunities for future global managers to work with, or manage, a multicultural workforce.
	I am based in the U.S., fly to Europe five or six times per year... The high point of this job is that I get to see different people, learn new things, experience new situations that help me grow as a person, and break the monotony of the daily office routine.
57	Build some type of meaningful, challenging expatriate assignment into their career paths within 3-5 years.
	I'm really at a threshold in my professional career, and I'm also at a turning point in my personal life. ... I've been here (in a domestic assignment) for almost 5 years, and I'm very eager and anxious to move on. ... I feel like culturally I'm so much better suited to be in an international environment, and to be able to use my language skills and other interrnational business skllls. ... I'm itching to make a move.

Table 3, continued

30	Develop mentor relationships between expatriates and people in the corporate headquarters for the purposes of social support, information exchange, and general career advice.
	The best advice I can give is to seek out others that have gone before; get as much information about your destination as possible. Before going abroad, be sure someone, such as a general manager or a vice president, will look out for you upon your return.
50	Plan ahead for a specific assignment for the returning expatriate, and provide opportunities for the repatriate to use the knowledge and skills learned overseas.
	In my company, expatriates are forgotten. When they come back to the home office, they usually get thrown into assignments that don't capitalize on their experience. (Top management) needs to spend more time planning international career paths.
29	Manage the career paths of international managers so that they are not relegated to the "slow track" because of their overseas assignments.
	In the few instances I've seen, companies do not 'manage' international careers. Often they choose people haphazardly to do foreign assignments and have no plans for them when they return.

The percentage reported is the percentage of respondents who are currently working in organizations using the listed human resource practice.

Managing a diverse workforce

The ethnic and gender composition of the workforce is becoming more diverse in numerous countries. In the United States, by the turn of the century the majority of new entrants to the labor force will be women and ethnic minorities. In Europe, France has increasing numbers of workers from Arab countries in North Africa, and Germany has an influx of workers from Turkey and the newly independent countries of Central Europe. These demographic changes require managers to develop skills in managing heterogeneous work groups. *Northern Industries* is a case about a firm in such a situation. The Massachusetts greeting card plant is staffed primarily by women, many of whom are African American or Thai. To date, management has paid little attention to issues relating to a diverse workforce. The company has been receiving complaints from customers about product quality and shipping delays and needs to diagnose the problems and propose solutions.

A second important issue in workforce diversity is the low percentage of women in managerial positions. The exercise, *Women in management around the world,* provides a framework for researching the status of women in management in various countries and for understanding the assumptions about women's role in management. In some countries the equity model may apply whereby women's contributions to work are assumed to be similar to men's. In other countries the complementary contribution model may apply such that women's roles are seen as different from men's in the work place. Regardless of which model prevails in a country, *Women: World-class managers for global competition* points out that women are an untapped resource in that they constitute a mere three percent of U.S. managers in international positions. The article argues that women can make important contributions to corporate global competitiveness by bringing skills and predispositions that can be effective in cross-cultural settings. In addition, the article dispells common stereotypes about women that often have been used as obstacles to prevent women from serving in managerial positions abroad.

Russia has one of the highest rates of participation by women in managerial positions in the world. As documented in *Women managers in the former USSR: A case of "too much equality?"*, virtually all women are employed, constitute half the labor force, and hold one-tenth of the top management positions (in the U.S. only one woman heads a Fortune 500 company). Yet, many Russian women still feel like second-class citizens. Seven factors affecting their access to managerial positions are presented in the article. These factors can also be used to analyze the career of Valentina, a professional woman in Moscow featured in the case, *Valentina on the verge.* Underutilized in her previous jobs as a technician in a government agency, and unfulfilled as a full-time homemaker, she becomes a manager in a foreign joint venture, only to find more career decisions to make.

Managing a diverse workforce

22. Northern Industries[1]

Northern Industries asked you, a consultant in organizational change and diversity management, to help them resolve some racial issues that, according to president Jim Fisher, are "festering" in their manufacturing plant in Springfield, Massachusetts. Northern Industries is a family-owned enterprise which manufactures greeting cards and paper and plastic holiday decorations. It employs 125 people full time, including Afro-Americans and Asians. About 80% of the full-time workforce is female. During the peak production months of September and January (to produce orders primarily for Christmas/Hanukah and Mothers' Day) the company runs a second shift and adds about 50 part-time workers, most of whom are women and minorities.

All orders are batch runs made to customer specifications. In a period of a week it is not unsual for 70 different orders to be filled, requiring different paper stocks, inks, plastics and set-ups. Since these orders vary greatly in size, the company as a long-term policy of giving priority to high-volume customers and processing other orders on a first-come first-served basis. Half a dozen of the company's major customers have been doing business with Northern for more than twenty years, having been signed on by Jim Fisher's father (now retired).

As you enter the attractive office suites, Beacon introduces you to Lily Soh, the receptionist. He smilingly points out that "Lily is really important to us because she can talk with the Thais in their own language." As you continue into the conference room, he adds, "She's our only way of communicating with them, really. Right before the holidays last year we hired nearly 60 percent Thais on second shift."

To begin your orientation to the company, Fisher asks his Production Manager, Walter Beacon, to take you around the plant. Beacon points out the production areas responsible for each of the various steps in the manufacture of a greeting card, from purchasing, to printing, to quality control and shipping. The plant is clean, but the two large printing rooms, each the workplace for about 25 workers, are quite noisy. You catch snatches of the employees' conversations there, but you cannot figure out what language they are speaking. In the shipping and receiving department you notice that most workers are black, perhaps African-American. Beacon confirms that eight out of ten of the workers in that department are black males, and that their boss, Adam Wright, is also African-American.

It has been previously arranged that you would attend this meeting of top management in order to get a flavor of organizational culture. The president introduces you as a diversity consultant and notes that several of his managers have expressed concerns about potential racial problems in the company. He says, "Each of the

---

1 Copyright 1991 by Rae Andre of Northeastern University. Used with permission.

minority groups sticks together. The African-Americans and Orientals rarely mix. Recently there has been a problem with theft of finished product, especially on the second shift, and we had to fire a Thai worker." Fisher has read a lot lately about "managing diversity" and hopes you will be able to help the company. Several managers nod their heads in agreement.

Fisher then turns his executive team to its daily business. The others present are the general manager, personnel manager (the only woman), sales manager, quality control manager, production manager (Beacon), and the shipping and receiving manager (the only non-white manager). Soon an angry debate ensues between the sales and shipping/receiving managers. It seems that orders are not being shipped quickly enough, according to the sales manager, and several complaints have been received from smaller customers about the quality of the product. The shipping/receiving manager argues that he needs more hands to do the job, and that the quality of incoming supplies is lousy anyhow. While this debate continues, the other managers are silent and seemingly uncomfortable. Finally one of them attempts to break up the argument with a joke about his wife. Fisher and the other men laugh loudly, and the conversation shifts to other topics.

Question:

What recommendations would you make to Northern's management toward successful management of diversity issues?

23. Women in management around the world[2]

purpose

To gain an understanding of issues with women in management
in various countries.

group size

Any number.

time required

25 minutes or more.

exercise schedule

Class # 1	unit time	total time
1 Introduction	10 min	10 min

Instructor goes over "Assumptions about Women's Role in Management" and
gives assignments to groups or individuals.

Class # 2	
1 Presentation (optional)	5 min per presentation

Groups or individuals report on what they found out about women in management in their particular country.

2 Class discussion	15 min

Instructor leads a discussion on women in management around the world.

assignment

Your instructor will assign a country to you (or alternately, you may choose one).
You are to find out as much as you can about women and work – and women
in management in that country. After you have done your research, try to
determine whether that country primarily uses the equity or the complementary
contribution model.

---

2 Copyright 1993 by Dorothy Marcic. All rights reserved.

Dorothy Marcic and Sheila Puffer, *Management International,* West Publishing, 1994.
All rights reserved. May not be reproduced without written permission of the publisher.
For more information, contact West Publishing, Publications Dept., 610 Opperman Drive,
St. Paul, MN 55164.

Assumptions about women's role in management[3]

Assumptions	Equity Model	Complementary contribution model
Fundamental Assumptions		
• Men's and women's contributions	Similarity Identical	Difference Complementary
• Fairness based on	Equity	Valuing Difference
Strategic Goal		
• Assessment	Equal Access	Recognizing/Valuing Differences
• Measured by	Quantitative Statistical proportion of women at each hierarchical level	Qualitative Assessing women's contribution to organizational goals
• Process	Counting women	Assessing women's contribution
Measurement of effectiveness		
• Women's contribution	Identical to men's	Complementary to men's
• Norms	Identical for men and women	Unique to men and women
• Based on	Historical "male" norms	Women's own contribution
• Referent	Men	Women
Acculturation process		
• Expected behavior	Assimilation	Synergy
• Based on	Standardized Male norms	Differentiated Female norms
• Essence	"Dress for Success" business suit	Elegant, feminine attire
Example	United States the "melting pot"	France "Vive la difference!"

These two models come from two completely different assumptions about the role of women in management. The equity model is based upon assumed similarities, while the other suggests a complementary contribution model based on assumed differences.

In the first model, women are expected to achieve what men do, the same way men go about it. Given these, the problem is then one of assimilation – just give women proper access and they will become like men in the workplace. In the second model, which is evident in all of Europe, but especially in Sweden, women are expected to make different, but equally valuable contributions in the workplace. In this scenario,

3 Adapted from *Women in Management Worldwide* by Nancy J. Adler and Dafna N. Izraeli. Armonk, NY: M.E. Sharpe Publisher, 1988, pp. 3-7. Used with permission.

Dorothy Marcic and Sheila Puffer, *Management International*, West Publishing, 1994.

statistical equity is not used as a measure of fairness (as it is in the other model), but rather effort is made to assure women's unique contribution is equally recognized in the organization. Instead of looking at how many women are at what ranks and how much money they earn, this model assesses the extent to which the organization allows and rewards women's contributions, and looks for synergistic ways to achieve that.

Both models view the other as heresy. From the viewpoint of the equity model, seeing women (or any minority) as different is the same as seeing them inferior. And from the perspective of the complementary model, not to see women's uniqueness is tantamount to negating their identity.

24. Valentina on the verge: A case of a Russian woman's career choice[4]

As usual, at 7 a.m. the alarm clock rang, but Valentina really didn't feel like getting out of bed. The night before she once again had got to bed late around midnight after helping her daughter with her homework, washing and ironing the clothes for the next day, and washing the dinner dishes. "Well," she thought, "I haven't even got up yet, and already I feel exhausted." With that, she fought off the urge to stay in bed and got up. While her husband was jogging, she started to make breakfast for the family. She put the food on the stove, tidied up the apartment, and woke up their twelve-year-old daughter and helped her get ready for school. By the time Valentina's husband returned and began to shower and shave, she was scurrying to finish the morning chores and barely had enough time to comb her hair and pull herself together before she had to leave for the office. Even though it was only a five-minute walk to the bus stop, there was a hitch. Lately the buses had been breaking down all too often, and this morning she had to wait an extra ten minutes, which made her late for work.

But lately cataclysmic changes were occurring in the country and her own family circumstances were in transition. At the end of 1991 the Soviet Union had ceased to exist and Russia had become an independent country free of the communist system.

While going about her daily routine in Moscow, Valentina often thought about her family, her job, her future, and her place in the scheme of things. But she never reached the point of making a decision to change things. Perhaps it was because she never had any real reason to change. Until recently, her husband's salary was sufficient to meet the family's needs, and this enabled her to continue working in a relatively low-paying but not very stressful job that would allow her to combine a career with family responsibilities.

The conversion to the market economy brought great upheaval, including price increases of 200 to 300 percent. On a personal level, in the summer of 1992 her husband left for a long-term assignment as a faculty member at an American university. As a result, Valentina was faced with having to bear the burden of work and family responsibilities with only his long-distance help and support. Valentina was particularly concerned that their daughter was requiring more attention as she started her teenage years. All these new problems, combined with the desire for a more interesting and challenging job, led Valentina to ask herself: "What do I do now?"

---

4   Copyright 1992 by Sheila M. Puffer and Anatoly V. Zhuplev. This case was prepared especially for this volume. The authors would like to thank Valentina for sharing her experiences and J. Hugh Fraser for his assistance in the preparation of this case.

Growing up in the Communist system

Valentina was born in 1955 in a small village outside Moscow. Her mother worked on the railroad and on a State collective farm (sovkhoz) and her father was a machinist in a peat moss processing plant. Valentina had two younger sisters. With little time or money to spare, her father graduated from the evening program of a technical institute and was promoted to the position of shop manager, and eventually chief of mechanical services. Valentina's mother, who shouldered all the family responsibilities, completed accelerated courses in bookkeeping and, shortly after Valentina's birth, took a job as a bookkeeper.

In Russia, particularly in rural areas, there is a lack of information on career counselling and guidance for young people and adults. Therefore, career choices are usually made on the basis of parents' advice or parents' jobs as a role model.

As commonly found in rural areas in Russia where there was little access to information, Valentina relied on three main sources of information: the media (especially government television), books, and the traditions and values held by the community, the school system, and the family.

This situation was true for Valentina. In his youth her father had enjoyed reading technical books and was always tinkering. He would invent and build things and prepare technical drawings and blueprints in his spare time. Encouraged by her father and following his example, she finished the eighth grade, and, at age fifteen Valentina enrolled in a two-year program at a vocational school and graduated with a diploma in drafting. In 1975, again under her father's influence, she enrolled in the full-time program at an engineering and construction institute in Moscow. Like the vast majority of women in the Soviet Union, Valentina went to work after graduation. For nine years she was employed in several large engineering and design offices in the building construction industry in Moscow.

For several reasons, Valentina's job had little appeal for her, and she did not seek advancement. First, the work ethic had lost its meaning in the 1980s in the Soviet Union. During that time under President Leonid Brezhnev, known as the period of "stagnation," people had become disillusioned about work and about society in general. There was little to buy in the stores and life consisted mainly of struggling to keep the family equipped with the bare essentials. At Valentina's office, as in most other organizations, people would spend one-third to one-half of working hours on activities unrelated to the work itself: they would pass the time drinking tea and socializing. In addition, when food, clothing and consumer goods turned up in the stores or on street corners, workers would slip out of the office to stand in the long lines.

They were guaranteed a job by the state and usually were paid regardless of how well or how poorly they performed. There was little encouragement of creativity and initiative and many people tended to do the bare minimum in their official state jobs.

Another reason for Valentina's low interest in her career was that her husband's salary was sufficient to meet the family's needs. Because her income was not essential, Valentina did not have to strain herself at work and was able to devote more attention to her family and her own personal needs. The burden of keeping a household going was heavy enough that it could easily consume all of one's time. Shopping for necessities took several hours a day, household tasks such as laundry, dishwashing, and cleaning were done without modern appliances, and few husbands felt obliged to participate in housework and childrearing. Typical of many educated middle- and upper-middle-class women in the Soviet Union, Valentina sacrificed her career for her family. Nonetheless, she still harbored thoughts of pursuing a fulfilling career.

Making a career move in a time of sweeping change in Russia

The reforms that President Mikhail Gorbachev introduced in the late 1980s under the policies of perestroika (restructuring) and glasnost' (openness) deeply affected the economic, social, and political landscape of the Soviet Union. Valentina and her family felt the impact of these changes directly. Soviet citizens were allowed to come into increasing contact with Westerners without the longstanding fear of reprisal or punishment by their government. Valentina's husband began working on academic research projects with Western scholars and through these colleagues and friends in 1989 he became a visiting professor at the business schools at Northeastern University in Boston and Loyola Marymount University in Los Angeles. Valentina and their daughter accompanied him and they lived in the United States for nearly two years. During that time, Valentina was away from her job and exposed to the American way of life and the lifestyles of American women. In this new environment Valentina began to re-evaluate her personal and professional situation and felt the need to further her career. Yet, she had no clear goal in mind.

As with the fall of the Berlin Wall in Germany in 1989, the economic, social, and political institutions in the Soviet Union had also collapsed. Economic factors began to play a more crucial role in daily life and professional and personal relationships, and everyone seemed to be preoccupied with money.

A new wave of nouveau-riche had amassed their fortunes by various means – some in the chaotic implementation of government reforms, others by dint of their own energy and drive, and some by breaking the law.

When the family returned to Russia in May 1991 at the end of her husband's contract in the United States, they discovered that their country was radically different from the one they had left two years earlier. Valentina noted with dismay that prices of goods and services that had remained stable for years now seemed to be increasing by the hour. Although her husband's income had increased significantly as a result of government wage adjustments and his additional expertise from having worked abroad, it couldn't keep up with galloping inflation. Nearly all the family income that they earned in rubles, including the twenty-five percent that came from her salary, was used for basic daily needs. Vacations, entertainment, purchases of durable goods, and putting money into a savings account were out of the question, as were luxuries such as buying a car or taking a short trip abroad.

As a result of worsening economic circumstances, Valentina was forced to look for a source of greater income. On her husband's advice, and in anticipation of making a career change, from September 1991 through January 1992 Valentina enrolled in a program to train people to become managers of private companies and joint ventures. The courses included principles of management, production operations, organizational behavior, and business protocol (business etiquette). Upon graduation Valentina sent her resume to several firms and was hired as office manager of a private Russian company specializing in wholesale trade inside Russia as well as import operations with a number of Western European companies.

Challenges and growing pains in the new job

Valentina was very happy in her new job. The company was conveniently located in the center of Moscow and had a well-equipped office as well as attractive dining and recreational facilities. She was offered a competitive salary that was substantially higher than in the state sector, bonuses, and benefits including medical and dental insurance, as well as other forms of extra compensation. She liked the fact that the company was run with the strong hand of the president who imposed order and discipline. Most of all, Valentina enjoyed the independence she had in planning and organizing the office as well as the opportunity to manage a small staff and to work with a computer, fax machine, word processor, and other office equipment.

At work Valentina's problems were mounting. She tried to make suggestions several times to the president to make the office more efficient and to reduce the need for overtime, but without success.

Although initially she did not find it easy to perform her new responsibilities, especially managing other people, she quickly developed the necessary skills and experience and proved her worth to the president, to whom she reported directly. Soon Valentina was given a raise. In addition, she derived a great deal of satisfaction from having her professional capabilities recognized, and felt the need for further career growth.

However, advancement wasn't that simple. When she first started working at the company the president would ask her to stay late occasionally to finish some urgent projects. As time went on, his requests became more and more frequent and Valentina began getting home from work two or three times a week at 9 or 10 p.m. instead of the usual time of 7:30. Sometimes she even had to go to the office on weekends. As a result she had little time to spend with her family, do the housework, or even relax and take care of herself. Her husband and mother-in-law supported her career aspirations and tried to help her as much as possible with the household responsibilities. Nevertheless, before long Valentina began to suffer from stress and exhaustion.

Moreover, several unpleasant aspects of the president's character were becoming more evident, particularly his authoritarianism, his suspicious nature, and his indifference to employees' personal and social needs. The president's behavior made Valentina personally uncomfortable and it also put her in a difficult position as office manager on a number of occasions. She became discouraged and resigned herself to thinking, "Given his suspiciousness and cruel relationship with his employees, it's hopeless to try to change anything."

The unpleasant relationship with the president and the long hours began to wear on Valentina's family. Her husband also had a demanding career and he would often be gone from 8 a.m. to 9 or 10 p.m. On such days, he was unable to look after their daughter or even stop by a store to buy bread and milk. So, some days the cupboard was bare since buying groceries required considerable time and effort that no one in the family could spare. By the end of the week so much housework had piled up that they couldn't catch up on the weekend. This led Valentina's husband to grumble, half in jest: "Here we go again. The dishes aren't washed, the apartment isn't cleaned up, and there is nothing to eat. You have to quit this job or we'll all die of starvation in a messy apartment before we ever lay eyes on you again!

To work or not to work?

"What should I do about my job?" Valentina began to ask herself more and more often. The satisfaction she had just started to enjoy from professional recognition and growth was becoming replaced by a feeling of inadequacy. The president failed to listen to her suggestions for improving the office, and seemed to dislike it when she began making more decisions on her own. Furthermore, inflation had eroded her salary, and her attempts to get a raise were unsuccessful. When Valentina asked to talk with the president about it, he replied with an anxious look on his face: "There's no time to discuss that now. Let's talk about it later." But later never came, and Valentina realized that the president had no intention of giving her a raise or even discussing the issue.

Deep down she still felt gratitude and loyalty to the president who had shown faith in her professional abilities by hiring her for her first managerial job.

In July 1992 Valentina received job offers from two companies that were clients of the firm for which she worked. The salary and benefits they offered were better than what she was currently earning, but Valentina had several reservations about changing jobs. The companies were located on the outskirts of Moscow and would involve a longer commute. They also lacked modern offices and office equipment. In addition, Valentina was bothered by, what to her was, an ethical issue. In her eyes she felt that, if she were to take a job with a client, she would be betraying the person who got her on her feet. It was a difficult decision for her even though the client was not a competitor of her current employer.

Seeing all this, Valentina's husband advised her to quit her job, relax and take care of herself. He suggested that she might take a course to learn a foreign language or to become more proficient with computers. He himself had recently accepted a job as vice-president of a private firm and his new salary was high enough to support the family. Although Valentina now had the option of quitting her job, she didn't want to lose her financial or personal independence. Having weighed the pros and cons, she had to make some kind of decision.

Discussion questions

1 What are the main factors influencing career choice and professional development in this case? Prioritize them from Valentina's point of view.

2 What differences do you see between the lifestyle and mentality of a woman manager in Russia and the United States?

3 What advice would you give to Valentina to help her balance her family and career responsibilities?

4 What can - or should - the following entities do to help Russian women make choices about family and career issues?

   a The Russian government
   b Private Russian enterprises
   c Western firms that have joint ventures in Russia

5 What decision would you make in Valentina's place and what factors would you take into account?

Women managers in the former USSR: A case of "too much equality"?[5]

Imagine a country in which women are granted equal rights with men under the constitution, have excellent professional and technical post-secondary education, comprise half the labor force, and are revered as the standard-bearers of the country's moral and social values. Furthermore, imagine that this country was founded on the basis of a grand social design whereby women were to be full participants in all aspects of society, and a department of women's affairs, headed by an influential and respected woman, was established to implement this policy. Who could ask for a better country for women to enter the management profession and to assume positions of power and responsibility in society?

The former Union of Soviet Socialist Republics fits the description of the country described above. With all these advantages supposedly granted to them, Soviet women have been touted for years by their government officials as being "the very happiest women in the world" [Mamonova, 1989, P. 139]. Yet, the typical Soviet woman will tell you that these conditions have brought her little happiness. The myth that they have done so has existed only in the propaganda of Soviet officialdom for the past seventy years. The reality experienced by the vast majority of Soviet women in their personal and professional lives is far different. Whereas the state officially proclaimed women's equality, many women complain, "We have too much equality" [cited in du Plessix Gray, 1989, Pp. 201, 202]. This ironic statement reflects women's dissatisfaction with having to fulfill society's expectations that they should work as well as be the primary person responsible for home and family.

An additional source of frustration for women aspiring to influential managerial positions is that their careers are often blocked in spite of the fact that they possess the requisite educational background and motivation.

The duality of women's roles

On the other hand, there is the view that women should devote more time to their nurturing role in the home and reduce their participation in the work force [Attwood, 1990].

As a result of the policy of glasnost or openness, in the past several years the role of women in Soviet society has become the subject of much debate. On the one hand, there is the position that women should have increased power and visibility at work, which would result in greater numbers of women in management. Women in the former USSR have clearly not advanced into managerial positions to the full extent of their training and abilities. The many factors responsible for this situation are rooted in the dual roles that women are expected to fulfill in society. This "double burden" has existed since the beginning of the Soviet state. The

5   By Sheila M. Puffer. This reading is an abridged version of the chapter by the same name published in *Competitive Frontiers: Women Managers in a Global Economy*, edited by Nancy J. Adler and Dafna N. Izraeli, Cambridge, MA: Blackwell, 1993. Reprinted by permission.

I am grateful to Nancy J. Adler and Dafna N. Izraeli for their many insightful comments that helped strengthen this article. I also express my appreciation to Professor Alexander Naumov, deputy director of the School of Management at Moscow State University, and Professor T. Anthony Jones of Northeastern University for providing useful background information and comments.

first constitution of 1918 "recognized work as a duty of every citizen of the Republic" and included the statement: "He who does not work shall not eat" [cited in Kiezun, 1991, P. 41.] At the same time women's role as wife, mother, and homemaker were officially hailed as critical to the moral and social development of Soviet society.

Background on the former USSR

The USSR was established after the communists, inspired by Marxist doctrine and led by Vladimir Lenin, seized power from Tsar Nicholas the Second during the Russian Revolution of 1917. Following the civil war of 1918-21 the new Soviet state was formed, composed of the nations that had been formerly part of the Russian Empire. With the annexation of the three Baltic republics of Latvia, Lithuania, and Estonia during World War II, the USSR consisted of fifteen republics and had a population in 1990 of approximately 280 million. The republics, which are diverse in terms of economic development, culture, and religion, range from the Central Asian republics in which the Moslem religion and eastern philosophy prevail, to the Slavic republics in which Christianity and European thought predominate. In 1985 President Mikhail Gorbachev initiated a break with the past through his policies of glasnost (openness) and perestroika (restructuring). These policies, which triggered the end of the communist dictatorship and marked the beginning of a politically free society and a market-based economy, culminated in December 1991 in the dissolution of the USSR and the independence of its republics. The world continues to witness extraordinary political, economic, and social changes in the republics of the former USSR. These epochal changes will take years to reach complete resolution.

It is important to keep in perspective the applicability of the information included here, in light of the turmoil and uncertainty in the former USSR. The statistics on labor force participation, education, and the like, refer to the diverse population in the fifteen republics of the USSR in the 1980s. However, there is a wide disparity throughout the various republics about the role of women in society and in the work place. For example, in the Central Asian republics few women hold managerial positions. The information about managerial and professional women refers primarily to the European republics of the USSR. My concluding comments about prospects for the future will be confined to women managers in the Russian republic.

Women in the labor force

Women's participation in the labor force in the former Soviet Union is strong in numbers but weak in status and influence. Before the communists took power in 1917, women constituted 10 percent of the work force and were employed predominantly as manual laborers in factory work and agriculture. Lenin advocated that women should have greater opportunities in the labor force and appointed Alexandra Kollontai as the head of the department of women's affairs. By 1922 women's participation in the work force had increased to 25 percent [Grigorieva, 1990, P. 7]. Today virtually all (92%) women of working age (16 to 54) in the former Soviet republics are employed or in school [Sanjian, 1991; Vaneyeva, 1991]. Since 1970 women have comprised more than half (51%) of the work force. One-tenth (11%) of top management positions are currently held by women [Zhenshchiny i Deti v SSSR, 1985].

The goal of the communists was to transform this multicultural group into the "new Soviet man," to build a society in which the individual was subordinate to the common good and the state would direct every facet of people's lives. Achievement of this goal was attempted through a repressive dictatorship and totalitarian state.

The managerial role

Being a manager in the former Soviet republics is a very demanding job. Many managers joke that they work an eight-hour day - from 8 a.m. to 8 p.m. [Puffer and Ozira, 1990]. Managers are responsible not only for the work organization, but also for meeting many of the social needs of employees including housing, childcare, food, and cultural enrichment.

According to communist ideology, there was no occupational or wage discrimination in the USSR. Legislation mandating equal pay for equal work came into effect shortly after the Russian Revolution of 1917. In reality, however, occupational and wage discrimination against women is widespread. The majority of women work in the most poorly paid sectors of the economy and in positions with the lowest wages and the most dangerous conditions.

Managerial work can also be frustrating. Under the communist regime managers were pressured to meet plans established by central authorities and were often denied the requisite resources. Managers had little latitude to negotiate with higher authorities, and were held accountable for results without having the authority to make policy decisions. It is little wonder that many people, men and women alike, decline management positions because they often pay less than nonmanagerial jobs and bring more headaches. Such people would rather earn extra money working overtime in their regular nonmanagerial job or a second job, often in the growing private sector where they can earn many times the salary paid in state organizations. To these people, the perks of a managerial position, such as prestige and preferred access to goods and services, are not worth the effort.

Under the communist regime a mandatory qualification for promotion to management was membership in good standing in the communist party.

Individuals who planned managerial careers typically became involved in party activities at an early age: they would join the Young Communist League (Komsomol) as teenagers, and in their twenties would become party members. Virtually all managers were party members, but it was not essential for professionals in nonmanagerial positions to be members. Preparation for senior managerial positions often included experience in an important role in the party organization away from the work place [Puffer and Ozira, 1990]. Traditionally, however, women were not well represented in party leadership positions, although they did have a presence at the local level [Sanjian, 1991]. Women's advancement into management was therefore hindered by their insufficient experience in communist party activity. Early in their careers they may have viewed party membership as unnecessary because they were oriented toward a professional rather than a managerial career.

No longer is the communist party the official ruling force in the independent Soviet republics. However, the vestiges of it will continue to have a negative impact on women for some time because the personal relationships developed among former party members will still be relied upon to do business, and women have been largely excluded from this network.

Women managers:
Where they are, what they do

They virtually monopolize the professional staff positions of bookkeeper (94% are women), engineer-economist and economist (89%) [economist includes a broader type of administrative work than the American definition as well as the specific profession of economist], rate-setting specialists (85%) [i.e., setting and measuring standards of output], technicians (84%), and chief and senior accountant (77%). These are staff positions not directly related to production and therefore are less influential and less likely to lead to top management positions.

In professional and technical positions women are concentrated at the bottom levels.

With respect to managerial positions, the greatest concentration of women managers is also in the services or staff sphere. The majority of women managers work in staff departments (39% are women). The more prestigious managerial staff positions in design bureaus and the like have far fewer women managers (16%). In line management women's participation is also greatest at the lowest levels, namely first-line supervisor or foreperson (30%), and managers of production departments and services (32%). There are only about half as many women at the next managerial level, namely shift managers and department managers in shops and laboratories (18%). Shop managers and their deputies are the next step up the ladder, and women managers comprise 12 percent of this group. The representation of women in top management positions is similar. Eleven percent of presidents of industrial enterprises are women, a percentage which also applies to women members of the top management teams (vice-president 8%, chief engineer and deputies 9%, and senior staff manager and deputies 13%) [Zhenshchiny i Deti v SSSR, 1985].

Overall the concentration of women in professional and managerial positions in the nonproduction sphere, and predominantly at the lower levels of these positions, indicates that women exercise little power in organizations despite their impressive numbers and educational qualifications.

Factors affecting Soviet women's access to managerial positions

Seven factors that have been identified by Adler and Izraeli [1988] as affecting women's access to managerial positions around the world will be discussed in the context of women in the former USSR.

1. The perception of management as a masculine domain

The extent to which women performing managerial work are held in ill regard has come to light in two recent studies by Komarov [1989] and Zhuplev [1988]. The studies, which surveyed both men and women, resulted in very similar images of women managers. Not only are women managers portrayed in an unflattering stereotype, but Zhuplev remarked that they are sometimes the butt of jokes spread by men and women alike, even by women managers themselves [Zhuplev, 1988].

Unquestionably, management has been considered a masculine domain in the former USSR, official communist dogma of equality of men and women to the contrary.

Komarov and Zhuplev's findings stand in marked contrast to the idealized image of working women portrayed in many official state publications. Both Komarov and Zhuplev took the position that there are gender differences in performing managerial work. In the words of Komarov: "The music of management is one and the same for everyone. But a man and a woman will play it differently." These attitudes are consistent with the complementary contribution model of assumed differences between men and women managers, as opposed to the equity model of assumed similarity [Adler and Izraeli, 1988, chapter 1]. The fundamental issue underlying the complementary contribution model is whether women's differences are considered a constraint or a valuable asset. The responses to Komarov's and Zhuplev's surveys reflect both views and create contradictions. It is important to keep in mind that the surveys contain many stereotypical questions, which may have contributed to construction of stereotypes by the respondents. What is sorely needed is to conduct research to observe the managerial behavior of men and women to determine the actual similarities and differences.

Perceived characteristics of the ideal woman manager

Based on his interview data, Komarov [1989] concluded that men and women consider the ideal woman manager to possess the following three sets of qualities: femininity, physical attractiveness, and charm; competence and professionalism; and the ability to deal with people.

Respondents rated femininity, physical attractiveness, and charm as top priority. They dislike sloppiness and excessive makeup and jewelry. Furthermore, some men lamented that there are too few beautiful women managers. Komarov [1989] offered the following explanation:

"I think it is very difficult for a very beautiful woman to be a manager. Beauty, as one might guess, requires a great deal of time and effort, as well as many admirers and amusements. A beautiful woman, if the author's observations have not deceived him, lives for her beauty, and for this reason remains a woman, ever a woman, in all respects. A businesswoman, it seems to me, is likable rather than beautiful, and is a manager who is also a woman, rather than a woman who is also a manager."

The second most important set of qualities in a woman manager, according to Komarov's survey, are competence and professionalism. However, there are different expectations of what constitute competence and professionalism for a woman manager as opposed to a man. Komarov's [1989] respondents put in third place the ability to deal with people as essential for women managers. Komarov claimed there are gender differences in the way managers interact with subordinates. Men pay little attention to how their managerial style affects women managers who report to them. In contrast, women managers are more sensitive to the effect they have on subordinates, and are more willing to change their style.

> Whereas aloofness, brevity, and sternness are considered normal in male managers, in women they are perceived as callousness.

Komarov [1989] argued that women are superior to men in four managerial skills: flexibility in using different approaches to completing a task, thoroughness in checking the facts with various sources, intuition in decision making, and personal stress management. Soviet women are sometimes called "our Japanese," because of their strong work ethic [du Plessix Gray, 1989, P. 35]. Such qualities make women prized employees at lower levels, but do not give them access to positions of power.

2. Cultural constraints

The cultural constraints on women's access to managerial positions can be traced far back in Russian history. Elvira Novikova, a prominent feminist and historian, contended that the Soviet media juxtapose two prototypes of women that are deeply rooted in Russian culture: "They've taken two basic images of women in our folklore – the Cinderella sweetie pie who sacrifices her life to family, and Baba Yaga, the wise independent witch who lives alone in the forest and is doomed to solitude. They ask us, 'Who do you want to be, Snow White or Baba Yaga?' The honey who must run around bringing man his slippers...that's the woman they're all pressing us to be, even after seventy years of our being fully employed in the work force!" [cited in du Plessix Gray, 1989, Pp. 88, 89].

These deep-seated images pull Soviet women in opposite directions, but the traditionally feminine role seems to be especially strong and serves as a brake on women's wholehearted launching into a managerial career. "The dominant theme in the current literature [on sex roles] is that women should 'choose' between work or family. However, genuine choice is hindered by stereotypical ideas about women's natural role, and by considerable psychological pressure to choose a family." [Attwood, 1990, P. 208].

The traditionally feminine role is a central theme of Russian culture and is found in nineteenth-century literature. The literary phrase "women's suffering as redemptive force" [du Plessix Gray, 1989, P. 39] depicted women as "priestess and redeemer, the chief repository of virtue in the form of agape....The desire for a woman savior is expressed in a constant adulation of the ethical strengths of the good woman and the refusal to consider the virtues of male heroism. She is 'whole' (tsel'naia), while man is neurotic, torn" [Hubbs, 1988, Pp. 230, 231]. Du Plessix Gray found that many women admitted that their "tradition of heroic self-sacrifice is a form of power play, a way of retaining their aura and their status" [P. 39]. This cultural norm may help account for why some women sacrifice a promising managerial career for the sake of their family or to maintain harmonious relations with male colleagues.

> Male identity is perceived as precarious, contingent, existing only in the ethereal world of ideas rather than rooted in the 'real' world. Woman, on the other hand, is regarded as the essence of stability, of life, of growth, of 'lichnost' (individuality) itself.

There are two points of view about women and work. On the one hand, some women would be happy to work less because they have been subjected to a decade of sex-role socialization on what it means to be a woman. "Many women agree that their full participation in the workforce has had negative consequences for the family, children and themselves, and seem happy to accept the notion that they are the repositories of a set of innate, traditionally feminine personality traits, however much at odds this is with their lived experience" [Attwood, 1990, P. 212].

On the other hand, according to surveys conducted in the 1970s some professional women have opposed reduced work hours and part-time work. Some research scientists who were surveyed feared that they would be expected in their own careers to be as productive as full-time professionals but at reduced pay, and professionals in industry feared that their career advancement would be jeopardized [Moses, 1983, P. 17].

3. Women's role in family life

Not only are Soviet women expected to work, but they are also held responsible for managing the household. A 1985 survey of 51,000 households found that women spend on average two to three times longer on household chores than men, and have 1.5 times less free time. Women typically spend several hours a day standing in line to buy food and other essentials. They wash clothes and dishes by hand because of the shortage of household appliances, and sew clothes for themselves and family members because of poor quality or overpriced apparel in stores.

Many women feel overwhelmed by the double burden of work and family, and the demands can lead to chronic fatigue. Panov [1987] found that fatigue was a common complaint of the women in his Ivanovo study who rated how they felt at the end of the work day. Although half of the women (48 percent) felt fine, one-third felt poorly, and 18 percent felt too tired to do anything once they got home.

So much ado is made about family responsibilities that one would assume that women had many children. Yet, few women in the European republics have more than one child. Cramped living quarters, scarce childcare facilities, divorce rates approaching fifty percent in urban areas of the Russian republic [Perevedentsev, 1985, P. 8], and emphasis on work are some factors that account for the small number of children. Since children do not appear to represent an inordinate portion of the family responsibilities, it is important to examine the uneven distribution of household tasks between the spouses as a more likely source of the woman's "burden."

On a typical work day women spend nearly seven hours on chores, while men spend less than two hours [Vestnik Statistiki, 1986, Pp. 68, 69]. This is in addition to putting in a full day at work. On weekends the time that women spend on household chores is even greater.

Several reasons have been suggested for the imbalance between men's and women's family responsibilities. They all revolve around power relations between the sexes. One view is that men are superior to women and should be indulged and pampered at home. This special treatment is to compensate for the emasculation of men as a result of serfdom in tsarist times and powerlessness in their jobs in modern times due to the centralization of decision making and authority under the communist regime. In addition, because of the great loss of life in the Second World War, many women who were fortunate enough to have husbands wanted to make life easier for them. An opposing explanation for the excessive family responsibilities performed by women is that women are superior to men and they manifest their superiority by taking on many tasks. Yet another factor is the high incidence of alcoholism among men, a condition that makes many men appear weak and unreliable in the eyes of women.

First, women take courses only half as often as men. This can be a serious drawback since the best management development programs are generally offered in large cities, and promising managers from around the country attend for several weeks or even months. Second, women's family responsibilities make it difficult for them to adopt the demanding schedules of typical managers.

There is little question that the heavy commitment of time to household and family responsibilities has interfered with many women's career advancement for at least two reasons.

4. Economic development of the republics

The republics of the former USSR are currently in a state of economic chaos. This crisis presents threats and opportunities for both men and women. The threats for women are manifold. One prediction is that, as a result of rationalization of the economy, approximately sixteen million people will lose their jobs, nearly all of them (fifteen million) being women

The argument is that women cannot be relied upon because their family obligations cause them to be absent from work and prevent them from taking courses to improve their skills [Egorova, 1990].

[Lebedeva, 1988]. Women will be hardest hit for two reasons. First, the jobs to be eliminated and replaced by technology are primarily in manual labor, a sector in which women predominate. Presumably, the managers of these women, who are often women themselves, will also lose their jobs. Second, some people, including some leading economists, believe that women are not full contributors in the work force. The best thing, according to some economists concerned about improving the economy, is to phase women out of the workforce by shortening their work day and improving maternity leave benefits. Cuts in state-run childcare are also forcing some women to stay home with their children.

Such measures, however, fail to take into account the rampant inflation in the republics. With wages rapidly losing their buying power, it is imperative to have more than one wage-earner in the family. Consequently, women may be forced to remain in the work force and seek well-paying jobs. However, this does not necessarily mean a managerial job. As discussed earlier, many people decline managerial positions in favor of other jobs that pay more money and require less responsibility. A counterargument, however, is that if there is less competition for managerial jobs, women should have a greater opportunity to be appointed to these positions.

On the positive side, the restructuring of the economy and the emergence of the private sector are creating new job opportunities for enterprising individuals. Since the opportunities for women exist within specific organizational contexts, they will be discussed in section 7 below (organizational context).

5. Social policy

Two fundamental social issues have had a major impact on women's roles and their decision to pursue management positions. One was the Soviet central government's concern about the low birthrate in the European republics in comparison with the Central Asian republics. The authorities were concerned for two reasons. First, it was argued that more children would be needed who would later join the labor force and support the growing number of retired people. Second, the central authorities gave the appearance of wanting to keep the European population dominant. Given that the birthrate is lowest in areas where women comprise a greater proportion of the labor force, some demographers warn that a population decline is likely unless women spend less time working.

The second major social issue affecting women is the patriarchal view that they must fulfill their natural role of mother and nurturer and leave the responsibility of providing materially for the family to men. Adherents to this view attribute the decline in moral values in society and the break-up of the family to women's neglect of their most important role. (It goes without saying that a more likely cause of this situation was the social policies implemented by the communist regime.)

Social legislation that has been suggested to address these issues include raising the status of motherhood, replacing the image of the emancipated working woman with that of the happy family characterized by distinct male and female roles, exempting mothers with more than two children from working, encouraging longer post-natal leave and more part-time work, and changing child custody rules to discourage women from seeking divorce [Attwood, 1990].

To popularize this view of women's roles the Soviet government developed a two-year course called "The Ethics and Psychology of Family Life" that was required for all students in the ninth and tenth grades of high school, beginning in 1984 [Attwood, 1990, Pp. 184-191]. The curriculum included the importance of the family as the basic cell of socialist society, the reverence of motherhood as women's "great mission," and the need to return to traditional sex-roles in which men are the breadwinner and women, although equal, put home and family before their jobs. The course was not offered in the Central Asian republics, presumably to avoid encouraging a higher birthrate there.

Another social policy that has the potential to restrict women's access to managerial positions is, ironically, the newly implemented legislation on maternity leave. Women are legally guaranteed their jobs for three years after having a baby. While this is a laudable policy, it also has a negative side. The women who are adversely affected by this policy are those seeking their first job. This includes recent college graduates who are interested in a managerial career. Many employers consider them a bad investment. They assume that these women will get pregnant and then take maternity leave, and therefore they are reluctant to hire them.

6. Access to higher education

Overall, women have more education than men, yet there is an underutilization of women's education in the work place. Women who have the same education and jobs as men at the time of entry into the work force are often paid less, and are promoted less frequently to senior positions. Women represent 60 percent of workers, both blue- and white-collar, who have a specialized secondary or post-secondary education. However, this level of education is not reflected in the type of work they perform. Specifically, 48 percent of men with post-secondary education hold managerial positions at various levels. The corresponding figure for women with the same education is 7 percent [Vaneyeva, 1991].

People gain access to management training in two ways. The traditional way is for their superior to nominate them. This can be a bottleneck for a woman. Their superior must recognize the woman's seriousness in pursuing a managerial career and her ability to be an effective manager. The immediate superior is more likely to know a female subordinates' abilities. This firsthand knowledge may prevent the superior from reacting stereotypically to them. Yet, the superior may also experience pressures from male supervisors or subordinates who prefer that men receive training instead. The second method is for people to apply to management programs independently and pay their own way. An increasing number of women are currently taking advantage of this opportunity, particularly those who are interested in entrepreneurship and the market economy. In the advanced management program for entrepreneurs women comprise 20 percent of the participants. Of the middle managers from a state-owned enterprise in the consumer products industry enrolled in a management program offered by MGU, one-third are women. Two women are among the five full-time students studying international business in the United States under the sponsorship of an American charitable foundation. Finally, in MGU's executive management program less than 2 percent of the participants are women. According to the deputy director of MGU's School of Management, Alexander Naumov, this distribution of women participating in management training programs is typical of management institutes in the Moscow area. What these data show is that women have fairly good access to management training at the entry and middle levels, but that they are highly restricted from training programs at the executive level. What is more, women are virtually absent in groups of managers sent abroad for training. Of the numerous groups of executives that have come to the United States for training in the last three years, I know of none that have included women managers.

For example, the School of Management founded in 1990 at Moscow State University (MGU) has a number of women enrolled in its programs. In the two-year full-time MBA program 40 percent of the students (12 out of 30) are women.

I believe several factors account for the minimal representation of women in executive management programs. First is the stereotype that management is a male profession. In my view this is the most serious impediment to women's access to the executive ranks. Second, almost all the gatekeepers of executive positions are men, and they are unaccustomed to thinking that their women subordinates may want such responsibilities. Third, the nature of the executive job, with its long hours and travel, may be considered by men and women alike as too onerous for women with heavy family responsibilities. Finally, executive programs, especially those offered in the West, provide the perks of foreign travel and knowledge of the market economy. Officials want a return on their investment from the executives they send abroad, and they may feel that men are a safer bet than women for the reasons cited earlier.

A promising development in the area of management training is the recent formation of business women's clubs, including The Association of Moscow Business Women and the club, Vera. These organizations offer management training programs for their members. In addition, a monthly column appearing throughout 1991 in the magazine, Soviet Woman, offered advice on how women can start their own businesses.

7. Organizational context

The dissolution of the Soviet state, and the concomitant fall of the communist regime and the dismantling of the centrally planned economic mechanism are creating unprecedented opportunities for enterprising and achievement-oriented men and women to start their own businesses. Privatization of the economy began on a small scale in 1983 when enterprises run by family members were legalized in Estonia. Since then thousands of private enterprises or cooperatives have been formed, a number of them by women. A survey of 586 owners of private businesses (cooperators) in ten large cities conducted in early 1990 included 14 percent women [Jones and Moskoff, 1991, P. 27].

Because they are a new organizational form and are relatively free from state control, cooperatives provide an organizational context more hospitable to women than state-owned organizations, and women have expressed more positive attitudes toward them than men have [du Plessix Gray, 1989, P. 195]. Cooperatives, which are private enterprises ranging in size from a few employees to many thousand, offer greater autonomy and flexible working conditions. Salaries are much better, and since pay is directly linked with performance, ability and initiative are recognized and rewarded, rather than connections and gender.

Women have begun to start cooperatives in traditionally male economic sectors and in niches that were previously nonexistent. Women's cooperatives are characterized by low capital investment and small size.

Professor Anthony Jones, a Western expert on Soviet cooperatives, recently told me about several cooperatives he encountered that were founded and managed by women. All were well educated professionals who had connections that enabled them to get the resources they needed. For example, a Moscow sociologist founded a for-profit journal of small business, another woman started a management consulting business with her husband, and a third became a "business facilitator" serving as an intermediary between foreigners and nationals, suppliers and customers. In the Komi region a group of women started a clothing factory, and a teacher founded a business school for teenagers. In Moscow a former journalism professor with connections to the Komsomol (the communist youth league) founded a monthly magazine for teenagers called Business and Culture.

The term *cooperative*, which is a holdover from the perestroika era, may be replaced by simply *private enterprise* as the free-market economy becomes established in the former Soviet republics. Regardless of what they are called, and in spite of the hazards, cooperatives or private businesses offer a new opportunity for women to prove themselves in an organizational context that is less likely to exhibit the sex-role stereotyping found in traditional state-owned organizations.

A serious drawback to working in a cooperative is that people who operate private businesses often face violence and bribery from the criminal element (mafia), which is a deterrent for women to start their own businesses. They often need police protection, security guards, and sometimes body guards.

Prospects for women in management in the former USSR

Surveys conducted over the past few years show that many Soviet women want to continue working and that there is a sizable number who seek advancement up the managerial ladder. According to one survey, 60 percent of women said they would continue working even if their husbands were to earn the sum of what they both currently earned [Novikova, 1985, P. 48]. This is similar to responses in the 1970s when 75 to 80 percent of women surveyed reported they would continue working even if they no longer needed the income. The proportion was higher for white-collar than blue-collar workers [Iankova, 1975, P. 73]. These findings suggest that work satisfies intrinsic needs of personal growth and development for many women, rather than simply being a source of economic sustenance. Work may also satisfy many women's need to be economically independent from their husbands.

The intrinsic satisfaction of work was also cited by women managers in the Ivanovo region where the textile industry predominates and the majority of employees are women. There Panov [1987] found that two-thirds of the women managers he surveyed there liked their jobs. Those who sought career advancement reported that they did so for the following reasons: to earn more money and improve their living standards (57 percent), to make decisions about bigger issues (54 percent), and to have more rights and opportunities at work (25 percent). However, three-quarters of those surveyed did not foresee any opportunities for career advancement, and 88 percent did not want a promotion. Work is not the only priority of professional women in the USSR. Surveys by Soviet sociologists have found that 90 percent of professional women polled rated equally the importance of their professional and familial roles [Novikova, 1985, P. 48]. Surveys also show that many women want to combine both sets of responsibilities and seek more respect for their efforts at home and at work [Antonov and Medkov, 1982]. Novikova summarized the view commonly expressed by professional women as follows:

"We're equally oriented toward family and career and that's our tragedy, we want to write our theses but we also feel we should be making pirozhki [turnovers]. Most of us end up compromising one or the other, or both....We've been brainwashed with the notion that our state has done everything for us to reconcile the two roles, but the state hasn't begun to provide for us." [cited in du Plessix Gray, 1989, P. 90].

These remarks leave little doubt that many Soviet women take their professional careers seriously. However, as described above, many barriers stand in their way. A few years ago the Center for the Professional Development of Sociologists in the USSR conducted a survey to determine managers' perceptions of barriers to women's advancement into managerial positions [cited in Andreenkova, 1987]. The sample consisted of 1,725 managers at various hierarchical levels in 103 large industrial enterprises in the USSR. Managers gave their opinions about women in general, rather than describing their own experiences. The factor cited most frequently as a barrier to women in management (by 62 percent of those surveyed) was women's family and domestic obligations. Other factors suggested by respondents were: that management is a male profession (28 percent), that women lack the necessary qualities to be a manager (19 percent), and that women are not sufficiently active themselves in pursuing managerial careers (15 percent).

Based on the results of opinion surveys as well as the analysis presented in this chapter, it is clear that action needs to be taken on five fronts if women are to become more prominent in managerial positions in the republics of the former USSR. First, an infrastructure of social services needs to be created to help women cope with the responsibilities of childcare and household tasks. This includes the provision of a greater number of reliable childcare centers and medical facilities, development of the retail sector to reduce shopping time, and production of a wide range of labor-saving home appliances. Second, a mass educational campaign needs to be conducted to eradicate sex-role stereotypes, including those that were introduced in the high school curriculum in the 1980s. Third, a concerted effort must be made to train women for positions at all managerial levels and to integrate them into networks of power and decision making. Fourth, the nature of the managerial job needs to be re-examined. The job would be more accessible to women if firms and managerial practices became more efficient, thereby resulting in a reduction of managers' work hours. Fifth, women need to organize and create pressure groups to gain greater control of the rules of the game in organizations.

As described above, these women face a multitude of obstacles in their pursuit of a managerial career. At home they have to juggle family responsibilities frequently without the benefit of adequate childcare, household conveniences, or supportive husbands. At work they are often subjected to wage discrimination and sex-role stereotyping. As many American professional women discovered in the 1980s, the pressures of being a "superwoman" can lead to burnout and disillusionment. It has also been recognized in the West that women alone lack the power to change this situation. Rather, fundamental changes in society must be undertaken through government and corporate policies as well as education.

Virtually every aspect of life in the republics of the former USSR is currently undergoing scrutiny and is ripe for reform. And there are bright spots for women managers in private businesses and management training programs. However, it is utopian to think that the conditions for women in management will improve in the near future to any significant extent. Attention to other "higher priority" economic and social issues, competition for scarce jobs, and the existence of deep-seated stereotypes about women make such developments unlikely in the short run. Furthermore, the reluctance of men to share power with women is recognized as a major obstacle by such influential women as Liudmilla Bezlepkina, who in 1990 was the deputy minister of the State Committee of the USSR for Labor and Social Issues. The following incident which she recounted vividly illustrates how strongly some men in high level positions feel about retaining power, and the incident suggests that power sharing with women will not occur overnight. Bezlepkina recalled:

> To be successful in management currently requires that women in the former USSR assume the persona of "superwoman."

"Recently one colleague asked another in my presence: 'Could a woman become the chairman of our Committee?' And he responded: 'Never.' I was surprised: 'Why?' He said: 'A chairman knows neither day nor night, holidays or days off.' 'But women are different and those who would consent to this post know about all its delights,' I objected. My colleagues shook their heads and smiled indulgently: 'No, a woman can't be, can't be and that's that'" [cited in Kopeiko, 1991, P. 5].

References

Adler, N.J., and Izraeli, D.N. (eds.) (1988) *Women in Management Worldwide.* Armonk, NY: M.E. Sharpe.

Andreenkova, N. (1987) "Kakim byt' rukovoditeliu," ("How to be a Manager,") *Argumenty i Fakty* (Arguments and Facts), 32.

Antonov, A.I., and Medkov, V.M. (1982) "Usloviia Zhizni Sem'i s Det'mi i Reproduktivnaia Motivatsiia v Krupneishom Gorode," ("Living Conditions for Families with Children and Reproductive Motivation in Large Cities"). In *Urbanizatsiia i Demograficheskie Protsessy.* (Urbanization and Demographic Processes.) Moscow, P. 83.

Attwood, L. (1990) *The New Soviet Man and Woman: Sex-Role Socialization in the USSR.* Bloomington, IN: Indiana University Press.

du Plessix Gray, F. (1989) *Soviet Women: Walking the Tightrope.* New York: Doubleday.

Egorova, I.A. (1990) Speech in Izvestiia, (June 30).

Grigorieva, N. (1990) "Zhenshchiny Vskryvaiut 'Paket'." ("Women Open the 'Package.'") Rabotnitsa, 5, Pp. 6, 7.

Hubbs, J. (1988) *Mother Russia: The Feminine Myth in Russian Culture.* Bloomington, IN: Indiana University Press.

Iankova, Z.A. (1975) "Razvitie Lichnosti Zhenshcheny v Sovetskom Obshchestve." ("The Development of the Female Personality in Soviet Society.") Sotsiologicheskoe Issledovanie (Sociological Research), 4, P. 43.

Jones, A., and Moskoff, W. (1991) *Ko-ops: The Rebirth of Entrepreneurship in the Soviet Union.* Bloomington, IN: Indiana University Press.

Kiezun, Witold. (1991) *Management in Socialist Countries: USSR and Central Europe.* Berlin: de Gruyter.

Komarov, E.I. (1989) Zhenshchina-Rukovoditel' (The Woman Manager). Moscow, USSR: Moskovskii Rabochii. An English translation of Chapter 3, "Kachestva i Stil' Zhenskogo Rukovodstva" ("The Qualities and Style of the Woman Manager"), was published in Soviet Education, Vol. 33, No. 11, November 1991, Pp. 56-81.

Kopeiko, V. (1991) "Destruction of a Stereotype, or a Monologue of a Woman About the Woman," *Soviet Woman,* 1, Pp. 4-5.

Lebedeva, M. (1988) "Poka Muzhchiny Govoryat ..." ("While the Men Are Talking...") *Izvestiia,* October 23, P. 6.

Mamonova, T. (1989) *Essays on Sexism in Soviet Culture.* New York: Pergamon Press.

Moses, J.C. (1983) *The Politics of Women & Work in the Soviet Union & the United States:* Alternative Work Schedules & Sex Discrimination. Berkeley, CA: University of California Institute of International Studies.

Novikova, E.E. (1985) *Zhenshchina v Razvitom Sotsialisticheskom Obshchestve.* (Women in Advanced Socialist Society). Moscow.

Panov, A.I. (1987) *Perestroika i Rukovoditel'.* (Perestroika and the Manager). Moscow, USSR.

Perevedentsev, V. (1985) "Interview with Perevedentsev." The New York Times, (August 25), P. 8.

Puffer, S.M., and Ozira, V.I. (1990) "Hiring and Firing Managers." Chapter 7 in P.R. Lawrence and C.A. Vlachoutsicos (eds.), *Behind the Factory Walls: Decision Making in Soviet and US Enterprises.* Boston: Harvard Business School Press.

Sanjian, A.S. (1991) "Social Problems, Political Issues: Marriage and Divorce in the USSR." *Soviet Studies,* 43 (4), Pp. 629-649.

Vaneyeva, N. (1991) "Politics and Business: Any Chance for Women?" *Soviet Life,* March, P. 16, 17.

Vestnik Statistiki (Statistical Review), (1986) Moscow.

Zakharova, N., Posadskaya, A. and Rimashevskaya, N. (1989) "Kak My Reshaem Zhenskii Vopros," ("How We Are Solving the Woman Question"), *Kommunist,* 4, 56-60.

Zhenshchiny i Deti v SSSR. (Women and Children in the USSR). (1985) Moscow, P. 30.

Zhuplev, A.V. (1988) "Zhenshchina-Rukovoditel': V Zerkale Mnenii i Problem." ("The Woman Manager: In the Mirror of Opinions and Issues.") In V.A. Arkhipov (Ed.), *Kak i Kem Upravliat': Opyt, Problemy, Mneniia.* (How and Whom to Manage: Experience, Issues, and Opinions.) Moscow, USSR: Moskovskii Rabochii, Pp. 206-229.

Women: World–class managers for global competition[6]

It is no secret that business faces an environment radically different from that of even a few years ago, the result of increasingly global competition. The Commerce Department estimated in 1984 that in U. S. domestic markets some 70% of firms faced "significant foreign competition," up from only 25% a decade previously. By 1987, the chairman of the Foreign Trade Council estimated the figure to be 80%. In 1984, U.S. exports to markets abroad accounted for 12.5% of the GNP; by comparison, Japan's 1984 exports were 16.5% of its GNP.[1] Global competition is serious, pervasive, and it is here to stay.

More stringent competition is an important result of this global economy. Because markets are increasingly interconnected, "world-class standards" are quickly becoming the norm. New products developed in one market are soon visible in markets around the world, as initial producers use their advantage, forcing competitors to meet the challenge or lose market share. Product life-cycle has been reduced by 75%. Product development and worldwide marketing are becoming almost simultaneous. For example, recent developments in superconductivity, initially demonstrated in Zurich, were quickly replicated in The People's Republic of China, the United States, Japan and in Europe. Similarly, U.S. automobile customers quickly learned to demand improved quality from U.S. automakers once the Japanese autos had demonstrated it. Standards for price, performance, and quality have been permanently altered worldwide.

The problem for Americans, who historically have enjoyed the luxury of a large and generally protected domestic market, is how to respond to all these changes. Global competition means much more than sending excess domestic production abroad.

New competitive strategies

Today, many formerly eager markets are contested by well-entrenched locals or by competing foreign companies. The new competition does not involve simply sales abroad, or even foreign competitors here and abroad. Rather, its varied faces are likely to include the following circumstances none of them typical for most business even a few years ago:

Extensive on-going operations within foreign countries. This means a vastly increased demand for sophisticated, multiculturally adept managers. Foreign operations and markets are neither temporary nor trivial, but essential for long-term survival.

Strategic management across cultures: Global management necessitates working in numerous countries at once. Yet what works at home, or in one foreign country, may not work in another. Cultural norms and expectations differ. Sensitivity and finesse must be brought to bear on strategic intentions, to transliterate them sensibly. In many cases a straight translation probably will not do, whether of a product name or the more complicated matters of market attack, strategic intent, or mission.

More foreign personnel throughout the company. Foreign personnel are both necessary and valuable to a firm seeking to penetrate global markets. Even within the United States a broadly pluralistic personnel pool with substantial ethnic identity most notably Hispanic and Asian, but others as well belies the mythical "melting pot" image of prior decades. Effectively managing the multicultural organization dynamics is a prerequisite for success today and tomorrow, not merely an indulgent gesture or a legal requirement.

---

6 Excerpted from Marrian Jelinek and Nancy J. Adler. *Academy of Management Executive*, 2(1), 1988, 11–19. Used with permission.

More joint ventures and strategic alliances to gain access to new technology, new markets or processes, and to share costs and lower risk. Indeed, not only are U.S. firms increasingly becoming involved in joint ventures with foreign firms, but more and more the U.S. firm is not the dominant partner. Today, "we" often need "them" as much as or more than "they" need "us." Thus, cross-cultural management is becoming increasingly critical to success – even survival.

Each of these new competitive strategies demands new skills. Improved ability to communicate across profound differences in approach and expectations, assumptions and beliefs to say nothing of languages is key. Because culturally based beliefs, perceptions, expectations, assumptions, and behaviors are deeply held, they are especially sensitive issues, requiring exceptional tact.

But can women make it, especially in foreign cultures that presumably do not consider them men's equals? Won't they be ignored, mistreated, or intimidated? Shouldn't we respect foreign countries' cultural norms – even if they appear discriminatory to us? And do American women managers really want to take on this challenge? These are valid concerns, and an emerging body of research suggests some surprising answers. We will look at the special skills women bring to the new global competition and at the results women are achieving abroad, particularly in the fast growing market in the world, the Pacific Rim. The conclusions may surprise you at first. However, upon reflection, they are utterly comprehensible and point to a powerful resource for a sustainable competitive advantage not readily available or duplicable in other cultures.

Melvyn Konner makes a strong argument that male aggression has biological roots in puberty, but thereafter, greater aggression may be a learned and socially reinforced pattern. He notes that males commit the vast majority of violent crimes in every known society. Women, whose biochemistry does not initially encourage aggression at puberty, according to Konner, tend to evolve behavior patterns that emphasize sensitivity, communication skills, community, inclusion, and relationships.[4]

A nontraditional (but increasingly valuable) resource

All cultures differentiate male and female roles, expecting males to behave in certain ways, females in others; anticipating that men will fill certain roles, and women others. In many cultures, including America's, the traditional female role supports many attitudes and behaviors contradictory to those defined as managerial. This has been one of the key barriers to women's entry into managerial careers in the U.S. domestic arena: it operates both in terms of self-selection and differential difficulty.

After two decades of women's liberation movements and despite legislation and education, women remain different from men, even in the United States, arguably one of the most assertively egalitarian countries in the world. Men are still typically raised to be more aggressive and independent; women are still typically raised to be social and more communal.[2] Of course, there have been visible changes in sex roles and norms in North America as elsewhere in the world. There is also substantial debate over how much of the difference in behaviors can be attributed to biology and how much to acculturation factors. Nevertheless, in general, men still tend to be more aggressive than women.[3]

Research on sex roles and managerial characteristics has tended to reinforce the rather limited view of management skills and leadership most of us have acquired, a view identifying leadership with power and potency with adversarial control. In study after study, undergraduates, MBAs, and managers (male and female) in the United States have tended to identify stereotypically "masculine" (aggressive) characteristics as managerial and stereotypically "feminine" (cooperative and communicative) characteristics as unmanagerial.[5]

Yet American women now make up about half the U.S. workforce, and occupy over a quarter (27.9%) of all managerial and administrative positions,[6] although as late as the mid-1980s they represented only 5% of top executives.[7] In international management, women are rarer still, less than 3%[8]. Yet their achievements call into question some widely held beliefs about women and about management. Their unconventional achievements suggest a resource difficult for others to match.

Women abroad

American women have been pursuing graduate education in management in increasing numbers, now accounting for about 50% of the enrollment at some large state schools and about a third of the enrollment at the most prestigious private schools. More and more are developing an interest in international postings. It would be surprising if they did not, as international business is so clearly "where the action is" in many companies today. To investigate the role of North American women as expatriate managers, Adler undertook a four-part study. In the first part, 686 Canadian and American firms were surveyed to identify the number of women sent abroad. Of 13,338 expatriates, 402 or 3% were female.[9] Other parts of the study sought to explain why so few North American women work abroad. The second part of the study surveyed 1,129 graduating MBAs from seven management schools in the United States, Canada, and Europe. Overall, 84% said they would like an international assignment at some point in their career; there were no significant differences between males and females.[10] While there may have been a difference in the past, today's male and female MBAs appear equally interested in international work and expatriate positions.

One need not depend on opinion or assumptions for assessing women's performance internationally; there are documentary research results. In the working world, women are beginning to be assigned abroad. In another part of the study a survey of 60 major North American multinationals revealed that over half (54%) of the companies were hesitant to post women overseas. This is almost four times as many as were hesitant to select women for domestic assignments (14%). Almost three-quarters of the personnel vice presidents and managers believed that foreigners are prejudiced against female managers (73%), and that prejudice could render women ineffective in international assignments. Seventy percent believed that women in dual-career marriages would be reluctant to accept a foreign assignment, if not totally disinterested. For certain locations, the personnel executives expressed concern about women's physical safety, hazards involved in traveling in underdeveloped countries and, especially for single women, isolation and potential loneliness.[11] These findings agreed with those of a survey of 100 top managers in Fortune 500 firms operating overseas: The majority believed that women face overwhelming resistance when seeking management positions in the international division of U.S. firms.[12]

No welcome mat?

There is certainly evidence to suggest that women are discriminated against as managers worldwide; women managers in foreign cultures are very rare indeed.[13] In many societies, local women are systematically excluded from managerial roles. Japan offers an excellent case in point; there are almost no Japanese women managers higher than clerical supervisors, especially in large, multinational corporations. Japanese society expects women to work until marriage, quit to raise children, and return, as needed, to low-level and part-time positions after age 40. In Japan, the workplace remains a male domain.[14] Similarly, while women from prominent families in the Philippines can hold influential positions in political and economic life, overall only 2.7% of working women hold administrative or managerial positions in business or government.[15] The picture is similar in India, where women are constitutionally equal to men, but are culturally defined as primarily responsible for the home and children. Women have fared somewhat better in Singapore, where government policy and a booming economy between 1980 and 1983 helped raise women to 17.8% of managerial and administrative positions, up from 7% in 1980.[16] Only recently, and as yet rarely, do women fill managerial positions in these countries.[17]

Women in international management

Clearly, it is the cultures of these foreign countries that perpetuate this scarcity of indigenous female managers in most Asian countries. If so, how can North American companies successfully send female managers to Japan, Korea, Hong Kong, the Philippines, the People's Republic of China, Singapore, Thailand, India, Pakistan, Malaysia, or Indonesia? Is the experience of these countries' women, most specifically their relative absence from managerial ranks, the best predictor of what expatriate women's experiences will be?

Research results suggest that local women's experience is not a good predictor of North American women's reception, experiences or success in Pacific Rim countries.[18] Indeed, it seems that North American predictions confuse the noun "woman" with the adjective "female," as in "female manager." The research disconfirms a set of North American assumptions predicting how Asians would treat North American female managers based on the North Americans' beliefs concerning Asians' treatment of Asian women. Confusing? Yes. Fundamentally important? Also yes. The problem with these assumptions, and the conclusions they lead to, is that they have been proven wrong.

Fifty-two female expatriate managers were interviewed while on assignment in Asia or after returning from Asia to North America as part of the larger study described earlier. Because of multiple foreign postings, the 52 women represented 61 Asian assignments. The greatest number were posted in Hong Kong (34%), followed by Japan (25%), Singapore (16%), the Philippines and Australia (5% each), Indonesia and Thailand (4% each), and at least one each in Korea, India, Taiwan, and the People's Republic of China. Since most of the women held regional responsibility, they worked throughout Asia, rather than just in their country of foreign residence. The majority of the women were sent abroad by financial institutions (71%), while the others were sent by publishing, petroleum, advertising, film distribution, retail food, electronic appliances, pharmaceuticals, office equipment, sporting goods, and soaps and cosmetic firms, and service industries (including accounting, law, executive search, and computers).

On average, the women's expatriate assignments lasted two and a half years, ranging from six month to six years. Salaries in 1983, before benefits, varied from U.S. $27,000 to U.S. $54,000 and averaged U.S. $34,500. The women supervised from zero to 25 subordinates, with the average being 4.6. Titles and levels varied considerably; some held very junior positions (such as trainee and assistant manager), while others held quite senior positions including one regional vice-president. In no case did a female expatriate hold her company's number-one position in any region or country.

The expatriate experience

These expatriates were pioneers. In the majority of cases, the female expatriates were "firsts," with only 10% having followed another woman into her international position. Of the 90% who were first, almost a quarter (22%) represented the first female manager the firm the firm had ever expatriated anywhere; 14% were the first women sent by their firms to Asia, 25% were the first sent to the country in question, and 20% were the first women abroad in their specific job.

Clearly, neither the women nor their companies had the luxury of role models; there were no previous patterns to follow. With the exception of a few major New York-based financial institutions, both women expatriates and their firms found themselves experimenting, with no ready guides for action or for estimating the likelyhood of success.

The companies decided to send women managers to Asia only after a process that might be described as "education." In more than four out of five cases (83%), it was the woman herself who initially introduced the idea of an international assignment to her boss and company. For only six women (11%) had the company first suggested it, the remaining three cases (6%) the suggestion was mutual.

> Overall, the women described themselves as having had to encourage their companies and their bosses to consider the possibility of expatriating women in general and themselves in particular. In most cases, they confronted and overcame numerous instances of corporate resistance prior to being sent.

The women used a number of strategies to "educate" their companies. Many women explored the possibility of an expatriate assignment during their initial job interview, and simply turned down firms that were totally against the idea. In other cases, women informally introduced the idea to their bosses and continued to mention it "at appropriate moments" until the assignment finally materialized. A few women formally applied for a number of expatriate positions before finally being selected. Some women described themselves as having specifically planned for international careers, primarily by attempting to be in the right place at the right time. For example, one woman predicted that Hong Kong would be her firm's next major business center and arranged to assume responsibility for the Hong Kong desk in New York, leaving the rest of Asia to a male colleague. The strategy paid off: within a year the company sent her, rather than her male colleague, to Hong Kong.

This cautiousness and reluctance are particularly interesting because they tend to create an unfortunate self-fulfilling prophecy. As a number of women reported, if the company is not convinced you will succeed (and therefore offers you a temporary position rather than a permanent slot for instance), this will communicate the company's confidence to foreign colleagues and clients as a lack of commitment. Foreigners will then mirror the home company's behavior, also failing to take the temporary representative seriously. Assignments can become substantially more difficult. As one woman in Indonesia put it, "It is very important to clients that I am permanent. It increases trust, and that's crucial."

Outcomes abroad: Did it work?

Ninety-seven percent of the North American women described their experiences as successful, despite the difficulties and the reluctance on the part of their firms. While their descriptions were strictly subjective, a number of objective indicators suggest that most assignments did, in fact, succeed. For example, most firms decided to send a woman abroad after experimenting with their first female expatriate. In addition, many companies offered the pioneer women a second international assignment upon completion of the first. In only two cases did women describe failures: one in Australia and one in Singapore. The Australian experience was the woman's second posting abroad, preceded by a successful Latin American assignment and followed by an equally successful post in Singapore. The second woman's failure in Singapore was her only overseas assignment to date.

Perhaps most astonishing was that, above and beyond their descriptions of success, almost half the women (42%) reported that being female served more as an advantage than a disadvantage in their foreign managerial positions. Sixteen percent found being female to have both positive and negative effects, and another 22% saw it as irrelevant or neutral. Only one woman in five found the professional impact of gender to be primarily negative abroad.

Advantages

The women reported numerous professional advantages to being female. Most frequently, they described the advantage of being highly visible. Foreign clients were curious about them, wanted to meet them, and remembered them after the first meeting. It was therefore somewhat easier for the women than for their male colleagues to gain access to foreign clients' time and attention.

In addition, many of the expatriates described a higher status accorded them in Asia. That status was not denied them as foreign female managers; on the contrary they often felt that they received special treatment not accorded their male colleagues. Clearly, it was always salient that they were women, but being women did not appear to prohibit them from operating effectively as managers. Moreover, most of the women claimed benefits from the "halo effect." Most of their foreign colleagues and clients had never worked with a female expatriate manager. At the same time, the foreign community was highly aware of how unusual it was for North American firms to send female managers to Asia. Thus, the Asians tended to assume that the women would not have been sent unless they were the best. Therefore, they expected them to be "very, very good."

Other companies made postings temporary, or shorter than the standard male assignment of two or three years. This temporary status was often an important detriment: One Tokyo banker warned potential foreign competitors, "Don't go to Japan unless you're ready to make a long-term commitment in both time and money. It takes many, many years.[19]

Managing foreign clients' and colleagues' initial expectations was a key hurdle for many of the women. Since most Asians had previously never met a North American woman in a managerial position, there was considerable curiosity and ambiguity about her status, level of expertise, authority, and responsibility and therefore the appropriate form of address and demeanor to be used with her. In these situations male colleagues' reactions were important. Initial client conversations were often directed at male colleagues, rather than at the newly arrived female manager. Senior male colleagues, particularly from the head office, became important in redirecting the focus of early discussions toward the woman. If well done, smooth, on-going work relationships were quickly established.

Business relationships and the effective development of "comfort levels" center on personal relationships and reliability over the long haul, especially in Japan, but also in many other "slow clock" cultures that focus on long term.[20] It takes time to build relationships, and time to learn the culture. The contrast to the infamous American emphasis on "fast tracks" and quarterly results could not be more stark.

The problems the women did experience were most often with their home companies rather than their Asian clients. For instance, after obtaining a foreign assignment some women experienced limits to their opportunities and job scope imposed from back home. More than half the female expatriates described difficulties in persuading their home companies to give them latitude equivalent to that given their male colleagues, especially initially. Some companies, out of concern for the women's safety, limited their travel (and thus their role and often their effectiveness), excluding very remote, rural, and underdeveloped areas.

Women as Gaijin

Throughout the interviews, one pattern emerged persistently. First and foremost, foreigners are seen as foreigners. Like their male colleagues, the female expatriates are categorized as gaijin (foreigners) above all, and not locals. Foreign female managers are not expected to act like local women. Thus, the rules governing the behavior of local women, potentially limiting their access to management and managerial responsibilities, do not apply to the expatriate women. The freedom of action this identification carries is substantial:

(Japan) "The Japanese are very smart: they can tell that I am not Japanese, and they do not expect me to act as a Japanese woman. They will allow and condone behavior from foreign women which would be absolutely unacceptable from their own women."

As Ranae Hyer, a Tokyo-based vice-president of personnel of the Bank of America's Asia Division said, "Being a foreigner is so weird to the Japanese that the marginal impact of being a woman is nothing. If I were a Japanese woman, I couldn't be doing what I'm doing here. But they know perfectly well that I'm not."[21]

Ultimately, of course, the firm's product or service and the woman herself must be acceptable in business terms. Simply sending a female will not carry an inadequate product or too-costly services:

(Hong Kong) "There are many expat and foreign women in top positions here. If you are good at what you do, they accept you. One Chinese woman told me, 'Americans are always watching you. One mistake and you are done. Chinese take a while to accept you and then stop testing you.'"

(Hong Kong) "It doesn't make any difference if you are blue, green, purple or a frog. If you have the best product at the best price, they'll buy."

Yet the traditional image of business as warfare and the character of the relationships based on it are increasingly dysfunctional. New modes of "collaborative competition" require traditionally "female" skills. The new competition is so challenging that only the best can stay in the game; we need all the advantages we can muster including full usage of the best of our resources, male and female.

Nevertheless, the incremental advantages of easier communication and visibility, greater facility at relationships per se, and greater trust and openness often allow a female expatriate to enjoy significant pluses in a highly competitive atmosphere. Perhaps even more important, women's advantage in succeeding abroad draws on characteristics that have traditionally been a fundamental part of the female role in many cultures their greater sensitivity, communication skills, and ability to establish rapport. Women need to buy into the competitive game. They can subtly shift the interaction out of the power and dominance modes so typical of business interchange and so highly dysfunctional in cross-cultural relations into the sort of cooperative, collaborative modes becoming increasingly important today.

Global competition is a tough game, and "world class" standards are a genuine challenge. Our opponents are worthy foes, strong competitors with numerous advantages. Foreign firms now control state-of-the-art technology producing top-quality, low-cost products and services that respond quickly and effectively to worldwide clients' rapidly changing needs. Moreover, they often enjoy lower costs for capital and personnel, concerted government support, and in some cases, nontariff, cultural barriers to foreign firms' entry into their domestic markets and long-established relationships with other foreign nations. These advantages must be overcome if North American firms are to prosper in the future.

Conclusion

Women who are successful abroad can provide role models and coaching for their male colleagues. This means that the women will have to be seen as resources, consulted and relied upon for their special expertise. Business school curricula can also help. Both specialized coursework and cross-cultural elements in all courses can highlight the importance of the international arena. Organizational behavior, organizational development, international management, and cross-cultural experiential activities can all present far broader perspectives than the standard BBA or MBA work focused completely on United States business practices.

Global competition is a tough league, so challenging that we must employ all our skills and advantages, and the best of our people. We believe women possess a crucial advantage in social relationship and communication skills. Increasingly, the best of our male managers too will be working to acquire and hone important skills formerly seen as "female," those centering on relationship communication, and social sensitivity.

American business already faces a global marketplace and global competition. This world is too small and too interconnected for "Lone Ranger" business practices; no single view encompasses all of its reality, and intolerance is a luxury we cannot afford. Traditional U.S. business approaches to competition as battle, which build arm's length business relationships on this basis, seem very risky indeed. Alliances, cooperative efforts, joint ventures, collaborations, and even business more or less as usual but carried out across cultural lines, can be facilitated by skills traditionally thought of as "female."

This paper draws extensively on research reported in Nancy J. Adler's "Pacific Basin Managers: A Gaijin, Not a Woman," *Human Resource Management* 26:2 (Summer 1987), pp. 169-192. The interested reader may find a more complete account of the research there; reprints may be ordered from John Wiley & Sons, Periodicals Division Reprints, 605 Third Avenue. New York, NY 10158: (212) 692-6025.

Endnotes

1.   Discussions of competition are widespread in the business press and current management literature. See, for instance, Thomas 1. Peters' "Competition and Compassion," California Management Review, 28(4), Summer 1986. pp. 11-26. Several sources for comparison figures on the U.S. economy and those of our trading partners can be found in Lester Thurow's *The Zero Sum Solution.* New York: Simon and Schuster, 1985; and Bruce Merrifield. U.S. Department of Labor, cited in Lester Thurow's "Why We Can't Have a Wholly Service Economy," *Technology Review,* March 1985.

For a thought provoking look at some of the changes, see also Thomas J. Peters. "A World Turned Upside Down," *Academy of Management Executive,* 1(3), August 1987, 231-242.

2.   Carol Gilligan, *In a Different Voice.* Cambridge, MA: Harvard University Press, 1982.

3.   See "Women, Men and Leadership: A Critical Review of Assumptions, Practices and Change in the Industrialized Nations," by Jeff Hearn and P. Wendy Parkin. *International Studies of Management & Organization,* v. 16 (Fall-Winter 1986), pp. 33-60, for a useful discussion from a thoughtfully international perspective.

4.   Melvin Konner, *The Tangled Wing: Biological Constraints on the Human Spirit.* New York: Harper Colophon, 1982.

5.   Gary N. Powell and D. Anthony Butterfield, "The 'Good Manager': Masculine or Androgynous?" *Academy of Management Journal* 22: 2 (1979). pp. 395-403.

6.   U.S. Department of Labor, 1982.

7.   A. Trafford, R. Avery, J. Thornton, J. Carey, J. Galloway. and A. Sanoff. "She's Come a Long Way Or Has She?", *U.S. News and World Report,* August 6,1984. 44-51.

8.   Nancy J. Adler, "Women in International Management: Where Are They?", *California Management Review,* 26(4), Summer 1984, 78-89.

9.   See Footnote 8 above.

10.   See Nancy J. Adler's "Do MBAs Want International Careers?" International Journal of Intercultural Relations, 10(3), 1986. 277-300; and "Women Do Not Want International Careers and Other Myths About International Management," *Organizational Dynamics,* 13(2), Autumn 1984.

11.   Nancy J. Adler, "Expecting International Success: Female Manages Overseas," *Columbia Journal of World Business,* 19(3), Fall 1984, 79-85.

12.   N. Thal and P. Cateora, "Opportunities for Women in International Business, ' *Business Horizons,* 22(6, December 1979, 21-27.

13.   There are a number of useful resources for information on women in Japanese management, including the following: Tracy Dahlby, "In Japan. Women Don't Climb the Corporate Ladder," *New York Times,* September 18,1977; M.M. Osako, "Dilemmas of Japanese Professional Women," *Social Problems,* 26, 1978, 15-25; Marguerite Kaminski and Judith Paiz. "Japanese Women in Management: Where Are They?" *Human Resource Management,* 23(3), Fall 1984. 277-292; and Patricia G. Stinhoff and Kazuko Tanaka, "Women Managers in Japan," *International Studies of Management and Organization,* 17(3-4), Fall-Winter 1987,108-132. Reprinted in Nancy J. Adler and Dafna N. Israeli (Eds.) *Women in Management Worldwide.* Armonk. NY: M.E. Sharpe, 1988.

14.   Blas F. Ople, "Working Managers, Elites," *The Human Spectrum of Development,* Manila, Philippines: Institute for Labor and Management, 1981.

15.   Audrey Chan, "Women Managers in Singapore: Citizens for Tomorrow's Economy," in Nancy J. Adler and Dafna N. Israeli (Eds) *Women in Management Worldwide.* Armonk, NY: M. E. Sharpe. 1988.

16.   Nancy J. Adler (Ed.) Women in Management Worldwide special issue of International Studies of Management and Organization, 17(3-4) Fall-Winter 1987; and Nancy J. Adler and Dafna N. Israeli (Eds.) *Women in Management Worldwide.* Armonk. NY: M. E. Sharpe. 1988.

17.   Nancy J. Adler. "Pacific Basin Managers: A Gaijin, Not a Women Human," *Resource Management,* 26(2), Summer 1987,169-192.

18.   Eric Morgenthaler. "Women of the World: More U.S. Firms Put Females in Key Posts in Foreign Countries," *Wall Street Journal.* March 16, 1978. 1, 27.

19.   Edward T. Hall and Mildred Reed Hall, *Hidden Differences: Doing Business with the Japanese.* Garden City. NY: Anchor Press/Doubleday, 1987.

20.   See Footnote 12 above.

21.   See Footnote 15 above.

Multinational parent-subsidiary and joint venture relationships

Many companies are extending their global reach by establishing subsidiaries abroad or creating joint ventures with partner firms in other countries. *Getting along with parents: A look at subsidiary relations* is an exercise that involves interviewing managers of an international subsidiary and analyzing the decision-making practices and operational procedures that are in place. The conflicts that can arise between headquarters and foreign subsidiaries are illustrated in *Rough times at Nomura*, a case about Nomura Securities Company in Japan and its American subsidiary in New York. American securities traders are frustrated by decision making that is centralized in Tokyo and career paths that are truncated. Furthermore, such policies have contributed to a decline in the company's earnings in the United States. The dramatic cultural differences inherent in American and Japanese business practices are explained in *The Japanese manager's traumatic entry into the United States: Understanding the American-Japanese cultural divide.* Seeing America from Japanese eyes is a dramatic way of presenting cultural differences, particularly the "negative surprises" in community life, business practice, organizational dynamics, and interpersonal dealings. A comparison of Japanese and American values and behavior patterns helps explain the source of these shocks. The Japanese manager's culture shock in America is even more understandable after non-Japanese experience aspects of Japanese culture, such as provided in the exercise, *Understanding Japan*, in Chapter 2.

The problems and prospects of joint ventures are presented in two case studies. *Misr Acrylic and American Standard*, a case that takes place in Egypt, describes an initial agreement signed by Misr Acrylic to produce a line of bathtubs to American Standard's specifications. Complications between the partners arose as sales increased, a new acrylic bathtub technology was introduced, and American Standard subsequently increased its share in Misr Acrylic from 25 to 40 percent. Issues of operational control and product quality had to be resolved. Latent conflicts also exist between the partners in *Ferox manufactured products*. The Czech enterprise, Ferox, a state-owned chemical equipment manufacturer, had a successful joint venture with Cryogas, an American-based international chemical company, to manufacture industrial gases. The partners were about to conclude a second agreement under the Czech government's privatization program mandated after the fall of communist rule. Under the new agreement the American partner would have a controlling interest of the former state-owned enterprise. Dramatic changes in the ownership structure may create conflicts over corporate strategy and management style, and both parties may experience difficulty during the transition to a market-oriented economy in the Czech Republic. Case studies of firms attempting to establish joint ventures in Hungary are applicable to the Ferox case. Like the Czech Republic, Hungary is in the process of transforming its economy to a more market-based system. Three cases of British firms are described in *Joint ventures in Hungary: Key success factors*. The article also provides a detailled outline of the major items to be included in a joint venture agreement as well as lessons learned from the two successful and one unsuccessful joint ventures in Hungary.

Chapter 6

Multinational parent-subsidiary and joint venture relationships

25. Getting along with parents: A look at subsidiary relations[1]

purpose

To examine problems and challenges of parents and subsidiary companies

group size

Any number of groups of 4-6 members

time required

10 minutes for each group presentation
and 15-20 minutes for total class discussion.

assignment

Choose a company which has a subsidiary in your geographical area, preferably one that has international connections. Set up interviews with several managers in this subsidiary and try to find out what it is like for the subsidiary to operate under the control of the parent company. You may ask the following questions, but do not limit yourselves to these alone:

1 What is the relationship of the types of business between parent and subsidiary? How long has your company been a subsidiary of this company?

2 Were you ever a subsidiary to another company? How was that different?

3 How large is the subsidiary related to the parent company? In sales, personnel or projected growth?

4 How often do staff from the parent company visit? Or telephone?

5 What types of policies are set by the parent company and what types does the subsidiary get to set on its own?

---

6   Who determines strategy decisions? How much input does the
     subsidiary have?

7   What happens when there are conflicts between parent and subsidiary?
     How are they resolved?

8   How similar or different are the cultures of the parent and subsidiary?

9   Do you feel there is equity in financial dealings?

10   Do you have enough independence from the parent company?

11   What do you think is the ideal relationship between the parent and
     subsidiary companies?

Your group should then prepare a 10 minute (maximum) presentation for the whole class
discussing the information you learned in your interviews.

Class discussion questions

1   What were the similarities in problems shown in the various
     subsidiary companies?

2   Which types of parent-subsidiary relationships seemed to work best?

3   If you were advising a parent company how to handle its subsidiaries,
     what would you propose?

26. Rough times at Nomura[2]

Additional topics covered: diversity management, corporate finance, organization structure, and customer relations.

The problem

George Rosebush sat at his desk pondering the magnitude of the decision he faced. He still couldn't believe what had transpired over the last year. It was July 1988, and he had been with Nomura Securities International (NSI), the American subsidiary of the Japanese giant, Nomura Securities Ltd., for exactly two years. During that time, George had acquired the skills necessary to be a successful stock trader. But he now felt blocked from using all his skills. NSI management, all Japanese personnel on assignment from the home office in Tokyo, had refused to give Americans such as George the latitude to aggressively pursue business. Like his predecessors, George was frustrated with coping with Japanese culture and business norms. In particular, the Japanese were slow in making decisions or changes, primarily because of their "consensus" method of decision making. Nomura was termed a "monolithic machine" where decisions emerged from "the system with little need for creativity." This was a significant impediment in the trading business where the ability of a trader to respond quickly to customer needs is vital to success. Furthermore, as a pure service industry, the ability to develop strong client relationships is imperative. Here again, Nomura insisted on doing things the "Japanese Way." Nomura was held back by Japanese tradition, inflexibility in negotiations, lack of imagination, little expertise in critical investment banking sectors, and weak relationships with U.S. and European institutional investors." [3] To make matters worse, the securities industry was suffering a major recession following the stock market crash of October 1987. Since the late 1970s, NSI's staff of 750 had increased tenfold.

> Yoshihisa Tabuchi, president and chief executive of Nomura Securities Company Ltd., stated: "The style and structure Nomura uses to sell securities in Japan cannot work well in the U.S. Nomura's traditional culture is as a Japanese brokerage firm, but, as it expands, it must become multicultural."

> Although the market downtown and changing Japanese trading habits had accounted for much of the problem, industry analysts said the Japanese had "...severely misjudged the difficulty of mounting major expansion drives overseas." [4]

---

2 By Allan Bird, Ron Dalbello, Richard Madigan, Jim Noble, and Prema Venkat. Used with permission.

3 *Dun's Business Month*, November 1986. "Nomura Securities Global Ambition," pp. 44-47.

4 William Glasgall, "Tokyo Brokers Beat a Retreat From the Street."

In the post-crash era, however, NSI experienced a larger fall in revenues and profits than other firms in the industry. This slump was particularly acute in George's department, Japanese Equities. George had made recommendations to improve business, but management refused to take the steps necessary to reverse the drop in market share and profits that George's department was experiencing.

Business had slowed so much that George and his colleagues did crossword puzzles to pass the time. Each day dragged slowly, and George eventually had to decide whether to quit or stay. He had started talking about job opportunities with other firms on the "Street."

Background Data

Nomura Securities, the world's largest stockbroker, continues to suffer from both host and home country regulatory pressures and related political risks associated with its globalization strategy. The Japanese securities industry, as in the United States, has undergone extensive deregulation over the past five years. Within this volatile environment, Nomura has continued growing, aggressively expanding into the London and New York markets.

> The strength of the Japanese stock market, combined with its partial deregulation, attracted many American money managers to invest in Japan.

Nomura's "growth phase"

Nomura was founded in 1878. It concentrated on high-quality research and the development of a worldwide financial network. It was the first Japanese securities firm to open an office in the United States (1927) and the first to become a member of the New York Stock Exchange.[5] Company operations suffered during World War II and did not re-establish an American presence until the 1950s. Trade between the two countries grew in the late 1960s and `70s, causing Nomura to increase its activities in the U.S. securities markets. Nomura's expansion led to the formation of a wholly owned subsidiary in the 1970s, Nomura Securities International. NSI's expansion required a large number of Americans to be hired. The company's intent was to rely on talented local professionals to further market expansion.[6]

Because Nomura now planned to serve American clients and compete directly with U.S. firms, the company needed Americans who could build the strong client relationships necessary for success. It is important to develop good working relationships with other firms in the industry. Americans were hired to be on the "front lines" and to lend credibility to the firm within the U.S. market.

> NSI however, retained two major competitive advantages over its rivals.

Setting the scene

Following the start of the bull market in 1982, the firm hired several recent American college graduates to work as traders. These new employees had no prior work experience in the securities industry. Nomura

---

5 *Corporate Decision & Reality*, October 1985. "The Many Worlds of Nomura Securities Company," pp. 422-424.

6 *Euromoney*, June 1989.

planned to let them learn on the job and gradually assume more responsibilities. By hiring inexperienced workers, Japanese firms kept down labor costs. New traders went through a learning phase, but they usually grasped the fundamental techniques of stock trading within a few months.

Mark Blanchard and Steve Montana were two traders who were hired directly out of college in 1982 to grade Japanese stocks. Neither had prior work experience in the industry. Before they were assigned to the trading desk, both Mark and Steve spent six months in Tokyo as part of Nomura's in-house training program. While in Tokyo, they learned about the Japanese stock market and local customs and cultural norms.

The fixed income department flourished. This was because of the tremendous placing power Nomura had in its home market where Japanese investors had an almost insatiable appetite for U.S. government securities. Nomura continued to increase its U.S. trading staff in order to become the primary Japanese dealer in American government securities.

In January 1983, Mark and Steve returned to New York and joined the trading desk. Their timing could not have been better. The primary international stock markets (including New York, London and Tokyo) were coming out of the prolonged "bear market" of the 1970s. The Japanese stock market was particularly strong, led by booming Japanese exports.

Fund managers flocked to Nomura for investment advice because it was the market leader in the Japanese securities industry. Clients wanted fast replies to inquiries and requests for bids and offers on block trades. Although Nomura could not deliver quickly enough for American clients, it still remained the best in the industry.

Both Mark and Steve played a central role in the firm's success. They dealt directly with the firm's clients and were an important information source for people who traded American stocks. As the Japanese stock market continued to grow in size and importance, investors in all markets began to show increased interest in the Japanese financial news. Mark and Steve kept the traders of American stocks up to date on special developments in Japan. The American stock traders passed this information along to their clients. In this fashion, the Japanese equities department helped attract business to the burgeoning American equities department.

As time passed, American and European firms began to trade and sell Japanese stocks in the United States. The deregulation of the securities markets in Japan helped expedite the process. As competition increased, NSI gradually lost market share to houses such as Saloman Brothers, Merrill Lynch, and S.G. Warburg. These firms could respond quicker than NSI to customer needs. NSI still had the best research, so most investors directed a portion of their business to NSI. But NSI needed to drastically improve the quality of its client relationships. It was no longer enough to merely retain Americans to interact with customers on the front lines. Nomura, in particular, faced two key issues: The company was operating in markets it should not be in, and it had failed to effectively run a foreign business.[7]

First, its parent company remained the major driving force behind the Japanese stock market. Being the market leader, Nomura dominated the already oligopolistic Japanese Securities market.[8] When it made a strong buy recommendation in Japan, the market usually responded accordingly. NSI's knowledge of which Japanese stocks were likely to be pushed was a tremendous client draw.

7 *The Economist*, Dec. 3, 1988. "Can Japan's Securities Firms Keep the Flag Flying?" pp. 85-86.

8 *Tokyo Business Today* (Japan), December 1988. "Omnipotent Big Four," pp. 12-17.

Second, with the market capitalization of Nomura at about $70 billion, its financial resources far exceeded those of its competitors. Potentially, NSI could tap into this vast source of funds as needed to attract business. NSI easily could have been a market leader in this capacity. Up until this point, however, it had lagged far behind its low-capitalized competition. This was primarily due to Nomura's high-risk aversion and slow client response time.

NSI's other New York departments were having mixed results. The firm's effort to become a major player in the U.S. equity market was proceeding slowly. Despite expanding its New York staff, NSI wasn't making any serious gains in market share. Departing from past practices, NSI hired several high-priced traders in the hope of boosting departmental performance.

> George had no experience trading financial securities. He found it very difficult to gain entrance into the trading business without that experience. Most of the opportunities he found were for lower operations positions.

By 1985, Mark and Steve were seasoned professionals. They had helped the business grow and established strong client relationships. They realized, however, that NSI's performance was rapidly deteriorating. They made frequent recommendations to management on how this trend might be reversed. Their suggestions were ignored, however. The traders in the U.S. equities department were also experiencing similar problems with management. Traders from both departments were becoming increasingly frustrated with policies that hindered their ability to perform. Their dissatisfaction with management's policies became so great that they went on a "wildcat strike" at one point, each trader calling in "sick." This was a drastic measure by the traders to demonstrate to management that their current policies were out of line. Additionally, it showed management the strength and solidarity behind their convictions. That day, NSI's trading operations in both Japanese and U.S. equities were halted. Not only were revenues lost, but the firm's reputation was tarnished. The traders, however, kept their personal relationships with clients. Customers were told the changes sought would benefit both the traders and their accounts by improving service.

Mark and Steve were grossly underpaid. Although experienced traders, their salaries were not much higher than when they joined NSI in 1982. Their counterparts at competing firms earned two or three times as much, worsening their morale.

At the end of 1985, Mark and Steve were seriously considering leaving the firm. That year, both had received specific promises regarding their bonuses that were subsequently broken. At the start of 1986, they continued talking with other firms about jobs. Annual salary raises at NSI were given out at the beginning of April. Once again, both Mark and Steve had been promised significant increases. Once again, they were both disappointed. This time they protested vehemently. The Japanese manager who had promised Mark a large salary increase responded, "We can't pay someone your age so much money." Mark left NSI in May to work for a European firm's New York subsidiary. A few weeks later Mark hired Steve at the firm.

> Mike was viewed by Japanese management as a renegade of sorts who was willing to test the limits of the Japanese business rules and hierarchy. He had an excellent understanding of the underlying forces driving the U.S. securities industry.

George's Tale

In June 1986, George wanted to enter the securities business, particularly to trade stocks. He quit his job at an employee benefits consulting firm to seek work in global finance. George had two brothers who worked in the securities industry. Both knew people who worked, or had worked, at NSI. George learned that Nomura needed traders to replace Mark Blanchard, Steve Montana and some traders from the American equities department who had resigned. George arranged an interview at Nomura to discuss trading opportunities at the firm. Before going on the interview, however, George spoke with Mark Blanchard about what working at Nomura was like.

ADRs (American Depository Receipts) represent Japanese stock that is held by a custodian bank in Japan. One cannot actually take delivery of Japanese stock, but can take delivery of ADRs. ADRs are denominated in dollars, which simplifies their purchase because investors do not have to make foreign exchange arrangements.

Prior to the July 4 holiday in 1986, George interviewed at NSI. Many of the cultural differences Mark had warned George about became readily apparent during the interview. George was greeted by the head of the sales department, Mr. Yoshida, and was whisked into a small conference room. They were joined by another Japanese manager and Mike, the head of the Japanese Equity Trading Department. Mike was a Japanese national, but instead of going by his last name – the custom in Japan – he adopted the American nickname "Mike."

The interview was a success and George was offered a job the next day. He started working for NSI on July 14, 1986.

George was joining a Japanese equity trading department that was in disarray. Mark and Steve had been gone for two months and no Americans were left in the department. Client relationships had deteriorated rapidly, and new traders were desperately needed. Francois Beaudreau, another new trader, also joined the department on July 14. Francois lived in France and the United States as a child and attended Columbia University in New York. Although he had some experience as a retail broker, he was essentially fresh out of college.

Neither George nor Francois had the experience necessary to immediately start trading with clients or other firms. To make matters worse, their boss Mike was the only other trader in the department. Mike was doing his best to keep the business going, which meant that he had little time to train George or Francois. Moreover, Mike was an introvert and did not enjoy interacting with clients.

Mike had been working in the United States for five years and was much more Westernized than his Japanese colleagues. Both George and Francois felt fortunate to be working for Mike, if they had to have a Japanese boss. Mike did not have the authority to make important policy decisions. They were made by senior Japanese managers. The senior managers were typically far removed from the daily operations of the firm, sometimes as far as 7,000 miles away in Tokyo.

Francois and George were initially instructed to sit with the traders in the American equities department. There they were supposed to "watch and listen" in order to learn the fundamentals of stock trading. After a few weeks, however, both felt they had learned as much as they could and were anxious to start trading on their own.

Management, however, did not feel George and Francois were ready for daily trading. George thought this was odd, considering the Japanese equity department was short-handed.

For six months George and Francois watched traders from the U.S. equities department. They did little all day except answer the telephone and relay information to the trading desk. George was growing restless and started to request additional responsibilities. To appease him, management allowed him to start trading Japanese ADRs and NASDAQ, the over-the-counter market.

NSI used to trade a few hundred thousand ADRs each day, but that number recently fell to just a few thousand. Before George could rebuild the client side of the ADR business, he first had to stimulate the firm's trading activity with other market makers on the Street. George gradually built good working relationships with the other major market makers of Japanese ADRs. Within a few months, George was making a modest but steady profit for the firm.

After George had been with NSI for about a year, he took on the added responsibilities of a sales trader for Japanese common stocks. Sales traders provide clients with daily market information and late breaking news, sent orders for execution on stock exchanges, and negotiate prices on trades.

> Even more damaging to the department was Mr. Yamaguchi's responsibilities for position trading for common stock. Because he had little experience in this area, trading losses began to mount. Two months later, his supervisor withdrew Yamaguchi's authority to make investment decisions on his own. In just three months, Mr. Yamaguchi had destroyed the trading operation of the Japanese equities department.

George found it difficult to provide clients with top quality daily Japanese market information. This information was available in New York, but only to those who spoke Japanese. Each morning, the most important news of the day was discussed in a conference call with the Tokyo headquarters. George and Francois had asked several times that the meeting be held in English. The request seemed reasonable, especially because all of the participants spoke English. Management refused to make the change, however.

To further complicate the situation, communication between salesmen and traders was poor. Important information discussed during the conference call was not relayed to traders.

This hindered traders' ability to effectively serve their clients.

George and Francois did their best to cope with the many internal problems at NSI. However, the decline of client interest in Japanese stocks made the situation more difficult and prompted them to seek new ways to stimulate business. Their proposals went unheeded.

Following the stock market crash of October 1987, the business climate deteriorated at NSI. Management began new austerity measures to reduce costs. Cuts were made across the board. The Japanese equities department did not suffer any losses associated with the crash, but it was not spared from cost-cutting measures. Even the department's subscriptions to the Wall Street Journal and the Financial Times were cancelled. The papers had provided information vital to running the trading operation. George and Francois found it difficult to comprehend the logic behind the decision to cancel the newspaper subscriptions.

In February 1988, Mike transferred to Tokyo and was replaced by Mr. Yamaguchi, a bond trader who had been working in Nomura's Hong Kong office for seven years. Because of delays in obtaining a work permit, Mr. Yamaguchi was not expected to arrive until April. During this two-month interim period, George and Francois took on more responsibilities and succeeded in stimulating new business. Their morale rose and for the first time in a long time they enjoyed their work.

This changed drastically, however, soon after Mr. Yamaguchi's arrival in New York. Mr. Yamaguchi had no previous experience trading stocks. Equally important, he was unfamiliar with American business and culture. Mr. Yamaguchi sat quietly and observed during his first few weeks on the job. Quite unexpectedly, however, he began widespread changes. First, in their role as market makers for ADRs and warrants, respectively, George and Francois were not allowed to take any positions unless specifically to fill a client's order. This eliminated almost all trading with other brokers, which effectively ended NSI's role as a market maker for these instruments.

As business in the Japanese equities department slowed to a virtual standstill, George and Francois once again became proficient at crossword puzzles. They found it nearly impossible to maintain a working relationship with their new boss. Mr. Yamaguchi would announce only in Japanese the location of department meetings. Not able to understand Japanese, George and Francois often missed meetings. When they failed to show up, Mr. Yamaguchi would be angry and demand an explanation.

George and Francois found it increasingly difficult to attract business. The sales and trading departments seldom cooperated, keeping each other in the dark about individual client needs and activities. NSI could not make bids and offers to clients upon request. Mistrust between Americans and Japanese hurt NSI's ability to build relationships, internally and externally.

Mr. Yamaguchi also wanted to change interaction with clients and other employees at the company. One incident, in particular, led to a heated confrontation between George and Mr. Yamaguchi. George was now responsible for covering NSI's other U.S. branch offices in Honolulu, Los Angeles, Chicago and San Francisco. These offices were small operations consisting primarily of retail brokers, support staff, and a few institutional salesmen. In addition to executing their orders, George provided each office with a daily market analysis. Mr. Yamaguchi informed George that he must give this information directly to Mr. Honda, the sales manager of the Honolulu branch. George's attempts to talk to Mr. Honda were a disaster. Mr. Honda's English was poor and he spoke with a heavy accent. Mr. Honda suggested to George that it might be easier to talk to someone in the office who spoke better English. George agreed, but Mr. Yamaguchi continued to insist that George speak directly with Honda.

Late one Friday afternoon, Mr. Yamaguchi brought up the subject again during a meeting with George and a Japanese salesman. Once again, George tried to explain the problem. Yamaguchi replied, "You must spend more time in Chinatown so you can learn how to understand people who speak English with an Asian accent." At first, George thought the remark was a joke, but he soon realized Mr. Yamaguchi was serious. Mr. Yamaguchi went on to explain to George that if he expected to become a "true businessman," he must overcome his inability to understand people with a foreign accent.

George was exasperated by Mr. Yamaguchi's failure to recognize the need for foreign nationals to respect the language and customs of their host country. He attacked Mr. Yamaguchi for his unprofessional behavior and lack of cultural respect. Mr. Yamaguchi was stunned that a subordinate would dare raise his voice, especially in front of another person. George returned to his desk to consider his options. He had some decisions to make.

Questions

If Nomura is to succeed in the United States, what changes in policies and procedures are necessary with regards to:

a   trading;

b   customer relations;

c   information distribution;

d   trader discretion;

e   diversity management;

f   and corporate finance, investment and structure?

Note: See "The globalization of business ethics: Why America remains distinctive," by David Fogel in Chapter 3 – Ethics *of this book for discussion of Nomura's ethical violations.*

27. Misr Acrylic and American Standard[9]

Additional topics covered: quality control, organizational culture, managerial decision-making.

Is corporate culture a function of the corporate lifecycle?

Misr Acrylic is an Egyptian company established in 1986 under law no. 159 as a private shareholding firm. With the increasing success of the company and the growing market for acrylic bathtubs, the firm entered into a joint venture with American Standard in 1988.

American Standard is a multinational corporation with a production facility in the 10th of Ramadan City. Instead of building a new factory for producing acrylic bathtubs, the company entered a 25 percent share venture with Misr Acrylic to manufacture them.

Industry and technology

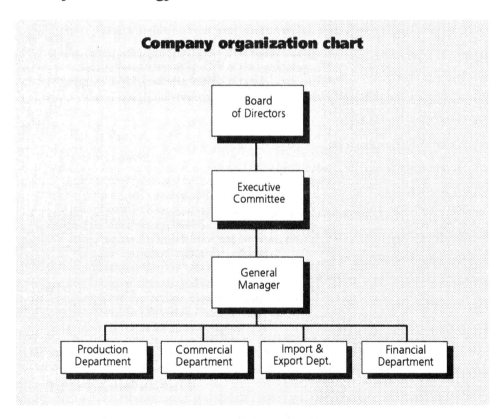

Company organization chart

Board of Directors → Executive Committee → General Manager → Production Department, Commercial Department, Import & Export Dept., Financial Department

---

9   By Dr. Tarek Hatem, Assistant Professor, and Maged Ayoub, graduate student, Management Department, American University, Cairo, Egypt. Used with permission.

The first acrylic bathtub was produced in October 1986. The local market at that time was dominated by imported bathtubs made of steel and cast iron. The Egyptian consumer was not familiar with the acrylic bathtub, and the company expected resistance because acrylic is perceived as plastic, while cast iron and steel are seen as metal.

Technology for manufacturing was transferred through an English consulting firm that supplied and installed the equipment and set up production.

Management Style

Due to the relatively young age of the general manager, his style of management followed the Lyckert's System 4 Style of Participative Management. All decisions were made in brainstorming meetings, where decisions are taken in a group.

History and culture

The company began with an entrepreneurial-dominated structure. A 30-year-old civil engineer was appointed general manager, and he reported to an executive committee that represented shareholders. Due to the location of the factory at the 10th of Ramadan City, many workers were hired from the Sharkiya governorate.

When production began, the general manager assumed a kind of informal division of labor. He developed excellent relationships with workers and encouraged them, especially when the company was getting on its feet.

The general manager spent most of his time on the shop floor talking to the workers and monitoring the progress of the various production runs.

Company Structure

With the increasing sales due to the company's pursuit of vertical integration strategy and product development, Misr Acrylic was entering stage II of its life cycle where it had to develop a functional structure.

The new production manager and import and export manager were friends of the general manager and believed in his style of promoting an informal company culture.

During the start up of the company, a 52-year-old commercial manager was appointed to plan the company's marketing strategy.

These problems were solved with one move. Acrylic sheets were stored as consigned stock (not paid) at the Port Said free zone area, which reduced purchasing time from three months to ten days. Thus, problems with cash flow and the backlog of unavailable sheets were solved.

The venture

From 1987 to 1988 the company sold its own brand of acrylic bathtubs. Sales were sluggish and expensive TV promotions were launched.

American Standard, a leader in the sanitary ware business, recently opened a factory in the 10th of Ramadam City to produce vitreous china. To complete its range of bathtubs, the company approached Misr Acrylic about producing acrylic bathtubs as part of a joint venture. American Standard purchased 25 percent of the company's shares in 1988.

The deal only included production of American Standard's range according to international specifications without any interference in Misr Acrylic's management.

The growth

After this venture, sales of American Standard products boomed because the well-recognized brand name created a perception of quality and luxury for acrylic bathtubs in the Egyptian market. Misr Acrylic, seeing a sales trend, created more luxurious models to capitalize on the change in consumer tastes.

The company sought international markets and secured deals for the supply of acrylic bathtubs in West Germany, Austria, France, Italy, and Holland.

> Misr Acrylic's general manager, fearing a loss of the prevailing culture that had been so crucial in the company's success, insisted on having a controlling share to prevent any further share purchases by American Standard.

Finance and raw material

The present management team at Misr Acrylic faced three problems:

1 Waits of up to three months for delivery of acrylic sheets.

2 Constant changing of models and colors to suit tastes in local and international markets. This made it difficult to forecast raw materials purchasing.

3 Cash flow problem because of long waits for delivery of raw materials and the credits given to clients.

International marketing

With these two major problems out of the way, the company continued to increase market share locally and internationally. Continuous innovations in new models and increased exports supported this growth. Sales of export improved from 3,000 units in 1989 to 9,000 in 1990 to 18,000 units in 1991. The company was establishing itself as a potential threat to European acrylic bathtub producers.

Technology change

Acrylic bathtubs in their current form were produced by vacuum thermoforming of the colored acrylic sheet. Then they were sprayed with fiberglass to reinforce the back of the bathtub.

American Standard, however, introduced a new technique that would make traditional manufacturing obsolete.

After convincing the board of directors of the need for changing the technology, American Standard increased its share in Misr Acrylic from 25 percent to 40 percent.

American Standard's culture

The company was a subsidiary of the American-owned MNC. Like all multinationals the subsidiary was totally autonomous and the division was considered as an investment center.

Profitability was heavily stressed. The general manager of the subsidiary presented monthly reports to the mother company about changes in the market and profitability. Headquarters attempted to coordinate its operating divisions through performance and results-oriented reporting systems and by stressing corporate planning techniques. Clear hierarchy and lines of command greatly reduced flexibility in decision-making.

Disadvantages of the MNC division:

1. Lack of strategic vision between employees, due to the large size of MNC.

2. Extreme pressures on employees because of the nature of achievement orientation, thus reducing informal relations.

Questions

1 What difficulties might Misr Acrylic encounter in implementing the new requirements and quality control techniques of the new bathtub manufacturing technology?

2 What impact will the new technology have on factory worker culture and on the

28. Ferox manufactured products[10]

November 1989, the Velvet Revolution

It was unusually cold for that time of the year, and the several hundred employees of Ferox Děčín who gathered in the yard could see their breath. Facing them, standing on an unloaded railroad wagon, was the managing director, Radek Malec.[11]
The time was exactly noon. Millions of people in Czechoslovakia stopped working that noon. Just as in Děčín, people gathered in meeting rooms, corridors, cafeterias, classrooms, and factory yards and went into the streets with one thing on their minds: making this the very last week of Communist rule in Czechoslovakia.

But few managing directors shared this goal, and even fewer were able to face their subordinates at this critical moment. Many of this elite group knew that it would be better not to show up. However, Radek Malec did face the volatile crowd at Ferox. After decades of mistrust between workers and managers, Malec knew that what he was going to say would be decisive for his own future, as well as for the future of Ferox.

October 1991

Radek Malec, managing director of Ferox, as gas and chemical company, has just read the Czech Republic's public announcement of Ferox's proposed privatization plan. Before proceeding with his plans, Malec had to wait for the U.S. company Air Products and Chemicals (APCI), to purchase controlling interest in Ferox and to allow for competing proposals to be brought forward. Although he has had little time to marvel at the monumental changes he and Ferox have experienced, he has devoted considerable energy to planning for the acquisition of Ferox by APCI.

---

10 By Jone Pearce and Michal Čakrt, *Managing in Emerging Market Economics: Cases from the Czech and Slovak Republics,* edited by Dan S. Fogel, 1994, by permission of Westview Press, Boulder, Colorado, pages 73-90.

11 The names of all the individuals in this case have been changed.

Background

Ferox is located in Děčín, a northeastern industrial city near the German border. The company was founded during World War II to produce chemicals and chemical equipment for the military. At the end of the war it was confiscated as Nazi property by the Czechoslovak government and began to produce simple agricultural chemical products.

Until 1989 Ferox was a component of one of the biggest Czechoslovak industrial trusts. In 1991, as a result of the first phase of the privatization process, it became a separate joint stock company with stock held by the government. By October 1991, Ferox was governed by an operating board that included people from the company (the chairman of this board was the deputy director for engineering), from other companies, and also from the government ministries. It was anticipated that in the second phase of the privatization the state would offer its shares to potential buyers.

At the time of this study, Ferox had three main product lines: cryogenic equipment, chemical equipment, and air-cooling systems for the chemical industry's long-distance pipelines. In January 1991, Ferox began selling gas, and this line was assumed by its joint venture with APCI. In 1991, the company was working with APCI on a new gas manufacturing joint venture.

Ferox's customers have been many and varied. Before the 1989 revolution, 40-45 percent of the company's market was dependent, either directly or indirectly, on the Soviet market. In 1991, only 1.5-2 percent of their sales came from that market because their former Soviet customers did not have the convertible currency to pay for Ferox purchases. In October 1991, Ferox had 1,350 employees organized into six functional departments: production services, production, commerce (included purchasing and sales), economics (accounting), personnel, and engineering (see Figure x.x). Ferox had annual sales of approximately $15 million.

Ferox formally submitted in October 1991 a privatization project to the Czech Republic Privatization Ministry and awaited approval. In accordance with the law, the proposal required that 3 percent of the shares would be set aside for a reserve fund for restitution to the original owners of companies. In addition, Ferox's proposal reserved 3 percent of the shares for employee purchase and 52 percent for purchase by APCI, with the remaining 42 percent of the shares allocated for purchase by Czech citizens through the government's voucher program. Shares purchased through vouchers must be held by the original purchasers for two years, until after the privatization of the entire economy is completed, before they can be traded. Revenue from the 55 percent of shares to be purchased by employees and by APCI would go to the National Property Fund.

Radek Malec, managing director

In other companies, the whole management was changed after the revolution, and those companies have had a lot of difficulties. Oftentimes they put researchers and design engineers in charge who are smart but don't really know how to run a company. They believed that all of the old contacts and relations would be useless, that people needed to be replaced because they could not change their behavior. The people expected big changes. We changed the government, why not change the management? They wanted to see blood. We at Ferox devoted a lot of energy to this transition. There was strong opposition to retaining top management, but people recognized quickly that we were playing an honest game. I believe our continuity was well chosen, and we have been able to change.

Since the very beginning of the revolution, I had close contact with the Civic Forum committee, the umbrella anti-regime movement, in this plant and we agreed to share information with each other. I kept emphasizing that we didn't want the different political factions fighting here. We have to cooperate at work. If two individuals who must work together in the production process are fighting, the work cannot go on. After the purges following the Soviet invasion of 1968, working relationships were disrupted for nearly ten years and cooperation was damaged. I knew that the company would bear the most unpleasant results for years to come if we had fighting here. I met frequently with the Civic Forum and emphasized the damage that would be done by the clashes here. I met often with the company's branch of the People's Militia and I tried to persuade them to remain calm and to accept that the situation had changed. I emphasized that everyone needed to respect that we were here for production and that the political changes should not destroy the company on which we all depended.

Certain people tried to use the political changes to advance their own positions. They really didn't care about the political changes or the company, only themselves. They tried to take advantage of the situation. Because the Civic Forum was a broad umbrella movement, anyone could say they were a member. We agreed to involve Civic Forum in the operation of the company by giving it a seat on the operating board of the company and by inviting its representatives trade union-management meetings, but because Civic Forum was participating in the running of the company, it had to be responsible for the behavior of its members. In this way we were able to prevent these opportunists from taking over the company. We even had a bulletin board that Civic Forum could use. It once posted a notice that was very critical of management, and a foreman took the notice down. I put it back up, I felt that if we agreed to let them have a bulletin board we had to live with whatever they put there. Later, we banned the participation of all political parties in the company. So, when the Civic Forum itself broke apart into political parties, it eventually lost its seat on these management committees too.

"Even during the most uncertain period of the revolution, we were able to keep production going with relatively little loss. People would start work a little later because they were busy exchanging news with each other when they arrived at the plant, and their breaks were a little longer for the same reason. But we had to be reasonable and couldn't take a hard line with them."

Not once have we in top management been caught lying. That was very important. People saw that management was working to protect the company from attacks. We had to show our people that we are here to protect their future. No one had to leave the company, and with the exception of one of my deputies, no one has left. I have had a job offer for more than double my salary here, but we all have a sense of responsibility to the company. When we had a problem with an order about one year ago, many people worked extra hours to save the good name of the company even though the problem was not their fault.

I first brought in CAPA consulting back in 1988 because I wanted to change two

"Under our old system, the scope of responsibilities for a company's managing director were much wider than in the West, but the authority was much narrower. We have different tasks to do every day. We are a typical Czech company: we have a kinder-garten; we own and maintain apartments for our employees; we have canteens. Up to five years ago, we were also responsible for our seventy-ton quota of dry hay."

attitudes in my managers: the system is perfect and problems are only created by people failing to carry out their jobs, and things don't change. I wanted them to know that the structure may change. Thanks to this cooperation [between CAPA and Ferox], we were able to anticipate, well before the revolution, the changes now being required of all companies.

Ten to fifteen years ago, the local authority discovered a shortage of hay. All companies in its region were made responsible for a quota of hay. Our assigned meadows were inaccessible for heavy mowing equipment, so we had to select those people from Ferox who understood how to work hand scythes. Our managerial problem was how to choose people who knew how to cut hay. Which employees were needed least that day? Who knew how to use scythes? Even our lawyer went out to cut hay. We had to provide lunches and transportation for them. Then the local authority decided that yields were too low, so we were invited to purchase a quota of fertilizer each spring. Later, the local authority decided that because we were contributing something of economic value to the agricultural cooperative, they should "pay us" for this work. So they paid us 40 koruny per ton – but our own cost was over 150 koruny per ton. After that, we bought a specialized machine to cut on these steep hillsides. A couple of years ago, this responsibility ceased, so now our problem is, who do we sell this equipment to?

Now we can laugh at it. It is the same as looking back on your experience as an army draftee: you look back and only see the comical aspects, you remember the amusing things. It was too crazy. We are here to produce chemical equipment. But then it was different – it was impossible to quarrel about it. It was horrible.

The procurement problem was much bigger than the sales problem. It was a dictatorship of the suppliers; now, this system is gone. We need to increase our sales department by two or three times, and we lack sales methodology and experience. At present, the situation in our country is still very unstable. Even trying to understand all of the information that comes out each week is hard. Nobody knows what will happen tomorrow. But we are firmly committed to the belief that this company will survive. We believe in our capability to find solutions to our problems. This belief has three pillars.

The first pillar is improvisation. Every day brings new information. One example of how we have improvised our management of the internal debt

"We have to spend a lot more energy to find new customers now. Someone from your system really cannot under-stand us. Five years ago, this was a strictly planned economy. The main problem was to organize production under conditions in which we were overloaded. The sales forecast was known two years in advance because the only customer was the state. The major problem was to meet the state's special requests for exports – through which the state hoped to make some extra hard-currency profits. Now, we have to find our own customers. Before, we had to take gifts to our suppliers in order to secure scarce deliv-eries; now, we take gifts to our customers."

problem. Today, we owe our suppliers about 60 million koruny, and our customers owe us 150 million koruny – this latter is the value of over three months of our production. Most of our suppliers retire their debt within the ninety-day period. We have only about five customers who have not paid us within ninety days. They are all big state-owned companies. One is the national railroad. It is impossible to know whether these are bad debts. We cannot imagine that the country will let the state-owned railroad go bankrupt. But we do now know whether a Western partner will come in and help any of these companies to become profitable. Everything is uncertain right now. Recently, we invoiced about 77 million koruny but received only 37 million koruny. Compared to the rest of Czechoslovak industry, we are in good shape.

Another example of how we have learned to improvise started with one of our suppliers. Our stainless steel supplier wrote us a letter saying, "You owe us five million koruny, so we have decided to postpone your next delivery for two months because you haven't paid us." When this letter arrived, we had to solve that problem immediately. So we discovered that we have knowledge of which companies owe money to other companies. We discovered that the steel mill is a supplier of pig iron to the stainless steel manufacturer, and the steel mill is one of our customers. We found a complete circle of debt. So we got all of the economics deputies for all three companies together and we agreed to simultaneously cancel as much of this circle of debt as possible. Each controller crossed the debt off the ledger and sent a fax to confirm.

> "The second pillar is privatization. There are several reasons we believe privatization is the most important precondition for reaching our long-term goal. First, we need investment money, and it is simply not available from local sources. We need new technology to modernize, to reach European technical standards. We need to improve our physical infrastructure to be more efficient."

This was so successful that we have tried to find other complete debt circles – some involve four parties, some even more. We have now hired one person whose sole responsibility is to try to clear debts in this way. But if there had been a computer network connecting us with all our customers and suppliers – which is not the case yet – we could be much more efficient. It is estimated that the entire Czechoslovak industry has 100 to 150 billion koruny of this internal debt, equal to one-third of the country's gross domestic product.

Second, we need know-how. What I mean by know-how is how to organize. We need information about how to conduct successful sales activities, to overhaul the financing system and the accounting system, and we need managerial know-how. The smallest difference between us and the West is the difference between our shop floor workers. Our welders are highly skilled. We need injections of knowledge, but we don't want to copy the West thoughtlessly. The West is the source of information, but it is up to us to use the information properly to reach our goals.

I feel that the biggest difference is in sales activities. Before I thought it was just: How do you sell something? Now, after working for a year with APCI, I see that it is much more than that. The main thing is to get customers who will be able to pay, and how we can help someone who is interested in buying find the means to pay.

"The third pillar for our survival is our long-term strategy. Our long-term goal is to become one of the most prosperous companies in the country by European standards. Privatization is our next objective but not our ultimate goal. It is not why we are here. It is a conduit, a tool to help us reach our goal. Privatization has taken a great deal of our time and attention, and we hope it will end soon. Now, we must wait for final approval. We don't want any agitation that might disrupt or slow down the government's approval of privatization."

At present, there is a coalition government and there is a great deal of political jockeying, as well as uncertainty about future political stability. We have an interim postrevolutionary parliament to guide the nation through the immediate postrevolutionary turmoil and develop a new constitution. Because we are a government-owned company, there is always the risk that the politicians will want to use us for political purposes. However, we are not very worried about this because we are in a relatively good shape economically and have a good privatization plan, and they have enough other things to worry about. We are trying to get away from political interference and be fully independent as quickly as we can, and we must be privatized to do that. Until we are privatized, we cannot do anything – we cannot sell property or reorganize.

As part of our privatization agreement, we have had numerous discussions with APCI about what we should do to reach our long-term goals. The agreement covers the training they will provide for our people in their facilities, know-how transfer, and so on.

We found APCI two years ago, before the revolution. As part of our 1988 strategic plan, developed with a consulting company, we began to look for Western companies with which to form a joint venture. Of course, we were too modest and vague at the beginning. We were just looking for someone to talk to us. We didn't know enough then. You can't create big plans without information. Before that, we had a bad experience trying to make contact with a Russian company, so we began to look for a Western company. We contracted the major companies in the industry. Only APCI was willing to sit with us then. During a conference in the United Kingdom, several of our researchers had an initial confidential discussion with several people from APCI. We offered them certain opportunities.

Then the revolution arrived and we realized very quickly that we would be facing economic reforms. We have been a monopolist supplier for most of our customers. We felt that this monopoly was neither sustainable nor desirable. Now we could see that the currency becoming convertible would not only allow foreign competition here but would also allow us to go international. We saw that we would soon be facing a normal market, and we did not have the know-how.

Of all the major companies we approached, APCI seemed the most flexible. About January or February 1990, we started our first real discussions. One of APCI's Western competitors had formed a joint venture with one of our customers. APCI expressed its interest in our gas separators and cryogenic units. In April 1990, I visited the company, but still not openly; it would have been dangerous to release information at that time.

In July 1990, we signed a letter of intent for the first joint venture, scheduled for the second quarter of 1991. This joint venture involves the new business, gas production, as well as the transfer of our existing cryogenic business to APCI.

In January 1991, we began our own gas business. We wanted to show APCI that we could get it started without them. We have only about 10 percent of the market, but because many of the customers who depended on us for necessary equipment also buy gas, we thought we would be able to influence more of them to do business with us in the future. Because our containers are 30 percent cheaper than any they can get elsewhere and are just as good, we hoped to retain and even increase our market share for both gas and equipment.

After more months of discussions we created the joint venture with APCI, which came into formal existence in April 1991. APCI owns 51 percent and Ferox, 49 percent. The joint-venture agreement also covers the distribution and sales of cryogenic equipment and liquified gases in Central and Eastern Europe, over which the joint venture has exclusive dealership.

Now we are working on the second joint venture, a large refinery that the first joint venture will need to produce the gas. It is a $70 million project that involves Ferox, APCI, and another Czechoslovak company. We signed the letter of intent in March 1991.

Finally, we agreed to the marriage of Ferox with APCI through the privatization program. They have controlling interest because they like to control what they are paying for. We had to show APCI that we were a good prospect. We have established markets. There is some synergy in the cryogenics area.

"Right now, neither APCI nor Ferox can pull out. This is a marriage with no possibility of a divorce. We are proud that we were able to get a company from the West, that we found the right worm for the hook. U.S. companies often appear too lazy and afraid. The Germans are the most aggressive here; they know the market, the territory, and our mentality."

Sometimes they don't understand how it is here. I was describing to Heinz Hoffman, the European vice president, and Bill Stoughton, the U.S. chief engineer, how we would use the dependence of our tank customers on us to influence them to buy gas from us. Stoughton put his head in his hands; he was so horrified by the rough way we do business here. But Hoffman, who fled East Germany years ago, said, "Good, good." He understood the situation and got the point right away. You in the West have developed an excellent system for yourselves over the years; you are used to shooting with a silencer on your guns. But we live in the real Wild East during this period here. You Americans can afford to be all polite and honest. If you act like that in this environment today, you won't get anywhere. It's a lot of trouble to explain.

APCI feels that we are a large company; Ferox will be its biggest manufacturing facility. APCI has 250 people in its U.S. plant and 250 in its UK plant. Its target is to increase our efficiency. We wonder what will be the effect on the other parts of our company, where APCI has no product expertise. Our agreement with APCI says employment will be kept at a reasonable level based on profit in all of the product lines. There is also another uncertainty: after privatization, what will we do with our service work? Some of it may be more efficiently provided by us, but each case has to be examined in detail. APCI wanted me to hire a security service. We have them now in Czechoslovakia, but they usually have only lazy, young people. These pensioners we have now are the cheapest, best solution for us.

For each of these services I will want to review options such as retraining it or leasing it. After privatization, I want to create a steering committee made up of high-

"APCI managers are very slow and careful. They evaluate projects step-by-step. They evaluate, then they estimate the finances; they check and check again. I can see how deeply interested the Americans are in the finances, so that even if an order is cancelled it will still make money."

level managers from APCI and Ferox to study these areas – people with sufficient knowledge to go through it all and to indicate our weak points. The chief of APCI's manufacturing facility told me, "Don't copy us."

Before, Ferox was a core manufacturing facility. All of the other kinds of tasks were done by others, for example, the foreign trade companies handled foreign sales. Now we are free to do this work ourselves, but we don't have anyone who understands how to write these contracts, issue letters of credit, conduct currency transfers, and so on. Today, we know about 50 percent of what it takes to make a good deal.

Now, I can see that a successful company is cautious, and why. What is the customers' ability to pay? Sometimes I have been disappointed in the cautious, slow progress in negotiations with APCI. It is their natural style. They must be sure of success. APCI has an entire system of making offers: stages one, two, and three. They protect their power and capability. Even after a U.S. group said that our second joint-venture plan was financially sound, the European Bank for Reconstruction and Development (to whom we have applied for a loan) requires yet another group of Western financial experts to examine the project. This project will have a firm base. Before the 1989 revolution, getting investment money was a grammar exercise. Who could paint the rosiest future? Or an important minister might have a pet project, and then after it was built, someone had to find a market for its production.

To inform the employees about the privatization program, we had to respond to their natural reaction: What will be the future of the company? In the spring, we started to organize meetings of employees, and we explained it to them – all that we knew and our intentions. We have been lucky to retain the trust of our people. We don't have any problems with public disobedience like they sometimes do elsewhere. Of course, the people here have mixed feelings about the relationship with APCI. Many are afraid of losing their jobs. APCI expects us to strictly reduce our staff because productivity is very low here.

There are different levels of employee interest in the privatization program. Some employees would like to talk about it all night. When we had our April meeting to explain the privatization project, we filled our largest canteen to overflowing. We always have our meetings right after the first shift. This was a very good turnout, almost a third of those who were not required to be at their stations. Many employees still take things lightheartedly. Management's job is to see that employees give 105 percent (the 5 percent is overtime for some extra income; employees don't want more overtime than that because it would cut into their free time). Many believe their only job is to show up at the start of the shift. Quality? Well, everyone makes mistakes. But most here have a sense of responsibility. If they are caught stealing or drinking on the job, they are fired immediately. The trade union supports this policy. APCI agreed to respect the trade union in the privatization agreement.

We are confident that we will have our approval for privatization by the end of

1991. Then we can begin to implement our privatization plan: restructuring the company and selling the support services and equipment we don't need. We need to provide a stable environment in the next three months. We want the image of a smoothly running company. The next couple of months is going to be decisive for many years to come.

Karel Nýč, Commercial Manager

In the past, we negotiated only delivery date and price. Now we negotiate much more. For example, we have added penalties for late payment. One of the ways I try to tell whether we are going to have trouble collecting payment from a potential customer is if they want to negotiate over the penalties. In addition, if it is a customer I don't know well, I ask our economics department to use its good connections with the banker to find out whether the company is in a good financial position.

Now, we have some completely new customers, but Ferox is unknown in the West. One new customer, a Japanese company, is making a purchase from us. Its representatives have just made their ninth visit to the plant in four months; they come twice a month. This Japanese company has very detailed rules for technical requirements. The require sixteen different checks on a flange. They require more detailed production plans and that these plans be provided very rapidly. I have to put more pressure on the technical department to get us information quickly to make a proposal.

Western customers want a quote back in ten days and will not even look at it if it comes in after that. Pressure from my department affects all areas. There is more pressure on the pricing department to provide information more rapidly.

"For this big Japanese project, after we had a firm order I called a meeting of all of the directors. Previously, this was completely unheard of. I wanted them to know that this was an important order."

We have not made these same changes for our old customers – we treat their orders as we always have. So far, we are closely tracking new accounts only because this still requires a lot of effort. But these new customers force us to make gradual changes in purchasing, planning, production, and control. We are not as computerized as APCI; we have many workers in purchasing and only two terminals. They must do their spreadsheets and economic analyses by hand. Due to these changes, other departments are under more pressure. There are lots of new activities emerging; many people have to do new things to change their jobs, and they complain. Under the old system, everything was petrified; everything was done the same way for decades. People do not know how to change, and they are reluctant. I know very well that they should get some training, but for the time being, we have to change on the go. Later, perhaps when APCI gets in, there will be more opportunity to work in a more structured fashion.

Another difference is that we have to make our own sales directly. Before the revolution, for foreign sales we went through one of the foreign trade companies. You know, before there was this almost insurmountable barrier between us and the outside world. In about six months we are going to have to establish a Ferox office

"All of these changes take time and money. I have to find a real manager for each activity. It's not easy to ask a fifty-year-old to learn German and to master a computer. Before, the customers always came to us. Now, the sales people have to visit the customers and they don't like to travel. Before, we were so overloaded with orders that the customers came to us. All of that has to change."

in Prague because we cannot get people with foreign-trade skills to move here. For some sales business, it is easier for customers to fly into Prague and for us to meet them there.

We cannot know what our focus should be in three years. Nowadays our best customer can change into our worst customer in six months. For example, Poland has changed its customs duties six times in the past year. Even the banks do not know what is really happening in the companies. For the next few years, the winners will be those who survive.

Jaroslav Mráček, Production Manager

We have one goal: to survive the next two years. We sacrifice everything for this goal. There are multiplying pressures for quality of production, especially for the blue-collar workers – the exempt workers were already working at a high standard. I will need two or three more managers in production. Some of my managers held party posts and were members of the so-called People's Militia. The new law forces me to remove them from management positions for the next five years.

Unfortunately, production has traditionally had a lower status than other areas; therefore, it has always been difficult to attract good people. It's a high-pressure job; managers have to resolve conflicts every day. They would rather escape to the laboratories.

The blue-collar workers are often so naive. They don't understand that if they want the same living standards as the Germans, they have to accept the whole package. The way I let them know that standards are higher now is by fully supporting the head of quality control. This is a big change. Previously, quality control was the enemy of the production department. I really need to support the quality-control manager because his people are even worse. Quality is the production supervisors' responsibility; they have the ultimate responsibility for quality. Now, the pressure on them is more accentuated. I have been in this job for a year, and my first and most important goal is to improve production quality.

Many of the employees understand, but some do not; it depends on their maturity. Some are much too self-confident. They agree, in general, that they need to improve themselves, but they want to start with someone else. They are used to comparing their work to that done in other companies in Czechoslovakia, and our work has always been good. Now that we are exposed to the West, we see poorer comparative results. The skill levels are high, but there is a lot of complacency.

We have been introducing the International Standards Organization Program for quality improvement that we received from APCI. It involves monthly meetings run by the production unit manager. Before, the meetings were always focused on party politics, but the employees now recognize that the accent has changed. I have asked the personnel manager to add more information on quality to the new employee training programs. I approached the local technical college to work with them [the college] to change their curriculum – we cannot wait for the Education Ministry.

The union has been flexible and supportive so far, although sometimes it can be unreasonable and want to have influence without responsibility. The union doesn't protect employees who are doing a bad job.

"APCI managers have voiced their dislikes. Our technical procedures are inadequate, our product line is too broad, and we need to focus. But in choosing which products to drop, we cannot make an error because it would involve the loss of many millions of koruny of revenue. APCI itself could be more diversified. There is no reason they cannot sell various equipment as we do. Different products would help them cope with instability in other lines. Not all in APCI have the same opinion. Some see far ahead and want the long-term prosperity of the company."

Our progress on quality improvement was reviewed by the chief APCI quality man the last time he was here, and he was not happy with our progress. He lives in quite another world. People who have spent some time here have adjusted better. We were given thousands of pages of English text to process. He says we are too slow; he has doubts about whether we are committed to change.

It's clear that whatever benefits APCI brings to us, it will also take care of itself. There are lots of completely new situations here. APCI managers have problems knowing who they can trust here. They will face the problem of picking the right people to run Ferox their way, people who have enough energy to turn it around. It will be an enormous amount of work for domestic people. We know that we are all being tested by them. They have been coming here for more than a year and are working around here freely, looking to see if the pace is fast enough. They are evaluating me and the commerce director especially.

I am convinced that APCI was the right company to make a deal with. We want to enter this marriage without debts and with no liabilities. We want our performance level as close as possible to APCI's even though that is almost impossible. As soon as we achieve that level, it will be easier for us.

We must manage ourselves. But APCI should tell us our goals – so we are moving in the right direction. I'm glad APCI is a U.S. company because I am uncomfortable with the way German business people behave here; the Americans have a milder style. I did not hesitate to support the choice of APCI because the U.S. market is larger and more dynamic and the United States is the technical leader in many respects.

When APCI management gets control of Ferox, we will learn a lot of things we don't know now. I fully understand that APCI cannot tell us everything freely yet.

Vladislav Petrovka, Personnel Manager

Everything in this department will be affected by APCI's involvement. This is because we have never had a real human resources department in Děčín. Recruitment, performance evaluation, professional development, career planning, civilized ways of handling retirement – all are undeveloped here. I can see hardly any area that will be unaffected.

In this department, we are responsible for all of the support activities – canteens, kindergartens, company flats, company-provided health care – as well as for seeing to building maintenance and for ordering office supplies, for example. At present, compensation and benefits are in the economics department, but we really feel they should be our business.

My biggest headache is dealing with the serious blow to the personnel department's staff in the aftermath of the November revolution. This department was a stronghold of the Communist party and despised by many. Here were stored the secret files on employees; and the employees were not supposed to be able to see them. This department was a refuge for many incompetent workers for whom the party found comfortable positions. Several people were removed in this department after the revolution. It was no tragedy that some of them left, given their attitudes and orientation.

> "The worst effect has been in the minds of the people: the assumption that we in personnel are dispensable. Many people think we are still doing the same political activities, for example, keeping secret files on people. Our real work – supervising the support activities – is less visible, and they don't see our role in those tasks."

With the exception of the managing director, the supervisors and managers are not interested in using this department effectively. If a supervisor needing a blue-collar worker comes in here, he tells us to get one and "don't you dare deliver one I don't like." But supervisors will not provide any details about their requirements. The delivery system must work, but quality isn't important to them.

It is a difficult task to teach every manager how to be more effective. Some supervisors mistreat their subordinates, so the best people sometimes leave. Some go to other companies, some decide to start their own businesses. Many bosses have no concept that they should take care of their employees' continuous development.

The burden of the past forty years is on our backs. Personnel policy is still something of a dirty word. There would be an uproar if I developed a succession plan – it would be seen as the restitution of the old "cadre reserve system" by which the party controlled positions. In that system, the party looked first for the most loyal people, then within that group, they tried to find the most suitable person for the position. Those in the personnel department were the party's mouth. The stink of the party's dead body is all over us.

Air Products and Chemicals, Inc.

Background

Air Products and Chemicals, Inc. (APCI) is an international gas products corporation of 15,000, headquartered in the United States, in Allentown, Pennsylvania, with $3 billion in annual sales. The APCI acquisition of Ferox was negotiated by a team of U.S., German, and British APCI executives. Initially, Nigel Chandler, a British APCI executive, was appointed as managing director of the new Ferox-Air Products joint venture. In the following interview, Chandler shares his experiences and observations on the challenges Western companies face in acquiring and forming joint ventures in the new Czech and Slovak republics.

Nigel Chandler, joint-venture managing director

I think you can see that Malec really runs Ferox. Last year in APCI there was a great deal of debate about the direction we were moving in forming this relationship with Ferox. You can imagine that it was a difficult decision. I genuinely believe it was the right decision. We will bring several important contributions to Ferox.

First, we bring know-how, which is a lot more than sheer technical knowledge. We bring specific know-how about the gas business. We know how to sell it commercially and where to make changes. We are a large successful gas company. Management skills that we bring are important also, but they're more difficult to define.

"Second, we bring financial and accounting skills. Quite clearly, the free market accounting system needs to be adopted – particularly pricing and costing systems, which barely exist now. Everything was done by rules under the old system. We are setting up our accounting systems with the hope that they will be in accordance with the new Czechoslovak tax laws, which are due in January 1993. But at this point we don't even know what kinds of business expenses will be deductible in computing taxes."

Third, regarding the privatization, APCI brings technological skills, as well as marketing skills. Ferox brings local knowledge and a low-cost manufacturing base. It also has an existing customer base. We want to be able to manufacture our products here and also to export our products from this plant to the West. Compared to our other plants, we can make the product significantly more cheaply here.

It is important to us that any acquisitions are made with the full support of local management. We need tremendous mutual cooperation. We think it is a good agreement, but we didn't undertake it lightly. It's not just the money, but the time. Heinz Hoffman, our European vice president, is spending a great deal of time on this project, and our senior legal people are spending a lot of time on it as well. It is a tremendous investment of our most valuable managerial resources. The senior managers are very involved.

Of course, we have had to sell ourselves to Ferox. Ferox had choices – we're quite aware of that. We want to drive it, but it's important to work together. The engineering staff at Ferox are very good. It was important that we bring our best engineering people out to talk to them.

After privatization we are clearly going to have to bring in a Western accounting person, a manufacturing person, and other staff. Probably they will need to be single, as it would be very difficult to move a Western family to Děčín. There are no English schools here in Děčín.

We will also move key individuals from Ferox into jobs in our Western plants for six months a year. We will actually place individuals in jobs for which they will be held responsible. We will be interchanging people.

"APCI has been in most countries in Western Europe for up to thirty years and has more recently developed business in the Pacific Rim. We have experience in starting businesses in developing countries, but we have no experience in a former Communist country. It is very important that a company such as ours understands that this is not a third world county. It is a developed, heavily industrial area that has been dormant for many years but that still has employees with high educational levels and well-qualified engineers. The industry is old, but there is a lot of production capacity."

It appears to be quite difficult to recruit the people we want. There are many good jobs in Prague, and people with the skills we need are unhappy to move to Děčín. It is partly cultural. People in Europe just don't move like Americans, and they value their leisure time more.

It is also important to a large multinational company to understand any extra liabilities that are taking on in the acquisition of a large manufacturing company here. For instance, any liability for previous environmental damage must be fully assessed and minimized by such actions as taking soil samples.

An apparent problem here is the lack of depth in managerial talent. Czech companies are very compartmentalized and are not very good at recognizing young talent; they don't think laterally.

One great concern to any Western company acquiring a Czech manufacturing facility is a general level of overstaffing compared to the West. This is particularly apparent in the administrative areas.

The employment ethic is amazingly harsh here compared to the Western standard. Of course, you know that the remuneration is very much lower and there have been no meaningful pay differentials. A welder may have a higher monthly salary than a salesperson. It is likely that Czechs with commercial and language skills will begin to command higher salaries as they gain experience.

Another example of the harsh personnel practices here is that a supervisor has the authority to cut an employee's bonus pay for what we would consider to be trivial things. At the end of the month he decides the employee didn't do a task he thought should have been done, and he cuts the bonus by 10 percent. Management here is based much more on fear as a motivation. Managers do not know how to motivate without fear. There is no concept at all of carrots, just of sticks. They have the concept of working hard but not the concept of achievement. However, we have built a fantastic commitment on our joint-venture team.

"One thing that any Western manager who comes here will have to understand is the cultural differences. I've learned that some aspects of the culture you have to keep."

For one thing, I sign a lot more paper here in Czechoslovakia. This is definitely a holdover from the old Communist system, where all commands were written. It is very difficult to travel here on business; you need written forms and permission to travel. If there is not prior written permission for a trip, the insurance company will not reimburse if there is an accident. Salespeople cannot just get in their cars and call on customers. I have tried to get rid of forms and to just talk to my employees.

The Czech government must first approve the privatization plan, which is expected in the near future. Then, the Ferox and APCI managers will be free to begin to make the changes necessary to meet their strategic objective, and the process of carrying out the acquisition by APCI will begin.

There are adjustments and changes in store for both companies in the future, but we are sure that Ferox will make a good partner.

Joint ventures in Hungary: Key success factors[12]

This paper examines the contrasting experiences of three British companies in attempting to establish joint ventures in Hungary. The cases highlight some of the important 'do's and don'ts' of setting-up joint ventures in previously centrally planned economies. Jim Hamill and Graham Hunt explain that the key to successful joint venture negotiations is sensitivity to the economic development needs of the host nation (e.g. technology transfer, modernisation, finance, training, etc.) without compromising the operating efficiency and profitability of the venture itself. Successful joint ventures can provide mutual benefits to both the foreign partner and host nation. In cases where major conflicts of interest arise, it may be better to break the courtship rather than enter into a troubled marriage.

Introduction

This paper examines the contrasting experiences of three British companies in attempting to establish joint ventures in one East European country, Hungary. The cases examined are:

United Biscuits' (UB) purchase of an 85 per cent stake in Gyori Keksz; Hungary's largest biscuit manufacturer

Thorn-EMI's unsuccessful attempt to establish a joint venture with the state-owned music company Hungaroton, and

APV's longer term and incremental approach to the Hungarian food and agricultural machinery market.

An important aim of the paper is to integrate the three case studies with the extensive volume of literature which exists on planning, negotiating, implementing, and controlling international joint ventures. The cases highlight some of the important problems in setting-up joint ventures in the former Eastern European bloc, state-run economies. The key to successful joint venture negotiations is sensitivity to the economic development needs of the host nation (e.g. technology transfer, modernisation finance, training, etc.) without compromising the operating efficiency and profitability of the venture itself. Successful joint ventures can provide mutual benefits to both the host nation and the foreign partner. Although in cases where major conflicts of interest arise, it may be better to resist the potential opportunities of the international joint venture.

12 By Jim Hamill and Graham Hunt, *European Management Journal*, 11(2), 238-47. Copyright 1993 Pergamon Press Ltd., Oxford, England. Reprinted with permission.

Joint ventures are sometimes viewed as a second (or even third) best option for supplying foreign markets; being used only when government regulations (e.g. ownership and import controls, restrictions on royalty payments, etc.) prevent the establishment of wholly owned subsidiaries, exports or licensing. Indeed, as will be shown later, there are major problems which arise in the planning, negotiation and management of international joint ventures which often result in a high failure rate.

Literature review

There is an extensive literature on the role of joint ventures in international business covering both (a) the strategic dimension, i.e. the use of joint ventures as a foreign market entry and development strategy; their advantages and disadvantages compared to the alternatives available such as exporting, licensing, wholly owned subsidiaries, etc., and (b) the managerial dimension, covering the problems involved in planning, negotiating, implementing and controlling joint venture agreements.

Joint ventures as a foreign market entry and development strategy

Despite such difficulties, it is widely recognised in the literature that there are important strategic and competitive advantages which may be derived from successful joint venture agreements and that such collaboration may be a first best option in certain circumstance (see Figure 1). A particularly important source of advantage is the potential synergistic effects of combining the complementary assets of the foreign and local partners. Thus, the foreign multinational will provide firm specific knowledge regarding technology, management and capital markets; the local partner provides location-specific knowledge regarding host country markets, infrastructure and political trends (see Figure 2). The pooling and sharing of firm and location-specific knowledge creates the potential for mutual benefit.

Figure 1

Advantages ot joint ventures as a foreign market entry and development strategy

- foreign market expansion with reduced financial commitment

- potential for synergy in the value chain activities of partners leading to cost savings, greater efficiency and enhanced international competitiveness

- foreign market expansion with reduced management commitment due to the contribution of local partners

- reduced political risk through involvement of local partners

- joint ventures allow a greater degree of parent company control compared to other forms of foreign market entry such as licensing and non-equity contractual agreements

- joint ventures may result in greater long-term penetration of foreign markets, e.g. promotion of local image, proximity to markets, etc.

Source: Young and Hamill, 1989

Planning, negotiating and managing international joint ventures

Although there may be mutual advantages to be derived from international joint ventures, inevitable tensions will arise in the operation of such agreements which often result in failure. The estimated failure rate in joint ventures is extremely high – 30 to 61% – with the incidence of failure being highest in joint ventures with developing countries and those involving government partners.

The causes of joint venture failure have been extensively discussed in the literature.[4] Tensions arise from the simple fact that there is more than one parent company and culture. This may lead to disagreement and conflict with respect to issues such as the setting of strategic objectives; the distribution of decision-making power; and day-to-day operational control. The two main reasons for joint venture failure identified in the literature are attempts by one of the partners to retain centralised control and disagreements over operating strategies, policies and methods. As regards the former, the retention of centralised control may be necessary to integrate the joint venture into the multinational's global strategy. (In two of the cases presented later – UB and APV – the Hungarian joint venture had an important role to play in the overall global/European strategy of the British partner.) The failure to delegate decisionmaking power, however, will be resented at local level and will create pressures for decentralisation. The multinational will be reluctant to delegate such power because of the interdependencies which exist between operating units in different countries. As regards operational issues, disagreements may arise in many areas including joint venture strategy; management style; financial management; accounting and control methods; marketing policies and practices; production policies and technology transfers; personnel and industrial relations policies; R & D; and government and trade relations. In addition, there may be other differences of opinion over the contributions of each party; the distribution of rewards and their composition (e.g. profits, royalty fees, etc.); and the time 'scale' of the venture.

The problems associated with joint ventures and their high failure rate implies that great attention needs to be paid to the effective planning, negotiation and management of such deals. While effective management of the joint venture process will never guarantee success, it will considerably reduce the likelihood of failure. As stated by Holton,[5] 'the rather dismal history of international joint ventures could be improved by more efficient planning, negotiation and management'.

Planning and managing successful international joint ventures will require attention to be paid to at least seven broad areas including:

- a clear statement of joint venture objectives and the time period over which they will be achieved.

- a cost/benefit analysis of the advantages and disadvantages of the joint venture compared to the alternative strategies for achieving the firm's objectives (e.g. licensing). These can be assessed against the financial commitment involved; management commitment; risk and control; synergy; long-run market penetration, etc.

- partner screening and evaluation to select the most efficient partner which best complements the firm's objectives. Partner selection is one of the most important criteria distinguishing successful and unsuccessful joint ventures

- achieving broad agreeemement between the partners on the business plan. This should not be a legal document, but rather is the basis for open and frank discussions. The United Nations Centre on Transnational Corporations (UNCTC)[6] has developed a comprehensive checklist of issues which should be discussed at this stage (see Figure 3)

- negotiating the final joint venture agreement based on the business plan

- incorporation of this agreement into a formally written and legally binding contact which should clearly specify the relationship between the two partners. The contract should be flexible enough to allow changes over time in the operation of the venture and should also specify the conditions under which the joint venture can be dissolved

- on-going performance evaluation of the venture to act as an early warning system

Figure 2

Contributions of Foreign and Local Partners to a Joint Venture

Contribution of:

Foreign MNE
- Technology
- Product know-how
- Patents
- Business & marketing expertise
- Technical training
- Management development
- Finance
- Access to international distribution channels
- Increased exports
- Improved competitiveness

Local Partner
- Knowledge of local political situation, economy and customs of the country
- General management
- Access to markets
- Marketing personnel and expertise
- Local capital
- Contacts and relationships with host country governments
- Plants, facilities and land of local partners
- Recruitment of local labour and trade union relationships
- Access to local financial institutions

Figure 3

Outline of Major Aspects of a Joint Venture Agreement

The following presents a comprehensive list of factors that could be included
in joint venture agreements. It should be pointed out, however, that all of these aspects
do not necessarily apply to every joint venture agreement.

1   Purpose and character of a joint venture:

a   major goals/strategy of joint partner

b   major goals/strategy of local partner

c   products/industries/markets/customers served

2   Contributions ot each partner:

a   capital

b   existing land, plant, warehouse, offices, other facilities

c   manufacturing design, processes, technical know-how

d   product know-how

e   patents and trade marks

f   managerial, production, marketing, financial, organisational and other expertise

g   technical assistance and training

h   management development

i   local relationships with government, financial institutions, customers, suppliers, etc.

3   Responsibilities and obligations of each partner:

a   procurement and installation of machinery and equipment

b   construction, modernisation of machinery and equipment

c   production operations

d   recruitment and training of workers and foremen

e   quality control

f   relationships with labour unions

g   research and development

h   general, financial, marketing, personnel and other management

i   continuous training of personnel

4   Equity ownership:

a   equity granted to foreign partner for manufacturing and product technology and
     industrial property rights

b   equity granted to local partner for land, plants, warehouses, facilities, etc.

c   ownership share of foreign partner

d   ownership share of local partner

5   Capital structure

a   equity capital

b   loan capital, national and foreign

c   working capital

d   provisions for raising future loan funds

e   loan guarantees by partners

f   future increase in equity capital

g   transfers of shares in stock, including limitations

6   Management

a   appointment/composition/authority of the board of directors

b   appointment and authority of executive officers

c   expatriate managers, technicians and staff

d   right of veto of appointment of officers and key decisions

e   development of local managers, including time schedule

f   organisations

g   strategic and operational planning

h   information system

i)   control procedures

7   Supplementary agreements:

a   licensing and technology agreements

b   management contracts

c   technical service agreements

d   allocation of foreign partner's corporate overhead to affiliate

8   Managerial policies:

a   declaration of dividends

b   reinvestment of earnings

c   source of supply of materials, intermediates and components, including price, quality, assurance of delivery

d   major marketing programmes, including product lines, trade marks, brand names, distribution channels, promotion, pricing, service and expenditures

e   export markets and commitments

f   executive compensation and bonuses

9   Accounting and financial statements:

a   accounting standards

b   financial statements in currencies of host and foreign countries

c   reporting requirements

d   audit and review of financial statements

10   Settlement of disputes:

a   board of directors and executive committee

b   mediation

c   arbitration

11   Legal matters:

a   relevant local laws, regulations and policies

b   governmental approvals required

c   articles and by-laws of incorporation

d   anti-trust considerations

e   tax laws and considerations

f   selection of legal counsel

g   use of courts of host country

Source: UNCTC (1987)

Hungary: Towards a Market Economy

Although it has been the radical reforms introduced since 1989 that have focused attention on the market opportunities available in Eastern Europe, the issue of economic and political reform has been on the agenda in Hungary for at least two decades. Four main phases in the evolution towards a market economy can be identified as summarised below:

Pre-1968, the period in which Communist ideology and power were at their strongest withthe economy being managed by traditional central planning techniques

1968-80, initial attempts at economic reform through the introduction of the New Economic Mechanism (NEM) which aimed at breaking the monopoly held by large state-owned enterprises in different sectors and to encourage greater competition. Success, however, was restricted mainly to agriculture

1981-88, the extension of NEM across most sectors of the economy and the gradual dismantling of tight central planning; legislation introduced permitting private and foreign investment; firms allowed to opt out of the central planning process; and the establishment of an economic, political and commercial framework within which a market economy could operate, e.g. the introduction of limited liability

1989 and beyond, the introduction of one of the most radical privatisation programmes of any East European country with the stated objective of transferring most State owned enterprises to the private sector within 5 years. The privatisation process is controlled by the State Property Agency (SPA). An important feature of SPA policy, and one which is relevant to the case studies presented later, is that price is only one of the criteria used in assessing bids. SPA is also concerned that the joint venture or takeover contributes to the long-term economic goals of the country involving an evaluation of the technology, management and financial aspects of the deal.

As a consequence of the reform process briefly described above, Hungary is now fully committed to a market orientated, outward looking (export-driven) economy. The attraction of inward foreign direct investment plays a crucial role in achieving these objectives and Hungary has been one of the most successful East European countries in this respect. Between 1972 and 1989, the country received less than $600 million in inward direct investment. This increased to approximately £2.5 billion in the two years 1990 and 1991, accounting for 60 percent of the total flow of foreign direct investment into Eastern Europe as a whole. There are now an estimated 13,000 joint ventures in Hungary involving foreign partners.

Case studies[13]

This section presents the three case studies covering the contrasting experiences of British companies in attempting to establish joint ventures in Hungary. Each case follows a similar structure covering a brief summary, the partners to the venture, joint venture objectives, the negotiation process, management structure and implementation. The final section of the paper pulls the three cases together by presenting a number of management guidelines for the successful negotiation of joint ventures in previously centrally planned economies, derived from the case studies and related to the literature review presented earlier.

1. United Biscuits (UB)

Summary

This case covers the purchase of an 85 percent controlling interest in Gyori Keksz – Hungary's largest biscuit manufacturer – by the British company United Biscuits (UB) in 1991. The Hungarian venture plays a strategically important role in UB's overall European operations, as well as providing a platform for entering and developing the Hungarian and other East European markets. The success of the venture can be attributed to the fact that agriculture and food processing has been identified by the Hungarian authorities as a priority development sector and by UB's willingness to invest capital and transfer technology to the venture.

The partners

UB is one of the largest food companies in the world with an annual turnover of approximately £3 billion (1991). Principal products of the company include biscuits, confectionary, snacks, frozen and chilled foods. The group has grown consistently over the last three decades or so, mainly through acquisitions. In 1973, UB established a major presence in the US market with the acquisition of the number two producer Keeblers. More recent acquisitions have focused on building brands and market share in Europe in the run-up to the Single European market. UB uses a number of clearly defined criteria when selecting an acquisition candidate, which are important to note since the same criteria were used in the choice of the Hungarian partner. The acquisition criteria used are:

---

13 By Jim Hamill and Graham Hunt, *European Management Journal*, 11(2), 238-47. Copyright 1993 Pergamon Press Ltd., Oxford, England. Reprinted with permission.

- the target company must be operating in UB's core business

- UB can bring something to the company, e.g. marketing, technology, etc.

- the target has good products and management, and

- the target has a large market share being either the market leader or in a strong number two position.

Gyori Keksz is Hungary's largest biscuit manufacturer. By Hungarian standards, it has the reputation of being an efficiently managed company with good products.

Joint Venture Objectives

The joint venture with Gyori Keksz was announced in April 1991 and involved the purchase of a 75 percent (later increased to 85 percent) controlling interest by UB. The purchase occurred at a time when the formalised legal framework for the privatisation of Hungarian industry was being put into place and this considerably aided negotiations. This contrasts with the more 'ad hoc' procedures faced by Thorn-EMI (see later).

In terms of strategic objectives, the joint venture with Gyori Keksz was aimed not only at gaining entry into the Hungarian market but was to play an important role in UB's overall European strategy. The three main objectives underlying the venture were:

The European food industry has traditionally been fragmented on a country-by-country basis reflecting national taste and cultural differences. In the last few years, however, the industry has become more panEuropean in scope with the growth of Euro-brands and the wave of crossborder mergers, acquisitions and strategic alliances amongst major producers. This trend has been reflected, too, in food retailing where major companies such as Aldi and Carrefour now operate a European network of stores and have a buying organisation that attempts, where possible, to buy for its European operations as a whole. These retailers demand large volumes and bulk discounts.

Market access

to a large extent, the purchase of a controlling stake in Gyori Keksz was motivated by UB's desire not to miss out on the huge (potential) opportunities likely to arise from the reform process in both Hungary and other East European countries. The purchase secured entry into the Hungarian market and could be used as a launch pad into closely related markets in East Europe. In many respects, it was a 'testing of the waters' before undertaking larger investments and more committed operations in the future.

Pan-Europeanisation

These trends had a major impact on UB's decision to purchase its controlling interest in Gyori Keksz. Some of UB's products such as 'Cream Crackers' and 'TUC' biscuits are pan-European. They are also commodity type products which require production in very high volumes at low cost. The Gyori Keksz venture is to occupy a strategically important position in this respect acting as a low cost sourcing base for such commodity products for major European retailers which are highly price sensitive.

Brand development

While the initial strategy was to use Gyori Keksz as a low cost production base, the longer term aim is to introduce UB's other snack brands into the highly developed Hungarian and East European markets. Gyori Keksz is seen as an excellent base for such future development.

Negotiations

In identifying Gyori Keksz as a partner, UB used the same criteria applied by the company to any acquisition or joint venture. As Hungary's largest biscuit producer, Gyori Keksz was clearly operating in the same business as UB and with a leading market position. By Hungarian standards at least, it was a well managed company with good products. Finally, there was considerable scope for improving value added through additional capital investment and through the transfer of UB technology, marketing and management skills. A significant capital investment programme is to take place involving the setting up of production facilities in five product segments – biscuits, wafers, snacks, peanuts and confectionery. Although R & D will be centralised at UB, significant technology transfer will occur (e.g. JIT); Hungarian nationals will be trained in marketing planning and broad management, new accounting and financial control procedures will be introduced; and a management information system installed. UB's proposals in these areas were crucial to the deal being accepted by the Hungarian authorities since agriculture and food processing has been identified as a priority development sector requiring the transfer of Western technology and skills. This resulted in a relatively lenient attitude being adopted by the principal negotiating body for privatisation – the State Property Agency – who were further encouraged by UB's willingness to establish an enterprise agency to help individual private businesses to develop. As a consequence, negotiations over the purchase proceeded smoothly with no major problems.

Management Structure

As stated above, UB initially owned 75 percent of the venture. The residual shareholding was divided between the local council (15%) and the State Property Agency (10%). The local council had a shareholding because they were the landowners on which the facilities were built. The SPA share will be reduced to 5 percent with the residual being offered to employees of the firm. UB have the option to buy the residual 25 percent within a year, and have since increased their share to 85 percent.

The board of the joint venture comprises three UB personnel from the UK; two employees of Gyori Keksz (a requirement of Hungarian law); and one other local Hungarian. The controlling stake of 85 percent allows UB to run the joint venture as a wholly owned subsidiary. Actual decision-making will, however, be as decentralised as possible. Gyori Keksz will be granted a high level of autonomy in decisions affecting the Hungarian market only. Decisions with wider implications for UB's overall European strategy will be more centralised.

Implementation

The successful implementation of the joint venture will be supported by the following policies:

- R & D – this will be centralised within UB but with the free flow of information and know-how to Hungary. Immediate applications will be on solving existing production problems and introducing new products to the Hungarian market

- Capital investment – a major capital investment programme to modernise plant and equipment is to be introduced covering five main areas – a complete biscuit production line; a new wafer production line; a new crisps production line; frying equipment for processing peanuts; longer term introduction of a confectionery production line. Such investment satisfies the main objective of the SPA to modernise the agricultural and food processing sectors

- Marketing – the introduction of Western marketing practices and brand management; and the training of local nationals in marketing

- Technology transfer – the major capital investment programme will involve the large scale transfer of technology from the UK

- Management accounting – transfer and training in modern management accounting techniques to align Gyori Keksz's accounting system with that of UB

- Management skills – ongoing training in areas such as negotiations, industrial relations and personnel management

- Market research – to better assess market potential in Hungary.

2. Thorn-EMI [14]

Summary

Unlike the previous case of a successfully established joint venture, Thom-EMI's proposal to establish a 50/50 joint venture with Hungaroton was aborted in August 1990. Major conflicts had arisen between the partners over the aims and objectives of the joint venture and their respective contributions. The Ministry of Education and Culture had viewed the venture primarily as a vehicle for promoting Hungarian musicians and culture rather than as a viable business entity in its own right. This proved unacceptable to Thorn-EMI.

The decision not to proceed with the venture attracted considerable publicity at a time when the government's mass privatisation programme was about to get underway. This led to major doubts being expressed by both Western industrialists and Hungarians themselves as to the government's willingness to relinquish control over industry. The feeling was that officially the government was in favour of privatisation, but psychologically it was reluctant to accept foreign investment. Clearly UB benefited greatly from the more formalised privatisation scheme introduced subsequent to the breakdown of Thorn-EMI's proposal. The case highlights the fact that it may be better to abort negotiations than to enter a troubled marriage.

The Partners

Thorn-EMI's principal business activities are the rental and retailing of electrical equipment; lighting; security systems; and music. The case presented here covers the music divisions which accounts for 27 percent of total group turnover of 113.7 billion (1990). EMI music is a globally integrated operation covering artist development and promotion, recording, manu-

---

14 By Jim Hamill and Graham Hunt, *European Management Journal*, 11(2), 238-47. Copyright 1993 Pergamon Press Ltd., Oxford, England. Reprinted with permission.

facturing, marketing and distribution of music. Major performers signed to EMI include – Cliff Richard, Paul McCartney, Duran Duran, Kate Bush, Queen, Tina Turner, Stevie Nicks, M.C. Hammer, Beach Boys and many others.

To understand the rationale underlying the proposed joint venture, it is necessary to briefly summarise key developments in the global music industry as they affect both partners. These include:

> Hungaroton is Hungary's largest music company with an 80 percent market share and major exports to other East European countries. Unlike Thorn-EMI, it is mainly a classical rather than popular music concern.

- overcapacity – especially in the production of vinyl records due to consumers switching to audio cassettes and compact discs. In 1991, Thorn-EMI made considerable provisions for the write-off of vinyl record pressing facilities surplus to requirements. Hungaroton is primarily a manufacturer of vinyl records with large pressing facilities

- classical/mainstream mix – classical music sales account for only 8 percent of total worldwide music sales revenue; and the same percentage of Thom-EMI's total music sales. Hungaroton, on the other hand, earns 80 percent of its revenue from classical music sales

- people business – a music company is only as powerful as the artists it has under contract. Actual manufacturing of the product (vinyl records, cassettes, compact discs) has little effect on competitiveness and there is an increasing tendency amongst the major music companies to subcontract the production process. In global terms, Hungaroton's artist portfolio is extremely weak compared to Thorn-EMI

- piracy and counterfeit products – this is a major problem for the world's leading music companies who invest heavily in promoting and developing artists only to have pirate manufacturers launch cheap, low quality products on to the market. It has been estimated that between 70 and 80 percent of all Western music sold in Eastern Europe is pirated and there are few legal supports for intellectual property.

Joint Venture Objectives

At least initially, the proposal was a 'textbook' example of mutual partner benefits through a joint venture. Major benefits to be derived by Thorn-EMI included:

- the establishment of a major presence in East European markets; with Hungaroton having an 80 percent market share in Hungary and well developed exports to other East European countries

- the growing market potential in Eastern Europe for Western music. Hungaroton would provide a 'bridgehead' through which Thorn-EMI could develop its popular music business in East European markets

- the two companies had a long history of cooperation through the licensing of artists which would be developed further by the joint venture

- Thorn-EMI would gain access to Hungaroton's classical music business for world markets

The Hungarian partner would gain access to ThornEMI's worldwide distribution, especially for the development of their large classical music portfolios. Hard currency would be earned to invest in modernisation of recording facilities and manufacturing operations – while the venture would provide access to Thorn-EMI's huge artist portfolio.

Negotiations

Despite these mutual benefits, the joint venture proposal failed. There was no single event which brought about failure. Rather a series of actions, and periods of inaction, that resulted in mistrust between the partners and conflicts of interest over the goals of the venture. Major contributing factors included:

- the fact that negotiations were handled by the Ministry of Education and Culture rather than the State Property Agency. The latter had been established to oversee the privatisation of Hungarian industry. Ideologically, it was pro-Western and pro-foreign investment. The Ministry, by contrast, was a relic from the past. Its ideology stemmed from the days of strict central planning and its primary function was to promote Hungarian culture rather than to encourage inward foreign investment

- one of the main reasons why Thorn-EMI was keen on the joint venture initially, was that they had worked before with Hungaroton's managing director Jenoe Bors and were very confident in his abilities. Two weeks before the deal was finalised, however, Bors was sacked and replaced by Istvan Ella, a well-known Hungarian organist, but with no previous business experience

- with the removal of Jenoe Bors, key elements of the original draft agreement were changed. Ella's main objective was to use the joint venture primarily as a means of promoting Hungarian musicians and culture, rather than as a stand-alone profit organisation

- finally, the original proposal envisaged that £14.8 million would be made available for investment in modernised production and recording facilities, with part going to the Ministry of Education and Culture. With the appointment of Ella, however, there were fears that the venture would become a vehicle for promoting Hungarian culture (e.g. the funding of two new orchestras) rather than as a viable business entity in its own right.

An important footnote to this case is that Quint, a company formed by Jenoe Bors, is rapidly stripping away Hungaroton's 80 percent market share and attracting many Hungarian musicians. Thorn-EMI is negotiating several cooperative ventures with Quint, following the breakdown of negotiations with Hungaroton.

3. APV[15]

Summary

Of the three cases examined, this one comes closest to the theory of internationalisation as an incremental process (stages of development approach), with the increasing involvement of a firm in a particular foreign market over time being accompanied by a shift towards more committed market development modes. APV's involvement in Hungary has evolved over a decade from the supply of plant, equipment and technical assistance to its current 60 percent joint venture, APV Ungaro. As in the UB case examined earlier, there was a complementarity of interests between APV and the Hungarian government. For the company, APV Ungaro has provided the base for developing the vast potential of East European markets. For the government, APV has provided the required technical know-how in food processing equipment which has been designated a high priority sector.

The Partners

APV is the world's leading supplier of process equipment to the food, beverage and food related industries, with an annual turnover of approximately £900m (1990). It is the only company supplying a comprehensive product portfolio to the whole spectrum of dry, liquid, frozen, fresh and animal food industries. The APV Ungaro joint venture is primarily concerned with the manufacture of equipment related to the liquid food sector of APV's operations which covers breweries, fruit juice plants and dairy product plants.

There are three Hungarian partners in the joint venture comprising a refrigeration company whose personnel are being trained by APV in the marketing of its products in Eastern Europe; a mining company, which provides buildings and labour; and the Hungarian Foreign Trade Organisation, which in the past was responsible for all imports of food processing equipment into the country.

Joint Venture Objectives

For APV, the Hungarian joint venture is the hub of the company's operations in East Europe, acting not only as a manufacturing and service facility, but also as a clear signal to other East European customers of their commitment to the region as a whole. The venture is mainly concerned with manufacturing activities which are labour intensive and require relatively low levels of technical inputs and know-how, e.g. stainless steel pipe manufacturing. The decision to form APV Ungaro was taken within the context of an overall strategic review of APV's worldwide operations involving a major rationalisation programme. As part of this review, several low-tech, labour intensive component plants in the UK were closed and production transferred to Hungary. The Hungarian plant has been integrated into APV's worldwide operations, supplying stainless steel components to all divisions of APV and receiving high technology components from the UK.

> The main objective of the Hungarian partners to the venture was to gain access to the technical know-how required to modernise the country's food processing industry.

15 By Jim Hamill and Graham Hunt, *European Management Journal*, 11(2), 238–47. Copyright 1993 Pergamon Press Ltd., Oxford, England. Reprinted with permission.

Negotiations

As stated previously, APV has adopted an evolutionary, stages of development approach to its involvement in the Hungarian market. This reflects the company's own increasing confidence in operating in the country, together with the progressive liberalisation of the Hungarian governments foreign legislation. The main stages in the company's involvement in the country were:

- International tendering – in the early 1980s APV was involved in tendering for the provision of large scale dairy plants to be operated by the state owned sector. The Hungarian government wanted to acquire Western technology for use in its dairy processing industry

- Representative office – the high level of technical back-up required in international tendering and recognition that agriculture and food processing were going to be key industries in Hungary's longterm development led APV to set up a representative office in the country. The office was headed by a technically qualified executive from the UK head office and provided advice to various government customers on the plant and equipment required for a particular job and made tenders on behalf of APV. The office was also used as a sales representative centre for markets in Czechoslovakia, Poland and the former Soviet Union.

- Minority joint venture (40%) – APV had always viewed its representative office as an intermediary stage towards a greater commitment to East European markets. In addition to its activities stated above, the office also undertook market research to identify possibilities for the establishment of some form of production facility. One of the main findings of this research was that many Hungarian and other East European commercial refrigerators had extremely short product life cycles, due mainly to problems with the compressor. This led APV to the next stage in its development in Hungary, namely the establishment of a 40 percent owned joint venture concerned mainly with the refurbishment of refrigerators using compressors shipped out from the UK.

At the time, the establishment of a minority joint venture was an ideal choice for APV since it allowed the company to supply a particular market niche without requiring high levels of capital investment which APV felt unwilling to make because majority owned foreign joint ventures were still prohibited and strict currency regulations controlling repatriation of earnings were still in force. Within a short period of time, however, it became apparent that the low cost labour available in Hungary provided major opportunities for APV in terms of its global strategy. This, combined with the progressive liberalisation of foreign investment legislation, led to the final stage – the establishment of a majority owned (60%) manufacturing joint venture.

Majority Owned, Manufacturing Joint Venture (60%) – Although in theory it was possible to operate a majority owned joint venture in Hungary since 1968, the reality of the situation made this extremely difficult in practice. It was not until 1988 that liberalisation had gone far enough for APV to feel confident in making a larger investment in Hungary. As stated previously, the new joint venture played an extremely important role in APV's overall global strategy responsible for the production of low tech, low cost components.

> Throughout this evolutionary process from initial tendering to the establishment of a majority owned joint venture, negotiations with the Hungarian government and other joint venture partners proceeded smoothly. This can be attributed to a number of factors – the government's identification of food processing as a priority sector, APV's strategy of sourcing locally whenever possible, the supply of technical assistance and so on.

Management Structure

In 1988, APV could have opted for 100 percent ownership, but preferred a 60/40 joint venture, believing that the long-term success of the venture required the active involvement of local partners in decision-making. As stated earlier, there were three main local partners participating in the venture.

Implementation

The major issues involved in implementing the joint venture included:

Management recruitment and training – despite considerable efforts to find a local manager to oversee the joint venture, it proved difficult to find anyone with the necessary skills. Start-up operations, therefore, were staffed by APV managers transferred from the UK. A large scale training programme, however, was introduced to develop the necessary skills of Hungarian nationals. APV has been in the forefront of management training and development in Hungary, including training for other Hungarian organisations in Western business methods

Joint ventures in Hungary: Key success factors

- Accounting procedures – two sets of accounts needed to be produced; one for APV and one to meet the requirements of the Hungarian government. Gradual integration of the two systems, however, will occur as Hungarian accountancy procedures are brought into line with Western standards

- Foreign exchange – hard currency targets are set for APV-Ungaro, that if met, bring a reduction in tax liability. This has been introduced by the government to promote exports

- Local sourcing – procurement policy of the joint venture is to source locally for low-technology components. Higher technology components such as sensors, thermostats and control panels are sourced from the UK. The willingness to source locally was welcomed by the government for stimulating local enterprises and reducing hard currency expenditure on imports.

Conclusions

The establishment of clearly defined joint venture objectives is a necessary prerequisite for successful negotiations. Both the UB and APV deals had clearly stated objectives covering the Hungarian market and the role of the joint venture in the groups' overall European strategy.

The case studies presented in this paper covered two successful and one aborted joint venture negotiations in Hungary. Although it is difficult to generalise from the small number of cases studied, taken together with the literature reviewed earlier a number of successful criteria can be identified for negotiating joint venture agreements in former centrally planned economies.

Significantly, there was flexibility in both UB and APV agreements allowing for an evolution over time in the product and market strategy of the Hungarian operation, and for the continuing upgrading of technology and management transfers. In the Thorn-EMI deal, major conflicts arose between the partners over strategic objectives.

Partner selection is a major determinant of joint venture success. In both the UB and APV deals, there was a clear strategic fit between the UK and Hungarian partners. This was not the case in the Thorn-EMI deal where the strategic objectives of the partners diverged.

According to Harrigan,[7] the outcome of joint venture negotiations is determined by the relative bargaining power of partners. Both UB and APV were in a strong bargaining position due to their control over technological know-how and the fact that they were operating in industries identified by the Hungarian authorities as 'priority' sectors. Neither company, however, abused this position, being very willing to contribute to the economic development goals of the country through technology transfers, etc. Thorn-EMI was in a less powerful position given that it was negotiating with a government ministry rather than the market orientated State Property Agency.

In conclusion, the key to successfully negotiating joint ventures or acquisitions in Hungary is the ability to cultivate good relationships with the authorities and venture partners. The way of achieving this is to match the requirements of the country for foreign currency, modernisation, technology transfer, exports and so on with the need for efficiency and profitability of the joint venture itself. While the latter must remain the ultimate goal of any deal, it will only be possible with sensitivity to the development needs of the host economy.

Political and economic reform in Eastern Europe will continue to create joint venture opportunities for Western companies. The success of these ventures, however, is by no means guaranteed and requires careful planning, negotiation and management.

References

A good summary of the literature can be found in: Young, S., Hamill, J., Wheeler, C., and Davies, J.R. (1989), *International Market Entry and Development: Strategies and Management,* Harvester-Wheatsheaf, PrenticeHall, Hemel Hempstead.

Beamish, P.W. and Banks, J.C. (1987), "Equity Joint Ventures and the Theory of the Multinational Enterprise," *Journal of International Business Studies*, 18(2).

Beamish, P.W. (1985), "The Characteristics of Joint Ventures in Developed and Developing Countries," *Columbia Journal of World Business*, Fall, 20(3).

Connolly, S.G. (1984), "Joint Ventures with Third World Multinationals: A New Form of Entry to International Markets," *Columbia Journal of World Business*, Summer, 19(2).

Contractor, F.J. (1984), "Strategies for Structuring Joint Ventures: A Negotiations Planning Paradigm," *Columbia Journal of World Business*, Summer, 19(2).

Contractor, F.J. and Lorange, P. (1988), "Competition vs. Cooperation: A Benefit/Cost Framework for Choosing Between Fully-Owned Investments and Cooperative Relationships," *Management International Review*, Special Issue, 28.

Friedman, W. and Kalmanoff, G. (1961), *Joint International Business Ventures*, Columbia University Press, New York and London.

Harrigan, K.R. (1984), "Joint Ventures and Global Strategies," *Columbia Journal of World Business*, Summer, 19(2).

Harrigan, K.R. (1985), *Strategies for Joint Ventures*, Lexington Books, D.C. Heath & Co., Lexington, Mass.

Holton, R.H. (1981), "Making International Joint Ventures Work," in Otterback, L. (ed.), *The Management of Headquarter-Subsidiary Relationships in Multinational Corporations*, Gower, Aldershoot.

Janger, A.R. (1980), *Organisation of International Joint Ventures*, Conference Board, New York.

Killing, J.P. (1982), "How to Make a Global Joint Venture Work," *Harvard Business Review*, May-June.

Kogut, B. (1988), "A Study of the Life Cycle of Joint Ventures," *Management International Review*, Special Issue 8, 28.

Lorange, P. (1988), "Cooperative Strategies: Planning and Control Considerations," Centre for International Management Studies, WP-512.

United Nations Centre on Transnational Corporations (1987), Arrangements Between Joint Venture Partners in Developing Countries, UNCTC Advisory Studies, No. 2, Series B, UN, New York.

Walmsley, J. (1984), "International Joint Ventures," paper presented at UK Academy of International Business Conference, Bradford, April, 4. Also see Walmsley, J.(1982), *Handbook of International Joint Ventures*, Graham & Trotman, London.

The Japanese manager's traumatic entry into the United States: Understanding the American-Japanese cultural divide[16]

Japanese executives routinely travel to the United States for business for periods extending up to several years. Their visits typically begin as a jarring experience for them and their families due to the substantial cultural differences they encounter. Despite the success of Japanese business worldwide and the growing presence of Japanese communities in many U.S. cities, Japanese individuals routinely face disorienting experiences in their dealings with Americans, encounters that impede their effectiveness and hamper the business they come here to manage. Such confrontations mirror in microcosm the tensions of contemporary U.S.-Japan relations. They reveal the presence of built-in cultural barriers to Japanese firms in the U.S. that constitute structural impediments every bit as real as the more widely criticized constraints on foreign business in Japan. They also highlight patterns of behavior that Americans must learn to bridle if they are to serve as key players in global institutions in the future.

Around a conference table in a large U.S. office tower, three American executives sat with their new boss, Mr. Akiro Kusumoto, the newly appointed head of a Japanese firm's American subsidiary, and two of his Japanese lieutenants. The meeting was called to discuss ideas for reducing operating costs. Mr. Kusumoto began by outlining his company's aspiration for its long-term U.S. presence. He then turned to the current budgetary matter. One Japanese manager politely offered one suggestion, and an American then proposed another. After gingerly discussing the alternatives for quite some time, the then exasperated American blurted out: "Look, that idea is just not going to have much impact. Look at the numbers! We should cut this program, and I think we should do it as soon as possible!" In the face of such bluntness, uncommon and unacceptable in Japan, Mr. Kusumoto fell silent. He leaned back, drew air between his teeth, and felt a deep longing to "return East." He realized his life in this country would be filled with many such jarring encounters, and lamented his posting to a land of such rudeness.

The newcomer's surprise

This scenario illustrates one of the disagreeable surprises Akiro Kusumo encountered when he first came to the United States a few years ago. As officer of a Japanese financial services firm, he was dispatched to serve a multi-year tour of duty with his firm's American operation. That assignment began a most uncomfortable period of adjustment. In his new role, he faced a round of challenges that far exceeded what his travel books and corporate training programs

16 Richard G. Linowes, *Academy of Management Executive,* 7(4), 1993, 21-38.
Used with permission.

had led him to anticipate. Though he had been engulfed with pictures and tales of America throughout his life, his experience of living and working with Americans as neighbors and employees proved to be far more unsettling than expected.

There were surprises in nearly all walks of life. City streets were a constant reminder that he lived in a strange and hostile environment, posing risks more frightening than anything he had known before. He was startled and alienated by Yankee assertiveness and bluntness. Though most Americans were friendly, he had trouble understanding routine conversations and serious difficulty knowing whom to trust. He longed for the structure, clarity, security, and peace of Japanese society.

Eventually Mr. Kusumoto learned to live well in America. He grew to enjoy its freedoms, diversity, comforts, and conveniences. But his U.S. experience was definitely a transforming experience, one that made his ultimate return to Japan both psychologically taxing and socially problematic for him and his family.

Forward-looking American managers are well advised to learn from Mr. Kusumoto's experience two key lessons that might improve their effectiveness in international dealings:

Mr. Kusumoto is not alone. Every year thousands of Japanese business professionals come to the United States to pursue business interests. Many have made the trip innumerable times, gaining invaluable experience in American styles of business, while others are relative newcomers. The newcomers' trials and tribulations shed light on the strengths and weaknesses of American society, and highlight ways in which Americans bear some responsibility for contemporary strains in American-Japanese relations.

1 There exist significant American cultural impediments to Japanese business. Americans need to be more sensitive to the challenges faced by Japanese when they tailor their traditional ways to the American experience. Difficulties between Americans and Japanese are in large measure the product of American conduct and habits of mind. A newfound awareness of American cultural impediments might temper their critique of Japanese ways, and form the basis for an improved, mutually respectful American-Japanese relationship. There is clearly room for improvement. According to a recent survey, only eight percent of Japanese believe Americans respect the Japanese, and only thirty-one percent of Americans think Japanese respect Americans.[1] Such suspicions do not bode well for multinational business, or any form of bilateral cooperation.

2 Some conventional American ways should be tempered in overseas dealing. Japanese impressions of Americans are relevant to matters that go well beyond Japanese trade, for in overseas settings American business people are being compared increasingly to Japanese people. From Malaysia to Thailand to Venezuela to Spain, local business people deal with both Americans and Japanese, sometimes choosing between the two. In such settings, relative differences between American and Japanese are most apparent. Since America's future in international business depends in part on the quality of these relationships, it is time to hold up a mirror to American ways, warts and all. In this article, trouble spots in "the American way" are examined by listing the disappointments faced by recently arrived Japanese business people. Their positive impressions are overlooked to highlight factors that make their American business dealings both awkward and uncomfortable. Drawing on the author's research on the cross-cultural encounters inside the U.S. subsidiaries of Japanese firms, this article offers a new synthesis of recognized differences between American and Japanese ways.[2] It then examines how these differences undermine the effectiveness of visiting Japanese business people. Though the presentation paints a more critical portrait of America than most Japanese might wish to convey, the findings are instructive for all engaged in global commerce.

Comparing American and Japanese Ways

To appreciate the shock of entry, the discussion begins with a pictorial summary of known differences between American and Japanese ways. Though Japanese and Americans share many similarities, they are different in critically important ways. Cultural traditions from each national heritage yield behavioral norms that are sometimes at odds with those from the other culture.

Exhibit 1 synthesizes these contrasts in visual form. Japanese values and behaviors appear on the left, while American values and behaviors appear on the right. Down the center appear the key contrasts reported over the years by keen observers, scholars, and the press.[3] The boldface print on both sides highlights fundamental differences: Japanese hold harmony as a social ideal, patience as a personal virtue, and hierarchy as an essential organizing principle. Americans, in contrast, hold freedom as a social ideal, action-orientation as a personal virtue, and equality as a fundamental organizing principle. Associated with each of these broad differences are the more specific paired contrasts appearing down the center. These contrasts are grouped by broad theme, but they are also linked sequentially from top to bottom. The .key contrast appears across the middle, once again in boldface print: Japanese focus on maintaining the group, whereas Americans focus on protecting the individual. The other contrasts illuminate areas where each society's traditionally sanctioned conduct differs markedly from that prescribed by the other culture.

Japanese society, in contrast, evolved in a self-contained fashion from a large homogeneous population based in communal villages and urban settings. Its thinking was shaped by the combination of Shintoism, Confucianism, and Buddhism, which taught a love for natural forms, social order, and self-denial, respectively. Through much of its history, it preserved social order by maintaining strict codes of social conduct and a rigorously observed sense of social hierarchy. Japanese recite the motto that "the nail that stands up gets hammered down."

Exhibit 1 helps one visualize the American-Japanese cultural divide. It can be considered an "Intercultural Reference Card," identifying memorable patterns in the contrasts between different cultural ways. It clarifies how the distinct social ideals of these two societies produce a known set of contrasting social behaviors.

The roots of these differences lie in the different historical and cultural traditions of each country. The amazing cultural and ethnic diversity of the United States was produced by waves of immigrants who came in search of better opportunities (though some were brought as slaves). They arrived in a country shaped by Judeo-Christian thinking that emphasized individual choice and clearly distinguished spiritual from commercial life. The founding heroes of this country declared their independence in a rebellion against authority, an act still esteemed as model behavior by succeeding generations. Americans recite the belief that personal dreams can be achieved though individual effort.

Both countries are undergoing significant change today, but the essential facets of each society remain resilient. "The general character of Japan cannot be changed, should not be changed and will not be changed," declared Yoh Kurosawa, chairman of Japan's largest bank.[4] Even though Japan has adopted many of the cultural trappings of the United States over the years, there remain inherent cultural barriers that limit the effective interaction of American and Japanese people. These barriers can be overcome – indeed, many have done so successfully – but the path is difficult and not commonly taken. It involves more than a "quick fix" of overseas travel and business protocol training. Improved relations will require significant willful adjustments by people on both sides of the Pacific.

Exhibit 1
Contrasting Japanese and American values and behavior patterns

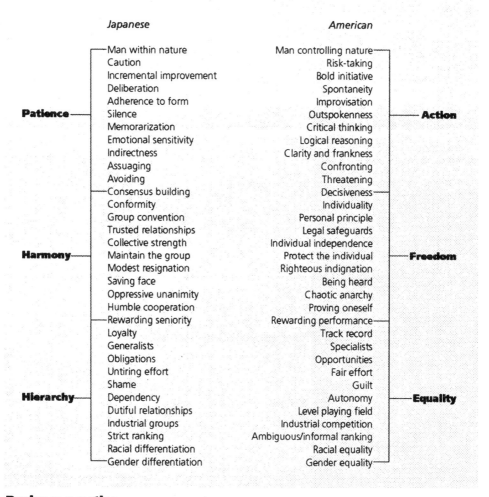

Japanese		American
	Man within nature	Man controlling nature	
	Caution	Risk-taking	
	Incremental improvement	Bold initiative	
	Deliberation	Spontaneity	
	Adherence to form	Improvisation	
Patience	Silence	Outspokenness	Action
	Memorarization	Critical thinking	
	Emotional sensitivity	Logical reasoning	
	Indirectness	Clarity and frankness	
	Assuaging	Confronting	
	Avoiding	Threatening	
	Consensus building	Decisiveness	
	Conformity	Individuality	
	Group convention	Personal principle	
	Trusted relationships	Legal safeguards	
	Collective strength	Individual independence	
Harmony	Maintain the group	Protect the individual	Freedom
	Modest resignation	Righteous indignation	
	Saving face	Being heard	
	Oppressive unanimity	Chaotic anarchy	
	Humble cooperation	Proving oneself	
	Rewarding seniority	Rewarding performance	
	Loyalty	Track record	
	Generalists	Specialists	
	Obligations	Opportunities	
	Untiring effort	Fair effort	
	Shame	Guilt	
Hierarchy	Dependency	Autonomy	Equality
	Dutiful relationships	Level playing field	
	Industrial groups	Industrial competition	
	Strict ranking	Ambiguous/informal ranking	
	Racial differentiation	Racial equality	
	Gender differentiation	Gender equality	

Business practice

Arriving Japanese managers must choose between emulating America business practice and continuing Japanese ways. Most attempt American ways, but they find the process taxing since it requires that they replace entrenched behaviors with foreign practices that seem rather unattractive. Tight control from Tokyo or Osaka corporate headquarters only complicates the issue.

Business operations in the U.S. are sometimes filled with arcane intricacies that are hard for newcomers, be they American or Japanese, to fully fathom. This is especially true in the securities industry, where Japanese lack of knowledge of American business ways has led one chief administrative officer in their employ to suggest that Japanese managers are "like children playing on the freeway; they have no idea what they have gotten themselves into." In the United States business world for just a few years, they rarely get beyond being rookies. Like a young son who inherits great wealth, they come dangerously close to exercising poor judgment.

Operational differences aside, Japanese are troubled by American ways of managing. The famed shortsightedness of American management is very frustrating and disappointing to Japanese associates. Americans seem unable to appreciate how business relationships can grow over time. Too often companies provide lackluster service and sell products of insufficient quality. Too often blase or inattentive sales personnel fail to treat customers as "honored guests." Americans are too quick to make deals, and too untrusting to engage in business without a brigade of attorneys to navigate through potentially catastrophic legal situations. Instead of working with people they know well, Americans will do business with most anyone, hiring lawyers to protect themselves.[5] Dangers lurk everywhere. Doing business in the U.S. can be very difficult.

Organizational dynamics

Within organizational contexts, entry problems are magnified. United States work settings resemble those in Japan, but American employees and Japanese managers hold very different work and career expectations. It is here that visiting Japanese businessmen often encounter their most unexpected and painful surprises.

In Japanese eyes, American work settings lack a spiritual quality. The fee of "collective specialness" carefully bred in Japanese organizations is largely absent in U.S. businesses. Gone is the sea of dutiful, talented subordinates who work without complaint to accomplish whatever management requests. American managers pursue personal careers and are willing to jump from place to place to obtain their next promotion. People are more concerned with personal job performance and compensation in narrowly defined jobs than overall organizational mission and success. People engage in political confrontations to protect their own interests, producing nasty turmoil and dissension in the ranks. In Japanese eyes, it is tragic the way harmony is wantonly violated.

Japanese are also surprised by the lack of loyalty in American institutions. Their experience has taught them that effective management depends on the richly woven, internal network of trusted relationships that takes years to develop. In Japan, people who moved from one company to another at an advanced stage in their working lives are traditionally viewed as difficult to mold and suspect in their loyalties. Today, lateral movement is much more common, but the U.S. situation is markedly different. This difference was dramatically illustrated by a Japanese executive's motivational talk that resoundingly backfired. Speaking to a group of American employees, the Japanese visitor informed them that the firm was losing money, and he admonished all present to redouble their efforts. An audience of dutiful Japanese would have responded with renewed diligence, but Americans heard the news differently. In the next few weeks, most sent out resumes seeking jobs elsewhere. Senior American and Japanese managers watched with dismay as many talented employees walked out the door.

Interpersonal dealings

On a personal level, newcomers face awkward moments relating to Americans. Many struggle just to communicate in a language not their own, but beyond this challenge lie the strains caused by broad differences. Americans appreciate Japanese politeness, but they are rarely aware how their conduct strikes the Japanese.

In contrast, Americans are usually forceful in their interactions. Rather than subtly reading interpersonal cues, Americans express their thoughts and feelings in frank, unencumbered ways. They have learned that through confrontation they can uncover truth and generate new ideas. Such behavior is an affront to most Japanese. They have heard stories about American assertiveness all their lives, but they are still surprised to encounter it.

This impression is exacerbated when Japanese meet Americans who particularly glib or egotistical. The free-flowing style of debate widely practiced in the U.S. is overwhelming to the Japanese. They cannot keep pace. They are largely unpracticed at such contests because

Among Japanese people, many things are left unsaid. Elaborate rituals of social reciprocity build trust and "institutionalize thoughtfulness."[6] People are taught to be indirect in conversation, carefully editing their remarks to reflect both good form and the concerns and status of their listeners. Ideally, superiors do not give orders, subordinates are sensitive enough to understand exactly what is wanted and to act accordingly.

they prefer to avoid the risk of offending other people. They further believe that especially talkative people cannot be competent. American displays of over-confidence seem shameless and contemptible to the Japanese. All displays of ego are severely punished in Japanese upbringing, and those of higher social standing are expected to display even greater modesty. Finally, Americans are impulsive, some frightfully so. They change direction and relationships much too easily. Impatient for the realization of their hopes and desires, they refuse to wait for developments to unfold naturally.

Taken together, American assertiveness and whimsy confuse the Japanese. Though most Americans are cooperative and trustworthy, trust is inhibited because Americans flagrantly violate Japanese social rules, even though as "foreigners" they are formally exempt from compliance. One Japanese described his quandary this way: "Eighty percent of Americans are wonderful people, but twenty percent are not, and I cannot tell the difference."

Impression shock, then, whether felt in communities, business dealings, inside organizations, or in personal relationships, encompasses the first round of surprises faced by newly arrived Japanese. As visitors to a foreign land, they witness the behavior patterns listed on the right side of Exhibit 1, and violate the precious Japanese values and behaviors shown on the left.

Integration shock

Once Japanese commence a daily routine in the United States, they experience a new round of surprises as Americans react to them in unexpected ways. American interpretations of Japanese behavior are often so different from Japanese intent that visitors are sometimes astonished by the American response.

Community life

The suburban communities in which many Japanese managers choose their homes are often the same bedroom communities in which upwardly mobile, prosperous American executives live with their families. In Japan, these towns are portrayed on Japanese television as the symbols of wealth and comfort of the American lifestyle. They represent much of the best that America has to offer – spacious homes, beautiful parks, cordial neighbors, and impressive shopping malls. With an automobile, everything becomes convenient and accessible.

But life in these communities can be extremely lonely for the Japanese. Accustomed as they are to close group relations, Japanese newcomers find themselves desperately seeking forms of group involvement not routinely felt by their American neighbors. In some locations, such as Scarsdale, New York, Fort Lee, New Jersey, and Grosse Ile, Michigan, the Japanese community has become a substantial force in and of itself, developing a very visible presence in schools and stores,

Though American reactions to Japanese newcomers are usually cordial, some Japanese ways seem a bit too strange, enough to trigger the concern and reprimand of the local community. Japanese-style parenting sometimes involves locking misbehaving children outside the home to punish their selfish behavior. The miscreant offspring cries outside the house begging his parents' forgiveness. Imported to the U.S., this technique has led well-intended neighbors to suspect child abuse. The resulting police intervention has proved very embarrassing for the authorities and most unsettling for the Japanese family.

on tennis courts and golf courses. Wary of the corrosive influences of American life – which can seriously jeopardize a child's reassimilation into Japanese society – Japanese parents sometimes establish special Japanese schools to teach Japanese language and formal social manners. Such groupish behavior in nearly all walks of life leads many Americans to criticize their Japanese neighbors as excessively aloof and clannish.

There is also a less than admirable side of life in these communities. Public outbursts decrying Japanese corporate acquisitions and visible real estate purchases galvanize fears of economic takeover. Many people feel resentment about Japanese business prowess and its presumed impact on the lagging American economy.[7] Some express latent hostility to any Japanese presence in the U.S., vestiges of wartime animosity and pockets of racism.

To address these problems, and to build better relations with American people, Japanese firms now offer their own versions of corporate American "good citizenship" programs, offering generous gifts to many U.S. communities. Japanese are then shocked to find these philanthropic gestures sometimes disparaged in the American press, where cynics overlook the spirit of these acts and see them only as self-serving conduct.

Business practice

Sometimes, however, it signals a polite refusal. Japanese traditionally avoid offending others to almost any degree possible, even if that means skirting the truth occasionally. Differences of opinion are usually downplayed to maintain good relations, often leaving associates without the whole story. Ironically, it is exactly this kind of conduct that makes Americans feel most offended or wronged.

Americans react very emotionally to Japanese business practices. Over the years, some have felt annoyed and even deceived by vague Japanese communications, and others have felt frustrated and even manipulated by Japanese time-consuming decision making. These reactions once seemed warranted from an American perspective, but today they are regarded as unfortunate and inappropriate responses to the natural workings of Japanese organizations. Some U.S. subsidiaries now move quite nimbly, but in general, slowness to act is a natural consequence of the Japanese consensus-building process.

Popular U.S. conceptions of Japanese business focus on overworked employees toiling away long after more family-minded Americans have headed home. Japanese do spend long hours at work, but largely out of work group devotion rather than blind ambition or fear of dismissal. Work relationships play a primary role in their lives. Forever attentive to their social obligations, they avoid being the first to break from the group at day's end. After-work soirees provide important opportunities to exchange information and nourish relationships. Americans have criticized Japanese "work obsession," and many Japanese firms are trying to modify their U.S. ways. Some distribute information to their U.S.-based Japanese employees on "enjoying a weekend, American-style." Some Japanese leaders even call for shorter work hours in Japan.[8]

Many Americans believe Japanese firms compete unfairly through their industrial groups.[9] Keiretsu members deal with each other extensively, reflecting the Japanese tendency to respect and honor long-established, trusted business relationships. Americans find fault with such cozy relations, and some get angry and demand market access. Ironically, their threats and arm-twisting create exactly the kind of tense emotional climate that is anathema to Japanese business relationships.

Japanese firms also appear to engage in the worst sorts of ethical violations: bribing officials, price fixing, paying off customers, and stealing industrial secrets. In Japan, such scandals routinely plague business as usual, for in some sense they are ill-fated extensions of traditional customs. Traditionally there were no "principles" that could not be compromised on occasion to build goodwill or maintain the group, even when moral issues might be involved.[10] The group's or leader's opinion more strongly influenced conduct than personal conscience. Individuals simply ignored their own ethical impulses for the sake of the group.[11] Depending on the situation, "bribery" and "pay offs" were justified to help solidify relationships; "rigged bidding" preserved interfirm harmony; "patent infringement" and "industrial espionage" protected a corporate group, or even the whole Japanese nation. However justified, such conduct today is roundly criticized in the industrialized world, and increasingly in Japan itself. Many Japanese now recognize that some of their traditional behavior patterns must be brought into alignment with Western ways if they will be received in international circles.[12]

Even so, Japanese feel jolted by American condemnation of Japanese political activities in the United States. In an effort to dissipate dark clouds of cultural misunderstanding, many Japanese feel they must make sincere efforts to educate American opinion makers and policymakers. Regrettably, these efforts are then sometimes denounced by American journalists and the public at large who condemn such attempts to influence officialdom.

The career paths of Japanese managers typically build broad generalist perspectives rather than indepth operational knowledge. As managers progress in their careers, they assume responsibility for tasks over which they have limited understanding and no direct experience.

Organization dynamics

Consensus decision making further exposes these gaps in experience. U.S. managers usually develop expertise in a functional area where they are granted autonomy to act decisively. Thus, when Americans join a Japanese management team, their contributions sometimes seem undervalued. They become just one voice in a group decision process, blending their advice with that of others who may have much less experience. Americans see this as a waste of time and talent.

The conflict between Japanese expatriate staff and local employees is actually the greatest concern Japanese managers face in globalizing their firms.[13] A closer look inside these firms shows why.

The career paths of Japanese managers typically build broad generalist perspectives rather than indepth operational knowledge. As managers progress in their careers, they assume responsibility for tasks over which they have limited understanding and no direct experience. In Japan, such transitions rarely pose a problem since managers can rely confidently on a devoted and diligent staff in the new setting to, in effect, "run" the business.

In the U.S., the same kind of organization is not in place. Many American employees are accustomed to traditional top-down decision making where they expect the man or woman in charge to more or less "run the show" and "call the shots." In this context, Japanese executives' limited operational knowledge can be problematic, even embarrassing. Some of the most basic elements of American management experience are missing from their background. Most likely they have never acted decisively, never hired or fired anyone, never given frank performance reviews, never resolved internal disputes – all standard practice in the U.S. They are surely not familiar with the challenges of working with a racially and ethnically diverse workforce. These gaps produce many painful experiences. Senior Japanese executives sometimes make suggestions that their experienced American subordinates know to be incorrect or inappropriate.

In American eyes, most Japanese are not "hands on." They avoid accountability. No one wants to make a decision. They forever send faxes to and from Japan. Americans feel excluded from the closed inner circle of Japanese management. Sometimes their decisions are overturned by Japanese superiors. They feel stifled by the lack of personal challenge at work and frustrated by the ambiguity of their career path. One U.S. executive complained that promotions in his Japanese company are like "waiting for a subway door to open exactly where you are standing."[14]

Career-oriented Americans seek professional challenges and a chance to grow in their jobs, and they seek out organizations that provide that kind of opportunity. Japanese employees are accustomed to organizational life where people blend together in harmony. They serve collectively. Individual differences are suppressed and managers are punished for their errors. People are obedient to supervisors who care for them paternalistically. Promotions come in recognition of maturity. There is little room to express personal feelings or to search for personal challenge. In such a work environment, unfettered American career ambitions seem awkwardly out of place. It is hard to pursue the American dream inside a Japanese bureaucracy.

Some problems end up in court. Japanese are shocked by accusations of racial and gender discrimination filed by angry employees who demand their rights. At recent Congressional hearings, Japanese firms were blasted as "outrageous and disgusting" because they "flout our values and principles" by "violating our labor, civil rights, and non-discriminational laws." Asking Japanese firms to offer in-house EEO training seminars "is like having Leona Helmsley instruct people on how to prepare a tax return. ... We are opening up an ugly chapter in Japanese-American relations. It won't close until this discrimination ends."[15]

> Rigid social hierarchies play a prevailing role in Japanese society. Language richly affirms them through an elaborate system of verb conjugations that communicate distinctions of rank. Years of service within an organization usually mirror hierarchical position. Obedience to seniors helps maintain social order, and maintaining social order is of paramount importance.

Interpersonal dealings

Japanese are further shocked by some American interpretations of the interpersonal encounters. Americans often feel offended by Japanese clannishness and apparent disdain. Yet this Japanese aloofness is partly a reaction to American assertiveness. That is, Americans in some sense evoke from the Japanese the behavioral qualities they find least attractive. Consider the following.

Americans violate this order regularly. They routinely speak their minds and pursue personal agendas. To the Japanese, therefore, Americans generally seem to be noisy, disruptive, and confrontational, often airing views that are better left unsaid. Americans may even walk out the door at a moment's notice. Such conduct is acceptable, even entertaining, among Americans, but once Japanese enter the picture it becomes problematic. In Japanese minds, socially unruly Americans must be dealt with cautiously and sometimes excluded from the group altogether. Since they are non-Japanese, such arms-length is acceptable in Japanese eyes. It takes a long time to develop trust with these foreigners. Americans see the situation differently.[16]

Most Japanese are probably unaware of these American perceptions. When they first learn of them, they are baffled and uncertain how to respond.

Integration shock, then, whether felt in communities, business dealings, organizations, or personal relationships, forms the second round of surprises Japanese face in America. Once they begin operating in this land of "foreigners," their well-entrenched values and behavior patterns listed on the left side of Exhibit 1 are often challenged and condemned as violations of American values and behaviors shown on the right.

Over time, Japanese visitors become more familiar with American ways. Events once shocking begin to lose potency. Japanese grow more accepting of America's great qualities, and some truly thrive in the new environment. America becomes a fertile ground for personal development. At some time in the future, however, when these individuals return home to Japanese society, they will most likely experience another painful and challenging transition.

> Some find the Japanese secretive, unwilling and unable to trust Americans. Others find them arrogant and conceited, quite willing to humiliate those of lower rank. Some get upset by the way Japanese hide their feelings and refrain from sharing personal thoughts. Japanese acquaintances seem overly cautious, and Japanese friends seem overly sensitive – too easily hurt by differences of opinion, and too fearful that disagreements will jeopardize friendships.

Conclusion

At a time when the American and Japanese economies are increasingly interlinked, little is served by a rise of xenophobia in either country. Trade imbalances may raise concerns that warrant business cooperation and joint government intervention across the Pacific, but the accompanying acrimony heard on both sides is ill-considered and terribly incendiary. It is hoped that this examination of American and Japanese culturally bred differences, seen from the viewpoint of the Japanese newcomer, will make people more aware and respectful of systemic differences and prevent their being hoodwinked by negative passions.

Most important, it is time for Americans to end the conversation of resentment. Negative mental habits beget negative results. It is unfair to condemn the Japanese for being unfair if they really harbor no unfair intentions. If they're just being Japanese, complying with the social tenets of their society that regrettably inadvertently smell of "foul play," then Americans should not rush to become confrontational. They should instead explain and encourage all necessary adjustments in the U.S. arena, maintaining goodwill toward Japanese associates throughout their rocky effort to learn American ways.

Similarly, in international settings, when questions arise over rules of trade, negotiators should consider using Japanese-style harmonious relations to all parties towards mutual accommodation. Contentious issues should be resolved while working to nurture relationships and opponents should see themselves as partners in search of common long-term benefits. Action-oriented, American-style threats and deadlines are often not the best option. Overseas partners find them annoying and shortsighted, and Americans risk squandering their hard-earned goodwill.

One thing is clear. In the words of Akio Morita, chairman of Sony, "both Americans and Japanese are being denied the benefits that could be gained from our unique and complementary relationship because it is fraught with political posturing and suspicion. This is a loss for our two countries, certainly, but even more, it is a loss for the world.... Japan is committed to a genuine partnership with the United States – one that has real, tangible benefits for both sides. ... Our goals are to cooperate and to gain and grow together."[78] To this, the chairman of Mitsubishi Electronics adds, "the cultural and social distance between Americans and Japanese remains huge, [but] it needn't be...

Americans and Japanese need to do more together.... Business relations [can grow. We must] aim for the highest goals and reach them one step at a time."[18]

A final word

What became of Mr. Kusumoto? After his initial, painful adjustment period, he learned to appreciate his life in America. He grew to enjoy its freedoms and spontaneity and love its spacious homes and gracious neighborhoods. He came to admire America's tolerance and even demand for independence in nearly all walks of life, and he now cherishes opportunities to act that way himself. In the office, he encourages subordinates to take bold initiatives, and he counts among his inner circle a few talented, modest Americans. In the community, he speaks out on matters that touch his interests and immerses himself in local affairs.[27] In modern parlance, Akiro Kusumoto came to America and "cut loose." Rumor has it he even joined a neighborhood amateur theatre group.

One hopes that he now displays the courage and confidence to share with others the social wisdom long developed in his native land. For if he can breed among his American colleagues the kind of mutually supportive, cooperative spirit so devoutly nurtured in Japanese organizations, then his U.S. sojourn will do more than just advance his business interests. He will make a social contribution to all those he meets, demonstrating the sense of peace and security that can be found in a network of harmonious relationships. In that way, he can inspire us to enrich our workplaces, our families, and our communities – even encourage us to strive more fervently to manage the world harmoniously. This then might become the real Japanese legacy.

See Instructor's Manual for notes and references.

Strategy

Developing a strategy that fits environmental conditions and enhances corporate competitive advantage is essential for any firm's survival and prosperity.
The turbulence of the international business environment, as well as the complexity of relationships with international subsidiaries and partners further accentuate the importance of corporate strategy. Four cases on strategy, three European and one Malaysian, are included in this chapter. *Saab-Scania's niche strategy: International management in the American automotive environment* outlines five challenges facing the Swedish auto and truck manufacturer Saab-Scania as it tries to penetrate the U.S. market: Saab's commitment to robotization of the workplace, their emphasis on niche market strategies, profitability and economies of scale, their relationship with Volvo, and the threat of protectionist legislation in the United States, Saab's largest export market. Their joint venture with General Motors presents a new host of potential opportunities and problems.

Critical incidents in international strategy examines numerous issues in strategy through a series of four caselets. *KNP, N.V.* is a case about Royal Dutch Papermills, who are developing an international business strategy in the context of the paper industry and the single european market. Having acquired firms in Germany, Italy and Spain, and exporting around the world, the company has considerable international experience. Aspects of globalization of their operations that need to be considered are acquisitions, market distribution, and ownership of shares. They are also contemplating the option of manufacturing in other locations, integrating forward into paper merchant operations, and upgrading technology. The decision to constantly innovate for competitive advantage, a major element in *The theory of competitive advantage* in Chapter 1, involves heavy investment and planning.

Oriental Crafts, Ltd. is profiled in the case *Formulating a strategy for a merchandising firm in Malaysia*. The small entrepreneurial firm's competitive position has worsened and an American-trained executive in the company sets a strategic direction and develops a plan by adapting American concepts of strategic management to the Malaysian context.

Forging alliances with other firms is an attractive way of implementing a global strategy. Once the initial benefits are gained, however, companies need to evaluate the relationship periodically. *Global strategy, competence-building, and strategic alliances* sets out seven stages of dependency in partnerships and warns companies to guard against the "hollowing out" of its core competencies by its partner who can eventually change from a collaborator to a competitor.

National differences in approaches to business strategy are discussed in *Great strategy or great strategy implementation – two ways of competing in global markets*. The strategies of eight semiconductor firms in the U.S. are compared with their counterparts in Japan. There are marked country differences with respect to emphasis on product uniqueness, decisions to withdraw from market segments, the role and sources of process technology, and the importance of vertical integration. These strategic decisions result in different competitive behaviors, with American firms developing unique strategies against other firms, and Japanese competing against rivals using very similar strategies. The advantages and disadvantages of the two competitive styles summarized in the reading can be considered in making recommendations for the cases in this chapter.

Strategy

29. Saab-Scania's niche strategy: International management in the American automotive environment[1]

Abstract

This paper analyzes Sweden's relationship to the international automotive market, the characteristics of Saab-Scania in this environment, Saab-Scania's history, and the current challenges. The original hypothesis was that Saab-Scania planned to expand to obtain the largest market share possible. Interviews and published materials indicated otherwise, however. Saab-Scania is pursuing a niche strategy for small growth and stable development, as seen most clearly in the marketing plan to sell upscale cars in the United States. The challenges discussed are (1) robotics, (2) protectionism, (3) niche strategy, and (4) relationships with Volvo.

Introduction

Multinational corporations face many challenges in today's turbulent international environment. Multinational automotive firms are no exception. Continuing development of automotive technology, shifting consumer demands, and differences in regulations and behavioral norms from one country to another make multinational automotive firms a dynamic subject to study.

At the 1986 Biennial Eastern Region Conference of the Association of Human Resources Management and Organizational Behavior, I presented a paper (Ramsey, 1986) on AB Volvo. While in Sweden in December 1986 and January 1987, I studied Sweden's other multinational automotive firm, Saab-Scania. The information is based on published materials and on interviews arranged by press officer Peter Salzer with managers of Saab-Scania.

1 By Richard David Ramsey, College of Business, Southeastern Louisiana University, Hammond, LA. Used with permission.

Sweden and the international automotive market

At first Sweden may seem an unlikely location for the headquarters of two multinational automotive firms. Situated in Scandinavia at the top of Europe and with a population of only 8 million, Sweden has harsh winters and labor costs among the highest in the world. The country, however, supplies automotive products on a global scale, has a strong work ethic, an abundance of competent technicians, relatively stable labor-management relationships, iron ore, and a foreign-affairs tradition of political neutrality that has escaped biases held against American, German, Japanese and Soviet products.

> The hyphenated name Saab-Scania reflects a division of the company's organizational structure. Saab designates the car manufacturer, one of the smallest multinational car-makers. Scania represents the world's fifth largest manufacturer of heavy trucks and buses.

Nonetheless, only 1 percent of the cars on the road worldwide today were made in Sweden, the vast majority of them Volvos. Surprisingly, the two Swedish firms make one-sixth of all heavy trucks (lorries) in the world. Volvo, with its American acquisition Volvo White, now Volvo White-GMC, has become the second-largest maker of heavy trucks on the planet.[2]

Characteristics of Saab-Scania

In 1986 Saab produced 120,000 cars. In the same year Scania produced about 26,000 buses and trucks. The company employs over 43,000 people and has manufacturing facilities in Sweden and Finland and marketing operations in 40 countries.

Saab and Scania do not share common characteristics with regard to the North American market. Saab, with 365 dealers in the United States and Canada, sold about 47,000 cars in North America in 1986, up from about 10,000 in 1976. But Saab neither seeks nor anticipates that this dramatic rate of increase (almost 18 percent per year) will continue (elimination of the deduction for car-loan interest in the United States is a factor). Rather, the company is implementing a niche strategy aimed at young urban professionals. This group includes consumers who like sporty, upscale cars with more avant-garde styling and zippy handling. The fact that the cars are made in Sweden is a marketing advantage. Saab hopes to increase North

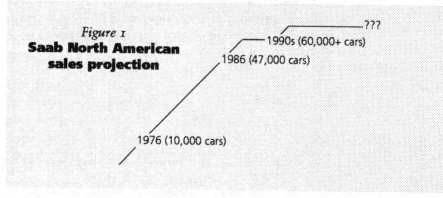

Figure 1
Saab North American sales projection

1976 (10,000 cars)
1986 (47,000 cars)
1990s (60,000+ cars)
???

---

2 Mercedes (Freightliner) is by far the largest. Navistar, the largest American manufacturer of heavy trucks, is almost as big as Volvo. See Gawell (1985) and Eriksson (1985).

American dealers to about 400, especially in the American Southwest where the car is less well established. Sales there should rise about 5 percent a year. Having purchased additional real estate in southern Sweden, Saab anticipates that its total car production will rise to 180,000, approximately one-third of which will go to the American market. These expectations are shown in Figure 1.

The objectives of Scania in North America look somewhat different. Despite its prominence in the bus and truck business worldwide, Scania has only a small nucleus of dealers in America, all in 10 northeastern states. Scania sold only about 100 buses and 100 trucks in America in 1986. Expansion of dealers beyond the Northeast will be essential if Scania is to appeal to long-haul needs. (It's one thing to sell a truck in Connecticut, quite another to service it broken down on a mountain pass in Colorado.) Because bus and truck design allows less creativity and because a niche strategy is harder to define along that line, Scania considers its foray into the American market exploratory. The company hasn't decided whether to go nation-wide with a network of dealers and an advertising campaign. The prospect for expansion is alluring, but the risks are great. Mercedes with its American affiliate Freightliner, and Volvo (White) may already have cornered the lion's share of the market for European truck companies in America. The recent problems experienced by Greyhound Corporation may indicate continuing non-reliance on buses for long-distance transportation. But a market may still exist for tour buses, which Scania is well-known for in Europe. Scania is concentrating on short-haul municipal vehicles, such as garbage trucks and city buses, that can be centrally serviced. Scania buses are, for example, used in Honolulu.

History of Saab-Scania, emphasizing Saab cars

Saab and Scania merged in 1969. Until then, Saab could claim only to be junior in age to its larger competitor Volvo. The 1969 merger, however, had the effect of making Saab-Scania 30 years older than Volvo (one of the oldest manufacturers of cars in the world) by virtue of the fact that Scania started as a car manufacturer in 1897, diversifying into trucks in 1902. Scania discontinued making cars in 1927, the year in which Volvo began marketing cars.[3]

> Throughout the history of Saab-Scania, cars have been more important than trucks in the company's development in America.

The history of Saab began in 1937. Perceiving, better than most, the gathering clouds of war, Sweden's government in 1937 established Svenska Aeroplan Aktiebolaget, hence SAAB, to produce military aircraft. The first plant or factory was near Trollhättan in western Sweden. The Trollhättan plant continues to be the largest Saab-Scania factory, but administrative offices were relocated to Linköping in 1939 when Saab acquired the aircraft division of Svenska Jarnavagsverkstaderna, the Swedish Railway Works. Lacking expertise in aircraft manufacturing, Saab at first hired U.S. engineers who strongly influenced the design of the company's first airplane. Today Saab makes military and commercial aircraft as well as missiles. The Saab Viggen is one of the most sophisticated fighter jets in the world.

---

3 For a history of Volvo see Ramsey (1986) and sources there. Useful sources for history of Saab-Scania include Chatterton (1980), Perret (1987), Robson (1983), and Sjögren (1984).

The concept of a Saab car began in 1945 when the war ended and the company sought to keep the workforce employed. At the suggestion of engineer Gunnar Ljungstrom, design-artist Sixten Sason designed Prototype 46, the teardrop ballistic shape that Saab retained into the 1970s. The shape was influenced by the manufacturer's aeronautical background. The first car offered for sale was the "92" in December 1949. During the 1950 model year, 1,246 Saabs of this type were made. Marketing was carried out by the Swedish retailing firm Philipsons, which already had a network of dealers. Saab continued this arrangement with Philipsons until 1960, when Saab took over its own marketing operations.

The 1950 model Saab 92 was a conversation piece. The car came only in green because the company was offered a good deal on camouflage paint left over from the war effort. The rear window was minuscule. There was no trunk lid. Access to the trunk was through the rear seat!

These and other unpopular features were changed by 1952. Saab advertising for several years in the 1950s often pictured the driver opening the trunk lid. From the start, however, one novel feature of the Saab never changed: front-wheel drive. Only Porsche can claim to have offered front-wheel drive earlier.

Saab's challenge in the 1950s was to build a bigger market share with as little overhead as possible. Consequently, Saab entered its cars in auto races where front-wheel drive had the advantage. In 1953, the first year Saab entered the Monte Carlo race, driver Grat Molander won the women's division. In the same year, Rolf Melde drove a Saab to victory in the Concours de Confort for cars with smaller engines. Swedish rally-racer Erik Carlsson won many races while behind the wheel of a Saab. Rallying was a fairly inexpensive way to advertise. The company also cut costs by declining to construct road-test facilities. Tests were instead conducted on the open road with Saab prototypes bearing the pseudonym Daihatsu, from a then-obscure Japanese manufacturer that had no operations in Europe.

The company gained important publicity in 1956 when a Saab won the Great American Mountain Rally. Sales rose fast. By 1959, more than 12,000 Saabs were in America. As with Scania, Saab attempted first to gain a toehold in the Northeast. The company's first American offices were in New York. Saab-Scania's American headquarters today are in Orange, Conn.

Before the 1969 merger with Scania, Saab pioneered development of the turbocharger. The market response to this and other innovations encouraged Saab-Scania management in 1972 to embark on a bold research and development program costing Skr 9.6 billion ($1.5 billion). The project culminated in 1984 with the introduction of the Saab 9000 Turbo.[4] The American yuppie was the primary marketing target for this model. At the same time, robots were introduced in Saab-Scania manufacturing facilities.

Saab recognized the need early to enter the American market. In 1956, a total of 250 Saab 93s were shipped to the United States.

---

4 Saab managers are not sure what to do next with the 9+ numbering system for their models: 90000 has to be ruled out because in Sweden, still a major part of Saab's market, this is the telephone distress number (like 911 in the United States).

Current challenges

Robotization not only affects job, but also the pressures in competitive international marketing; a robot will do the same quality of work in Trollhättan as in Tokyo or Detroit. Its performance will be as effective on a Yugo as on a Saab. The effect of this perception on international marketing is not yet clear. Saab intends to prepare for any uncertainty by robotizing on a scale second to none.

Robotics represents perhaps the most salient of several current challenges at Saab-Scania, which may be the most robotized car-marker in the world.

Another challenge is the threat of protectionist legislation under consideration in the United States, where more Saabs are sold than anywhere, including Sweden. Saab managers are not as concerned as one might think. They believe Americans buy Saabs for prestige and quality, not price. Some are concerned, however, that protectionist tariffs in one country would cause a ripple effect that could stagnate international markets. Even so, Saab's export managers feel that customs inspectors in the United States and other countries often raise needless complaints at the point of entry to protect domestic business.[5]

The niche being pursued with Saab cars is yuppies enchanted by such features as Saab's airplane-influenced design and turbocharged engines. It remains to be seen whether the company can carve out a corresponding niche for Scania trucks, which in America must meet long-established tight competition.

A third, but related, challenge is Saab's niche strategy. The general strategy was summarized by Saab-Scania president Georg Karnsund as follows: "Think small, think niches."
(Kapstein, 1986, p. 54).

The idea of merger seems even more enticing, given the niches these two manufacturers seek to fill are different. Volvo may appeal to the yuppie, but primarily to one who has a family. Saab dropped the station wagon from its inventory in 1978 after nearly 20 years. But the station wagon continues to be Volvo's most popular model in the United States. The chief barrier to a merger of the two companies seems to be their pride in building and marketing their own products. A merger was widely discussed and then dismissed in 1979.

Finally, although neither Saab nor Volvo seems enthusiastic, there is the possibility of a partnership. The two companies have much in common.[6] Some wonder whether Sweden can forever have two multinational automotive firms.

Conclusion

In conclusion, students may see Saab-Scania as a multinational entrepreneur among automotive firms and as a company bent on success measured not in overwhelming quantities of sales but in qualitative terms of how to prosper along moderate objectives in an upscale market niche. One may be fascinated with the company's metamorphosis from an airplane manufacturer into a highly robotized car-maker while being blessed with some impres-

---

5 In 1989, Saab sold 31,306 cars in Canada and the U.S.; in 1990, 26,245 cars; and, as mentioned, in 1991, 26,014. Therefore, the decline in sales seems to be abating. See Saab-Scania Group (1991 and 1992).
6 As well as other relationships which are less obvious: for example, Volvo Flygmotor makes engines for Saab aircraft.

sively farsighted decisions: front-wheel drive, rally-racing as a means of advertising, development of the turbocharger, investing heavily in research during a time in which other manufacturers (American Motors, Chrysler, Jaguar) were worried about survival, and adopting a niche strategy and pursuing it successfully in an upscale American market despite Japanese competition.

In any event, the multinational orientation of Saab-Scania is a commitment stated by Karnsund in words fitting to end this analysis:

> We are international. Nine out of every ten trucks are exported, as are three out of four cars. Furthermore, Saab-Scania has extensive cooperation with leading aircraft and aerospace manufacturers outside of Sweden, with the result that more than 62% of our production is exported.

> This is only to be expected. After all, our domestic market is small and our products are competitive even on international markets. At the same time this adds another dimension to our products and our field of activity.

> Our expansion – our future – is on the international market. In my view, the internationalization of Saab-Scania has only just begun. In the future, more than ever before, we will have to measure ourselves against the best the world can offer. To cope with that challenge we not only need skill in marketing, we will also need to be in the forefront in quality and technical development. Testing our "art" to its limits.

> (Karnsund, 1985, p. [1])

Questions

1 What is the future of Scania trucks in America: Should Saab-Scania pull out of this market, go coast-to-coast with it, or follow the example of Mercedes and Volvo and tie in with an American manufacturer?

2 Should Saab-Scania and Volvo merge, even if only in their international (non-Swedish) operations?

References

Chatterton, M. (1980). *Saab the Innovator*. Newton Abbot, Devonshire: David & Charles.

Eriksson, I. (1985). "Scania – What It is and What It Stands For," In "Saab-Scania Kicks Into High Gear" (*Report of the Saab-Scania Management Conference*, 1985, March 25-28, Linköping) pp. 13-14. Linköping: Saab-Scania.

Gawell, J. (1985). *Sweden's Automotive Industry*. Stockholm: Association of Swedish Automobile Manufacturers and Wholesalers.

Herman, D.J. (1990, February). "David J. Herman charts Saab Automobile AB course," (Press Information, No. 0290:07). Orange, CT: Saab-Scania of America.

Kapstein, J. (1986, December 16). "Saab's Well-Engineered Entry Into U.S. Trucking," *Business Week*, p. 54.

Karnsund, G. (1985). "Art in Technology," (Publication No. U.8533E[20]). Linköping: Saab-Scania.

Perret, P. (1987, May 19). "The Saab 900: Formula Still Works," *Times-Picayune* (New Orleans), p. D5.

Ramsey, R.D. (1986). "Volvo Corporation's Strategy for International Business: The View From the Home Office," Gothenburg, Sweden. In W.A. Hamel (Ed.), *1986 HRMOB Biennial Eastern Region Conference HRMOB Proceedings*. (pp. 125-129). Virginia Beach, Va: Maximilian Press.

Robson, G. (1983). *Saab Turbo 99 and 900 Series; 3,4,5-Door*. London: Osprey Publishing.

Rossi, S., & Nobile, K. (1989, December). "General Motors and Saab-Scania sign agreement: joint ventures in passenger and engineering businesses," (Press Information No. 1289:82). Orange, CT: Saab-Scania of America.

Rossi, S., & Nobile, K. (1990, March). "Final closing of Saab-Scania, AB/General Motors joint venture announced," (Press Information, No. 0390:15). Orange, CT: Saab-Scania of America.

Saab-Scania Group. (1991). *Saab-Scania annual report 1990*. Linköping: Saab-Scania.

Saab-Scania Group. (1992). *Saab-Scania annual report 1991*. Linköping: Saab-Scania.

Sjögren, G.A. (1984). *The Saab Way – The First 35 Years of Saab Cars, 1949-1984*. Nyköping: Gust. Österbergs Tryckeri.

30. Formulating a strategy
for a merchandising firm in Malaysia[7]

Additional topics covered: family businesses, motivation, human resource management, organizational structure.

Introduction

Hambrick and Lei (1985) have categorized three substreams in the area of strategy. (1) The first is the situation-specific view that treats strategy as a future oriented plan that juxtaposes the firm and its market environment. Often labeled as the field study approach, this method has the clinical attribute. More recently, longitudinal case studies (Mintzberg and Waters, 1982, 1985; Prasad, 1986) have attempted not only empirical descriptions, but have also proposed typologies and hypotheses. (2) Another is the universal approach, which implies that universal "laws" are applicable to all situations. The limits to this view, however, are extensively demonstrated (Hall and Howell, 1985). (3) The third is the contingency view. "Contingency theories state that the appropriateness of different strategies depends on the competitive settings of businesses." (Hambrick and Lei, 1985, p. 765).

These and other approaches will no doubt have limitations (Duncan, 1979). Moreover, we tend to think the approach a researcher takes itself is contingency. For example, the case study approach, including the longitudinal dimension, is feasible if the researcher has some consulting or other relationship with a firm or firms (e.g., Ferdows and Spray, 1985; Hamel and Prahalad, 1985; Prasad, 1985). Similarly, the cross-sectional statistical type of contingency approaches to studying strategy depends upon the access to data banks such as PIMS (e.g. Galbraith and Schendel, 1983; Hambrick and Lei, 1985; Harrigan, 1985). Yet we do not see these approaches as mutually exclusive. We view them as complementary. Given our present access to data and information on the Malaysian firm, we have taken the field study approach.

Because the firm is more than 100 years old and has remained under the control of the founding family, it is reasonable to assume that it will remain a family enterprise in the future under George Chen, who has an engineering degree and an MBA with a concentration in strategic management.

Purpose and method

The purpose of this paper is not to test any hypothesis. Rather, it is to examine a small Chinese merchandising firm from a clinical perspective. The rapport between researchers and the firm was established when a third-generation member of the

7 By S.B. Prasad, Ohio University and Central Michigan University; Ellsworth Holden, Ohio University; and Michael Heng, Promomark Inc. Used with permission.

founding family (whom we call George Chen) became associated with us. The purpose of Chen's research was to examine which concepts and tools of strategic movement would have the most relevance to the firm of which he was going to be the managing director. We focus, in this paper, only on a small number of dimensions that we believe are critical to the future success of this firm, Oriental Crafts Ltd. The extent to which George Chen succeeded in introducing any of the strategic conditions he felt were important in repositioning the firm in Malaysia will be discussed in the final section. In the initial two sections, we narrate the origin and scope of the firm as well as the changing dynamics of the firm's marketing environment.

Exhibit 1
Oriental Crafts, Ltd.

Quantifiable Goals	Present	Intended in the Future
Return on net worth	4.8%	10%
Sales growth (per year)	2.3	10
Profit margin (after tax)	3.0	5
Earnings per share	$.1	.27

Non-quantifiable Goals	
Innovation	To be in the forefront with regard to the firm's product – market scope
Management Performance	To become professional
Consumers	To place emphasis on meeting consumers' needs; provide 'value' for thier money
Employee Attitudes	To foster participation, in steps
Market Posititon	To regain the Number One position by emphasising the service attributes of a 'generational' firm
Productivity	To enhance it in a measurable way

notes:
1 Present return on net worth is upon 1983 figures
2 Sales growth at present is based on 1981-1984 year moving average
3 Earnings per share assumes that privately issued shares will remain constant

---

Oriental Crafts: A brief history

Oriental Crafts Ltd., began more than a century ago in the old bazaar section of Kuala Lumpur, the federal capital of Malaysia. The original business imported antiques from China and marketed them in Malaysia. Prior to the country's independence in 1957, Malaysian Chinese were the primary customers of Oriental Crafts. Tourists from around the world were a second tier of customers.

Oriental Crafts markets antiques, curios, souvenir items and the like in two retail outlets adjacent to each other. Chen said the purpose of Oriental Crafts was to "cater to the needs of discerning customers of quality interior items, both functional and decorative, throughout Malaysia." This new definition was considered broad enough not to preclude any lucrative opportunities in the future. Chen felt that a

Exhibit 2
Oriental Crafts, Ltd.

	1980	1981	1982	1983	1984*
Chinese Heritage	n.a	5	31	29	30
Oriental Crafts	38	34	22	21	21
Asian Arts	14	15	12	13	14
Other Competitors	48	46	55	37	35
Total M$ volume (in millions)	2.7	3.3	4.6	4.8	5.1

M$ – Malaysia dollar or ringgit

five-year plan was the most reasonable for his business because no extenuating characteristics in the firm's environment proved otherwise. His conviction was that the ability to do the right things at the right time would be enhanced in a five-year plan. Past performance and the history of the company, although interesting, were downplayed by Chen who felt the organization culture of the firm and those in the industry might inhibit rational approaches. The present and the intended future was operationalized in quantifiable and non-quantifiable terms as shown in Exhibit 1.

George Chen realized there was turbulence in the once-stable industry, caused primarily by new entrants. Oriental Crafts now had to cope with a more complex environment. This was not an isolated case. Chen decided to begin a market and customer analysis in terms of the three SBUs he identified earlier.

The concept of SBUs is expressed in terms of some distinction within the firm. For example, according to Pains and Naumes (1982): "Various strategic business units (SBUs) – divisions, bureaus, profit centers, product lines, departments – may be identified independently if they sell a distinctive set of products or services to an identifiable group of customers or clients..."; Bryars (1984): "SBUs are units within a larger organization that sell a product or service to an identifiable and distinct group of customers or clients." George Chen found the concept of SBU relevant to his firm, although it was a small company. He recognized that identifying a small number of SBUs within Oriental Crafts would help him analyze and understand the varying nature of the different markets, competition and environmental factors therein. He identified three SBUs that represented the total product-market scope of the firm:

SBU Product/Services

a) *Retailing of antiques and reproductions*

b) *Retailing of linen, lace and curios*

c) *Wholesaling of linen, lace and curios*

Unlike a large U.S. retailing company, however, certain resources of Oriental Crafts Ltd., such as management and finance, were indivisible in terms of the identified SBUs. Yet, SBU-A was the cornerstone of the firm. Chen concentrated on the competition and market share dimensions of SBU-A as shown in Exhibit 2.

In preparing Exhibit 2 and focusing on the distinct competence of Oriental Crafts, Chen found the approach of Tourangeau (1981) to be the most helpful. The industry that includes Oriental Crafts has about 12 firms. Of these, three account for a major share of the market. Oriental Crafts is the oldest of the three. The other two are Chinese Heritage Company and Asian Arts. Market share estimates by Chen suggest that Oriental Crafts has been losing the share mostly to Chinese Heritage. What about Asian Arts? For a number of years in the 1960s and 1970s, Asian Arts was an affiliate of Oriental Crafts. But Oriental Crafts recently emerged as a major competitor. Most of the enterprise, contacts, suppliers and other competencies that Asian Arts possessed were drawn from Oriental Crafts. Furthermore, Asian Arts in late 1983 acquired additional space at its present location and opened a branch in the suburbs of Petaling Jaya. Its product line included household brass ornaments. The firm has shown some clout in marketing that line in recent years.

Chinese Heritage was a relatively new entrant in the industry. Formed by a Hong Kong antique dealer in collaboration with a smaller dealer in Malaysia, Chinese Heritage's greatest strength was finding first-choice antiques and reproductions from mainland China, according to Chen.

The marketing approach of Chinese Heritage was also novel. Regular display shows or exhibitions were held in major hotels in Kuala Lumpur and other cities in Malaysia, aimed primarily at foreign residents and visitors to the country. At least half a dozen firms took the same route to market entry, but they were not successful.

Market and Customer Analysis

Antiques and reproductions (SBU-A)

Customers for antiques were generally well-educated people. Most of them were professionals (architects, lawyers, doctors and senior business executives). From his company's historical records, Chen estimated that per capita sales ranged between M$1,000 to M$4,000. Customers were also sophisticated. They had good knowledge of antiques and the reasonable trade-offs between rarity, uniqueness, and price. A further segmentation was along the lines of genuine antiques, foreign reproductions, and local reproductions. Profit margins were high in antiques, but sourcing had become more difficult than before. Although margins were low, volume was high for reproductions. A boom in the late 1970s and early 1980s in housing, especially luxury apartments and flats, and the emergence of "interior decorating" had a mixed impact on Oriental Crafts.

Linen, lace and curios (SBU-B and SBU-C)

The market for linen, lace and curios was broader than for antiques. The country's social structure was a major factor. Malay people (Bumiputras) are artistically inclined: they take great pride in decorating their homes and are fond of intricate lace and linen. Chinese and Indians, except for professional elites, are less conscious of their homes and are not willing to pay higher prices for good quality linen and lace products.

> Oriental Crafts operated on the assumption that it had a divine right to operate profitably forever – a management attitude that was nurtured by the past growth and success of the firm. Chen wanted that attitude to change. He preferred close linkages with customers, suppliers, government officials, bankers and friendly competitors so that Oriental could foresee changes in the market. He wanted his key subordinates trained in the art of raising the "right questions."

The curio segment also includes handicraft products. The market for these was similar to that of linen and lace products, but also included expatriates and foreign tourists. Chen considered the wholesaling of these products as a separate and distinct business.

Framing a strategy for Oriental Crafts Ltd.

For George Chen, planning a proper strategy was important. He was familiar with strategy problems in American companies, and he had studied the Japanese concept of the two-sided coin: formulation on one side and implementation on the other. He was convinced that the latter was a good strategy for his company. In identifying the SBUs, he had noted that certain organizational resources were indivisible among the three. Nonetheless, the distinctions made between the three SBUs were analytically very helpful. In his scanning of American professional literature, he was impressed with the writings of Professor Robert Hayes of Harvard. He agreed with Hayes' notion of means-ways-ends sequence identified earlier and more fully expressed recently (Hayes, 1985).

The following is the strategy, expressed in general terms, by George Chen:

> To strive for market leadership and to practice a focused strategy in a profitable segment of our company's business, the thrust of our strategy should be in rebuilding our name and reputation. To be an effective retailer-wholesaler, the driving force of Oriental should be responsive, alert and swift reactions to market contingencies.

Chen had recognized two key factors in the family organization. First, he believed that human resources were of paramount importance in the antique/curio business. Second, he wanted to instill a sense of commitment throughout the organization. His predecessor had mistakenly assumed that the existing alliance between Oriental and Asian Arts would never change. Because Oriental was dominant and more established, he never envisioned Asian Arts emerging as a competitor.

As noted earlier, Chen did not only plan strategy; he considered how to implement it.

Implementing strategy at Oriental Crafts

George subscribed to the premise of Bourgeois and Browdin (1984), which resembled the traditional business policy and strategic planning model. In this model the chief executive officer uses economic and competitive analyses to plan resources for achieving objectives. It contains a strong normative bias toward centralized direction. Chen attempted to cast this model against the backdrop of his firm's culture as well as the societal culture in Malaysia. He concluded that a centralized mode would be the most appropriate first step for Oriental Crafts.

Preparing to implement the strategy was another important step for Oriental Crafts. Chen noted five areas that he should rework in detail before initiating the strategic management process. These areas were:

(1) controls and checkpoints to ensure that the strategy was appropriate and on the right track;

(2) innovative ways of compensating the employees;

(3) reliance on earnings per se as the indicator of success, not as an absolute;

(4) reward for non-profit achievements, such as developing personal skills, identifying market signals, setting up competitive barriers, providing good customer relations on a continued basis, and being alert to governmental rules and regulations.

These were considered essential to the achievement of the strategy of Oriental Crafts. Even though Oriental Crafts may not achieve its goal during the first three years, it should not revert to the old way of doing business because the environmental/competitive conditions have drastically changed. Chen also did not rule out a future alliance, such as a merger with Asian Arts.

> Chen recognized that the most pivotal step in implementing the strategy was to clearly explain the objectives to key employees in the company. While the company's objectives provided purpose and direction, he wanted employees to rethink their roles with the firm. He preferred not to get into the nuts and bolts of the plan because he feared that would only distort the overall perspective gained by his subordinate managers.

Questions

1 Review the ways in which changes in competitive and other conditions have changed the strategy of Oriental Crafts to date. Especially in light of globalizing trends, how might conditions change in the near future and what changes in strategy might be adaptive to such future conditions?

2 How does this case suggest an internationalized role for strategic thinking as an alternative to sophisticated planning performed by large departments or staffs?

References

Ansoff, Igor H. (1965). *Corporate Strategy*. New York: McGraw-Hill Book Company.

Borgeois III, L.J. and Brodwin, David R. "Strategic Implementation: Five Approaches to an Elusive Phenomenon," *Strategic Management Journal*. Vol. 5 (3): pp. 241-264.

Bryars, Lloyd L. (1984). *Strategic Management: Planning and Interpretation*. New York: Harper and Row Publishers.

Duncan, Robert B. *Qualitative Research Methods in Strategic Management*. Schendel. D.E. and Hofer. C.W. (eds.), Boston: Little, Brown and Company. pp. 424-447.

Ferdows, Kara and Spray, C. (1985). "Honeywell Pace: Cases A and B," *Journal of Management Case Studies*, Vol. 1. pp. 60-73.

Hall, Graham and Howell, S. "The Experience Curve From the Economist's Perspectives," *Strategy Management Journal*, Vol. 6 (3) pp. 197-211.

Hambrick, Donald C. and Lel, D. "Towards an Empirical Prioritization of Contingency Variables for Business Strategy." *Academy of Management Journal*, Vol 28 (24) pp. 763-788.

Harnel, Gary and Prahalad, C.K. (1985). "Do You Really have a Global Strategy?" *Harvard Business Review*, Vol 86 (3) pp. 139-148.

Harrigan, Kathryn R. (1985). "Strategies for Intrafirm Transfers and Outside Sourcing," *Academy of Management Journal*, Vol 28 (4). pp. 914-925.

Hayes, Robert H. (1985). "Strategic Planning – Forward in Reverse?" *Harvard Business Review*, Vol 63 (6) pp. 111-119.

Minztberg, Henry, and Waters, J.A. (1982). "Tracking Strategy in an Entrepreneurial Firm," *Academy of Management Journal*, Vol. 25 (3) pp. 465-499.

Ohmai, Kenichi. (1982). *The Mind of the Strategist*. New York: McGraw-Hill Book Company.

Paine, Frank T. and Naumes, W. (1982). *Organizational Strategy and Policy*. New York: The Dryden Press.

Prasad, S.E. (1985). "Acquisition Strategy of an Irish Firm," *Managing in a Global Economy*. Sanders P., and Yanouzas J.N. (Eds.), Tilburg, The Netherlands. pp. 75-81.

Tourganou, Kevin W. (1981). *Strategy Management*. New York: McGraw-Hill Book Co.

31. KNP, N.V.[8]

Additional topics covered: production management, transportation and plant site costs.

Koninklijke Nederlandse Paperfabrieken, N.V. (KNP), or Royal Dutch Papermills, produces and sells paper and board products to printing and packaging industries throughout the world. The firm originated in 1850 as a small papermill in Maastricht, the Netherlands. One of the firm's three papermaking mills operates in the city today. Another papermill is located across the Maas River in Belgium. The firm also produces packaging materials at various European locations and has investments in paper merchant operations in a number of countries.

The company's headquarters are in a modern office building in a newer section of the ancient and historic city of Maastricht. It is here that Wilmer Zetteler, the commercial director of KNP België, ponders the emerging international business strategy of KNP and the decisions that will be necessary to meet the challenges faced by the firm.

KNP and the world paper industry

The evolution of the papermaking industry and the emergence of the modern European economic system have shaped KNP. In the year following World War II, the relatively undamaged but depreciated plant at Maastricht produced only 10,000 tons of paper. By 1950 the firm was pioneering the production of coated paper. KNP was the first European producer of such papers to use technology obtained under a license from the Consolidated Paper Company in the United States. A companion plant that produces top grade coated paper for brochures, art books, and catalogues is located at Nijmegen on the Waal River. Another mill at Meerssen, a town outside Maastricht, produces colored and watermarked paper.

The oil price shock of 1973 led the firm to reconsider its fundamental strategy and further specialize in the production of high-grade coated papers to gain prominence in international markets. The firm was already well known for this specialty, but managed to expand its position. A mill was constructed at Lanaken, across the Maas in Belgium, just north of the Albert Canal, to produce more lightweight coated paper. This paper is used for magazines, brochures, catalogues, and promotional material.

---

8 By Alan Bauerschmidt, University of South Carolina, and Daniel Sullivan, Tulane University. Used with permission.

A separate packaging division of KNP has nine plants that produce various forms of carton board for the packaging industry and other industrial applications. These products include solid, folding, corrugated, and other board products for making boxes. In addition, the plants at Oude Pekela and Sappemeer produce a greyboard for jigsaw puzzles, books and various types of deluxe packaging.

The plant at Oude Pekela in The Netherlands also produces solid board that is used in making boxes for shipping flowers, vegetables, fruits and various exports. This board product is manufactured on machines similar to those that make paper, but the board machines at KNP use wastepaper rather than virgin pulp as a raw material in the manufacturing process. The firm owns and operates eight wastepaper collection firms that handle 250,000 tons of raw material a year. Some 30,000 tons of capacity were added in 1986 when two more firms were purchased.

> This product of KNP's "Verpakkingsgroep" is exported to 35 countries. The Kappa board trade name and the firm is one of the world's largest manufacturers of this product.

A factory in the Dutch town of Eerbeek produces folding box board. The pharmaceutical and food industries use this product, which also is manufactured from wastepaper. Overall, KNP processes 500,000 tons of wastepaper a year.

KNP acquired in 1986 the German firm of Herzberger Papierfabrik Ludwig Osthushenrich GmbH and Co. KG, which manufactures boxes in four locations in western Germany. The Oberstot plant, gained in the Herzberger acquisition, also produces liner and corrugated board used in boxes and other packaging applications. The Herzberg and Oberau plants that were acquired also produce the corrugated materials used in box converting operations. These acquisitions increased the capacity of the packaging division of KNP by 60 percent.

Figure A

KNP Plant locations

In addition to the four German packaging plants, KNP owns box-making operations in The Netherlands, Italy, and Spain. Each is supplied with board stock manufactured by other divisions of the firm. KNP also has a joint venture with Buhrmann-Tetterode, nv in operating a mill that can produce 350,000 tons of paper for the manufacture of corrugated board. With the addition of a fourth machine at the mill in 1986, this joint venture has become one of the principal suppliers of packaging paper of the European market.

KNP began a series of acquisitions of paper merchants beginning in the late 1970s. Each acquisition was a defensive strategy to prevent competitors from capturing existing channels of distribution of KNP products. KNP has paper merchant operations in Belgium, France, and the United Kingdom. The firm also owns a 35 percent interest in Proost en Brandt, one of the two largest paper merchants in the Netherlands, and a 51 percent share in Scaldia Papier B.V. in Nijmegen.

Exhibit 1 displays the group structure of KNP, while Exhibits 4 and 5 summarize the plant capacity of the principal divisions of the company. Exhibits 2 and 3 provide a financial summary of the firm, based on current annual reports. Figure A shows the location of facilities in the Netherlands.

Internationalizing of the firm

KNP's activity outside the Netherlands is not surprising. As with most Dutch manufacturers, the firm has always been an exporter and maintained an international perspective. The market for paper in the Netherlands is insufficient to support a plant. Europe is KNP's principal market. In 1986, 75 percent of its paper and 45 percent of its packaging materials were sold outside the Netherlands.

The firm has progressively increased the capacity of its plants to meet growing demand. Such demand can only exist in a nation or an integrated group of nations with a modern and sophisticated economy. The European Community is an example of such a market. The emergence of the Community in the years following World War II paralleled the development of KNP's international ventures.

The modern manufacture of paper products depends upon machines that produce large volumes. KNP has state-of-the-art technology that can produce such volumes.

The Netherlands has a population of 15 million, not nearly enough people to support a single modern paper manufacturing plant. On the other hand, the European Community has a population of about 275 million and a modern economy that can easily support a number of competing paper firms. Figure B shows the makeup of the European Community.

In most European countries, paper is traditionally marketed through paper merchants who distribute products to converters and printers. These merchants serve national or sub-national markets.

Yet sometimes market development is not straightforward. When the demand for lightweight machine-coated paper emerged in the United States, KNP had a paper merchant on each coast for other products of the firm. But the lightweight coated product required a more direct approach to the printing customer. KNP skirted traditional distributors and developed an exclusive relationship with the Wilcox-Walter-Furlong Paper Company, a paper merchant in Philadelphia that stocked KNP's product in the eastern United States. In the western United States, the firm marketed its product through the offices of MacMillan Bloedel, a firm with a 30 percent stock interest in KNP.

KNP's foreign activities can be divided into two segments and two stages. Part of the first stage has existed since the firm began exporting to adjacent nations in the early 19th century.

The second stage began with the development of the European Community, which was an important factor in the growth of KNP. The development of the company after World War II was typical of other manufacturers in Europe. Management knowledge and skill was necessary to seize the opportunity provided by the reconstruction of the European economy.

The European Community is designed to break down barriers that prevent economic activity. As the community emerged, paper firms and other businesses used skilled sales agents who were proficient in dealing with the new market. Firms succeeded in extending their markets by meeting the needs of each nation.

Language was not a barrier at KNP, where executives typically speak a number of European languages. Cultural differences also were not a factor.

Outside Europe, KNP initially exported specialized products to Africa and the Middle East. In the early 1980s, the company began exporting to Australia and the Far East and began testing markets in the United States and Canada. No special cultural and language barriers emerged because of the company's previous experience in exporting to European nations.

KNP penetrated the United Kingdom market by working through a sales agent with contacts in the printing trades. Later, the company solidified its position in the United Kingdom by hiring an English paper merchant, Contract Papers Limited, to distribute its products. KNP now owns 45 percent interest in the company.

KNP today is one of Europe's largest exporters of coated paper and a leading producer of board. According to KNP's 1986 annual report, 31 percent of sales were in the Netherlands, 55 percent elsewhere in the European Community, and 14 percent elsewhere in the world.

Figure B

KNP Plant locations

Globalization of the firm

KNP cannot be considered a fully globalized company because it does not manufacture products in the markets it serves.

While the specialized paper products of KNP are global products, their manufacture does not fit the global integrated strategy as described by Yves Doz and other theorists of international business. Therefore, KNP would be best described as following a multi-focal international business strategy.

The paper industries of Europe and North America have different configurations. American firms tend to be more fully integrated vertically and horizontally in respect to the full range of forest products. European firms, with the exception of the Scandinavians, have little opportunity to buy extensive woodlands in their home countries. Because North American firms have woodlands and a large domestic market, it is difficult for European firms to become established in the market. The Swedes and Finns, on the other hand, have forest resources, but they are handicapped by poor markets for finished paper in their countries.

The KNP has acquired foreign paper merchants with connections in various world markets. KNP owns Papetries Libert S.A. in Paris. The firm has a 51 percent holding in Saldiaa Papier, N.V. in Wilrijk, Belgium, and a 45 percent stake in Contract Papers (Holdings) Ltd. in London. In The Netherlands, KNP has a 35 percent interest in Proost en Bandt, N.V. in Amsterdam, and a 51 percent interest in Scaldia Papier B.V. in Nijmegen.

These acquisitions were made in 1978 and 1979 as a defensive move against competitors in the European Community. Competitors had begun acquiring paper merchants that sold KNP products and threatened to use them to promote their own products. Meanwhile, the paper merchants acquired by KNP continue to stock a full range of goods, including those produced by competitors.

In terms of global distribution, KNP is among the leading firms in Europe.

No distinct figures are available on KNP's foreign revenues. Overall, distribution provided 2 percent of operating results, while the paper group provided 62.9 percent of operating revenues and 71.7 percent of operating results. The packaging group produced 29.2 percent of operating revenue and 26.3 percent of operating results. These figures ignore the influence of internal transfers, which made up 8.2 percent of the total operating activity of the firm.

Other aspects of globalization

While the purchasing of paper merchants was a major thrust into the international market for KNP, the firm took steps to globalize earlier. Twenty years ago, the company purchased shares in Celupal S.A., a manufacturer of paper products for the packaging industry in Spain.

In many respects, the creation of KNP België, N.V. in Lanaken is a prime example of the establishment of a greenfield manufacturing operation in a foreign country. The Lanaken paper manufacturing operation was established at the point when the business strategy of the firm shifted toward the production of special grades of coated paper for the printing trades. This decision, just before the energy crisis in the early 1970s, enabled the firm to exploit those grades of specialty paper that had a higher value added in manufacture. The creation of the greenfield operation at Lanaken supported an offensive European niche strategy, while the acquisition of paper merchants in France, Belgium and the United Kingdom was a defensive maneuver to prevent erosion of existing channels of distribution that supported the more extensive range of products produced by KNP.

The plant that was finally constructed at Lanaken had to be located somewhere in the heavy industrial triangle of northwest Europe to minimize transportation costs to key European markets. The Liege-Limburg-Aachen area is close to the heart of this triangle and has the necessary infrastructure for paper production. The nearby Albert Canal provides direct access to the facilities of the port of Antwerp and pulp shipments from worldwide sources.

The situation is somewhat different at the packaging materials operations of KNP in Germany, Italy, and Spain. Raw materials are shipped from KNP operations in the Netherlands and Germany. These locations are strategically situated to minimize transportation costs.

Future globalization

A more important question is whether KNP would ever consider harvesting forest resources, given the limited opportunity to manufacture pulp in the Netherlands. In contrast, some American and Japanese firms have been enticed by less developed nations to develop and harvest forests so that they have sure sources of pulp. This is one example of globalization. Another example is shipping antiquated paper machines or converting equipment to less developed countries where labor and energy costs are lower.

Given its history, KNP will adopt whatever production and distribution strategy is necessary to remain competitive in the global market. KNP, however, will not enter the American market in the near future because a temporary supply shortage exists there and the capacity of the firm is temporarily underutilized. It must be ready to make long-term commitment to the U.S. market before launching exports.

Future strategic developments

The top management team at KNP is aware of these developments in the world paper industry. Zetteler will take these features into account as he helps plan KNP's future, as marketing and production strategies in the industry are already showing signs of change. For example, the firm in early 1987 started a 70,000 ton capacity chemi-thermomechanical pulp line in at the Lanaken mill. This is KNP's first integrated production operation that uses softwood drawn from the Ardennes, instead of the chemical pulp purchased in the international commodity markets. The firm is considering doubling this integrated capacity with a second pulp line in the next few years.

The emergence of KNP and other firms of integrated European producers of special papers would enhance competition in various world markets. The U.S. market has already been penetrated because of the declining value of the dollar and the superior quality of certain European paper products. Any firm that entered the U.S. market, however, would have to consider transportation costs and the advantages of U.S. producers that have forest resources.

KNP also appears to have no intention of marketing specialized production components in various parts of the world. The industry is limited in the amount of global specialization that can be practiced. On the other hand, the firm does specialize in the production of board and its conversion into packaging materials in various countries.

Questions

1 Should KNP manufacture in other national locations to obtain economies of transportation in raw material and final product?

2 Will competitive pressures require further forward integration by KNP into paper merchant operations?

3 What potential impact (and in what time frame) will new technology have on KNP plant placement production methods and materials producing?

Exhibit 1
KNP, N.V.
Group and Divisional Organization

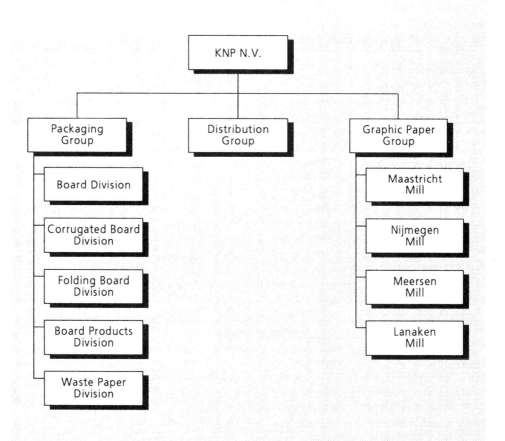

Exhibit 2

KNP, N.V. Balance Sheet
(Figures in Thousands of Dutch Guilders)

	1986	1985	1984	1983	1982	1981	1980	1979	1978	1977
ASSETS										
Tangible Fixed Assets	1156529	606237	433024	397588	384692	382035	341651	332083	323274	334550
Financial Fixed Assets	51848	55252	43826	7337	17752	20067	18603	19720	43716	54239
Inventories	289363	201059	203194	182381	178384	185376	163377	157340	130188	117327
Accounts Receivable	418355	260556	261031	227434	203701	199923	162865	162105	123938	116868
Cash	185307	195864	10938	8311					5471	9572
	2101402	1318968	958013	823051	784529	787401	686496	671248	626587	632556
LIABILITIES AND EQUITY										
Issued Share Capital	82810	74180	70943	70943	59185	56909	56909	56909	56909	56909
Share Premium Account	103691	58784	41644	41644	31420	33696	33696	33696	33696	33696
Other Reserves	421543	330634	255009	206545	173966	168820	165382	165322	168871	164501
Shareholders Equity	608044	463596	367596	319132	264571	259425	255987	255927	259476	255106
Minority Interests in Group Companies	104918	70786	2215	123	123	140	106	103	103	103
Equalization Fund (Subsidiaries)	180434	70858	61451	47677	39464	34135	22325	10037	3894	
Group Equity	893396	605242	431262	366932	304158	293700	278418	266067	263473	255209
Provisions	198743	102802	105403	92809	118259	117348	109842	114348	112826	118911
Long Term Liabilities	535398	271398	137988	147820	166002	147535	110017	121448	130684	108578
Current Liabilities	473865	339526	283360	215490	196110	228854	188219	169385	119604	149858
	2101402	1318968	958013	823051	784529	787437	686496	671248	626587	632556

Exhibit 3

KNP, N.V. Profit and Loss Statement
(Figures in thousands of Dutch Guilders)

	1986	1985	1984	1983	1982	1981	1980	1979	1978	1977
Net Sales	1581491	1616344	1496887	1213461	1174308	1164384	1065293	950886	816592	717514
Changes in Inventories	4079	11301	3587	-9165	8870	8387	4236	11504	5439	2762
Own Work Capitalized	7191	6573	4077	5274	5609	5782	5214	3573	2879	1263
Other Operating Income	8672	2583	475	796	2241	1331	652	2318	1949	529
	1601433	1636801	1505026	1210366	1191028	1179884	1075485	968281	826859	722068
Raw Materials and Consumables	885784	917468	944217	717926	722904	742812	627443	524025	419638	411239
Work Subcontracted and other External Costs	89073	82489	63485	59173	52316	51036	53421	50912	42925	33238
Labor Costs	316833	314731	288278	283633	290399	287311	289270	273932	250956	205788
Depreciation of Tangible Fixed Assests	74809	71547	55113	54758	52836	51524	51290	50132	47685	44675
Other Operating Costs	69786	59666	49572	42649	38245	39891	39842	36867	32136	25563
Total Operating Costs	1406285	1445901	1400665	1158139	1156700	1172574	1061266	935868	793340	720503
Operating Results	195148	190900	104361	52227	34328	7310	14219	32413	33519	1565
Profit on Financial Fixed Assests	131	167	201	0	0	0	0	0	0	900
Interest Income	5101	11558	3437	2139	2609	2527	1478	1351	1297	784
Interest Expense	13871	27624	18443	17603	22236	19854	15716	14200	12226	6564
Results on ordinary operations before taxes	186509	175001	89556	36763	14701	-10017	-19	19564	22590	-3315
Taxes thereon	68720	66140	27643	10457	4014	-5959	-143	10284	9637	-3245
	117789	108861	61913	26306	10687	-4058	124	9280	12953	-70
Share on Results of Partly-owned companies	15103	8397	1481	-1672	-2070	-2128	55	1813	920	1446
Results on ordinary operations after taxes	132892	117258	63394	24634	8617	-6186	179	11093	13873	1376
Extraordinary income (expense net)	0	0	0	11764	-97	0	-14443	0	0	0
	132892	117258	63394	36398	8520	-6186	-14264	11093	13873	1376
Minority Interests	297	-21	-16	0	0	0	0	0	0	0
	132595	117279	63410	36398	8520	-6186	-14264	11093	13873	1376

Exhibit 4

KNP, N.V.

Plant Capacities of Packaging Group

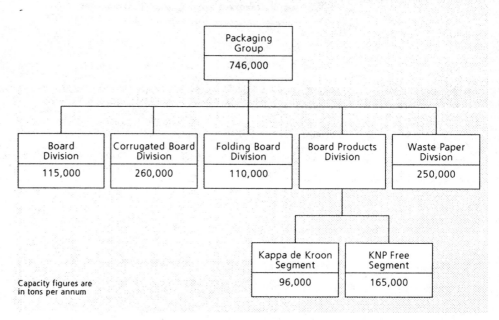

Capacity figures are
in tons per annum

Exhibit 5

KNP, N.V.

Plant Capacities of Graphic Paper Group

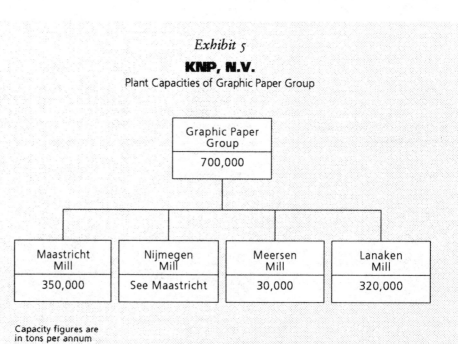

Capacity figures are
in tons per annum

32. Critical incidents in international strategy[9]

purpose

To problem-solve various business strategies for international corporations.

group size

Any number of groups of 3-6 members.

time required

20 minutes or more.

exercise schedule

1 Read critical incidents and develop strategy (pre-class)

2 Small groups discuss (optional)   20 min

Groups of 3-6 members try to identify the main strategic issues in each of the cases and try to achieve some kind of consensus on which strategy to use.

3 Class discussion   20+ min   20 min

Instructor leads discussion on strategic issues. Are there some common issues which need to be addressed in international dealings? How can managers be more sensitive to issues in international business?

Critical Incidents[10]

Although strategic decision-making is often quite complex and filled with many issues, the caselets below are simplified examples of composite companies, based on true business cases. The idea is to discuss the few issues in these caselets, without all the complexity which occurs in longer cases.

1 A clothing manufacturer has been losing business because of a competitor's lower prices and must take some action soon before the balance sheet looks worse. One idea would be to locate a new plant in Mexico where wages are cheaper. It has been estimated this could save the company enough to reduce the price of clothing by 15%, which would once again make it competitive. However, one of the top managers has mentioned that a shoe factory was just recently relocated to the area in question and it has been hit with higher turnover and lower productivity than expected. He read that the shoes are expected to cost 12% more than former estimates had predicted. Should the company relocate this factory to Mexico? If not, what other strategies could be employed?

2 Equip, Inc., is interested in buying 70% of a large heavy machinery company in one of the former Soviet bloc countries. With a purchase price of $40 million and updating costs of $10 million, Equip figures it can realize a profit within three years, with a decent return for investors. However, the government has balked at Equip owning 70%, and instead wants to sell 35% at $20 million and expects the company to put in $8 million for renovations. Although it has not been explicitly stated (and no direct answer to questions has been given), the international department expects the company to resist laying off the 30% of inflated workforce. This would greatly change the profit picture. Still, if the market proceeds as expected, the company could be earning a respectable profit within five years. Inside information suggests the government will not sell more than 49%, no matter what. Yet, this is the type of machinery you want to get into and know you can develop this market further than almost any other company.

3 Your development and construction company put in a $60 million bid to build the new airport in one of the South American capital cities. The government has decided to privatize the airport. You know the other companies who bid and know you are the most competent. Your idea is to reduce the number of employees at the airport from 2000 to 85, with most work being contracted out to small businesses. Calculations show this to be the most efficient way to run the airport. Figures show this project will mean a net profit of $2 for the company, assuming no major unforseen problems. However, a Canadian firm is given the job, a company you know is on the brink of bankruptcy. You also know the government minister in charge of awarding the contract had spent six months in Canada a couple of years ago. Two years later you are not awarded the contract, and after the Canadian firm goes under, the government comes back to you and offers you the contract. However, because the Canadian firm made promises to keep the 2000 employees and to hire several less than efficient sub-contractors, you are not certain you can

10 Copyright 1993 by Dorothy Marcic. All rights reserved.

make a profit on this venture (for it looks quite difficult to get out of those promises). It even looks like you will lose about $1 million. However, you know that several other major governments considering new airports around the world are looking at this project to see who does it and with what quality, and they are also looking at a few other similar projects now under construction by other companies.

4 You run a large mail order and television ordering business which has enjoyed enormous success in recent years. However, several of your key managers feel it is time to branch out into lesser-developed countries, for there is virtually no competition in these places. They argue that even though profits would be low for several years, your company would have itself firmly established when the market would surge (assuming it in fact would). Other managers do not disagree with that. On the contrary, they feel these are strong reasons to enter such markets. What they argue against are basically the problems of low income and uncertain economic futures in these countries, particularly in four of the countries. Two of the eight proposed even have some political instability (though admittedly not much). They also argue that these countries have poor phone systems, making it difficult for phone calls to get through and most of them do not have any capability of an 800-type system, though a few governments are said to be "thinking it over." Two of the countries are in the Pacific Rim region and are projecting tremendous rates of economic growth in the next five years. However, they are not yet consumer societies and there is some disagreement when and if they will become so. What do you do?

Global strategy, competence-building and strategic alliances[11]

Companies must learn how to better utilize strategic alliances as vehicles for learning new technologies and skills from their alliance partners while simultaneously protecting themselves from being "deskilled" and "hollowed out." Deskilling creates an external dependence for components, supplies, and new designs and technologies. As the rising costs and risks of new product development and new production processes permeate industries, strategic alliances will become even more prevalent. To sustain competitive advantage, companies must learn and assimilate new sources of manufacturing technologies, tacit skills, and core competencies that will become the basis of future industry and technology initiatives.[1] Many firms do not understand the inherent complexities involved in formulating and implementing a strategic alliance and simply seek to cut costs and thereby reduce their commitment to investing in new product development and manufacturing technologies. In effect, firms that rely on strategic alliances as an outsourcing mechanism to secure access to competitive products may find their internal skill sets deteriorating as they become "locked out" from learning new skills and technologies critical to participating in industry evolution.[2]

Alliances are co-alignments between two or more firms in which the partners hope to learn and acquire from each other the technologies, products, skills, and knowledge that are not otherwise available to their competitors. Yet, without clearly understanding and identifying the risks inherent in alliances, collaboration may unintentionally open up a firm's entire spectrum of core competencies, technologies, and skills to encroachment and learning by its partners. There is an old Chinese saying: "One bed, different dreams." When managers of joint ventures "dream different dreams," a lack of mutual understanding can develop, which can then result in the demise of the joint venture. According to Kevin Jones and Walter Shill, members of McKinsey & Company staff in Tokyo, the foreign partner's dream is usually to make good money, while their Japanese partner's dream is to learn new skills. Unfortunately, this arrangement does not lead to the building of a business for the Japanese firm's foreign partner.[3] For example, the dream of the Japanese firm Sumitomo Chemical has never been purely financial, rather it has aspired to be a leader in the pharmaceutical and chemical industries as a basis for future growth. Forming alliances is just one way for Sumitomo Chemical to gain the skills needed to achieve its goal. Many Japanese firms that enter into alliances work hard to learn and digest the skills of their partner. As one Japanese manager stated, "We are ashamed that we have to go out for help. Therefore, it is our duty to learn these skills as fast as possible."[4]

> Alliances can be used as an indirect strategic weapon to slowly "deskill" a partner who does not understand the risks inherent in such arrangements. Collaboration within alliances leads to a competition both in learning new skills and in refining firm capabilities in other products and processes. Although collaboration and competition do go hand-in-hand, how managers approach this duality will significantly affect the firm's propensity for learning and developing new skills.

11 David Lei and John W. Slocum, Jr. Copyright 1992 by the Regents of the University of California. Reprinted from the *California Management Review*, 35(1), 81-87. By permission of the Regents.

The growing ranks of industrial dependence

Table 1 illustrates how dependent many U.S. firms have become on foreign partners, especially Japanese ones, for critical components and production processes in six key industries. In consumer electronics alone, no U.S. manufacturer produces its own color television sets, VCRs, stereo equipment, or compact disc players. All electronics products sold under the Eastman Kodak, General Electric, RCA, Zenith, or Westinghouse brands are made by their foreign alliance partners and imported into the United States.[5] The electrical power generation and distribution industry (which manufactures capital-intensive products such as steam turbines, generators, and nuclear power equipment) is also becoming the domain of Japanese competitors (such as Hitachi, Toshiba, and Mitsubishi Heavy Industries) as well as a European competitor (Asea-Brown-Boveri). General Electric and Westinghouse, which once dominated the world in the power distribution industry, are now becoming distributors for their own firm's products, especially in the small motors and turbines markets that utilize a high level of microelectronics and precision manufacturing. A similar trend is being repeated in the factory automation and numerical controls industry.[6]

In many of these industries, American firms originally held a commanding position across design, production, distribution, and marketing skills. Yet over the past two decades, they have steadily lost their initiative and in many cases have become second-tier players to strong competitors from Japan and Europe. Although Japanese firms have steadily invested in these areas on their own, what they have learned from their alliance partners has contributed immeasurable insight and skills that have accelerated their development. In most cases, the American firm has unwittingly helped this learning process by letting critical technology flow out of the corporation through misunderstood or poorly implemented alliance mechanisms. Joint ventures, outsourcing agreements, and co-production arrangements can effectively transfer away initiative and learning from the firm to its alliance partner if managers are not cognizant of the different goals held by their alliance partners or if they are not careful about the interrelationships that involve converging technologies.

Alliances, learning, and new sources of competition

Most of the foreign partners shown in Table 1 have successfully used an alliance mechanism to effectively learn new technologies, core skills, and capabilities from a partner. Whether alliances involve licensing, co-production, joint venture, or consortia mechanisms, they all pose the same fundamental risks to firms regarding the flow of information and technologies. By their very nature, alliance mechanisms create direct and indirect windows of opportunity for gaining access to a partner's skills, technologies, core competencies, and even strategic direction.[7]

Technological interrelationships

Although many alliances (particularly joint ventures and consortia) are intended to share costs, reduce risks, obtain economies of scale, and gain access to new markets, one of the partners could find that the costs of sharing technology or skills significantly outweigh the potential benefits. Sharing risks or improving cost position usually requires that both partners share their

The problem is that few products, designs, or production processes are limited to a narrow product/market scope. The growing levels of technological or production-based interrelationships between such once disparate industries as computers, communications, and optics means that collaboration with an alliance partner on one specific product often opens up the firm's entire array of related skills and technologies that may have direct applications to other fields.

Table 1

Areas of Growing U.S. Dependency

Consumer Electronics

GE-Hitachi (TVs)

Westinghouse-Toshiba (TVs)

GE-Samsung (microwave ovens)

GE-Matsushita
(room air conditioners)

Kodak-Canon
(photographic equipment)

Kodak-Matsushita (camcorders)

Kodak-Philips (photo-CD players)

Heavy Machinery

Allis Chalmers-Fiat-Hitachi
(construction equipment)

Ford-Fiat (farm equipment)

Caterpillar (growing outsourcing)

Dresser-Komatsu
(construction equipment)

Deere-Hitachi (farm equipment)

Clark-Samsung (forklift trucks)

Power Generation Equipment

Westinghouse-ABB
(heavy power equipment)

GE-Toshiba (nuclear equipment)

GE-Hitachi (nuclear equipment)

GE-Mitsubishi (steam turbines)

Westinghouse-Mitsubishi (motors)

Westinghouse-Komatsu
(motors, robotics)

ABB-Combustion Engineering
(power equipment)

Composite Materials

GE-Asahi Diamond
(industrial diamonds)

Corning Glass-NGK Insulators
(high energy ceramics)

Hercules-Toray (specialized chemicals)

Armco-Mitsubishi Rayon
(composite plastics)

Factory Equipment

GE-Fanuc (controllers)

GM-Fanuc (robotics)

Bendix-Murata (machine tools)

Cincinnati Milacron (semiconductors,
automated equipment)

Kawasaki-Unimation (robotics)

Fujitsu-McDonnell Douglas (CAD/CAM
systems)

IBM-Sankyo Seiki (robotics)

Houdaille-Okuma (machine tools)

Allen Bradley-Nippondenso
(programmable controls)

Bendix-Yasegawa Tools (robotics)

Office Equipment

ATT-Ricoh (fax machines)

Kodak-Canon (mid-range copiers)

Fuji-Xerox (small copiers)

3M-Toshiba (copiers)

Apple-Toshiba (printers)

RCA-Hitachi (PBX controls)

Hewlett Packard-Canon (laser printers)

Xerox-Sharp (low-end copiers)

knowledge and technological skills concerning the immediate product or manufacturing process under development. For example, the extensive use of carbon fibers and hybrid composites in the aerospace industry has led to more efficient process technologies that allow such materials to be used in sporting equipment, electrical insulators, automobile engines, and even medical equipment. Thus, alliance formation to gain economies of scale in one industry cannot be easily confined to the original technology or specific product class. Because highly interwoven production and technological relationships based on a core competence can provide the means for entering new and different markets, a technology-sharing alliance can undermine a firm's long-term potential in a particular industry.

> Managers and technical specialists working with their foreign counterparts often divulge important technical or design information in incremental amounts that do not seem to matter much at any one time, but which cumulatively represent a rich body of information. Thus, every alliance mechanism provides the opportunity for learning a partner's array of core competencies and skill sets.[9]

Faster learning

Because alliance implementation depends upon frequent day-to-day contact between employees and managers, it is difficult to seal off the many unforeseen gateways and opportunities for a partner to learn about a firm's technologies. The alliance negotiations cannot specify the type, rate, and flow of information that occurs once the partners implement the alliance. One-time technology transfers, such as those initiated through blueprints and design sketches, are not nearly as effective (or dangerous) a learning mechanism as the partner's working with a host's skilled engineers and development people. Tacit information and knowledge that cannot be easily transmitted or expressed in written form is passed on in day-to-day contact.[8] The greatest potential for fast learning is at the plant or design site where the two firms' employees interact daily.

Outsourcing and supply arrangements

Domestic firms often believe that alliances serve ultimately as outsourcing or long-term supply agreements to free up capital for R&D, new products, or higher dividends to stockholders. However, the alliances may actually be creating new competitors in those fields which they eventually intend to enter. Firms entering into outsourcing and supply arrangements often assume that design, manufacturing, and marketing are separable functions that can be delegated to entities outside the firm. Consequently, many firms have concentrated their efforts on designing, distributing, and marketing new product ideas, only to have the production of these products take place in a partner's manufacturing facilities. In numerous cases, this division of labor results in a steady deterioration of the firm's production skills and technologies that are important sources of organizational learning. Consumer electronics firms, such as General Electric, Westinghouse, and Zenith, often enter into supply arrangements through formal alliances with Japanese and Korean partners because of their inability to build low-cost, hi-quality components at home. High domestic costs, exchange rate fluctuations, and the prospect of higher quality encouraged these firms to look abroad for alternative labor and component supply sources. Under these conditions, outsourcing may actually accelerate the "hollowing out" of a domestic industry precisely because foreign partners are able to develop the kinds of human resource skills and technologies that are needed to eventually enter into the industry on their own. This has been the case with General Electric's outsourcing relationship with Samsung of South Korea in microwave ovens.[10]

Collaboration as competition

Although there are numerous problems with strategic alliances when they are poorly under-stood, many firms can still benefit from their alliance partners if they understand that collaboration is in many ways another form of competition. In many instances, the alliances were never intended to survive for more than a few years. Under these conditions, firms must regard their source of sustainable competitive advantage to be their capability for learning and improving their skills. Over time, the direction and flow of knowledge and skills across partners is a significant indicator of each partners' strengths, as well as the alliance's likely evolution. While many alliances are often predicated around securing entry into new markets, sharing of technological risks, or joint product/process development, collaboration often involves both partners' simultaneously competing to learn new skills and capabilities from working with one another.

Table 2
Elements of Initiative

Technological	Strategic
Core competencies that extend to a range of different products	Management focus on activities and skills, rather than price/performance character-istics for rewards
Self-generated innovation to nurture growth and promising technologies	Tolerance of ambiguity and uncertainty
Modern, flexible manufacturing skills that respond fast to change	An understanding of indirect approaches and competitor's unorthodox behavior
Sound, large domestic market base	Looking for opportunities away from home market
Organization embedded skills	Perception that scarcity is around the corner; prosperity is illusory

Building initiative: core competencies and the indirect approach

Building initiative refers to a firm's ability to direct resources that build and refine core competencies, skills, and capabilities in a way that creates competitive advantage. Initiative provides a firm wide latitude to choose its own growth path and to freely maneuver in a fast-changing environment. Alliances can seriously undercut a firm's initiative not only by draining its unique core competencies and skill sets, but also by limiting the firm's strategic choices for managing its environment. Strategic alliances, which were once considered important for building competitive advantage, could actually encumber a firm's ability to move quickly on its own.[11]

Table 2 presents the critical elements of initiative that encompass both technological and strategic dimensions. Because of fierce global competition, senior management must under-stand not only the technologies but also their competitors' motives. Building and maintaining initiative requires that firms focus on a competitor's strengths and weaknesses in all activities.

An understanding of both core competencies and the motives of prospective partners helps each partner's business interests. As Lord Palmerston said long ago about Great Britain's relations with other nations, "We have no eternal allies nor enemies. Our interests are eternal and perpetual and it is our duty to follow these." If each party understands the other's strengths and weaknesses, then an initial balance can be achieved. However, strength and weakness need to be periodically reviewed if an alliance is to survive for a long time.

Elements of initiative

The single most important ingredient of initiative is continuous organizational learning that is focused on core competencies. This focus allows a firm to develop multiple and overlapping technologies and skills into future generations of new products. In addition, this process can be augmented by investments in key skills, such as flexible manufacturing and total quality management.

Another important aspect of building initiative is redirecting the corporate focus away from product/performance characteristics and towards upstream (manufacturing) activities and skills. Maintaining the initiative requires senior management to search for all possible ways to learn new technologies, skills, and competencies from a variety of sources, including strategic alliances. An overly narrow view of the firm as an agglomeration of disparate, distinct products severely undercuts the identification and nurturing of core competencies, which are necessary to the formulation of a learning-based strategy. When managers do not understand how competencies and skills relate to products, then their use of strategic alliances will likely be misunderstood and misguided.

Stages of surrendering initiative

Table 3 shows the various stages of dependency that emanate from a poor understanding of core competencies and of alliance partners' motives. The seven stages of growing dependency reveal the dangerous role alliances can play for those firms that do not understand their partner's dreams.

In the first two stages of dependency, firms seeking to reduce costs look to outsource simple assembly and low-value-added, labor-intensive tasks or components to other countries. This usually involves simple tasks such as wiring assembly, packaging, and other processes whose high labor costs discourage the firm from performing these activities domestically.

Table 3
Stages in dependency on partnerships

stage one:	outsourcing of assembly for inexpensive labor
stage two:	outsourcing of low value components to reduce product price
stage three:	growing levels of value-added components move abroad
stage four:	manufacturing skills, designs and functionally related technologies move abroad
stage five:	disciplines related to quality, precision-manufacturing, feeling, and future avenues of product derivatives leave
stage six:	core skills surrounding components, miniaturization, and complex systems integration move abroad
stage seven:	competitor learns the entire spectrum of products and skills related to the underlying core competence

Stage three involves the manufacturing and assembling of key components abroad, including core components or items that represent the essence of the product itself. At the large European consumer electronics firm N. V. Philips, its compact disc players use miniature lasers and controls developed and produced by Matsushita Electric of Japan. In this case, the groundwork for further transfer of technical knowledge to Matsushita has been established.

Stage four is the turning point. It is where the domestic firm loses initiative and the foreign partner ascends into a commanding position in technology and manufacturing. The U.S. automobile industry's reliance on foreign partners in Japan and Korea for small compact cars typifies a stage four dependency. In this case, GM, Ford, and Chrysler drastically cut back their participation in designing and manufacturing the next generation of small cars. Isuzu, Suzuki, Toyota, Hyundai, and Daewoo are rapidly moving down the learning curve and building future initiative in this industry while GM, Ford, and Chrysler retreat and rely upon alliances as long-term supply agreements.

Stages five and six reflect the growing disarray in the firm that has lost its initiative to learn. When manufacturing skills have been relegated to the alliance partner, the firm ceases to invest in most upstream activities. This is currently the situation with Zenith in color television sets. Zenith still maintains investment and interest in future HDTV technology, but has completely abandoned all manufacturing and design of color television and VCR technology to its Korean partner Goldstar. Although Zenith gets an infusion of cash for both equity and licensing, plus a Korean partner with plants in Asia, the Middle East, Europe, and the U.S., Goldstar will gain valuable access to a new digital-based HDTV system that Zenith is developing in the United States. This HDTV system is considered by many experts to be superior to the older Japanese analog system.

Stage seven typifies a complete exit or divestiture of the business, while the foreign partner begins to apply its long-tenn acquisition of core competencies to other industries and arenas. General Electric's growing dependence on Samsung to develop and produce even smaller, more lightweight microwave ovens not only compromises GE's position in the domestic home appliance industry, but also encourages Samsung to pursue other GE consumer electronic markets.

Some strategic tools create the illusion of building a competitive advantage, but they may actually encourage managers to enter into alliances too quickly. These can undermine corporate efforts to focus on and renew core competencies, while discouraging careful thinking and strategizing of prospective partners' intentions.

Strategic control

Once they realize how dangerous alliances can be if they don't understand their partners' motives, firms can avoid becoming "hollowed out." However, much of the conventional wisdom and strategic analytic tools used by senior managers today actually encourage impulsive alliance formation. These practices aggravate the dependency process.

Separating design from manufacturing and marketing

One fallacy regarding the decision to outsource production to the alliance partner is that design, manufacturing, and marketing are separable tasks. In many products, ranging from machine tools to plastics to jet aircraft, design and manufacturing have become so tightly interwoven that development and commercialization occur in a "seamless" value chain in which it is nearly impossible to determine where one activity ends and another begins. CAD/CAM systems, information networks, and flexible manufacturing platforms are among a growing array of technologies that allow firms to organize their design, manufacturing, and marketing activities concurrently rather than sequentially. Organizing value-added tasks in this manner allows the firm to engage in faster learning.[12] A firm's ability to practice doubleloop learning becomes increasingly important when many underlying product technologies and characteristics are merging together. Firms that excessively outsource their manufacturing activities to an alliance partner unwittingly give their partner significant insight into the firm's operations elsewhere in the value chain.

Product portfolio matrices

Competitor analysis tools, such as the BCG and GE product portfolio matrices, may actually damage corporate efforts to rebuild competitiveness. The focus of these tools is to examine the flow and use of cash across disparate businesses. However, these businesses are in many cases becoming more related through converging technologies and growing interrelationships across product features, distribution channels, or customers. Allocating cash along traditional portfolio lines deters investment into "low-growth" businesses which have the potential for undergoing a renaissance later (e.g., Black and Decker's power tools). Low-growth businesses are also natural entry points for foreign competitors who use alliances to learn about these markets and eventually enter them (Stages One through Three of Table 3).

The use of product-portfolio matrices encourages and rewards managers to think along discrete product lines of businesses, which in turn makes collaborative alliances attractive. However, many products emanate from a common set of core competencies and value-adding activities that are not reflected in the matrix.

Divisional and SBU organizational lines

Firms that organize themselves along SBU lines often encounter great difficulty in building the necessary critical mass to justify investments in converging and related technologies. For example, at United Technologies Corporation, products such as helicopters, elevators, heating and cooling systems, jet engines, and hydraulics share several technologies, such as microelectronics, avionics, motion control, and closed-loop electrical designs. An excessive corporate focus on evaluating Sikorsky, Otis, Carrier, and Pratt and Whitney as separate SBUs may actually be undermining each of these businesses' efforts to generate future products based on shared corporate core competencies. Sikorsky has now begun working with a Korean partner to develop a new generation of lightweight helicopters, while Pratt and Whitney is considering a series of foreign joint ventures to co-develop and co-produce the next generation of turbofan engines. Carrier has already been working with a Korean partner in small room air-conditioners for over a decade. Moreover, a corporate organization design for discrete business units may indirectly encourage SBU managers to enter into a wide network of outsourcing or joint technology development alliances to locate and secure financing for future products that are not forthcoming from sister divisions or headquarters. Thus, each division of the corporation and its underlying technology becomes open to predatory alliance partners willing to provide financing and markets in exchange for learning and technology transfer. This has already happened to varying degrees with General Electric in its consumer electronics, power generation, jet engines factory automation, and industrial materials businesses.

Using alliances to renew competitive advantage

Defining core businesses – The first step managers must take to better understand competitor/partner motives is that alliances in themselves represent a temporary coalignment of current interests. The value of each partner's contribution is relative, not absolute. Each alliance mirrors the other partner's options and capabilities at a point in time. The most attractive partner in the short run is likely to be a company that has a leading share of the market, but needs to learn some new technological skills. In the long run, however, the best partner might be the one that does not have a dominant share of the market or isn't even in the industry.[13] The latter case offers much greater opportunity for both partners to maintain a healthy balance of contribution and dependency.

Although there are numerous problems with strategic alliances when they are rashly formulated and implemented, firms still can still learn from their alliance partners. Successful alliances share some common elements that permit them to leverage their skills across multiple centers of competence.

The first step is to establish an external "friendly" relationship with the foreign partner. In most cases, the only way for two companies to avoid the shifts of balance in this relationship is to commit all their managerial resources to the establishment of a new venture, such as Fuji Photo Film and Xerox did. The second step is to help build up the partner for a period of time without "giving away the store." For example, Hoechst's joint venture with Mitsubishi Kaisei in dyestuffs began by selling its products through the Mitsubishi salesforce. During the mid-1980s, still half of its sales were sold by its own salesforce in Japan. Recently, the two companies combined their salesforce into a joint venture by itself. The third step is to complete a specific task. Corning Glass Works uses this strategy to learn of potential improvements in designing and manufacturing different glass and ceramic-based products with over 14 different alliance partners in Europe, Asia, and Latin America to penetrate new markets and share the risks of technological development. With Ciba-Geigy of Switzerland, it concentrates on medical diagnostics. The partnership with Siemens of Germany produces fiber optics. The alliance with NGK Insulators of Japan focuses on ceramics for catalytic converters and pollution control equipment. Corning's successful alliance strategy is based on its management's careful understanding of each partners' motives, their technological scope, and the alliances' implications for two-way knowledge flows.[14]

As a practical matter, senior management should be able to sense and detect over time a future partner's willingness and determination to learn. For example, a prospective foreign partner willing to supply high-quality components at a deep discount evinces a very strong learning propensity. Alliances conceived around an upstream/downstream division of labor often indicate potential trouble.

The examples of small cars and consumer electronics show how alliances originally predicated around joint development and production eventually become long-term supply agreements in which the alliance partner outlearns and seizes the initiative away from the original technological leader. The more willing a partner is to supply the components or end-products, the more intent it probably is upon eventual entry and seizure of the initiative from the original firm. This was the case with Mitsubishi Motors and Chrysler.

Human resource practices

Determined to boost short-term financial results, companies minimize the number and tenure of people they assign to the joint venture. As a result, little corporate memory of how to compete is built up, and no base for sustained learning is created. Indeed, the original objectives of the joint venture are often forgotten as new waves of managers seek to reach their own goals. There is little reward for learning in such a system because the other partner knows that managers will be replaced as soon as they learn everything. There are exceptions, such as Ciba-Geigy and Corning Glass Works, which keep managers in place for an extended period of time. The virtue of keeping the same people in the alliance is that they can establish a network that can pick up rumors and solve minor problems before they become large. In most Japanese alliances, managers are assigned to it for the lifetime of the venture. Because the Japanese partner in the alliance stays in close contact with the staff it assigns to the venture, it usually understands in detail what is going on. In most U.S. companies, the average tenure is less than five years. Therefore, the newcomers don't have the time to really understand their partners well enough to know where the roadblocks are or to trust them well enough to tell them. Moreover, short time-horizons in the managerial and technical staffing of the alliance limit the firm's ability to learn tacit knowledge that can only be transmitted through continuous exposure and practice. IBM and BASF, for example, have consciously transferred some staff and senior managers in charge of an alliance permanently in order to improve their ability to conduct business with their partner. In the future, strong interpersonal linkages will be required to sustain learning and to provide the glue for keeping an alliance together.[15]

> Some common practices in these programs are to give newcomers an early assignment outside their home country, assign them to international taskforces, and place them as a general manager in an alliance outside of their home country in the first five years. This systemic human resources development process usually takes ten years or more to accomplish.[16]

One of the major sources of competitive advantage for any alliance is its ability to attract talent from anywhere in the world. Thus, a systematic international management development system is vital. Companies such as Unilever, IBM, Whirlpool, Ciba-Geigy, and British Petroleum are experimenting with various human resource activities as a means of developing sources of competitive advantage.

Ignorance and lack of experience are often at the root of alliance problems and failures. Many alliance partners believe that if they have of a shareholding position, they have control. While legal control may be important for managers who do not have a deep understanding of their alliance partner's dreams (or their own firm's dreams), the amount of "legal" control is irrelevant. Knowledge flow and rate of learning occur independently of legal structure and control. The successful alliances between Kellogg and Ajinomoto of Japan, as well as between Hewlett-Packard and Yokogawa Electric, are based on the integration of day-to-day processes and an understanding of corporate values and not on legal ownership.

Lean superstructures

Once an alliance has been formed, managers can design a structure to implement the alliance's strategy. Group headquarters – the level that oversees the several alliances – become meaningless. Since managers in the alliance are responsible for manufacturing/marketing strategy and coordination with other responsible departments, there is little value-added potential for another structural layer. Value-driven superstructures rather than bloated corporate headquarters should oversee the day-to-day operation of the alliance. Where necessary, shared resources should be organized as profit or cost centers.

In the future, the internal structure of the alliance will be shaped by the exigencies confronting it. A firm's ability to experiment and learn new skills and technologies will emanate from the underlying strength and durability of the alliance's organization. Tight integration of product development teams across value-adding functions can enable faster learning by encouraging managers to better understand and practice new techniques, such as value engineering, continuous improvement, and modular manufacturing. The need to instill rapid learning and faster time-to-market of new products will demand an organizational format that enhances value-adding activities concurrently, as opposed to traditional functional-based structures.[17] Traditional functional-based structures impede a firm's ability to learn knowledge and skills from its partners because information does not flow freely from design to manufacturing to marketing.

A type of structure that is replacing the traditional functional-based form is the "horizontal" organization. In this form, work is primarily structured around business processes such as new product development, manufacturing technologies, or integrated logistics, as opposed to areas of functional expertise. It is these processes that link employees to the needs and capabilities of suppliers and customers in a way that improves performance. In horizontal organizations an alliance's core processes are owned by teams. Each team is responsible for a process's performance and ensures that its performance objectives are congruent with other processes and with the strategy of the alliance. The technical expertise to support these teams is housed in each parent.

Many organizations, such as Kodak, Motorola, and Xerox, have been able to make these teams self-managing. However, to be effective, teams must have the authority, information, resources, and motivation to evaluate and to change when, how, and with whom they do their work. Team members must hold themselves accountable for agreed-on goals and be rewarded for the attainment of them.[18]

Summary

Building successful alliances requires identifying the core competencies of both partners and developing the strong interpersonal skills and values needed to manage them. Experience has shown that few companies have understood or anticipated the problems they would have to face in the day-to-day operation of alliances.

Companies that have been successful with their alliances understand that their alliance partner can facilitate the achievement of their own goals in the long run. This perspective requires that the company get its "dreams" clearly focused. These "dreams" help each partner understand what they are supposed to contribute and learn from the alliance. The process of thinking through this duality of simultaneous collaboration and competition provokes questions that need to be raised before the alliance can be structured and the reward system fashioned.

Many companies did not envision the alliance as an integral part of their corporate strategy, but pursued it as a quick fix to raw material or technological problems. They expected to gain financial benefits in the short run, but never intended to learn from their alliance partner about the industry or how to successfully build a competitive advantage. Consequently, these firms did not view their collaboration with other firms as another form of competition.

Endnotes

1. C. K. Prahalad and G. Hamel, "The Core Competence of the Corporation," *Harvard Business Review*, 68 (May-June 1990): 79-93. See also G. Hamel and C. K. Prahalad, "Strategic Intent," *Harvard Business Review*, 67 (May-June, 1989): 63-76.

2. D. Lei and J. W. Slocum, Jr.. "Global Strategic Alliances: Payoffs and Pitfalls," *Organizational Dynamics, I* (1991): 44-62. See also R.A. Bettis, S.P. Bradley and G. Hamel. "Outsourcing and Industrial Decline," *Academy of Management Executive*, 6 (February 1992): 7-22.

3. K. K. Jones and W. E. Shill, "Allying for Advantage," *McKinsey Quarterly*, 3 (1990): 85.

4. B. Stronach. *Defining Nationalism in Contemporary Japan* (Niigata, Japan: The International University of Japan Press, 1991).

5. See Harvard Business School Case #9-389-048, "General Electric: Consumer Electronics Group," for a discussion of how the consumer electronics industry migrated from the U.S. to the Far East.

6. *Fortune*, "Japan's Robot King Wins Again," May 25, 1987, pp. 53-57.

7. J . L. Badaracco, Jr., *The Knowledge Link* (Cambridge, MA: Harvard Business School Press, 1991).

8. R. Reed and R. J. DeFillippi, "Causal Ambiguity, Barriers to Imitation and Sustainable Competitive Advantage," *Academy of Management Review*, 15 (1990): 88-102.

9. Badaracco, op. cit. See also H. Kahalas and K. Suchon, "Interview with Harold A. Poling, Chairman, CEO, Ford Motor Company," *Academy of Management Executive*, 6 (1992): 71-82.

10. I.C. Magaziner and M. Patinkin, "Fast Heat: How Korea Won the Microwave War," *Harvard Business Review*, 63 (January-February 1989): 83-93. See also "Korea's Tigers Keep Roaring," *Fortune*, May 4, 1992, pp. 24-28.

11. Prahalad and Hamel, op. cit.

12. M. McGill. J.W. Slocum, Jr., and D. Lei, "Management Practices in Learning Organizations," *Organizational Dynamics*, (Summer 1992): 5-17.

13. K. Harrigan, *Strategies for Joint Ventures* (Boston, MA: D. C. Heath, 1983). See also S. Goldenberg, *Hands Across the Ocean* (Boston, MA: Harvard Business School Press, 1988).

14. "Corning's Class Act: How Jamie Houghton Reinvented the Company," *Business Week*, May 13, 1991, pp. 68-72. See also "Partnerships Are a Way of Life for Corning," *Wall Street Journal*, July 12, 1988, p. 6.

15. K. Jones. "Competing to Learn in Japan," *McKinsey Quarterly*, 1 (1992): 45-57.

16. R.S. Schuler, "Strategic Human Resources Management: Linking the People with the Strategic Needs of the Business," *Organizational Dynamics* (Summer 1992): 18-32.

17. K. Jones and T. Ohbora, "Managing the Heretical Company," *McKinsey Quarterly*, 3 (1990): 20-45.

18. F. Ostroff and D. Smith, "The Horizontal Organization," *McKinsley Quarterly*, 1 (1992): 148-168. See also C.C. Snow, R. E. Miles and H. J. Coleman, "Managing 21st Century Network Organizations," *Organizational Dynamics* (Winter 1992): 5-20.

Great strategy
or great strategy implementation –
two ways of
competing in global markets[12]

Many business analysts have attributed the loss of U.S. market share in the semiconductor industry to unfair Japanese practices, including trade barriers and "dumping" of goods in export markets. Egelhoff draws from a study of sample semiconductor firms to argue that the market share losses have also been influenced by the distinctly different competitive modes that U.S. and Japanese firms use U.S. firms tend to compete by developing a unique business strategy; Japanese firms tend to compete by implementing not-so-unique strategies better than anyone else.[1] He shows how these two competitive styles have implications for a range of business activities and for other global industries as well.

> On 19 April 1775, British troops (Redcoats) marched toward Concord, Massachusetts, to destroy military stores that had been collected by the American revolutionaries (Minutemen). At Lexington Green, a large, flat, open area, the Redcoats met the Minutemen in the first battle of the day. Both sides employed a similar battle strategy, firing at each other in the open from closed ranks. It was the dominant battle strategy of the day. The Redcoats quickly prevailed, and the Minutemen dispersed after a few volleys and a number of casualties.
>
> Later in the day, as the Redcoats returned to Boston, a second battle developed. At various points along the road, Minutemen fired upon the Redcoat formations from inside houses and behind stone fences. When the Redcoats charged these positions, the Minutemen withdrew into the countryside and reappeared farther down the road. The Minutemen's skirmish tactics took a heavy toll on the massed and extremely vulnerable Redcoats, who could do little but set fire to the buildings the Minutemen had already abandoned.

Like the Minutemen, competitors frequently don't compete the way one expects them to. This is one of the key difficulties for managers trying to understand, prepare for, and manage global competition. Western firms, and U.S. firms in particular, generally try to compete through some kind of strategic advantage. That is, they often try to develop a unique business strategy that will allow them to outmaneuver competitors. Yet many global Asian firms appear to compete successfully without much attempt to develop distinctive business strategies. Instead, they try to implement not-so-unique business strategies better than competitors and thereby to gain competitive advantage.

> The two battles between the same opponents on the same day produced two very different results. It seems reasonable to suggest that between the two battles the Minutemen made a fundamental shift in their battle strategy, and this new strategy, rather than luck or chance, produced the significant difference in results.

---

12 Excerpted from William G. Egelhoff, *Sloan Management Review*, Winter 1993, 34(2), 37-50. Used with permission.

Implications for global competitiveness

In this section I will attempt to generalize from the specific findings and limited hypotheses about the broader implications for global competition. The globalization of an increasing number of U.S. markets has brought many U.S. firms into direct competition with foreign firms. Many of these foreign firms, especially those based in the Pacific Rim countries, primarily compete through superior strategy implementation. At the same time, the maturing of many product categories has made it more difficult to compete with unique product-market strategies. In many cases, it has been impossible to consistently stay a step ahead of a determined competitor that possesses superior strategy implementation capabilities. As technology curves flatten out, time is on the side of the better implementer.

Attempting to gain strategic competitive advantage through frequent repositioning of one's product lines and market segments seems to work best when one's competitors also believe in this principle and are playing the same game. When one's competitors are not playing this game, frequent strategic repositioning may not lead to long term success.

Compared to Japanese firms, U.S. firms have fairly flexible business strategies and are quite adept at realigning product lines and market segments to reflect changes in competitive advantage. This kind of continuous strategic maneuvering has worked well for those companies that can maneuver the best. Competitors generally understand the meaning of being outmaneuvered and back off quickly, either going into other areas or licensing the winner's technology. A good example of this has been Intel, which has consistently focused its resources on developing the next product before others, quickly coalesced a group of customers and suppliers around the new product to make it an industry standard, and retreated from old products and markets as they have matured and become too price competitive.

But Japanese firms do not play this same game of frequently repositioning product lines and market segments. It is more difficult for a Japanese firm to alter strategy and very hard to withdraw from products or markets when one has been outmaneuvered or lost competitive advantage. A good example of this has been NEC's persistence over the years in developing and establishing its own line of microprocessors, despite the dominance of the Intel and Motorola designs. The typical Japanese response is to refocus its efforts on catching up. Toshiba committed itself in 1982 to catching up in DRAMs and in 1988 became the largest and most successful producer of the one-megabit DRAM. Japanese firms do not generally attempt to leapfrog new developments in either product or process technology, the way many U.S. firms do. Thus, when a Japanese firm falls behind, it can generally catch up by simply working harder at implementing the existing strategy. Conversely, when a U.S. firm fails at implementing an overly ambitious strategy (such as leapfrogging a product improvement), it tends to fall so far behind that it frequently must exit this segment of the market.

Overall, the frequent strategic repositioning of U.S. firms seems to have a definite impact on the strategies of other U.S. firms but relatively little impact on the strategies of Japanese competitors. The Japanese firms are busy implementing product line and market segment strategies that are longer term, less flexible, and not subject to being judged on short-run profitability. When faced with a poor competitive situation, the Japanese firm is much more likely to alter the nature or intensity of strategy implementation than the strategy itself.

This kind of competitive behavior raises questions about the efficacy of strategic repositioning as a means of gaining competitive advantage. Most strategies based on frequent repositioning rely on competitors recognizing and backing away from firms in strategically more favorable positions. For awhile, at least, this leaves the fruits of the abandoned product line or market segment to the winner. If, however, the competitor fails to yield and insists on competing (even at a loss), the expectant winner will not realize the full benefits of its strategic advantage. In fact, if the competitor displays superior strategy implementation capabilities and has staying power, it is probable that the early winner will even lose much of the product line or market segment as the initial advantage wanes. This is because competitors with superior strategy implementation capabilities can usually catch up once they target a product or market segment in which a dominant product design or industry standard already exists. For example, U.S. firms were early leaders in SRAMs and once dominated this market.

Now they only dominate the very fast SRAM segment, where technology development has been most rapid and unique designs abound. Japanese firms hold the bulk of the SRAM market and dominate those segments in which product technology has matured. If firms are not deterred by short-run losses and do not confront an unassailable mobility barrier, such as a patent or trade barrier, strategies based on implementation can probably negate the advantages of strategies built on frequent strategic repositioning.

It is probable that competing through superior strategy works only over a limited period of time in an industry's life. Unless a firm can drive out all competitors while it possesses the superior strategy and raise entry barriers sufficient to keep them out, it must at some point change its competitive style to one stressing superior strategy implementation.

It is important to recognize that both modes of competing – creating a unique and superior business strategy and excelling at strategy implementation – constitute strategic behavior. It is not that one is strategic while the other is tactical or operational, although strategy implementation frequently involves getting tactical and operational behavior to strongly support key strategy elements. Both competitive modes can fundamentally influence or alter the firm's strategic position in its competitive environment. The overall strategic management of a firm needs to be viewed as some combination of these two modes of competing, although it appears that most firms tend to emphasize one more than the other. While this tendency is undoubtedly influenced by industry and technological maturity, it also appears to be influenced by national culture. If this is true, it is a disturbing complexity for those who deal with global industries, and especially for those who seek to achieve "fairness" or a "level playing field" in global competition.

I conclude with three implications, as shown in Table 1. In the increasingly global competitive system, more U.S. firms will need to shift their way of competing from relying on superior strategy to developing superior strategy implementation capabilities. Superior strategy worked well for the Minutemen and for most industries during the early periods of product life cycles. Their experiences have helped to create a myth that this is the most successful and profitable way to compete. Unfortunately, flattening technology curves and global competition have made this myth out of date for many industries.

Table 1
Implications for U.S. competitiveness

- More firms need to shift from relying on superior strategy to developing superior strategy implementation capabilities.

- Education, reward systems, and cultural values need to facilitate this shift.

- Otherwise, the United States will have to establish barriers and avoid direct confrontation. Trade would have to be more confined to regional and intracultural competitive patterns, and it would have to be more carefully regulated across these regional and cultural differences.

Education, reward systems, and cultural values need to change to facilitate this shift toward strategy implementation. U.S. business education has strongly touted the virtues of strategic maneuvering, breakthroughs and rapid success, outflanking rather than confronting competitors, and high early profits. If the United States cannot become more competitive in terms of strategy implementation capability, it will probably have to establish trade barriers to protect itself from foreign competitors that excel at this competitive mode. Trade will have to be more confined to regional and intracultural competitive systems, and it will have to be more carefully regulated across these regional and cultural differences. To some extent, this is the pattern that may be developing in Europe.

> The constant, incremental improvement of a company's operations and performance is generally viewed as a boring way to compete; it is not the route to the cover of *Business Week*. Somehow, reward systems need to change.

Porter argues that a competitive home environment is a prerequisite for global success. This article points out that national environments can be competitive in different ways. It suggests that the U.S. environment is not necessarily insufficiently competitive but that it is more used to a different kind of competition than the Japanese environment. Porter's notion of competitive and noncompetitive home environments may be too simple to fully capture the reality of global competition when fundamentally different modes of competition are involved.

The framework and hypotheses in this article present a somewhat different perspective of global competition than previous articles.

This perspective was suggested by an examination of the business strategies and competitive styles of firms in an industry that has recently become global. Most attempts to explain global competitiveness and international trade problems have employed industry and societal-level factors such as industry spending on R&D, differences in interest rates, and government policies. This new perspective needs to be seen as augmenting, not replacing, the existing perspectives. It suggests, however, that international competitiveness problems exist at multiple levels of analysis and are unlikely to be successfully addressed by simple, single-level solutions.

Appendix

This article is based on a major study of strategy and strategy implementation in twenty-three semiconductor firms. Eight were in the United States, eight were Japanese, and seven were European (the latter are not used here). I used information from public sources to choose companies that represented the strategic diversity of the industry in each geographical area.

I conducted structured interviews during 1986 and 1987 at each company's headquarters and often at additional company sites. The interviews generally involved the general manager, R&D manager, manufacturing manager, and marketing manager, as well as others. In all but a few instances in which individual managers objected, I taped the interviews. The tapes facilitated the later quantification and coding of certain data and the transcription and analysis of qualitative data.

Although many of the variables and concepts I measured were suggested by prior work, the thrust of the study was exploratory. The central idea presented in this article evolved out of a comparative analysis of the firms' various strategies.

Endnotes

1. The research is described in more detail in: R.N. Langlois, T.A. Pugel, C.S. Haklisch, RR Nelson, and W.G. Egelhoff, *Microelectronics: An Industry in Transition* (Boston: Unwin Hyman, 1988).

2. M.E. Porter, "The Competitive Advantage of Nations," *Harvard Business Review*, March-April 1990, pp. 73-93. Reprint 3423.

Chapter 8

Financial and political risk

Companies doing business internationally must be prepared for the wide variations in political stability of various countries, the financial risks of foreign currency markets and foreign investment, and world events that can have a major impact on business operations. For example, in the past five years a number of major world events have dramatically affected business conditions, not to mention social conditions and political relationships among countries. The fall of the Berlin Wall, the collapse of the Soviet Union, and passage of the Single European Act are but a few dramatic examples. The exercise, *The wave that shook the world: An exercise in global interdependency*, provides a way of tracking the effect of a world event on a specific product in various countries. The object of the exercise is to help understand how an event in one place can have an effect on business in other parts of the world.

While financial and political risk exist worldwide, this chapter focuses on doing business in developing countries where serious political instability and large foreign financial investments are often present. The countries included here are the Sudan, the Dominican Republic, Peru, and Belize.

The Sudan, the largest country in Africa, has a highly unstable political environment that erupted into civil war and resulted in a famine that killed 250,000 people in 1988 and also destroyed the country's economic base. The case, *Textiles in the Sudan: Financial and political problems faced by developing nations,* describes the general problems associated with doing business in the Sudan and chronicles the history of the company, Cotton Textile Mills, which was founded in 1978. The current problems for the company are to finance a textile mill and attract investors to set up a production facility. The case also requires calculating repayment of a loan.

The other three cases take place in Latin America. *GOMEP: A manager's day in a developing country* profiles a firm in the Dominican Republic that manufactures and sells household products, pharmaceuticals, and toiletries under license from American firms. In developing a strategic plan, the company must take into account the prospect of a new government, a devalued currency, and low worker productivity, as well as the advantages of licensing compared to alternative business arrangements. The investment climate in the Dominican Republic is compared with other countries in the Caribbean and Central America in the reading, *Managers' views on potential investment opportunities*. This article reports ratings by American business people of the favorability to investors of nearly two dozen incentives typically offered in these countries. In addition to country differences, the desirability of incentives is influenced by the size of the investment, type of product, and market orientation.

Belco Petroleum is the Peruvian subsidiary of a U.S. firm. The Peruvian government has threatened to nationalize Belco's local operations if agreements with Petroperu do not work out. Belco executives must decide a course of action to deal with this threat from the political environment. Nationalization or expropriation can be a serious threat when new political parties come into power. Other factors constituting political risks are listed in *What executives should know about political risk*. Companies need to periodically evaluate a broad range of potential political risks when conditions change in a country in which they are currently operating, or when contemplating entry into a new country.

Hondo River Enterprises, a broom, shoe and garment manufacturer in Belize, takes its name from the Hondo River, which forms the border with Mexico. The owner was considering several expansion opportunities, including seeking a long-term contract to provide brooms to the U.S. military, marketing brooms in the U.S. retail market, acquiring a broom manufacturing plant in Mexico, and operating twin Mexican-Belize factories modeled after U.S.-Mexican maquiladoras. Issues of financing expansion and economic policies in the three countries need to be considered in the decision. The reading, *Competitiveness and the "global capital shortage,"* provides background on international funding sources and flows. The impact of free trade in North America on Hondo River's decisions should also be considered. *NAFTA: The fight and facts*, as well as *The Mexican automobile industry and the North American Free Trade Agreement* in the next chapter provide background information on this topic.

Chapter 8
Financial and political risk

33. The wave that shook the world: An exercise in global interdependency[1]

purpose

To understand how an event in one place can affect life in a distant country.

group size

Any number of groups of four to six members.

time

30+ minutes, depending on number of presentations.

exercise schedule

	Unit time	Total time
1 Instructions	**10 min**	**10 min**

Instructor goes over requirements for assignment, as shown above.

2 Presentations (optional)	**5 min per individual or group**

Each person/group gives evidence of the effect. Overhead transparencies, hand-outs or other visuals are helpful.

3 Discussion	**20 min**

Instructor leads a discussion on the ripple effect of various events on companies and life around the world. What evidence does this give of a more global economy and world?

Instructions

This assignment may be done individually or in groups.

Each person/group will be assigned a different country.

The whole class will have the same world event and the same product effect to work with.

For example, the instructor may say:

"Depending on your country, you will need to find the effect of the fall of the Berlin Wall on the sales of a particular soft drink in that country." or "Find out the effect of the demise of the Soviet Union on sales of heavy construction in your assigned country."

Examples of world events to use:

Fall of the Berlin Wall

End of the Soviet Union

War with Iraq

Civil war in Yugoslavia

End of the civil war in Ethiopia

*Winning of the election
by religious fundamentalists in Algeria and subsequent
emergency called by government*

End of legal apartheid in South Africa

Inter-tribal warfare in Somalia

Israel-Palestinian peace process

Yeltsin's imposition of martial law in Russia

Russia's 1993 elections and the move away from democracy

Increase of fundamentalism in the Sudan

Organized crime in Central and Eastern Europe

Loss of press freedom in Central and Eastern Europe

*North Korea's withdrawal from the
Treaty on the Nonproliferation of Nuclear Weapons (NPT)*

China's imminent takeover of Hong Kong

Japanese market crash

*China's economic development and changing attitudes toward
totalitarianism/democracy*

Other current world events

34. Textiles in the Sudan: Financial and political problems faced by developing nations[2]

Additional topics covered: Financial management, production scheduling, and infrastructure difficulties.

International business is a topic often approached from the perspective of companies in industrialized nations. The problems faced by non-industrialized nations as they attempt to enter world markets are different from those encountered by industrialized states. These problems may include the following:

An unstable political environment
Lack of a unified culture

- Cultural values not supporting an industrial state

- Lack of technology and electricity for production

- Inefficient distribution systems

- Low gross domestic product

- Currency trade problems

- Currency devaluation

This case focuses on a textile manufacturer in the Sudan. Many of the problems discussed, however, may be generalized to other developing nations. For example, in many non-industrialized nations, unstable political environments are manifested by on-going civil wars, which not only deflect resources available for productive enterprises, but often literally destroy production facilities. Recent civil wars have hampered economic development in the Sudan, Ethiopia, Liberia, Peru and Angola. Similarly, nations with low gross domestic product do not have the economic resources to recover from natural disasters, such as the Bangladesh cyclone and the Peruvian cholera epidemic.

The textile industry is particularly appropriate for a discussion of these problems, as textile manufacturing is often one of the first major industries formed in a developing country. Nearly every country has a textile industry. Apparel manufacturing is also common to most countries.

This case focuses on the political and financial problems that have contributed to the Sudan's difficulties in developing a viable economic base. The results of borrowing money from foreign sources to finance industrial development are discussed specifically. Each of the problems mentioned above will be discussed below as they relate to the Sudan. Following this discussion and a brief description of the cotton textile industry in general, a case involving a textile manufacturing firm, Cotton Textile Mills, will be presented.

---

2 By Claudia Harris, University of Scranton. Used with permission.

The Sudan

In terms of land area, the Sudan is the largest country in Africa. Significant trade benefits accrue to the Sudan because it is bordered on the north by Egypt and on the east, across the Red Sea, by Saudi Arabia. The Nile River, flowing north through the Sudan and Egypt into the Mediterranean Sea, provides a trade route, water to an otherwise arid region, and a potential source of electrical power.

During the Cold War, the United States attempted to maintain friendly relations with the Sudan, both to protect the headwaters of the Nile in support of Egypt and to avoid the creation of an unfriendly pathway from the Red Sea to the Mediterranean Sea. This situation changed when Soviet support for the Ethiopian government ended and Ethiopian rebels toppled their repressive government.

The United States had provided the Sudan with $400 million in military and economic aid in 1985. In 1990, aid to the Sudan was discontinued, although food shipments and medical aid continued under non-governmental auspices. This reduction in aid reflected a shift in the U.S. position due to a lack of cooperation by the Sudanese government and rebel forces in distributing aid. The Sudanese government's refusal to negotiate an end to its devastating civil war also was a factor. Both Britain and the Netherlands cut aid to the Sudan for the same reasons.

The White Nile and Blue Nile rivers join in central Sudan to form the Nile River, which flows north into Egypt. The valleys surrounding these two rivers contain 200 million acres of arable land, only 5 million of which are now cultivated.

An unstable political environment

From 1969 until 1985, the Sudan was governed by a repressive military dictatorship under the leadership of Major-General Jaafar al-Nimeiri. Nimeiri's government mismanaged the economy, causing the emigration of large numbers of professionals, technicians and skilled workers. In 1985, the dictatorship was toppled in a bloodless coup. With broad-based support, Prime Minister Sadiq al-Mahdi assumed power. Unfortunately, Sadiq al-Mahdi was an ineffective leader, and his regime degenerated as a series of coalition governments dissolved. He was overthrown in June 1989 by a group of military officers led by Brigadier General Omar Hassan Ahmed Bashir.

Bashir's regime combines militarism and Islamic fundamentalism in its domestic policies. He has a policy of torturing and killing Sudan's non-Muslim groups by bombing refugee camps, burning towns, and massacring refugees from the southern areas of the country. Africa Watch, a human rights organization, accused Bashir of torturing political opposition in a manner "that surpasses the worst excesses of the long-time military government that ruled from 1969 to the mid-80s."

Bashir was initially seen as a political moderate who remained unaligned with any foreign power. But he banned the Sudan's myriad political parties and trade unions and closed down the press. The civil war continues, and new economic policies are not clear. Therefore, local and foreign investors remain cautious in spite of promises by Bashir to improve the investment climate.

The move toward fundamentalist Islamic policies

by Bashir has also turned away potential allies in the Arab world. The Sudan did not join the coalition against Iraq
in the Gulf War, which angered its traditional allies, Egypt, Saudi Arabia, and Kuwait. In addition to changes in its central government, the Sudanese political situation is lacking in stability as a result of its continuing civil war. Essentially, the peoples of the south of the Sudan, primarily Christians and animists (traditional African religions), led by John Grang, a U.S.-educated Dinka, are fighting against Moslem rule.

To further exacerbate the problem, both the national government and the rebel army have obstructed shipments of food from relief agencies, each claiming that the food will benefit their enemies.
The International Monetary Fund found that the Sudanese government had sold large amounts of its grain abroad in order to generate currency, which it used to purchase weapons from China to continue the civil war.

In 1983 Nimeiri ignited the civil war by imposing strict shari'a, the Islamic fundamentalist legal code that imposes amputation of the hand of a thief, public whipping, stoning and hanging for other crimes, prohibition of interest charges on loans, a total ban on alcoholic beverages, and covering the heads and faces of women. The shari'a has become a rallying point for the south. The rebels want changes in the Khartoum government's cultural, political, and economic policies.

The civil war devastated the already struggling economic system and has destroyed the base of the southern economy. People who had subsisted by herding animals and growing crops have been pushed from their land and have crowded into towns that are unequipped to deal with large numbers of refugees.

As a result of the civil war, an estimated 250,000 people died of starvation in 1988, and the Save the Children Foundation estimated that 10 million people were in danger of starvation in 1991. Neither the Red Cross nor the United Nations is able to determine with any accuracy the number of people in South Sudan who have died of starvation or in mass killings by the Sudanese government or who have fled into Ethiopia, Uganda, or northern Sudan.

Lack of a unified culture

The civil war is a manifestation of the religious and cultural differences within the Sudan that hamper the development of a unified culture. That the Sudan has 500 tribes that speak 200 different languages is a good indication of the enormity of the unification task. This resulted in regionally-based government policies and poor national communication and transportation services.

Although both northern and southern Sudanese would be identified as black people, the southern Sudanese refugees who have escaped the civil war by moving north into Khartoum are easily identifiable. They are extremely tall and their skin is darker; men in Dinka and Nuer tribes have intricate tattoos on their heads; and southern women do not veil themselves in the Moslem tradition. These physical differences single out southern Sudanese for abuse and maltreatment, and they are relegated to living in camps outside the city.

Cultural values that do not support an industrial state

In addition to the wide diversity of Sudanese cultures, many of the subgroups of the Sudanese peoples are nomadic, which does not lend support to industrialization. For members of nomadic groups, ownership of livestock is a sign of wealth and provides high status. Living in a town or being tied to one area of land is unappealing and is considered to be the result of lacking enough wealth to own livestock.

Lack of technology and electricity for production

Poor economic conditions and an unstable political environment in the Sudan have encouraged the exodus of trained personnel, which has not only deprived the country of their skills but also removed the social strata of a potential middle class that valued modernization of the economy and society.

Due to a lack of productive facilities, the Sudan has been linked to the world economy as an exporter of cotton and oil seeds and as an importer of manufactured goods. While cotton is a major Sudanese export, some thread and yarn are produced within the country. One of the largest problems for textile production in the Sudan is a lack of electrical power. While hydroelectric power generation has been used in the Sudan since 1925, it is limited and service is erratic.

Another major problem for industrial production is a lack of machinery and equipment, which must be imported along with replacement parts. As a result of these problems, the Sudan's industrial plants operate at about 30 percent of capacity with some as low as 4 percent and others closed entirely.

Inefficient distribution systems

In addition to technology and electricity for production, distribution systems are a necessary part of the infrastructure needed to support a productive economy. In the Sudan, the distribution of goods within the country is not only hampered, but almost made impossible by its lack of transportation systems. The rail system is antiquated, and airstrips in most areas function only sporadically. Road and river transport is unreliable and vulnerable to both armies of the civil war. No paved roads connect the north and the south. With a land area one-fourth of the United States, the Sudan has less than 500 miles of paved roads.

Low gross domestic product

Despite its potential for productivity, the Sudan remains a poor country with annual per capita income of less than $400. Actually, this figure means little; many Sudanese exist in a non-monetary economy based on food production and barter for goods. Both the civil war and other climate conditions – drought and then flooding – have created serious famine problems.

The government has been spending about $1 million per day to pursue the war and an additional $300 million per year on arms, totalling more than the total export earnings of the entire nation.

In addition, the civil war continues to drain economic resources. As a result of drought, flooding, and the civil war, many southern Sudanese people have fled into neighbouring countries. The daily cost of the war does not include the cost of human suffering, nor does it include the cost of opportunities lost.

Currency trade problems

Two aspects of financing that restrict production in a developing nation are currency trade problems – the difference between official exchange rates and black market exchange rates – and a currency that is not traded in international markets.

Developing nations that wish to invest in production facilities must often repay loans in the currency of the country from which the loan was obtained. Essentially, the exchange rate is set when the loan is obtained. If the exchange rate fluctuates, loan repayment in dollars, francs or British pounds may require increasing amounts of the borrowing country's currency.

Another currency problem is the difference between the official rate and the market exchange rate. For instance, in September 1987, the official exchange rate was 2.5 Ls Sudan per $1 US; at that time 4.5 Ls Sudan could be obtained per $1 US on the black market. Because of this difference in exchange rates, local producers who are paid according to the official rate have a disincentive to produce goods or services for export.

The currencies of most developing nations are not traded in established markets, so the usual means of securing investments by purchasing futures contracts on the currencies involved (hedging) is not available to investors in these countries.

Currency devaluation

Two more aspects of financing that affect production in a developing nation relate to inflation: the effects of devaluation of the local currency in international markets and the effects of devaluation of the local currency in local markets.

Currency devaluation, or inflation, in the local economy would be expected to improve the competitiveness of domestically produced goods by raising the price of imports. However, the purchasing power of local buyers is decreased by inflation. For the exporting producer, inflation increases the cost of local inputs, including labor.

Toward the end of the 1970s and into the 1980s, most non-oil-producing developing nations experienced serious balance of payments difficulties. Increases in oil prices, increases in interest rates, and slides in primary commodity prices led to the devaluation of the Sudanese pound. For instance, the exchange rate between the Sudanese pound and the U.S. dollar between 1978 and 1988 increased by 900 percent (see Table 1). The difference between a 1978 U.S. dollar and a 1988 U.S. dollar was about 140 percent. As a currency is devalued, payments that producers receive in local currencies become less valuable.

The cotton industry

Participants in the world cotton industry, whether producers of raw cotton, textiles or apparel, face several common problems. While demand for cotton remains high, the fortunes of the cotton market are dependent on the whims of the world fashion market. The textile industry exists in a more competitive environment than the apparel industry. Buyers of textiles for apparel production can purchase goods from a wide variety of firms, choosing them based on quality and price. The products of competing apparel firms are viewed as distinct and are therefore less likely than textile goods to be sensitive to changes in prices.

The demands for both textiles and apparel, however, are sensitive to the business cycle. Sales of textiles and apparel rise during economic expansions and decline during economic contractions. Because of this sensitivity, competition in the textile and apparel industries is intense during a general economic downturn.

The health of the cotton industry also depends on the supply of cotton and, as a result, on the prices that it can bring. Sudanese farmers have become increasingly reluctant to grow cotton. Initially, the already impoverished farmers must provide expensive chemicals, both as fertilizers to treat the land and as a protection against insects to treat the plants. Then, while exporters themselves are paid in foreign currencies for the cotton they export, they, in turn, pay the local farmers in Sudanese pounds based on the official international trade rate, which is considerably lower than the market conversion rate.

Cotton Textile Mills

Cotton Textile Mills was formed in 1978 to produce cotton textiles primarily for local consumption, although it was hoped that the industry would grow into exporting. This production would provide an import substitute for Sudanese nationals. In the Sudan, the demand for cotton textiles remains high. The climate of the Sudan encourages wearing cotton, as Khartoum is one of the hottest cities in the world. The Muslim population of the north characteristically wears clothing that requires many yards of cloth, as an abundance of fabric is considered a sign of wealth. The Cotton Textile Mills plant is located near cotton-growing areas and is connected to cotton ginning factories by both a paved highway and a railroad. Modern textile industry in the Sudan is more than 20 years old, and many textile engineers, technicians and skilled workers are available locally. The only expatriates needed are for the senior technical and managerial jobs.

The company was established with contributed capital of 6.5 million Sudanese pounds and loans of $23 million at an average interest rate of 10 percent, financed mainly by the Sudan Development Corporation and the International Finance Corporation. The loan was to be repaid in ten annual installments after the plant became fully operational. Interest was charged on the loan beginning Jan. 1, 1979, but this interest was not to be paid until the plant was fully operational and was to be spread over the 10-year payment period. The plant was completed and became fully operational beginning in 1982. As shown in Table 1, the 1978 rate of exchange between the Sudanese pound and the U.S. dollar was .5Ls; by the end of 1984, it was 2.5Ls per dollar. In fact, the situation was worse than that because the Sudanese banking industry had no dollars for sale at the official rate. Any dollars purchased would have to be obtained at the market rate, which by 1989 was 171 percent higher than the official rate.

> The Sudanese pound had been relatively stable to the dollar for approximately nine years, so there was no real evidence that it would change as radically as it did. The subsequent volatility in the value of the Sudanese pound reflected a general instability in the world economy that could not have been controlled locally.

The company had revenues and expenses shown in Table 2. The company did not cease production in spite of the difficulties it faced. These difficulties included the following:

- *Shortages of reliable and continuous electricity;*
- *Shortages of gas and oil for standby gas generators;*
- *Lack of foreign exchange to finance the imported spare parts, dyes and chemicals;*
- *Very high labor turnover due to the emigration of skilled workers to Saudi Arabia and other Gulf states;*
- *Smuggling of textiles and dumping in the local market from Eastern Europe and Asia;*
- *Unrealistic government policy regarding pricing local textile products and cotton for local mills;*
- *Sharp and continuous devaluation of the Sudanese pound in international markets;*
- *Continuing high local inflation.*

Cotton Textile Mills could not increase its prices to fully offset the effect of the exchange losses because large quantities of textile goods were smuggled into the country and because the decrease in real income of potential local buyers had reduced the size of the market. In addition, in response to the generally declining economic situation, the Sudanese government enacted price controls, freezing the prices at which the cotton goods could be sold.

In 1984, faced with losing a potentially productive facility, the Sudanese government enacted the following actions to prevent bankruptcy:

Table 1
Exchange rates
for Sudanese
pound and United
States dollar
(per $US)

1970	0,348
1971	0,321
1972	0,371
1973	0,348
1974	0,348
1975	0,348
1976	0,348
1977	0,348
1978	0,500
1979	0,800
1980	0,800
1981	1,170
1982	1,300
1983	2,500
1984	2,500
1985	2,500
1986	2,500
1987	4,500
1988	4,500

- *Controlling illicit imports and smuggling of textiles;*
- *Relaxing price controls for goods produced;*
- *Reducing the price of cotton for use by local mills;*
- *Allocating foreign currency through the Bank of Sudan (the central bank) for the purchase of spare parts, dyes, and chemicals at the official exchange rate, which remained at less than 50 percent of the market rate;*
- *Keeping the debt service at the original rate of exchange, with the Bank of Sudan paying the difference;*
- *Helping indirectly to provide power by implementation of the national supply project.*

Simultaneously, the company was obligated to find some sources of short-term financing. The Sudan Development Corporation agreed to make a loan in local currency at an 18 percent interest rate. Other lenders agreed to freeze debt service until the financial position of the company improved. As a result, Cotton Textile Mills has continued to function, producing cotton cloth for local market consumption.

Exercises

1 The "Debt Obligation" shown in Table 2 is the actual amount that Cotton Textile Mills owed. This amount varied as government policy changed to help the company continue functioning. Construct a chart based on the original $23 million loan. The purpose of this exercise is to underscore the dramatic difference between projected payments and the payments that resulted from devaluation of the Sudanese pound. Use the following assumptions to construct a loan repayment schedule:

a Calculate 10 percent simple interest on the amount due in each year. Assume payments made at the end of the year.

b 10 percent interest accrues for the years 1979 through 1981, but this interest is then spread out equally over the 10-year repayment period.

c The first payment is made in 1982 and payments continue through 1991.

d In each year payments include one-tenth of the interest accrued from 1979-1981, one-tenth of the original $23 million loan, and 10 percent interest on the amount owed prior to the current year's payment.

e   After calculating the amount of each year's payment in U.S. dollars, calculate the payment in Ls Sudan using the expected exchange rate of .5 Ls = $1.

f   Recalculate the loan payment schedule using the exchange rates shown in Table 1; assume that the exchange rate remains constant at 4.5 Ls = $1 from 1989-1991.

2 Use the periodicals database in your library (eg., INFOtrack, ABIinform) to find an article relating to small business development in developing nations. These may include plans where payments in goods are accepted in lieu of cash, international small business development agencies, development funds of nations that hope to reap benefits from increased production, etc. What avenues of financing are available for Cotton Textile Mills that would avoid the problem of having to repay the loan in the lender's currency?

3 How could the government of the Sudan make establishing production facilities more attractive to potential investors? Which elements of the Sudan's culture will have an influence on these choices?

Table 2
Income from operations
(percent of total market)

	1988	1987	1986	1985	1984	1983	1982
	(000)	(000)	(000)	(000)	(000)	(000)	(000)
	Ls	Ls	Ls	Ls	Ls	Ls	Ls
Sales	18,273	23,278	22,269	12,856	12,837	8,986	8,767
Cost of Sales	16,183	13,638	16,434	5,876	10,335	7,234	6,978
Gross Profit	2,090	9,641	5,836	6,980	2,503	1,752	1,789
Selling and Administrative Costs	2,237	1,694	2,909	2,314	1,756	1,351	980
Income Before Other Expenses*	27	8,018	3,099	4,698	777	422	849
Debt Obligation	19,074	16,276	15,155	10,107	5,617	5,350	2,729

*These are actual income figures obtained from the company.
Income cannot be determined by subtracting Selling and Administrative Costs
from Gross Profit because the income was adjusted to reflect changes
in the debt level, which rose and fell according to variations in goverment policies.

35. GOMEP: **A manager's day in a developing country**[3]

Additional topics covered: Strategy, production management, infrastructure problems, foreign monetary exchange, worker productivity, licensing agreements.

In June 1989, Miguel Palmero, general manager of Maxim Gomez P., C por A. (GOMEP), sat at his desk contemplating the future of the company. GOMEP enjoyed a strong reputation in the Dominican Republic, where many of the company's products additional brand leadership positions in their respective markets.

Despite GOMEP's success and healthy financial condition, Palmero was uneasy about the future of the firm. "Our primary strategic goal at GOMEP is steady, controlled growth," he explained. "Growing too quickly is dangerous, and stagnation or decline are even worse." But steady growth was difficult to achieve under the political and economic conditions that prevailed in the Dominican Republic.

"How can I develop a strategic plan under these conditions?" Palmero wondered. "Our environmental conditions are so volatile it's difficult to anticipate our opportunities and threats a month from now, let alone five or ten years from now. And economic forecasts–forget it!" The economic climate of the country had deteriorated during the past few years. The stability of the political environment was not much better, especially with the Dominican presidential election scheduled for May 1990.

Business conditions in the Dominican Republic

The Dominican Republic (DR) occupies the eastern two-thirds of the island of Hispaniola in the Caribbean Sea between Puerto Rico and Cuba. Haiti occupies the western third of the island. The capital is Santo Domingo (population 1.7 million), the oldest city in the Western Hemisphere, founded in 1492 by Christopher Columbus. Table 1 provides an overview of the country.

The economic environment

Economic conditions in the Dominican Republic are traditionally unstable, and the economy has weakened in recent years. The Dominican economy is heavily dependent on agriculture, with 41.2 percent of the working population employed in this sector. Table 2 provides statistics on the nation's gross domestic product (GDP). The table shows that the Dominican per capita GDP of $757 has slipped in recent years.

---

3 By Stephen J. Porth, Associate Professor of Management and Chair of Management and Information Systems Dept. at St. Joseph's University in Philadelphia. Used with permission.

Table 1
Country profile: the Dominican Republic

Location:	The Dominican Republic is located between Puerto Rico and Cuba in the Caribbean Sea.
Population:	6.9 million 1989 with annual growth of 2.3%.
Government:	Democracy, with presidential elections every four years.
Language:	Spanish. English is widely spoken in the business community.
Currency:	The Dominican peso, indicated by the $RD.

Source: *The Dominican Republic, The Europa Year Book, Europa Public Limited,* Vol. 1, 1988.

The Dominican Republic has been ravaged by inflation, with an inflation rate exceeding 60 percent in 1989. Unemployment is also a problem. The island nation has an ample supply of unskilled and semi-skilled labor, with a total workforce estimated at 2.9 million. There is, however, a shortage of skilled workers and technicians. The unemployment rate reached 29.6 percent in 1989, with estimates of the combined unemployment and underemployment rates exceeding 50 percent. Inflation and unemployment rates are given in Table 3.

Labor unions represent approximately 12 percent of the country's labor force. Union activity is weak and divided into at least eight competing national confederations. The country's high unemployment and underemployment rates also tend to diminish the strength of the labor movement.

Table 2
The Dominican economy: Gross Domestic Product (GDP)

	1986	1987	1988	1989
GDP (in billions, current $RD)	17.5	21.7	31.4	38.3
Real GDP (billions, 1988 $US)	4.81	5.04	5.28	5.22
Real per capita GDP (in $US)	752	764	787	757

Source: Oliveira, Ana. *Country Marketing Plan for the Dominican Republic,* United States Embassy, Santo Domingo, 1990.

Table 3
Inflation and unemployment in the Dominican Republic

	1986	1987	1988	1989
Inflation (CPI % charge)	6.5	25.0	57.6	62.0
Unemployment (avg. % per year)	28.7	26.3	28.6	29.6

Source: *Oliveira, Ana. Country Marketing Plan for the Dominican Republic, United States Embassy, Santo Domingo, 1990.*

The labor code of the Dominican Republic, Codigo de Trabajo, establishes employment policies and procedures. Wages and salaries are established through mutual consent, subject to the minimum wage scales that are dictated by the government for each type of industrial and commercial activity. During 1989, the private sector minimum wage rate was increased from 500 pesos ($80) to 700 pesos ($111) per month and the public sector minimum wage was raised from 400 pesos ($64) to 500 pesos ($80) per month. This translates into a minimum wage rate of less than 50 cents an hour.

Foreign exchange is another problem faced by Dominican managers. The Dominican government Central Bank manages the money supply and controls foreign exchange reserves. The Central Bank requires that all requests to purchase dollars in excess of $10,000 per year be channeled to and authorized by the Central Bank. Transactions subject to these controls include payment for imports of goods and services, and profit and royalty repatriation.

> Because the Central Bank frequently lacks a sufficient supply of foreign reserves to cover demand, some Dominican companies resort to buying dollars on the black market, usually at a significantly higher cost than the official exchange rate.

During 1989, foreign exchange availability was unpredictable due to a shortfall in foreign exchange reserves. As a result, during September 1989, all foreign exchange allocations by the Central Bank were postponed for one month. The economic conditions described above are reflected in the weakening of the Dominican peso relative to the dollar and the growing shortage of foreign exchange reserves. Table 4 provides data on Dominican exchange rates and foreign exchange reserves. The table shows that from 1986 to 1989 the peso lost more than half its value to the dollar.

The political environment

With a presidential election in May 1990, political conditions were uncertain. The incumbent, Dr. Joaquin Balaguer, was bidding for a sixth term in office and his second consecutive four-year term. He was challenged by fellow octogenarian, Juan Bosch. Balaguer, 83, who was blind, promised to increase national productivity if re-elected. He also would take other economic measures to rein in inflation and address a shortage of such imported goods as medicines, rice, and milk. Bosch, who was a Marxist president of the country in 1962 and 1963 before being ousted by the military, called for the industrialization of the nation. Some Dominican business managers were uneasy about the election, fearing widespread change in government policies toward business, particularly if Bosch was elected.

Table 4
Foreign exchange

	1986	1987	1988	1989
Foreign Exchange Reserves *(millions)*	6.5	25.0	57.6	62.0
Average Exchange Rate *($RD_____= $1 US)*	28.7	26.3	28.6	29.6

Source: Oliveira, Ana. Country Marketing Plan for the Dominican Republic,
United States Embassy, Santo Domingo, 1990.

Public utilities and infrastructures

Electricity supplies in the Dominican Republic are inadequate, posing a major obstacle to business firms and consumers. Less than half of the nation's electricity demand is currently being met by the state-owned Dominican Electricity Corporation (CDE).

Dominican businesses face other challenges as well. Postal service is inefficient, and mail frequently gets lost forever. Communication systems may be unreliable and expensive. For instance, telephone connections may be cut off at any time for no apparent reason, and telephone service is so expensive that some companies use CB radios to communicate with their sales force in the field.

Electricity outages occur on a daily basis, often several times per day, and may last for a few seconds or for hours. For businesses, the outages disrupt the flow of work and contribute to low levels of employment productivity. To circumvent this problem, firms generally install private emergency generators, increasing both investment and operating costs.

History of GOMEP

GOMEP was established in 1927 and incorporated in 1942 by Don Maximo Gomez Pina. Under licensing agreements with companies throughout the world, GOMEP manufactures, distributes and sells household products, cosmetics, toiletries and pharmaceuticals in the Dominican Republic and Haiti. Among the firms represented by GOMEP are Mennen, Scott Paper, Chesbrough Ponds, Faberge, Pfizere and other worldwide leaders in the consumer products and pharmaceutical industries. A list of companies represented by GOMEP and the length of each business association are presented in Table 5.

Key executives and organizational structure

GOMEP stock is closely held, primarily within the Gomez family. Since 1960 Mrs. Mariana Gomez Franco, daughter of the founder of the company, has served as president of GOMEP. Management directs a staff of approximately 200 permanent employees, plus temporary factory workers.

GOMEP is structured on a functional basis with centralized decision-making. Five functional managers (i.e., the manager of Finance, Marketing, Industrial Management, Human Resources, and Maintenance and Security) report directly to the general manager (Miguel Palmero), who in turn reports to the president. The Finance, Marketing, and Industrial Management Departments are further subdivided as described below.

Table 5
Companies represented by GOMEP

Company	Year appointed
The Mennen Company	1927
Northan Warren Corp. (now Chesebrough Pond's Int., Ltd.)	1927
Scott Paper Company	1927
Pond's Extract Company (now Chesebrough Pond's Int., Ltd.)	1928
White Laboratories (acquired by Schering Corp.)	1930
Schering Corporation	1934
Lanman & Kemp-Barclay & Co.	1939
Chemway Corporation (acquired by Cooper Laboratories, Inc.)	1942
Pfizer Corporation	1952
Allergan Pharmaceuticals	1963
Meyer Productos Terapeuticos (Venezuela)	1967
Fabergé Incorporated	1968
Rayette-Fabergé, Inc.	1968
Scripto, Inc.	1969
Andrea Raab Corp.	1970
Wilkinson Sword, Inc.	1971
Miles Laboratories, Inc.	1971
Laboratorios ELMU, S.A. (Spain)	1971
Tip Top Division (Fabergé, Inc.)	1971
Lancome-Paris	1974
Laboratorios Liade, S.A. (Spain)	1974

Industrial Management Department

The Industrial Management Department, headed by Raul Gorrea, is divided into three subgroups–Materials, Production, and Quality Control. The Materials manager oversees purchasing of supplies and materials, and storage of finished inventory. The purchasing process is cumbersome and bureaucratic; raw materials are often not delivered on time. GOMEP must import most ingredients for manufacturing. Imported goods then must go through customs in the Dominican Republic, often a paperwork nightmare involving banks, agencies from two governments, freight companies, and insurance companies. The cost and time commitment are considerable.

Production Department

The Production Department is managed by Luis Pimentel, who supervises the formulation of products (i.e., the mixing of ingredients), filling, and packaging processes. Production runs are scheduled on a monthly basis using sales forecasts developed by the marketing department. The production facility is 462 square meters and is staffed primarily by temporary personnel. The temporary production workers are contacted by GOMEP's Human Resources Department when they are needed for a production run. They are paid minimum wages. When the production run ends, temporary workers are dismissed.

Because of the nature of its products, quality control is a critical function at GOMEP. As part of the licensing agreement, GOMEP promises to manufacture products according to exact specifications outlined by the licensor.

Eleven production lines are devoted to filling (e.g., bottling) and packaging. With the exception of the Q-Tip cotton swab, all products are mixed, bottled, labeled and packed manually. These lines produce a total of 403 different products, including talcum powder, creams, pastes, aerosols, liquids, polishes, lipsticks, colognes, and shampoos. At any one time, however, there are rarely more than two or three different products produced simultaneously. Production rarely exceeds 20 percent of capacity and is now running at about 15 percent of capacity.

Quality control is regulated by GOMEP chemists and by the licensor, which periodically inspects GOMEP's plant and operations. The quality control department monitors production, not only by monitoring the formulas used, but also by testing raw materials and inspecting manufacturing, packaging and storage.

Marketing Department

The Marketing Department has four divisions – Consumer Products, Pharmaceuticals, Market Research, and Sales. Each division reports to Marketing Director Consuelo Sanchez. The managers of the Consumer Products and

Pharmaceuticals Divisions are responsible for the marketing of their respective brands. Table 6 lists some of the brands produced under license and marketed by Consumer Products. After phasing out its own brand of toothpaste (Combate) in 1987, GOMEP no longer produces any products under the GOMEP brand name.

The Marketing Research and Sales Departments work in conjunction with both product divisions – consumer and pharmaceutical. There are two sales zones – the Santo Domingo zone, which has 13 sales representatives, and the Santiago zone, with 10 representatives. Clients called on by the sales force include drugstores, food stores and small retails. GOMEP's role in the marketing process is extensive. For instance, GOMEP managers work with the licensor to jointly decide the products that GOMEP will produce and distribute in the Dominican Republic. In addition, the Marketing Department is responsible for planning market strategies, devising promotions for new and existing products, determining sales forecasts, pricing, coordinating advertising efforts with the licensor, maintaining customer relations, and bringing expired materials back to the plant for credit. Sales representatives also collect payment from clients.

GOMEP's advertising agency, McCann Erickson, assists in many of these activities. In addition, the licensor often provides GOMEP with cooperative advertising money. In exchange for development of the product and use of the brand name, formula, and marketing support, GOMEP pays a royalty on sales to the licensor.

Table 6

Brands – Consumer Products Division

Chesebrough Pond's Int., Ltd.
Dreamflower
Cold Cream
Dry Skin Cream
Cutex Removedor
Vaseline Intensive Care Lotion
Vaseline Petroleum Jelly
Odorono
Q – Tips

Prince Matchabelli
Catchet

The Mennen Company
Soft Stroke
Skin Bracer
Mennen Roll-on
Push Button
Speed Stick
Baby Magic

Fabergé Inc.
Brut 33
Brut Regular
Babe
Fabergé Organics

Parera
Varon Dandy
Agua Profunda
Andros

Louis Phillipe
Patrichs

Lanman Kemp – Barclay
Agua de Florida
Jabon de Reuter
Tricofero Barry

Finance Department

Director of Finance Ramon Taveras oversees data processing and the office of the controller. The controller, in turn, supervises the accounting sections and the Collection and Credits Department. There are seven accountants, each responsible for different aspects of operations. For instance, one accountant handles payroll, another deals exclusively with the liquidation of imports, and another with disbursements.

Foreign exchange is a different problem faced by finance managers at GOMEP. Most of the raw materials used in production are imported by the company. Royalties and fees must also be paid to GOMEP licensors. GOMEP is obligated to make these payments in U.S. dollars. An insufficient supply of dollars from the Dominican Central Bank has forced GOMEP, at times, to purchase dollars on the black market at a cost of up to three times the official exchange rate. This, coupled with the devaluation of the Dominican peso, has had a significant negative effect on GOMEP profitability.

Conclusion

Miguel Palmero, general manager of GOMEP, understood the magnitude of the challenge faced by his company. Achieving GOMEP's strategic goal of controlled growth, given current business conditions in the Dominican Republic, would not be easy. With a presidential election looming in the near future, political and legal conditions were uncertain and could change overnight. Economic conditions were poor and showed no signs of near-term improvement.

Perhaps Palmero's biggest frustration, however, was knowing he was powerless to change business conditions in his country. "I simply have to work within my constraints," he said. "It's just another day in the life of a Dominican manager."

Questions

1 Compare and contrast the business conditions faced by Miguel Palmero with business conditions faced by American managers in comparable positions.

2 The productivity of GOMEP production workers is low compared to U.S. standards.

    a   What may be the reasons for low productivity rates at GOMEP?

    b   How should production managers at GOMEP increase employee motivation and productivity?

3 Identify two threats to GOMEP resulting from foreign monetary exchange. Explain the impact of these threats on firm profitability.

4 How can GOMEP minimize the impact of foreign exchange threats?

5 Consider licensing agreements as international business strategies.

    a   What are the advantages and disadvantages of licensing to GOMEP? To GOMEP's licensors?

    b   Put yourself in the place of one of GOMEP's licensors (e.g., Scott Paper Co.). Based on the information provided in the case, explain why Scott Paper choose to use a licensing strategy to compete in the Dominican market rather than establishing a subsidiary

36. Belco Petroleum[4]

Additional topics: decision–making, parent-subsidiary relationships, strategy

Belco Petroleum Corporation of Peru was founded in 1959 by Arthur B. Belfer and his son, Robert A. Belfer, as a wholly-owned subsidiary of Belco Petroleum Corporation, a U.S. company. Belco's extensive operations included exploration, drilling and production, construction of platforms, and the laying of flow lines between platforms and the shore. Belco also owned a 1.1 million barrel oil storage facility and a submarine oil loading line.

Belco was purchased for approximately $769 million by InterNorth Holdings, an international energy corporation, on Aug. 1, 1983. Robert Belfer took over for his father at the time of the sale. Both were appointed to InterNorth's board of directors. Belco operated as a wholly-owned subsidiary of InterNorth and was charged by InterNorth to develop known reserves and conduct exploratory drilling. InterNorth purchased political risk insurance.

Belco's Peruvian operations – 1984

Belco had three production sharing agreements with Petroperu, the government-owned oil company. These agreements expire between 2006 and 2012. Belco was obligated to sell its pro-rata share of oil production required for domestic consumption to Petroperu. The remainder was exported at world market prices. Any amount received for such exports that exceeded the current domestic prices by more than $10 per barrel was required to be shared by Petroperu on a 50-50 basis.

Under the terms of Belco's natural gas agreement with Petroperu, Belco received base prices ranging from $1.50 to $3.00 per gross MCF delivered. Prices escalated with deliveries in excess of 15 MCF of gas per day and were determined on a monthly basis. Deliveries in excess of 20 MCF per day qualified for the maximum contract price. Base prices were subject to BTU adjustment and to fluctuations in the average price of the reference crude oil used to adjust the price for domestically sold oil.

Internorth merger – 1985

In July the stockholders of Houston Natural Gas Corporation (HNG) approved an "Agreement and Plan of Merger" that resulted in the merger of Houston Natural Gas Corporation and InterNorth to form HNG/InterNorth Gas Corporation and InterNorth to form NG/InterNorth. The merger had no effect on the way Belco was to operate.

---

4 © Copyright 1992 by Gary A. Lombardo, School of Business, Economics and Management, University of Southern Maine, Portland. Used with permission.

Belco operating highlights – 1985

For the six months ending June 30, operating revenues and net income were $243,171,000 and $60,347,000. Earnings reflected lower oil prices in Peru. The decline in average oil prices was the result, in part, of the OPEC agreement to lower prices. This was reflected in the price Belco received under its sales agreement for oil sold within Peru. Spot market prices were also lower, affecting export sales.

During the second quarter, Belco had to curtail deliveries of natural gas due to striking Petroperu employees. Average daily gas production for the quarter was 15 percent below the previous year's level.

Peru's 1985 presidential election

President Belaunde's term had been marred by deep recession, spiraling inflation, crushing foreign debt, a growing narcotics industry, and a brutal counter-insurgency campaign against the Shining Path.

Alan Garcia Perez, Belaunde's rival and victorious candidate of the American Popular Revolutionary Alliance, projected a more modern Social Democratic image that appealed to many young voters. He offered vague prescriptions for economic revival and promised protection from foreign competition. Garcia would not discount nationalization as a means of stabilizing Peru's economy.

Speculation circulated among industry experts about Petroperu's technical expertise and whether it could operate its highly advanced exploration and extraction equipment if indeed Belco's assets were expropriated. Belco was given until Dec. 27 to renegotiate its contracts with the Peruvian government.

Garcia was elected in April. Within 30 days of his July inauguration, Garcia announced plans to take control of three foreign oil companies, including Belco, if new operating agreements could not be reached within 90 days with Petroperu. This 90-day period was subsequently extended to Dec. 27.

Garcia described the action as settling accounts with the oil companies. Garcia asserted that Belco owed $50 million in back taxes for the 1980-1985 period. This was not the first time that Peru had either threatened or actually taken control of foreign-owned companies. Several disputes involving foreign companies occurred.

Belco's future in Peru

Belco was HNG/InterNorth's most profitable foreign operation. Belco denied that the company violated any contracts with Peru. According to Belfer, "We haven't even used all the credits we're entitled to." He added that Belco had informed Peru that a contract renegotiation was necessary in the wake of falling world oil prices.

Question

What are Belco's options and which one should it choose?

0

37. Hondo River Enterprises[5]

Additional topics covered: Plant locations, human resource management, foreign currency exchanges.

For many years, Emilio Monte had waited for the legislative approval and international agreements that would permit the operations of the free trade zone, but it had not yet happened. Thus, in terms of operations as well as physical location, the firm was in a marginal position, and Emilio was constantly reminded of this because his home was located within the main factory.
At the moment Emilio was considering several expansion opportunities.

An approaching holiday – 1988

Emilio noticed that the traffic across the border was already very busy as he walked along the second floor balcony of his main factory. The next day would be the five-day Easter holiday, 1988, and families would want to be together. Mexican immigrants and workers on a visa would travel to Chetumal or one of the dozens of rural villages in the new Mexican state of Quintana Roo. Belizean workers in Mexico, likewise, would be travelling home for the holidays–perhaps to the border town of Santa Elena or Corozol Town, the center of the northern district of the Central American country of Belize. The space occupied by Emilio's establishment was originally set aside as a free trade zone by Belize and was located on the southern bank of the Hondo River, the actual border between Mexico and Belize. On the north side of the river was the Mexican immigration and customs checkpoint and to the south of Emilio's establishment were the Belizean checkpoints.

After studying the process closely, he discovered that as many as four different businesses were involved in the manufacturing, distribution and sales of the Mexican broom–each adding to the cost of the item.

Broom factory beginnings – the 1960s

Emilio's business was developed from a hunch about a common household product–the corn straw broom. He had always known that brooms were an essential item in rural Belizean homes because of dusty roofs made of palm branches and windows always left open to catch the cool nighttime breezes. All homes needed them, and they had to be inexpensive. As a young entrepreneur, he also noticed that brooms used in Belize were manufactured in Mexico. All he needed to compete successfully against the Mexican manufacturers was machinery, a reliable supplier of broom corn and a master broom maker. Inexpensive broom corn was found in North Carolina, where it could be reaped more efficiently than in the tropics. A joint venture was formed. A master broom maker was found in Monterrey, Mexico, through an informal network of business acquaintances. With the help of family resources, two machines were purchased:

The first production run was sold in the local market and was immediately successful – priced below the Mexican product but of equal quality – and provided a substantial profit.

5 By Steven K. Paulson, Department of Management, Marketing and Logistics, College of Business Administration, University of North Florida, Jacksonville. Used with permission.

Dorothy Marcic and Sheila Puffer, *Management International*, West Publishing, 1994.

one that held the handle and bound the straw to it and another that sewed the strands together.

Initial supplies of pine handles, thread wire, red paint, hand tools and product labels were acquired, also through family resources. Additional machines were bought, employees were trained by the master, and Emilio spent his time developing the sales and distribution network that soon covered the entire Belizean market. Emilio's business was established. In a short time, nevertheless, the business leveled off. The market of 40,000 households had become saturated and the business essentially became one of broom replacement sales – providing adequate cash flow, but not enough for capital expansion. Not satisfied, Emilio turned his attention to other possibilities.

> The businesses were very successful, in part, because of the deterioration of the Mexican economy. More importantly, they thrived because Emilio stayed involved in every aspect of the business and because he paid close attention to subtle shifts in international relations and consumer preferences.

Re-export commercialization – the 1970s

Until it achieved statehood, the Mexican province of Quintana Roo operated much like a free trade zone with minimal tariffs on small quantities of imported goods and no duty on personal goods brought into the country. Given the favorable rate of exchange for Belizean currency prior to 1982, Emilio believed a business could succeed by selling consumer goods to Mexicans who would spend one day a week shopping in Corozol or Orange Walk. A loan was obtained and a 30,000 square foot supermarket was constructed. For several years, Emilio bought large quantities of dry and canned goods from the U.S. and several European countries, especially Denmark. He sold them in his supermarket and in small lots to other supermarkets in nearby Mexican communities. This business, along with the broom business, provided him with flexible two-way international activity that he managed personally through one-to-one relationships with customers and employees.

Peso devaluation and diversification – the early 1980s

During the early and mid-1980s, Emilio's Mexican business declined substantially due to the devaluation of the peso and the corresponding loss of purchasing power by Mexicans. During this time, Emilio searched for a way to adapt his workforce and core technology to a more successful activity. Given that broom manufacturing involved the sewing of straw, he looked into alternative product lines requiring a sewing process. As a more speculative activity, a small shoe assembly process was also begun using hand tools and four to six workers who cut canvas and sewed and glued it onto rubber soles purchased abroad. Both sewing activities were labor intensive – each worker produced a single item, from start to finish.

> The popularity of T-shirts and similar garments with Belizeans was one possibility. He had no major competitors in the domestic market, a variety of foreign sources of cloth, and an available workforce. After much searching, a number of used sewing machines were located. Production began on a regular basis in 1986.

Management and marketing opportunities - 1988

Emilio employed 20 people in the sewing-related enterprises of broom, garment and shoe manufacturing. All of Emilio's employees were Belizeans. They worked a single shift of 48 hours during a six-day work week, which included three hours at an overtime rate. The workers were, for the most part, young men (shoes, brooms) and women (garments). Although some had family financial responsibilities and all were conscientious workers, Emilio had trouble keeping them for long. He knew that once workers saved enough money, they often left to live off the savings and to look for jobs with shorter work weeks. One particularly frustrating and ironic problem was the high rate of literacy and bilingualism of the local population. Once they had some work experience, they could move to cities in the U.S. and earn a great deal more as interpreters, receptionists or supervisors.

One of Emilio's dreams was to expand and market the brooms through retail outlets in the United States. Hardware store chains in Florida had shown some interest, but they preferred to buy entire lines of brooms, mops, brushes and rakes. On price alone, he believed, his brooms were competitive with the Chileans and Hungarians – his chief competitors for the North American market. For him, the most efficient export unit was the 40-foot container that held approximately 1,000 dozen brooms.

The continuing loss of employees to the U.S. concerned Emilio, who on several occasions discussed the problem with U.S. Embassy officials. During these conversations, Emilio learned of the possibility of negotiating a contract for selling brooms to a U.S. military supply division. Emilio estimated that his facility was operating at 25 percent of its capacity. He knew that the master broom maker could easily train workers and have the factory operating at full capacity within two weeks. The military contract represented a realistic expansion opportunity, but he had others plans to consider as well.

Another one of Emilio's enduring ambitions was to operate a Belize-Mexico version of the "maquiladoras" that line the US-Mexican border–twin factories that are responsible for different parts of the manufacturing process as determined by the differential wage rates, labor availability, currency values and market access of the two nations. Another possibility was buying a small broom manufacturer in Merida, Mexico, some 600 kilometers to the north.

The approaching holiday was a good time for Emilio to reflect on the current status of his sewing enterprises. The businesses were holding their own, but just barely. As an entrepreneur, he was willing to do what was necessary to develop the business.

Question

Which of these opportunities should Emilio undertake?

What executives should know about political risk[6]

Life was simple. For decades the American business community had conducted its international activities within the cozy confines of U.S. foreign policy. Out there were the good guys, the bad guys and an amorphous and constantly changing middle group representing various gradations of risk.

The Cold War defined much of what the U.S. corporate executive could accomplish abroad; it qualified the countries in which a company could invest and those with which it could trade, as well as the goods that could be sold. If Washington's policy changed toward a traditionally hostile nation, then that country suddenly became an immediate opportunity for the business community. After President Nixon's visit in 1972, China was transformed from frog to shining prince to the ensuing regret of a number of firms that pursued this prospect without first conducting a realistic appraisal.

In this environment American businesspeople were satisfied with the simple political measure of "safe" and "unsafe" and were secure in selecting foreign projects against traditional commercial and financial benchmarks. Little or no effort was made to probe and analyze the political equation within a country or region in terms of how events might affect the success of the venture.

The astounding political changes of recent years, however, are forcing the U.S. business community to face up to new and confusing uncertainties. For example, the naive but happy presumption that the end of the Cold War meant the end of political conflict was quickly laid to rest by the Iraqi invasion of Kuwait and the eruption of intramural violence in Eastern Europe and the USSR.

Fallen powers

These changes began well before the unleashing of perestroika and glasnost. The seemingly sudden demise of the powerful and friendly Shah of Iran at the hands of what was assumed by many to be a small minority of religious fanatics is a case in point. Iran had been an eager, cash-up-front customer of American goods and services, and the end of the Shah's regime adversely affected many American companies that had assumed that profits from Iran were an eternal phenomenon.

Remember, also, how the markets of Mexico, Nigeria and other OPEC members expanded geometrically under the beneficence of upwardly spiraling crude oil prices? That is, until mismanagement, corruption and the decline of oil prices destroyed their economies and caused irreparable harm to foreign creditors, foreign suppliers and foreign investors.

Fortunately, companies are beginning to recognize the impact of political issues upon international ventures, and that a sure-fire opportunity in a foreign country can deteriorate into a tremendous headache – affecting the safety of personnel as well as of profits – if political factors are not measured and provided for along with traditional market and investment perspectives.

---

6 By Benjamin Weiner. President of Probe, International Inc., a Stanford, Conn, research firm specializing in political evaluation for corporations. Reprinted by permission. The article previously appeared in *Management Review*, January 1991, 19-22.

Let's identify a variety of issues that fall within the political rubric, and then consider what a company can do on its own to identify and cope with these problems.

Political problems range from catastrophic events such as revolution or war, through a broad range of destabilizing issues including endemic corruption, labor unrest, crooked elections, religious violence, coups d'etat and incompetent economic management by government agencies, and then on to narrow but nevertheless dangerous matters such as the political leverage of your competition or ethnic conflict within a specific worksite. All of these phenomena spell trouble if not considered in advance.

Identifying these issues within a country and measuring their impact on political and economic stability requires an alertness to changing events and a healthy respect for reality. This becomes self-evident when we realize that more than one-third of the world's governments change hands each year, many by processes that would not qualify as democratic.

At the top of the scale is the potential for armed conflict with a neighbor or a civil war within a country's borders. In this category are perennial issues such as the India-Pakistani crisis and problems in the Middle East, and now the emerging ethnic-driven crises in Eastern Europe and the USSR that also signal potential bloodshed, terrorism and lingering instability.

These seeds of instability within a country thrive on any number of identifiable issues – historical, tribal, religious, linguistic, social, political or economic in nature. The questions are obvious:

Is conflict predictable and is it imminent?

Would it affect production and access to raw materials, and would it affect the marketplace?

What about your workforce? Does it comprise different ethnic groups and are they compatible?

Whose side are they on?

On a more specific note, it is incumbent upon the corporate executive to make certain that a prospective agent or joint venture partner fits into the political and ethnic equation in which he will be operating. This in turn requires an understanding of the ethnic and religious composition of the nation in question.

For example, an approach to the Nigerian potential could prove disastrous were an Ibo or Yoruba tribesman chosen to head an operation that was primarily concerned with the Hausa-Fulani region, or vice versa. In Pakistan one must understand the differences between Punjabi and Sindi. In Malaysia it is essential to recognize the special economic relationship between Chinese and Malay. In the Philippines it is important to understand the significant and sometimes lead financial role played by Filipino-Chinese.

Political issues

If we were to select a "most important" political phenomenon, it would be ethnicity. It is the dominant engine behind current and potential instability throughout the world and will remain so for decades to come. Many of the conflicts attributed to struggles between political groupings are in fact the result of ethnic differences. And it is a vital issue for management to understand because it affects specific operations as well as general instability in a given country.

Ethnic violence is shaped by two factors, one historical and the other relatively recent. In some countries ethnic rivalries go back for hundreds of years and have managed to resist the influences of modern nationalism. (Perhaps the two most important components of ethnicity are religion and language, as we can see from events in Yugoslavia, Lebanon and the USSR.)

More recently, large numbers of foreigners with alien religions and customs have established themselves in wealthier nations. the result of the imbalance between labor-short Western industrial nations and labor-surplus Third World countries. Accordingly, France suddenly finds itself burdened with 3 million Muslims, Germany with nearly as many and England with between 1 million and 2 million. These new alien communities represent a source of political and social instability.

It is worth looking at the ethnic issue in terms of its impact upon a number of countries:

Canada. French-speaking, Roman Catholic Quebec has maintained its identity for some two centuries despite its being part of English-speaking, Protestant Canada. In recent decades the Quebecois have begun to assert their singular identity and position themselves as distinct from the remainder of Canada. It is possible that this trend will lead to partial or complete separation for the Province. In turn, this could lead to the further disintegration of Canada with the western provinces, for example, seeking economic and perhaps political union with the United States. The impact of this political dissolution upon U.S. interests depends on where the American company is located and the nature of its Canadian markets.

Soviet Union. The dissolution of the Soviet Union into autonomous or independent republics is generally along historical ethnic lines. This creates two problems. One is that although the new republics may possess all the political attributes of independence, some may not be able to function effectively as independent economic units, either because of the absence of raw materials or the inability to access foreign markets or markets within the other republics.

Second is the painful reality that there may be groups of differing ethnic background within many of the new republics, and they may resist integration. This is the case with the Abkhazian people within Georgia, who inhabit prime coastal territory in Georgia and seek autonomy. Then there is the problem of the Shi'ite Meskhetians in Sunni Uzbekistan. Nor can we ignore the tensions between the Catholics and the Orthodox in the Ukraine. All of these issues represent potential friction, instability and bloodshed.

South Africa. The problem is no longer just black/white. It now is also black/black, with thousands of blacks killed in recent years as the result of struggles between two dominant tribes in that country, the Zulus and the Xhosa. For some reason the media hesitate to describe the bloodshed as tribal or ethnic in origin, but rather prefer to describe it in political terms as if the violence stemmed from profound ideological differences, for example the Inkatha Party versus the African National Congress (ANC). The reality, however, is that the Inkatha is almost exclusively Zulu, whereas the ANC is dominated by the Xhosa.

Tribalism in Africa is the paradigm of ethnicity. It not only encompasses the fundamentals of creed and language but also dictates for individuals the clothes they wear, the food they eat, how they dance, where they work, whom they marry and for whom they vote. In this context and until the tribal issue is resolved, American companies had best practice caution before renewing or establishing operations in South Africa.

Political analysis is rapidly becoming an integral element of the procedure by which companies evaluate foreign prospects. It's about time, given the chaotic political changes in play around the world.

But whether a company conducts its own research or contracts out for analyses, two important ground-rules must be observed: Focus on political issues before they become headlines; it's too late if you first learn about a problem on the evening news. And never, ever try to shape the outcome of political events in a given country. The consequences can be painful. The task of political evaluation is to protect a venture against the impact of political developments, or to take advantage of them if they signal opportunity.

Lessons learned

Specific, narrow political events – the kind that affect a particular venture rather than the nation as a whole – are difficult to categorize. However, a few examples get the message across rather quickly:

In the '60s, Mack Truck established an assembly plant in Pakistan but eventually left because of complications generated by its principal Pakistani competitor, whose managing director happened to be the son of the dictator. Lesson: Assay the political strength of your competition as well as of your own potential venture partner or agent. Mack Truck apparently failed to do this and paid the price.

Initially dazzled by the publicity surrounding EC 1992 (remember all those conferences?), an American manufacturer took the time to measure local political attitudes within the Common Market. It turned out that his product line would remain constrained by local customs and local regulations and that he was better off operating on a country-by-country basis despite the advent of a unified marketplace. Lesson: Don't always believe what the experts are proposing.

A West Coast manufacturer was invited by a group of Saudis to establish a joint venture in Saudi Arabia. They claimed impeccable credentials. The lead "Saudi" was named George, which piqued the curiosity of one of the company's executives, since it was a Christian name not normally used by a Saudi Arabian. After a discreet investigation it turned out that George was a Lebanese passing as a Saudi to foreigners. The manufacturer wisely terminated discussions. Lesson: Learn the ethnic equation early on.

A guide to political evaluation[7]

The following is an abridged version of Probe's Political Agenda Worksheet, which may serve as a guide for corporate executives initiating their own political evaluations.

External factors affecting subject country

prospects for foreign conflict

relations with border countries

regional instabilities

alliances with major and regional powers

sources of key raw materials

major foreign markets

policy toward United States

U.S. policy toward country

Internal groupings (points of power)

Government in Power

key agencies and officials

legislative, entrenched bureaucracies

policies – economic, financial, social, labor, etc.

pending legislation

attitude toward private sector

power networks

Political Parties (in and out of power)

policies

leading and emerging personalities

internal power struggles

sector and area strengths

future prospects for retaining or gaining power

Other Important Groups

unions and labor movements

military, special groups within military

---

7   By Benjamin Weiner. President of Probe, International Inc., a Stanford, Conn, research firm specializing in political evaluation for corporations. Reprinted by permission. The article previously appeared in *Management Review*, January 1991, 19-22.

families

business and financial communities

intelligentsia

students

religious groups

media

regional and local governments

social and environmental activists

cultural, linguistic and ethnic groups

separatist movements

foreign communities

potential competitors and customers

Internal factors

power struggles amongst elites

ethnic confrontations

regional struggles

economic factors affecting stability (consumer inflation, price and wage controls, unemployment, supply shortages, taxation, etc.)

anti-establishment movements

Factors affecting a specific product

(Custom designed for each project)

Managers' views
on potential investment opportunities[8]

Is your company considering investing overseas? Given the competition among countries seeking to attract investment from abroad, firms are faced with many different types of incentives. Fry (1983) identified 51 different incentives offered by developing countries to foreign investors. These include such items as tax holidays, subsidization of local wages, and cash grants for part of the investment cost.

Not all incentives, however, are preferred equally by investors. The characteristics of the investment – size, product, market orientation – will affect some of the incentives desired.
For example, a firm making an investment requiring a large amount of equipment may rate accelerated depreciation provisions very high.

Because of the large number of incentives offered by host countries, investors comparing investment locations are often faced with a confusing array of incentive choices. To assist managers in their analysis of investment incentives, we report the experiences and opinions of 103 managers concerning incentives offered by countries in the Caribbean region. The managers' responses may be helpful when your company has to evaluate the variety of incentives offered.

Methodology

The countries and areas selected for this study border on the Caribbean Sea. These include Central America, northern South America, the islands of the Caribbean, and Mexico. Countries in this area that were not included in the study were Cuba and U.S. territories. Cuba has not permitted a U.S. firm to invest in the last 30 years. Possessions of the U.S. were not included because U.S. firms were to be contacted about foreign incentives. The total population of all countries selected is almost 175 million people.

The Caribbean area was chosen for several reasons. First, a majority of the countries use incentives as part of their package to attract foreign investment. Second, the countries included in the study and the types of investments made in these countries are diversified. Third, since the passage of the Caribbean Basin Initiative there has been an increased interest in this region. This initiative exempts most products from Central America and the Caribbean Islands from U.S. customs duties. Finally, Mexico is the third largest trading partner with the United States. Export-oriented investments have been attracted to the border regions of these two countries.

Table 1 lists the countries included in the study and the number of responses received from firms operating in 18 of the 35 countries in the region. The countries that did not respond

---

8 Mark McCarthy, Martha Pointer, David Ricks, Robert Rolfe, *Business Horizons*, July-August 1993, 54-58. Used with permission.

were smaller, with few U.S. investments. Based on the information provided by the Department of Commerce, more than 80 percent of the companies investing in the region made their investments in the countries that responded.

Participants

The participants for the survey were managers of 891 U.S. firms with operations in the Caribbean region, obtained from *The Directory of American Firms Operating in Foreign Countries* (1987). The questionnaire was addressed to the foreign operations officer for each company so that the manager most familiar with the foreign investment could complete the survey.

Of the 891 questionnaires mailed, 103 usable responses were returned, indicating a response rate of 13 percent. A response rate of this level is consistent with previous findings that surveys addressed anonymously tend to have response rates in the low teens (Kanuk and Berenson 1975). In addition, 31 questionnaires were returned as undeliverable and 60 were returned as not applicable.

Questionnaire

The questionnaire asked for information about the firm's most recent investment in the Caribbean area. Each participant responding to the survey was asked to rate how desirable each of 20 incentives (listed in Table 2) would have been for its investment. The attractiveness of each incentive was measured using a nine-point scale, with "1" indicating "not very desirable" and a "9" indicating "very desirable."

Each participant indicated whether its most recent investment in the Caribbean region was start-up, expansion, or acquisition. The majority of the investments were expansion (57), whereas start-ups accounted for 26 and acquisitions for 13 of the investments (seven participants did not respond).

There was also a mix in the responses concerning the target area of the investment. Sixty-six of the new investments targeted the local market, whereas 31 were for production and export. The remaining six indicated both local market and export as the target.

Of the questionnaires received, 97 of the managers listed the year of their firm's last investment. The timing of the investments ranged from 1960, when there were two (2.1 percent), to 1990, when there were six (6.2 percent). However, 74 investments (76.3 percent) were made in the 1980s. Of those, 50 were made in 1989.

Items related to the size of the investment and the number of jobs created were also included in the questionnaire. Overall, the investments were small, with 65 of them less than $1,000,000. In addition, 81 of the investments created fewer than 100 jobs. The criteria for grouping firms based on size of investment and number of new jobs created were based on statistics; of recent Caribbean investments reported in *Caribbean Basin Investment Survey* (1988).

Finally, the participants were asked to indicate the type of product or service for which the investment was made. Most investments were for manufacturing 83 in all while the remaining 17 were service investments. Three participants did not indicate the type of product or service.

Table 1

**Caribbean region countries
responding to the survey**

country	number of responses*
Antigua and Barbuda	2
Colombia	10
Costa Rica	2
Dominican Republic	8
El Salvador	1
Grenada	1
Guatemala	7
Haiti	1
Honduras	4
Jamaica	5
Martinique	1
Mexico	41
Netherlands Antilles	1
Panama	2
St. Kitts-Nevis	1
Trinidad and Tobago	2
Venezuela	14

*The following small countries had few investments
and no responses to the mailed survey:
Anguilla, Aruba, Bahamas, Barbados, Belize, Bermuda, British Virgin Islands,
Caman Islands, Dominica, French Guiana, Guadeloupe, Guvana, Montserrat Nicaragua,
St. Lucia, St Vincent, Sunnam, and the Turks and Caicos Islands.

Table 2
Ranking of incentives by mean values

incentive	rank*
No restrictions on other intercompany payments	7.69
No controls on dividend remittances	7.17
Import duty concessions	7.15
Guarantee against expropriation	6.91
Tax holidays	6.83
Exemption from dividend withholding tax	6.71
Tax treaty with United States	5.95
Cash grants for fixed assets	5.90
Accelerated depreciation	5.45
Subsidized loans	5.43
Real estate tax concessions	5.07
Capital gains tax exemption	4.83
Job training subsidies	4.76
Tariff protection from competition	4.41
Loan guarantees	4.39
Wage subsidies	4.14
Land grants	3.97
Quota protection from competition	3.84
Assistance in feasibility studies	3.16
Research and development subsidies	3.08

*Scale 9 = Very Desirable; 1 = Not Very Desirable

Follow-up telephone interviews

In addition to the mail responses, all managers who identified themselves on the questionnaire were interviewed by telephone. The interviews, which lasted from 15 to 30 minutes, helped gain additional insight into managers' incentive preferences.

Findings

Managers ranked the importance of 20 different incentives. These results are reported in Table 2. The rankings indicate that foreign exchange restrictions and taxation of profits are a primary concern of investors. Six of the ten most important incentives were related to either income taxes or foreign exchange restrictions.

The incentives ranked first and second – no restrictions on non-dividend payments and no controls on dividend remittances – reflect managers concerns about foreign exchange restrictions. Many of the host countries have strict foreign exchange laws limiting the amount of profit repatriated to the firm's home country. In most cases, the country's central bank has a monopoly of foreign exchange. A comment made by one manager in a follow-up interview was that foreign exchange restrictions can change "overnight," making foreign exchange risk management very difficult.

Another incentive preferred by managers is import duty concessions. This ranking reflects the high level of import duties found throughout the region. One manager stated that import duties in some cases can easily exceed 70 percent of an asset's value.

Managers were also concerned with political instability. Some of the countries in the Caribbean area, such as Nicaragua and Haiti, have experienced great instability. Ranking fourth is government guarantees against expropriation, reflecting managers' concern with the political situation in the host country.

A previous study by Aharoni (1966) concluded that incentives that reduce the cost of the initial investment are the most important. These include cash grants for fixed assets, land grants, and assistance in feasibility studies. However, managers rated these types of incentives as only moderately desirable or not desirable at all. Managers contacted by telephone suggested that this was the case because in many situations grants are not offered at all or are offered for investments in very underdeveloped areas of the country.

Tax holidays rated fifth in the survey. However, several managers in the follow-up interviews expressed their frustration with tax holidays. In many cases, the holiday exemption period expires just when the project becomes profitable. The feeling of the managers telephoned was that the high ranking of the tax holiday incentive reflected their desire to have longer holidays.

Finally, the low ranking of job training subsidies (number 13) and wage subsidies (number 16) reflect that these incentives are not very attractive. The managers interviewed by telephone agreed with the low ranking of wage subsidies, noting the low cost of labor in the region. In addition, because many operations do not require skilled labor, training is not an expensive operation.

So far we have reported overall impressions, experiences, and opinions. However, the 103 managers reporting were quick to add that their ranking of the importance of various incentives really depended upon the situation. We therefore asked them what influenced their ranking and how it altered their preferences. The executives indicated that incentive preferences depended upon market orientation, location, product type, and size of the investment.

Size of investment

Investment size (less than $1 million versus greater than $1 million) yielded more differences among managers than any other incentive. Managers rated nine incentives differently. Smaller investment firms preferred relaxed restrictions on dividends and interfirm payments. The managers of larger investments rated cash grants, land grants, job training subsidies, real estate tax concessions, accelerated depreciation, and tax holidays higher. In follow-up interviews, most managers reported that the foreign exchange incentives are rated higher by smaller firms because changes in foreign exchange affect small firms much more than large firms.

Start-up versus expansion

Managers of firms with start-up operations rated cash grants and accelerated depreciation incentives as less desirable than did managers of expansion operations. In follow-up telephone interviews, several managers noted that the small size of start-up operations typically reduces the amount of benefit these incentives can provide.

However, as an operation becomes profitable, it may expand; as such, the desirability of these incentives might increase.

Country of Investment[9]

Managers with investments in Mexico rated accelerated depreciation higher than managers with investments in other countries. This difference is explained by the fact that Mexico is the only country in the region that does not offer tax holidays. Therefore, deductions that reduce taxable income are much more important for Mexican investors than investors in other countries.

Market orientation

Managers of export operations rated import duty concession the highest; managers investing in local market operations rated import duty concessions fourth. This incentive is rated high by export operation firms because many of the components and equipment are imported. These ratings demonstrate that government programs waiving import duties, such as the free trade zones of the Dominican Republic and the maquiladora program of northern Mexico, are providing the incentive deemed most important by their targeted investors.

Managers of mining investments preferred tax holidays, import duty concessions, and guarantee against expropriation. Two equally important incentives for mining operations were guarantees against expropriation and tax holidays. These rankings reflect the nationalization experience of the industry and the high level of taxation generally imposed on extraction operations.

Product I type

Four categories of products were studied: mining, light manufacturing, heavy manufacturing, and service. Each category was compared with the others to determine any differences in incentive preferences.

Mining versus manufacturing (light and heavy). In comparing mining with manufacturing, four incentives were rated differently among managers: tariff protection, tax holidays, import duty concessions, and guarantee against expropriation. In a follow-up telephone interview, one manager expressed concern over the high import duties for mining equipment. These rates can change overnight, rendering a project suddenly unprofitable. Concession of these duties can, therefore, make the operation much more profitable.

9 In these rankings, Mexico was compared to all other countries in the survey. This was because Mexico differs from the other countries in several significant ways. First, it is by far the largest country studied, with a population exceeding 84 million. Second, it is the only country in the survey that borders the United States. Third, it has the most diversified economy of all the countries examined.

Manufacturing versus service. Managers of manufacturing firms placed more importance on land grants than did service firm managers. This finding was not surprising; many service operations rent their space and require little or no land. However, in both cases land grant incentives were not rated very desirable.

Light manufacturing versus heavy manufacturing. Managers of heavy manufacturing companies rated cash grants higher than did managers of light manufacturing. However, cash grants were not one of the more desirable incentives for either type of manufacturing company. In addition, light manufacturing companies rated wage subsidies higher. These types of firms tend to be more labor-intensive than heavy manufacturing firms. In both cases, the incentive was not rated as one of the most desirable to gain.

> Naturally, any firm considering an overseas investment should therefore look for opportunities that offer the most desired incentives. However, before making a final investment decision, the firm needs to consider its unique situation.

Most countries offer a vast array of incentives to attract foreign investment. The findings of this study demonstrate that experienced investors do recommend some incentives more than others. The overall importance placed on each incentive is reported in Table 2.

Table 2 identifies desirable incentives to seek, but the exact nature for each firm needs to be taken into account. Basically, preferences of incentives are a function of the type or investment, the countries involved, the market orientation of the investor, the type of product, and the size of the investment.

The responses indicate that investors need to evaluate the characteristics of their investment and then seek the incentives best suited for that investment. For example, if your firm is making a large investment, it should focus its efforts on incentives that are a function of the amount of investment, such as cash and land grants, accelerated depreciation provisions, and subsidized loans.

From the overall rating of incentives, any type of investment should be concerned with host country foreign exchange restrictions. It must be noted that the responses from this survey are from the Caribbean region. Therefore, even though the area has received significant investment in the past ten years, it may not be totally representative of investments in other regions.

Finally, this study looked only at investor preferences for incentives. In most investment transactions, the host country may also impose various performance requirements such as regulations on local content or minimum local ownership. These items should also be considered when making a foreign investment.

> In recent years many countries have relaxed their foreign exchange policies; this should be welcomed by investors. In addition, the incentives offered in free trade zones, import duty concessions, income tax holidays, and no foreign exchange restrictions appear to match well the preferences of export-oriented investors. This may explain in part the popularity of the free trade zone systems in the Dominican Republic and Costa Rica.

References

Y. Aharoni, *The Foreign Investment Decision Process* (Boston: Harvard University, 1966).

Caribbean Basin Investment Survey, Bureau of Economic Analysis (U.S. Department of Commerce, 1988).

Directory of American Firms in Operation in Foreign Countries, World Trade Academy Press (New York: Uniworld Business Publications, Inc., 1987).

E. Fry, *The Politics of International Investment* (New York: McGraw-Hill, 1983).

L. Kanuk and C. Berenson, "Mail Surveys and Response Rates: A Literature Review," *Journal of Marketing Research*, November 1975, pp. 440-453.

Competitiveness and the "global capital shortage"[10]

To exercise influence over economic policy, it is first necessary to keep discovering alarming new "crises" that need to be fixed. This is why interest groups with completely opposite positions will nonetheless welcome and embrace such notions as a loss of U.S. "competitiveness" or a "global capital shortage." Ill-defined issues such as these can easily be cited as reasons for free trade agreements or protectionism, for tax incentives or tax increases, for tight money to keep inflation down or easy money to sink the dollar. These solutions remain the same; only the problems change.

> There is no point in rehashing the many efforts to define "competitiveness." The words imply means different things to different people. The U.S. economy can certainly do better, regardless of how it stacks up against other countries. And there are surely some new and promising industries we would not want to lose.

Unfortunately, the political need to exaggerate problems in order to divert attention from numerous other issues and interests that compete for news and legislation has led to a grossly distorted perception of what has actually been going on in the U.S. and world economies. In particular, there is a common impression that most U.S. manufacturing industries have been in a state of chronic decay, facing "deindustrialization" and leaving only "hollow corporations" with offices here but factories abroad. It is likewise widely believed that most U.S. businesses can't compete on world markets, leaving this country importing more and more while exporting less and less.

The Index of U.S. Manufacturing Output primarily consists of physical measures, such as numbers of vehicles or tons of steel. It differs from the total index for industrial production because it excludes utilities and extractive industries (such as oil and coal, which have been hurt because of low prices and high costs). For comparisons with Japan, which has a much smaller mining sector, manufacturing output is more appropriate. From 1981 to 1989, manufacturing output rose by 5.2 percent per year, up from 2.8 percent in 1971-80. The 1981-89 gains were twice as large as in Germany (2.6 percent) and only slightly below Japan (6.7 percent) (see Figure 1).

> Looking at the economy as a whole, rather than at separate industries, it is quite clear that U.S. manufacturing grew very rapidly in the past eight years, and that exports likewise boomed for the past five.

Figure 2 shows U.S. exports, taken from the GNP statistics; it likewise speaks for itself. They figures are adjusted for inflation, and they show the real volume of exports up more than 50 percent from any previous peak, and nearly doubling from the bottom of the 1982 recession. Exports continued to soar during the mini-recession of late 1990 and early 1991.

With manufacturing and exports way up, those who want to whip up some anxieties about "competitiveness" have had to keep redefining the problem that requires their pet solution. A favorite trick is to point to a long-term decline in the U.S. share of exports to the "world." Unfortunately, the United States is a very large part of the "world" import market, and the U.S. is the only country that cannot possibly export to the U.S.!

10 Alan Reynolds, *Business Horizons*, Nov-Dec 1991, 34(6), 23-26. Used with permission.

The U.S. economy grew faster than most other economies in 1983-87 (4.2 percent a year, even faster than Japan's 3.9 percent) – sucking in a lot of imports of capital equipment and industrial components and materials. U.S. industries were then busy supplying the needs of a rapidly expanding economy (such as aluminum and paper) and had no spare capacity for exporting. Yet such growing shipments from one domestic firm to another, rather than to foreign branches (as in the 1970s), were obviously not counted as exports. The U.S. share of exports to the rest of the world – aside from the U.S. – itself has held up quite well. From 1986 to 1989, for example, U.S. exports to non-OECD countries rose by 19.2 percent per year, compared with 11.3 percent for Japan and 9.3 percent for Germany.

> Another source of confusion is that shares of world trade are measured in U.S. dollars, so the dollar's decline in 1990 appeared to give Germany a slightly larger share of world exports than the U.S. (Japan, surprisingly, is not even close). But the dollar's dramatic rebound in early 1991 likewise means Germany and Japan once again have a much smaller share of the dollar volume of world exports. Yet another problem with "shares of world exports" is that the U.S. share naturally declined after 1973, simply because OPEC oil claimed a much larger share.

A seemingly straightforward definition of competitiveness might be growth of real GNP. On this criterion, the common impression is that the economies of Japan and Europe have been speeding up, while the U.S. has slowed down. That was true of the past two or three years, but it is not true over any reasonable time frame, nor is it expected to be true in 1992. Looking at trends over a longer period give a quite different picture (see Figure 3).

Although the Japanese economy continues to grow more rapidly than more mature economies, particularly since cutting tax rates in 1987, growth rates in Japan have slowed to only a third of what they were in the 1960's. For all the fuss over "Europe 1992," the EC economies clearly grew far more slowly than that of the United States in the past decade. The EC average would look even worse were it not for a 4 percent growth rate in Britain following the Thatcher tax reforms of 1984-87. Economic growth in 1983-87 averaged only 2 percent in West Germany and was much slower than that in Belgium, Austria, and the Netherlands. All of these economies perked up after cutting marginal tax rates late in the decade, though Germany reversed that policy in early 1991. Compared with past performance, though, it is clearly Japan and Europe that have slowed down – not the United States.

An alternative criterion of "competitiveness" is living standards, which can be measured by the OECD index of real consumption per capita, adjusted by purchasing power parity (to avoid distortions from unstable exchange rates). On an index scale in which the OECD average equals 100, the U.S. rose from 138 in 1982 to 143 in 1989 – 43 percent above average. Japan rose from 89 to 91 in the same period, but that still left average living standards about 35 percent below the U.S. level. Britain rose from 88 to 95 percent of the OECD average. Germany dropped from 92 to 84. Clearly, on the basis of delivering the goods to consumers, the U.S. is far ahead, and (unlike during the 1970s) has been gaining on most other major economies in the past decade.

Much of the anxiety about trade, of course, refers to the large and rising U.S. current account deficit in 1984-87 and corresponding surpluses in Japan and Germany (see Figure 4). The U.S. economy was growing more rapidly than the other two at that time, so Japan and Germany were exporting capital equipment to the U.S. rather than investing their savings at home. In any case, the so-called "imbalances" in trade have been shrinking rapidly since 1987.

> The claim that the U.S. has been slipping in competitiveness thus turns out to be difficult to pin on growth of manufacturing, GNP, exports, or living standards. Even trade deficits, which are a meaningless measure at best, are shrinking fast.

Perhaps the inconvenience of all this evidence accounts for the excessive attention paid to labor productivity. From 1980 to 1989, cumulative increases in U.S. labor productivity in manufacturing were 42.9 percent, up from 26 percent from to 1970 to 1979. A 42.9 percent rise over nine years compares well with a 22.3 percent rise from 1980-89 in Germany, and even with a 59.3

percent rise in Japan. After all, employment increases were far more rapid in the U.S. than in any other major country (see Figure 5). If productivity were all that mattered, and jobs didn't, then we could raise average productivity by simply firing all new and inexperienced workers.

Moreover, the productivity of capital matters too, and OECD estimates show capital productivity falling by 1.7 percent a year in Japan from 1979 to 1988. Some of the apparent rise in Japanese labor productivity may actually reflect undercounting of the contribution of capital. Yet it is nonetheless plausible that new capital investment in Japan may not be yielding much "bang for the buck," considering high real estate and labor expenses. In view of the loose talk about a global "capital shortage" (which mainly means growing export markets for U.S. capital equipment), it is instructive that the OECD estimates that rates of return on capital in the U.S. will be more than competitive with those in Japan (see Figure 6).

Actually, what matters for "competitiveness" is the combination of productivity and pay, called "unit labor costs." On this score, the U.S. has few rivals (see Figure 7). Productivity gains have been brisk while compensation remained moderate, partly thanks to relatively low marginal taxation of pay increases.

Thus, the U.S. looks very competitive indeed in labor costs, return on capital, manufacturing growth and productivity, and real exports. This surely does represent a "competitiveness" problem – all those books about declining U.S. competitiveness may have to be recalled, due to shoddy workmanship.

References:

OECD Economic Outlook, December 1990, p. 157.

OECD, National Accounts, Vol. 1 (Paris 1990), p. 146.

U.S. Department of Labor, Monthly Labor Review, March 1991, p. 92

Alan Reynolds is the Director of Economic Research
at the Hudson Institute in Indianapolis, Indiana.

Figure 1

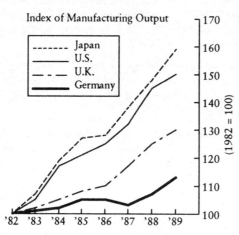

Figure 2

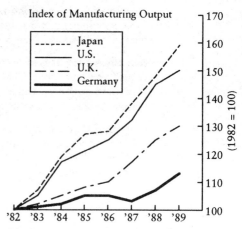

Figure 3

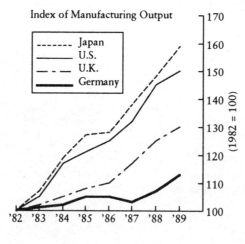

Figure 4

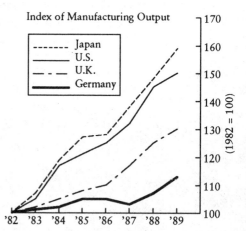

Figure 5

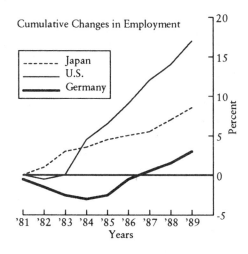

Cumulative Changes in Employment

Figure 6

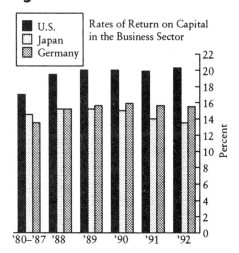

Rates of Return on Capital in the Business Sector

Figure 7

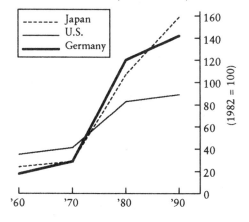

Unit Labor Costs in Manufacturing: Trends Over Decades (in U.S. Dollars)

European and North American integration

Despite considerable opposition from various groups, free trade is becoming a distinct possibility within Europe as well as in North America as countries on these continents integrate their economic systems and remove many barriers to doing business across international borders. In 1993, leaders of the European Community ratified the Maastricht Treaty in October and the U.S. Congress passed the North American Free Trade Agreement (NAFTA) in November, having ratified the free trade agreement with Canada earlier. A third significant event during that period was continuation of the Uruguay round of the General Agreement on Tariffs and Trades (GATT) talks, which would result in decreasing economic protectionism in dozens of countries.

Companies cannot afford to ignore the implications of free trade for the way they do business. Free trade offers such opportunities as improved access to markets, but also creates threats by eliminating government subsidies and protective tariffs. This chapter examines how three firms – one European, one Canadian, and one Mexican – are developing their strategies for growth and expansion and how they are poised to take advantage of free trade. The United Kingdom based firm *Cadbury Schweppes, PLC* is an international manufacturer of confectionery and soft drink products with a long British tradition dating back to its founding in 1831. Faced with increased competition and cost pressures, the company must develop a new strategy by evaluating opportunities for mergers and acquisitions, as well as new product development and the prospects for market expansion in Europe, North America, and other countries. *Strategic alliances: Gateway to the new Europe?* argues that forging alliances with firms already established in the European market may be an attractive strategy for many firms. The article cautions firms to carefully consider five motivational factors for forming alliances as well as ten environmental conditions under which such alliances are appropriate. The life cycle model of strategic alliances presented at the end of the reading can be compared with the stages of dependency outlined in *Global strategy, competence-building, and strategic alliances* in Chapter 7.

Mr. Jax Fashion Inc., a Canadian manufacturer of women's clothing, is seeking growth opportunities in order to achieve its goal of becoming a major international apparel company by the end of the century. Having saturated the Canadian market and diversified through several acquisitions, the firm is poised to enter the large U.S. market under the benefit of the recently ratified free trade agreement. The company was evaluating the pros and cons of several ways of entering the U.S. market. *NAFTA strategies for Canadian manufacturers* discusses two methods of restructuring industrial production – consolidation of production facilities and relocation – that must be considered in order to remain competitive under conditions of North American economic integration.

The Mexican automobile industry and the North American Free Trade Agreement provides information to evaluate the attractiveness of Mexico as a potential location for international automobile manufacturers. The case presents background on the Mexican economy, the maquiladora industry, and a history of government regulation of the auto industry in Mexico. The major international automobile manufacturers are profiled and their options are considered in light of NAFTA. The pros and cons of NAFTA presented in *NAFTA: The fight and the facts* can be compared with the arguments presented in this case.

Chapter 9
European and North American integration

38. Cadbury Schweppes, PLC[1]

Additional topics covered: International expansion, strategy, joint ventures.

> *"All large (food) companies have broken
> out of their product boundaries.
> They are no longer the bread, beer, meat, milk
> or confectionary companies they were
> a relatively short time ago –
> they are food and drink companies."*
>
> Sir Adrian
> Cadbury Chairman (retired)
> Cadbury Schweppes, PLC

In the early 1990s, Cadbury Schweppes, PLC embodied the archetypical modern food conglomerate. With extensive international operation in confectionery products and soft drinks, the company maintained a diversified global presence. Although Cadbury had enjoyed a relatively stable competitive environment through much of the company's history, contemporary developments in the international arena presented Cadbury management with many diverse and critical challenges.

The history of Cadbury

The company began in 1831 when John Cadbury started processing cocoa and chocolate in the United Kingdom for beverages. The company became Cadbury Brothers in 1847. It enjoyed its first major achievement when the second generation of Cadburys found a better way to process cocoa in 1866. By using an imported cocoa press to remove unpalatable cocoa butter from the company's hot cocoa drink mix instead of adding large quantities of sweeteners, Cadbury capitalized on a growing public concern about adulterated food.

The company further prospered when it later found that cocoa butter could be used in recipes for edible chocolates. In 1905, Cadbury introduced Cadbury Dairy Milk (CDM) as a challenge to Swiss firms' virtual monopoly in British milk chocolate sales. A year later, the firm scored another success with the introduction of a new hot chocolate drink mix, Bournville Cocoa. These two brands provided much of the impetus for Cadbury's early prosperity.

---

1 By Franz T. Lohrke, James C. Combs and Gary J. Castrogiovanni, Louisiana State University, College of Business Administration, Baton Rouge. Used with permission.

Cadbury faced rather benign competition throughout its early years. In fact, at one point, Cadbury provided inputs for the UK operations of the American firm, Mars, Inc. Cadbury also formed trade associations with its UK counterparts, J.S. Fry and Rowntree & Co., for the purpose of, among other things, reducing uncertainty in cocoa prices. The company later merged financial interests with J.S. Fry, but spurned offers to consolidate with Rowntree in 1921 and 1930.

Facing growing protectionist threats in overseas markets following World War I, Cadbury began manufacturing outside the UK, primarily in Commonwealth countries (see Figure 1). This international growth was also prompted by increased competition. For example, by 1932 Cadbury management considered the Swiss company Nestle as their primary competitor in the international arena.

In 1969, Cadbury merged with Schweppes, the worldwide maker of soft drinks and mixers. The merger offered both companies an array of advantages, both defensive and offensive. First of all, both companies faced potential takeover threats from larger firms, so the merger placed the new company in a better defensive posture to ward off unwanted suitors. On the offensive side, the marriage allowed the new company to compete better on a worldwide scale. Cadbury had invested primarily in Commonwealth countries, and Schweppes had branched out into Europe and North America, so the new company enjoyed greater geographic dispersion. The increased international presence also allowed the company to defray product development costs over a wider geographic base. Furthermore, the new company enjoyed greater bargaining power with suppliers. For example, following the merger, Cadbury Schweppes became the largest UK purchaser of sugar.

Figure 1

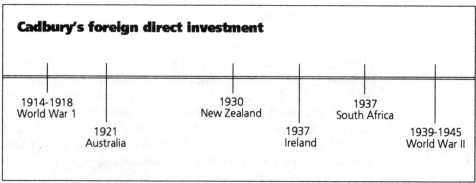

The British confectionery companies historically pursued a different strategy than their American counterparts. While companies from the United States, such as Mars, Inc., manufactured narrow product lines and employed centralized production, Cadbury maintained 237 confectionery products until World War II forced the company to scale back to 29. While faced with a lack of intense competition, Cadbury's brand proliferation strategy could be undertaken. As rivalry heated up in the mid-1970s, though, Cadbury's share of the UK chocolate market fell from 31.1

to 26.2 percent between 1975 and 1977. Management then began to realize that the lower cost American-style strategy of rationalized product lines and centralized production provided the only viable means to compete.

The environment

As is the case with several products in the food industry, many of Cadbury's product lines enjoyed very long product life cycles. (See Table 1 for assorted confectionary products of Cadbury and its rivals.) Food and beverage companies derived substantial benefit from their long-established products, such as Cadbury's CDM bar. The occasional new product introductions often required little in the way of technological investment. The food companies, therefore, competed primarily by cutting costs through process improvements such as automation, by finding alternatives to expensive cocoa, and by introducing creative packaging and marketing (see Table 1).

Along with its many leading products, Cadbury had also become famous for its unique management style. "Cadburyism," which drew influence from the founders' Quaker heritage, included providing for worker welfare and cultivating harmonious community relations. Following Cadbury's reorientation toward core products and rationalized production, though, the company's old management style underwent a transformation. Confectionery manufacturing personnel were reduced from 8,565 to 4,508 between 1978 and 1985. In the process, management's traditional close relationship with workers began to erode as jobs disappeared at the company.

Successful new production introductions remained sporadic, though, and many of the most successful confectionery products, such as Mars Bar and Rowntree's Kit Kat, had been around since the 1930s. Some unsatisfied demand seemed to persist, however, as was evidenced by Rowntree's successful 1976 launch of its Yorkie bar, Mars' profitable introduction of Twix a few years later, Cadbury's notable 1984 launch in the UK of its Whispa bar, and Hershey's 1988 introduction of Bar None.

Nevertheless, new brand introductions required immense investments in development and marketing costs with only limited possibilities for success. For instance, various research suggests that approximately 60 percent of new food product introductions have been withdrawn inside of five years, and this figure may be an under-estimate. Consequently, established brands with customer loyalty are crucial assets for food and beverage companies.

Modern Cadbury Schweppes

Expansion was the key to Cadbury's plans to improve its international position. Chief Executive Officer Dominic Cadbury commented, "If you're not operating in terms of world market share, you're unlikely to have the investment needed to support your brands." In 1986, Cadbury shared third place in the world with Rowntree and Hershey, each having approximately 5 percent of the market. Nestle held second place with about 7.5 percent, while Mars dominated internationally with approximately 13 percent.

To generate its necessary worldwide expansion, Cadbury had two primary markets in which to gain positions. Enjoying a dominant position in its home market, the company realized that the United States and the remaining countries of the European Economic Community (those besides the UK) provide critical markets for a worldwide standing. Terry Organ, director of international confectionary, said: "Rightly or wrongly ... we decided to tackle the U.S. first." Earlier, Cadbury had taken steps toward competing more vigorously in the U.S. by acquiring Peter Paul in 1978. By 1980, however, the company still controlled only about 3.5 percent of the U.S. confectionery market, far eclipsed by its bigger rivals, Hershey and Mars.

In the U.S., Cadbury did not have sufficient size to employ the sales force of its competitors. The company, therefore, had to rely on food brokers to push products to wholesalers, which left the firm far removed from the consumer. Further, the company could be easily outspent in advertising by its two larger rivals.

To compound problems, the company also committed two marketing blunders in the U.S. market. When Cadbury introduced Whispa, the company's marketing success of the decade in the UK, management did not realize that distribution channels in the U.S. were much longer than in the UK. Consequently, the candy bars aged seven to nine months by the time they reached test markets in New England, and consumers reacted accordingly.

The company's second mistake occurred following an effort to standardize its candy bar size across countries. When Cadbury first introduced its CDM bar in the U.S., the bar cost more than its U.S. rivals. Since CDM was also larger than U.S. competitors' regular bars, consumers often were willing to pay a little extra. When Cadbury reduced the size, however, management soon discovered that given the choice between CDM and American confectionery products of equal size and price, U.S. consumers usually chose the more familiar American products. According to one former Cadbury executive, "What happened in the U.S. was a gigantic, gargantuan cock-up, and the fact that London (Cadbury headquarters) did not know what was happening is a sheer disgrace."

Table 1
Assorted major brand names of Cadbury Schweppes and its confectionary competition

Cadbury Schweppes

Cadbury Dairy Milk (CDM)	Roses
Mild Tray	Whole Nut
Crunchie	Fruit and Nut
Whispa	Trebor

Nestle

Nestle's Crunch bar	Polo
Kit Kat	Quality Street
Smarties	Yorkie
After Eight	Aero
Rolo	Black Magic
Dairy Box	Fruit Pastilles
Butterfinger	Baby Ruth

M&M/Mars, Inc.

Mars Bar	Galaxy
Twix	Maltesers
Bounty	Milky Way
M&Ms	Snickers

Hershey

Hershey Bar	Reese's Peanut Butter Cup
Hershey Kisses	Reese's Pieces
Mounds	Almond Joy
Bar None	

Philip Morris

Milka
Toberlone
E.J. Brachs candy

Not all the news from the other side of the Atlantic was bad for the UK company, however. Although Peter Paul-Cadbury only controlled a small piece of the U.S. chocolate market, some products such as Coconut Mounds and York Peppermint Patties dominated their segments. Cadbury's Cream Eggs also enjoyed seasonal success. Moreover, the company's acquisition of Canada Dry from R.J. Reynolds provided Cadbury Schweppes with a strong position in the carbonated mixers market in the U.S. and many other countries (see Table 2 for U.S. market shares). For example, although Cadbury Schweppes only commanded about a 3 percent market share in the $43 billion U.S. soft drink industry, the company sold Canada Dry, the No. 1 ginger ale and club soda in the U.S., and Schweppes, the leading tonic water in the American market. Additionally, the cola giants, Coca-Cola and PepsiCo, did not (as yet) vigorously market products in segments dominated by Cadbury Schweppes. Overall, though, the company faced a struggle in many segments of the U.S. market.

In an effort to remedy some of the company's problems in the U.S. confectionery market, Cadbury sold its manufacturing assets to Hershey in 1988, catapulting the Pennsylvania company to the dominant position in the U.S. market (see Table 3).

Table 2
Top five soft drink companies in the United States
(percent of total market)

	1986	1987	1988	1989	1990
Coca-Cola, Co.	39.8	39.9	39.8	40.0	40.4
Classic	19.1	19.8	19.9	19.5	19.4
Diet Coke	7.2	7.7	8.1	8.8	9.1
Sprite	3.6	3.6	3.6	3.6	3.6
PepsiCo	30.6	30.8	31.3	31.7	31.8
Pepsi-Cola	18.6	18.6	18.4	17.8	17.3
Diet Pepsi	4.4	4.8	5.2	5.7	6.2
Mountain Dew	3.0	3.3	3.4	3.6	3.8
Dr Pepper	4.8	5.0	5.3	5.6	5.8
Dr Pepper	3.9	4.0	4.3	4.63	4.8
Seven-Up	5.0	5.1	4.7	4.3	4.0
7-Up	3.5	3.4	3.1	3.0	2.9
Diet 7-Up	1.4	1.0	1.0	.9	.9
Cadbury Schweppes	4.2	3.7	3.5	3.1	3.2
Canada Dry	1.4	1.4	1.4	1.3	1.2
Sunkist	.9	.7	.7	.7	.7
Schweppes products	.5	.5	.5	.6	.6
Crush	1.4	1.0	.8	.6	.6
Total Market Share of Top Five					
	84.5	84.5	84.5	84.6	85.2

(Source: Standard and Poor's Industry Surveys, 1991)

Cadbury also granted Hershey licenses to manufacture its Peter Paul products, including Mounds, Almond Joy, and York Peppermint Patties. Under this arrangement, Cadbury gained Hershey's marketing muscle behind the Peter Paul products.

Cadbury also faced challenges to building market share across the Atlantic in the European Economic Community (EEC). Similar to the U.S., Schweppes beverages enjoyed success on the continent, but Europe's confectionery industry proved difficult to tap because the market remained dominated by family-owned firms and suffered from overcapacity. Successful expansion in the EEC, however, was crucial to Cadbury remaining a dominant player in the worldwide food and beverages industries.

Contemporary challenges

The 1990s brought radical shifts in the industries in which Cadbury Schweppes competed. First, corporate leaders (and stock markets) discovered that food and beverage enterprises with established brand names were not mundane investments offering only lackluster financial returns. Purchasing popular brands or taking over companies that had portfolios full of well-known products often provided a safer and more economical avenue for growth than attempting to develop entirely new products. In 1985, for instance, Philip Morris acquired General Foods for $5.75 billion, approximately three times book value, while R.J. Reynolds laid out $4.9 billion for Nabisco Brands.

These attempts to acquire popular brands were also dictated by dramatic industry-wide changes that altered the nature of competition faced by the international food and beverages industry. First, the push by the 12 countries of the EEC to remove trade barriers among the member nations by 1992 sparked a buying frenzy of European food companies with established brand names. (See Table 4 for a comparison of the North American and EEC market.) Many non-European companies feared that the EEC would eventually increase tariff barriers for products from outside the community, which would have effectively closed foreign companies out of the market. This anticipation of "Fortress Europe" sent companies without EEC operations scurrying to acquire European enterprises.

Second, the common perception that only the largest companies could survive long-term in most European and global industries also contributed to the takeover hysteria. To expand very quickly, companies began aggressively acquiring rival food companies. For example, Nestle scored a major victory in July 1988 when it outbid its Swiss counterpart, Jacobs Suchard, to acquire Cadbury's longtime UK competitor, Rowntree. In the process, Nestle moved from a minor status in the EEC confectionery market into a first-place duel with Mars. In the UK market, Nestle's acquisition positioned the company in a second place battle with Mars and within striking distance of the first place Cadbury. In January 1992, Nestle continued its acquisition binge by launching a hostile takeover bid for the French mineral water company, Source Perrier.

Table 3
Top five companies in the $8 billion U.S. confectionary market

1980

company	market share
Mars	17.0
Hershey's	15.3
Nabisco	7.1
E.J. Brachs	6.4
Peter/Paul Cadbury	3.5

1988

Hershey's	20.5
Mars	18.5
Jacobs Suchar	6.7
Nestle	6.7
Leaf	5.6

Table 4
The United States
and the European Economic Community

	U.S.	EEC
Population	243.8 million	323.6 million
Gross National Product (GNP) (in 1987 $US)	4.436 trillion	3.782 trillion
Per capita GNP	$18.200	$11.690
Inflation	3.7%	3.1%
Unemployment	6.1%	11.0%

(Souce: House, 1989)

Note: EEC members include the UK (England, Scotland, Wales, Northern Ireland),
Ireland, Denmark, Germany, France, Belgium, the Netherlands, Luxembourg, Portugal, Spain, Italy and Greece.

Other major food conglomerates, such as Philip Morris (U.S.) and Unilever Group (UK/Netherlands) were also rumored to be on the prowl for acquisitions in Europe (See Table 5). These heavyweights not only presented medium-sized food and beverage companies such as Cadbury with increased competition in the marketplace, but also represented potential bidders in any acquisitions attempted by Cadbury. This increased competition threatened to drive up acquisition prices through cutthroat bidding for popular brand names. In fact, as the takeover battles became more heated, stock market analysts speculated that Cadbury and other medium-sized companies could find themselves targets of acquisition attempts.

The European food and beverage industries were undergoing other changes along with the acquisition binges. At the end of the food and beverage distribution pipeline, for example, many European supermarkets were also consolidating. In April 1990, eight EEC grocery chains formed an alliance to combine buying power and promote house brands. As these supermarket companies combined forces, they greatly enhanced their bargaining power against the food and beverage companies. This increased power threatened future profits of food and beverage companies since the grocery chains' ability to demand price concessions from the companies was enhanced by the stores' consolidations. Furthermore, because supermarkets only wanted to carry the top two or three brands for each product type, food and beverage companies had to acquire popular brands or risk losing shelf space in stores.

Table 5
Food sales-Europe
(including the UK, in billions $)

Nestle	15.1
Unilever	12.2
Philip Morris*	8.0
BSN	7.8
Mars	4.1
Cadbury Schweppes	3.1

*includes Jacobs Suchard

(Source: Templeman & Melcher, 1990)

In response to these massive changes in the industry, Cadbury also began acquiring name-brand products and searching for strategic alliances. In 1986, for example, the company ended its bottling agreement with Pepsi to form a joint venture with Coke in the UK. In 1990, Cadbury purchased the European soft drink operations of Source Perrier, and in 1991, the company formed a joint venture with Appolinarus Brunnen Ag, a German bottler of sparkling water. (See Table 6 for Cadbury Schweppes worldwide sales figures.)

Table 6
Cadbury Schweppes' 1990 worldwide sales
(in millions of pounds*)

region	total sales	confectionery	beverages
United Kingdom	1,746.0	715.4	760.6
Continental Europe	638.0	195.6	442.4
Americas	403.7	18.3	373.5
Pacific Rim	49/5.5	# n/a	n/a
Africa and other	132.9	91.2	38.8

* one pound = $1.93
# sales primarily in Australia/New Zealand
n/a: not available

note: total sales will not always equal confectionery plus beverages. In the U.S. (Americas region), for example, Cadbury Schweppes also generated sales from its Mott's subsidiary.

(Source: Compact Disclosure; Wall Street Journal)

Analysis

With the competitive environment heating up, Cadbury management faced a number of crucial questions. Could the company continue to compete independently against the food and beverage mega-corporations that were forming, or should Cadbury merge with another company before being faced with a hostile takeover attempt? Did Cadbury have the resources to acquire more brand names, or should management continue to investigate the joint venture route? Should Cadbury keep its emphasis on Europe, or should the company's attention shift to possible opportunities in the underdeveloped Asian market? Regardless of the decision, Cadbury Schweppes management had to move quickly. The choices of popular name brand food and beverage products on the table were being cleared away fast.

Discussion questions

1 Define Cadbury's primary product categories. How does the firm match up against competitors in each market segment?

2 What, if anything, is Cadbury's competitive advantage? What are the key threats to future expansion in the EC? How can Cadbury's competitive advantage be used to overcome those threats?

3 How should Cadbury be organized? What organizational structure would best facilitate future geographic and product line expansion? Keep in mind that the firm's tight margins suggest that efficiency is a major concern. How might Cadbury organize to gain (a) the flexibility needed for expansion and (b) the efficiency needed to compete within each local product market?

Financials
(in thousands of pounds*)

Balance sheet

fiscal year ending	12/29/90	12/30/89	12/31/88
Assets			
cash	62,600	57,400	41,300
marketable securities	118,00	33,300	200,700
receivables	554,100	548,200	434,500
inventories	328,200	334,800	253,400
TOTAL CURRENT ASSETS	1,062,900	973,700	929,900
net property, plant, equip.	978,800	822,500	602,200
other long term assets	320,700	332,600	20,700
TOTAL ASSETS	2,362,400	2,128,800	1,552,800
Liabilities			
notes payable	60,100	57,400	92,200
accounts payable	272,100	263,900	409,500
current capital leases	76,200	76,300	21,900
accrued expenses	320,900	305,900	52,100
income taxes	78,200	95,800	81,800
other current liabilities	154,700	143,600	118,800
TOTAL CURRENT LIABILITIES	962,200	942,900	776,300
long term debt	407,900	381,400	124,700
other long term liabilities	108,401	124,000	74,600
TOTAL LIABILITIES	1,478,500	1,448,300	975,600
preferred stock	300	n/a	3,300
net common stock	174,400	173,600	150,400
capital surplus	95,800	36,700	33,000
retained earnings	115,800	167,600	88,800
miscellaneous	381,600	217,400	210,500
TOTAL SHAREHOLDERS EQ.	767,900	595,300	486,000
minority interest	116,000	85,200	91,200
TOTAL LIAB. & NET WORTH	2,362,400	2,128,800	1,552,800
one pound =	$1.93	$1.61	$1.81

39. Mr. Jax Fashion Inc.[2]

It was 6:30 a.m., Monday, January 16, 1989. Dawn had not yet broken on the Vancouver skyline, and Louis Eisman, President of Mr. Jax Fashion Inc., was sitting at his desk pondering opportunities for future growth. Growth had been an important objective for Eisman and the other principle shareholder, Joseph Segal.

In the future, Eisman felt continued growth would require a different approach. A good option appeared to be expansion into the U.S. market. Strong growth was forecast in the women's career/professional market, Mr. Jax's principle market segment, and the recently ratified Free Trade Agreement (FTA) provided an excellent low tariff environment for expansion into the U.S. Yet, Eisman wanted to ensure the appropriate growth strategy was selected. He was confident that, if the right approach was taken, Mr. Jax could become a major international apparel company by the end of the next decade.

Initially, the company had focused on the professional/career women's dresses, suits and coordinates market, but by 1986 it had virtually saturated its ability to grow within this market segment in Canada. Growth was then sought through the acquisition of 4 companies: a woolen textile mill and 3 apparel manufacturing companies. The result of this decade-long expansion was a company that had become the sixth largest apparel manufacturer in Canada.

The Industry

The apparel industry was divided into a variety of market segments based upon gender, type of garment and price points. Based on price points, the women's segments ranged from low-priced unexceptional to runway fashion segments. Low-priced segments competed on a low-cost manufacturing capability, while the higher quality segments tended to compete on design and marketing capabilities. Companies in the higher priced segments often subcontracted out manufacturing.

The professional/career women's segment ranged from the medium to medium-high price points. During the late 1970s and early 1980s, this segment had experienced strong growth due to the demographic growth in career-oriented, professional women. In the U.S., it had grown by 50% annually during the first half of the 1980s, but had slowed to about 20% in 1988. Experts predicted that by the mid-1990s, growth would drop to the rate of GNP growth. The U.S. professional/career women's segment was estimated to be $2 billion in 1988. The Canadian market was estimated to be one tenth this size and growth was expected to emulate the U.S. market. Yet, the exact timing of the slowing of growth was difficult to predict because of extreme cyclicality in the fashion industry. During difficult economic times, women tended to delay purchases, particularly in the mid-priced, fashionable

---

2 Dr. J. Michael Geringer, Associate Professor of Strategy and International Business, California Polytechnic State University, San Luis Obispo and C. Patrick Woodcock, University of Western Ontario, London, Canada. Used with permission. Copyright © 1991 by J. Michael Geringer and The University of Western Ontario.

market sectors. Then, during times of economic prosperity, women who would not otherwise be able to afford fashionable items tended to have more resources to devote to these items.

Competition

Some of the more prominent Canada-based companies competing in the professional/career women's segment included:

Jones New York of Canada, a marketing subsidiary of a U.S.-based fashion company, was thought to share the leadership position with Mr. Jax in the Canadian professional/career women's market. The company focused exclusively on marketing clothes to this market segment. Manufacturing was contracted out to Asian companies.

The Monaco Group had become a major Canadian designer and retailer of men's and women's fashions during the 1980s. By 1988, the company had sales of $21 million and a rate of return on capital of over 20%. The company designed their own fashion lines, which were merchandised through their own retail outlets as well as major department stores. Manufacturing was contracted out to Asian companies. Recently, the company had been purchased by Dylex Inc., a large Canada-based retail conglomerate with 2,000 retail apparel stores located in both Canada and the U.S.

Nygard International Ltd., with revenues of over $200 million, was Canada's largest apparel manufacturer. Approximately one-third of their sales and production were located in the U.S. This company had historically focused on lower priced clothing, but they had hired away Mr. Jax's former designer to create the Peter Nygard Signature Collection, a fashion line aimed at the professional/career women's market. This new line had been out for only six months, and sales were rumored to be moderate.

Additional competition in this Canadian segment included a wide variety of U.S. and European imports. These companies generally manufactured garments in Asia and marketed them in Canada through independent Canadian sales agents. Historically, most had concentrated their marketing resources on the rapidly growing U.S. market, yet many had captured a significant share of the Canadian market based upon strong international brand recognition. Prominent U.S.-based competitors included:

Liz Claiborne, as the originator of the professional/career women's fashion look, had utilized their first-mover advantage to build a dominant position in this segment. This company, started in 1976, grew tremendously during the late 1970s and early 1980s, and by 1988 they had sales in excess of $1.2 billion (U.S.), or nearly two-thirds of the market. Claiborne generally competed on price and brand recognition, a strategy copied by many of the larger companies which had begun to compete in this segment. To keep prices low, Claiborne contracted out manufacturing to low-cost manufacturers, 85% of which were Asian. The company's large size allowed them to wield considerable influence over these manufacturing relationships. Recently, the company had diversified into retailing.

J.H. Collectibles, a Milwaukee-based company with sales of $200 million (U.S.), had one of the more unusual strategies in this segment. They produced slightly upscale products which emphasized an English country-sporting look. Using facilities in Wisconsin and Missouri, they were the only company to both manufacture all of their products in-house and to produce all of them in the U.S. In addition to providing stronger quality control, this strategy enabled J.H. Collectibles to provide very fast delivery service in the U.S. Limiting distribution of their product to strong market regions and retailers also enabled them to maintain production at levels estimated to be at or near their plants' capacities.

Jones of New York, the parent company of Jones New York of Canada, was a major competitor in the U.S. market. In fact, the majority of their $200 million (U.S.) in sales was derived from this market.

Evan-Picone was a U.S.-based apparel designer and marketer which had become very successful in the slightly older professional/career women's market. This company contracted out their manufacturing, and had annual sales in excess of U.S. $200 million.

In addition, there were a myriad of other apparel designers, marketers and manufacturers competing in this segment. They included such companies as Christian Dior, Kasper, Pendleton, Carole Little, Susan Bristol, J.G. Hooke, Ellen Tracy, Anne Klein II, Perry Ellis, Adrienne Vittadini, Tahari, Harve Bernard, Norma Kamali, Philippe Adec, Gianni Sport, Regina Porter, and Herman Geist.

Profitability in this segment had been excellent. According to data from annual reports and financial analyst reports, Liz Claiborne led profitability in the apparel industry with a 5-year average return on equity of 56% and a 12-month return of 45%, and J.H. Collectibles had averaged over 40% return on equity during the last 5 years. This compared to an average return on equity in the overall apparel industry of 12.5% in the U.S., and 16% in Canada during the past 5 years.

Distribution

The selection and maintenance of retail distribution channels had become an important consideration for apparel manufacturers in the 1980s. The retail industry had gone through a particularly bad year in 1988, although the professional/career women's segment had been relatively profitable. Overall demand had declined, and retail analysts were predicting revenue increases of only 1-2% in 1989, which paled beside the 6-7% growth experienced in the mid-1980s. The consensus was that high interest rates, inflation, and somewhat stagnant demand levels, were suppressing overall profitability.

Although initially considered a mild downturn, recent market indicators suggested that this downward trend was relatively stable and long lasting. Industry analysts had begun to suspect that permanent market changes might be occurring. With baby boomers reaching their childbearing years, further constraints on disposable income might result as this group's consumption patterns reflected increasing emphasis on purchases of homes, or the decision by many women to permanently or temporarily leave the workforce to raise their children. In addition, the effects of rampant growth in the number of retail outlets during the 1980s were beginning to take their toll. Vicious competition had been eroding margins at the retailer level, and the industry appeared to be moving into a period of consolidation.

The principal components for success in the retail apparel industry were location, brand awareness and superior purchasing skills. The apparel companies which had integrated successfully into retailing were the more market-oriented firms, such as Benetton and Esprit.

As a result of these developments, a shift in power from the designers to the retailers appeared to be underway.

To counter the retailers' increasing power, some apparel designers had been vertically integrating into retailing. The attractiveness of this option was based on controlling the downstream distribution channel activities, and thus enabling an apparel company to aggressively pursue increased market share.

The Free Trade Agreement

Historically, developed nations had protected their textile and clothing industries through the imposition of relatively high tariffs and import quotas. Tariffs for apparel imported into Canada averaged 24.5%, and 22.5% into the U.S.. Tariffs for *worsted* woolen fabrics, one of the principal ingredients for Mr. Jax's products, were 40% into Canada, and 22.5% into the U.S.. Import quotas were used to further limit the ability of developing country manufacturers to export to either country. Despite these obstacles, Canadian apparel imports had grown from 20% to 30% of total shipments during the 1980s, most of which came from developing countries. Shipments into Canada from the U.S. represented an estimated $200 million in 1988, while Canadian manufacturers exported approximately $70 million to the U.S.

The FTA would alter trade restrictions in North America considerably. Over the next 10 years, all clothing and textile tariffs between the two countries would be eliminated, but stringent "rules of origin" would apply. To qualify, goods not only had to be manufactured in North America, but they also had to utilize raw materials (i.e., yarn, in the case of textiles, and fabric, in the case of apparel) manufactured in North America. Unfortunately, these "rules of origin" favored U.S. apparel manufacturers, as 85% of the textiles they used were sourced in the U.S., while Canadian manufacturers utilized mostly imported textiles. To ameliorate this disadvantage, a clause was appended to the agreement which allowed Canadians to export $500 million worth of apparel annually into the U.S. that was exempt from the "rules of origin" but would have a 50% Canadian value-added content. There was much speculation as to how this exemption would be allocated when, in approximately 5 years, exports were projected to exceed the exemption limit. Experts expected the companies successfully demonstrating their ability to export into the U.S. would have first rights to these exceptions.

Overall, Eisman considered the FTA a mixed blessing. Competition in Canada would increase moderately over time, but he felt that the lower tariff rates and the company's high-quality, in-house woolen mill presented an excellent opportunity for expansion into the U.S. market.

Many industry experts had contemplated the consequences of the FTA. There was some agreement that in the short-term, the FTA would most severely impact the lower priced apparel segments in Canada because of the economies of scale which existed in the U.S. market (i.e., the average U.S. apparel manufacturer was 10 times larger than its Canadian counterpart). Yet, long-term prospects for all segments were restrained because the industry was slowly being pressured by the Canadian government to become internationally competitive. The question was when international negotiations would eliminate more of the protection afforded to the industry. It was with this concern in mind that Eisman had been continuously pushing the company to become a major international fashion designer and manufacturer.

Mr. Jax Fashions

In 1979, a venture capital company owned by Joseph Segal acquired a sleepy Vancouver-based apparel manufacturer having $3 million in sales, 70% of which was in men's wear. Segal immediately recruited Louis Eisman, a well-known women's fashion executive, who proceeded to drop the men's clothing line, and aggressively refocus the company on the career/professional women's market segment.

Eisman's energy and drive were also critical in establishing the merchandising and distribution network. He personally developed relationships with many of the major retailers. He hired and developed sales agents, in-house sales staff, and in 1983, recruited Jackie Clabon, who subsequently became Vice-President, Marketing and Sales. The sales staff members were considered to be some of the best in the industry. Clabon's extensive Canadian sales and merchandising experience, combined with Eisman's design and marketing strength, provided Mr. Jax with considerable ability in these critical activities.

Initially, acceptance by Eastern fashion buyers was cool. The fashion "establishment" was highly skeptical of this new Vancouver-based apparel designer and manufacturer.

Thus, Eisman focused on smaller independent retail stores, which were more easily swayed in their purchasing decisions. As Mr. Jax gained a reputation for high quality, classical design and excellent service, larger retail chains started to place orders. By 1988, Mr. Jax's products were sold in over 400 department and specialty stores across Canada. Major customers included The Bay, Eaton's, Holt Renfrew and Simpson's and, although initial marketing efforts had been aimed at the smaller retailer, the majority of Mr. Jax's sales were now to the larger retail chains. The apparel lines were sold through a combination of sales agents and in-house salespersons. Ontario and Quebec accounted for 72% of sales. In addition, two retail stores had recently been established in Vancouver and Seattle; the Vancouver store was very profitable, but the Seattle store was not. Industry observers had suggested a number of factors to explain the two stores' performance differences. These factors included increased competition in U.S. metropolitan areas due to increased market density, lower levels of regulation and other entry barriers, greater product selection, and more timely fashion trend shifts compared to the Canadian market, which often exhibited lags in fashion developments of 6 months or more. Mr. Jax also had a local presence in Vancouver, which was believed to have helped their store by way of reputation, ancillary promotions, and easier access to skilled resources.

Eisman appreciated the importance of fashion, and for the first 3 years he designed all of the new lines. In 1982, he recruited an up-and-coming young Canadian fashion designer, yet he continued to influence the direction of designs considerably. He travelled to Europe for approximately 2 months annually to review European trends and procure quality fabrics appropriate for the upcoming season. He personally reviewed all designs. The combined women's fashion knowledge and designing abilities provided Mr. Jax with a high-quality, classically designed product which differentiated it from most other Canadian competition. In 1989, the designer resigned, and Eisman recruited a New York-based fashion designer, Ron Leal. Leal had excellent experience in several large U.S. design houses and, unlike the previous designer, he brought considerable U.S. market experience and presence.

Many industry experts felt that Mr. Jax's product line success could be attributed directly to Eisman. He was known for his energy and brashness, as well as his creativity and knowledge of the women's fashion market. In his prior merchandising and marketing experience, he had developed an intuitive skill for the capricious women's apparel market. This industry was often considered to be one of instinct rather than rationality. Eisman was particularly good at design, merchandising and marketing. He worked very closely with these departments, often getting involved in the smallest details. As Eisman said, "It is the details that make the difference in our business." Although he concentrated a great deal of his effort and time on these functions, he also attempted to provide guidance to production. The production function had been important in providing the service advantage, particularly in terms of delivery time, which Mr. Jax held over imports. By 1988, Mr. Jax's professional/career women's fashion lines accounted for $25 million in revenues and $3 million in net income (exhibit 1).

Diversification through acquisitions

In 1986, Segal and Eisman took Mr. Jax public, raising in excess of $17 million although they both retained one-third equity ownership. The newly raised capital was used to diversify growth through the acquisition of four semi-related companies.

Surrey Classics Manufacturing Ltd., a family-owned Vancouver-based firm, was purchased in 1986 for $2 million. This company was principally a manufacturer of lower priced women's apparel and coats. The acquisition was initially made with the objective of keeping the company an autonomous unit. However, the previous owner and his management team adapted poorly to their position within the Mr. Jax organization and, upon expiration of their non-competition clauses, they resigned and started a competing company. Unfortunately, sales began to decline rapidly because of this new competition and the absence of managerial talent. To stem the losses, a variety of designers were hired under contract. However, Surrey's poor cash flow could not support the required promotional campaigns and the new fashion lines faired poorly, resulting in mounting operating losses.

Several administrative functions were transferred to Mr. Jax, including design, pattern making, sizing and scaling operations. Marketing and production continued to be independent operations housed in a leased facility just outside of Vancouver. Surrey Classics now produced a diversified product line which included Highland Queen, a licensed older women's line of woolen apparel, and Jaki Petite, a Mr. Jax fashion line patterned for smaller women. During this turnaround, Eisman himself provided the required industry specific management skills, which demanded a considerable amount of his time and attention. Eisman kept in daily contact and was involved in most major decisions. During this time Surrey's revenues had declined from $12 million in 1986 to $10.8 million in 1988, and net income had dropped from $100,000 in 1986 to a loss of approximately $2 million in 1988. Eisman felt that, in the next two years, Surrey's operations would have to be further rationalized into Mr. Jax's to save on overhead costs.

In late 1988, Eisman reassigned Mr. Jax's Vice-President, Finance as interim manager of Surrey Classics. As Eisman stated, "The company needed a manager who knew the financial priorities in the industry and could maximize the effectiveness of the company's productive capacity."

West Coast Woolen Mills Ltd. was a 40-year-old family-owned, Vancouver-based worsted woolen mill. Mr. Jax acquired the company for $2.2 million in 1987. Eisman was able to retain most of the previous management, all of whom had skills quite unique to the industry. West Coast marketed fabric to customers across Canada. In 1986, its sales were $5 million, profits were nil, and its estimated capacity was $10 million annually. The company was the smallest of three worsted woolen mills in Canada, and in the U.S. there were about 18 worsted woolen manufacturers, several being divisions of the world's largest textile manufacturing companies.

Both Mr. Jax and West Coast had mutually benefitted from this acquisition. The affiliation allowed Mr. Jax to obtain control of fabric production scheduling, design and quality. In particular, Mr. Jax had been able to significantly reduce order lead times for fabric produced at this subsidiary, although the effects of this on West Coast had not been studied. West Coast benefitted from increased capital funding which allowed it to invest in new equipment and technology, both important attributes in such a capital intensive industry. These investments supported the company's long-term strategic objective of becoming the highest quality, most design-conscious worsted woolen mill in North America. This objective had already been reached in Canada.

Mr. Jax was presently fulfilling 30-40% of its textile demands through West Coast. The remainder was being sourced in Europe. By 1988, West Coast's revenues were $6.5 million and profitability was at the break-even point.

Olympic Pant and Sportswear Co. Ltd. and Canadian Sportswear Co. Ltd., both privately owned companies, were acquired by Mr. Jax in 1987 for $18.3 million. The former management, excluding owners, was retained in both of these Winnipeg-based companies.

Combined revenues for these companies had declined from $35 million in 1986 to $30 million in 1988. Both of these companies had remained profitable during this period, although profits had declined. In 1988, combined net income was $1.2 million. Management blamed declining revenues on increased competition and a shortage of management because of the previous owners' retirement.

Olympic manufactured lower priced men's and boys' pants and outerwear as well as some women's sportswear. Canadian Sportswear manufactured low-priced women's and girls' outerwear and coats. Canadian Sportswear was also a certified apparel supplier to the Canadian Armed Forces and, although these types of sales made up a minority of their revenue base, such a certification provided the company with a small but protected market niche. The disparity in target markets and locations between these companies and Mr. Jax dictated that they operate largely independently. The expected synergies were limited to a few corporate administrative functions such as finance and systems management.

The corporation's present situation

Diversification had provided the company with excellent growth, but it had also created problems. The most serious was the lack of management control over the now diversified structure (exhibit 2). By 1988, it had become quite clear that without the entrepreneurial control and drive of the previous owners, the companies were not as successful as they had been prior to their acquisition. Therefore, in late 1988, Eisman recruited a new CFO, Judith Madill, to coordinate a corporate control consolidation program. Madill had extensive accounting and corporate reorganization experience, but had limited operating experience in an entrepreneurial environment such as the fashion industry.

Eisman had always maintained that one of Mr. Jax's competitive strengths was its flexibility and rapid response time. He thought increased administrative overhead would restrict this entrepreneurial ability, and that extra costs would severely restrict future expansion opportunities. Thus, he had limited the administrative expansion to two industrial accountants for the next year.

Madill suggested that corporate personnel, financial, and systems management departments be established to integrate and aid in the management of the subsidiaries. Eisman was not completely convinced this was the right approach.

Consolidation was also occurring in the existing organization. Eisman was trying to recruit a vice-president of production. Mr. Jax had never officially had such a position and, unfortunately, recruiting a suitable candidate was proving to be difficult.

Originally, production had been located in an old 22,000-square foot facility. By 1986, it had grown to 48,000 square feet located in four buildings throughout Vancouver. Production flow encompassed the typical apparel industry operational tasks (exhibit 3). However, the division of tasks between buildings made production planning and scheduling very difficult. Production problems slowly accumulated between 1986 and 1988. The problems not only restricted capacity, but also caused customer service to deteriorate from an excellent shipment rate of approximately 95% of orders to sometimes below the industry average of 75%. Mr. Jax's ability to ship had been a key to their growth strategy in Canada. Normally, apparel manufacturers met between 70% and 80% of their orders, but Mr. Jax had built a reputation for shipping more than 90% of orders.

Consolidation had begun in the latter part of 1987. An old building in downtown Vancouver was acquired and renovated. The facility incorporated some of the most modern production equipment available. In total, the company had spent approximately $3.5 million on upgrading production technology. Equipment in the new facility included a $220,000 Gerber automatic cloth cutting machine to improve efficiency and reduce waste; $300,000 of modern sewing equipment to improve productivity and production capacity; a $200,000 Gerber production moving system to automatically move work to appropriate work stations as required; and a computerized design assistance system to integrate the above equipment (i.e., tracking in-process inventory, scheduling, planning, and arranging and sizing cloth patterns for cutting). The objectives of these investments were to lower labor content, improve production capacity, and reduce the time required to produce a garment.

There were relatively few experienced apparel manufacturing executives in North America. Furthermore, Vancouver was not an attractive place for fashion executives because it, not being a fashion center, would isolate him or her from future employment opportunities. Higher salaries, as well as lower taxes, tended to keep qualified individuals in the U.S. Yet, a manager of production was badly needed to coordinate the internal production consolidation program.

In the last quarter of 1988, Mr. Jax had moved into this new head office facility. The building, which was renovated by one of Italy's leading architects, represented a design marvel with its skylights and soaring atriums. The production department had just recently settled into its expansive space. However, the move had not gone without incident. The equipment operators had difficulties adapting to the new machines. Most of the workers had become accustomed to the repetitive tasks required of the old technology. The new equipment was forcing them to retrain themselves and required additional effort, something that was not appreciated by many of the workers. In addition, the largely Asian work force had difficulty understanding retraining instructions because English was their second language.

To further facilitate the implementation of the consolidation program, an apparel production consultant had been hired. The consultant was using time-motion studies to reorganize and improve task efficiency and effectiveness.

An example of a problem which had resulted from the move was the need for integration between overall production planning, task assignment, worker remuneration, and the new Gerber production moving system. If these elements were not integrated, the new system would in fact slow production. Unfortunately, this integration had not been considered until after the move, and the machine subsequently had to be removed until adjustments were made. The adjustments required converting workers from a salary base to a piece rate pay scale. The consultants were training all the workers to convert to piece rate work and to operate the necessary equipment in the most efficient manner. Three workers were being trained per week. The conversion was expected to take two years.

Despite these ongoing problems, production appeared to be improving and operational activities were now organized and coordinated with some degree of efficiency. Eisman was hopeful that production would gain the upper hand in the fight to remedy scheduling problems within the next six months.

Opportunities for future growth

Despite problems such as those detailed above, Mr. Jax's revenues and profits had grown by 1,500% and 500%, respectively, over the past 8 years. Further, Eisman was very positive about further growth opportunities in the U.S. market. During the past two years, Eisman had tested the Dallas and New York markets. Local sales agents had carried the Mr. Jax fashion line, and 1988 revenues had grown to $1 million (U.S.), the majority of which had come from Dallas. Follow-up research revealed that retail purchasers liked the "classical European styling combined with the North American flair."

This initial success had been inspiring, but it had also exposed Eisman to the difficulties of entering the highly competitive U.S. market. In particular, attaining good sales representation and excellent service, both of which were demanded by U.S. retailers, would be difficult. Securing first-class sales representation required having either a strong market presence or a promising promotional program. In addition, Mr. Jax had found U.S. retailers to be extremely onerous in their service demands. These demands were generally a result of the more competitive retail environment. Demands were particularly stringent for smaller apparel suppliers because of their nominal selling power.

U.S. retailers' demands ranged from very low wholesale prices to extremely fast order-filling and re-stocking requirements. Eisman recognized that Mr. Jax would have to establish a focused, coordinated and aggressive marketing campaign to achieve its desired objectives in this market.

Eisman had studied two alternate approaches to entering the U.S. market. One approach involved establishing a retailing chain, while the other involved starting a U.S.-based wholesale distribution subsidiary responsible for managing the aggressive promotional and sales campaign required.

Establishing a retail chain would require both new capital and skills. Capital costs, including leasehold improvements and inventory, would be initially very high, and an administrative infrastructure as well as a distribution and product inventory system would have to be developed. Yet, starting a retail chain did have benefits. The retail approach would provide controllability, visibility and rapid market penetration. It was the approach taken by many of the aggressive apparel companies in the women's professional/career market segment, such as Liz Claiborne, Benetton, and Esprit. Furthermore, Mr. Jax's marketing strength fit well with this approach. It was estimated that the initial capital required would be about $10 million to open the first 30 stores, and then cost $300,000 per outlet thereafter. Sales revenues would grow to between $300,000 and $750,000 per outlet, depending upon the location, after 2 to 5 years. Operating margins on apparel stores averaged slightly less than 10%. Experts felt that within 5 years the company could possibly open 45 outlets; 5 the first year, and 10 each year thereafter. In summary, this option would entail the greatest financial risk, but it would also have the greatest potential return.

The alternative approach was to establish a U.S. distribution subsidiary. This alternative would require capital and more of the same skills the company had developed in Canada. In general, the company would have to set up one or more showrooms throughout the U.S. The location of the showrooms would be critical to the approach eventually implemented. (Exhibit 4 illustrates regional apparel buying patterns in North America).

An advantage to the regional approach was that regional retailers demanded fewer and smaller price concessions compared to the larger national chains. The obstacles to this approach included the large sales force required and the superior service capability. Even though Mr. Jax had utilized this strategy successfully in Canada, success was not assured in the U.S. because of the very competitive environment. These factors made this approach both difficult to implement and slow relative to other approaches. Experts estimated fixed costs to average $1 million annually per region, of which 75% would be advertising and 25% other promotional costs. Additional operating costs would consist of sales commissions (7% of sales) and administrative overhead costs (see below). Revenues would be dependent upon many factors, but an initial growth rate of $1 million annually within each region was considered attainable over the next five years. In summary, this approach would minimize Mr. Jax's risk exposure, but it would also minimize the short term opportunities.

A wholesale distribution approach could be carried out in one of two ways: either on a regional or national basis. A regional approach would involve focusing on the smaller regional retail stores. These stores tended to attract less competitive attention because of the higher sales expense-to-revenue ratio inherent in servicing these accounts. The approach required the new distributor to provide good-quality fashion lines, and service the accounts in a better manner than established suppliers.

The national approach was also a viable option. The greatest challenge in a national strategy would be the difficulty in penetrating well established buyer/seller relationships. Floor space was expensive, and national chains and department stores tended to buy conservatively, sticking with the more reputable suppliers who they knew could produce a saleable product and service large orders. They also tended to demand low prices and rapid re-order terms. In summary, the national approach provided significant entry barriers, but it also provided the greatest potential for market share growth. Clearly, if economies of scale and competitive advantage in the larger North American context was the desired goal, this had to be the eventual strategy.

The principal costs of this approach would be the advertising and promotional expenses. National apparel companies had advertising expenditures of many millions of dollars. In discussions with Eisman, industry advertising executives had recommended an advertising expenditure of between $3 and $5 million annually in the first 3 years and then, if successful, increasing it by $1 million annually in the next 2 successive years. Additional operating costs would be required for sales commissions (7% of sales) and administrative overhead (see below). The results of this approach were very uncertain and two outcomes were possible. If the approach was successful, Eisman expected that 1 or 2 accounts grossing $1 to $2 million annually could be captured in the first two years. Eisman felt the sales would then expand to about $5 million in the third year, and increase by $5 million annually for the next two years. However, if the expected quality, design or service requirements were not sustained, sales would probably decline in the third year to that of the first year and then virtually disappear thereafter.

Both the national and regional approaches would require an infrastructure. Depending upon the approach taken, the U.S. head office could be located in a number of places. If a national approach was taken, Mr. Jax would have to locate in one of the major U.S. apparel centers (e.g., New York or California). Eisman estimated that the national approach would require a full-time Director of U.S.

Operations immediately, while the regional approach could delay this hiring until required. Such a managing director would require extensive previous experience in the industry, and be both capable and compatible with Mr. Jax's marketing, operating and strategic approach. To ensure top-quality candidates, Eisman felt that a signing bonus of at least $100,000 would have to be offered. The remuneration would be tied to sales growth and volume, but a continued minimum salary guarantee might be necessary until the sales reached some minimum volume. In addition, a full-time sales manager would be required. Eisman estimated that the subsidiary's administrative overhead expense would be $500,000 if a regional approach was taken, versus $1 million for a national approach in both cases. These overhead costs would then escalate by approximately $500,000 annually for the first five years.

Both the national and regional approaches would require an infrastructure. Depending upon the approach taken, the U.S. head office could be located in a number of places. If a national approach was taken, Mr. Jax would have to locate in one of the major U.S. apparel centers (e.g., New York or California).

Eisman had now studied the U.S. growth options for over six months. He felt a decision had to be made very soon, otherwise the company would forgo the window of opportunity which existed. The new FTA environment and the growth in the professional/career women's market segment were strong incentives, and delaying a decision would only increase the costs as well as the possibility of failure. Eisman realized the decision was critical to the company's evolution toward its ultimate goal of becoming a major international fashion company. The challenge was deciding which approach to take, as well as the sequencing and timing of the subsequent actions.

Question

Which approach would you recommend taking?
Explain sequencing and timing of all subsequent actions.

Exhibit 1
Mr. Jax Fashion Inc.
financial statements
Income statement (000s)

	1981	1982	1983	1984	1985	1986	1987	1988
							9 months	
Sales	4,592	4,315	5,472	7,66	13,018	24,705	53,391	72,027
Cost of sales	2,875	2,803	3,404	4,797	7,885	14,667	38,165	49,558
Gross profit	1,717	1,512	2,068	2,869	5,133	10,038	15,226	22,469
Selling & gen. admin.	1,172	1,117	1,458	1,898	2,434	4,530	9,071	18,175
Income from operation	545	395	610	971	2,699	5,508	6,155	4,294
Other income	22	25	25	10	16	564	418	117
Loss from discontinued operation								(554)
Income before taxes	567	420	635	981	2,715	6,072	6,573	3,857
Income taxes–								
Current	150	194	285	432	1,251	2,874	2,746	1,825
Deferred	47	2	(5)	28	24	57	245	(195)
Net income	370	224	335	521	1,440	3,141	3,582	2,227
Share price range						$7.5-$11	$8-$18	$7.5-$14

Note: In 1987, the accounting year end was changed from February 1988 to November 1987.
    This made the 1987 accounting year nine months in duration.

Balance sheet (000s)

	1981	1982	1983	1984	1985	1986	1987	1988
Assets								
Current assets								
Short–term investments	–	–	–	–	–	5,027	1,794	495
Accounts receivable	709	874	961	1,697	2,974	6,430	16,113	14,923
Inventories	464	474	684	736	1,431	3,026	15,431	16,914
Prepaid expenses	11	15	20	22	201	398	404	293
Income taxes recoverable	–	–	–	–	–	–	–	1,074
Prop., plant & equip.	318	349	424	572	795	4,042	7,789	13,645
Other assets	–	–	–	–	–	273	526	513
Total assets	1,502	1,712	2,089	3,027	5,401	22,196	42,077	47,857
Liabilities								
Current liabilities								
Bank indebtness	129	356	114	351	579	575	1,788	4,729
Accounts payable	490	435	678	963	1,494	3,100	4,893	6,934
Income taxes payable	126	58	86	153	809	1,047	546	
Deferred taxes	84	86	81	109	133	217	462	267
Shareholder equity								
Share equity	127	7	13	5	4	12,252	26,577	26,577
Retained earnings	546	770	1,125	1,446	2,347	5,005	7,811	9,350
Total liabilities	1,502	1,712	2,097	3,027	5,401	22,196	42,077	47,857

Note: Years 1981–84 were estimated from change in financial position statements.

Exhibit 2
Mr. Jax Fashion's
Organization Chart

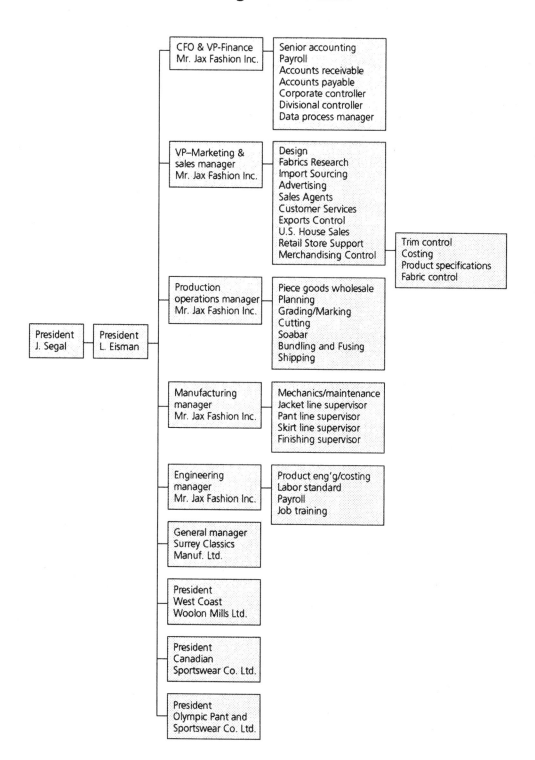

Exhibit 3
Mr. Jax Fashion's
Production Flow Chart

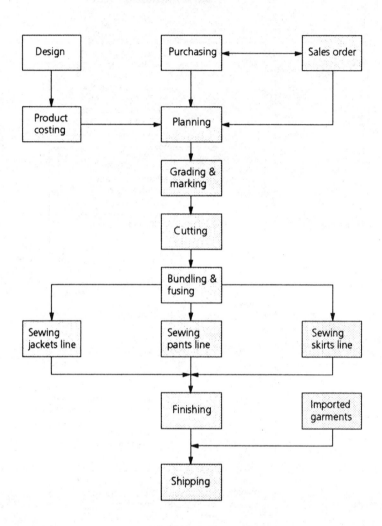

Exhibit 4
North American Apparel Consumption by Region

40. The Mexican automobile industry and the North American Free Trade Agreement[3]

> *"There is an enormous growth potential here...*
> *It's a market of 88 million consumers who have*
> *been economically depressed for years as a result*
> *of the 1980s oil bust. And now it is opening up....*
> *The real opportunity here is to support the growing*
> *domestic market, rather than exporting cars*
> *to the United States."*
>
> Nicolas Scheel,
> president of
> Ford Motor Repair,
> 1991[4]

The automobile industry in Mexico

The Mexican government has used five decrees to control the automobile industry.[5] The 1962 decree required that 60 percent of the Mexican vehicles had to incorporate components produced by Mexican manufacturers. Engine imports were stopped in September of 1964. As a result, a number of European firms abandoned the Mexican market including: Volvo, Austin, Peugeot, and Fiat. Only the main American producers stayed: Ford, General Motors, and Chrysler. With time, other firms entered the market: Nissan, Volkswagen, Renault, American Motors, and Borgward. Borgward closed its doors in the early 70s, and Renault stopped selling cars in 1986 but stayed in the parts business. Renault and VAM (a subsidiary of American Motors) had merged in 1984.

The decree of 1972 required that all Mexican vehicles should use Mexican parts and components as long as their cost did not exceed 25% of the cost of imported parts. With these policies the Mexican government was trying to develop a national industry.

The 1977 decree imposed some export "performance requirements" instead of the content requirements previously emphasized. It allowed vehicle assemblers the importation of components as long as they exported a compensating amount of automotive products. The 1983 decree required automobile manufacturers to reduce the number of passenger car lines and models. Only one line with five models was to be allowed in 1987. It was expected that by specializing the producers, the necessary economies of scale would be achieved in both the terminal and component industries to attain more competitive pricing for the vehicles.

---

3 By Carlos Alcerreca-Joaquin, Instituto Tecnologico Autonomo de Mexico, Howard D. Feldman, University of Portland, and Pochara Theeratorn, Memphis State University.

4 Lindsay Chappell, "South of the border," *Automotive News*, April 1, 1991, p. 1.

5 Stephen Downer, "String of five government decrees steers industry down bumpy road," *Automotive News*, April 1, 1991, p. 20.

The 1989 decree removed the restrictions on lines and models, and allowed for the first time in 30 years, the import of new vehicles. Up to 40% of the surplus in the commercial balance of the firm could be used to import these products.[1] That is, for every dollar worth of imports, assemblers must export $2.50 worth, this number will drop to $2 for every $1 of imports in 1992 and 1993, and to $1.75 per dollar of imports beginning in 1994. Besides, they will be able to sell to each other the portion not used of this capacity. In the first five months of 1991, 5,303 units were imported under this concept.

Due to the improved perspectives generated by the oil boom of the late seventies, the automobile car assemblers built plants in order to comply with the export requirements and take advantage of the expected increase in the domestic market.

However, the 1982 crisis contracted the sales of durable goods and the attractiveness of the Mexican market. Sales of cars in the internal market peaked in 1981.

The Mexican automobile industry seems to be on its way to becoming integrated in the globalization process, however, several threats exist. First, Asian car manufacturers continue to gain market share in the USA, and they are increasingly doing so with production generated in the USA territory.

In the 1980s the Mexican peso was kept undervalued, providing an incentive for automobile exports. The plants located in northern Mexico increased their productivity and quality and became successful exporters. The assembly plants located in central Mexico were about half the size of the typical plant in other countries and were older, however, they began to export to the US and Carribean countries. The number of units exported increased from 15,819 in 1982 to 276,866 units in 1990. About 86% of the exports went to the USA, and 14% to other American nations. The automobile industry has become the second largest exporter after the oil industry. In 1990, the automobile industry exports were for $4.5 billion dollars, almost one third of the manufacturers' exports during the year.

There seems to be a trend in which major car manufacturers will establish production facilities in all major world regions: North America, Europe, and East Asia in order to take advantage of the commercial preferences given to those firms producing inside each economic block. For example, Honda has an installed capacity of 510,000 units in Marysville, Ohio, and since 1982, has captured 9.3% of the USA market. Besides, since 1986 Honda operates a plant in Alliston, Ontario to take advantage of the US-Canada Free Trade Agreement. This plant has had problems that may impact the future exports of Mexican plants to the U.S.. The U.S. Customs Service has indicated that the Canadian plant of Honda has had problems with the origin rules (50% of the direct cost of the product must be incorporated in Canada) and dumping since the cost of the units is $1,500 higher than their price to the public.

Second, as a consequence, the amount of imported units decreased in the USA since 1986 due to slow growth of demand, and the high price of each unit. This may be due to the voluntary export quotas that some foreign producers have adopted to avoid formal import restrictions.

The Mexican foreign investment regulation includes a law issued in 1973, and the by-laws issued in May of 1989.[6] The regulation establishes the amount of foreign direct investment allowed by the industry. In the automobile industry, only a minority foreign participation (below 49%) is allowed, the Department of

Commerce and Industrial Development of Mexico (SECOFI) will review exceptional cases. The law does not require established firms with 100% foreign capital to sell 51% of their shares to Mexican nationals, but requires authorization of any additional investments. Investments made for the export market do not require previous approval. Indirect foreign investments, through the stock exchange, are handled with a trust system. Besides, U.S. auto makers already employ 75,000 Mexicans along the border in "maquiladora" factories.

Car imports from Mexican subsidiaries have continued to increase in the face of import reductions from other countries. This may be due to location, quality, and productivity of the northern Mexico plants.

Maquiladoras allow U.S. firms to import components or raw materials into Mexico, to process or assemble them, and to re-export the final product to the U.S. without paying import duties. In 1989, the average hourly compensation of automotive industry workers was $21.51 in the US, $17.74 in Canada, and $3.12 in Mexico. Maquiladora wages are as low as $1.00 per hour.[7] Labor conflict is common in Mexico. In 1990, labor grievances interrupted production at Ford's Cuautitlan assembly plant for months after a worker was murdered in an internal union dispute.

Competition[8]

Chrysler. Chrysler de Mexico SA, began producing vehicles in Mexico in the 1940s. In 1988 employed 19.7 thousand people in Mexico. In 1990, Chrysler built 73 thousand units for the United States market. Chrysler operates a plant in the city of Toluca. It had 143 distributors in 1990. It has a financing plan for car buyers: down payments from 25% to 50% and 12 to 24 months to pay the difference.[9] In 1990, it sold 89.8 thousand vehicles. The units with the highest sales were: SPIRIT 4-DOOR, PICK UP D-250, PICK UP D-350, SHADOW 2-DOORS, AND RAM CHARGER. It intends to produce convertible shadows for the export market.

Daimler-Benz. The firm acquired 49% of the Fabrica de Autotransportes Mexicana SA de CV (FAMSA) in 1985. This truck plant had 942 employees in 1989, had 52 distributors, and the capacity to produce 15,000 commercial trucks. Its sales in 1990 were 5,941 units, an 84% increase over 1989. In 1990, Daimler-Benz announced that it would increase its participation to 80% of the stockholders' equity. Mercedes-Benz has announced that it will begin assembling 1000 automobiles of the 300 model series in 1993 in its plant in Santiago Tianguistengo (State of Mexico) for

---

6 "Industria del Automovil," *Examen de la Situacion Economica de Mexico*, Banco Nacional de Mexico, January 1990, p. 28-36.

7 Asociación Mexicana de Distribuidores de Automotores, A.C. "El sector automotor, el segundo generador de divisas en Mexico," *Reporte Semanal*, May 13-17, 1991.

8 "Acuerdo de libre comercio: Reglas de origen," *Examen de la Situacion Economica de Mexico*, Banco Nacional de Mexico, August 1991, pp. 370-372.

9 AMDA, *Analisis Ejecutivo*, June 1991.

the domestic market. Mercedes-Benz assembles automobiles in Germany, Indonesia and South Africa, but only the German cars are exported to other countries.[10]

Dina. Diesel Nacional, SA has 65 truck distributors in the country. In 1990, their sales increased 46% to 7,314 units. Navistar International owns 5% of this firm and is expected to increase its participation to 17%. It employed 2,500 persons in 1991.

Ford. Ford Motor Company SA de CV was established in Mexico in 1925, in 1932 inaugurated its La Villa plant which is still in operation. In 1964, Ford established the industrial complex of Cuautitlan, a suburb of Mexico City, which includes foundry, engine plant, quality control labs, offices, and test track. In 1983, the engine plant of the northern city of Chihuahua was inaugurated, and in 1986, the stamping and assembly plant of the northwestern city of Hermosillo (Sonora) began operations destined to the export market. Ford employs 22 thousand people and has 124 dealers in the country.[12] Ford invested $750 million dollars in the Hermosillo plant in 1990 in order to expand its capacity. This plant is able to assemble 170,000 Escorts and Tracers per year, destined to the American market. Ford is closing its

General Motors. General Motors de Mexico, SA de CV began operations in Mexico in the 1940s. In 1990, it sold 90.3 thousand units in the domestic market and built 40 thousand vehicles for the export market. Its most popular models were: PICK UP C-20, CUTLASS, CAVALIER, PICK UP P-30 AND PICK UP C-15. Besides its Mexico City plant, it operates 26 component parts in the country. It has 133 distributors in the country.

Kenworth Mexicana; SA de CV. Kenworth is a truck manufacturer that had 675 employees in 1987. It was able to sell 2,406 trucks in 1990, a 33% over the sales of 1989.

Nissan. Nissan Mexicana, SA de CV has a plant in Cuernavaca, and will invest $1 billion dollars in Mexico in the next six years, including $330 million to construct a new plant in Aguascalientes, which will build 120,000 Sentras for the domestic and export markets. It has 162 distributors in the country. Its most popular lines were: TSURU (SENTRA) SEDAN 4 DOOR, TSURU SEDAN 2-DOOR, TSURU STATION WAGON, PICK UP LONG BED, and PICK UP SHORT BED. The firm does not have a sales financing plan.

V.W.. Volkswagen de Mexico. SA de CV established a plant close to the city of Puebla in 1962, where it employs 19,600 persons.[11] The firm will invest $1 billion dollars between 1990 and 1994 to increase its production capacity to 334,000 units per year. Mexico is the North American base of VW, which plans to supply Golfs and Jettas for the US and Canadian markets from this plant. It had 214 distributors in 1990. The firm sold 147.7 thousand vehicles in 1990, an increase of 72% over 1989. The most popular models were: SEDAN JETTA 4-DOORS, GOLF 2-DOORS, GOLF 4-DOORS, and the COMBI WAGON. Its sales financing plan involves a down payment of 50% with the difference to be paid in 6 months at a rate of 1.9% monthly interest, or if paid in 12 months with a rate of 2.4% monthly interest. The sales financing plan was credited with bringing them back to the unit sales leadership, a position they'd not held since 1986.

---

10 "Produccion de autos de Mercedes Benz," AMDA, *Reporte Semanal,* July 15-19, 1991.

11 "Volkswagen crece con Mexico," AMDA, *Reporte Semanal,* July 1-5, 1991.

Chihuahua plant for two years in order to double its production capacity to 500,000 engines per year beginning in 1983, this will require an investment of $700 million dollars.[13] The models with the highest sales in 1990 included: TOPAZ 4-DOOR, PICK UP F-200, PICK UP F-350, PICK UP F-150, and COUGAR. They also produced the only car classified in the sports category in Mexico: the THUNDERBIRD. Ford's sales financing plan in 1991 included 1.6% for 12 month loans, and 1.9% for 18 month loans.

For commercial vehicles: a down payment of 30% and the difference to be paid in 12 months without interest.

Industry forecast

The Mexico model developed by Wharton Econometrics projected that in 1991, the GDP will grow 3.4% in constant pesos, the inflation rate will be 17%. The assumptions for the automobile industry include an average price increase of 19.2%, the importation of 24,000 vehicles with an average price of $18,700 US dollars. The expected exports in 1991 will be 311,750 units, a 25.1% rate of increase over 1990, domestic sales are expected to increase 8.03% to 596,580 units (381,120 cars and 215,460 trucks), while the level of production is expected to increase to 883,930 units.[14]

Since 1983, a liberalization process began which included the privatization of most public enterprises, including the telephone company and the banks.

In August of 1991, N. Scheele of Ford of Mexico indicated that Mexico could become the fourth largest automobile producer in the world after the USA, Japan, and Germany, due to its geographic location, its labor force and competitiveness.[15]

The Mexican economy

The government budget deficit, as a percentage of the gross domestic product, has declined from 17% in 1982 to 3.5% in 1990, and its is forecasted to be 1.9% in 1991 thanks, in part, to the good prices of oil in the first part of the year. Interest rates have been declining due to the debt reduction agreement, the improvement on the government deficit, and the reduction in the inflation rate. In July 1985, the import permits, which were required for about 50% of the goods were substituted for tariffs. In November of 1986, Mexico became incorporated to the GATT (General Agreement on Trade and Tariffs), and established a liberalization of the trade calendar. A pact of economic solidarity between government, businessmen, and workers had kept stable prices and wages. Current government economic policy involves reducing inflation and interest rates, maintaining a stable foreign exchange rate, moving toward allowing market forces to determine prices and wages, and enforcing tax and expenditure laws and policies. The mid-term elections of August

12   Susana Ostolaza,"Mundo Automotriz: Trayectoria de Ford," *Economia Nacional,* March 1991,pp.49-50

13   "Inversiones del sector automotor en Mexico," AMDA, *Reporte Semanal,* July 29-August 2, 1991, p.1.

14   Reported by AMDA, *Analisis de la Industrial Automotriz de Mexico,* 1990, source: CIEMEX – WEFA, *Perspectivas Economicas de la Industria Automotriz,* December 1990.

15   "Agenda Ejecutiva: Sector Automotor," AMDA, *Reporte Semanal,* August 12-16, 1991, p.5.

1991 gave a strong victory to the government party PRI, which indicated general public support for the government economic policies in spite of the slower pace of the political reforms, and a weakening of the leftist parties in spite of the decrease in real income suffered by Mexican workers in the 1980s, the slow growth of the economy, which resulted in high levels of unemployment and sub-employment, and an undervalued peso which made expensive the acquisition of imported goods.

The free trade agreement

There are several forms of international trade association:

(1) preferential trade clubs have some preferential tariffs between the participating members,
(2) free trade areas eliminate import taxes between them but keep differential taxes with other countries,
(3) custom unions eliminate import taxes between them, and keep common tariffs with respect to other countries,
(4) common markets allow the movement of products, capital, and labor between the participant countries, and
(5) economic unions also maintain common fiscal and monetary policies.[16]

The U.S. and Canada signed a free trade agreement in 1988, which began to operate January 1, 1989. The liberalization calendar establishes that the elimination of tariffs will be accomplished in ten years. The agreement included not only products, but also services such as financial services and telecommunications. It does not require common tariffs to the rest of the world, but has incorporated rules of origin.

Article XXIV of the GATT establishes that a free trade agreement between two countries is acceptable if it is consistent with the multilateral system, does not increase tariff to third countries, includes rules of origin (minimum value added required to avoid tariffs), and includes most productive sectors of each nation.

In 1991 Mexico began to negotiate a free trade agreement with the U.S. Later, Canada requested to be included in the negotiations. In spite of the small international trade between Canada and Mexico, the existence of an independent agreement between Mexico and the U.S. created the possibility of Mexico getting more concessions than Canada, displacing trade and investment flows originally directed towards Canada to Mexico. Mexico and Canada compete for the U.S. market, particularly with respect to machinery, electric equipment, automobiles and their parts. However, Mexico does not have the trained labor force that Canada has, so it may be expected that different kinds of investment will occur in the two nations.[17]

The FTA will not deal with labor flaws or impose common tariffs to other countries, or force common monetary or fiscal policies, although some consistency may be

---

16 "Ante la integracion de bloques comerciales en el mundo," *Examen de la Situacion Economica de Mexico*, Banco Nacional de Mexico, May 1990, pp. 245-253.

17 "Otros acuerdos comerciales internacionales," *Examen de la Situacion Economica de Mexico*, Banco Nacional de Mexico, March 1991, pp. 127-134.

necessary, but will decrease tariff and non-tariff barriers to trade through time among the three countries, allowing stable access to the external markets, a critical element to plan long-term investments directed to the foreign markets. It will impose rules of origin based on costs or value added, will impose rules for foreign direct investments, will implement a mechanism to solve controversies independent of the political system of each country avoiding unilateral actions, and should recognize the asymmetries existing among the three countries, and promoting the opportunities for economic synergy that may exist. Negotiations began June 12, 1991 with a meeting of the Commerce Department representatives of the three nations. In the meeting, an action plan was developed which involved the creation of 17 negotiation groups, including one that will discuss market access for the automobile industry. It is expected that the agreement will be signed in 14 to 18 months. It is possible that the signature of the agreement will require changes in the internal laws of Mexico.

Mexican business will need to modernize their installations, and design a careful market strategy to retain their market share. Furthermore, the overall impact of the FTA on the Mexican economy is expected to be positive, increasing the size of the Mexican market.

Potential impact of the free trade agreement

With the FTA, the currently captive Mexican market will be progressively open to any models and brands produced in the US and Canada. The result will be more competition in prices, advertising, and financial conditions. Mexican producers see this as an opportunity and a challenge.

The Mexican Association of the Automobile Industry (AMIA) has recommended emphasis on eliminating dumping and other disloyal competitive practices, elimination of import permits, standardization of quality norms among the three countries, and the governmental approval of technical assistance contracts which allow subsidiaries to pay parent firms for the concept technical assistance received from them.[18]

American car manufacturers are concerned with the use of Mexico as a platform for European brands to attack the U.S. market, and the simplification of their operations in Mexico.[19] Canadian experts believe the new FTA may negatively impact the Car Pact that Canada signed with the U.S. in 1965.[20]

Early indications of the impact of the FTA signed on Canada during 1990 suggest that mergers and acquisitions increased, many firms went through restructuring processes, subsidiaries were purchased, and plants were relocated. For example, Unisys closed a plant in Montreal and laid-off 230 of its 3,000 employees. Cheesborough Ponds of Canada closed some installations in Canada, laid off 150 employees, and tried to consolidate Canadian and American product lines. General Electric will buy back shares of its Canadian subsidiary to consolidate it with the multinational. It is also going to specialize its Canadian production. GE will estab-

---

18 Roy Ocotla, "Nombres y noticias," *Mexico Automotriz*, June 17, 1991, p. 3.

19 Lindsay Chappell, "Industry: Free-trade pact must limit use of off-shore parts," *Automotive News*, April 1, 0991, p. 22.

20 Roy Ocotla, "Nombres y noticias," *Mexico Automotriz*, June 17, 1991, p. 3.

lish a plant in Montreal to produce washers and dryers for the North American market. Xerox is going to produce copier toner in Ontario for the North American market. Whirlpool will substitute the Canadian washer model for an American model, and will close one plant and lay off 650 workers. For some American firms, the lack of import taxes in Canada reduced the incentive to locate there in order to avoid them.[21]

MIT Professor J.P. Womack, co-author of the book "The machine that changed the world,"[22] believes that U.S. manufacturers could reclaim the low-end segment of the market by using Mexico as a stage for building its own low-end cars again. These low-end cars are currently being produced in Asia without UAW participation.

The UAW believes has lost many jobs to Mexico and stands to lose many more. The Canadian Auto Workers have also decried the proposed FTA. However, the U.S. Council of the Mexico-U.S. Business Committee made a study that suggests that the FTA could create 400,000 jobs in the U.S. during its first 5 or 6 years, since the original U.S. investment will return in the form of new sales for U.S. firms given that Mexican-assembled cars contain U.S.-made components.

However, up to now, U.S. manufacturers have not seen large benefits from their Mexican imports because they do not have a fully integrated Mexican production strategy. Currently, most of the vehicle value is incorporated in the U.S., for example, Mexican Escorts have a 78% North American content level. Unless the production is integrated in Mexico, a lot of money will be paid on transportation, infrastructure and other costs that reflect U.S. economics. MIT's International Vehicle Program indicates that it costs GM $625 less to deliver a Celebrity made in Mexico to U.S. dealers, than a Celebrity made in the Oklahoma City plant.[23]

Note: NAFTA was passed into law by the U.S. government on November 17, 1993.

---

21 "ALC Canada-EUA: Estrategias de Negocios," *Examen de la Situacion Economica de Mexico,* Banco Nacional de Mexico, October 1990, p 497-500.

22 Womack, J.P. Jones, D.T. & Roos, D. *The machine that changed the world,* Rawson Associates, 1990.

23 Lindsay Chappell, "South of the Border," *Automotive News,* April 1, 1991, pp. 1, 20, 21.

Chronology of Major Economic Events in Mexico, 1976-1990[24]

September 1, 1976.
Mexican peso devalued about 42%, it is allowed to float. IMF austerity plan imposed as condition for IMF loans.

December 1, 1976.
Jose Lopez Portillo (JLP) is sworn in as President of Mexico.

September 1, 1977. JLP announces improvement in Mexico's oil revenue. Exploitation of oil reserves and retirement of IMF loans, with the elimination of IMF austerity constraints. Oil-financed boom starts.

February 17, 1982. Peso is allowed to float freely without government support. This results in a devaluation of 30%, the first since 1976. A package of economic measures accompanies the devaluation.

May 10, 1982. Alfa Industries Group, the largest private firm in Mexico, declares it is unable to pay its foreign debts.

August 5, 1982. Second major devaluation of the peso. A two-tiered foreign exchange rate is imposed: free and controlled exchange rates. The controlled rate is used for necessary imports and to repay foreign debts.

August 12, 1982. Foreign exchange controls are imposed for the first time. All foreign currency accounts (Mexdollars) are converted into pesos.

September 1, 1982. Government nationalizes all (53) private banks. Additional exchange controls imposed.

September 7, 1982. Foreign debt principal payments are suspended. Interest payments are continued.

November 10, 1982. Mexico accepts a new IMF austerity program.

December 1, 1982. Miguel de la Madrid Hurtado (MMH) is sworn in as president of Mexico and announces a 10-point economic program. Foreign exchange controls are relaxed.

December 20, 1982. Peso is devalued 53%. Third devaluation since August.

May 10, 1984. Government sells 339 companies swept up by 1982 bank nationalization.

September 1, 1984. MMH rejects defaulting on the foreign debt in consonance with other Latin American countries.

July 24, 1985. Banco de Mexico (the central bank) announces a 20% devaluation of the regulated peso rate.

August 1, 1985. Announcement of regulated float of newly devaluated peso. Allows daily changes but prevents wild fluctuations.

September 19, 1985. Major earthquake strikes Mexico. $4 billion dollars in damages are estimated.

---

24 Elaborated with data from: "New York: Facts on File," several years.

December 9, 1985. Mexico decides to formally seek membership in GATT (General Agreement on Tariffs and Trade).

July 22, 1986. Third major rescue package for Mexico is signed in Washington. A new IMF economic program is approved.

November 6, 1987. U.S.-Mexico Trade Pact signed. Similar to Canada's and Israel's. An executive agreement, no congressional approval necessary.

November 18, 1987. Government halts support of pesos's value, resulting in a devaluation of 59%.

December 15, 1987. An Economic Solidarity Pact (PSE) is signed between labor, industry, and public sector to maintain stable wages, salaries, and foreign exchange rates. Official exchange rate is devalued by 22%. Tariffs are reduced.

December 1, 1988.

Carlos Salinas de Gortari (CSG) is sworn in as president of Mexico.

October 4, 1989. U.S. and Mexico sign broad economic agreement to enlarge trade and investment between the two countries.

February 4, 1990. Mexico signs agreement with foreign bank creditors to cut debt burden by as much as $20 billion. Debt-service reductions are linked to market-oriented economic adjustment programs.

March 7, 1990. Government accelerates privatization program by deciding to privatize the iron and steel industry.

May 13, 1990. Chamber of Deputies votes to approve a constitutional amendment returning control (66% of the stockholders' equity) of the commercial banks to private hands.

June 12, 1990. U.S. and Mexico agree in principle on negotiating a free-trade agreement.

February 6, 1991. Canada will be incorporated into the free trade conversations in order to create a single North American free trade zone.

April 23, 1991. Only 269 public firms remain in Mexico. In 1982 the government owned 1,155 enterprises.

November 17, 1993. NAFTA is passed by U.S. government

Strategic alliances:
Gateway to the new Europe?[25]

A form of corporate renewal, strategic alliances are attractive in the context of the single European market. With the prospect of a more unified Europe, the development of alliances among firms without an established manufacturing and service operation in Europe is more urgent than ever. The potential for a 'two-track' program for Europe also suggests that firms located in nations from both tracks. However, before taking the plunge, companies should assess the longer term implications of any alliance. Not all alliances are the same, and many alliances are of only limited duration. What types of alliances are possible? And, what forces lead to their formation and dissolution? This article addresses these questions and what they mean for strategic alliance activity in Europe in the 1990s.

'Strategic alliance' is a fairly new term which is applied to organizations co-operating and forming coalitions based on mutual needs. Originally, the most notable arrangements were those between large industrial firms and smaller, entrepreneurial firms possessing some form of technology.[1] In recent years, however, giants such as AT & T and Philips, Siemens and Fujitsu, and General Motors and Toyota have formed alliances to strengthen their competitive positions. An example of this kind of relationship is the Ford-Mazda connection, which has led to joint projects in Canada, the United States, Japan, Europe, Mexico, Taiwan, and Korea.[2] Philips, based in Holland, is also attempting to participate in global markets through the use of strategic alliances. Philips' activities in this area: Philips has formed partnerships with AT & T, Sony, Bull, ICL, Siemens, Olivetti, Victor Company and Control Data. More recently, strategic alliances have been identified as a vehicle through which mid-sized firms can compete more effectively against large companies.[3] Finally, strategic alliances can be used to circumvent trade restrictions and allow an organization to enter a market very quickly, without the time lag and investment of funds in building new plants and obtaining equipment. Such an arrangement could easily serve as a path or gateway to Europe as it increasingly becomes more unified.

Strategic alliances are being regarded as the latest phase in the search for innovation, entrepreneurial spirit, and globalization among organizations.[4] As low-cost world class competition makes inroads into companies with outdated plants and technologies, inferior products, and inefficient organizational structures, many new approaches have been used to trigger corporate renewal efforts.[5] These include internal development, external acquisition, internal venturing, corporate spinoffs, and strategic alliances.

Among these, strategic alliances are viewed as one of the most attractive ways to restore the balance in competitiveness. In today's fast changing world, the traditional competitive model, which is essentially adversarial in its orientation, may no longer suffice. Rather than striving to beat all comers, management are recognizing the effectiveness of more co-operative approaches.

Today the strategic challenge of doing more with less leads corporations to look outward as well as inward for solutions to the competitive dilemma, improving their ability to compete without adding internal capacity. Lean, agile, post-entrepreneurial companies can stretch in three ways. They can pool resources with others, ally to exploit an opportunity, or link systems in a partnership. In short, they become better 'PALs' with other organizations – from venture collaborators to suppliers, service contractors, customers, and even unions.[6]

This is not a universal view of course. Some management teams see strategic alliances as potential traps, which, if employed as a broad-based strategy, will lead inexorably to mediocrity.

25 Excerpted from Edwin Murray and John F. Mahon. Reprinted with permission from *Long Range Planning*, 26 (4), 102-111, 1993. Pergamon Press Ltd, Oxford, England.

Dorothy Marcic and Sheila Puffer, *Management International*, West Publishing, 1994.

Whether viewed as an important new way forward or a problem area to be avoided, strategic alliances are increasingly being formed. To deal with the phenomenon, some have offered guidelines for success in the development and management of alliances.[8] However, before embracing the concept of alliances, we think it is prudent to examine more carefully two key questions:

How genuinely useful are strategic alliances?

Are they appropriate vehicles for entering into and/or managing in the unified Europe yet to come?

Alliances with foreign companies have become another managerial fad and cure-all: they represent a tempting solution to the problem of a company wanting advantages of foreign enterprises or hedging against risk, without giving up independence. In reality however, while alliances can achieve selective benefits, they always exact significant costs; they involve coordinating two separate operations, reconciling goals with an independent entity, creating a competitor, and giving up profits. These costs ultimately make most alliances short-term transitional devices rather than stable, long-term relationships.[7]

U.S. firms are realizing that the best way to invade markets like Europe and survive global competition may lie in the development of *Keiretsus* and Strategic Alliances. Through the use of strategic alliances, firms can gain entry to markets without investing capital in plants and equipment. It allows an organization to move quickly into a market. Ford, for example, has developed a *keiretsu*-like arrangement (cross-shareholdings, networks of individuals linked together by common interests, etc.) through purchase of equity positions in Mazda (Japan), KIA Motors (Korea), Aston Martin Lagonda (Britain), Autolatina (Brazil), and IVECO Ford Truck (Britain). The arrangement enables Ford to buy cars from Mazda for sale in Japan, and could also allow Ford or Mazda to buy cars from one another for sale in Europe. Strategic alliances abound in the automotive industry and include arrangements between Volvo and General Motors, and Toyota and General Motors. These alliances allow the firms involved to either develop or expand their presence in a given market.

Competitive advantage

Ghemawat[9] argues that there are three sources of sustainable competitive advantage, and the more of these sources an organization possesses, the greater the likelihood that it will be able to maintain a premier position in its industry. The three sources are size, access, and control of options.

Size has three components: (1) economy of scale, that is, becoming bigger does yield advantages. But economy of scale can also be an advantage in terms of geographical selection of manufacturing and service sites that squeeze the competition (for example Wal-Mart). (2) Experience effects or as Ghemawat describes it, 'size over time.' (3) Economies of scope. These economies deal with the advantages accrued from activities in interrelated markets.

Access advantages are independent of size and centre on the control of access to resources or customers. This access can be based on superior know-how and ability, control of inputs or supplies, and limits of entry to particular markets. As Europe moves toward unification, access advantages will assume growing importance in the battle for competitive supremacy. Indeed, Japan has been frequently charged with deliberate limitation of access to its home markets. That limitation, it is further argued, has led to Japan's increasing economic power in international markets. Presumably, European countries as a bloc could yield to the same temptation, thus raising the spectre of a 'Fortress Europe.'

The recent economic troubles in Europe have affected the voting on the Maastrict Treaty. Some have argued for a dual track approach to European unity, with those countries possessing stronger economies and currencies opting for a closer union. The other European nations would follow a slower path and presumably join the fast track group at a later time. However, this dual track would allow for the development of differential governmental

The Wal-Mart example is particularly instructive here. Wal-Mart avoided big cities and major competitors by focusing on small towns in the United States. This focus on small towns allowed the organization to develop regionalized distribution centres to serve several stores and thereby reduced its costs of transportation, storage, and stock-outs. This advantage in storage, purchasing and logistics goes beyond mere scale and reflects the interrelated effects achieved from 'scope' activities.

policies that could favour the industries and firms of the fast track nations over those of the second track. Options also can be exercised in the area of sunk costs. If entrenched competitors are now restricted in their flexibility and capability by fixed past investments, competitors can build more capacity that yields significant competitive advantages. For example, one fallout from the move toward EC unity has been the increased Japanese investment in Europe. Ford has publicly acknowledged competitive difficulties arising from recent Japanese initiatives.

Life cycles

Any alliance begins with the ritual courtship stage, where the partners investigate each other, a strengths and weaknesses, develop initial contacts and negotiating positions, and critically evaluate what benefits and costs will arise out of this particular alliance. This is to minimize costs and organizational disruption at later stages of the alliance. If the courtship stage goes well, then the individual organizations enter into detailed negotiations to hammer out a contractual agreement. If this stage goes well, then the start up phase begins where joint activity occurs. For participants, any ambivalence about the alliance is preferably addressed explicitly in these early stages. This apparently never occurred in the Peveo-Thyssen alliance.

From the standpoint of a competitor seeking to foil the formation of an alliance, action should be taken in the courtship and negotiation stage. This is advisable for two reasons. First, the possibility of disrupting an alliance in the early stages of formation is greater with much less cost than at later stages. Indeed, the parties entering into an alliance are not yet committed and have not invested a significant amount of resources beyond talking and meeting. Second, once startup operations have begun, the organizations are committed, and so too are individuals within those organizations. This makes withdrawal by either of the parties personally embarrassing and organizationally disruptive. The costs to a competitor of breaking the alliance at this point are considerable, although there remain other ways to affect the success of a given alliance once formed.

Once the startup phase is completed, the organizations involved will generally move to the maintenance phase. It is possible, however, that if the startup phase is a failure, organizations will move immediately to the endings stage. In the maintenance phase, routinization of operations and reporting relationships occurs, and the organizations experience one another on a continuing, operational basis.

As we have noted, endings are crucial to a given organization's future alliance activity. There are three possible endings: (1) the end of the specific relationship with extensions into other areas of mutual interest; (2) an amicable separation and completion of the alliance with no further immediate

Figure 1

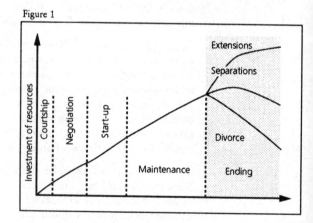

relationships among the partners; and (3) a hostile or bitter divorce.

The final ending stage, divorce, is just what it implies. The parties to the alliance break the relationship over serious disagreements and interpretations over results, actions, and commitments. The divorce can be public, messy, and involve the careers of individuals as well. Organizations ending alliances in this fashion will be very careful in the future about the development and commitment to alliance activity. The specific firms' culture may even perpetuate a failed alliance in its myths and folklore. This would make future alliance activity extremely difficult, if not impossible.

Conclusions

This paper has attempted to fill a gap in the literature, and to contribute to management's understandinding of strategic alliances. A definition of strategic alliance was developed, and the motivations fo entering into an alliance were analysed. Three major alliance types were examined, and the organizational and environmental conditions, and other factors influencing alliances were assessed. Th major alliance types were described in an explanation based upon relative strengths, resources, and leadership. Finally, we proposed that alliances follow a life cycle, and that an organization's past experience with an alliance, especially the way alliances ended is crucial to future alliance activity

This analysis was made in the context of the change and uncertanties surrounding the coming of a united Europe in the 1990s. This is a window of opportunity which exists for American and Japanese firms to enter Europe. It is equally a 'window' of limited duration for European firms as they prepare themselves for increased pressures from internal and external competitors. We have just begun to see an acceleration in the use of strategic alliances on a global scale by multinational corporations. This trend will demand responses by smaller domestic firms and may even trigger political action by national governments to protect domestic producers.

Endnotes

1   B. G. Posner, *Strategic Alliances*, Inc., 74-78, 80, June (1985).

2   N. Kobayashi, Strategic alliances with Japanese firms, *Long Range Planning*, 21 (2), 29-34 (1988).

3   R. L. Kuhn, Japanese-American strategic alliances, *The Journal of Business Strategy*, 51-53, March/April (1989).

4   S. Urban and S. Vendemini, *European Strategic Alliances*, Blackwell, Oxford (1992) .

5   R. H. Waterman, Jr, *The Renewal Factor: How the Best Get and Keep the Competitive Edge*, Bantam Books, New York (1987).

6   R. M. Kanter, Becoming PALs: Pooling, allying, and linking across companies, *Academy of Management Executive*, 3 (3) 183-193 (1989).

7   M. E. Porter, *The competitive advantage of nations*, Harvard Business Review, 73-93, March-April (1990).

8   See, for example, G. Devlin and M. Bleakley, Strategic alliances – guidelines for success, *Long Range Planning*, 21 (5), 18-23 (1988).

9   P. Ghemawat, Sustainable advantage, *Harvard Business Review*, 53-58, September-October (1986).

NAFTA strategies for Canadian manufacturers[26]

Trading blocks such as NAFTA are forcing Canadian manufacturers
to produce higher value-added products

NAFTA IS NOT about Mexico; it is about remaining competitive in the U.S. market. North America is a "hub and spoke" economy, with most trade flows going to and from the U.S. Therefore the Mexican challenge for Canadian manufacturers will not come in the Canadian market, but in the U.S. market. The fundamental issue for Canadian manufacturers under NAFTA is where, geographically, to compete. Companies face a choice between defending their existing markets in the home and the hub, pursuing new markets in the Mexican spoke and other Latin American spokes, or competing in all markets. Facing limited resources, the average mid-sized Canadian manufacturer may have to choose between offense (penetrating new markets) and defense (defending existing markets).

The emergence of Mexico in the North American economy is a key issue for Canadian manufacturers. But many companies are in danger of developing the wrong strategies because they do not understand the issues. This article outlines the key issues managers must consider in developing their responses to NAFTA.

Of course NAFTA brings opportunities as well. The Mexican economy is booming, making it an attractive export market. In addition, the economy is restructuring after 50 years of protectionism, and many companies need capital and technology to survive. This makes Mexico an attractive market for Canadian foreign direct investment. There are also export opportunities for some industries – industrial machinery for example. And Mexico may provide gateway to what could eventually be a continental free trade area. Nevertheless, the value of Canadian trade and investment with Mexico is dwarfed by that with the U.S.

NAFTA is about the U.S. market

The "Growth in Export Flows" figure illustrates that the largest NAFTA trade flows are between Canada and the U.S., while Mexico-U.S. trade is growing quickly. Indeed, at current growth rates, Mexico-U.S. trade will approach the level of Canada-U.S. trade in roughly 10 years. Much of this trade is in manufactured goods, and many of these products are high value-added items, such as automobile engines. Canada-Mexico trade is growing, but is only 1.3% of Canada-U.S. trade. The profile of trade flows highlights that the key challenge facing Canadian companies under NAFTA is defense of their U.S. markets.

Restructuring inevitable

If Mexico is to become more integrated into the North American economy; what impact will this have on Canadian industries? In a world where capital is highly mobile, we are probably moving to an integrated North American economy, where Mexico competes in many of the traditional industries of Canada and the U.S. As is the case today, the U.S. will be the hub of this economy, with the other countries competing for exports into the hub and for capital investment from the hub. Indeed Mexico's major manufactured exports to the U.S. are already the same as ours: automotive vehicles and parts. Moreover, Mexico is the fourth largest exporter of automobiles to the U.S. and is the fastest growing.

---

26 By Dave Fraser. Reprinted by permission of *Business Quarterly,* published by the University of Western Ontario Business School, London, Ontario. Summer 1993, 84-92. Used with permission.

If Mexico's integration is inevitable, then so is restructuring in Canadian and U.S. industries. Restructuring is a widely used term, but here I mean only the reconfiguration of production activities. There are two ways in which production may be reconfigured. The first is to alter the scale of production by either consolidating or fragmenting it. The second is to relocate production, independent of any change in scale. The two types of restructuring may occur separately, or together.

Under NAFTA, we might expect consolidation in the pharmaceutical industry, as harmonization of regulatory standards permits greater scale of production. We might expect continued relocation in the wire harness industry as companies take advantage of Mexico's comparative advantage in labor-intensive manufacturing. And we might expect both types of restructuring in the automobile industry as automotive companies seek to further consolidate North American production and expand capacity in the quickly growing Latin American market.

Many factors drive restructuring

The extent of restructuring will differ by industry; this seems intuitive. But how do we anticipate the extent of restructuring by industry? How much consolidation? How much relocation? The chart "Factors Driving Restructuring" highlights the key factors that will drive consolidation and relocation. As a start, managers should identify the factors that apply to their industries.

The next step is to identify the interplay between these factors under NAFTA. The current integration of an industry gives us a sense of how these factors have played out in the past and may play out under NAFTA. Beginning with consolidation, the graph, "North American Export Ratios by Industry", shows the ratio of trade between the three NAFTA countries to their total production, and is a measure of North American consolidation. Industries at the bottom of the figure are not highly traded: production is oriented to the domestic markets. Industries at the top are highly traded, and are more likely to be achieving scale in production.

We can use the chart "Factors Driving Restructuring" to explain these differences in trade ratios, and to anticipate how much additional consolidation might occur under NAFTA. It appears that trade and investment barriers will play a significant role. Contrast the trade ratios of automotive products and pharmaceuticals: both are industries where economies of scale are important, but trade and investment barriers differ significantly between the two. In the automotive industry, the Canada-U.S. auto pact and the maquiladora program have permitted companies to achieve scale and a trade ratio of 42%. In pharmaceutical, regulatory differences have led to fragmentation of production and a trade ratio of 4%. Similarly, tariff barriers help explain the low trade ratios in the textile and footwear industries.

In response to falling barriers, we can expect consolidation in industries with low trade ratios. Does this mean that all industries will become as integrated as the automotive industry? Unlikely. Falling trade and investment barriers alone are not sufficient to result in consolidation; other factors must be present. In industries where economies of scale are not important, significant consolidation seems unlikely. A large segment of the metal fabricating industry, for example, makes customized products for which scale would be counter-productive. Similarly, differences in local preferences and distribution channels will limit the level of consolidation that will occur in this industry. And products with low value-to-bulk ratios (ratios of price to cost of shipping) will not pay to ship over large distances, limiting the amount of consolidation that will occur in such industries as paper products. It becomes apparent that no one factor is sufficient to cause consolidation, and that the particular interplay of factors will vary by industry.

Again, it appears that trade and investment barriers play an important role in production location, and therefore will play a role in relocation under NAFTA. In the automotive industry, for example, Mexico's integration is lower than Canada's because automotive trade and investment between Canada and the U.S. is more liberalized. As NAFTA brings Mexico under a new auto pact, we would expect Mexican integration to move nearer the Canadian level.

Factors driving relocation

There is both a supply side and a demand side to relocation. On the demand side, the best measure of the potential for relocation is to compare various attributes of market demand across countries: growth rates, price levels and so on.

On the supply side, one way to anticipate the extent of relocation is to decompose the previous trade ratios into ratios for Canada-U.S. and for Mexico-U.S. In most industries, Canada is more integrated into the U.S. economy than is Mexico, highlighting the potential for Mexican integration and relocation under NAFTA.

Does this mean that as trade and investment barriers fall we should expect Mexico's integration into the U.S. economy to approach Canada's? Again, falling trade and investment barriers will not be sufficient to result in greater integration. Mexican comparative advantage, for example, will also be a critical factor. Canada has a strength in industrial machinery for resource industries such as mining and forestry equipment. It is unlikely that Mexico will have comparative advantage in this industry, limiting the degree to which Mexico will become a production base for the U.S. market. Higher factor costs in some industries will also limit the extent of integration. In pharmaceuticals, the cost of establishing North American plant capacity in Mexico that would meet North American regulatory requirements would be prohibitive, especially when such capacity already exists in the U.S. Finally, products such as steel commodities with lower value-to-bulk ratios will not pay to ship from Mexico across North America.

A word of clarification on relocation is now required. Relocation need not involve dislocation of Canadian production to be a threat. In the automotive industry, much of the relocation of automaking capacity to Mexico will come from Asia, not from Canada or the U.S. While

Unfortunately, there is no formal calculus to anticipate the type and extent of restructuring that will occur in a particular industry under NAFTA. What is apparent is that no one factor is sufficient to drive restructuring; a combination of supply-side and demand-side factors must typically be present to result in significant restructuring. Managers must identify the factors that apply to their industries, and anticipate the interplay between these factors. Correctly anticipating the type and extent of restructuring then forms the foundation of an appropriate NAFTA strategy.

General Motors is slashing jobs in Canada, it is not replacing them with jobs in Mexico. Nevertheless, the emergence of Mexico as an automotive nation may reduce future investment in Canadian automaking capacity. And what of the auto parts suppliers? As automakers increase production in Mexico, they will source more from Mexican parts suppliers, who will increase their scale and quality, and become more competitive in the U.S. market. Regardless of whether there is dislocation of Canadian vehicle assembly and parts production, relocation to Mexico will mean more competition for Canadian automotive companies.

Sustain Competitiveness in Existing Markets

How do Canadian manufacturers compete under the different kinds of restructuring? Under consolidation, prices will likely fall as manufacturers achieve scale. The same will be true of relocation when it is driven by such supply-side factors as the attempt to lower factor costs or capitalize upon higher comparative advantage in Mexico. The immediate challenge for Canadian manufacturers under these two kinds of restructuring will be to sustain competitiveness in existing markets.

As the accompanying figure shows, there are many combinations of location and non-location changes open to companies. The simplest location change is to procure from Mexico. To stay competitive with Mexican clothing imports, a Canadian apparel maker for example, may choose to source cheaper material from Mexico. Should the Canadian company desire greater control over production, it may choose to pursue a joint venture with the Mexican supplier, injecting capital and technology to ensure better quality. Depending upon the degree of desired vertical integration and the risk aversion of the Canadian company, it may go so far as to move to Mexico, even to establish a greenfield site. These location shifts would exploit differences in comparative advantage between Canadian and Mexican textile industries.

In the range of non-location changes open to companies are tactics for competing on price through a lower market structure. For example, a company may attempt to lower its costs through some combination of plant retooling, plant redesign or rationalization of raw materials, products and end-user markets. Alternatively, a company may decide to move into higher value-added markets and products. A number of lumber mills in B.C., for example, through a combination of market research, new products and plant investment have successfully moved off commodity products into higher value-added goods for the Japanese market.

Companies that decide to move production to Mexico should beware. There is the obvious problem that while labor rates are low, so is productivity. There is the less obvious problem that comparative advantage must be sustained to justify relocation. More than one company has been burned by shifting labor-intensive manufacturing to Mexico, expecting to capitalize upon Mexico's absolute advantage over the U.S. or Canada, but because productivity growth in the industry lagged behind the national average, the product became overpriced. Some European companies have had the same experience in Spain, where their productivity increases did not keep up with the appreciation of the peseta, making their investments unprofitable.

It becomes apparent that it is an error to reduce NAFTA a strategy to a decision on whether or not to move to Mexico. Before moving to Mexico, companies might ask what can be done to existing operations to improve the competitiveness. A second error is to be unclear on the reasons for moving to Mexico. Is it to buy or to sell? Is it to capitalize upon differences in comparative advantage and factor costs? Or is it to capitalize upon differences in demand conditions? These are just different ways of asking whether a company is defending or attacking.

Growth in Latin America

How do manufacturers compete in industries that are relocating to take advantage of growth in Latin America? This second type of relocation, driven by demand-side factors, brings a completely different challenge. In these industries, there will be competitive pressure to follow the expansion in Latin America. An auto parts supplier, for example, will feel pressure to follow its customers who expand capacity in Mexico. While supply-side consolidation and relocation compel companies to defend existing markets, demand-side relocation compels companies to penetrate new markets. Here the issue is offense.

Again, companies will face a range of location changes and non-location changes for penetrating new markets. Location changes will now involve exporting rather than importing, and would extend to include the establishment of operations in Mexico, just as before. Now, however, the company moves to Mexico not to lower costs, but to sell into the Mexican market. The range of non-location changes would be the same, but again for a different purpose. An industrial machinery manufacturer that wishes to ride the wave of retooling in Mexico may first need to refine its products and end user markets to position itself properly for the Mexican market. It may also need to reduce its costs to sell to Mexico, where lower purchasing power makes some foreign goods prohibitively expensive.

Choose Between Defense and Offense

Many mid-sized manufacturers will not have the resources to pursue both offense and defense. Given the over-whelming size of the U.S. economy, over 25 times Mexico's market, the home and hub would seem the obvious priority. Exceptions will apply. In some industries, industrial machinery for example, growth in Mexico and Latin America will likely be much higher than in the U.S. and Canada. Where demand conditions and company strengths warrant, Latin American markets are worth pursuing. Nevertheless, for many Canadian manufac-turers, the priority under NAFTA will be defense of

Most industries will experience some consolidation as trade and invest-ment barriers fall, and will also experience some relocation – not necessarily dislocation – as companies expand their capacity in Latin America. Managers will probably face competing challenges: defense in existing markets (home and hub) and offense in new markets (Mexican spoke, another Latin American spoke). Therefore the first element of any NAFTA strategy is the geographic decision on where to compete.

Large companies with financial resources may not need to choose; their strategy will be to secure market share in the Americas, which involves offense in some markets and defense in others. A company like Magna would fall into this category – it is following customers into Mexico while focusing on its existing markets.

Some manufacturers may not enjoy choice in the first place; Canadian subsidiaries may have their strategies chosen for them by their parents. To provide bargaining room, they may develop a product specialty that will make them key to both offense and defense.

There will be industries where manufacturers cannot afford to simply defend existing markets. In industries that become highly integrated at a North American level, it may be difficult to compete in the mainstream of the industry without pursuing the Latin American market. For example, given significant relocation in the automotive industry, a Canadian parts manufacturer may not be able to ignore Mexico. Autoparts suppliers that do not follow their customers to Mexico may jeopardize their position in the home and hub. Therefore, in highly integrated industries, it will be difficult to separate offense from defense. Companies with limited resources must focus by product and end user segment to maximize the return on their resources. Moreover, they should pursue offense only to the Deloitte & Touche. He has made presentation extent necessary to maintain existing customer relationships.

Regional Trading Blocs Important

Managers can easily develop the wrong strategies if they do not think about NAFTA within the proper framework. Many people view NAFTA as a Mexico issue; they think it is about moving or not moving into Mexico. They are right to reduce the issue to geography, but wrong, for two reasons, to focus upon Mexico.

First, North America is a hub and spoke economy, and the imperative for most companies must be defense of the home and hub. For companies of limited resources, fortification of market position in existing markets will command their financial resources and managerial energy. This does not mean that only companies with strong U.S. positions should be moving into Mexico. Moving some operations to Mexico can also be part of a defensive strategy – but to buy rather than to sell.

The second reason it is wrong to focus upon Mexico is that this obscures the many non-location changes that may be an important part of a NAFTA strategy. Competing in Mexico, or defending against Mexico, may depend more upon improving existing operations such as plant re-tooling than upon establishing new operations in Mexico. Managers should consider a full range of location changes and non-location changes, regardless of whether they are pursuing offense or defense.

With or without NAFTA, Canadian manufacturers must deal with one of the most significant trends in the world economy: the emergence of regional trade blocs, built on alliances between developed and developing countries. The developed countries offer capital and technology, the developing countries offer lower labor costs and growing markets. Both may benefit from the relationship, but not without restructuring. The developing countries will be competitive in traditional industries, forcing the developed countries into higher value-added production. Latin America will chase us up the industrial ladder; Canadian managers must prove themselves worthy of the challenge.

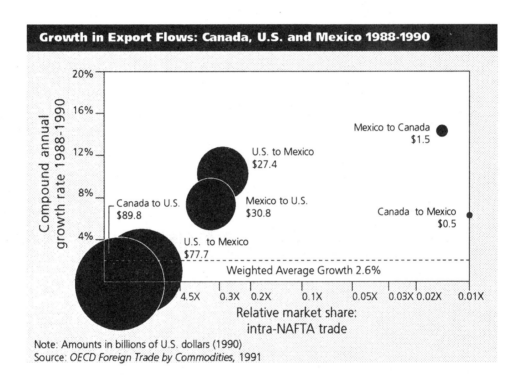

Growth in Export Flows: Canada, U.S. and Mexico 1988-1990

Note: Amounts in billions of U.S. dollars (1990)
Source: *OECD Foreign Trade by Commodities,* 1991

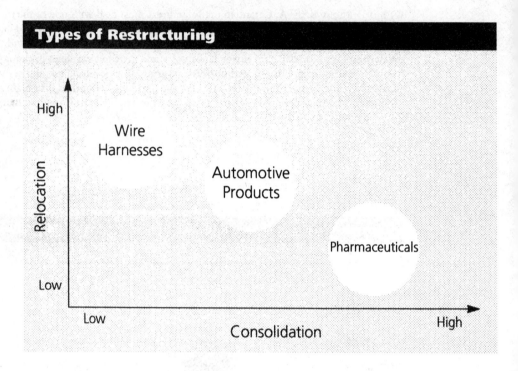

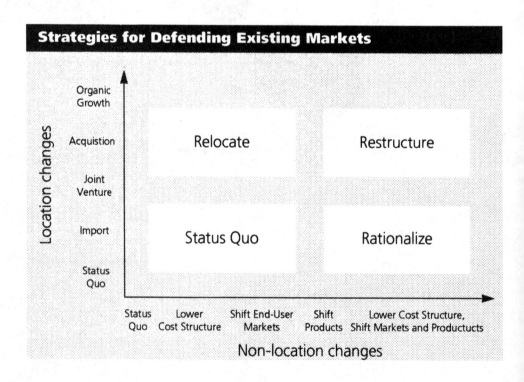

Factors Driving Restructuring

Factor Contributing To Restructuring	Implications	Industry Where Factor Applies	Industry Where Factor Does Not Apply
Consolidation			
Supply-Side Factors			
Importance of Economies of Scale	NAFTA allows greater scale in production and distribution	Automotive manufacturing	Business services, metal fabrication
Falling Trade and Investment Barriers	High pre-NAFTA barriers may spell significant consolidation	Pharmaceuticals	Few industries have no barriers
High Value-to-Bulk Ratios	Cost effective to produce in one country and ship over large distances to other countries	Pharmaceuticals	Some paper products
Demand-Side Factors			
Similarities in Products and Local Preferences Between Countries	Product standardization facilities, rationalization of production	Auto parts	Many consumer goods, metal fabrication
Similarities in Distribution Channels Between Countries	Consolidation of operations	Appliance parts	Metal fabrication
Relocation			
Supply-Side Factors			
Falling Trade and Investment Barriers	High pre-NAFTA barriers may spell significant relocation	Electrical equipment	Few industries have no barriers
Differences in Comparative Advantage Between Countries	Relocation may occur in industries where Mexico has a comparative advantage	Wire harnesses	Pharmaceuticals
Differences in Factor Costs Between Countries	Location shifts for labor-intensive activities	Electrical equipment and other labor-intensive industries	Segments of industrial machinery
High Value-to-Bulk Ratios	Cost effective to produce in one country and ship over large distances to other countries	Some auto parts	Paper products
Demand-Side Factors			
Differences in Demand Conditions Between Countries	Differences in price levels and market growth create market opportunities	Life insurance industrial machinery	Few industries

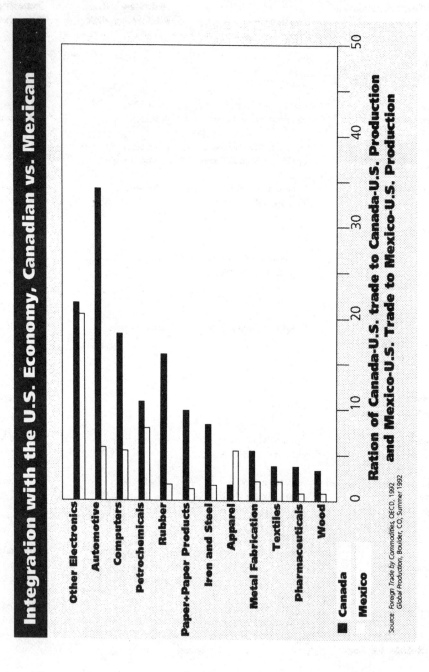

Integration with the U.S. Economy, Canadian vs. Mexican

Ration of Canada-U.S. trade to Canada-U.S. Production and Mexico-U.S. Trade to Mexico-U.S. Production

■ Canada
□ Mexico

Source: *Foreign Trade by Commodities*, OECD, 1992.
Global Production, Boulder, CO, Summer 1992

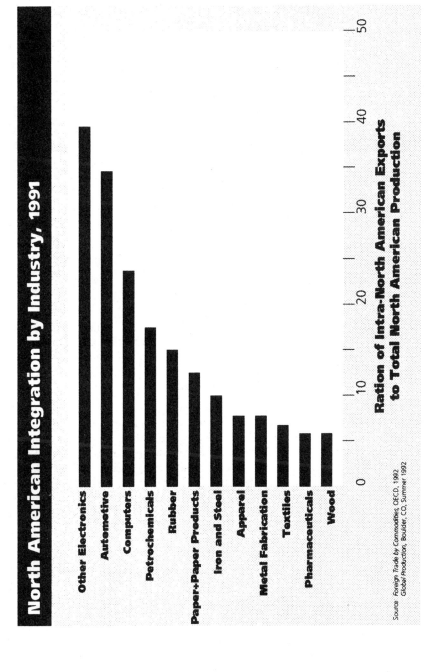

North American Integration by Industry, 1991

Other Electronics
Automotive
Computers
Petrochemicals
Rubber
Paper+Paper Products
Iron and Steel
Apparel
Metal Fabrication
Textiles
Pharmaceuticals
Wood

0   10   20   30   40   50

Ration of Intra-North American Exports
to Total North American Production

Source: Foreign Trade by Commodities, OECD, 1992.
Global Production, Boulder, CO, Summer 1992

NAFTA: The fight and the facts[27]

A place to begin: the overall importance

pro

NAFTA is a historic turning point for the U.S. akin to the creation of NAT0 or post-Second World War trading system. Economically, it would establish a vast, single market from Canada to Mexico. Politically it would reaffirm U.S. leadership of an open capitalist world.

con

NAFTA would cau.s.e massive loss of U.S. jobs to cheap Mexican labor. It would accelerate the income stagnation and declining living standards that have afflicted the U.S. economy for the last two decades.

A closer look

The economic consequences of NAFTA have been overstated by both supporters and detractors. Largely lost in the debate has been the fact that the U.S. economy is 10 times as large as Canada's and 20 times as large as Mexico's ($5.9 trillion in output last year, compared to $570 billion and $280 billion, respectively). Result: the pact is unlikely to have a major economic effect on the U.S. one way or the other.

The political and foreign policy consequences are much harder to judge. Mexico and other Latin American nations have been lifting govemment economic controls at least in part to foster closer trade ties with the U.S., and would be badly shaken if the U.S. rejected the deal. Bargaining over GATT, a separate and much larger treaty that fixes the rules for world trade, has stalled, and, some warn, could collapse altogether if NAFTA is defeated. Other economically advanced nations – most notably Germany and Japan – have entered or are considering trade agreements with neighbors, and some analysts think the U.S. mu.s.t do the same or be outpaced. Finally, there may be an important symbolic issue at stake: whether the U.S. decides to turn outward to the post-communist world or retreat inward.

---

27 By Peter G. Gosselin. Reprinted courtesy of *The Boston Globe.* Published by *The Boston Globe.*, November 14, 1993, p. 1.

Jobs

PRO: The U.S. has lost millions of jobs to cheap foreign labor. NAFTA would help control further losses, which will occur anyway, by funneling many to a nation that buys from u.s..

CON: The U.S. has lost millions of jobs to cheap foreign labor. Like the other trade deals that hurt the U.S., NAFTA would make it easier for jobs to flee abroad, raising unemployment and driving down wages.

A CLOSER LOOK: The NAFTA debate has been almost exclu.s.ively about whether the U.S. would lose jobs to Mexico. Largely missed has been the fact that even pessimistic forecasts predict losses that are small by comparison with the size of the American labor force and the U.S. economy's job-producing powers. For example, the Economic Policy Institute, a Washington think-tank that opposes the pact, says the U.S. would lose 500,000 jobs over 10 years. But the U.S. economv produced more new jobs than that in the last 10 months alone. Opponents say the iosses would be seriou.s. anyway becau.s.e they would be concentrated in certain regions and be the kind of high-paying, indu.s.trial jobs the U.S. has already lost millions of. Proponents counter that losses in some indu.s.tries would be made up by gains in others, and overall the U.S. would come out ahead 35,000 to 170,000 jobs over 10 years again a small number compared to the economy as a whole.

> More broadly, some studies suggest that U.S. job losses in recent decades have had deeper causes than cheap foreign labor and bad trade deals. MIT economist Paul Krugman and Harvard economist Robert Z. Lawrence recently concluded that the source of U.S. economic troubles since the early 1970s has been "overwhelmingly domestic." If true, NAFTA would make little difference one way or the other.

Wages

PRO: Though Mexican workers are paid much less than Americans, they also produce much less per worker so there is no big incentive for U.S. firms to move operations and jobs south. NAFTA does not add to existing incentives.

While wage disparity and the looser rules might seem an irresistable lure for US businesses to move jobs, most mainstream economists dismiss their importance. The economist's reasoning: wages are only part of what goes into a product and all the other things – from proximity to suppliers to access to a good phone system – make Mexican workers less productive than American ones.

CON: Mexican workers are paid so little and have such poorly enforced labor standards, they will underbid American workers, dragging them down to their level. No indu.s.trialized nation has opened its borders to another with such a wide disparity.

A CLOSER LOOK: This has been the crux of the debate, and opponents have several key pieces of evidence on their side. First, the gulf between the U.S. and Mexican pay is indeed wide. While U.S. workers made an average of $16.17 an hour in wages and benefits last year, Mexican workers made $2.35.

Secondly, the difference is substantially greater than in other instances when rich nations opened their borders to trade with poor ones. It is far greater than when the poor nations of Greece, Spain and Portugal entered the EC. In that case, the gap was three-to-one, according to economist William Spriggs. In this, it is almost seven-to-one.

Thirdly, there is the Maquiladora program, Mexico's 28-year old effort to attract foreign investment to manufacturing zones along the U.S.-Mexican border. By last year, more than half of the 2,522 "maquiladora" plants were at least partially owned by U.S. firms, according to the Congressional Budget Office. Virtually all paid less than comparable U.S. plants, and many operated under much looser labor and environmental laws than they would if they were in the U.S.

Some cite a recent study by Congress' Office of Technology Assessment, which found that while a car made in the U.S. contains $700 in wages and the same car made in Mexico contains only $150, the final cost of building and delivering the former to a buyer was $300 or more lower than that of the latter.

Concerning the maquiladora, NAFTA supporters say that companies moved operations there before the pact was ever devised, and would still able to do so if it was rejected. They argue the agreement offers the U.S. its best chance for raising wages and tightening standards in Mexico.

Tariffs

PRO: Mexico now has an advantage over the U.S. becau.s.e it imposes 10 percent tariffs on U.S. goods Mexicans can buy, but only has to pay four percent tariffs on goods it sends here. NAFTA would correct the imbalance by removing all tariffs

CON: The most important effect of removing tariff barriers would be to make it cheaper for U.S. firms to move jobs to Mexico.

A CLOSER LOOK: Tariffs have been a major focu.s. of discu.s.sion, at least in part becau.s.e they are one of the most easily graspable parts of NAFTA. However, it is unclear whether removing them would make all that much difference.

Ultimately, say some economists, the wage gap between the two countries and other differences in costs of doing business are more important than tariffs in determining whether U.S. companies send jobs to Mexico. Furthermore, the fundamental demand for each countries' goods is more important than the slight addition to costs from tariffs in determining how much trade occurs.

Supporters make two basic arguments: First, it is simply unfair for Mexico to charge so much more than the U.S., and the pact would correct that. Secondly, by removing tariffs, the agreement would encourage exports, and studies show U.S. export indu.s.tries pay workers on average 17 percent more than other bu.s.inesses. Detractors argue that since most trade with Mexico wiil cost U.S. jobs, removing tariff barriers, which would increase it, is wrong. They say that cutting Mexican tariffs would make it cheaper for U.S. bu.s.inesses to send machinery to Mexico to set up factories, and cutting U.S. ones would make it cheaper to send products back to the U.S. for sale.

Immigration

PRO: By helping Mexico prosper, NAFTA will ease pressure for illegal immigration into the U.S.. The pact is the cheapest alternative for coping with the problem.

CON: Illegal immigration will increase, not decrease, under NAFTA

A CLOSER LOOK: Even NAFTA supporters agree there would be some increase in illegal immigration if the pact is approved. The reason is that tariff reductions on U.S. farm goods, plus. Mexico's independent dismantling of its agricultural subsidies, would drive many Mexican farmers out of bu.s.iness, and some wowld likely head north in search of jobs. The supporters say the increase would be small and short-lived; opponents warn it could be substantial and long-lasting.

Environment

PRO: NAFTA would give the U.S. new tools to help force clean-up of the indu.s.trial mess across the border.

CON: NAFTA would encourage U.S. companies to do what many have already done, which is escape stringent U.S. environmental laws by moving plants south.

A CLOSER LOOK: All sides agree the border region is, in the words of the American Medical Association, "a cesspool," and that it got that way without NAFTA. The pact does set a new precedent by including environmental provisions in a trade agreement. Supporters emphasize the recently negotiated environmental side-agreement provides $2 billion for border cleanup, and establishes a system for the U.S. to investigate lax enforcement of Mexican environmental laws. Opponents complain the system is weak, requiring hearings that can take more than a year and permitting only $20 million in fines, which they say is peanuts. "It's really just a marginal improvement over what we have now," Daniel Seligman, an official with the Sierra Club, which opposes the agreement.

The future

The goal of Management International has been to prepare you for the challenges of being an effective manager in international settings. With this preparation finished, you are now about to take your knowledge into deep space. As the title of this concluding exercise shows, *Management in the Year 2200* is an opportunity to simulate what it would be like to apply your knowledge two hundred years from now. You are assigned the role of a middle-level manager in a large conglomerate based on Earth. Your task is to develop a strategy for exploiting an ex-colony in the Orion cluster. To decide what strategy to propose, you will need to make judgments about the characteristics of Orions, how they structure their activities, and how they do business. A thorough analysis will be sure to include a discussion of the topics covered in Management International.

Epilogue
The future

41. Management in the year 2200[1]

purpose

To explore issues in management in other cultures.

group size

Any number of groups of four to six people.

time required

50 minutes

exercise schedule

1   Pre-class

Read background and answer questions.

		unit time	total time
2	**Group discussions**	**20 min**	**20 min**

Groups of four to six answer questions.

		unit time	total time
3	**Class discussion**	**30 min**	**50 min**

Groups report results and instructor leads discussion
on issues of "cross-cultural" management.

Background

The year is 2200 A.D. During the past two centuries, Earth has achieved interstellar
travel at faster-light warp speed. Because of overcrowding and depletion of resources
on Earth during the second half of the 22nd century, we began to colonize other
planets in other star systems. People were sent out to assist in civilizing uninhabited

---

1   Hiroaki Izumi, Dept. of Business Management, City Polytechnic of Hong Kong.
Used with permission.

planets and to extract their resources for shipping back to the industries in our home solar system. About 100 years ago, a major political upheaval on Earth put most of the colonies out of touch with us for about 75 years. They no longer were able to ship resources to Earth so they began interstellar commerce amongst themselves. They continued to extract resources but they also began some limited industrialization themselves. The level of development on these colonies could be compared to that of the LCDs on Earth during the 20th century, but at a much higher level of technological sophistication.

Recently, about the year 2175, when contact was re-established with the Earth colonies, interstellar trade with them was also re-established. Earth is trying to regain the lost commercial trade that existed prior to the political problems and loss of contact. But the situation has changed. The colonies no longer act as colonies, but more like nations on their own. They have tariff barriers, their own commercial laws and codes based on the old common law ideas, political parties and full governments, their own corporations and business infrastructures, their own educational systems, and their own market structures. In fact, during almost one generation of separation from Earth, each of the colonies began to develop their own human subcultures based on the conditions that existed on their planet.

> Earth, surprisingly, has not changed much in how we do business, our diversity of political parties and ideologies, our lifestyles, our mores and norms, and our knowledge of how to deal with strange cultures. We still tend to be slightly xenophobic, too concerned with making money, living for the short term with emphasis on quick return on investments (though there is some improvement in favoring long-term investments among some groups), and we haven't improved our production and marketing skills much. We've only improved our production methodologies.

One planet that recently regained contact with Earth is in the Orion constellation of stars. It is the only colony in that area, so the colony is known as the Orion colony and the people on the planet as Orions.

The Orion colony is rather strange by Earth standards. The planet is relatively new in geological terms and still has Ice Age conditions. The climate is very harsh due to the cold weather. It is, however, rich in certain rare elements trapped in pockets in the ice. Before losing contact with Earth, the Orions traded in the rare elements that they extracted from the ice by mechanical means. The equipment is highly sophisticated and fully automated. Unfortunately, even automated equipment must be maintained and serviced. Furthermore, the ice must be prospected using labor-intensive methods in which individuals must go out on the ice and run specialized sensing equipment, which has a very limited life-span.

Because of the cold weather and great physical endurance needed for prospecting and servicing and maintaining the equipment, most of the field workers are women who are much better suited to the work. Women's better physical heat retention, smaller size, greater manual dexterity, and greater muscle endurance provide them with physiological advantages that cannot be matched by men. Having recognized these qualities early on, Orion women were better technically educated than Orion men. Because of their technical expertise and educational advantages, they also quickly took over control of much of the organizational management positions, with women generally being the top executives. The men were relegated to lower-level positions in the large mining organizations, the small-business market system, lower level education system, clerical work, or house-husbands. In fact, one could say that the traditional Earth-type sex relationships were reversed on the Orion colony.

This has led to some interesting conditions concerning the Orion culture. First, a strong feminist culture exists. Women like to be seen as individualistic, independent, and stoic, but at the same time very feminine in appearance. The frontier mentality of individualism and independence runs strong in both the female and the male population. Small nuclear families that often stay together for many years are the norm.

The language is the same as the Interlingua used on Earth, so they have no real communication problem. People from Earth do find the common usage of the language a little strange. Instead of the subject-verb-object sentence structure used on Earth, Orions tend to leave out the subject and start sentences with verbs. A linguist from Earth might consider this a sign of a high level of action orientation in the society. Orions say it is because they generally know who they are talking to during a conversation.

> The Orions spend much of their free time trying to achieve higher self-actualization through greater education. You might even say they have a thirst for exploration of new territories, new ideas, new levels of understanding, and their own minds.

Everyone is literate and highly educated through the education system based on lesson transmission to children at home. Children receive their lessons on the three-dimensional holographic, interactive television network, which is the same system used for entertainment in the home and communication with those outside. Because education is free and widely available, it could be depreciated. But survival on the ice, work, and independence depends on good education, so it is appreciated and even valued. With its wide availability, everyone has achieved a high level of education for a colony in the boondocks.

> The nuclear families of a dwelling module is the core of the culture, and each modular group of families tries to be as self-sufficient as possible because they could easily be cut off from the rest of the district or city by a major disaster. The people in each module are so close that they often share child-care duties, work duties, religions, and sometimes even spouses.

They live in underground family dwellings that are connected to others by 3-D holographic video-telephone, computerized delivery systems connected to all major stores and services, and computerized pneumatic shuttle service-like individualized train compartments. Dwellings are grouped in sets of three called a module. These sets of three dwellings are, in turn, connected to a more widely spaced grouping of three other family modules. These sets of three modules are called blocks. Nine blocks make up a district. Some districts are made up on strictly commercial units, also structured in the modular system of modules-blocks-districts. An indeterminate number of districts make up one Orion city. Everything in these cities is underground, but the high-technology infrastructure allows for rapid communication, transport, and intra-city commerce. Unfortunately, this superb infrastructure tends to break down in inter-city commerce. While communication over the ice is no problem most of the time, transportation across it is often interrupted by icestorms, shifting ice and icequakes, electromagnetic storms, and static-electricity storms.

In terms of the old Hofstede culture analysis, the module dwellers would be described as moderate in Individualism, low in Power Distance, low in Uncertainty Avoidance, and high in Femininity. This means that they have slight collectivist tendencies based on the modular dwelling system. The low Power Distance characteristic arises from the individualistic and equalizing tendencies of the frontier culture; out on the ice, your status doesn't matter. They have to have low Uncertainty Avoidance. It's a risky life in the colonies, especially on the Orion ice. High Uncertainty Avoidance people wouldn't last. The high Femininity level results from the frontier mentality also. Because they have to always look out for each other when people are working on the ice, they tend to be greatly concerned for others and their own quality of life. They also emphasize relationships over acquisition of money and material goods because they have most of what they need. They also have learned that being too assertive on the ice can be fatal.

The tendency for family modules to be somewhat private towards other modules or strangers allows them to hold many different philosophical beliefs without conflict between philosophies.

As for other value dimensions, they believe in harmony with nature (especially the ice), have a "present" Time Orientation (They really don't have much of a past and they don't know what is going to happen in the future), and a "doing" Activity Orientation (They like to work and accomplish things). Living on the ice with a high Femininity Behavior Orientation, they have come to believe that people are generally good. They have a slight Group Orientation in their belief concerning people's relationship with others due to their modular dwelling system. The modular dwelling system has also contributed to their "mixed" Conception of Space. In one module, there is really little private space. But with those outside, they tend to stress privacy.

Their religions are generally eclectic and very individualized. There is no real common system of religions. The only consistent religious factor is that families in one module tend to hold similar religious or philosophical beliefs. In general, people from one module will not ask people from another module about their private lives, but will accept people on face value. A cultural norm, though, is that if you are visiting another module where the values differ from your own, you will accept the values, beliefs, and behaviors of that module as your own as long as you are a guest in that module. Thus the beliefs and values of the people must allow for adaptability and tolerance. You cannot visit another module and push your values and behaviors on them, nor can you use them yourself. Such behavior would constitute a gross violation of social norms. You would no longer be welcome in that module.

The government of Orion colony is based on a modular structure of city-states. Each Orion city-state has its own separate form of democratic government, but they all send representatives to a planetary council in the largest city of Intbus.

The demographics of Orion colony show that the mean age of the people is about 50 Earth years and they have a life span of about 150. So the population pattern tends to be tulip shaped. They normally don't start families until at least 40 Earth years. Starting families is not a problem because the sexes are almost evenly balanced. The tulip-shaped demographics and equal number of sexes resulted from the Orions' belief in birth control to regulate population and sex of children.

Within each city-state, the exact form of government can vary, but they are generally democratic structures based on representation by districts. Districts usually have no need for government, per se, but they usually do have ad hoc working committees to get things done on a group basis. These ad hoc committees spring up and then disband on a need basis. The lack of a strong governmental tendency at the district level can be attributed to the Orions' general dislike of extensive government interference. Modules like to be left alone, as do districts. If anything needs to be done on a group basis, the people would rather solve the problem on an ad hoc consensus and involvement basis. So committees for special projects are always springing up and then disappearing. They can work in an ad hoc manner because of the highly accommodative nature, low Power Distance, high Femininity Behavior Orientation, present Time Orientation, slight Group Orientation, and "doing" Activity Orientation of the Orions.

These business modules are highly flexible in that a single functional module from the support core could be transplanted into another business organization without much trouble. Production modules, which constitute the technical core of industrial organizations, could be easily assigned to produce different products if they were provided with the correct equipment. Geographic business modules of the marketing function could easily be reassigned responsibility for a different geographic region without too much trouble. Thus Orion business organizations are highly flexible and loosely connected.

Their business systems also tend to be highly modular. Even the large firms are based on a modular structure, with each module handling a function, production, or geographic area.

Each major business organization is made up of a central core module that coordinates the work of all other modules; functional, production, and geographic modules; and sourcing modules. Within these modules, the workers generally work in teams with very little hierarchy. The modules can be said to have lean, flat structures with little bureaucracy. Usually everyone is on the same level and the leadership works in a facilitative rather than directive manner.

The functional modules are normally production, marketing, finance, and accounting. The only type of function that they really lack is the Research and Development (R&D) function. Businesses in the Orion colony do not conduct R&D because they have not yet produced significant technological research expertise. The sourcing modules are closely interlinked modules that supply resources and materials to the technical core of the main organization. Each of these sourcing modules are smaller organizations in their own right. They are linked with the major business organization through a commonality in organizational missions, philosophies, goals, and objectives. These smaller sourcing modules are, however, expendable to the major business organization. If they are no longer needed because the major business organization has changed its business or its organizational mission, the services of the sourcing modules may be sold to another major business or they may be left on their own. An illustration of this type of structure is shown in the appendix.

Production systems in businesses tend to be highly modular. The production equipment is fashioned to take advantage of the flexible manufacturing systems technology. One piece of equipment can often be used for manufacturing several different items. All of this equipment is fully automated. The work of production team members is to service, maintain, control, and modify the equipment to obtain the best performance from the equipment.

The Orion economy is dominated by the major conglomerate businesses that extract rare elements. Using mining as their cash cow, these businesses have diversified into industrial goods production, consumer goods production, and services. Surrounding these major conglomerates are many medium-sized sourcing modules. Servicing these sourcing modules are small-sized independent firms. Other specialized services and goods are provided by other small independent firms. For consumer retailing, boutiques or small shops are the norm. The only exception is food, which is centrally produced and distributed directly to homes. Most of these businesses can be considered relatively young, except for the major conglomerates, which got their start when the planet was colonized.

People shop when they have to. Foodstuffs are delivered to their homes, so weekly grocery shopping is unnecessary. Clothing and other household goods are bought at the small boutiques in the shopping districts. Purchases are made on an electronic credit transfer system through the central city computer. Purchases are usually made by males, who often stay home and raise children. Open hours of the stores differ by district, and at least one shopping district is open at any time of the day since being underground means there is no night or day.

Industrial goods are purchased by firms directly from other firms using the electronic credit transfer system of the central city computer. Supply contracts are usually not used. Deals are often consummated by a simple shake of hands. These agreements are generally renegotiated every six Earth months. Distribution of industrial goods occurs through a separate underground transportation network than is used by commuters or retail goods. The transportation system is fully automated, very efficient, and reliable.

Shipping bulk goods to Orion colony takes two Earth months, but small packages and people can get there in two Earth weeks. Communication with Earth is even quicker. Electronic messages sent by subspace radio can reach Earth in two days. This does not indicate, though, a lag in communication – it is not instantaneous.

Research of the Orion colony has shown that they have a desire to trade with Earth for new Earth clothing fashions, educational material, fresh Earth foods brought to Orion in stasis chambers that keep them fresh forever, the latest industrial equipment, the latest consumer technology, and the latest transportation technology.

Question:

You are a middle-level manager in a large conglomerate based on Earth. You have been given responsibility for the exploitation of an ex-colony in the Orion star cluster. The top management directive to your department is to develop a strategy for the commercial exploitation of the Orion colony. They want you to tell them how to go about benefitting from Earth's recent contact with this planet; how should they invest their time and money? What kinds of problems are they likely to face in dealing with these people? And what can you do to overcome these problems? Remember, you'll have to come up with some hypotheses concerning how Orions do business. You'll have to make some intelligent and supportable guesses at how they structure and carry out various business functions.

From "Comrade's dilemma"[1]   Chapter 4

Directions to workers

All members of your group are Workers. Your role is to produce whatever State (the other group) asks you to produce to the best of your ability. The State's role is to provide you with whatever you need.

After five minutes the State will request a list of what you need and will give you a "Five Minute Plan" with a job assignment and production quota. You should spend the remainder of this first five minute period preparing your list of needs.

Your groups should request the following for each worker:

> *A house*
>
> *One art work*
>
> *One health care treatment*
>
> *One dental treatment*
>
> *Two books*
>
> *Seven servings each of meat, bread, vegetables, dairy products and fruit.*
>
> *One each of a suit, blouse, belt, hat, television, refrigerator, washer/dryer, stereo and automobile.*

When you are asked to produce something, sketch the object (or something that represents the object) and label it. Each sketch equals one unit produced. For example, if you are asked to produce 10 houses, sketch 10 houses on a piece of paper with the word "house" under each sketch. Of course, as a Worker, you are proud of what you do and strive to produce high-quality sketches. A sample sketch

---

1 By John E. Oliver and Julia T. Connell. Used with permission.

of each item is provided on the next sheet as a guide.

If you are asked to produce aircraft, fold pieces of paper into paper airplanes. Missiles are a half-sheet wadded into a ball. These are the only products that are actually made and not drawn.

You will work in five minute periods, and will be given a Five Minute Plan to guide you during each period. From time to time you may be asked by the State to provide a new list of your needs.

Keep all production that the State redistributes to you. Sit on it (literally).
It is your wealth.

Workers needs

We, the Workers, would like the State to provide us with the following goods and services. We, of course, realize that we will have to produce them. We will do our best to produce whatever quotas the State Planning Group deems necessary.

Our needs are for:

____ *houses*

____ *art works*

____ *health care treatments*

____ *dental treatments*

____ *books*

____ *servings of meat, bread, vegetables, dairy products and fruit*

____ *suits*

____ *blouses*

____ *pairs of shoes*

____ *belts*

____ *hats*

____ *televisions*

____ *refrigerators*

____ *washer/dryers*

____ *stereos*

____ *automobiles*

Sample Sketches

fruit

washer and drier

auto

refrigerator

house

books

meat

dental care

health care

bread

dairy products

dress

ship

television

radio

suit

vegetable (beet)

shoe

art work

Directions for state

Your group is the State. Your role is to manage the economy and to defend the homeland. You manage the economy by telling the Workers what to produce and by distributing their production equitably. You defend their homeland by ensuring that the military has a continuing supply of aircraft, ships, and missiles.

Half the members of your group should be designated Military Officers and should wear symbols of authority. They should spend their time playing war games with their aircraft, ships and missiles, while the Workers (the other group) perform their duties. If a worker is dissatisfied, the Military must ask the worker to accompany one of the Officers out of the room. The rebelling worker will be told he or she is exiled and that the game is over when out of the room. Out of the room is the equivalent to Siberia. If a rebellion is uncontrollable, Military has the authority to draft the worker into the military. The worker can be returned to the workforce at any time by the original (ranking) Military officers. If Workers are caught cheating on their quotas or re-using goods produced in an earlier period, they too may be sent to Siberia. Members of State who cheat should also be sent to Siberia. Military should watch for cheating.

The half of your group that is not Military is the Planning Group. The Planning Group creates Five Minute Plans that assign workers as Builders, Farmers, Doctors, Clothiers, Artists, Manufacturers, Teachers and Defense Industry workers. Builders produce housing. Farmers produce food. Doctors produce health and dental care. Clothiers produce clothes. Artists produce art works. Manufacturers produce appliances and automobiles. Teachers produce books. And Defense Industry workers produce military goods. Planning Group may set whatever priorities it chooses except for military production, which is the highest priority.

Initial worker assignments should include one Builder, one Artist, one Doctor, and one Teacher, with the rest of the workers evenly distributed as Defense workers, Farmers, Clothiers, and Manufacturers. (If group size is not sufficient, the Artist, Doctor and/or Teacher assignments may be eliminated).

The initial quota for each worker classification is determined as follows:

Defense workers
(First priority)
Produces a number of aircraft, ships and missiles equal to the total number of participants. For instance, 10 Workers and 10 State = 20 aircraft, 20 ships and 20 missiles.

Builders
Produce a number of houses equal to the total number of participants.

Artists
Produce a number of art works equal to the total number of participants.

Doctors
Produce a number of health and dental treatments equal to the total number of participants.

Teachers
Produce a number of books equal to the total number of participants.

Farmers
Produce one serving each of meat, bread, vegetables, dairy products, and fruit for each participant.

Clothiers
Produce 1 suit, 1 blouse, 1 pair of shoes, 1 belt, and 1 hat for each participant.

Manufacturers
Produce 1 television, 1 refrigerator, 1 clothes washer/dryer, 1 stereo, and 1 auto for each participant.

Following the initial Five Minute Plan, **ALL** Five Plans **MUST** produce the minimum below:

Defense	Same as initial quota.
Houses	No minimum. Houses can be shared.
Art	No minimum.
Health/Dental	No minimum.
Books	No minimum.
Food	Minimum of one serving of everything per participant.
Clothes	Minimum of one of everything in every other plan.

A Five Minute Plan is provided for your convenience.

After five minutes, you will be asked by the instructor to give Workers your first Five Minute Plan and to receive from Workers their list of needs. Workers will then spend five minutes producing while you compile a list of worker needs and prepare a new (second) Five Minute Plan with new worker assignments and quotas. Remember, Military needs come first. You may set other priorities as you see fit, with the goal of maximizing the well-being of your society. You must also be sure to feed, clothe, house, etc. the Military and Planning Group.

After five minutes, the instructor will ask Workers to deliver their production to you (State) and for you to deliver your second Five Minute Plan assignments and quotas to workers.

During the next (third) five minute period, Workers will produce while you determine how to distribute equitably what has been produced. All participants - workers, military, planners - should literally sit on their distributions. It is their wealth. It is against the rules to re-use production that has been distributed by the State.

After the third five minute period, you will again collect production. Then, for five minutes, you will determine how to distribute it and will prepare a third Five Minute Plan with new assignments and quotas. Workers will be taking a five minute vacation while you do this.

After the fourth five minute period,

you will distribute products to the Workers along with your third Five Minute Plan. Then you will spend the next (fifth) five minute period creating a fourth Five Minute Plan while Workers produce according to the third Five Minute Plan.

At the end of the fifth five minute period, the instructor will tell you to collect production from Workers and give them new assignments. Then, Workers will produce while you determine how to distribute what has been produced and create a fifth, and last, Five Minute Plan.

After five minutes, the instructor will ask Workers to give their production and you to give the Workers your new Five Minute Plan.

You then distribute the latest production while Workers produce. After five minutes, the instructor will tell all participants to stop all production and planning activities. You will collect and distribute the final production.

Do not destroy anything created during the exercise. Keep everything you have distributed to yourselves (sit on it, literally) at the end of the activity. It is your wealth.

Five Minute Plan #1

job	names	quota	product
Defense workers			Aircraft
			Ships
			Missiles
Builders			Houses
Artists			Art Works
Doctors			Health treatment
			Dental treatment
Teachers			Books
Farmers			Meat Servings
			Bread Servings
			Vegetable Servings
			Dairy Servings
			Fruit Servings
Clothiers			Suits
			Blouses
			Shoes
			Belts
			Hats
Manufacturers			Televisions
			Refrigerators
			Washer/Dryers
			Stereos
			Autos

Five Minute Plan #2

job	names	quota	product
Defense workers			Aircraft
			Ships
			Missiles
Builders			Houses
Artists			Art Works
Doctors			Health treatment
			Dental treatment
Teachers			Books
Farmers			Meat Servings
			Bread Servings
			Vegetable Servings
			Dairy Servings
			Fruit Servings
Clothiers			Suits
			Blouses
			Shoes
			Belts
			Hats
Manufacturers			Televisions
			Refrigerators
			Washer/Dryers
			Stereos
			Autos

Five Minute Plan #3

job	names	quota	product
Defense workers			Aircraft
			Ships
			Missiles
Builders			Houses
Artists			Art Works
Doctors			Health treatment
			Dental treatment
Teachers			Books
Farmers			Meat Servings
			Bread Servings
			Vegetable Servings
			Dairy Servings
			Fruit Servings
Clothiers			Suits
			Blouses
			Shoes
			Belts
			Hats
Manufacturers			Televisions
			Refrigerators
			Washer/Dryers
			Stereos
			Autos

Five Minute Plan #4

job	names	quota	product
Defense workers			Aircraft
			Ships
			Missiles
Builders			Houses
Artists			Art Works
Doctors			Health treatment
			Dental treatment
Teachers			Books
Farmers			Meat Servings
			Bread Servings
			Vegetable Servings
			Dairy Servings
			Fruit Servings
Clothiers			Suits
			Blouses
			Shoes
			Belts
			Hats
Manufacturers			Televisions
			Refrigerators
			Washer/Dryers
			Stereos
			Autos

Five Minute Plan #5

job	names	quota	product
Defense workers			Aircraft
			Ships
			Missiles
Builders			Houses
Artists			Art Works
Doctors			Health treatment
			Dental treatment
Teachers			Books
Farmers			Meat Servings
			Bread Servings
			Vegetable Servings
			Dairy Servings
			Fruit Servings
Clothiers			Suits
			Blouses
			Shoes
			Belts
			Hats
Manufacturers			Televisions
			Refrigerators
			Washer/Dryers
			Stereos
			Autos

Directions for free enterprise

Workers are free to be whatever they choose: Farmer, Clothier, Manufacturer, Defense Worker, Builder, Artist, Doctor, Teacher, or any other job that might be in demand. As the game progresses, they may change jobs as often as they like, change or improve the product they produce, start their own company, hire out to someone else's company, or even take an extended vacation. Just remember that workers must feed, house, and clothe themselves. If they do not, they will die, and that violates the rules of the game. There is no welfare. The State will not provide workers with anything other than what they have when the game starts.

Today, the Grand Comrade, Head of State, decided a change was needed in the economy. There will be no more central planning or Five Minute Plans. The Planning Group has been turned into a Central Bank with authority to create Rubarbs (money). Initially, the Central Bank must distribute ten Rubarbs to every worker. An amount equal to twice the total for all workers must be kept by the Central Bank. (For example, 10 workers would have a total of 100 Rubarbs and the Bank would have 200 Rubarbs).

Half the Bank's initial reserve Rubarbs must be given to the Military for defense, including feeding, housing, and clothing the Military. As the exercise progresses, the Military may request more Rubarbs from the bank. The Central Bank can continue to produce as many Rubarbs as necessary throughout the exercise to fulfill its missions.

The Military must buy its goods from workers. If the Military cannot feed, clothe and house its members, some will be released from service to become workers.

Workers may do whatever they like with their Rubarbs. They may place them in savings accounts with the Central Bank and collect interest, buy products, loan them to other workers, hold them or even give them away.

When the exercise begins, your goal is to maximize your own well-being. This will be measured by the amount of goods, services, and money you accumulate. The Free Enterprise exercise will last 30 minutes. All participants must obtain the following minimum products to live (and survive):

Security (as indicated by a minimum defense posture)

A house (Nicer is better. Vacation homes are nice, too)

One art work (More is better. Quality counts)

At least one health treatment (More is better)

At least one dental treatment (More is better)

Two books (More is better)

Seven servings of all foods (More is better)

Three complete sets of clothing (More is better. Quality counts)

Each of one appliance (Quality is important)

One automobile (More is better. Quality counts)

Innovation is possible. Luxury and/or low-cost items may be in demand. Inventions might combine several products such as a refrigerator/freezer or entertainment console. Supermarkets, convenience foods, or special clothing packages may sell (or may not). You are in a free enterprise economy. Innovate and differentiate.

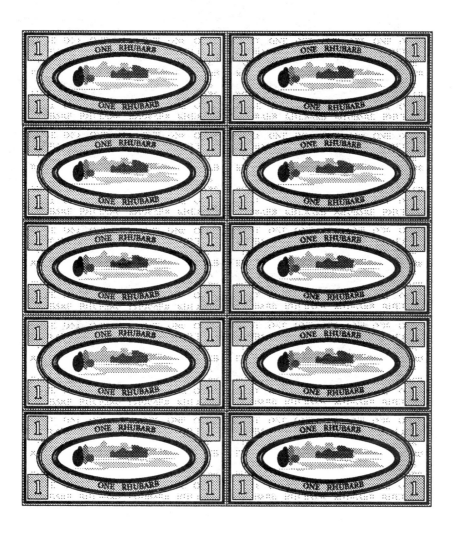

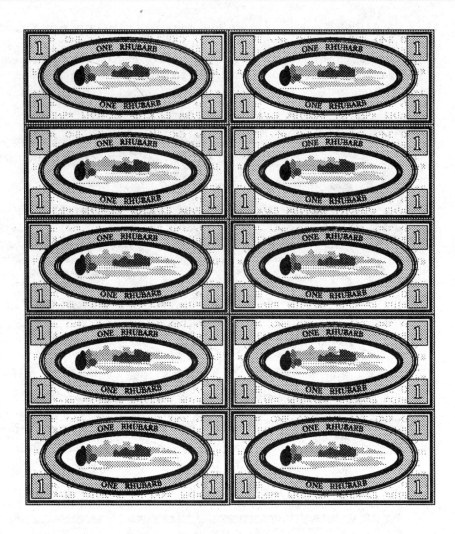

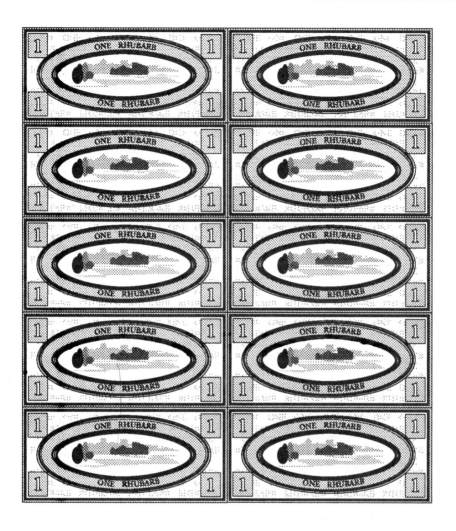

Appendix B

From "Understanding Japan"[2] Chapter 2

Questions

Membership:

Who was the most "in" and who the most "out"? What seemed to be the basis for membership? How did membership relate to the stated task? How did membership relate to other tasks that the group created?

Status:

Who seemed to be the most valued group member? Did different subgroups have different status? Were there wide divergences between high- and low-status members or was status relatively equally dispersed? Was there competition for status? How did status in the group relate to the task given to it?

Communication:

Who communicated to whom in the group? Was there a consistent pattern of communication between group members? Did certain members communicate with only one or two others, or was everyone involved more or less equally?

Leadership:

Who seemed to be the leader of the group? Did some bids for leadership fall short? Why do you think they failed? How was effective and ineffective leadership affected by the task that was defined by the professor? Did you notice any "followership" in the group? Were people willing or unwilling to follow?

---

2 By Bill van Buskirk. Used with permission.

From "H.B. Fuller"[3]   Chapter 3

I.
La Gaceta – Republic of Honduras –
Tegucigalpa, D.C., April 17, 1989

Text of legislation

WHEREAS, the inhalation of certain products utilized in shoemaking, carpentry, offices, or in domestic or school activities, on the part of children, youths, and adults, has become a serious danger for our society, and,

WHEREAS, the drug addiction resulting from these behaviors, instead of diminishing, tends to increase, involving children and youths, who in other circumstances would be in conditions to become a part of the national productive process, and to reach their full development as useful individuals both for their families and society as a whole; and,

WHEREAS, it is the duty of the government of Honduras, as representative of the State, to watch over the safety, security and happiness of our children and youths, through the promulgation of preventive dispositions which can avoid further deleterious afflictions for the health and personal integrity of the populace;

THEREFORE,

DOES DECREE:

ARTICLE 1:
The prohibition of the introduction into the country of contact adhesive products whose formulation does not include Allyl Isocyanate (oil of mustard).

ARTICLE 2:
The Secretariat of Public Health shall oversee that the products introduced prior to this disposition are sold pursuant to the prescriptions of the present Decree.

ARTICLE 3:
National producers of articles known generically as rapid setting contact cements, adhesives, or glues, and whose composition includes volatile organic solvents, and

---

3 From case study by Norman E. Bowie and Stephanie A. Lenwy. Used with permission.

which due to their penetrating odor are susceptible to being inhaled, must incorporate a proportion of oil of mustard in their composition, so that the content thereof becomes repulsive for human aspiration.

ARTICLE 4:
This Decree will become effective upon publication in the Journal of Official proceedings La Gaceta.

II.

Brief history of the H.B. Fuller company

The H.B. Fuller company was founded in 1887 by Harvey Fuller in St. Paul, Minnesota as a manufacturer of glue, mucilage, inks, blueing and blacking. The founder was an inventor of a flour-based wet paste that paperhangers found especially effective. Harvey's eldest son Albert joined his father in 1888 and the company grew rapidly, making its first acquisition, the Minnesota Paste Company, in 1892.

Harvey continued to invent new products including an adjustable leg scaffolding and a dry wall cleaner that could be mixed with cold water. By 1905 H.B. Fuller was international with customers in England, Germany and Australia. Harvey Fuller imprinted on H.B. Fuller a business philosophy that was customer based, growth oriented, and international in scope.

Harvey's third son, Harvey, Jr. joined the company in 1909 and succeeded his father as president of the company upon Harvey, Sr.'s death in 1921. Although the company's fortunes had declined in the early 1920's, Harvey, Jr. reversed them by entering the industrial adhesives market. The hiring of chemist Ray Burgess was especially fortuitous. Although, he had no formal degree in chemistry, he developed dozens of new products and the company prospered. Another hiring decision was even more momentous.

Andersen became sales manager the year the company celebrated its 50th anniversary. Despite the addition of new products and new acquisitions during the 1930's, by 1938 the depression began to take its toll on sales. In 1939 Harvey, Jr. suffered a stroke from which he never fully recovered. In 1941 H.B. Fuller received an acquisition offer from Paisley Products. But Elmer Andersen, using his savings, a loan against his house and financial help from his wife's family, purchased the company.

The defense needs for adhesives turned H.B. Fuller's financial fortunes around. Under Andersen's leadership the company grew rapidly as it built facilities throughout the country and became an industry leader. But financial success was not sufficient for Elmer Andersen. He wanted H.B. Fuller to be known as a socially responsible company. H.B. Fuller's mission statement reflected Elmer Andersen's corporate philosophy. In 1959 the company had $10 million in sales, nine affiliated companies, over fifteen plants from coast to coast, and sales in all parts of the world.

While serving as president of H.B. Fuller, Elmer Andersen also served in the Minnesota Senate from 1949 to 1959. In 1960 Elmer Andersen was elected governor of Minnesota and Al Vigard became president of H.B. Fuller. The company continued to prosper. In 1952, the 75th anniversary, sales totaled $14.2 million. Vigard also reported a 57% increase in contributions to the employee profit sharing plan.

After losing the election for a second term as governor by .007 % in 1962, Elmer Andersen returned to H.B. Fuller as Chairman of the Board. Vigard remained as company president. At this point H.B. Fuller initiated a series of international joint ventures and acquisitions. In 1967 it acquired Kativo Chemical Industries Ltd.

In 1971 Elmer Andersen stepped down as president and his son Tony became president of H.B. Fuller at the age of 35. Elmer became Chairman of the Board. Both hold the same positions today. Tony Andersen's business philosophy is in the tradition of his father's. Tony Andersen's business priority is acquisition and growth, particularly in the international arena.

In pursuit of this goal, he travels incessantly throughout the world. He also intended to double the company's sales every five years. 1971 brought joint ventures with Japan. In 1971 H.B. Fuller was listed in Fortune's top 1,000 corporations. In 1982 H.B. Fuller acquired Asar-Rokall Chemie, a division of Schering AG, West Germany, enabling it to triple its European sales from $30 to $90 million. In 1984 it was listed in the Fortune 500. In 1985 H.B. Fuller signed a joint venture with Guangdong province, China.

During the 1970s and 1980s H.B. Fuller developed its philosophy of corporate responsibility. Employee benefits were broadened. A truly unique feature was the bonus vacation time on the 10th anniversary of employment plus a substantial check so that employees could travel and see the world. H.B. Fuller joined the 5% club in 1976 (a group of Minnesota corporations that contribute 5% of their pre-tax profits to the community). In 1983 it opened the energy efficient environmentally sensitive Weldon Lake research center. H.F. Fuller continually wins awards for its responsibility to the environment.

The year H.B. Fuller made the Fortune 500, it also made Fortune's "Best 100 Companies to Work for in America." As Elmer Andersen said at the celebration gathering, "We always wanted to grow and be large but we also wanted to be good."

III.

Political Profile of Honduras

The Honduran government has been unable and in some cases, perhaps unwilling, to address the poverty issue. A democratically elected government headed by Roberto Suazo Cordova took power in 1982. After his election a liberal newspaper, El Tiempo, wrote that Cordova's election was "a vote against corruption and the presence of the military in power (Acker, 1988:124)." After taking office Cordova implemented an austerity program at the suggestion of the International Monetary Fund (IMF) and the U.S. government. By 1983, Cordova wrote President Reagan in request for aid.

The austerity measures are contributing toward increasing unemployment. We greatly fear that if this situation continues it will become a politically destabilizing factor and weaken our people's belief in the capacity of the democratic system to resolve the problems that we are trying to remedy through these economic policies (Acker, 1988:128).

This request resulted in $2.3 million in U.S. aid to Honduras. The aid which was both for the military and economic development exacerbated dependency and corruption within the Honduran government. Alison Acker writes that by 1987, there were hunger marches to the capital, and strikes for a reasonable wage. Clinics and schools closed for lack of supplies or money to pay staff. Glue-sniffing was rampant among Tegucigalpa's street kids, who could not shine shoes because that was now the job of grownups who could find no other work. (Acker, 1988:29).

Jose Axcona Hoyo, a Liberal Party member, elected in November 1985, proved no more able than Cordova to bring Honduras out of its economic decline. In 1988 credit remained very tight because of the government's tight monetary policy and the growth in the economy was made possible by U.S. aid.

By 1989, to avoid raising taxes and implementing a currency devaluation during an election year, Axcono refused to sign an agreement for more foreign aid with the IMF. As a result with Honduras $248 million in arrears on its foreign debt payments, negotiations over $300 million in aid from the IMF, the World Bank and the U.S. were suspended. Also in 1989, senior officers in the Honduran armed forces accused General Humberto Regalado Hernandez of misappropriating millions of dollars in U.S. military aid. The officer claimed that Regalado treated the military equipment as personal gifts and sold it to units under his command (New York Times, 10/15/89).

In November 1989, Rafal Leonardo Callejas of the conservative National Party won the general elections. The aims of the Callejas government included the renegotiation of the foreign debt, the reduction of the fiscal deficit, and privatization of state owned enterprises. On March 3, 1990, the Honduran government passed new legislation that included: devaluing the currency from L2 = $1 to L4.5 = $1, a reduction in tariffs, and income tax reforms. Whether or not these policy decisions will be successful remains to be seen.